THE TWENTIETH-CENTURY MIND
II
1918–1945

THE TWENTIETH-CENTURY MIND

in three volumes

THE
TWENTIETH-CENTURY
MIND

History, Ideas, and Literature in Britain

EDITED BY

C. B. Cox and A. E. Dyson

II
1918–1945

OXFORD UNIVERSITY PRESS

LONDON   OXFORD   NEW YORK

1972

Oxford University Press

LONDON OXFORD NEW YORK
GLASGOW TORONTO MELBOURNE WELLINGTON
CAPE TOWN IBADAN NAIROBI DAR ES SALAAM LUSAKA ADDIS ABABA
DELHI BOMBAY CALCUTTA MADRAS KARACHI LAHORE DACCA
KUALA LUMPUR SINGAPORE HONG KONG TOKYO

Paperback edition ISBN 0 19 281123 1
Clothbound edition ISBN 0 19 212192 8

First published as an Oxford University Press paperback,
and simultaneously in a clothbound edition, by
Oxford University Press, London, 1972

*Printed in Great Britain
by Richard Clay (The Chaucer Press), Ltd.,
Bungay, Suffolk*

CONTENTS

Introduction

We continue here the policy outlined in our introduction to the first volume, 1900–1918. We have invited a number of well-known scholars to write about developments in their own subject in the twentieth century. We have asked them to emphasize the climate of thought in Britain, but suggested that in certain cases extended treatment should be given to developments overseas. The history, philosophy, and literature chapters are largely confined to Britain. We have again made an exception in the case of drama, and Mr. Stein includes detailed treatment of playwrights such as Brecht and O'Neill, who have had a major influence on the British theatre.

In psychology and the sciences, new discoveries become part of the international scene, and so in these chapters the authors give a general survey of the whole field. Many of the most stimulating changes in theology took place in Europe, and these are included by Mr. Sykes. Mr. Raymond Plant provides an essential chapter on European social thought, particularly on the Marxist and Fascist ideologies which in this period so changed Western civilization. We have encouraged contributors not to adhere rigidly to the dates, 1918–1945, but to begin and end as appropriate to their subjects (at least as far as possible). Developments in the biological sciences do not fall in any sensible way into our chronological divisions. In the first volume, Professor Waddington brought his account up to the 1920s; he continues up to the present day in a chapter we have decided would be more appropriate in volume III (1945–1965). In each volume Mr. Edward Lucie-Smith ends with a general survey of the non-literary arts.

Our approach, therefore, is not comprehensive. There are major gaps, such as European and American literature, but we have preferred to allow our contributors to write extensively on selected areas. The alternative would be three pages on Rilke, three pages on Thomas Mann, one page on E. M. Forster, and all of them treated far too simply. We hope that our approach may provide a more intimate sense of each subject and its method of discourse, and that students will be encouraged to move on afterwards to areas not covered here. These books are intended as background reading, particularly for students and readers interested in knowledge outside their own specializing, and for students of general courses. The danger of the general course is that it provides too much superficiality, and persuades the student he can comprehend the ideas of

Freud, for example, when he has not read any of Freud's own works. We hope that students will proceed from these chapters to their own reading of the original texts. We believe that usually it is best in unfamiliar fields of study to begin with a detailed survey of British developments, rather than, for example, to attempt a reading of Thomas Mann with students who have no German, and who have not read *Ulysses* or *Four Quartets*. These essays should be taken as a series of beginnings; in the twentieth century it is obviously impossible to study all subjects in depth. We hope the individual chapters will make a useful start as students begin the life-long task of trying to comprehend the richness and diversity of twentieth-century thought.

The period from 1918 to 1945 is dominated by memories of war and fears of war. It begins with the founding of the League of Nations, and ends with the dropping of atom bombs on Nagasaki and Hiroshima. In *After the Deluge* (1931), Leonard Woolf writes:

Civilized people had at the beginning of the twentieth century almost come to believe that it was neither necessary nor probable that they should in great masses slaughter one another or die of plague and pestilence or starve to death. A certain amount of disease, a certain amount of poverty, a certain amount of mass misery in some classes of the population, were regarded as inevitable concomitants of civilization and a healthy national life, but normally public opinion demanded and ensured that misery and violent death should be confined within certain limits. From 1914 to 1918 these limits were completely abolished, and, since in Europe, which was the centre of the combatants' operations, the population was far greater than at any previous stage in the world's history, the sum of concentrated human misery was during those years probably greater than human beings had ever experienced before.   (Chapter 1)

Numerous writers similarly testified to the overwhelming impact of the 1914–18 war on imagination and thought. We think of Robert Graves's *Good-bye to All That* (1929), F. Scott Fitzgerald's *Tender is the Night* (1934), Ford Madox Ford's Tietjens saga, or T. S. Eliot's *The Waste Land* (1922). In his chapter on the other arts, Mr. Edward Lucie-Smith points out that the pre-1914 glorification of war by artists such as Marinetti did not survive the reality of the trenches. The irrational manifestations of Dada, so influential in subsequent decades, began in Zürich in 1915 largely as a simple protest against the criminal folly of the war. Professor Jones describes how *The Waste Land* confronted contemporary Britain with its own spiritual and cultural desolation. The war seemed to have marked the end of an era, the breakdown of religious, moral, and social traditions, and many artists were profoundly pessimistic about the future of civilization. Oswald Spengler's *The Decline of the West* was first published in 1918; he argued that all civilizations pass through a life-cycle, and that Western civilization had passed the climacteric and must inevitably dwindle to its death. Visions of an approaching apocalypse are to be found in writers such as Yeats or D. H. Lawrence, and in the 1930s the sense of impending disaster found warrant in the growing menace of Hitler.

The liberal faith in rational progress, so powerful in the late Victorian period, seemed bankrupt. E. M. Forster is a typical figure. His artistic talent had been fertilized by Edwardian England and by optimistic belief in the natural goodness of man. Both the society and the liberalism appeared to have been extinguished by the war, and, except for *A Passage to India* (1924), Forster wrote no more fiction. Liberalism came under heavy attack in this period, though, as Mr. Plant shows, it was sufficiently resilient to remain a powerful influence after 1945.

In this world of confusion and turbulence, the ordinary man was beset by fear of unemployment. Professor Mowat and Dr. Lovell both examine in detail the effects of the great depression, after the American slump in 1929, which finally ended all attempts to restore the pre-war international economic order. For Britain, the inter-war period was one of great sadness, as we think of the dole queues, the Jarrow marchers, or the conditions described by George Orwell in *The Road to Wigan Pier* (1937). It was in this climate that so many left-wing intellectuals turned to Marxism and Russian Communism as a solution to the malaise of capitalism. Their sympathies in many cases were soon to be alienated by the purges in Russia and by the German–Soviet pact of 1939. As Dr. Lovell shows, new ideas were emerging that would help the post-1945 governments to solve the problem of unemployment. He sees this period as a watershed between the old industrial regime of the pre-1914 era, and the new industrial economy of post-1945. The impact of the new technology was growing apace, and there was huge progress in the development of the radio, the cinema, the motor car, and electricity. John Wren-Lewis outlines major discoveries in chemistry, among the most wonderful the finding out of the medicinal qualities of penicillin. J. M. Keynes's *The Economic Consequences of the Peace* came out in 1919, and in subsequent works his views on national finance laid the foundations of the welfare state. Amidst the tragedies of the Second World War, the Beveridge Reports and the 1944 Education Act offered new answers to the social problems of pre-1939. During our period, the Liberal party fell into permanent decline; 1945 saw the triumph of the Labour party.

The history of thought in this period is complicated and contradictory, and we can offer here only headlines for the following chapters. Marx and Freud dominate the thought of the post-1918 world. Their dual influence can be seen in men as different as Auden, the poet, and Namier, the historian. Their names crop up again and again in this volume; there is Freud's influence on surrealism and literary criticism, or Marx's influence on sociology and historiography. In his chapter on drama, Walter Stein suggests that essential components of modern experience were Utopian aspirations and fascinated fixations on their collapse. This mixture of hope and despair is reflected in the diverse influence of Freud and Marx. To many people, Freud offered liberation from Victorian repressions. The work of educationalists such as A. S. Neill brought forward new optimistic ideas for child-development. In his book describing his controversial school at Summerhill, A. S. Neill wrote: 'Freud showed that every neurosis is founded on sex repression. I said, "I'll have a school in which there will be no sex repression".' Freud himself, particularly in *Civilisation and its Discontents* (1930), was much more pessimistic than many of his followers. Perhaps most important, his revelation of the power of sexual urges and the unconscious mind reduced confidence in the moral will. In volume I, Professor Hearnshaw showed how psychoanalytic teaching undermined the orthodox belief of Western man, established since Greek times, in the priority of reason. It is not surprising, as Professor Zangwill points out in this volume, that academic psychologists have been distrustful towards the claims of psychoanalysis. But the influence on fundamental attitudes has been enormous. Lytton Strachey was influenced by Freud, and in his *Eminent Victorians* (1918) achieved fame by debunking the pretensions of the eminent. The emergence of the anti-hero in the novel, and of what G. S. Fraser in his chapter on the novel calls Menippean satire, were in many ways consequences of new doubts about the rationality of human action.

Marxist doctrines seemed to offer high hopes for future society, but here too there were causes for pessimism. The emphasis on human consciousness as a product of social conditioning implied that man is determined by his environment. In this way Marxism seemed to contribute to the growing sense of the futility of moral action. All these trends, which we mention so superficially, created doubt about traditional values. Professor Cole continues his analysis of the physical sciences, in which the idea that things are seen relatively, rather than absolutely, to a particular observer, is at the centre of recent research. John Wren-Lewis tells how the use of poison gas cast a shadow upon the new world being created by science and technology. Aldous Huxley's *Brave New World* (1932) prophesied the eventual horrors which would result from scientific conditioning.

In philosophy, under the influence of Wittgenstein, A. J. Ayer proposed that there was no longer any scope for grand theories of goodness, truth, and beauty. Professor Atkinson describes the enormous intellectual effort of contemporary philosophers to dispose of metaphysics, and to prove that statements in ethics, theology, and aesthetics have no meaning. As the threat of totalitarianism grew, philosophy and history abandoned their claims to solve the problems of living. It was left to literary criticism, dominated by Dr. Leavis, to offer saving values for its initiates. One reason for the considerable popularity of literary criticism in the 1930s and 1940s was that Dr. Leavis propounded clearly and forcibly, if one-sidedly, the social and moral power of literature. It remains indisputable, however, that the main movements in the humanities were towards narrower and more rigid perspectives, which excluded most of the moral and spiritual values of Christian Europe. Arguably, this warping of knowledge towards materialism proved more damaging to the humanities than 'narrow specialism', which is often adduced as the villain.

In the non-literary arts, Mr. Lucie-Smith traces the conflict between reason and unreason, the search for forms appropriate to the twentieth-century experience. Perhaps the period is best summed up by Picasso's 'Guernica'. This anguished outcry at the cruelty of the Spanish Civil War is surrealist in its nightmare disorder, yet its energy and passion still testify to the power of the human imagination.

Suggestions for further reading will be found at the end of most chapters. An excellent collection of original writings is *The Modern Tradition: Backgrounds of Modern Literature,* ed. Richard Ellmann and Charles Feidelson, Jr. (1965).

C. B. Cox
A. E. Dyson

June 1971

History: Political and Diplomatic

C. L. MOWAT[*]

I

Anyone contemplating the 'inter-war years' and the period of the
Second World War from the vantage-point of the third quarter of
the twentieth century must feel that they were very unsophisticated
times. Nuclear fission, the atom and hydrogen bombs, rockets and
intercontinental missiles were not to be found in the armoury of war.
(The war just ended in 1918 had been an infantry war, differing
from past wars chiefly in the weight of numbers and losses, the use of
high explosive shells and the machine gun, and in a limited way the
introduction of the tank.) There were few military innovations until
the mid-thirties. Aviation was still in its infancy. In medicine there
were no antibiotics, no penicillin, no contraceptive pill; tuberculosis
was still a heavy killer. There were no computers, no transistors, no
miniaturization, there was no knowledge of lasers or neutrinos
(though the groundwork of nuclear physics was laid in these years).
The one new piece of equipment in everyday life was the wireless
receiving set; and sound broadcasting developed at first rather
slowly after the British Broadcasting Company was formed in 1922
(the Corporation succeeded it in 1926). Electricity more and more
replaced gas and oil for lighting; telephones were more numerous;
and the private car ceased to be an expensive novelty and came to be
accepted as a desirable amenity in middle-class families, while the
lorry and light van and the bus undermined the railways' near-
monopoly in public transport. Electric trams still provided unob-
structed movement in the cities.

The war had both changed things and left them the same. Some
changes soon ceased to be remarkable or were absorbed into the
system: the 'lost generation' of the three-quarters of a million
soldiers and sailors of the United Kingdom killed in the war;
increased public debt, expenditure, and taxation; the growth of big
government, reflected more in the increase in the clerical grades than

---

[*] Professor Mowat's unfortunate death in 1970 prevented him from making
final preparations of this chapter for the printer. Full documentation can be
found in his book, *Britain Between the Wars, 1918–1940.*—Eds.

in the administrative class of the civil service. Whether in science and technology, in politics and industrial relations, in policy and movements of opinion concerning the British empire (as it then was called), in diplomacy and foreign policy, or in matters such as social welfare and education, the contrasts between the Edwardian age and the postwar were smaller than the similarities; war accelerated what was already in train.

Thus the inter-war years came to look old-fashioned, a period piece, static in its quality. The class structure remained little changed: aristocracy, county people, the middle classes of the professions, industry, and business, and the working class with its many gradations but still with an essential solidarity. King George V (1865–1936), who was almost forty-five when he succeeded to the throne in 1910, was already a sort of father-figure, brought closer to the people by the war, by his visits to the front and to military hospitals, and by his industrial tours which had preceded the war; he was a symbol of continuity, though he was far from unadaptable to the times.

None the less, change was to be seen in almost every aspect of life within this period, reflected in the politics of the time and shaped by events and pressures from outside: Europe, Russia, the United States, the dominions and colonies of the British empire. It was these outside pressures, the world depression of 1929 onwards, the ambitions of the dictators and particularly of Hitler as Fuehrer of Nazi Germany, which made the thirties noticeably different from the twenties. In economic and social policy the government was forced into a somewhat more active role; at the same time foreign policy and the questions of rearmament and collective security forced people to think anew about politics and to become involved in them, often in a spirit of revolt. The Second World War, like the First, did not so much add anything new (at least, the changes it wrought only became clear in the years afterwards) as increase the pace of change. Over the whole period continuity is at least as marked as change; changes were gradual, and large only when their cumulative weight was seen in retrospect.

This was true of politics. Before the war there were two major parties, Liberal and Conservative, and two lesser parties, Labour and the Irish Nationalists (the party of Home Rule). At the end of the war the Government was a coalition of Conservatives, Liberals, and Labour headed by David Lloyd George (1863–1945). Lloyd George and the Conservative leader, Andrew Bonar Law (1858–1923), agreed that coalition was equally indispensable for the problems of peace, and appealed to the country in a general election (December

1918) in which Conservative and coalition candidates were given joint endorsement (the 'coupon', as Herbert Asquith (1852–1928), the Liberal leader, contemptuously called it in reference to wartime ration coupons). The Labour party resumed its independence. The election returned the coalition to power: coalition, 484 members (Conservatives 338, Liberals 136, others 10), Labour 59, Asquith Liberals 26, Irish Nationalists 7, Sinn Fein 73, independents and Conservatives outside the coalition 57. A second look reveals the changes. The great Liberal party was split, and its Asquithian wing decimated: Asquith himself lost his seat and did not return to Parliament until 1920. The decline of the Liberal party was to be the most significant fact in the politics of this period. The obverse of this was the advance of the Labour party, whose popular vote in 1918 (2·3 millions) was not reflected in its parliamentary representation (the coalition vote was 5 millions, the Asquith Liberals' 1·3 millions). And the Irish had virtually disappeared from Parliament: the Home Rulers were reduced to seven, while the revolutionary Sinn Feiners never took their seats. Party politics settled down—this was clear by the general election of 1922—into the rivalry of Conservatives and Labour, with increasingly ineffectual interventions by the Liberals. Most of the leaders and rank and file were of the pre-war generations, and it is tempting to speculate that it was the absence of the 'lost generation' which accounts for a certain lack of *élan* in the politics of the time. Three members of the generation which fought in the war who entered Parliament between 1922 and 1924 were Clement Attlee (1883–1967), Anthony Eden (b. 1897), and Harold Macmillan (b. 1894).

Lloyd George's postwar coalition has had a bad name since its fall in 1922, but it wrestled with multifarious and daunting problems and it is unlikely that any other government would have done better; its positive achievements are not always remembered. Elaborate plans for a smooth transition from war to peace and for the reshaping of government and society had been drawn up by the various committees of the Ministry of Reconstruction; but few ever left the shelves. The arrangements for demobilization of the troops (based on industrial skills rather than length of service) were scrapped after demonstrations in the camps at Folkestone, Kempton Park, and elsewhere, and the principle of first in first out was applied. A sudden boom in industry removed the fears of unemployment caused by the run-down of work in munitions, and reinforced the demands of business leaders to be allowed to get on with the job free of wartime controls. Decontrol and the dismantling of wartime ministries (such as Munitions, Shipping, Food) were pushed ahead, though coal-mining and the railways were not decontrolled until 1921. Instead of the nationalization of basic industries which had been assumed to be the natural consequence of the wartime experience of pooling and large-scale production (even the *Observer* had declared the nationalization of the 'inseparable Triad' of transport, electricity, and coal to be inevitable), the old world of free enterprise and competition returned, though the railways were grouped into four large companies by the Railways Act of 1921. Decontrol of the mines on 31 March 1921, accompanied by the offer of greatly reduced wages, led to a coal strike and, beyond that, to an imminent general strike in which the railwaymen and transport workers would have supported the miners under the terms of the 'Triple Alliance' of 1913; but on 'Black Friday' (15 April) the railwaymen and transport men withdrew their support when the miners rejected a move towards a settlement. This was, as it happened, almost the last of the great strikes which had threatened civil peace since January 1919, when a general strike in Glasgow in support of a forty-hour week had led to the 'battle of George Square', police charges, arrests, and the military 'occupation' of the city. A police strike in London (August 1918), a railway strike in October 1919, small strikes and larger threats from the miners and other workers had all faced the Government with embarrassing decisions. Against the railwaymen it had begun to enrol 'Citizen Guards', but thought better of it and offered a wage settlement which the men could accept. Conciliation, even deception, had got the country safely round a dangerous corner: the miners' demands for nationalization bought off by a grand inquiry into the industry, the Sankey Coal Commission, the trades unions in general placated by a short-lived National Industrial Conference of employers and union leaders intended to be a 'parliament for industry'. Lloyd George and his colleagues got no thanks for thus keeping the peace: working men felt tricked by promises evaded, the comfortable classes alarmed by the strikes and apparent surrenders to the strikers.

A postwar government can hardly be popular for long, as the Labour government of 1945–51 showed anew. When the speculative boom and the inflated prices of 1919 collapsed towards the end of 1920 unemployment became the aching question it was to remain for the next two decades: the number of unemployed was 1·3 millions in March 1921, 2·1 millions (17·8 per cent of insured workers) in June 1·5 millions a year later. An economy drive, known from the chairman of the committee, Sir Eric Geddes (1875–1937), as the Gedde axe, cut the armed services and education; the wails of the axed mingled with businessmen's prophecies of national bankruptcy. Yet in its social legislation the government was in reality quite progressive. The Unemployment Insurance Act of 1920 extended the provisions of previous measures to almost all categories of workers. The Housing Act of 1919 began the social revolution of the 'council house'—working-class housing with some approximation to middle-class amenities; the local authorities were required to build houses with the aid of national subsidies.

To many people, however, it was not the Government's record at home that caused shame or anger, it was its responses to a host of external problems, in Ireland, in India, at the Paris Peace Conference and later international meetings. Its fate was to suffer blame as much for its good deeds as for its bad.

This was especially the case in its dealings with Ireland. Ireland ended the war in a state of revolt. The Easter rising in Dublin in 1916 had been suppressed, and with no more than fifteen victims of the army's firing squads. This number of martyrs was sufficient: the population turned sullen towards British authority and was ready to give at least passive support to those demanding independence and the republic (proclaimed to the world in 1916). The Irish Republican Army and the Sinn Fein party worked together. The Sinn Feiners elected to Parliament in December 1918 turned themselves into the Irish Parliament, Dail Eireann, which met in Dublin and published a declaration of independence (21 January 1919); a government was set up, which gradually superseded the official authorities. The leaders were mostly young men such as Eamonn de Valera (b. 1882), lecturer in mathematics, and Michael Collins (1890–1922), ex-bank clerk; Arthur Griffith (1872–1922), a journalist, was rather older. When the declaration of independence was ignored, guerrilla war was begun: shootings, ambushes by flying squads of the I.R.A., attacks on police barracks. There was inevitably a 'bloody Sunday', 22 November 1920, when fourteen British officers, said to have been secret service men, were murdered in their hotel rooms in Dublin in the early morning. The Government determined to restore order, and hardly needed the urgings of its Conservative members who, as Unionists, had been fomenting the Ulster rebellion against Home Rule in 1912–14. The police were reinforced by new drafts of men, mostly ex-servicemen from England, soon dubbed the Black and Tans, and the regular army forces were increased. Terror was met by terror: Black and Tan raids on villages and farms and creameries, the burning of buildings (including part of the city of Cork in

December 1920), looting and shooting, were the reply to the murders and ambushes of the Irish gunmen. On the very evening of 'bloody Sunday' the Tans opened fire on a football crowd in Croke Park, Dublin, killing twelve persons and wounding sixty. In northeast Ireland, the loyalist parts of Ulster, fights between Orangemen and Roman Catholic nationalists cost 62 lives in Belfast in July 1920 and over 100 in 1921; Irish losses in the south in thirty months have been put at 752 persons killed and over 800 wounded.

It was a war which neither side could win, and which put the Government morally in the wrong. In Parliament and the press there were constant protests against Black and Tan tactics and American opinion, to which the Government was sensitive, seemed wholly to favour Irish independence. A Home Rule bill (the Government of Ireland Act) was passed in 1920, but this gave Ireland not one parliament but two, partitioning off the six northeast counties from the remainder. The war continued until the King's visit to Belfast to open its new parliament with a conciliatory speech provided the occasion for truce talks which ended the war on 11 July 1921. Lloyd George had, in fact, been negotiating secretly with the Irish leaders for some time through intermediaries in Dublin; he was never one to rely on one course alone, and his flexibility and quickness made him ready to cut his losses and seize on the chance of a settlement. The devious negotiations in London which began in October between a delegation from the Dail government and a delegation of Cabinet ministers ended in a treaty in the small hours of 6 December. Ireland, less Northern Ireland, won its independence as a dominion within the British Commonwealth of Nations, the Irish Free State, enjoying the same status as Canada. It was a triumph and a tragedy. It ended the conflict of centuries, after a squalid war. To Unionists it was a betrayal; to liberals it was marred by the preceding orgy of violence; to the Irish as a whole it denied unity, and to the republicans it denied the republic. De Valera supported the anti-Treaty faction of the I.R.A. in the civil war which followed (1922–3), which was far more destructive than the Black and Tan war had been, and in which the Free State government was forced to turn into gaoler and executioner of its recent comrades before its authority was established. Arthur Griffith died suddenly; Michael Collins was shot in an ambush. De Valera and his followers boycotted the Dail, but later took their seats and, on winning a majority, formed a government in 1932.

All this now looks like the whimpering beginning of the end of the British empire. At the close of the war little seemed changed, though the contribution of the Dominions to the war effort had been recognized by the holding of meetings of an Imperial War Cabinet of British ministers and Dominion prime ministers in London; at the Paris Peace Conference the Dominions had their own delegations, and they became individual members of the League of Nations. The new association between Britain and the Dominions was provided with a name, the British Commonwealth of Nations, by General J. C. Smuts (1870–1950) of South Africa; and its existence made possible the assimilation of Irish independence with the British connection. The Imperial Conference of 1926 accepted a formula defining the freedom and association of the Dominions; the Statute of Westminster gave this legislative form in 1931; the Irish Free State used it to opt out of the Commonwealth (to all intents and purposes) in 1937; the British Government ratified this by the Irish Relations Treaty in 1938. But there was still the colonial empire of crown colonies and protectorates in Africa, the Pacific, the West Indies, as yet little affected by winds of change. Native representation in legislative councils was increased in the next twenty years, and native interests were declared to be paramount, which led to loyalist-rebellious talk by white settlers in Kenya in the middle twenties. (Southern Rhodesia had been governed by the settlers since 1923.) These were mere ripples on the surface of empire. There was still the brightest jewel of all, the Indian empire. But here, too, was ingratitude and revolt. The Government of India Act of 1919 increased the share of Indians in both central and provincial government, yet sedition and rioting, product of war-inflamed nationalist feeling, continued until at Amritsar on 13 April 1919 soldiers fired on a crowd which had failed to disperse: the dead numbered 379. The Congress Party, under the leadership of Mahatma Gandhi (1869–1948), started its campaign for Indian independence, using non-violent non-resistance; violence and arrests ensued in 1922. The British Raj lasted on uneasily (E. M. Forster's *A Passage to India*, published in 1924, really depicts its pre-war phase), to be modified once again, after the Round Table conferences of 1930–2, by the Government of India Act of 1935. As an imperialist Winston Churchill (1874–1965) was quite right to sever himself from his Conservative colleagues over this issue in 1931.

Towards Europe, by contrast, Lloyd George's policy was not one of disengagement: it was the Conservatives in his government who favoured a course of withdrawal. Eventually they got rid of Lloyd George on this very issue and carried the country into the placid waters of non-involvement in the middle twenties. At the Paris Peace

Conference the Versailles Treaty was hammered out between January and May 1919. Lloyd George led the British delegation and, with President Woodrow Wilson, Clemenceau, and Orlando (the Italian premier), was one of the 'Big Four'. The Treaty imposed terms on Germany—loss of territory, limitation of arms, liability to pay reparations, the demilitarization of the Rhineland and the temporary occupation of the left bank of the Rhine by Allied forces for fifteen years. By these means France was promised the security against future attack which she sought, but the additional protection offered her, a guarantee treaty binding herself, Britain, and the United States, lapsed when the American Senate rejected it. The real security was, however, to be collective, provided by the League of Nations, whose covenant was part of the Treaty, and which Wilson, in particular, fought for. Lloyd George's role was that of mediator. He tried to limit the punitive terms against Germany and to prevent the figure for reparations being set impossibly high. For his pains he received a telegram from 233 Conservative M.P.s protesting against any leniency.

The Treaty of Versailles and the accompanying treaties with the other defeated powers were only a beginning. Europe was exhausted, the old empires of Austria and Turkey fragmented in the new succession states, the old Tsarist empire in the grip of Lenin and the Bolshevists, though the civil war in Russia was not over until 1920. Bolshevism or communism was a new source of insecurity, and spawned revolts in Hungary and Germany (the Spartacist movement). Thus Lloyd George, who remained in office after the rest of the Big Four had retired, was impelled to spend much of the next three years (1920–2) in a series of conferences to restore tranquillity, to satisfy France while saving the new democratic regime in Germany from breaking under excessive demands for reparations, and at last simply to keep the peace. This diplomacy by conference kept him much away from Parliament and led his enemies to accuse him of delusions of grandeur. When it seemed to fail—at the Genoa Conference (April–May 1922) which German and Russian delegations attended along with those of twenty-seven other European states—Lloyd George's own reputation suffered. Already the Conservatives were restive in supporting a government whose policies they could not control although they provided its majority. They revolted when war nearly broke out anew in Turkey in September 1922. Mustapha Kemal's nationalist forces had overthrown the rule of the Sultan, and had driven out the Greek armies occupying Smyrna and much of Anatolia, and they now reached the neutral zone on the coast of the Sea of Marmora occupied by British and French troops and briefly entered it at Chanak on 23 September. Lloyd George, Churchill, and other ministers were convinced that this threat to the whole peace settlement must be met by force. They appealed by telegram to the Dominions for help, and received chilly replies, while the French, with whom relations were at their worst, threatened to withdraw altogether. The danger passed, and a settlement was later made with the new Turkey; as Robert Boothby (b. 1900), then a young Conservative candidate, wrote in his autobiography, *I Fight to Live* (1947), putting it in italics, '*It was the last occasion on which Great Britain stood up to a potential aggressor before the outbreak of the Second World War.*' It was too much for Tory nerves. At a meeting at the Carlton Club on 19 October 1922, Conservative M.P.s voted by 187 votes to 87 to withdraw from the coalition. As soon as Lloyd George heard the news he resigned.

Thus ended the coalition and the years of T. S. Eliot's *The Waste Land*, which was published in 1922. In politics it had been an abnormal period, dominated by leaders a little larger than life: at least this was true of Lloyd George and Churchill (still a Liberal), and of Lord Birkenhead (1872–1930), Austen Chamberlain (1863–1937), and Lord Curzon (1859–1925) among the Conservatives. Lloyd George was at the height of his powers: dynamic, confident, quick, intuitive, a charmer, untrammelled by class or friendships or convention, a natural force and a genius. None of these qualities made him loved; and the defects of his virtues, unscrupulousness, ruthlessness, a certain carelessness in the lavish distribution of honours, and perhaps the rumours of his amorous proclivities (though nothing of this was known to the public at large until years after his death) made him distrusted if not hated by many. No wonder Stanley Baldwin (1867–1947), sitting silently in Lloyd George's cabinet, wondered if England 'would ever be clean again'. Lloyd George's weakness was that he had no political base; he was leader without a party, for the coalition Liberals were an unstable group and the party machine remained in the hands of the Asquith Liberals. His hopes for a new anti-socialist centre party had taken shape in the 'fusion' movement in 1920, but had come to nothing. He never held office again after 1922, though he remained a force in politics until 1940, rejoined Asquith's wing in 1923 and led the Liberals from 1926 to 1931.

II

There followed the era of the 'second-class brains' or, as Churchill later called it, the Baldwin–MacDonald era. Bonar Law headed the Conservative government which succeeded the coalition and which was confirmed in office by the general election of November 1922, the first of three in three years. On his retirement through illness the next May he was succeeded, not without some surprise, by Baldwin. Curzon, the Foreign Secretary, ex-Viceroy of India, was the other candidate, but was passed over on grounds of personality and peerage; and with Austen Chamberlain in opposition for the moment Baldwin, the Chancellor of the Exchequer, was the only possible choice. He was not a natural leader, but a quiet, shy man of country tastes who had lived outside Bewdley, Worcestershire, in charge of the family iron works, until he succeeded to his father's seat in Parliament in 1908 at the age of fifty-three. He spoke seldom, but had been taken up by Bonar Law and was President of the Board of Trade in 1921. His speech at the Carlton Club, warning of the dangers to the party of Lloyd George's 'dynamic force', put him in the forefront, and from then until his retirement in 1937 he embodied, if he did not always dominate, the Conservative party. He was easy-going but not indolent, easily tired so that energy and collapse alternated within him in any crisis. He was a man of goodwill and honesty, a little left of centre, anxious to promote 'peace in our time' and to avoid class war; he sought to moderate extreme Tory views and to adjust the party to serve a society in which privilege and the right of certain classes to rule counted for much less than it had done in his youth. At times he was thrown off course by his colleagues; and his reputation has suffered also from his retention of office in the thirties, when a more vigorous leader was needed. At his best he was a latter-day Walpole. The long tenure of power which the Conservatives enjoyed from 1922 to 1940 (except for short intervals) owed much to the feeling for Baldwin in the country as a man you could trust, who was in politics for unselfish ends.

The Conservatives' hold on power also owed much to the lack of a strong alternative. The Liberals made several attempts to regain their position as a major party, particularly in the election of 1929, yet their record was one of decline: 117 M.P.s elected in 1922, 158 in 1923, 42 in 1924, 59 in 1929; by 1931 the new splits within the party make the figures not comparable. Their popular vote was much larger than their representation: 5·3 millions in 1929 when Conservatives and Labour had over 8 millions each. Certainly the war-time split in the party, when Lloyd George supplanted Asquith as Prime Minister in December 1916, was a source of weakness which was prolonged until reunion was patched up for the 1923 election. The real reasons for the party's failure to convince the electorate that it offered a valid alternative to the Conservatives were two: that the Labour party now offered another choice, and that the Liberals seemed old-fashioned, their radicalism a matter of Home Rule for Ireland, disestablishment of the Church in Wales, and social legisla-tion, of which the last was appropriated by the other parties and the others belonged to 'old, unhappy, far-off things, and battles long ago'. The war, the negation of liberalism, had been their undoing, though there had been signs of decay before that.

Equally the war had done much to strengthen the Labour party. It had joined the two coalition governments and several of its leaders had held office. The trades unions, its industrial wing, had grown in strength as the demands of wartime production increased their importance. At the end of the war Arthur Henderson (1863–1935), its leading organizer, and Sidney Webb (1859–1947), the Fabian theorist, had drawn up a new programme of moderate socialism (nationalization was, after all, assumed to be a natural part of 'reconstruction') and a new constitution which widened the party's appeal. Soon disillusioned Liberals, some of them M.P.s and peers, swelled its middle-class support. Its leader after 1922, Ramsay MacDonald (1866–1937), embodied the moderate, non-doctrinaire character of the party as much as Baldwin embodied the new Con-servatism. From lowly origins he had become a writer and lecturer, an early Fabian, first secretary and later chairman of the Labour party before the war. He had opposed the war, and suffered much vilification for this until his return to Parliament in 1922. His aristo-cratic bearing and manner, though later a handicap within his party, was an asset to a national leader. He was a practised orator, a good administrator, and an able parliamentarian.

The general election of November 1922 showed the new con-figuration of politics: 347 Conservatives were returned, 142 Labour, and 117 Liberals (roughly divided between Lloyd George's sup-porters and Asquith's). Baldwin suddenly decided to ask for a dissolution of Parliament in November 1923, claiming that he needed a mandate for a protective tariff to combat unemployment. The move reunited the Conservatives, and also the Liberals, but produced a stalemate, in which Labour for the first time took office under Mac-Donald (January 1924), though it needed the Liberals' votes for its majority (Labour 191, Liberals 158, Conservatives 258). The Labour government was an unhappy one, too moderate for its left-wing members, and unable (or was it a useful alibi?) to experiment while dependent on the Liberals. MacDonald, who combined the offices of Prime Minister and Foreign Secretary, had his successes in the latter capacity; and he and his colleagues at least proved that Labour could govern as well as any other party. They fell over a minor incident, but had lacked the vigour in legislation (except over housing) or administration which might have given them a longer term of office. In the final election of the series (October 1924) the voters plumped for stability by returning the Conservatives with 415 seats to Labour's 152; Labour increased its total vote, and it was the Liberals, with 42 seats, who were the real victims. A Red scare, the 'Zinoviev letter' (a letter, probably forged, published just before the election, in which the Russians were apparently urging the British Communist party to increase its revolutionary activities) may have helped to swell the Conservative majority.

Baldwin now had his longest term of office, 1924–9, and brought both Churchill, as Chancellor of the Exchequer, and Austen Chamberlain, as Foreign Secretary, into his government. It was, with the large exception of the General Strike in 1926, a quiet time. The Government's social policy was progressive, partly under the energetic planning of Neville Chamberlain (1869–1940) as Minister of Health: old-age pensions were extended on a contributory basis and widows' pensions introduced; the voting age for women was reduced to twenty-one (votes for women at the age of thirty, if qualified on the local government franchise, had been conceded in 1918). The B.B.C. and the Central Electricity Board were established as public corporations in 1926, more on technical grounds than as pieces of 'Tory socialism'.

In foreign affairs a time of harmony had arrived. The French claims to reparations payments, and Germany's failure to meet them, had led to the French occupation of the Ruhr in January 1923. A change of government in France had helped MacDonald to play the peacemaker at the London Conference of July 1924, at which a new scheme for reparations (the Dawes plan) was accepted by Germany and the other powers and the occupation of the Ruhr brought to an end. The Labour government put great faith in the League of Nations—MacDonald was the first British Prime Minister to attend the Assembly—and wished to see its power to maintain peace strengthened by the adoption of 'the Protocol' (Protocol for the Pacific Settlement of International Disputes). The powers subscribing to the Protocol would be pledged to submit all disputes to arbitration and to apply sanctions (already provided for under article 16 of the Covenant of the League) against an aggressor. The Conservatives, when they returned to power, rejected the Protocol but substituted a security pact, the Locarno Treaty (October 1925) by which Germany, France, and Belgium promised not to make war on each other and Germany's western frontiers were guaranteed by Britain, France, and Italy. Germany joined the League of Nations. The 'Locarno spirit' was much lauded at the time as a harbinger of peace; but disarmament, which it promised, lagged behind, and a three-power conference on naval disarmament (Britain, the United States, Japan) in 1927 was a failure. Already, however, the three chief naval powers had agreed to limit their fleets at the Washington Conference (November 1921–February 1922). Britain cut back all three branches of the armed services, as much for economy reasons as any; Churchill, at the Treasury, was ruthless. The 'ten-year rule', that no war was to be expected for ten years, was renewed annually until 1932. It was a policy of withdrawal, or at least of limiting one's commitments, which was part of the spirit of the time. It also assumed that the old pre-war order had returned, and this was confirmed when the pound was restored to the gold standard in April 1925. Unfortunately, Britain's trading position was not as strong as it had been in 1913 and by restoring the pre-war parity of pound to dollar ($£1 = \$4·86$), the pound was overvalued by about 10 per cent, a further handicap to exports.

The first effect was the General Strike of 1926. That this was the one dramatic event of the mid-twenties was no accident—or rather, the General Strike was itself an accident, an exception to the general tenor of the times. Industrial unrest had died away after 1922 as prices fell and unemployment remained steady at around one million persons out of work. The coal miners, the most volatile part of the labour movement, had even benefited from an improved wage settlement in 1924 reflecting the increased exports of coal caused by the interruption in supplies from the Ruhr. By 1925 this windfall was finished, exports slumped, and the owners demanded wage cuts or a return to an eight-hour day. The miners refused, the Government arranged a truce by providing a subsidy, and a new inquiry into the industry was held (the Samuel Commission). When the subsidy ran out the owners again offered cuts and longer hours, and the coal strike, or lockout, began on 30 April 1926. There was, to say the least, no finesse in the negotiations on either side: owners and miners were equally obdurate. The General Council of the Trades

Union Congress tried to find means to avert the coal strike; their leaders were all moderate men, J. H. Thomas (1874–1949), a railway-man M.P. and ex-Cabinet minister, Ernest Bevin (1881–1951), secretary of the Transport and General Workers Union, and Walter Citrine (b. 1887), secretary of the T.U.C. They were, however, pledged to support the miners in 'resistance to the degradation of the standard of life of their members', believing that the owners' terms were the beginning of a general attack on wages. A conference of trades union executives was summoned for 29 April; but mean-while the Industrial Committee of the General Council negotiated with Baldwin and a committee of the Cabinet over ways of calling off the coal strike and preventing it from leading to a general strike. On the night of Sunday 2 May these negotiations were on the point of success when they were broken off by Baldwin on the ground that the general strike had already begun: the Cabinet had heard that the machine men at the *Daily Mail* offices had refused to print an editorial branding the threatened strike as a 'revolutionary move-ment'. Why Baldwin used this trivial incident to throw away the chance of preventing a general strike has never been made clear: exhaustion probably led him to surrender to the 'strong men' in the Government, such as Churchill and Neville Chamberlain, who were thirsting for action. And the Government had been preparing emergency arrangements for a general strike over the past nine months of the coal subsidy.

The General Strike lasted nine days, from May 4 to 12. Although the Government demanded unconditional surrender before negoti-ations over the coal strike could be resumed there were, in fact, continuous negotiations behind the scenes, and when the General Council of the T.U.C. felt it had received sufficient assurances of fair treatment for the miners (though the miners did not agree) they called off the strike. The coal strike dragged on till the end of the year, when the men went back to work beaten. The General Strike, while it lasted, was a complete success: the railways, road transport, the docks, the printing trades, building, iron and steel, metals and chemicals were all paralysed. Volunteers got some emergency trans-port going, and essential services were kept up, but the local strike committees in every town and district maintained control. Churchill edited an official news sheet, the *British Gazette*, which excelled in misinformation and provocative exhortations to the hundreds of new special constables; the Government attempted to turn the strike into a 'challenge to Parliament' and an attack on 'constitutional government'. Fortunately the good sense and the discipline of the strikers prevailed, helped by fine weather which made the occasion almost a holiday. There were some disorders but no lives were lost. There were, however, over 3,000 prosecutions for incitement to sedition and for violence arising out of the strike.

The outcome was paradoxical. The feeling of workers was one of pride, of the leaders that they had found the 'limitations of industrial power' and must countenance no repetition. Thus the Government's punitive legislation, the Trade Disputes Act of 1927 which tried to ban a general strike, was quite unnecessary; the next several years were remarkably free of strikes. One reason for this was that there was no general attack upon wages; so perhaps it was not only the trade unions to whom the General Strike taught a lesson. The remainder of the Government's life was dull: tiredness set in. The next general election, in May 1929, resulted in its defeat. It offered little except its record. The Liberals under Lloyd George put on a great campaign based on a programme of national development and public works, *We Can Conquer Unemployment*. Labour, claiming it could do as well, won the largest number of seats, though again lacking a majority (Labour 287 seats, Conservatives 261, Liberals 59).

MacDonald's second Labour government lasted longer than the first, but was no happier. It had the ill fortune to coincide with the beginning of the world depression, which can be dated from the Wall Street crash of October 1929. As the number of unemployed mounted towards 2·7 millions (June 1931) the Government's inability to find any remedy became more obvious. The one large proposal before it, a memorandum prepared by Sir Oswald Mosley (b. 1896), a junior minister, was rejected; it argued for a protective tariff, import controls, industrial reorganization, and public control of banking and credit. The Liberals, ready to accept vigorous measures, found their patience wilting; by the middle of 1930 a group of them under Sir John Simon (1873–1954) were splitting off from the rest and moving towards the Conservatives, ultimately to become indistinguishable from them under the name Liberal National.

The Government came to a sudden and bitter end in August 1931. A financial crisis arose, partly from the pessimistic forecasts of budget deficits in an official report published just as Parliament rose for the summer. There was a flight from the pound, and the Bank of England, having exhausted new credits obtained from Paris and New York, demanded a reassuring gesture from the Government (though much of the trouble was of the City's own making, from the volume of short-term deposits it had accepted while its assets abroad were frozen in long-term loans: 'lending long and borrowing short'). MacDonald, backed by his flinty Chancellor of the Exchequer, Philip Snowden (1864–1937), was ready for drastic economies all round, including cuts of 10 per cent or more in unemployment pay and the wages and salaries of government employees, teachers, police, the armed services. The Cabinet was split, a majority of eleven accepting the total savings proposed while nine balked at cutting the slender payments to the unemployed. The General Council of the T.U.C. offered advice, leading to the strange accusation that it was dictating to the Government (were not the bankers also doing so?); it suggested that other means, such as a tariff, re-examination of the gold standard, suspension of sinking-fund payments—all measures subsequently adopted by the 'National' government—be considered for balancing the budget. The gap between the two sides in the Cabinet was no more than £12¼ millions; all agreed to economies totalling £68½ millions.

MacDonald decided that the Cabinet, so evenly split, must resign, and the members agreed. Instead, however, of being succeeded by a Conservative–Liberal government, as would have been both 'normal' and practicable, the Labour ministers were told next morning (24 August) by MacDonald that he had accepted the King's commission to form a 'National' government of all parties, as a temporary measure to overcome the emergency. Baldwin and Sir Herbert Samuel (1870–1963), the latter speaking for the Liberals in Lloyd George's absence after an operation, had agreed when consulted, on MacDonald's advice, by the King. The King's part in the crisis was controversial, but not unconstitutional. MacDonald's was ambiguous: had he plotted this, to save the country as a national leader freed from the narrowness of his lifelong but uncongenial colleagues? (Only four ministers, including Thomas and Snowden, followed him into the new Government.) There is no evidence of a plot. MacDonald believed that his course was the best for working people and the people generally, saving them from financial ruin; and he was carried away by the emotions of the moment, after a hectic fortnight of meetings and negotiations. To the Labour party, which expelled him, he seemed a traitor, and the bitterness engendered by this 'treachery' affected Labour's thinking and policies for years to come. There was also the feeling that Labour had been forced out of office—and always *would* be forced out of office if its policies were unorthodox—by a 'bankers' ramp'. The real trouble was that the Cabinet had not the courage or the knowledge to be unorthodox over finance; it allowed Snowden to insist on the classical, pre-Keynesian policies of economy and deflation and then balked at the consequences.

But the National government had come to stay. It appealed to the country in October and won a smashing victory in a panicky election campaign: Snowden called his ex-colleagues' policies 'Bolshevism run mad'; someone else told voters that they would lose their savings in the Post Office Savings Bank if Labour was returned. The 'National' government received a majority of 497 seats: its 556 members included 472 Conservatives, 33 Liberals (under Samuel), 35 Simonite Liberals, 13 National Labour. Most of Labour's long-time leaders were defeated, including Henderson, who had temporarily replaced MacDonald. Labour, though it polled 6·6 million votes to the Government's 14½ million, had only 46 M.P.s: they were joined in opposition by Lloyd George and three members of his family who were returned to Parliament.

III

The crisis of August 1931 was a turning point in Britain's history between the wars, not only for its effects at home but because it coincided with the beginning of the world crisis which ended in the Second World War: the resort of Japan to foreign aggression, of Germany to terror and intimidation within and outside its boundaries. The Japanese invasion and occupation of Manchuria began with the Mukden incident on 18 September 1931. This was the first large challenge to the power of the League of Nations to prevent or punish aggression, and within a year and a half it was obvious that the League had no such power; the integrity of Chinese territory had not been preserved, Japan had not withdrawn from her conquests but merely from the League. In Germany democratic government was never very strong under the Weimar Republic and was weakened in the mad inflation of 1923 (at the time of the occupation of the Ruhr) when the mark fell to 22,300 millions to the the pound sterling from a parity of 20 to the pound; it finally collapsed as the world depression engulfed it. Hitler and the Nazis, playing on fear of communism and resorting to tactics of terror, gained power when Hitler was appointed Chancellor on 30 January 1933; at once he seized dictatorial powers, crushing all opposition, persecuting the Jews, rearming (against the provisions of the Treaty of Versailles) and preparing: for world conquest, or for the absorption by force or guile of neighbouring territories with or without war—who knew? Mussolini, in power in Italy since 1922, had already given the world a foretaste of modern dictatorship and the glorification of war. It was only in the thirties, however, that threats, violence, and terror became the daily challenge to peace and order, might was right, and collective security and economic sanctions were vain hopes.

It was the National government which had to face this challenge. It was ill-equipped for it. It was elected to overcome the domestic crisis of the depression, not to decide on policies of peace and war, defence and rearmament. Its huge and largely Conservative majority meant that it was not under the spur of dangerous criticism—though criticism was loud and continuous, in and outside Parliament. Labour, in spite of its small representation, proved effective in Parliament under the leadership of the old-time pacifist George Lansbury (1859–1940) and after 1935 of Clement Attlee. For the Government a large majority meant not vigour but caution, bred of an equal fear of pacifist feeling, which seemed strong, and of the 'warmongering' of realists such as Churchill. The leadership was old: MacDonald was ailing and his speeches often seemed designed to compound confusion, Baldwin's strength was easily taxed and he preferred to exercise influence from behind, as Lord President of the Council. In the general election of November 1935 the National government won a reduced majority and was more than ever Conservative in all but name; Baldwin had replaced MacDonald as Prime Minister earlier in the year. Baldwin's last two years of office coincided with critical issues of foreign policy—over the Abyssinian war, the German remilitarization of the Rhineland, the Spanish Civil War. There was some progress in rearmament. The main event at home was Edward VIII's abdication in December 1936, after a reign of eleven months; Baldwin was at his best in his tactful and—in the main—honourable handling of this sudden crisis. After the coronation of George VI in May 1937 Baldwin was succeeded by Neville Chamberlain. He was only two years younger (sixty-eight), but much more vigorous and decisive. Appeasement may have been misguided, but it was positive and was pursued with persistence. Chamberlain's very resentment of criticism made the choices clearer, and led to the great decisions for war in 1939 and 1940.

The Government had three main concerns during these years (1931–9): depression * and recovery, foreign policy, armaments. All were interwoven with each other. Before the depression passed into

---

* The problems of depression are dealt with by John Lovell in the next chapter.

history it left its deposits: bitter memories for many, but also some growth of knowledge for the rest. Social consciousness and an interest in politics (not necessarily in party politics) were stirred by reports from the depressed areas; undergraduates, for example, did voluntary work in the summer in educational centres such as Maes-yr-Haf in the Rhondda. University departments undertook social surveys. Planning became a respectable idea. The poems of the new poets, W. H. Auden (b. 1907), Stephen Spender (b. 1909), and C. Day Lewis (b. 1904), the satirical plays of Auden and Christopher Isherwood (b. 1904), the novels of George Orwell (1903–50) expressed a new concern with the evils of the time, whether at home or in Spain where General Franco's Nationalist forces were winning the Civil War. Others embraced Marxism. Anything seemed better than to do nothing, silent under the spell of the old men at Westminster.

Foreign policy was even more contentious. On the face of it, it was clear enough: full support for the League of Nations. But the League had no power of its own. The big Disarmament Conference (1932–4) failed. Japanese aggression in China continued unchecked. Germany left the League of Nations and began rearming openly, particularly in the air. Meanwhile, there was still much faith in the League, shown by the unofficial Peace Ballot in 1935 in which 11½ million people voted. A three-to-one majority favoured the imposition of sanctions, economic but also if necessary military, against an aggressor. The Government won the 1935 election on a programme of support of the League and rearmament. The election coincided with Italy's war on Abyssinia which began in September 1935. The League at once voted for economic sanctions against Italy. They proved ineffective, and in December Sir Samuel Hoare (1880–1959), the Foreign Secretary, was persuaded by the French Foreign Minister, Pierre Laval, to agree to a deal by which Italy would be bought off by the cession of two-thirds of Abyssinia. This betrayal of the League was too much for the public to stomach (Hoare resigned, to be replaced by Anthony Eden). Then in March 1936 Hitler ordered the German army to reoccupy the Rhineland. Britain and France were unwilling to oppose this by force. The League could do nothing; nor could it later in the year when the Spanish Civil War began, with Germany and Italy openly aiding and abetting Franco's forces against the legal Republican government.

The need for a new policy was not met until Neville Chamberlain became Prime Minister, in May 1937. It had two sides: rearmament, which had begun as early as 1934, and 'appeasement'. Appeasement consisted of negotiations to remove grievances which might lead to war—a not unreasonable policy if the negotiations were fairly and freely conducted. An alternative policy would have been one of withdrawal: if Hitler demanded the re-incorporation of Germans within the Reich (and his large but imprecise ambitions seemed to be the most likely cause of war), let him go ahead, as he did in the invasion of Austria in March 1938. The difficulty was that the next destined victim seemed to be Czechoslovakia, where the Sudeten Germans constituted a considerable minority. If Germany attacked Czechoslovakia France was bound by treaty to intervene, and Britain, if only as a fellow-member of the League, could hardly stand aside. Hence Chamberlain's extraordinary essay in personal diplomacy (not he, but Lord Halifax (1881–1959) was now Foreign Secretary), in September 1938, to prevent a war breaking out over Czechoslovakia by 'negotiations' in which the Czechs were threatened and bullied into yielding up the Sudeten areas which Hitler demanded before he took them by force. Chamberlain's dramatic flight to see Hitler at Berchtesgaden, his second visit to Godesberg, and the four-power conference at Munich (Britain, France, Italy, Germany), did produce 'peace for our time' as Chamberlain told the crowd in Downing Street on his return. 'Munich' was overwhelmingly popular at first. Then came second thoughts, uttered all along by Churchill, several Conservatives, and most Labour members. Was it, as Chamberlain had also said, 'peace with honour'? The sacrifice was Czechoslovakia's alone, underlined by the instant nature of the occupation of the Sudeten areas, where a new persecuted minority of non-Germans now existed.

It was the sense of humiliation which Munich evoked, coupled with the belief that Hitler's appetite was still unsatisfied, which led to the intensification of opposition to the Government in the winter of 1938–9. Many thought that Chamberlain's policies were too much influenced by *The Times* (arch-appeaser in the press) and the 'Cliveden set' of important persons who met at week-ends at the country house of Lady Astor (1879–1964). Among the Conservatives several members were critical: Churchill, Eden, Macmillan, Leopold Amery (1873–1955) among others. Labour was equally critical, but handicapped by its opposition to rearmament, based chiefly on distrust of the Government's intentions. The real ferment, however, was outside Parliament and indeed outside the parties. It was a matter of articles and paperback books (Penguin books began to appear in May 1937), meetings, processions, and independent candidates at by-elections. The 'revolt of the Left' owed much to sympathy with the Spanish Republicans and the stories of the atrocities of the Nationalists. It owed much to sympathy with the 'Russian experiment' (despite the 'purges' of the mid-thirties) and the belief that Chamberlain would gladly do a deal with Hitler at Russia's expense: a holy war against Russia would divert Hitler's attentions from the West. It owed something to the British fascist movement led by Sir Oswald Mosley, after he had left the Labour party in disgust at the rejection of his ideas in 1930. The British Union of Fascists staged demonstrations against Jews and 'communists' in the East End of London, in which the police seemed readier to protect the fascists than their victims. In the mobilization of the Left the Left Book Club, founded in May 1936, played a large part, not only by the books it circulated each month but by discussion circles among its 50,000 members.

By the time of Munich many people on the Left were ready for war in place of further retreats and surrenders to threats or violence. The Government, however, persisted in its belief in appeasement, while betraying its scepticism by accelerating rearmament—later given as a justification of the Munich settlement—though the extra time was of equal value to the Germans. The build-up of the Royal Air Force was pressed on, not only in bombers but with the Hurricane and Spitfire fighters. A tardy effort was made to speed up the mechanization of the army, and by September 1939 four divisions were ready to serve as an expeditionary force. Most important, perhaps, was the development of the chain of radar stations and the beginning of Air Raid Precautions (A.R.P.).

In the end Hitler himself forced Chamberlain's hand. The sudden occupation by the Germans of Prague and the absorption of the remainder of Czechoslovakia on 15 March 1939, convinced Chamberlain that appeasement alone would not keep the peace: it must be backed by clear warnings of action against future aggression. Since the next victims seemed likely to be Romania or Poland they were offered guarantees of assistance, and a little later negotiations were begun with Russia to draw it into a pact of mutual assistance with Britain and France. But Stalin had decided to seek safety in another way, and on 23 August the Russo–German treaty was signed in Moscow. At the same time Hitler increased his pressure on Poland for the surrender of Danzig and other concessions. There was the chance of another Munich, but Hitler began the invasion of Poland on 1 September 1939, before any conference could meet. When Germany ignored an ultimatum, the British and French governments declared war on 3 September in fulfilment of their promises to

Poland. Chamberlain told Parliament, ' . . . everything that I have worked for, everything that I have hoped for, everything that I have believed in during my public life, has crashed in ruins'.

IV

To these years the Second World War was the epilogue, though to the fifties and sixties it was the prologue. The 'phoney war' of 1939–40 was a continuation of appeasement: Hitler completed his blitzkrieg conquest of Poland while making peace offers to Britain and France, whose forces remained on the defensive along the French borders. This phase ended with the German invasion of Norway and Denmark on 9 April 1940, followed on 10 May by the invasion of the Netherlands and Belgium and the attack upon France. On that day Churchill became Prime Minister in a truly national government of Conservatives, Labour, and Liberals. Chamberlain had decided to resign after his majority in a debate on the failure of the British expedition to Norway fell to 81: some 40 Conservatives had voted against him and over 80 abstained. The fall of France, the evacuation of British and French troops from Dunkirk, the 'battle of Britain' (July–September) in which the *Luftwaffe* failed to secure mastery over the skies of Britain, did not shake the country's determination. A German invasion seemed imminent; in fact Hitler had made inadequate preparations for it, not believing that the British would refuse to come to terms. Britain continued at war, alone with the Dominions except Ireland, through the 'blitz' (the big air raids in the winter of 1940–1); the only theatre of operations was in Egypt and Libya.

After the German invasion of Russia in June 1941 and the American declaration of war against Japan and Germany after the attack on Pearl Harbor on 7 December 1941, the remainder of the war was an anticlimax for Britain. There was a greater mobilization of men and women and resources than in any other country; there were the long days of work in the factories and the fields, the long nights of the blackout, the daily peril of the seamen from the U-boats, whether in convoy or in ships sailing alone; there were the see-saw campaigns in Egypt where the Italians and Germans invaded and were repulsed, returned and withdrew, advanced again under Rommel, and were finally driven back by General B. L. Montgomery's Eighth Army. After the decisive second battle of El Alamein (October 1942) Britain's role was secondary. British troops shared in the invasions of North Africa, of Sicily and southern Italy and in landings in Normandy on D-Day (6 June 1944) after the build-up of American forces in Britain. They both took part in the liberation of France and the invasion of Germany across the Rhine. They fought in Burma after the Japanese seizure of Malaya. British bombers blasted the great German cities, Hamburg, Cologne, Berlin, and the raid on Dresden in February 1945 which took perhaps a quarter of a million lives; retaliation for the big German raids on London, Coventry, Bristol, Hull, Birmingham, Plymouth, Swansea, Exeter, and elsewhere. The brunt of the fighting, the weight of numbers and metal, was borne by the Russians and, particularly in the Pacific, by the Americans; beside the two super-powers Britain's status inevitably declined. The development of the atom bomb and its use by the Americans at Hiroshima and Nagasaki in August 1945 only made this clearer: the initial work was done in Britain, but in 1941 the Americans began development on their own and quickly pushed ahead while Britain turned cool towards co-operation. When the Government changed its mind it was too late, and British scientists were kept at arm's length from the secrets until some co-operation was restored by the Quebec agreement of August 1943. This alone shaped much of the pattern of the postwar world: more so than the conference at San Francisco in April 1945, before the war had ended, at which the United Nations was established.

For the British people during the war one thing was clear. There must be no going back to the dreary life of the thirties. The Beveridge Report of December 1942 outlined a comprehensive 'welfare state' based on national insurance, guaranteeing minimum well-being for all 'from cradle to grave'. The common experience of the blitz, which spared neither rich nor poor and which only the state services could relieve, was a great persuader for a better, more equal society. For this a new government was needed. The general election of July 1945 gave Labour for the first time a majority of its own: 393 Labour members to 213 Conservatives, 12 Liberals, and 22 Independents. Labour was given its opportunity and put to the test in a postwar period far more daunting than that of twenty-five years before.

FOR FURTHER READING[*]

The best book describing this whole period is A. J. P. Taylor, *English History 1914–1945* (Oxford, 1965), which combines political, economic, and social history in connected narrative. His coat-trailing asides and footnotes may be

[*] Place of publication, in this and following reading lists, is London unless otherwise indicated.

ignored. C. L. Mowat, *Britain between the Wars, 1918–1940* (1955), is much
fuller for all aspects of the period it covers. Both books have extensive bibliographical references. L. C. B. Seaman, *Post-Victorian Britain, 1902–51* (1966),
is an up-to-date political history, sharp in its judgements. W. N. Medlicott,
Contemporary England 1914–1964 (1967), is solid and comprehensive. There is
no adequate history of the Conservative party, but there is useful historical
material in R. T. McKenzie, *British Political Parties* (1955), and J. P. Mackin-
tosh, *The British Cabinet* (1962). For the Liberals Trevor Wilson, *Downfall of
the Liberal Party 1914–1935* (1966), is useful for the coalition period but is far
from providing a full explanation; Lord Beaverbrook's *Decline and Fall of Lloyd
George* (1963) deals only with 1921–2 and is really special pleading for its author's
conduct. By contrast, much has been written on the Labour movement: G. D. H.
Cole, *History of the Labour Party from 1914* (1948), is comprehensive and
authoritative; Henry Pelling's (1961) is the best of the shorter histories (he has
also written short accounts of the British Communist party and trade unionism).
Ralph Miliband, *Parliamentary Socialism* (1961), presents a critical view of
Labour's history.

There are few important biographies. For Lloyd George the best and briefest
is by Thomas Jones (1951); Frank Owen's *Tempestuous Journey* (1954) is fuller
and windier. G. M. Young's life of Baldwin (1952) is inadequate; A. W.
Baldwin's *My Father: The True Story* (1953) is useful. A full life, *Baldwin: A
Biography*, by J. Barnes and R. K. Middlemas (1969), appeared while this
chapter was being written. R. Blake, *The Unknown Prime Minister* (1955), is an
excellent life of Bonar Law. Keith Feiling's *Life of Neville Chamberlain* (1946)
is important and much more revealing than Iain Macleod's (1961). Harold
Nicolson, *King George the Fifth* (1952), is a model biography of high value. Roy
Jenkins's *Asquith* (1964) is fairly charitable. For Labour leaders Alan Bullock's
Life and Times of Ernest Bevin, I (1960) is outstanding. Colin Cross, *Philip
Snowden* (1966), is useful. The ten-year supplementary volumes of the *Dictionary
of National Biography* have sound lives of most of the figures of the time.

The most lively sources for political history are the memoirs, of which thi
generation produced a large crop. Churchill is his own memoirist in *The Worl*
Crisis, of which *The Aftermath* (1929) deals with the immediate post-war years
after 1918, and his *Second World War* (6 vols., 1948–54), which includes a goo
deal on the 1920s and '30s in its first volume, *The Gathering Storm*. The mos
useful autobiographical works are Snowden's *Autobiography* (1934); A. Fenne
Brockway's *Inside the Left* (1942); L. S. Amery's *My Political Life* (3 vols.
1953–5); Hugh Dalton's *Memoirs* (3 vols., 1953–62); A. Duff Cooper, *Ol*
Men Forget (1953) and Harold Nicolson's *Diaries and Letters 1930–1939* (1966
both valuable for Munich; Thomas Jones, *Diary with Letters 1931–1950* (1954
useful for Baldwin and the Cliveden set; Lord Citrine's *Men and Work* (1964
for the T.U.C.; Beatrice Webb's *Diaries 1912–1924* and *1924–1932* (1952, 1956
and Mary Agnes Hamilton, *Remembering My Good Friends* (1944), whic
contain shrewd (Mrs. Webb's, somewhat malicious) sketches of Labour figure
Lord Templewood, *Nine Troubled Years* (1954), Sir Samuel Hoare's memoir
is the best apologia for the policy of appeasement. Of Eden's *Memoirs* tw
volumes, *Facing the Dictators* (1962) and *The Reckoning* (1965), cover this perio
but not very illuminatingly. B. H. Liddell Hart's *Memoirs* (2 vols., 1965) tell th
story of disarmament and rearmament along with vivid sketches of men an
events.

For the rebellion and civil war in Ireland see the bibliographical references i

Mowat, especially p. 72. There has been much work on this period recently in Ireland (though mostly concerning the Easter rising of 1916), much of it in paperbacks. See Desmond Williams, ed., *The Irish Struggle 1916–1926* (1966); Edgar Holt, *Protest in Arms* (1960); Eoin Neeson, *The Civil War in Ireland* (Cork, 1966); Frank Gallagher, *The Anglo-Irish Treaty* (1965). The later history of the Irish Free State is best studied in D. O'Sullivan, *The Irish Free State and its Senate* (1940), and W. K. Hancock, *Survey of British Commonwealth Affairs*, I (1937).

Foreign policy stimulated much writing at the time and has continued to do so, especially over Munich. A full account will be found in F. S. Northedge, *The Troubled Giant* (1966). A. J. P. Taylor's *Origins of the Second World War* (1961) spreads the blame on others besides Hitler: there is some change of emphasis in the Penguin edition, 1964. On appeasement the best books are J. W. Wheeler-Bennett, *Munich* (1948), M. Gilbert and R. Gott, *The Appeasers* (1963), and Gilbert's *Roots of Appeasement* (1966), which surveys policy since 1918 and suggests some revision of his earlier views. The general history of these years is treated in the *New Cambridge Modern History*, XII (rev. ed., 1968).

Books on particular topics: For the General Strike see the bibliography in Mowat, p. 331. Julian Symons, *The General Strike* (1957) is useful for the accounts of participants which it draws on. R. W. Lyman, *The First Labour Government* (1957), and R. Bassett, *1931: Political Crisis* (1958), deserve mention; the latter is strongly biased in defence of MacDonald's conduct. Much has been written on Edward VIII's abdication: see references in Mowat, p. 587, to which Lord Beaverbrook's account, *The Abdication of King Edward VIII* (1966), should be added for some new chinks of light it lets in.

On the Second World War the literature, especially in generals' memoirs, is already immense. Taylor's *English History* has a good selective bibliography, including the titles in the two official British series of histories, the United Kingdom Military Series and United Kingdom Civil Series. L. Thompson, *1940* (1966), stands out amid a mass of journalistic works for its thoroughness and insight. Ronald Blythe, *Components of the Scene* (Penguin, 1966), is a most useful anthology of prose and poetry of the war. Margaret Gowing's *Britain and Atomic Energy 1939–1945* (1964) tells a disheartening story of success and bungling and Anglo-American non-co-operation.

2

History: Economic and Social

JOHN LOVELL

This chapter begins and ends with the termination of a world war. The intervening period includes six years of total war, and twenty-one years of peace. The period of peace was hardly one of unbroken prosperity, including as it did the most severe economic depression in modern times. It would be an exaggeration to view this period as one of continual crisis, but it was scarcely a normal time. The point was well put by W. A. Lewis, who, writing in 1949, said of the interwar years: 'There can have been few periods of twenty-one years into which so much experience has been packed, and most of us will hope that at any rate we and our children shall not have the privilege of seeing such exciting times again.'[1] The abnormality and complexity of this period make the historian's task most difficult, and in this chapter nothing approaching a comprehensive survey of the economic and social developments of these years can be attempted. Instead, attention will be drawn only to what the writer regards as the most outstanding features of the time, and much that is interesting and worthy of note will necessarily have to be omitted. It is proposed to divide the period into three parts, and to deal with each in turn, as follows:

(1) 1918–29—The Postwar Decade
(2) 1930–9—World Depression and Recovery
(3) 1940–5—The Second World War.

The Postwar Decade

The two great conflicts of the first half of the twentieth century are in a class apart in the history of warfare. They placed a strain upon the economies and societies of those nations involved which went far beyond anything previously experienced, and resulted in either the collapse of existing institutions or their transformation—at least for the duration of the war.[2] In all essential respects Britain had had a free enterprise economy prior to 1914. The role of the government in the economy had been increasing, it is true, but it remained basically confined to finance, commercial relations with foreign powers, and social policy (a fast-growing sector). With the outbreak of the First World War the ruling class exhibited a great reluctance to depart from this pre-war pattern, but depart it did none the less, and in the last two years of the war the free market economy of Edwardian times disappeared under a welter of government controls. It might have been expected that this dramatic break with the past would have had important and lasting consequences. In fact this was not to be the case. The elaborate apparatus of economic control was dismantled as quickly as it had been constructed, and by the middle of 1922 decontrol was complete.[3] It would be wrong to suggest that the massive state intervention in the wartime economy had no permanent impact on society. Thus, for example, although the government decontrolled the railway industry in 1921, refusing to take it into permanent public ownership, it did impose on the railways a scheme for rationalization, whereby the numerous companies were grouped into four large concerns. This was obviously a direct result of wartime experience. In other less tangible ways, too, society was perhaps rendered more sympathetic to various forms of state intervention. But, in the main, the wartime experience was discarded, and the nation's rulers showed a marked desire to restore the pre-war pattern of economic activity as quickly as proved practicable. In this they were no doubt encouraged by the boom that developed immediately following the Armistice.

Unfortunately the freedoms of pre-1914 were to prove incompatible with the social reform that many had anticipated in the aftermath of the war. The exact nature of the relationship between war and social reform has been the subject of much debate among historians and others, but suffice it here to say that there appears to be some connection between the proportion of the total population engaged in the war effort and the strength of the demand for social change.[4] The First World War made enormous demands on British manpower, both for combat purposes and on the industrial front.

By all past standards the level of social involvement in the Great War was revolutionary. In Britain 5 million men were under arms and as many more were working on war production under government supervision. It was a war in which popular participation in the war effort not only was for the first time the critical condition of victory, but was felt to be so by politicians, civil servants, trade unionists and the press.[5]

The crucial importance to the nation of its least privileged groups—that is the working class and women generally—could not have been more powerfully demonstrated, and it was not surprising that the war should generate demands that the political, social, and economic status of these groups should in the future reflect the contribution that they had made to victory. Quite apart from this generalized pressure for social reform, there was also the fact that the war had in some respects actually exacerbated pre-1914 social evils. It had done this particularly in respect of education and housing. In the former case, the war had resulted in children being withdrawn from school prematurely in order that they could take up industrial employment, and educational standards had suffered grievously as a result. In the case of housing, the war had resulted in a cessation of new building, so that an acute housing shortage developed; in the period between the census years 1911 and 1921 there accumulated a deficit of 805,000 houses.[6]

The wartime Ministry of Reconstruction certainly recognized the critical situation in education, housing, and other spheres that had arisen as a result of the war. It also recognized the more general feeling in the country in favour of social reform, a feeling that grew out of the sacrifices made by the still underprivileged and deprived sections of the community. The magnitude of the social problem generated and exposed by total war necessitated drastic action, and there was in the Government a certain readiness to accept the proposition that the state should intervene in the sphere of social reform on a far larger scale than pre-1914. Thus in 1918–20 the Government came forward with its programme of social legislation. In 1918 there was the Education Act, and the following year brought the Ministry of Health Act and the Housing and Town Planning Act. In 1920 there was the National Insurance Act. Meanwhile on the industrial relations front, the state had moved to implement the report of the Ministry of Reconstruction's Whitley Committee, in favour of Joint Industrial Councils with greater worker participation in the running of industry. It had also convened an Industrial Conference in 1919, with the ostensible purpose of bringing management, workers, and the state together to discuss the general problems affecting the status and conditions of the worker in industry. It was all very promising, yet it came to very little.

The problem was both an economic and an ideological one, and is perhaps best seen with reference to the postwar housing problem.[7] The Housing and Town Planning Act of 1919 imposed upon local authorities the duty of surveying the housing needs of their areas and making and carrying out plans for the provision of the houses needed. The programme was to be financed by Treasury subsidies to local authorities, enabling the latter to fix rents at a level which those most in need of accommodation could afford. This Addison

Act—named after Christopher Addison (1869–1951), the Minister of Health—represented a radical extension of government responsibility in the social sphere, for hitherto the state's interest in housing matters had been largely confined to the public health problem of slum clearance. The Act was not, however, a success. Only 214,000 houses were built under its auspices between 1919 and 1923, and this number was nothing like sufficient to cover even the backlog that resulted from the war. The immediate difficulty was finance. As might have been expected, the demands made upon the building industry after the war were intense. The demand was not only for houses but for factories and offices as well. Given the fact that skilled labour and building materials were in short supply, costs in the industry rose alarmingly, and the houses built under the scheme were excessively expensive. In 1921 the Government took fright, and drastically cut the number of houses scheduled to be built. The same year saw government cuts in the education programme and elsewhere. The failure of the scheme, and with it the promise of 'homes fit for heroes', was closely related to the question of decontrol. Without the deliberate control of building resources by the state the scheme was bound to be undermined, for local authorities were forced to compete with other bidders in order to obtain sufficient resources to carry out their plans, and given the postwar scarcities this process was bound to involve tremendous expense. The reformers in the Government were in fact willing the end, but not the means. They desired that the state should accept the responsibility for increasing the supply of cheap housing, but they shrank from maintaining the wartime economic controls which alone would have enabled them to carry their programme out.[8] They were inhibited by an ideological barrier, which made them loath to sanction anything in peacetime which might be construed as meddling with the 'natural' workings of a private enterprise economy.

The housing programme was the most obvious casualty in the period of rapid decontrol after the war, but other programmes were affected in a less direct manner. After allowing the postwar boom to run its inflationary course for many months after the Armistice, the Government introduced a deflationary budget in April 1920 just when the boom was beginning to sag of its own accord. The result was to intensify an already rapidly deteriorating situation, and as a consequence the level of employment and industrial activity dropped with alarming rapidity. The deflationary policy introduced in 1920 administered the *coup de grâce* to what remained of the

Government's social programme. There were the drastic cuts in housing and educational expenditure mentioned above, and the Government washed its hands of responsibility for the coal and agricultural industries now that the collapse in world prices threatened it with heavy subsidy payments. To modern eyes government budgetary policy after the war seems singularly ill-timed, and it must have exacerbated what was in any case the extremely difficult problem of postwar readjustment. The Government had run a budget deficit in the immediate aftermath of war, thus intensifying the inflation which it should have been restraining, and it had begun its efforts to restore a surplus at precisely the time when the boom was already faltering. The result was to intensify the boom/slump cycle which characterized the world economy in the aftermath of war, and the violent swings of this cycle necessarily removed any hopes of implementing to the full the generous plans that had been made for social reconstruction. Certain measures did, however, survive this economic onslaught, and it will be as well to look briefly at these before examining the rationale behind the deflationary course upon which the Government embarked in April 1920.

Although the Addison programme of house construction largely failed, it did at least establish the principle of state intervention in the supply of cheap houses, and subsequent inter-war governments were able to carry on where Addison left off. In all, between 1919 and 1939 over 1 million houses were built by local authorities. As one writer has said: 'This was perhaps the most outstanding peacetime experiment in state intervention in this country in the provision of a necessity of life, which had formerly been supplied almost exclusively by independent private enterprise.'9 (It must be said, however, that the expansion of publicly provided housing was to some extent overshadowed by the great boom in private building that developed in the 1930s.)

Apart from housing, by far the most important legacy of the post war coalition Government in the social sphere was unemployment insurance. Social insurance in Britain had made a tentative start i Britain before the war. However, while the pre-war health insuranc scheme covered a very large slice of the working population—about 13 millions in fact—unemployment insurance had been much mor selective, covering only $2\frac{1}{4}$ million workers or one-sixth of the indus trial labour force. The number insured against unemployment wa increased in 1916, but it was the Unemployment Insurance Act of 1920 which transformed the position. Under this measure th number insured was raised to 11 million, and while this still le important groups outside—domestic servants and agricultural labourers, for instance—it was none the less a great step forward. It is a nice question as to whether the step would have been taken had it been realized at the time that Britain stood on the verge of a prolonged period of mass unemployment. However, the important point was that the state, having once embarked on a policy of near-universal insurance against unemployment, was obliged to maintain this commitment during the period of massive unemployment that ensued. In America, for example, things were very different, and the great crash of 1929 found the industrial workers of that country entirely unprotected against unemployment.

On the industrial relations front the record of the immediate post-war years was bleak indeed, with an unprecedented degree of conflict, but one institution created at this time did in fact survive and was later (at the time of the Second World War) to be introduced on a large scale. This was the Joint Industrial Council, recommended by the wartime Whitley Committee of the Ministry of Reconstruction. The formation of these Councils, representative of unions and management, was actively encouraged by the Government in a number of industries immediately after the war.[10] In the short term, however, their success was extremely limited. There were numerous reasons for this, but it was in any case useless to look for a stable and harmonious relationship between the two sides of industry at a time when violent fluctuations in the level of prices led to constant demands for readjustment in wage levels—upwards during the inflation of 1919–20 and downwards in the slump of 1921. Any improvement in the climate of industrial relations after the war would have needed, just as a basis for further development, a government able and willing to do something to control the more extreme fluctuations in domestic price and employment levels. Without this, talk about harmony in the industrial sphere was so much waste of time. In one respect, however, the immediate aftermath of war did see a permanent change for the better in the condition of the industrial wage earner, although this owed more to the direct actions of trade unions than to the Government. During the course of 1919 the unions were successful in achieving a reduction in the length of the working day without loss of wages. In most industries hours per day were reduced from nine or more to eight, and this gain proved to be permanent: it has been described by one author as 'perhaps the most valuable permanent gain from all the high hopes of postwar reconstruction.'[11]

The deflationary policy upon which the Government embarked

in 1920 had its origin in the recommendations of the Cunliffe Committee on Currency and Foreign Exchanges. The final report of this Committee appeared in December 1919. The Committee regarded an early return to the gold standard at the pre-war parity as a vital prerequisite to successful recovery from the effects of the war. Without the monetary stability implied by the gold standard, it was felt that the intricate fabric of world trade could not be successfully pieced together once more. The problem arose, however, not so much over the question of the restoration of the gold standard as such, as over the question of restoration at the pre-war parity of the pound to the dollar. The pound had greatly depreciated as against the dollar during the war and its immediate inflationary aftermath. In order to permit a return to gold at the pre-war parity the British price level would have to be drastically deflated. The Government accepted the viewpoint put forward in the Cunliffe Committee Report, and initiated in 1920 a sternly deflationary policy with the object of forcing down prices to a level at which the pre-war parity could be restored. The bank rate was raised, government expenditure was slashed, the budget was brought into balance, and the short-term debt and note issue reduced. The wisdom of this policy was questionable, to say the least. In 1920 the postwar boom broke, as we have seen, and a severe depression was ushered in. 1921 was one of the bleakest years in Britain in the whole inter-war period, with over 2 million men out of work. Deflation would hardly appear to us today to be an appropriate policy at such a time, but it was adhered to none the less. It was the orthodoxy of the age. The policy was justified on the grounds that the depression resulted from the dislocation of the world economy caused by the war. Recovery, it was argued, was only possible when currencies were once more placed on a sound basis, thus reviving confidence and with it world trading activity. The 'sound basis' was assumed to be the pre-war position, hence the single-minded pursuit of the pre-war parity.

In the period that followed 1920 the level of domestic prices, costs and wages was considerably reduced, but not far enough. The downward pressure on wages was strongly resisted by the trade unions, and the power of resistance of these bodies was perhaps strengthened by the existence of unemployment insurance, a factor weakening the deterrent effect of a high unemployment rate. On the side of capital cartel arrangements operated to make the downward movement of prices extremely sticky. Home costs, despite the great reductions that had taken place, remained at a level about 10 per cent too high None the less, in 1925 the return to the gold standard at pre-war parity was announced by Mr. Winston Churchill as Chancellor of the Exchequer. Britain's lead in the restoration of 'sound money' was followed by a large number of other countries, though not all of these returned to gold at the pre-war parity. The long-awaited return to gold did not, however, usher in an era of great prosperity for the British economy. Things had certainly been improving since the bleak year of 1921. Production had been restored to the pre-war level and the number of unemployed considerably reduced. In 1925, the year of the return to gold, world trade was back at its pre-war level, and it was to rise above this level in the years that followed. The last five years of the twenties were in fact the most prosperous the world was to know between the wars. Yet Britain shared in this prosperity less than some other nations. This does not mean that there was a depression in Britain in the later twenties. On the contrary, the current research being undertaken on this period tends to emphasize the substantial growth that took place.[12] But there were two striking features on the British economic scene that caused disquiet after 1925. In the first place there was the level of unemployment, which although lower than earlier in the decade, remained none the less much higher than the pre-war average. Secondly, there was the decline of Britain as an exporter, both in relative and absolute terms. These two features were of course related, in that it was in the export industries that unemployment was largely concentrated.

There were those at the time (and there have been many more since) who argued that the restoration of the gold standard at the pre-war parity, far from creating a necessary framework for expansion, in fact inhibited that expansion. J. M. Keynes (1883–1946), an economist whose epoch-making *General Theory* was to appear in 1936, argued that Mr. Churchill had overvalued the pound by 10 per cent as a result of the adoption of the pre-war parity. As a consequence of this, Keynes claimed that British exports would be rendered uncompetitive in international markets. In this situation he predicted that employers would be forced to embark upon a drastic campaign to reduce costs (and therefore wages) to a level at which they could once more compete with rivals abroad.[13] Given the strength of trade unionism in the export industries, and especially in the coal industry, such a campaign was likely to be fiercely contested. Demands for wage reductions in coal-mining did in fact produce a major crisis. Workers in other industries supported the miners in their resistance to cuts, fearing that if the employers' attack was successful in coal it would spread soon enough to other industries. The result was a nine-day general strike in May 1926. Viewed in terms of its immediate objectives the strike was a failure, for the employers succeeded in the end in enforcing drastic wage reductions upon the coal miners. However, the reductions in coal did not lead to any general lowering of wage levels throughout industry; to an extent therefore the strike may have been successful in deterring employers from a general assault on wages. The nature of this success needs to be qualified. If the pound was overvalued at the pre-war parity, the maintenance of existing wage levels was likely to mean the mainten-ance also of a high level of unemployment, and the percentage of insured workers out of work in fact remained at about 10 per cent for the remainder of the decade. Given the overvaluation of the pound, wage levels could be preserved only at the cost of mass unemployment.

In the above analysis the Government's foreign exchange policy appears as the villain of the piece. Yet some historians have ques-tioned whether the return to gold at the pre-war parity really made that much difference.[14] In the case of the coal industry it can be argued that it was the recovery of the German mines from the effects of the French occupation of the Ruhr that precipitated the coal crisis of 1925-6, rather than the return to gold. But beyond this there were in any case more profound, long-term, causes of the malaise in the British export industries. British exports were made up of products for which world demand was rising only slowly, if at all.[15] They were often products, such as cotton textiles, which newly developing countries were increasingly able to manufacture for themselves. Or they were products whose market was being eroded by technological change, as, of course, in the case of coal and some branches of engineering. The trend against these products was no new thing in the 1920s, it had been apparent before 1914. But the war had accelerated developments. It had forced primary producing countries, cut off by the impact of war from their usual suppliers of manufactures in Britain, to develop their own industries and move towards self-sufficiency or alternatively to buy from other countries closer at hand, such as Japan. The war also speeded up certain technological developments which affected the demand for British products. The postwar world was thus bound to be a difficult one for traditional British exports, although the reality of the situation was at first obscured by the re-stocking boom of 1919 and 1920. Even after the onset of mass unemployment in 1921 the real nature of the problem facing the country was not understood. The depression of the major export industries was regarded as a purely temporary phenomenon, a result of the uncertainty caused by the collapse of the continental currencies, and certain to be remedied once sound money was restored. Only after 1925 did the nation awake to the fact that her basic export industries were afflicted by a permanent contraction in demand. Recognition of this unwelcome fact was signalled by the introduction of the Government's industrial transference scheme, which aimed to move unemployed workers out of the older industries into newer lines of production.[16] It was gradually realized that far-reaching structural changes were required in British industry, entailing the running down of certain industries, and the expansion of others to take their place. The problem was especially acute for Britain because of the country's 'overcommitment' to the older lines of production.[17] Coal and textiles were sick industries in other countries besides Britain, but they absorbed a much smaller proportion of these countries' productive resources, and readjustment was consequently much easier. Quite simply Britain, for historical reasons, had too many eggs in one basket.

If the major cause of the heavy unemployment in Britain during the later twenties was this deep-seated structural problem, it may well be asked whether we need after all take much account of government monetary policy as a factor influencing the situation. Pre-war parity or no, would not the basic problem still remain? The need for structural changes in British industry was inescapable, and a more favourable exchange rate for British exporters would not have cured the problems of industries suffering under the impact of long-term shifts in world demand. However, it is possible that a different policy might well have rendered the task of readjustment easier than in fact proved to be the case. If the pound had been devalued the *newer* industries would have found it easier to expand, both in the home market (because competing imports would have been dearer) and by increasing exports. As it was the price of British manufactures was too high relative to foreign prices, and the development of new lines of production to compensate for the declining sectors was thus correspondingly more difficult.[18]

Unemployment has given the twenties a sombre image, but the postwar decade was not in its later stages depressed in the strict sense of the term. Although as we have seen exports declined, and a tenth of the nation's labour force was idle, industrial production rose well above the level of 1913. Such a situation was made possible by improved productivity in industry and by the development of markets at home. In the period 1924–9 the economy was growing at a rate faster than in Edwardian times, and at approximately the same pace as in the second half of the nineteenth century.[19] It was thus not so gloomy a picture. One factor behind the process of growth was the impact of new technology. Innovations, pioneered before the war, were now being introduced on a considerable scale, and were, among other things, beginning to make possible the marketing of 'high-cost' consumer durables on the home market. Motor-cars form a good example.

Improvements of the product were continuous—better carburettors, more efficient combustion chambers, self starters, windscreen wipers—and, just as important, the techniques of production were steadily improved so that costs fell and better cars were made cheaper. A twelve-horsepower Austin in 1922 cost £450–£490: in 1928 the same car, but bigger, faster, more economical, more reliable, more comfortable and more refined, cost £325–£335. This was made possible by better engineering, larger outputs and flow production.[20]

Another important area of innovation and development in the twenties was the electrical products industry, and the future prospects of this industry were immensely strengthened by the passing in 1926 of the Electricity (Supply) Act which authorized the construction of a national grid system. Electrical products, automobiles, synthetic fibres—these were to be very much the growth industries of the twentieth century. Britain's stake in the manufacture of products such as these had been very limited at the beginning of the postwar decade, but by its end the position had changed considerably. Production of cars, for instance, had more than trebled. Furthermore, the foundations had been laid for a much more rapid expansion in these sectors in the 1930s. It was true, of course, that the development of new techniques and products and the greater attention paid to realizing the potentialities of the domestic market had not been on a scale sufficient to wipe out the unemployment derived from the stagnating or declining sectors. As we have seen above, the Government's foreign exchange policy may well have been an inhibiting factor here. But far-reaching structural change was none the less under way. In the phrase of a recent writer on the period, the twenties may be regarded as 'a watershed between the old industrial regime of the pre-1914 era and the new industrial economy of the post-1945 period'.[21]

World Depression and Recovery

For the world as a whole the later twenties were in the main years of optimism and hope. The world economic system appeared to have recovered from the dislocation caused by the war. Yet appearances proved to be deceptive, for there lurked beneath the surface fundamental instabilities, instabilities which were shortly to plunge the world into the most severe and prolonged depression of modern times.[22]

One of the most important problems concerned the primary producing countries. During the war agricultural production had contracted in Europe and expanded outside that continent. When the war was over the non-European output continued to expand, while inside Europe production was gradually restored to pre-war levels. By 1925 the restored European agriculture combined with the greatly expanded overseas output to bring about a situation of serious overproduction. The position was worsened by two other factors. Firstly, on the supply side, improved technology resulted in an increased yield per acre and a reduction of costs. Secondly, on the demand side, the population growth of the industrial countries (which were of course heavy consumers of primary products) began to slow down. The combination of the above factors seriously depressed prices, and, as if this was not enough, an exceptionally good harvest in 1928 intensified the glut of foodstuffs on the world market. Now this situation had serious implications for the economies of primary producing countries, and therefore for the world at large. In the first place, of course, the falling incomes of these countries reduced their capacity to purchase manufactured goods, and this affected the prosperity of industrial producers. Secondly, there was the heavy indebtedness of the primary producers. Placed in a precarious situation by the prevailing glut these countries, rather than adopt deflationary policies, went in for heavy borrowing from overseas in order to finance their mounting stocks. In this way agricultural producers became heavily reliant upon continued injections of foreign capital. Here then was one major area of instability in the world economy of the later 1920s.

A further source of instability was to be found in the international financial structure of the twenties. After 1925, when numbers of countries returned to the gold standard, it might have seemed as if the period of postwar dislocation was ended. But the new gold standard was, in many cases, not the same as of old: it was a gold exchange standard. This meant that a number of countries held as reserves foreign exchange in addition to or instead of gold. This placed a strain on the world's two major financial centres, New York and London, for they needed to hold sufficient gold both to meet their own needs and to cover the reserves of countries on the exchange standard. London, being continually threatened with gold losses as a result of the overvaluation of the currency, was not equal to this strain, and, as events were quickly to show, was not able to withstand any serious loss of confidence. Here then was one source of instability under the new arrangements. There was another also. A number of countries on the gold-exchange standard accumulated their reserves through short-term loans rather than through an export surplus. This placed them in a highly vulnerable position, for a loss of confidence was liable to result in the withdrawal of the loans, thus depleting their reserves and forcing them off the standard. It thus appears that the damage done by the war to international currency arrangements had not been satisfactorily repaired.

There remains one further point to be made, on the subject of international lending. Before the war London had been the focal point of the world's financial system, and it was from London that capital flowed overseas to finance the development of international trade. After the war was over the City imagined that it could resume its former role, and indeed overseas lending did take place on a considerable scale in the twenties. But the country no longer had a sufficient surplus on current account to make such a policy viable, and the City was reduced to the expedient of attracting short-term funds to London in order to provide the wherewithal for large-scale overseas loans. This latter practice was in itself to prove a serious source of instability, as events were to show in 1931. The important point to notice, however, is the eclipse of London as the world's chief financial centre. The weakness of her trading position and her loss of overseas capital assets as a result of the war had combined to bring about this situation. But the void left by the demise of London had to be filled, and it was natural that New York, as the hub of the world's most powerful economy, should fill it. Yet the shift of the centre of gravity of financial power from one side of the Atlantic to the other almost certainly decreased the stability of the world economy. It was not that the United States did not lend heavily overseas; this she certainly did. But whereas Britain in her heyday had pursued a policy of free trade, admitting imports, and thereby allowing interest payments by debtor nations to be made easily, America tended towards protection which had, of course, the reverse effect. Furthermore, owing to inexperience a good deal of American lending was of a somewhat unfortunate character. This was particularly true in the case of loans to Germany, a country which indulged in borrowing on a massive scale in the twenties. Loans made to Germany did little to enhance that country's capacity to export and therefore make repayment, being diverted instead to other uses, and interest payments were only kept up by resort to further borrowing from overseas. In this respect, as in so many others, the world economy lived dangerously.

In the last resort, the precarious prosperity of the 1920s hinged upon one factor: the continuance of the great American boom. The boom in the United States had begun in 1922. To many it seemed as though it would continue indefinitely. And so long as it did the instabilities which have been dealt with above could be glossed over. As long as America continued to expand and continued to lend these things did not matter. But in 1929 the great boom in the United States came to an end. The reasons for its collapse cannot be our concern in this chapter; suffice it to say that they were purely domestic in character. However, if the collapse was caused by purely internal factors, its consequences externally were massive indeed. 'In 1929 the U.S.A. made available to the rest of the world through imports and investments the sum of 7,400 million dollars; this sum contracted in 1932 by 5,000 million dollars to as little as 32 per cent of what was made available in 1929. It is hardly necessary to look much further for the causes of world-wide depression.'[23]

In view of the instabilities mentioned above the impact of the American slump was far more serious than it would otherwise have been. Primary producing countries were, of course, among the first to be seriously affected. The drying up of American loans left them with the problem of how to meet their interest payments. They were forced severely to restrict their imports and expand their exports. This, however, inevitably had the result of depressing prices still further. In the end many were forced to devalue, yet this in itself had the effect of further reducing the flow of capital. The rapidly deteriorating position of these countries reacted in its turn upon industrial producers, whose exports were affected by the falling incomes of agrarian nations and their resort to import restrictions. In a world where economic interdependence was so highly developed difficulties in one sector were inexorably passed on to others, and so the level of economic activity spiralled downwards. Europe, so recently the victim of the disruption of war, was especially vulnerable. The cessation of American lending produced a major financial crisis. Beginning with the failure of the great Credit Anstalt Bank in Austria, the crisis quickly spread to Germany, the country which above all others had been dependent on American capital. Nor was London immune. Some of the weaknesses of the City's position have already been mentioned, and in 1931 these came home to roost. The prevailing atmosphere of panic had affected confidence in

London, and there began a rush on gold which resulted in a loss of a quarter of the country's gold reserves in the space of three weeks. Despite the formation of a coalition government to deal with the crisis, Britain was none the less forced to abandon the gold standard in September 1931.

For Britain above all nations the great depression which began in 1929 represented the ending of an era. It was not that Britain herself was the worst hit by the slump (America and Germany perhaps suffered most among nations), indeed in a *relative* sense the impact of the slump in this country was mild as we shall see below. The point is that the great depression ended finally the attempts that had been made to restore the pre-war international economic order. Faced by disaster, the nations of the world, Britain included, now turned in upon themselves. The world economy was shattered and each country now sought to insulate itself as far as possible from external influences. They shored up their economies with a battery of trade and currency restrictions—tariffs, quotas, exchange controls.[24] There was to be no return in the thirties to the levels of international trade and lending characteristic of the pre-depression period. The break with the past was greatest in the case of Britain because Britain more than any other nation had in the past allowed herself to become heavily dependent on world trade. She had furthermore geared her financial institutions to meeting the requirements of borrowers from overseas. Now all this was changed. The country withdrew from its earlier free trade position, instituting heavy tariffs in 1931 and virtually prohibiting the foreign borrowing of long-term capital in the same year. At the Ottawa conference in the following year a system of imperial preference was inaugurated, something that had been impossible in the past when free trade policies prevailed. Britain also embarked on a policy of providing subsidies for her industries. The nineteenth-century economic order was now well and truly buried.

The catastrophe that overtook the world in 1929 manifested itself in the industrial nations in a massive increase in the level of unemployment. The financial crisis which spread outwards from Wall Street to Vienna, Berlin, and London may have seemed remote and unintelligible to the mass of industrial workers, but the 'breadlines' of the unemployed were an all too tangible sign that things had taken a drastic turn for the worse. In Britain unemployment was less than in America and Germany; furthermore there existed in this country from the beginning some form of provision for those out of work. It was a grim experience none the less. Of course unemployment had been high in Britain even before the onset of the depression. In the years 1927–9 between 9 and 10 per cent of insured workers had been out of work. After the crash in the United States the numbers out of work in this country gradually mounted, and the peak was reached in August 1932, when 23 per cent were without work. Including those outside the insurance scheme, there were probably $3\frac{1}{2}$ million unemployed at this time.

As experienced by Britain, the great depression was essentially a phenomenon imported from the outside world: it did not derive from the collapse of a domestic boom. What happened was that the slump in America and among the primary producers transmitted itself to Britain through a fall in the demand for our exports. These, of course, had been scarcely buoyant before 1929. The further contraction in demand reduced them to a very low ebb and, of course, the fall in production in the export sector affected other areas of the economy. Industrial production fell by about 11 per cent between 1929 and 1932. But if the causes of the depression were external in origin, it is equally certain that recovery was initiated, and sustained, by internal factors. The recovery was in fact fairly rapid. Industrial production had ceased to contract by the third quarter of 1932, and a steady upward rise began in 1933. By 1935 business activity had surpassed the pre-depression level, though unemployment still remained high. What were the internal influences at work in this revival? This is necessarily a complex matter, and has indeed been the subject of a recent full-scale study.[25]

The most important single factor present in the situation was the position of the so-called new industries. These were the industries, mentioned in the previous section, which arose out of technological developments in the late nineteenth and early twentieth centuries: their products included such items as motor-cars, cycles, aircraft, rubber tyres, electrical machinery and household appliances, radios, and rayon and other synthetic fibres. It is meaningful to group all these products together because the industries involved in their manufacture were to a large extent interrelated.[26] Some fairly obvious examples of this spring to mind: motor-cars and rubber, radio and plastics, electrical supply and household appliances. The industries arose out of a common pool of innovations pioneered around the turn of the century, and in their growth they tended to feed upon each other. As a group, however, their pattern of growth tended to vary as between different industrial countries, and it is at this point that their significance for Britain's recovery becomes apparent. In some nations, as in America especially, these new industries made rapid headway in the early years of the twentieth century so that by the end of the twenties they accounted for a very considerable share of total industrial production. In Britain this was not the case. It was only in the twenties that these industries began to make their presence felt, and while great strides were made, as we noted in the previous section, the output of the new industries at the end of the decade still remained small in relation to the total. What has been called Britain's 'overcommitment' to an industrial structure based on nineteenth-century technology had inevitably acted as a drag on development in the newer spheres.[27] None the less, by the end of the twenties the new industries had progressed sufficiently to be on the verge of a period of great expansion.

It might have been expected that the onset of the world slump would have cut short this expansion. Instead the reverse happened, for the new industries supplied an impetus sufficient to carry the British economy out of the trough. How could this have happened, given the fact that a depression means falling income and therefore, one might presume, falling purchases? The presumption is, however, false. A fall in total income need not mean a fall in total consumption, since the share taken by consumption may rise. Such an increase in the aggregate propensity to consume may result, for instance, from transfers of income as between different sections of the population. Certainly in Britain the level of aggregate consumption tended to remain steady in the depression. This may reflect in part the transfer of income away from upper income groups (whose propensity to consume was low) to wage earners and lower-paid salary earners (whose propensity to consume was high). This transfer resulted from the fact that during the slump prices (and therefore business profits) declined faster than money wages. Because prices fell faster than wages, the latter rose in real terms, thus placing more purchasing power in the hands of wage earners. Of course against this gain for those in work must be set the loss of earnings of the great numbers thrown out of employment. However, those out of work received unemployment benefit, paid by the government, and all of this necessarily went into consumption. The preceding argument must be seen in the context of improving terms of trade, resulting from the fall in the prices of primary products, for this boosted the real income of those wage earners both in and out of work. In the main, however, the effect of the above developments was to benefit the upper stratum of wage earners and the lower-paid salary workers at the expense of the middle classes and the unemployed.

A stable aggregate level of consumption obviously operated to moderate the impact of the slump, but it went further than this, because a stable aggregate was made up of rising expenditure on some commodities and declining expenditure on others. It is at this point that the new industries emerge as crucial. They had reached a stage at which they were able to put on the market a wide range of relatively cheap durable consumer goods which were attractive to those groups whose purchasing power had been boosted during the depression. Radios were a good example of this. Until the late twenties radio sets were for the most part assembled by people in their own homes; manufactured sets were too costly. However, the introduction of mass production methods at the end of the decade greatly altered the situation. A relatively new, attractive, durable consumer good was now brought within the reach of a large sector of the population. Sales rocketed, and the number of radio-licence holders increased by 973,000 in 1930–1 alone.[28] What was true of radios was true of other consumer durables to a slightly lesser extent. The demand for these goods was reinforced by long-term trends in population growth. The rate of population growth fell off between the wars, and the size of families tended to be reduced. Fewer children made possible a reallocation of family income. Less expenditure was needed on food and clothing, more could be devoted to the purchase of luxury articles, and in this connection the new consumer durables were of the greatest significance.

The expanding demand for the products of twentieth-century technology was a major factor in Britain's recovery. Rising demand in this sector induced new investment in key sectors of the economy such as steel and engineering. It remains to consider the role played by the building industry in lifting Britain out of the depression, for the 1930s witnessed a private housing boom of very considerable dimensions. House building revived earlier than most other activities (in 1931), and surged forward after 1932. Furthermore, because of the sheer size of the industry, the fact of an early revival and subsequent rapid progress obviously had important stimulating effects upon the rest of the economy. It seems, however, that it would be wrong to seek to explain the recovery of the thirties as something springing directly from the boom in house construction. It has been argued that it is more useful to see the roles of house building and the mass production industries as being complementary.[29] While factors such as cheap money and the expansion of building societies played an important part in the housing boom, the attractiveness of new houses to potential buyers derived from modern industrial developments. The motor-car made possible the location of houses in areas at some distance from centres of employment. The development of electricity supply made possible new forms of lighting, heating, and household equipment (vacuum cleaners, for example). Another form of the relationship between housing and the mass-production industries arose from the fact that the latter tended to develop in the Midlands and the South, away from the older centres of production in the North, and this of course set up a demand for new housing. Finally, the booms in house construction and in consumer durables responded to the same stimuli, such as changes in population structure and in purchasing power. Taken together, the expansion in the newer industries and in house building seem to have been the main factor in lifting Britain out of the slump. Expansion in these areas owed relatively little to government policy, although the introduction of cheap money and protectionist policies were not without some effect. One thing about the slump and recovery in Britain is certainly clear, namely, that while the depression was caused by external factors, the recovery was domestically based. Recovery in fact owed everything to the expansion of demand at home.

How complete was the recovery from the slump? Business activity certainly rose consistently from 1932 to 1937 and after a short recession began to move upwards again in the autumn of 1938. 1937 was the peak year of the thirties, and in that year industrial production had reached a level one-third higher than at the previous peak of 1929. Recovery then was substantial, yet in one respect at any rate it seemed to many to be incomplete. While the level of unemployment was reduced substantially during the thirties, falling from 22·1 per cent in 1932 to 10·8 per cent in 1937, it remained well above the pre-war average throughout the decade. In effect 10 per cent was the best that the thirties could do, and this represented well over 1 million unemployed. The resemblance to the previous decade was marked and in the peak years of both (i.e. 1929 and 1937) the level of unemployment was roughly the same.

It has been argued that the unemployment remaining in 1937 was not of a cyclical kind, being rather technological or structural in character, and that it does not therefore detract from the success and vigour of Britain's recovery from the slump.[30] Thus the newer industries were more capital intensive than the old, and were not able to absorb all the labour shed by the latter. Furthermore, productivity was rising in new and old alike, so that total output grew much faster than employment. Then there was the immobility factor. The expanding sectors of the economy in the 1930s were mainly concentrated in the Midlands and South, away from the coalfields where the bulk of the industrial labour force had been located in the past. It can be argued that inadequate mobility from declining to expanding regions boosted the unemployment rate; certainly rates were much higher in the older industrial regions of the North and Wales than they were in the Midlands and South. Against this, however, is the fact that unemployment was by no means inconsiderable even in expanding areas and industries. Thus in 1937, at the peak of the recovery, London, the South-east, and the Midlands had unemployment rates of 6·3, 6·7, and 7·2 per cent respectively. These were the most prosperous regions in the country, yet their unemployment levels had not been reduced below the pre-war *average* of about 6 per cent. Regional figures, of course, reflect the industrial composition of the area, and if unemployment in particular industries is considered a similar picture emerges. While rates were highest in the contracting industries, they were by no means negligible in expanding ones. Unemployment rates in six expanding industries in 1937 were as follows: building, 13·8; motor vehicles, 4·8; electrical engineering, 3·1; food industries, 12·4; hotel, services, etc., 14·2; distributive trades, 8·8.[31] In twelve major growth industries the numbers unemployed in 1937 were greater than at the previous peak of 1929, although owing to increases in the labour force the actual rates of unemployment may not have changed or may even have declined. Thus in view of the considerable amount of unemployment even in growth sectors it may be questioned whether immobility of labour was really a major source of the heavy unemployment in the 1930s.[32] Had there been widespread shortages in expanding sectors the case would of course be different. As it was such shortages were felt only in certain skilled occupations. Returning to the question of the extent of the recovery from the slump, it seems that while it can be argued that recovery was complete, this must certainly not be taken to imply that Britain's economic performance in the thirties was in some way superior to that of the twenties. The rate of unemployment in 1929 and 1937 was almost identical, as we have seen, furthermore the overall growth rate of the economy was no higher in the thirties than it had been in the twenties. Certainly productivity in manufacturing accelerated in the thirties, but against this must be set a deceleration in most other sectors.[33]

In the above paragraphs the unemployment problem has been seen primarily in economic terms, but it has of course another dimension. It was a social evil of the greatest magnitude. Viewed

from this angle the unemployment problem in the thirties was something very different from what it had been in the twenties. In the
twenties there was relatively little long-term unemployment. Although during that decade one man in ten had been continuously
out of work there was 'no considerable section of the population
which was permanently "tenth man" '.[34] Thus in September 1929
less than 5 per cent of the unemployed had been continuously out of
work for a year or more. This 5 per cent was largely concentrated in
one industry—coal—and outside of that there were only 15,000
long-term unemployed in the country. The onset of the great
depression brought a profound change. By the beginning of 1932
the number of long unemployed (more than a year) had passed the
300,000 mark, and it continued to rise even when the general tide of
unemployment had begun to recede. Despite the general improvement in the employment situation in the mid-1930s the number of
long-term unemployed remained obstinately high: in 1936 it was
still around the 300,000 mark—or one-quarter of the total out of
work—and it remained very high until the outbreak of war. Long
unemployment as might be expected was a problem that was very
unevenly distributed over the country, and it was in the most
depressed regions that the number of long-term unemployed bore
the highest proportion to the total. In Wales in 1937 nearly two out
of every five persons unemployed had been out of work for more
than a year. It was this long unemployment that gave to the chronically depressed areas their sadness. Here there were thousands of
workmen who had been out of work for years and knew that they
would almost certainly never work again. It was a tragedy that
afflicted older men in particular. The extent of long unemployment
could reach extraordinary proportions. In Crook, in Durham, 71 per
cent had had no work for five years or more. This was in 1936.

How did this problem affect people? Long unemployed persons
tended to lose the capacity for sustained effort and their physiques
deteriorated. Furthermore, there can be no doubt that prolonged
unemployment brought real privation to the worker and his family.
They suffered from malnutrition and the health of the children was
naturally affected adversely. Also the poverty they endured degraded
the quality of their life. George Orwell has described the wretched
conditions in Wigan where unemployed miners were forced to
scrabble about on the coal tips for waste coal, coal that they could not
afford to buy.[35] Finally, there was the hopelessness that sprang from
the sense of being redundant, surplus to society's needs, merely a
burden on the rates. For men who had once been proud of their

skills, for whom work had been the central feature of their life, such a fate could be heartbreaking. Some became bitter against the society which permitted them to exist in idleness, others determined to make the best of things—they cultivated their allotments, kept their poultry, and worked on schemes to improve the amenity of their areas. This latter reaction was perhaps most typical in Durham. An oldish man in Crook who occupied himself working on local amenity schemes told an observer: 'I like to be tired. Before I had this, I used to go out and lie in the sun and come back again and do a thing or two and not know whether I was tired. Now I can come in and smoke my pipe and have my bit of grub and go to sleep.'[36]

Long unemployment was at its worst in the chronically depressed areas, but it existed everywhere in the thirties. There were 10,500 long unemployed even in London in 1937, though of course this was small in relation to the total unemployed of 137,000. But unemployment in more prosperous areas could bring misery of a kind not found in the depressed localities. Because unemployment did not dominate the area, men out of work sometimes became ashamed of their position. They concealed their unemployment from their neighbours and isolated themselves from the rest of the community. There was a feeling here that unemployment indicated failure.

Long unemployment, and indeed mass unemployment as a whole, was a problem that was not solved during the inter-war years. It required for its solution a drastic reappraisal of the role of government in the economy. In the two inter-war decades the state accepted no responsibility for the maintenance of full employment, and the demand for labour was left to find its own level. The only way forward lay in a government undertaking to meet any deficiency in the total demand for labour by a programme of public spending, financed if necessary by a budget deficit. Of course, state intervention with the object of generating sufficient total expenditure to absorb total labour supply would not of itself wipe out all unemployment because of obstacles to labour mobility. But since it may be argued that immobility was not the major source of mass unemployment, it may also be presumed that intervention of this kind would have gone a long way to solve the problem.[37] Public spending as a cure for unemployment was not, however, seen as a feasible policy by inter-war governments, entailing as it did the likelihood of an unbalanced budget. Such a policy was too unorthodox for governments which were not in the last resort prepared to regard unemployment as *the* problem, overriding all others, and demanding urgent and drastic measures for its cure.[38] Not until the work of J. M.

Keynes had percolated into government departments, providing a theoretical justification for policies hitherto considered to be rash and ill-conceived, was the state willing to undertake responsibility for the maintenance of full employment. But this happened during the Second World War. Before 1939 governments contented themselves with providing a subsistence for those out of work while making half-hearted efforts to encourage the movement of industry into the hardest hit regions—designated after 1934 as special areas.

Prolonged mass unemployment inevitably darkens the image one has of the inter-war years. But to do the period justice it must be said that this was by no means a stagnant episode in our history. In whatever light they are viewed it remains true that the two inter-war decades did profoundly modify the structure of the British economy and society. During this period the economy was growing at the same rate as in the later nineteenth century, and this growth in the inter-war years involved substantial changes in the nation's economic structure. Foreign trade became less important and the industries that had been heavily dependent upon it in the past tended to stagnate or decline. In their place there developed the more modern mass production industries, which were essentially oriented towards the home market. This shift in relative importance among British industries created in its turn new regional disparities as the manufactures of the Midlands and South-east prospered while those of the North and the West decayed. As a result some areas, such as the counties around London, increased their populations by well over half, while others, like the counties of Glamorgan and Monmouth, actually fell in numbers. Growth also brought significant changes in occupational structure, as the numbers of those in white-collar occupations expanded relatively to those employed in manual work. So far as Britain is concerned it is in the thirties that one gets the first glimpses of the age of high mass consumption. It had not yet arrived, but it was clearly foreshadowed. There were the cars, filling stations, new style factories, motor-coaches, wireless sets, cinemas, dance halls, classless ready-made clothes, household gadgets, and hire purchase. Many of the great industrial giants of the post-1945 world first appear in their modern guise in the twenties and thirties: I.C.I., Unilever, Vickers Armstrong, Guest, Keen and Nettlefold, and so on.[39]

There is, however, one sphere in which the legacy of the inter-war years is especially apparent—housing. In twenty years over 4 million new houses were built in Britain by private and public enterprise. This amounted to about one-third of the total number existing in

1939.[40] In most areas of Britain today one does not have to look very far to see evidence of this great housing boom. Our towns and cities are ringed by acre upon acre of semi-detached houses dating from the inter-war years, and in addition to this private suburban development there are also the vast municipal housing estates. Council housing and sprawling middle-class suburbia, these were the characteristic products of inter-war Britain. They serve to remind us that this was in fact a time of improving living standards and amenities, for the majority who were in employment. For the minority who were not, particularly for those who were relegated to the human scrap heap of the long-term unemployed, the period was frankly tragic.

The Second World War

Britain attained, as we have seen, a reasonable level of prosperity in the later thirties. In a sense, however, it was an unreal prosperity in that it was achieved in the midst of a rapidly deteriorating international situation. The thirties were allowed to pass by without thought for the future, without thought for the day when a re-armed Germany would be ready to take on her conquerors of 1918. The British in the interests of a quiet life deceived themselves as to the nature and intent of the Nazi regime that had taken power in 1933. Only towards the end of the decade was serious thought given to rearmament, and meanwhile the Nazis were allowed to mop up the Rhineland, Austria, and Czechoslovakia, with all the strategic advantages that possession of these territories gave. Because resistance to the Fascists was put off so long, it was all the harder to undertake in the end. Even when war was finally declared, in September 1939, the nation deluded itself as to the real nature of the sacrifices that would be required for victory. Certainly the Government was more realistic than its predecessor of 1914 had been in appreciating the need for drastic economic controls, but it considered the country immune from direct attack and was content to plan for a relatively leisurely expansion of munitions production which would give Britain superiority over Germany in three years' time.[41] The fall of France in 1940 changed all this. It made it abundantly clear that the nation faced nothing less than a struggle for survival, and that nothing short of total commitment to the war effort would suffice. The normal course of the country's economic development was brought to a halt.

The total commitment that was required to secure victory was certainly forthcoming. The economy was geared by the state to this one single end; almost everything else was sacrificed. It was a remarkable fact that the British economy was subjected to a greater degree of state supervision and control than was the case with totalitarian Nazi Germany.[42] Control over the economy was exercised not so much by direct government takeovers of private enterprises as by indirect methods, above all by the allocation of raw materials and labour. As the war effort got under way it became clear that it was manpower that constituted the limiting factor (the unemployment of the thirties was quickly eliminated). This remained so even after the Government took in 1941 the unprecedented step of conscripting women. Labour being the scarce factor, its allocation became the principal method by which the Government controlled the balance of the economy. A system of manpower budgeting was evolved, and by the end of the war these budgets had become 'the main force in determining every part of the war effort from the number of heavy bombers raiding Germany to the size of the clothing ration'.[43] Of course central allocation of manpower was reinforced by control over the use of raw materials. In allocating labour and scarce resources there were three broad sectors to be considered: 'the Services, industry working for the Services, and everything else'.[44] 'Everything else' came last on the list. Consumption was cut back ruthlessly and living standards dropped. Food and clothing were rationed, and production of many goods curtailed. Many consumer goods were only manufactured according to standardized 'utility' specifications. Inevitably there were scarcities of basic items. There were, of course, limits to the cutback in non-essentials. The maintenance of morale required some concessions, as for instance in the continuance of tobacco supplies, horse-racing, and cinema shows. None the less, the cut in living standards was very considerable.

While most peacetime industries were forced to contract there were two which were greatly expanded—agriculture and engineering. Both were, of course, closely related to the war effort. By increasing home production of food much valuable shipping space could be saved. The area under arable cultivation was raised from about 12 million to 18 million acres. Hand-in-hand with this increase in acreage went the wholesale mechanization of British farms, the number of tractors, for example, increasing from 56,000 to 203,000 during the war years.[45] The engineering industry was central to the production of war materials and was expanded in all its branches. New methods of mass production and design and quality control were introduced. The industry was also affected by the large-scale deployment of scientists on problems of war production. The results achieved in terms of output of aircraft, tanks, lorries, and ships were remarkable. Production of aircraft, for example, rose from 8,000 in 1939 to over 26,000 in 1943 and 1944, and this underestimates the achievement as it takes no account of the greater complexity and weight of the finished product.[46]

Not the least important aspect of war-time economic controls was the financial. By distorting the normal pattern of production the war-time economy generated, as in 1914–18, serious inflationary pressures, and unless controlled these pressures could have had a disastrous impact upon industrial relations and civilian morale generally. By a variety of means, however, the rise in the cost of living was limited to less than 50 per cent. Key items were subsidized, price controls and rationing were introduced, and spending power was cut back by high levels of taxation and the mobilization of savings. In all this the government made use of the new methods of economic analysis associated with the name of Keynes. Keynes and other prominent economists were in fact brought into the Treasury in 1940, after the shocks of that summer had created an appetite for new and radical thinking. The budget introduced by Sir Kingsley Wood (1881–1943) in April 1941 was the first to reflect the new approach. The level of government spending was now related to the level of spending in the economy as a whole, rather than being simply assessed against the government's revenue. The budget ceased to be an exercise in balancing government income against expenditure, and became instead an instrument for influencing the level of activity in the whole economy. This new approach, conceived in national income terms, was to have great significance not merely in the war-time emergency, but in the postwar world that was to follow.[47]

Despite the total commitment to the war effort it was a feature of the Second World War that thought was given at an early stage to the problems and possibilities of postwar reconstruction. As the official historians of the war economy point out, however, there was a sense in which plans for reconstruction may be regarded as themselves being an integral part of the war effort.[48] The conflict required as we have seen very real sacrifices by the entire population. Such sacrifices were willingly borne because it was assumed that at the end of the day victory would make possible a better and more just society. People expected the Government to make preparations to ensure that this aspiration would be realized. The proposals which perhaps as much as any others caught the imagination of the war-time public were those contained in Sir William Beveridge's (1879–1959) report on *Social Insurance and Allied Services*, which appeared in 1942. The Report proposed to erect a comprehensive system of social security, making provision for unemployment, sickness, disability, accident, old age, and most other eventualities. It also assumed that a comprehensive health service would be established, available to all. The Report in short took all the piecemeal welfare schemes that had been enacted in the previous half-century and welded them into a unified and intelligible whole which covered everybody. The Report was a best-seller at the time of its publication and became, of course, the foundation upon which the postwar Welfare State was subsequently erected. Two years later Beveridge produced another report, *Full Employment in a Free Society*, in which it was shown how the state might regulate the level of economic activity in such a way as to insure full employment. The Report naturally drew heavily on Keynesian economic analysis. Since unemployment had been the principal curse of the inter-war years, the attention given to the problem was not surprising, and in the same year as Beveridge's Report on the subject (1944) the Government issued its own *Full Employment White Paper*, pledging itself to maintain the level of employment at a high level. A revolution had been accomplished in people's understanding of the potential role of government in the economy. Numerous other proposals relating to postwar reconstruction were put forward and so far as education was concerned plans were actually translated into legislation before the peace. The 1944 Education Act made secondary education free to all and raised the leaving age.

The planners of the postwar world recognized that it was not sufficient to think in purely national terms. The inter-war period offered evidence enough of the consequences that followed failure to restore the world economy from the ravages of war. Thus, beginning in 1941, the British and American governments gave consideration to the question of international economic co-operation in peacetime. There was this time no question of a desire to restore the pre-war situation, such as had characterized the post-1918 period. The economic nationalism of the 1930s was not a climate to which people wished to return. One of the factors that had led to the disastrous downturn of international trade after 1929 had been the trade restrictions imposed by countries suffering from balance of payments difficulties. The reserves of such countries had not been sufficient to enable them to weather the crisis without resort to restrictive measures. Proposals were therefore put forward during the war aimed at creating an international body which would provide credit to nations in payments difficulties. The outcome of these proposals was the agreement, reached at the Bretton Woods conference in 1944, which set up an International Monetary Fund. The I.M.F. was only concerned with short-term credits, but the nations involved in the Bretton Woods conference considered also the possibility of setting up a fund to provide longer term capital. Such an institution was in fact set up in 1946. It was known as the International Bank for Reconstruction and Development, or World Bank. The question of co-operation in removing restrictions on trade was also discussed during the war, although in the event it was not until 1947 that a General Agreement on Tariffs and Trade (G.A.T.T.) was reached. It was signed by twenty-three countries.[49]

The consideration given to postwar reconstruction, both nationally and internationally, kept alive the hope that the effort involved in winning the war would not be in vain. But there could be no denying the cost of victory for Britain. Everything had been sacrificed to this end. We have seen how living standards were cut back, but this was only part of the cost. The stock of capital in Britain was allowed to run down, as resources normally available for replacement and upkeep were diverted to other uses. Britain in fact began to consume her capital. Annual net non-war capital formation in the United Kingdom fell from 5 per cent of net national income in 1938 to −12 per cent in 1940–5. The above figures make allowance for the expansion in agriculture and engineering and they represent, as one historian has written, 'a staggering cumulative total of neglect, decline and loss of efficiency in many vital industries and services'.[50] The railway and coal industries in particular were badly hit. All this loss was, of course, in addition to the direct damage caused by bombing. Then there were our foreign assets. The raw materials necessary for the war effort had to be paid for, and although the lend-lease arrangement with the U.S.A. introduced in 1941 was of tremendous assistance, in that it postponed payment for the duration of the war, not all our requirements could be obtained through lend-lease. Britain was thus obliged to sell many of her foreign capital assets, deplete her reserves, and of course run into debt. 'The final result was that Britain emerged from the war having sold over £1,100 million of capital assets, reduced her gold and dollar reserves by £150 million, and increased her external debt by almost £3,000 million.'[51] Finally there were our exports. Lend-lease relieved Britain from having to try to pay for her massive imports by a dollar-earning export drive, so that production for export was cut right back to make room for war production. By 1944 the volume of British exports was less than one-third what it had been in 1938.

In all these ways long-term considerations were sacrificed in the interests of the immediate task of military victory. The task of re-capturing export markets, replenishing the stock of capital, repaying debts, and at the same time restoring and improving upon pre-war living standards once peace returned was a daunting one indeed. America by contrast emerged from the war stronger than before. Her living standards, capital formation, and foreign trade had been unimpaired; had in fact expanded. There was indeed a parallel between the situation of the U.S.A. at the close of the Second World War and the situation of the United Kingdom over a hundred years before, at the close of the Napoleonic wars. The official historians of the British war economy drew attention to this parallel in their closing paragraphs.

Despite all the contrasts of technology and of economic magnitude between the wars of the Napoleonic Age and those of the twentieth century, there are some striking parallels between the situation of the United Kingdom in the earlier age and the situation of the United States in the later one. Each of these two countries, in its own fortunate time, was able to use the expansion of its exports as an instrument of war; each found itself, at the conclusion of war, in some degree compensated for its efforts and sacrifices by an immense enhancement of its comparative economic strength among the nations. But the United Kingdom in the twentieth century found itself in quite the opposite situation. The nation's struggle after the Second World War to overcome the con-sequences of an effort which had so heavily overtaxed its economic strength was bound to be a long one.[52]

NOTES

[1] W. A. Lewis, *Economic Survey 1919–1939* (1949), 11.
[2] For a study of the impact of the war see A. Marwick, *Britain in the Century of Total War* (1968).
[3] See R. H. Tawney, 'The Abolition of Economic Controls, 1918–21' *Economic History Review*, XIII (1943).
[4] See P. Abrams, 'The Failure of Social Reform: 1918–20', *Past and Present* XXIV (1963), 45–6.
[5] Ibid. 46.
[6] M. Bowley, *Housing and the State* (1945), 11–12.
[7] Ibid. ch. ii.
[8] Abrams, *Past and Present* (1963), 56.
[9] Bowley, *Housing and the State*, vi.

[10] W. A. Orton, *Labour in Transition* (1921), 124, 144, 173, 180–4.
[11] S. Pollard, *The Development of the British Economy 1914–1950* (1962), 91.
[12] See, for example, J. A. Dowie, 'Growth in the Inter-War Period: Some More Arithmetic', *Economic History Review*, 2nd ser., XXI (1968).
[13] J. M. Keynes, *The Economic Consequences of Mr. Churchill* (1925).
[14] See in particular R. S. Sayers, 'The Return to Gold', in L. S. Pressnell, ed., *Studies in the Industrial Revolution* (1960).
[15] Lewis, *Economic Survey*, 77–9.
[16] K. J. Hancock, 'The Reduction of Unemployment as a Problem of Public Policy, 1920–29', *Economic History Review*, 2nd ser., XV (1962), 330.
[17] H. W. Richardson, 'Over-Commitment in Britain before 1930', *Oxford Economic Papers*, XVII (1965).
[18] Lewis, *Economic Survey*, 41–2.
[19] Dowie, *Economic History Review* (1968), 97.
[20] A. J. Youngson, *The British Economy 1920–1957* (1960), 47.
[21] D. H. Aldcroft, 'Economic Progress in Britain in the 1920s', *Scottish Journal of Political Economy*, XIII (1966), 298.
[22] Lewis, *Economic Survey*. ch iii.
[23] Ibid. 57.
[24] A. Harrison, *The Framework of Economic Activity* (1967), 51–60.
[25] H. W. Richardson, *Economic Recovery in Britain 1932–39* (1967).
[26] Ibid. 95.
[27] Richardson, *Oxford Economic Papers* (1965).
[28] Richardson, *Economic Recovery*, 120.
[29] Ibid. 179–81.
[30] Ibid. 22–3, 313.
[31] Pollard, *Development of the British Economy*, 245
[32] See W. H. Beveridge, *Full Employment in a Free Society* (1944).
[33] Dowie, *Economic History Review* (1968), 101.
[34] Pilgrim Trust, *Men Without Work* (Cambridge, 1938).
[35] G. Orwell, *The Road to Wigan Pier* (1937), 91–3.
[36] Pilgrim Trust, *Men Without Work*.
[37] See Beveridge's analysis, *Full Employment*.
[38] For a detailed analysis of government unemployment policy see the recent study of the second Labour Government: R. Skidelsky, *Politicians and the Slump* (1967).
[39] E. J. Hobsbawm, *Industry and Empire* (1968), 212.
[40] C. L. Mowat, *Britain between the Wars 1918–1940* (1955), 458–9.
[41] Pollard, *Development of the British Economy*, 301.
[42] Harrison, *Framework of Economic Activity*, 73–4.
[43] W. K. Hancock and M. M. Gowing, *British War Economy* (1949), 452.
[44] Youngson, *British Economy*, 146–7.
[45] Pollard, *Development of the British Economy*, 315–16.
[46] Ibid. 312.
[47] Harrison, *Framework of Economic Activity*, 76–81.
[48] Hancock and Gowing, *British War Economy*, 541.
[49] Harrison, *Framework of Economic Activity*, 83–6.
[50] Pollard, *Development of the British Economy*, 308.
[51] Youngson, *British Economy*, 148.
[52] Hancock and Gowing, *British War Economy*, 555.

FOR FURTHER READING

General histories: The best general account of the period (as far as 1940) remains C. L. Mowat, *Britain between the Wars* (1955), although this study embraces fully political as well as economic and social matters. On the more economic side there are a number of useful works. As a book of reference S. Pollard, *The Development of the British Economy 1914–50* (1962), is invaluable: shorter, but more readable, is A. J. Youngson, *The British Economy 1920–57* (1960); E. J. Hobsbawm, *Industry and Empire* (1968), is also very readable but covers a period much longer than that with which we are concerned and is consequently less detailed than the above books. A. Marwick, *Britain in the Century of Total War* (1968), is rather disappointing as a study of the impact of war upon society, but is useful as a general social history of the period. Finally, W. A. Lewis, *Economic Survey 1919–1939* (1949), while rather dated, remains an invaluable introduction to the complexities of the international economy of the period.

Specialized studies: A. Harrison, *The Framework of Economic Activity* (1967), is a short, simple, but admirably lucid exposition of the role of governments in the world economy during our period. A. Bullock, *Ernest Bevin*, I (1960), is much more than a biography, being a superb study of the inter-war trade union movement. H. W. Richardson, *Economic Recovery in Britain 1932–39* (1967), is not light reading, but is *the* book on economic revival in the thirties and I have drawn on it heavily in the preceding chapter. W. K. Hancock and M. M. Gowing, *British War Economy* (1949), is the authoritative study of the war economy. W. H. Beveridge, *Full Employment in a Free Society* (1944), illustrates admirably the impact of Keynesian economic analysis upon thinking about unemployment. Pilgrim Trust, *Men Without Work* (Cambridge, 1938), brings home the meaning of long unemployment.

3

Historiography

B. J. ATKINSON

History reflects the age in which it is written. It should not surprise us therefore that the years from 1918 to 1945 produced a mixed crop. Hope and despair were both overwhelmingly present. The hope sprang from the triumph of liberal-democracy in the Great War and from the building of a new world in Russia as Soviet communism, heir to the high-flown aspirations aroused by the victory of 'freedom' over 'tyranny', established itself amidst the ruins of the Tsarist empire. But hope was soon betrayed. Out of plenty came the depression; out of Soviet communism came a tyranny at least as terrible as any which had preceded it; out of Germany and Italy came another totalitarianism, that of the Right. Liberal-democracy, with its values of tolerance and understanding, seemed to be played out. Culture and civilization themselves were threatened. In such circumstances, history lost confidence in itself. It was no longer easy to believe, as many Victorians had done, that history had a meaning, that it was the story of how man had progressed until he had reached the peak of the present day.

Though historians were less sure of where they were going, more people than ever before wanted to become historians. The subject attracted ever-increasing numbers of students at universities, with a strengthening of the trend away from classics and towards history as the modern liberal discipline. At the same time the subject was becoming professionalized. The gifted amateur, the gentleman-historian with the money and leisure to pursue his researches within a broad cultural pattern and present his findings stylishly, in a manner readily understood by all educated people, was becoming extinct, slaughtered by graduated taxation. University teachers were dominant and as their numbers increased they could afford to concentrate on ever narrower specialisms. This increasing confinement within universities and within specialisms was dangerous. Those responsible for writing history were used to teaching students, who were themselves specialists. The art of communication with the general public was being lost.

The trend towards specialization was partly the result of the growth in the amount of material available. As more archives were opened, more collections of private papers saved, more institutions regarded as fair game for historical explanation, the subject became overwhelmed by the richness of its sources. Historians responded by increasing their output of publications. Mastery of more than a small field in history's vast territories seemed no longer possible; specialization was the only answer. But as the historian confined himself to an ever smaller period he realized how unqualified he was to generalize about periods outside his own. Too many historians were too busy studying the trees to set about charting a path through the wood. Yet it was the broad path of explanation for which the general public was searching, and unable to get satisfaction from historians, it turned elsewhere. So we have two schools of history: one continued to seek salvation in specialization, piling up facts in the fashion of a Bury,* not because it expected to find thereby an over-all pattern but because it saw no other way in which the profession could retain its honesty; the other seeking to provide meaning, to supply a philosophy of history.

Some historians had no difficulty in finding meaning in history. For those who believed in the Marxist interpretation, history was the story of the class struggle; its meaning lay in the contribution it made to the eventual—and inevitable—triumph of the proletariat. Here Clio's virtue was in danger; history might too easily be bent to serve the interests of the guardians of the Marxist state.

Marxism did more for history than lay a snare, however; it provided valuable insights. As economic and social ends began to replace political and constitutional ones, historians turned to economic and social interpretations of the past. As the downtrodden of former ages began to claim their inheritance—it was in the 1920s that the first Labour government was formed in Britain—so historians who sympathized with such broad social movements began to investigate the past in terms of the origins of modern industrial society, often emphasizing the hardships experienced by the poorer sections of the community and thereby providing emotional ammunition for the political reformers of their own day. Historians no longer said with E. A. Freeman: 'History is past politics.' History was past experience and to interpret the vast wealth of that experience historians called to their aid the learning and tools of the social sciences; of economics, sociology, and psychology. This was a trend

* J. B. Bury (1861–1927), who once said: 'A complete assemblage of the smallest facts of human history will tell in the end.'

going back far beyond 1914—Sidney and Beatrice Webb* had published their *History of Trade Unionism* in 1894—but it gathered
force after the Great War. The Webbs continued to pour out a vast
number of publications dealing with social history and local government, the Hammonds† contributed their studies of the town and
village labourers, bemoaning the adverse effects which they argued
the Industrial Revolution had had on working-class life, and the
Coles,‡ especially G. D. H., were even more prolific than the Webbs.
The most significant of these social historians was R. H. Tawney
(1880–1962). Tawney brought to social and economic history the
analytical tools of Marx and of the German sociologist Max Weber.
But, equally important, he brought to his writings a personal sympathy with the underdog—though never at the expense of historical
accuracy, for Tawney was a fair man who believed in giving the
devil his due. His sympathy was not reserved exclusively for the past.
An ardent Christian Socialist, he wrote pamphlets for the Labour
party and was of invaluable service to the Workers' Educational
Association. But it is by his historical works that he will be remembered, especially *Religion and the Rise of Capitalism* (1926), which
laid the foundation stone of religious sociology in this country.
Tawney had the power of analysis and the capacity to express his
findings in challenging prose, putting forward fruitful hypotheses
for discussion and modification. Out of the controversies thereby
aroused came knowledge. Tawney was also able to give the past
meaning for the present; for him, the task of history was 'to summon
the living, not to make a corpse, and to see from a new angle the
problems of our own age, by widening the experience brought to
their consideration.'[1] After him, social history was much more than
'history with the politics left out'.

Meanwhile in France a group of social historians, among whom
Marc Bloch (1886–1944) was prominent, was attempting to syn-
thesize the data of the social sciences in order to build up a broader
and more human history. In a bid to escape from the growing
emphasis on the subjective nature of historical judgement, Bloch
sought to show how the historian could learn from actual tangible
remains of the past, such as field patterns and linguistic characteristics. Bloch saw himself as a craftsman, not re-enacting the past in

---

* Sidney Webb (1859–1947), President of the Board of Trade in the first
Labour government, Secretary of State for the Colonies in the second, created
Baron Passfield 1929; Beatrice Webb (1858–1943).
  † J. L. Le B. Hammond (1872–1949); Barbara Hammond (1873–1961).
  ‡ G. D. H. Cole (1889–1959); Margaret Cole (b. 1893).

his mind but explaining with a technician's skill the visible remains of history.

These two trends—the introduction of new tools from the social sciences and the increase in available historical material—combined to exercise a fragmenting influence on history. Economic history began to develop along independent lines, showing a greater interest in statistics than was common among other branches of history and moving closer to the social sciences. Separate specialisms grew up within the subject, such as diplomatic history, which developed out of the conjunction of the mass of archive material released after the First World War and the interest generated in it by a desire to justify or attack the Treaty of Versailles and to find out what had caused the war.

Within the mainstream of the subject the great debate as to whether history was an art or a science withered away. Science itself was no longer the confident discoverer of immutable laws; it now proceeded warily by means of hypotheses continually liable to modification. History was thus able to achieve its independence. Discussion turned instead to the proper relationship between the past and the present. Benedetto Croce (1866–1952), the Italian philosopher and historian who had triumphantly asserted the autonomy of history, argued that all history was contemporary history in the sense that every historical judgement was reached through the action of the historian's mind upon his material, and that mind was affected by the circumstances of its own times. History was thus an active interrelation between present and past. R. G. Collingwood (1889–1943), the Oxford philosopher and historian, developed this idea. He saw the past not as a collection of dead material to be observed, ticketed and explained, but as a living thing to be experienced. History consisted of understanding the thought behind past actions, and this could be attained only by the historian re-enacting that thought for himself.

To see history in terms of imaginative reconstruction seems more praiseworthy than measuring the past by the standards of the present or meting out judgement in accordance with a strict moral code (as Lord Acton (1834–1902) was wont to do). Perhaps this is merely to say that it was an attitude well suited to an age which was losing confidence in its values, which was not sure of where it was going but which was still sufficiently honest to realize that easy judgements of past epochs would be hypocritical. However, one must not minimize the dangers which such a view of history presents. It is an easy step from imaginative understanding to excusing. If history is to be an autonomous subject, it must either have objective standards of its own whereby the material of the past can be interpreted, or it must recognize that there will be almost as many standards as there are historians. In this case history can still be study of the past in search of truth, but its findings will have little relevance beyond the borders of the subject itself, for they will be so various, so relative, that they will convey an infinity of meanings, and thereby present to the outsider no meaning at all. On the other hand, if meaning has to be sought from outside history, whether from an all-embracing philosophy such as Christianity or Marxism, or from a present which instead of taking part in a dialogue with the past merely extracts that which seems relevant to itself, then history is in danger of being perverted.

While Collingwood was pondering over the intricacies of a philosophy of history, Herbert Butterfield (b. 1900) at Cambridge had already produced an exposé of the dangers of historical interpretation being influenced by the needs of the present. In *The Whig Interpretation of History* (1931) Butterfield attacked the Whig–Protestant approach to the past, the tradition of Lord Macaulay and Sir G. O. Trevelyan among others, which loved to trace back religious liberty to Luther, political liberty to the 'Glorious Revolution' of 1688, and to interpret succeeding events as a succession of struggles between the allies of progress, among whose ranks the historians themselves enlisted, and the supporters of reaction whose efforts they condemned. By looking at the past in this way the historian lost perspective:

If we turn our present into an absolute to which all other generations are merely relative, we are losing the truer version of ourselves which history is able to give, we fail to realise those things in which we too are merely relative, and we lose a chance of discovering where, in the stream of the centuries, we ourselves, and our ideas and prejudices, stand.[2]

Butterfield felt that bias crept in when the results of many pieces of particular research had to be rendered comparatively briefly and in general terms. Butterfield's answer to this problem looks dangerously like selling the pass:

In the last resort the historian's explanation of what has happened is not a piece of general reasoning at all. He explains the French Revolution by discovering exactly what it was that occurred; and if at any point we need further elucidation all that he can do is to take us into greater detail, and make us see in still more definite concreteness what really did take place. . . . The last word of the historian is not some fine, firm general statement; it is a piece of detailed research.[3]

Butterfield, at this time, conceived of history as a means not of solving problems but of making people realize how complicated they were. As a rationalization of what some historians were doing, this emphasis on detailed research and the absence of any broad sense of meaning was admirable. To the public, however, already confused enough, this portrayal of history, not as a tour along a broad highway leading to general truths but as a series of journeys along minor roads meandering into the middle of a dense forest, was depressing.

The most significant British historian of these years was Sir Lewis Namier (1888–1960), a Polish Jew. He resembled great historians of the past in that he was a cosmopolitan, and his greatest work was written when he was not an academic* but a private scholar. But Namier was also a man of his age, uniting in himself the dominant historical traits of the time. The influence of Marx was revealed in Namier's belief that a man's attitude could be traced back to the way he earned his living; from Freud, Namier acquired an abiding sense of the importance of psychology in history. Finally, Namier appreciated that the vast mass of historical material, which was appearing in a never-ending stream, could be used in a positive way; in this he was unlike some who feared that the subject would be crushed to death by such a weight of source material.

Namier has been accused, among other things, of taking mind out of history. The basis for this comment is to be found in his profound distrust of ideologies; as he wrote, 'the less man clogs the free play of his mind with political doctrine and dogma, the better for his thinking.'[4] Namier was a true conservative. He was also a psychologist. He had learnt to look beneath the surface of events and of theories. He taught historians to consider not what a man said, but what he did, to go behind the public record to the private papers.

Namier turned his attention first to a period of history most suited to his preconceptions, the eighteenth century, an era free from the religious and political upheavals which had characterized the previous two centuries and free also from the ideologies released upon Europe by the French Revolution. He was convinced that interpretations of eighteenth-century British history in terms of party and principle were wrong. He showed this by examining in minute detail the politics of a few years around the accession of George III, collating a vast amount of miscellaneous detail, building up biographies of the people involved—not just of the leaders but of as

* Namier was Professor of Modern History at the University of Manchester, 1931–53.

many Members of Parliament as possible. So Namier was able to expose the real connections, those of finance and family, which for him explained far more about the politics of that day than the traditional historian's terms, Whig and Tory, Crown and corruption. This book, *The Structure of Politics at the Accession of George III* (1929), not merely made his name but gave it to a whole method of historical research.

Namier revolutionized the study of history. He had shown how the historian could use the mass of material at his disposal, rather than wilt under the challenge it presented. This was detailed research directed to an end, the construction of a coherent picture of a segment of the past. Namier had also shown how institutions could be studied through compiling biographies of the people who composed them, and observing the interplay between those people, their words and their deeds. His methods were widely applied to other periods of history by his followers. History was being 'Namierized'. Historians, who had previously been rather solitary creatures, began to hunt in packs; many people were needed to do the research required to build up the detailed pictures which Namierization found necessary. Namier, himself rather an astringent man, was helping to make the historian a social animal.

Namier's achievements were not confined to eighteenth-century studies. His origins and his Jewish ties drew him to European history. His essays reveal a mind capable of summing up the vast sweep of a man's life in a few pages, informed with psychological insight and expressed in a pungent, sometimes almost brutal, style.

Namierization illuminated many facets of history, but its dangers were not inconsiderable. Some of Namier's imitators, though not Namier himself, have tended to underestimate the influence of ideas and principles upon men's actions, forgetting that what was true of the eighteenth century might not always be generally applied. Namier himself, rather than his method, may have caused another fault. Though he could use the microscope and telescope with equal effect, he found the middle range of narrative beyond him. *The Structure of Politics* had been intended as the groundwork for the more descriptive treatment of *England in the Age of the American Revolution*, but of that work only one volume ever appeared. If Namier, with his insight and skills, found it difficult to express the results of his researches as a whole, how easy it must be for lesser mortals to become immured in warrens of research with little to show for their infinite labours. There is a moving picture of the death of Namier; after spending his last years as an editor of the *History of*

Parliament, compiling hundreds of biographies of eighteenth-century M.P.s, it was not until the day before his death that he could say: 'Yesterday was the first time I saw in my mind's eye the survey of Parliament as a whole.'[5] History is a cruel discipline: it denies to even its greatest practitioners the satisfaction of perfect mastery.

From one of the most significant historians we now move to one whom many would regard as one of the least. Lytton Strachey (1880–1952) saw it as his task to save history from the dullness which was threatening to envelop it:

> The first duty of a great historian is to be an artist. The function of art in history is something much more profound than mere decoration; to regard it, as some writers persist in regarding it, as if it were the jam put around the pill of fact by cunning historians is to fall into a grievous error; a truer analogy would be to compare it to the process of fermentation which converts a raw mass of grape-juice into a subtle and splendid wine. Uninterpreted truth is as useless as buried gold; and art is the great interpreter.[6]

Strachey exploded on to the historical scene in 1918 with the publication of *Eminent Victorians*, four biographical studies of leading nineteenth-century personages. In brilliant prose, shot through with sparkling shafts of wit, Strachey savaged his chosen subjects. He forced his material to serve his preconceived end, the debunking of smug Victorianism, in a manner so entertaining as to compel attention. *Eminent Victorians* was an instant success.

But was it history? Strachey's own words did little to allay the doubts of the profession. In the preface to *Eminent Victorians* he wrote: 'Ignorance is the first requisite of the historian—ignorance, which simplifies and clarifies, which selects and omits, with a placid perfection unattainable by the highest art.' Such a demeaning attitude was hardly likely to enhance Clio's image. Nor were certain passages of *Eminent Victorians*, especially where, in the essay on Cardinal Manning, Strachey's attempt to transform history into entertainment carried him beyond the bounds set by the need to respect one's sources. Nevertheless, *Eminent Victorians* and its kindlier and more affectionate successor, *Queen Victoria*, reached a vast public and brought to the art of biography a critical approach and an appreciation of psychology. Strachey could at least consider that he had redeemed English biography from Carlyle's criticism: 'How delicate, decent it is, bless its mealy mouth!'[7]

Other writers chose a different way of restoring history to communion with a wider public and, like Strachey, received bitter criticism for their pains from the professionals. They sought to pro-duce what one might term macro-, as distinct from micro-history. The first of these writers was Oswald Spengler (1880–1936). As a German who had lived through the First World War, it is not per-haps surprising that he should take a gloomy view of the prospects of civilization. In July 1918 he produced the first volume of his work *Der Untergang des Abendlandes* (The Decline of the West), which established him as the first modern historical prophet of doom. Spengler called his book a study in historical 'morphology'. Instead of seeing human experience as a story of progress towards modern civilization, he compared present civilization with those that had preceded it. By viewing history comparatively, Spengler claimed to establish a time-scale showing the life cycle through which every civilization must pass, including the contemporary Western one, for which the prospects were not favourable. The West had passed through its creative phase, the period of Culture, and had entered the age of Civilization and World cities, a period of decay.

Spengler, as befitted a man trained as a natural scientist, saw his civilizations in terms of the biological process: they were born, grew old, and died. Arnold J. Toynbee (b. 1889), as befitted a Professor of History in the University of London, was more flexible in his ap-proach. Rejecting Spengler's mechanistic philosophy, Toynbee, after much hesitation, endowed his civilizations with free will. But the two men were alike in this: they saw history in terms not of nations and states but of civilizations and they sought to extract meaning from a comparative study of them.

In his great work *A Study of History*, six volumes of which appeared in the 1930s, Toynbee identified more than twenty civiliza-tions and in a remarkable *tour de force* he moved freely among all of them, showing mastery not only of their history but also of their literature, calling to his aid concepts from philosophy, psychology, and sociology and expressing his findings in vivid and compelling language. This was indeed history in the grand manner. But despite its wealth of learning and illustration, the *Study of History* was as-sailed by more conventional historians. As Toynbee swept through the scattered pieces of territory of the specialists he was open to their separate attacks: he had got his facts wrong here, he had not taken account of all the material there. So the credibility of the work could be chipped away. Nor were more fundamental and wide-ranging criticisms lacking: Toynbee had claimed that his work was an empirical study, that is the plan had emerged from consideration of his source material. To many it seemed, on the contrary, that, like

Strachey, he had drawn up the plan first and had then selected such material as would fit into it.

The *Study of History* drew more acclaim from the general public whose craving for meaning and explanation it satisfied. What did Toynbee tell them of the present and the future, for after all what people generally wanted from the past was some guidance as to what they could expect in their own lifetime? Toynbee was more comforting than Spengler, but only just. Western civilization was in process of disintegration, but it had not yet reached the stage of the universal state; Western man still had that period of peace, the Indian summer of his civilization, to look forward to. Beyond that, Toynbee in the first six volumes of his work could only offer a return to faith in God: 'we may and must pray that a reprieve which God has granted to our society once will not be refused if we ask for it again in a contrite spirit and with a broken heart.' [8]

Toynbee and Spengler had tried to restore meaning to history. They had not satisfied the majority of historians. The paradox remained; more historians were working at more material, but the result was not more enlightenment. Phrases like 'the lessons of History', 'the judgement of the past', were less fashionable than ever. But this is not to say that history had not developed. It had responded to the stimuli of Marx and Freud and had accepted aid from the social sciences generally. It had, through Namier, developed ways of handling the mass of material at its disposal and it had appreciated that the past could speak not only through documents but through inanimate objects too. History was extending its boundaries to include the whole of life. The price it had to pay was fragmentation and specialization. This alone made generalization more difficult, but the destruction of 'meaningful history' is to be attributed to two different factors: a loss of confidence, part of the general crisis of Western civilization, and a greater maturity, the realization that history, like life, was complex.

There were still historians who found patterns among the complexities. Just as in previous periods those who believed in progress or Christianity traced the fortunes of their belief through the ages, so in the inter-war years the followers of economic determinism wrote history in the Marxist image. But there was a danger that they would succumb to the same temptations as Toynbee and bend their material to suit their pattern. The risk was greatest where the state was determined to insure that history should be made useful by being made to serve the government's interest. In this event we leave history and enter the realm of myth.

NOTES

[1] R. H. Tawney, *Religion and the Rise of Capitalism* (1966 ed.), 19.
[2] H. Butterfield, *The Whig Interpretation of History* (1931), 63.
[3] Ibid. 72.
[4] Quoted in E. H. Carr, *What is History?* (1965 reprint), 39.
[5] Lady Namier, quoted in Ved Mehta, *The Fly and the Fly-Bottle* (1965 reprint), 222. Since this chapter was written, Lady Namier has published a life of her husband: *Lewis Namier, A Biography* (1971).
[6] M. Holroyd, *Lytton Strachey* (1968), II. 262.
[7] Quoted in E. L. Woodward, *Studies in History* (1966), 309.
[8] A. J. Toynbee, *A Study of History* (1939), VI. 321.

FOR FURTHER READING

Several of the books mentioned in volume I (p. 112) as being useful for the period from 1900 to 1918 retain their value for the inter-war years. I will just instance A. Marwick, *The Nature of History* (1970), which has the merit of being reasonably comprehensive and recent, and the virtue, for the general reader, of being aimed at him rather than at the professional historian. I would add to the list H. Stuart Hughes, *History as Art and as Science: Twin Vistas on the Past* (New York, 1964), a short work which may be of advantage to some; P. C. A. Geyl, *Debates with Historians* (1955), especially valuable for those interested in Toynbee; M. Bloch, *The Historian's Craft* (Manchester, 1954), an unfinished record of how a great historian saw history, published posthumously after his death in the war; V. P. Mehta, *The Fly and the Fly-Bottle* (1963; paperback ed. 1965), which shows that certain historians are human beings as well; and finally, for those who are still wondering what it is all about, E. H. Carr, *What is History?* (1961; paperback ed. 1964).

4

Social Thought

RAYMOND PLANT

In August 1914 something happened in the world. This happening lasted only four years, though the ripple of its events continues over the world's surface.[1]

So observed Leonard Woolf in 1931. The First World War and its aftermath provoked during subsequent years a succession of crises in the fabric of European social and political life, and a series of theories connected with these crises. Although most social and political thought articulates a response to, or rationalization of, some malaise in the social environment of the theorist, the fact that the historical circumstances which gave rise to theories no longer obtain does not thereby entail that they have become outmoded. Such theories, far from being mere *pièces de circonstance*, rather embody an element which transcends the particular problems which generated them.

The social and political thinking of the period 1918–45 presents a tangled skein which it will be the task of this essay to unravel. Some points can, however, be made in a programmatic manner: the shattering of complacent liberal nostrums by the war; the economic recession in Europe at the end of the twenties and during the thirties; the Russian revolution; the rise of Fascism and National Socialism and the continuing process of industrialization, all claimed the interest and attention of theorists. Indeed, socialism in the Soviet Union, Fascism in Italy, and National Socialism in Germany were all connected to bodies of articulate social and political doctrine, and the political leaders of these states were moved to produce substantial works of theory to justify or to rationalize their particular political positions. Seldom has there been such a close relation between political theory and practice. Lenin and Stalin both produced works which at once developed and amended the Marx–Engels canon; Mussolini wrote an exposition and defence of Fascism in the *Enciclopedia Italiana* in 1932; and between 1925 and 1927 Hitler produced *Mein Kampf*, which includes passages of considerable importance for the understanding of National Socialist political doctrine. The ideological popularity of both Communism and Fascism posed a threat to the Catholic understanding of man and his place in society, and as a result the Roman Church was constrained to formulate its social and political doctrine with some precision. This was done by Pope Pius XI in two encyclicals: *Quadragesimo Anno* and *Divini Redemptoris*, and in a series of letters to the heads of churches in politically troubled countries. At the same time T. S. Eliot struggled to formulate a Christian doctrine of social life in *The Idea of a Christian Society* and elsewhere. The 1930s in Britain, as is well known, produced a deluge of Marxist analysis, diagnosis, and prediction. This somewhat uncharacteristic manifestation was the result of a number of factors. In particular the economic recession seemed to give some credence to Marxian economics; the 'discovery' of the Soviet Union by prominent radicals showed the feasibility of what was considered to be a genuine socialist society; and the rise of Fascism led to the view that Communism was the only force of sufficient ideological power to challenge it. For intellectuals in this particular situation, Marxism had a great deal of appeal, and a significant amount of creative work was done by John Strachey, Stephen Spender, and Christopher Caudwell. At the same time, however, other left-wing intellectuals remained unseduced by the blandishments of Marxism. Douglas Jay and Evan Durbin argued in favour of the advance of socialism through democratic channels, and in fact this tradition of socialist thought had the greatest influence in the long term. The Fabian tradition on the British Left was too firmly ensconced for a temporary swing to Marxism to alter fundamentally the structure of British politics. The polarization of politics during this period led to a decline in the vitality of liberal theory, a style of thought which had in the previous century been dominant. In an age of extremes, the man who holds the middle ground is execrated on all sides. Marxists considered that liberalism was basically allied to Fascism in that both accepted the capitalist order, whereas the Fascist derided the liberals' commitment to individual freedom and the conception of the state which secured this freedom. It was only towards the end of our period that there was anything like a revival of liberal thought, particularly in the work of Karl Popper and F. A. Hayek.

Although the crisis in Europe occupied many social and political thinkers, other problems too were at the centre of interest, in particular, the continuing process of industrialization. Here the guild socialist movement carried on the humanistic critique of industrial society to be found, for example, in the work of thinkers such as William Morris and John Ruskin in the previous century.

This critique of industrialism found perhaps its most influential expression in Tawney's *Acquisitive Society*, and in some novels and essays of D. H. Lawrence. The development of psychoanalytical theory had a great influence on social thought. Psychoanalysis changed man's conception of himself, and therefore his conception of society, and a theory of society from this point of view is articulated in Freud's *Civilisation and Its Discontents*. The period was, as a whole, one of tremendous vitality for social and political thought, and it is interesting to notice that during such a period, professional philosophers were becoming increasingly sceptical about the viability of social and political philosophy. This scepticism was most lucidly expressed by A. J. Ayer in *Language, Truth and Logic* (1936). During the whole of this period there was no work on social and political thought done by a professional philosopher who shared the central philosophical presuppositions of the time, with the exception of Bertrand Russell—and his work on social and political problems was not closely related to his philosophical position. The only really systematic thinkers in the political field during the period were Michael Oakeshott and R. G. Collingwood, both of whom were indebted more to the idealists than to the native form of empiricism, and consequently they stood apart from the mainstream of philosophical activity during the period.

Fascism

> ... Fascism, besides being a system of government, is also
> and above all a system of thought.
>
> Benito Mussolini, 1932[2]

It would be wrong to make the claim that Fascism in Italy was consciously built upon a body of political theory, despite the implication involved in the statement of Mussolini (1883–1945) cited above. Indeed it was not until 1929, at the earliest, that any coherent body of theory emerged from the Fascist movement, and in fact theorizing was to some extent despised. It seems more likely that a body of theory was built up to stimulate and develop a political impulse and had the same function as a Sorelian myth, a point which seems to be borne out by Mussolini's insistence in 1929 that Fascism must provide itself with a doctrine in the two months preceding the meeting of the National Congress of the Fascist party! The political theory of Fascism is then not so much an academic intellectual construction as, rather, a myth to stimulate political action.

However, whatever the role of Fascist philosophy in the creation and consolidation of political power in Italy during the 1920s and '30s, by 1932 a reasonably coherent body of theory had been developed which received both definitive and authoritative expression in Mussolini's *The Doctrine of Fascism*, published in the *Enciclopedia Italiana*. In this article Mussolini discusses the fundamental ideas of Fascism, and develops in its most systematic fashion the theory of the corporate state which embodies the Fascist conception of the role of the state *vis-à-vis* individuals and groups within society. Although Mussolini's conception of the state owes something to the work of Hegel, particularly as it was mediated through Giovanni Gentile, it should be stressed that there are major differences. Hegel, for example, was a constitutional monarchist with a respect for individual freedom, although he did not regard this as the ultimate political value, whereas Mussolini was a totalitarian dictator who had no conception of the value of individual freedom at all. Also, perhaps Hegel was too much of a nationalist to approve of imperialism, which denies the nationhood of other states; however, no such scruples seem to have preoccupied Mussolini before the invasion of Abyssinia. It is perhaps also significant that the *doyen* of Italian Hegelians, Benedetto Croce, always stood aloof from Fascism and cast doubts upon the Hegelianism of Gentile.

In *The Doctrine of Fascism*, Mussolini stressed the falsity of individualism, and liberalism, the cognate political creed. Liberalism made the individual the unit of political and historical meaning and value, whereas Mussolini argued that man is moulded both by his contemporary social experience in the family, in social groups, and in the nation; and by history and tradition made manifest in the language, the mores, and the institutions of the community. The abstract individual is a chimera; he cannot be separated from the social nexus which nurtures him, gives him language, culture, and ideals: consequently liberalism, which builds up a conception of politics, of the power and the role of the state, on the basis of this abstract individual, is in fact false. Mussolini did not deny that in the eighteenth and nineteenth centuries liberalism, though based upon a false assumption, had played a useful role in the challenge which it presented to outworn absolutist regimes, but the social and political conditions which gave liberalism its historical importance no longer obtained. In particular, Mussolini pointed to the changing role of the state in those countries which had adhered to the principles of liberalism. The recurrent economic crises had, he argued, forced state intervention in the economic life of such countries in ways which were not sanctioned by the ideologies to which these states subscribed.

The individual cannot then be the unit of political meaning, the ultimate political value. In Mussolini's view this is the role of the state. The state is the embodiment of the experience, the standards, and the ideals of the nation. It is the guardian of its history and the interpreter of its traditions. Since the individual can only find himself in and through his social experience, it follows that he can only really become conscious of himself through his experience as a citizen of a state which makes concrete the experience of the nation. Because the state embodies the spirit of the people it follows that it is in some sense a spiritual entity, a point which Mussolini emphasizes:

The state as conceived by Fascism and its acts is a spiritual and moral fact because it makes concrete the political, juridical and economic organisation of the nation, and such organisation is in its origins and its development a manifestation of spirit.[3]

As the supreme embodiment of the spirit of the people, the state is the highest form of social reality, and it has to determine the other modes of social experience within the community, to give them a structure and a role consistent with its own interpretation of the spirit of the people. The state has therefore to be totalitarian in that it has to determine the life of both the individuals and the groups which fall within the national community.

Although the Fascists vehemently rejected liberalism and the notion of the pure individual, they came to accept at least a modified form of capitalism, the form of economic structure usually associated with liberalism. Although some statements by the Fascists seem to indicate a rejection of capitalism, these criticisms were directed more against the capitalist ethos, its commercialism and materialism, than against capitalist economic organization as such. In mature Fascist doctrine, although the private enterprise economy is subordinated to the national purpose as interpreted by the state, so long as an industry is working for the social good, the capitalist remains responsible for it and receives the profits from his enterprise. This link between Fascism and capitalism was used by some Marxists to argue that liberalism and Fascism are in fact allied, for both accepted capitalism and would, if the occasion demanded have formed an explicit alliance to fight socialism.

The Fascist critique of liberalism was, at the time at which it was made, outmoded. Certainly the individualism which Mussolini criticized so trenchantly, and with some justice, was one strand in the complex liberal tradition, but the kind of critique which he offered had already been assimilated by liberal theorists. T. H. Green had provided for a liberal theory of the state while at the same time accepting the critique of individualism propounded by Hegel in terms very similar to those used by Mussolini. The Fascist critique of liberalism was at this time an attack against a straw man in that extreme individualism was no longer a cornerstone of liberal theory.

National Socialism

The National Socialists shared certain ideas with the Fascists, in particular the hatred of liberalism and the unheroic commercial tone which they regarded as its concomitant, a virulent nationalism, a belief in the virtue of social discipline, and a view that political and social theory is a myth designed to stimulate and to rationalize a political response. But there is one major difference between the two styles of thought. For the Fascist, as we have seen, the state is the embodiment, the articulation, of the spirit of the people, and the ultimate value; the same is not true of the National Socialist. For the National Socialist the *Volk* (the racial people), not the state, is the basic unit. The state is an instrument of the Volk and does not embody it in an absolute manner.

The basic texts for understanding National Socialist theory are Hitler's *Mein Kampf* and Alfred Rosenberg's *Der Mythus des 20 Jahrhunderts*, although it is possible to see some of the basic ideas of National Socialism in a seminal but unsystematic form in the works of some of the 'New Conservative' philosophers who wrote during the 1914–18 War and during the early years of the Weimar Republic. The work of Werner Sombart, *Händler und Helden* (1915), included an attack on individualism and bourgeois commercialism which he saw as the dominant ethos of the British people and which in the war stood counterpoised to the heroic spirit of the German people with its emphasis on discipline and obedience. Attacks on liberalism in this vein became a *leitmotif* of subsequent National Socialist literature. It is also of interest that Thomas Mann in *Betrachtungen eines Unpolitischen* (Reflections of an Unpolitical Man) supported the old German values against the individualistic and materialistic ethos of the liberal states. Sombart also formulated a concept of *Volksgemeinschaft* (a community of racial folk) based upon a form of authoritarian collectivism which would be suited to the spirit of the German people. Similar ideas were propounded by Oswald Spengler in *Prussentum und Sozial-ismus* (1920), in which he argued that the authoritarian ethos of Prussianism, with its emphasis on command and obedience, was in fact implicitly allied to socialism, for both rejected anarchic, individualistic liberalism. He pointed to the need to develop a state which would combine the collectivism of socialist theory and the authoritarian nature of Prussian practice.

This emphasis on the need to attack liberalism and its ethos seems to be far more opportunist than the comparable critique in Fascist theory. It was an attempt to take the measure of the ideological enemy, in this case Britain, and to identify the nature of the political and economic system which had led to Germany's defeat. This point was made very explicit by Moeller van den Bruck, who urged that the liberalism which had defeated Germany and was now eating its way into the fabric of German life should be rigorously combatted. He advocated some form of socialism based upon the 'best and noblest traditions of the German people'.[4] The work of these thinkers prepared a good deal of the ground which led to the wide acceptance of National Socialism. The latter merely generalized, and made more explicit, doctrines which had been in the air for some time. It is clear that these theorists were socialists only in a very Pickwickian sense; they had nothing in common with Marxian socialists, or with social democrats. They were socialists only in that they were concerned to emphasize the primacy of the *social*, the claims of the community on the individual, and to reject the view that the state was to guarantee the individual's freedom.

The conception of the Volk as the basic or ultimate political unit cannot be understood outside of National Socialist racial theories. These theories were propounded most clearly in Rosenberg's work cited above. The conception of the Volk and its role in political and social life is a deduction from certain biological facts which Hitler regarded as constituting 'iron laws of nature'. These facts concerned the ways in which races arise and develop. It was argued that each beast naturally mates with a member of its own race, or species; when it does not then deleterious consequences follow, in that the resulting offspring is inferior both physically and mentally to the offspring of a racially pure liaison. The crossing of racial stock leads therefore to a decline in the mental and physical power and vitality of the race. It would seem then that nature sanctions racial purity. The second component of the theory was that not only is there an impetus in nature to racial purity, but also some races have in fact dominated the world. Rosenberg argued that the most important of these was the Aryan race. All that has enduring value in human life and culture has been the product of the Aryans.

These were the two basic ideas of National Socialist theory: the whole of history was regarded as being explicable not in terms of the development of freedom or of class conflict, but rather in terms of racial struggle and racial development, and in history the dominant race was conceived as having been the Aryan. These ideas constituted the *Volkisch Weltanschauung* which corresponded in function to the Sorelian myth. Once the *Weltanschauung* had been formulated, it was thought to be necessary to give it some kind of concrete embodiment in a militant party; different world views were envisaged as being engaged in a struggle for acceptance. This struggle had to be violent in that such basic differences in world views cannot be settled by rational argument, and this view was put forward by Hitler in *Mein Kampf*. The concrete articulation of the National Socialist world view was the National Socialist Workers' party and the S.A.,* its para-military wing.

The Volk was the living embodiment of the traditions and values of the race, and all the ends of life had to be subordinated to the needs of the Volk. This applied also to the state. The state was not the embodiment of the spirit of the people, as in Fascist theory, but rather the instrument of that spirit. This point, at which National Socialist and Fascist theory part company, was made by Rosenberg: 'Today we see the State no longer as an independent ideal before which men must bow the knee, but only as a means of representing the people. . . . The authority of the Volk is above that of the State. The person who does not see this is the enemy of the people.'[5] This difference in emphasis between the National Socialist and Fascist theories can perhaps be best explained by looking at the social and political backgrounds which gave rise to the theories. Before the advent of the Fascists, Italy did not possess a strong and efficient state structure; it had no mature and disinterested bureaucracy, no efficiently controlled administrative machinery, and its economy was, relative to the economies of Britain and France, backward. The almost religious glorification of the state and the subordination of all other ends to the state therefore played an important ideological role in the Fascists' attempt to create a strong united state in Italy. The situation in Germany was totally different. Since the time of Bismarck Germany had possessed a strong

---

* The S.A. (*Sturm Abteilung*) was led originally by Röhm. The S.S. (*Schutzstaffel*) grew out of a disagreement between Hitler and Röhm over the S.A. The S.S.'s function was to guard the party dignitaries. It was eventually reformed by Himmler and became a kind of police force within the party.

state structure which even the defeat in 1918, and the abdication of the Kaiser, had not basically weakened. There was therefore no need on the part of the Nazis to lay the same kind of stress on the state. The emphasis on the development of racial pride and racial consciousness on the contrary played an important role in that it enabled the Nazis to pose as the champions of the traditional German values which the machinations of the liberals and Jews during the Weimar Republic had undermined.

The aim of National Socialism was to build a *Volksgemeinschaft* (folk community), based upon racial purity, and upon the historic German soil. These two features of *blood* and *soil* explain the major preoccupations of National Socialist internal and external policies. Internally, the aim was to promote and develop racial purity as a pre-condition of the full creation of a folk community. Such a community had to be racially pure and based upon racial unity, and conse-quently the state had to expel all those elements which were racially poisonous. This point accounted for the Reich Citizenship Law of 1935, and the Law for the Protection of the German Blood and Honour of the same year. Article Two of the Reich Citizenship Law stated: 'A citizen of the Reich is only that subject of the Reich who is of German and kindred blood.'[6] The aim of racial purity, as one of the components of developing a racial community based upon old German virtues, explains the persecution of the Jews, the eugenic legislation of 1935, the effect of which was to rid society of mental and physical defectives, and the emphasis upon increasing the birth rate, which seems at first sight to conflict with the major aim of German foreign policy during the period, namely the achievement of *Lebensraum* (living space) for the German people.

Externally, the aim of the National Socialist government was to secure to Germany its historic lands so that the folk community could be based upon the totality of German soil. The concern for the Sudeten Germans and their lands in Czechoslovakia is accounted for by this theoretical notion of a racial community, and concepts such as 'cultural landscape' and 'folkish soil' were used by propa-gandists to justify German claims in the East. Indeed, the marching slogan of the Sudeten Germans under their leader, Heinlen, was '*Ein Volk, Ein Reich, Ein Führer*'.

It is clear that National Socialism was a totalitarian political doctrine in that the party and, more importantly, the Führer articulated the spirit of the people, and everything else in the community had to be subordinated to this. All moral, cultural and educational activities were under the control of the state as the instrument of the people and the content of these activities was to be subordinated to the development of racial consciousness. Trades unions were emasculated to form the Labour Front which was in fact an extension of the party, and the government intervened often and directly in industry, while as far as cultural activities were concerned Rosenberg's comment can stand: 'The Totalitarian state does not recognise the separate existence of art. It demands that art should make a positive contribution to the Nation.'[7]

The sociology of the Nazi movement is interesting, and fails to bear out the Marxist claim that the movement was the ideological embodiment of monopolistic capitalism. S. M. Lipset in *Political Man* (1960) argues that, initially at least, Hitler's support came from shop-keepers, small farmers, and self-employed artisans, not from the representatives of big business and the finance capitalists. He also points out the fallacy of the view that it came largely from the ranks of the unemployed. Although both the unemployed and big business came to support him at a relatively late stage, the power base of the National Socialist movement was the lower middle class.

Socialism

The most important developments of the period which influenced socialist thought were the First World War, the Russian revolution in 1917, and the economic recession in 1929. The First World War and the revolution in Russia in March 1917 led Lenin, and to some extent Bukharin, to develop in a very impressive manner elements of traditional Marxist thought. Lenin's *Imperialism: The Highest Stage of Capitalism* and Bukharin's *Imperialism and the World Economy* both extended the Marxian theory of capitalism to take account of developments leading up to the war; while *The State and Revolution*, by Lenin, was occasioned partly by what he considered to be the un-Marxist ideas of influential theorists such as Kautsky, and partly by the essentially bourgeois nature of the March revolution in Russia. The failure of the war to lead to the overthrow of the capitalist system elsewhere induced Stalin to propound the related theories of 'socialism in one country' and 'capitalist encirclement', theories which, as Trotsky showed, were in direct contradiction to the explicit thesis of Lenin's work on the imperialist stage of capitalism. This dispute led to the ideological break between Stalin and Trotsky, the overtones of which are still with us long after the deaths of the figures associated with the theories. The development of the Russian revolution had a very

profound impact outside the Soviet Union, for it seemed to demonstrate the viability of socialism, and to give the lie to those who
claimed that all socialist blueprints were Utopian. This apparent
success of socialism in the Soviet Union, coupled with the pilgrim-
ages made there by the left-wing intellectuals, at least partially
explains the astonishing hold which Marxism had over British
intellectuals during the 1930s.

The two major theoretical contributions of Lenin (1870–1924) to
socialist thought in this period were *Imperialism: The Highest
Stage of Capitalism* (1917) and *The State and Revolution* (1917–18).
The theory of capitalistic imperialism was clearly influenced by
Lenin's need to provide a Marxist understanding of the causes of
the First World War, and in particular of working class reaction to
it, which was largely chauvinistic. The thesis of *Imperialism: The
Highest Stage of Capitalism* was that capitalism had developed in a
monopolistic manner, and this, of course, entailed that capital was
concentrated in the hands of a very few people, in particular banks
and financiers. This centralization of capital in the hands of a small
body of men from the capitalist class led to a corresponding change
in the function of the state, which, in Marxian thought, is conceived
as the instrument whereby the capitalist class manages to control
the proletariat. The basic incentive of capitalism, the need to maximize profits, led to the development of monopolies and consequently to the state direction of the economy in the interests of
the monopoly capitalists. One way in which the state served the
interest of monopoly capital was through the acquisition of colonies.
In order to maximize profits colonies were needed as sources of
cheap labour and raw materials, and as retail outlets. The increase
in profits derived from imperialist expansion was thought to have
been partly used to 'buy off' the leaders of the proletariat:

The receipt of high monopoly benefits by capitalists in one of the numerous branches of industry, in one of the numerous countries, etc., makes i*
economically possible for them to bribe certain sections of the workers
and for a time a fairly considerable minority of them, and to win them to
the side of the bourgeoisie.[8]

This process duped the working class into thinking that its econ
omic interest lay in supporting imperialist policies, and this, i
Lenin's view, explained the support given by large sections of th
working class to the First World War, which he regarded as essenti
ally an imperialist war. It was an imperialist war between state
controlled by monopoly capitalists for the control of colonies an

empire. Imperialist wars up to this point had led to the emergence of certain capitalist super-powers who regarded it as basically in their interests to live peaceably because their economies had become interlocked largely as a result of the export of capital for foreign investment. Economically, then, peace was in the interest of monopoly capital, but this ignored the reality of national feeling which generated wars which then turned into struggles for empire. This tension reached breaking point in 1914. Because of the war the whole interlocking nature of the world economy was strained and from this strain world-wide revolution was to follow. This provided the theoretical underpinning for the theory of world-wide revolution which Stalin was to modify. It must be said that Lenin's ideas on this point are not entirely original; a very similar thesis had been argued by Bukharin in *Imperialism and the World Economy*, written during 1915–16.

World revolution seemed inevitable as a result of this world-wide imperialist war and indeed revolution occurred in 1917 in the Soviet Union when the Mensheviks and Socialist Revolutionaries under the leadership of Kerensky, Avksentyev, and Chernov seized power in March 1917. Profoundly dissatisfied with this revolution which he regarded as merely bourgeois, Lenin was moved to produce *The State and Revolution*, which constitutes a brilliant exposition of the Marx–Engels theory of the state. He criticized the opportunism of both the Mensheviks who had taken power in Russia in 1917 and other Social Democrats, particularly in Germany, such as Kautsky, Ebert, and Legien, and propounded his own theory of violent revolution rather than socialist gradualism. Lenin supported the view that the state had become an instrument of class oppression, and that a socialist society could not be achieved without smashing the bourgeois state and its institutions, for these were the instruments whereby the proletariat was oppressed. He went on from the theory of revolutionary transition to elaborate on the nature of the dictatorship of the proletariat and the conception of the 'withering away' of the state. Lenin pointed out that Marx and Engels were clear that the state was not, as some Social Democrats observed, an instrument for class reconciliation, but rather for class domination, in particular the domination of the proletariat by the capitalists. He pointed out that the Mensheviks implicitly accepted that the state was not like this, for they merely took control of the apparatus in 1917 without trying to get rid of it. Lenin, however, argued that if the state was an instrument of class control, then, if a classless society was to be achieved, the state structure had to be broken, not merely controlled.

A further feature of the Marxian theory of the state, which Social Democrats had obscured for their own purposes, was the notion of the 'withering away' of the state. This was interpreted by Social Democrats as meaning that when the state structure had been appropriated by the proletariat, eventually, with the development of the classless society, its functions would become otiose. Lenin argued that this was a deliberate falsification of Marxist theory for opportunist ends. Marx and Engels contended that the bourgeois state had to be smashed by revolutionary means, and that in its place would develop the 'dictatorship of the proletariat' which would act as the instrument of the proletariat to control and extirpate the remnants of the capitalist class. Eventually, however, with the dispossession of the capitalist, and the decline in capitalist consciousness, a classless society would be achieved. At *this* stage the proletarian state would wither away because there would be no need for the oppression of one class by another. Lenin insisted, therefore, that a violent revolution was necessary for the achievement of a genuine socialist society, and that the first stage of socialist society would in fact be characterized by the oppression of the capitalists by the proletarians. Although Lenin's pamphlet is a brilliant piece of Marxist exegesis, its purpose was more immediate. It was to provide a Marxian justification for the violent revolution in October 1917. This would overthrow the Menshevik regime which paid lip service to Marxism, and used Marxist theory to justify its bourgeois aims. *The State and Revolution* also provided the theoretical justification for the strong party dictatorship which Lenin was to introduce after the October revolution, a dictatorship necessitated by the existence of counter-revolutionary elements within society, but which would wither away when these elements had been eliminated.

One of the most ardent advocates of Lenin's theory of worldwide revolution, which as we have seen was the message of *Imperialism: The Highest Stage of Capitalism*, was Leon Trotsky (1879–1940). By 1924 Lenin, however, was dead and the world communist revolution had not materialized. In particular, the failure of the K.P.D., the German Communist party, to seize power immediately after the war, the final failure of the party in the Bamberg rising at the end of October 1923, and the right-wing attempt by Hitler and Ludendorff to topple the government in November of the same year, considerably weakened the force of the world revolutionary idea with which Trotsky was so closely identified. The ideological validity of this idea became a factor in the struggle for succession

after the death of Lenin, and late in 1924 Stalin embraced the twin
theories of 'socialism in one country' and 'capitalist encirclement'.
Socialism could be achieved in one country, in Stalin's view, even
though that country was surrounded by hostile capitalist neighbours, provided that the country was not dependent upon the
capitalist countries for raw materials. The major difference between
socialism in an individual country and socialism achieved on a
world-wide scale was that in an individual country, the dictatorship
of the proletariat, or the socialist state apparatus, could not wither
away even though bourgeois elements within the country had been
overcome; a strong state was still necessary to combat ideological
subversion from without. Trotsky regarded this theory as both
deviationist and counter-revolutionary, and clearly it does undermine the theory enunciated by Lenin about the interlocking nature
of capitalist economies in his theory of imperialistic capitalism. So
began the quarrel between Stalin and Trotsky, the ramifications of
which continue to this day. It might be argued, for example, that
the Soviet Union's present leadership sees its task in essentially
Stalin's terms—to establish internal socialism and to wait for the
inevitable collapse of capitalism—whereas the Chinese are nearer
to the Lenin–Trotsky emphasis in their insistence that socialism
is not a matter of the organization of one country or power bloc,
but rather has to be a world-wide movement if it is to be anything
at all.

Apart from Lenin and Trotsky, the Marxist thinker who had the
most influence during this period, and indeed since, was undoubtedly Georg Lukàcs (1885–1971). The reason for this influence is one
work published in 1923, and composed during the previous four
years. The book, *Geschichte und Klassenbewusstsein*, is important for
two reasons. In the first place, Lukàcs's work profoundly altered
the conventional view of Marx: in place of the severely scientific economic analyst, Lukàcs describes a morally committed
humanitarian who had developed certain concepts in Hegelian
philosophy into a radical critique of capitalist industrial society,
and who used economic and historical analysis as a tool to provide
backing for his social theory. Secondly, Lukàcs's work is important
in that it provided an impetus for the development of the sociology
of knowledge by Karl Mannheim and others.

In order to understand the importance of Lukàcs's humanistic
reading of Marx, it is necessary to realize that until 1927 Marx's
early works were not available (the more important ones indeed
not until the early 1930s[9]), and that the conventional reading of

Marx was based upon his mature writings, in particular *The Communist Manifesto*, *The 18th Brumaire of Louis Napoleon*, *A Contribution to the Critique of Political Economy*, and *Capital*. All these works were contributions either to economic analysis or to elucidating points in the materialist theory of history. These were the texts which the major expositors and interpreters of Marx's thought, such as Lenin, Kautsky, Rosa Luxemburg, and Plekhanov, had used as a basis for their theorizing. It seems clear that they were not aware of the existence of Marx's early writings. The central problems in Marxian thought at this time were concerned with economic determinism and the interpretation of contemporary economic and political conditions using the analytical tools which Marx had forged. Marxism was widely regarded as a scientific, not a moral analysis of capitalist society, and its historical development. Lukàcs's interpretation of Marx, which was borne out by the publication of works such as *The Economic and Philosophical Manuscripts of 1844* and *The German Ideology* during the early 1930s, profoundly altered this view. He demonstrated the intellectual debt which Marx owed to Hegel, and in particular argued that Marx had taken over the Hegelian notion of alienation, or man's feeling of the loss of himself in objects and institutions. This conception of alienation became in Marx's work, so Lukàcs argued, the basis of his moral critique of capitalism. In capitalist production man's spirit becomes objectified in his labour, and the product which should express this spirit in its concrete form is appropriated by the capitalist. Man becomes a commodity as a result of the wage system because his labour, his basic mode of being in the world, is bought. Capitalism distorts human nature, but because alienation is tied to capitalism it can be overcome when the economic and social conditions which have generated alienation are destroyed. Not only, then, is there a moral element in Marx's critique of capitalism; there is an element of eschatology too. The economic and historical studies of Marx's maturity represent not a departure from his morally based earlier work but rather constitute an analysis of the development and structure of capitalist society in order to understand more fully the possibility of its overthrow, and the subsequent development of a truly human community.

Lukàcs's writing seemed to vindicate the humanitarian concern of Marx, but at a cost, namely that of undermining its scientific status. The economic and historical studies become an instrument for elucidating this moral critique, and for providing empirical backing for the eschatological element. This change in emphasis which seemed to many to destroy the Marxian distinction between Utopian and scientific socialism did not appeal to the official keepers of Marxian orthodoxy in the Soviet Union, probably because the emphasis on the scientific nature of Marx's critique of capitalism had considerable appeal to a newly socialist country surrounded by mature capitalist societies. As Ernst Bloch said: 'Some will say of it that Marx had not placed Hegel on his feet so that Lukàcs can put him back on his head.' In the early 1930s after Hitler's rise to power Lukàcs took refuge in the Soviet Union and he made a somewhat abject recantation of his idealistic and deviationist tendencies. However, whatever the opinion of Lukàcs of his own work and that of the upholders of Communist orthodoxy, his brilliant championship of Marx's humanism at this time had a profound influence; it provided the initial impetus for the development of the kind of humanistic socialism which plays such a large part in New Left discussions today.

In developing a solution to the problem of the logical status of Marxism in Marxist terms, Lukàcs was concerned with the particular problem of whether Marxism itself has an absolute or merely relative validity. It is a part of the Marxist thesis that all forms of knowledge are determined by a nexus of social and economic conditions: 'It is not the consciousness of men which determines their existence, but, on the contrary, the social existence determines their consciousness.'[10] It follows from this that when the social conditions which determine consciousness and ideology change, then the forms of consciousness and ideologies related to them become outmoded. But if all human consciousness and knowledge is parasitic upon social and economic conditions, and has this merely limited validity, the problem arises of what becomes of Marxism, which surely is itself a form of consciousness. Has Marxism, then, purely limited validity? Engels faced this problem and argued *a priori* that certain logical laws and Marxism were true in an unconditional manner. Lukàcs, too, wanted to vindicate the superiority of Marxism over merely ideological systems, but he does not take this somewhat simplistic view of Engels. In fact his theory is anything but simple. He argued that ideologies other than Marxism are implicitly one-dimensional in that they take the given structure of the social world as absolute, and here the work of the social scientist is important in that he tries to bring social *facts* under *laws*. In taking the social world as given in this sense the existing state of social affairs is reified.

However, ideological insight at this level is not able to fit contemporary social patterns into the totality of historical development.
In order to do this there is a need to transcend these one-dimensional
ideologies which lack this historical orientation in order to achieve
a level of understanding of social life which can in fact fit contemporary social experience into an overall historical pattern. Marxism
embodies this higher standpoint. The trouble with this is that it
seems to make Marxism too absolute, because Marxism has also to
be articulated in the consciousness of the revolutionary proletariat,
but this consciousness has to be socially determined because social
existence in every case determines consciousness. On the one hand,
Marxism has to present itself as an absolute system, not as some
merely relative ideology; on the other hand it has to be given concrete
expression in the consciousness of the proletariat, a consciousness
which is structured by a particular nexus of social and economic
circumstances. Lukàcs solved the problem in a complicated fashion.
In order to fulfil its theoretical role of a *complete* break with bourgeois society, and therefore *with all forms of alienation*, the proletariat has to see all bourgeois ideology as a form of false consciousness, as a form of reification. To do this it needs to be in possession
of a theory which shows up this relative and undistorted nature
of bourgeois ideology—proletarian consciousness is not ideological
in that it does not itself embody distortion and false consciousness.
Marxism is not therefore ideological and distorted and it is still
capable of being articulated as the consciousness of the proletarian
class because the consciousness of the proletarian class cannot
itself be distorted if the complete break with reification is to be
achieved. Lukàcs's position on this problem had invidious personal
consequences. He accepted the view that the Communist party
of the Soviet Union articulates in its most complete form the consciousness of the proletariat, but this Communist party condemned
Lukàcs's work, and, accepting the logic of his position, he recanted.
    Apart from the particular intellectual problem with which
Lukàcs was concerned, his theory had a considerable influence
upon his one-time collaborator Karl Mannheim (1893–1947), the
sociologist. Mannheim argued that all knowledge, except the
knowledge derived from natural science, logic, and mathematics
is socially determined. All knowledge is related to the practical
interests pursued in a particular society. Indeed, Mannheim thought
that even the basic categories in terms of which we structure our
experience are socially determined. In *Ideology and Utopia* he
argued that the task of the sociology of knowledge was to 'analyse

the relationship between knowledge and existence'[11]—to observe how and in what form intellectual life at a given historical moment is related to the existing social and political forces. No ideology can therefore be judged in terms of correspondence, or lack of correspondence, to reality, because there is no reality outside the socially structured conception of it. An ideology is not so much true or false as *fitting* to a situation, or correct for a particular nexus of social circumstances (*situation gerecht*). Mannheim applied this doctrine to Marxism; it, too, became socially relative, structured by a particular set of economic and social conditions. The sociology of knowledge in the hands of Mannheim commits us to an extreme social form of Pythagorean relativism. The truth or falsity of an ideology cannot arise in the sense of its congruence to reality; all that can be asked is whether it fits closely the social conditions to which it is related. Epistemologists, for example Kant, regarded their categories as given and immutable, whereas they are in fact relative and subject to change. Therefore, the theory of knowledge as a philosophical discipline was to be superseded by the sociology of knowledge.

The extraordinary popularity of ideological politics following the First World War is a puzzling phenomenon. Most commentators on the period see it as in some sense an attempt on the part of those whose values and mores had been destroyed by the war to identify with a definite and clear-cut political creed, an attempt to escape from the waste land of conflicting values, or of no values at all. Arthur Koestler, for example, makes this point extremely cogently in *Arrow in the Blue:*

There was after the war a mass migration of the sons and daughters of the European bourgeoisie trying to escape from the collapsing world of their parents. The inflation years which had followed the first world war were the beginning . . . and the depression years which came a decade later accelerated the process; the second world war completed it. The economic and moral disintegration of the middle strata of society led to the fatal process of polarisation. The active elements among the pauperised bourgeoisie became rebels of the left or the right: Fascists and Communists shared about equally the benefits of the social migration. The remainder who found no consolation in hatred lived on pointlessly like a swarm of tired winter flies crawling over the dim windows of Europe, members of a class displaced by history.[12]

The speed of this process varied from country to country, and was largely related to the economic climate of the countries in question. In Italy, for example, the middle classes began to espouse the extreme politics of Fascism as early as 1922, in Germany a few years later, by which time unemployment had reached 4,500,000. In Britain the predilection for ideological politics came later in the 1930s. In the early twenties intellectuals seemed to be virtually apolitical, certainly if the testimonies of some of the most aware minds of the period are to be believed. Hugh Gaitskell in his contribution to *Essays in Labour History* has, for example, written about politics in Oxford during the early twenties:

The political and economic anxieties of the immediate postwar years were over. The gloom of the great depression and the horrors of the Nazis were yet to come. Nobody had heard of Hitler. The Spanish civil war was ten years off. Mussolini strutted about the stage but was regarded as a minor blot. There were still hopes that the League of Nations might work. . . . Politics to tell the truth were rather at a discount. . . . we were suspicious of general ideas.[13]

Gradually the situation changed. The development of the recession after 1929 made a profound impact among intellectuals of the period, an impact which was perhaps best expressed by Stephen Spender's vision of the unemployed:

> They lounge at corners of the street
> And greet friends with a shrug of the shoulder
> And then they empty pockets out,
> The cynical gestures of the poor
>
> .   .   .   .
>
> They sleep long nights and rise at ten
> To watch the hours that drain away.[14]

The inauguration of the Five Year Plan in the Soviet Union in 1928 seemed to point the way to the solution to these problems which capitalism developed but could not solve. The reports brought back by influential socialists such as the Webbs, who visited the Soviet Union under the direction of Intourist, added credence to the view that a new and better world was being created in Russia. Soon the politics of the extreme left began to make an impression on British intellectuals who, losing their penchant for empiricism, soon began to take Marxist theories with immense seriousness. This reached the stage when C. Day Lewis was able to sum up and encapsulate the mood of many of his contemporaries in the lines:

> Revolution, revolution
> Is the one correct solution.
> We've found it and we know it's bound to win
> Whatever's biting you, here's a something to put life into you.[15]

John Strachey, Christoper Caudwell, and Stephen Spender took the view that Marxism was the answer to the problems thrown up during this period. Their analyses of the fundamental postulates of contemporary British society were not so much radical as revolutionary. In *The Coming Struggle for Power* (1932) Strachey (1901–1963) argued that a revolution in Britain was both necessary and desirable, and in *The Theory and Practice of Socialism* (1936) he explained at some length the economic and social philosophy of Marxism with the avowed aim of developing a revolutionary consciousness on the part of the proletariat, so that they could understand the real nature of the economic and political crisis facing the country. This claim to be educating the proletariat had some substance in that Strachey's works were published by the Left Book Club which at this time had very nearly 60,000 subscribers and nearly 500,000 copies of Left Book Club works had been sold. In *The Theory and Practice of Socialism* Strachey argued the need for the development of a united workers' party which would be guided in its programme and action by the scientific theories of social change enunciated by Marx and Engels. He argued that capitalism could not be transformed from within, but rather had to be abolished; the mission of a united workers' party would be to wrest control of industrial enterprises from the capitalist class. The mechanics of this transition from capitalism to socialism could not be decided in advance, but would depend upon circumstances:

Nor does a knowledge of the science of social change enable us to foretell the exact character of the process; to foretell to what extent it may be violent, or at what point in it our existing capitalist institutions will have to be remoulded. The British and American working class movements will strive with all their might to minimise the degree of violence which will accompany the abolition of capitalism. But they will not do so at the cost of choosing the incomparably greater violence which is certain to accompany the continued existence of British and American capitalist imperialism.[16]

The case for Communism was argued on somewhat different lines by Stephen Spender (b. 1909) in *Forward from Liberalism* (1937), in which he argued that in fact Communism was the true heir of all that was valuable in the liberal tradition. Liberalism had been correct in its emphasis on the individual and his right to self-realization, but for the majority of working-class people within the *laissez-faire* societies which had underpinned liberalism, this notion of freedom and self-realization had meant very little. A communist society would secure social justice and an equitable distribution of resources and therefore an environment in which the ideals of liberalism would be realized.

Christopher Caudwell (1907–1937) was preoccupied with cultural rather than with directly political analysis in the style of Strachey and Spender, although of course he would have denied that there was a meaningful distinction between the two. This cultural emphasis is shown particularly in the works *Studies in a Dying Culture* (1938)[17] and *The Crisis in Physics* (1938). In *Studies in a Dying Culture*, Caudwell was concerned to work out a Marxist aesthetic, to see central problems in cultural life as basically problems in social relationships, which in turn are bound up with the means of production and the relations of production in capitalist society. The work of D. H. Lawrence, the concept of Love, and of Freedom are subjected to this sort of analysis. Lawrence, in Caudwell's view, gave a brilliant diagnosis of the sickness of contemporary Western European society: he characterized its possessiveness, its acquisitive nature, its fascination with function, and its distortion of human relationships, particularly sexual relations. Lawrence's solution to this problem, however, was both irrational and impossible. He solved it in his own life by a retreat into primitive forms of life and experience, a fact which accounts for his interest in the Etruscans, and for his decision to go and live in Mexico. A solution of this sort is impossible. In the first place it undermines the artist's social integrity, for he does nothing to alleviate the situation which he has described, and secondly because he cannot, with a highly developed even though distorted consciousness, return in a complete way to primitive modes of life and forms of experience. The problems which Lawrence saw as characteristic of contemporary society can only be solved by changing social relationships, and the economic relations which underpin them: 'Social relations must be rebuilt. The artist is bound for the sake of his integrity to become a thinker and a revolutionary. . . . Social relations must be altered not so as to contract consciousness, but to widen it.'[18] Social relationships, however, cannot be altered by mere willing, as Caudwell pointed out in his study of Liberty. It is also necessary to know the underlying causes of these distorted relationships, and the way these causal factors are developing. This is the role of Marxist philosophy which provides both the tools for social analysis, and an indication of the direction of change in society.

Indeed, so strong seemed to be the Marxist analysis of contemporary capitalism that it seduced some of the central figures of the Fabian Society, such as Sidney and Beatrice Webb and Harold

Laski. After a visit to the Soviet Union in 1935, during which time, as Beatrice characteristically remarks, 'We spent our energies by our practised methods in studying the political, economic, and cultural organisation of the U.S.S.R.',[19] the Webbs published *Soviet Communism—A New Civilisation?*, a work which was republished two years later without the question mark as an indication of their total conversion to Communist theory. This was not, as some may have thought, the result of senile decay, but rather a reaction to the changing world and the seeming inability of capitalism to cope with its own crises. Laski (1893–1950) too became convinced during the thirties of the correctness of the Marxist analysis. He thought that historical events demonstrated the impossibility of Fabian gradualism, and he argued that the immediate postwar German experience, and that of the two Labour governments in Britain, proved his contention. The time had come, he argued, for a general attack on capitalism and for wholesale nationalization. He explicitly put the argument in terms of an absolute alternative, an exclusive choice between Soviet Communism and Fascism, in *Liberty in the Modern State* (1930), and pointed out that if democracy was incompatible with the abolition of poverty and needless unemployment, then democracy must be sacrificed.

Despite what must have seemed to be *trahison des clercs* on the part of these prominent Fabians, their tradition was ably represented by the younger generation of socialists, and in fact by the 1940s it had again become dominant. Three factors help to explain this. In the first place the development of Keynesian economic theory seemed to provide the key to the correct management of capitalism so that the final crisis the Marxists had predicted could be avoided.[20] The development of the thesis of 'the managerial revolution'[21] seemed, perhaps unjustly, to undermine the Marxian conception of the ruling class, for the ownership of economic power was thereby divorced from the control of industrial enterprises; and finally, the Russo-German pact of 1940 was to many a betrayal on the part of the Communist bloc of all that it had stood for during the rise of Fascism in the thirties. By allying itself with what months before it had denounced as the last desperate stand of the monopolistic stage of capitalism it forfeited a great deal of plausibility. Two works in particular stand out at this time as reasserting the Fabian tradition, Evan Durbin's *The Politics of Democratic Socialism* (1940) and Douglas Jay's *The Socialist Case* (1937). So strong indeed seemed to be the arguments of Jay in particular, and so strong was the sense of Soviet betrayal that John Strachey, the

most influential Communist theorist, rejoined the ranks of the
Labour party with his work *Programme for Progress*. Certainly
the gradualist tradition had the most influence in the long run, and
it dominated the Attlee government in the immediate postwar
years.

The Liberal Tradition

It is difficult not to feel a large amount of sympathy for liberal
political thinkers in this period, in that their ideas seemed to most
of their contemporaries to be based upon presuppositions whose
social and economic basis had fallen away. A great many of the
notions which had characterized liberal thought seemed to be
destroyed by the Great War. Liberal thinkers seemed by and large
to lose their nerve—not surprisingly. Capitalism, the economic
system to which liberalism had historically been allied, seemed to
be in a state of permanent crisis, a condition which many regarded
as fatal. The social and economic conditions which in Edwardian
days had made liberalism such a powerful and palatable creed had
disappeared, and many regarded it as being thereby outmoded.
Further confusions concerned the role of liberalism in the rise of
Communism, and the development of Fascism. T. S. Eliot, for
example, regarded the popularity of Communist doctrines during
the 1930s as a direct result of the prevalence of liberalism. Indeed
such a view was not without a certain plausibility, for, as we have
seen, Stephen Spender saw Communism taking over liberal ideals
without having to accept the inhuman economic system which had
underpinned these ideals in the past. The contrary thesis was however argued by Marxists, and in particular by Herbert Marcuse
(b. 1898) in an article called '*Der Kampf gegen der Liberalismus in der
Totalitaren Staatsauffassung*'.[22] In this article, published in *Zeitschrift für Sozial Forschung* in 1934, Marcuse put forward two
reasons why Fascist attacks on liberalism were not to be taken at
their face value. First, in a crisis liberal and Fascist would unite
against socialism in the name of saving European culture; and,
second, liberalism led to Fascism in that liberalism was the style of
politics relevant for the individualistic, competitive stage of capitalism, whereas Fascism is the political structure of more advanced
monopoly capitalism, the stage which would follow, of necessity,
from the individualistic stage. Faced with these contradictory interpretations of their precise role in history, it is not surprising that
liberals felt somewhat diffident in defence of their beliefs.

The problem confronting liberalism seemed to be that of combining, in the words of E. M. Forster, the 'new economy with the old morality',[23] planning for material resources with freedom for the mind. It was argued by critics such as Laski in his *The Decline of Liberalism* (1940) that liberal theory had historically been allied to *laissez-faire* economic policies; but uninhibited capitalism, Laski maintained, involved a denial of freedom to the vast majority who did not own the means of production and were exploited by the capitalists. Liberalism had declined, he held, because it had failed to come to terms with the necessity of economic planning in order to secure to the vast majority the economic conditions of freedom. In support of his thesis he pointed out that the major opposition to Roosevelt's New Deal policies in fact came from these unreconstructed *laissez-faire* liberals who failed to realize that planning was necessary in order to make individual freedom a *real* possibility for the masses.

It would be wrong however to assume that no attempt had been made by liberal theorists to overcome this problem; in fact various writers during the 1930s were concerned with precisely this question. Ramsay Muir in *The Future of Democracy* (1939) argued that liberalism was incompatible with the monopoly capitalism which was developing in Western European countries and state socialism which was developing in the Soviet Union. The future of the liberal tradition depended upon the possibility of a *via media* between these two extremes. Eliot Dodds in *Ownership for All* (1939) suggested a substantial amount of state interference in economic life in order to secure the material conditions of liberty to all people in society. He argued that the ownership of property was basic to the exercise of freedom, but that in 1939, 60 per cent of the property in Britain was owned by 1 per cent of the population. What was required was a redistribution of property in order to give everyone the material basis for the exercise of freedom, since a real democracy 'can only be made out of free men who enjoy the independence of ownership'. It must be said, however, that these books had little influence at the time, and the attitude towards liberalism among large sections of the community was that it was allied to an order which was in its death throes. To seek to modify the theory of liberalism in these peripheral ways was, in Auden's vivid line, 'Lecturing on Navigation while the ship is going down'.[24]

During the final years of the Second World War, however, a significant revival in liberal thought was seen, especially in the work of Karl Popper (b. 1902) in *The Open Society and its Enemies*, and in the very robust view advocated by F. A. Hayek (b. 1899) in *The Road to Serfdom* (1944). In *The Open Society and Its Enemies* (1945), Popper advocated what he called piecemeal social engineering as opposed to utopian political activity which involved planning directed towards the ends to be achieved. Popper rejected any eschatological political doctrines which involved the precise directing of all areas of activity in the service of some moral or political plan. In their place he advocated a 'goalless' view of political activity with minimizing misery rather than maximizing happiness as the basic political impulse. In Popper's view people here and now have claims which should be met and not sacrificed for some dubious long-term political end. In its conception *The Open Society* can be seen as a conscious reaction against the ideological style of politics which had dominated the political scene for so long, and against the political messianism and moral futurism which had recently brought such disaster to Europe. Hayek's theory is more extreme than Popper's. He would, I think, disagree with Forster's formulation of the liberal dilemma because it made too many concessions to the socialist-minded critic such as Laski. The problem of liberalism is not the planning of material resources with freedom for the mind, because in Hayek's view planning is incompatible with freedom if more is meant by planning than the removal of severe physical deprivation and hardship. Once planning becomes an instrument of a political ideology or plan then freedom disappears. Free competition with help for those who are very sorely oppressed by the system is the only real guarantee of freedom.

The Second War ended with a resurgence of two traditional styles of thought, democratic socialism and liberalism. The resurgence of the third major tradition, the conservative, which had lain dormant to some extent during the inter-war years, except for Harold Macmillan's somewhat singular *The Middle Way* (1938), was to take a little longer. Michael Oakeshott, the dominating figure of conservative thought, published his major contributions in the late 1940s and early '50s and consequently an analysis of his writings falls outside our period.

Social and Political Order: The Christian Approach

The growth of Fascism, National Socialism, and Communism obviously presented a challenge to the Christian view of man and his relationship to society, and at this time several leaders of Christian thought attempted to restate traditional doctrine in a way that could be made relevant to the contemporary crisis. This was attempted by Pope Pius XI in his encyclicals *Quadragesimo Anno*

(1931), and *Divini Redemptoris* (1937), and in various letters to the heads of churches in particular countries, the most important of which, *Mit brennender Sorge* (1937), was dispatched to the Roman Catholic Church in Germany. In Britain at the same time T. S. Eliot sought to restate the idea of a Christian society in contrast to the materialistic secularism which surrounded him.

The Catholic teaching on the relationship between man and society had been formulated with a great deal of vigour and clarity during the latter years of the nineteenth century by Pope Leo XIII in his encyclicals *Immortale Dei* (1885), *Libertas* (1888), and *Rerum Novarum* (1891). Given the fact that these were issued *ex cathedra* they constituted, as it were, the co-ordinates in terms of which Pius XI formulated his own teaching in the 1930s. Not unnaturally at this time the Church was particularly concerned with the role of the state *vis-à-vis* the individual, and on this point Leo XIII was quite unequivocal in *Immortale Dei*. In this encyclical he argued that the state had a necessary role in human life since man could not become a man as opposed to a brute without society, and society had to be held together by the state. The state in turn, however, derived its authority from the power of God: 'From this it follows that there can be no public power except from God. For God alone is the true and supreme lord of the world.'[25]

This statement would seem to imply that the Church would have to condemn any political ideology which postulated the state or the nation as the supremely spiritual object. The Church did not lay down what kind of political structure a particular community should have, only this formal requirement was made, that whatever the political structure, it should always be regarded as subordinate to the will and purpose of God. A similar point was made by Pius XI in *Mit brennender Sorge* in which he argued that the utility of the people or the state could not be the ultimate political value because it mattered whether the needs of the people were morally right, and this was fixed by the will of God. The autonomy of associations or corporations within society was also insisted on up to a point, provided that they were not evidently bad, unlawful, or dangerous to the state. *Prima facie*, groups within society should be tolerated and their autonomy respected. The onus was thus on the politician who wished either to dispense with them or to undermine their autonomy to demonstrate that they could be considered bad, unlawful, or dangerous. Clearly a great many of these points were relevant for the guidance of those who accepted the Pope's authority when confronted at this time with totalitarian ideologies of the right or the left.

In Britain the Christian teaching on man and society was expounded most clearly by T. S. Eliot (1888–1965) in *The Idea of a Christian Society* (1939) and to a less systematic extent in *For Lancelot Andrewes* (1928). In *The Idea of a Christian Society*, Eliot made clear that he regarded himself as characterizing something like a Weberian Ideal Type. He disputed the vulgar view that the Western democracies were Christian in any real sense of the word. In fact Eliot asked with an almost Burkean resonance whether contemporary society could be regarded as existing for any reason other than the maximization of economic utilities, and whether it had any beliefs more essential than: 'A belief in compound interest and the maintenance of dividends.'[26] A truly Christian society would be organized on beliefs and attitudes which postulated certain transcendent, not merely material ends of life. This would not mean, Eliot agreed, that all the activities of such a society would be based on this transcendent aim. Rather the basic characteristic of a Christian society would be the development of a truly human community in which virtue could flourish, but also one in which those who had eyes to see could, in their social existence, pursue a supernatural end. Eliot's aim was to delineate the kind of society in which man as a citizen and a member of a human community would not be at odds with himself as a child of God, a society in which a man's religious claims would not clash with his social duties. Eliot saw the main obstacle to the achievement of these aims as industrialism and the predominance of the profit motive in large areas of human life and activity.

Between the Scylla of decline, which Eliot thought the most likely course, and the Charybdis of a reconstructed secular society, Eliot suggested a positive Christian society based upon the establishment of a church which, in Britain, would be the Anglican Church. Anglicanism he claimed, controversially, to represent the traditional form of Christian belief and worship of the great mass of the people in the country, and its establishment to be sanctioned by tradition. If Eliot's theory is generalized, he seems to be arguing that truly Christian national states could only grow if the traditional form of Christianity in that country were to be established and permeate the social relations of those who lived in the nation. It seems on the basis of this that for all his Anglo-Catholicism, Eliot was basically a latitudinarian in that he was not willing to lay down *a priori* restrictions on what was to count as a truly Christian church. The only criterion which he proposed seems to have been the tradition of the society concerned. Against this however it must be said that

he had ecumenical hopes that church unity might lead to the formation of a universal church and therefore to an international or supra-
national Christian society.

Industrial Society and Its Critics

A continuing thread of social and political thought was the critique of industrial society developed in the previous century by
Ruskin, Morris, and Carlyle, and more immediately by the early
guild socialists such as Orage, Penty, and Hobson. The early guildsmen provided a moral, humanistic critique of industrial capitalism,
but their practical political and economic proposals seemed to many
to be both utopian and vague. Penty urged a return to the medieval
guild system advocated originally by William Morris, whereas
Orage and Hobson argued that the human dimension of work could
only be recovered when the wage system, which distorted the relationship between the producer and the product by treating labour
as a commodity and not as an expression of human creative activity,
was done away. Because the wage system distorted man's creative
activity and made him into a passive labourer instead of an active
producer, the quality of life throughout the community, and particularly the quality of its political life, suffered. A change in the relations of production would profoundly affect the whole social and
political fabric of the country. These arguments were taken further
by G. D. H. Cole, a professed guild socialist, and R. H. Tawney, a
sympathizer. Both Cole and Tawney were more capable than the early
guildsmen of translating a humanistic ideal into a practical political
and economic programme for the reform of industrial capitalism.

Cole (1889–1959), who was an academic political philosopher, an
economist of note, and a superb propagandist, concentrated his
efforts on three fronts: fronts which in a sense reflected these differing capacities. He was concerned with the dissemination of guild
socialist propaganda through the National Guilds League which he
founded in 1915. This propaganda was particularly aimed towards
the trade unions, and socialist groups. He pursued research into the
productive relations in particular industries in works such as *Labour
in War Time* (1915), *The Payment of Wages* (1918), and *Trade
Unionism on the Railways* (1917). This research was indispensable
if a practical political and industrial programme was to be developed
out of the guild socialists' humanist ideals. Finally, and possibly
most importantly, Cole developed a more concise theory of the
political and industrial organization of a guild socialist society. This
political and economic philosophy was developed primarily in *Guild*

Socialism Restated (1920), *Self Government in Industry* (1917), and
Social Theory (1920). In these works, Cole sought to describe the
organization of the industrial structure of guild socialism, the
political organization which would take account of this new structure, and how the transition from industrial capitalism to guild
socialism would come about. The early guild socialists, particularly
Hobson and Orage, had concentrated solely upon the role of industrial action in the achievement of a guild socialist society, whereas Cole was concerned to show that the political structure could not
be ignored. In fact, in his view, the state had a central role to play
in the transition from one form of social order to another. Cole's
argument was that if industrial control could be wrested from the
capitalist by purely industrial action, organized labour could not, as
a result of the debilitatingly passive role which it had played in
capitalist society, immediately take over the management of industry. There would be a need for an interregnum when workers, freed
from their passive role in production in the capitalist system, would
be able to prepare to assume control of industry. Nationalization of
industry by the state was necessary during this period. This would
insure that industrial enterprises were not returned to capitalism,
and would mean that there would be no industrial anarchy before
the workers were able to exercise their newfound responsibility.
Nationalization was, however, a form of industrial organization
which was anathema to the early guildsmen. So strong was Cole's
argument that the view that state control of industry was a necessary
expedient during the transitional period was adopted as official
policy by the National Guilds League in 1921.

Such was Cole's theory of transition, but he went beyond this to
formulate clear plans for the industrial organization which would
enable workers to be fully in control of their enterprises, and a
theory of political structure which would take account of the new
relationships of production. For each industry there would be a
particular guild which was to be organized democratically with a
committee for each factory elected by men on the factory floor.
From these factory-based committees would be generated district,
area, or regional committees, elected partly by the factory committees and partly by the workers themselves. An executive committee responsible for the broad national affairs of the guild would
be elected and certain permanent national officials would be appointed by the national executive. The management of each factory,
as well as other officials, would be elected by the whole body of
workers in the factory. In this way the industrial structure of society

would be profoundly changed; and clearly a different political system would be required to take account of the new social structure. Cole's political theory was profoundly influenced by the political pluralism of writers such as Figgis and Maitland. The pluralists attributed to groups a status in society of such importance that the state was concerned as little more than a referee, arbitrating between different group interests. In *Guild Socialism Restated* Cole utilized the pluralist conception of society in his guild socialist philosophy. The country was to be divided into areas, both urban and rural, which would be ruled by groups or communes in which local guild committees and local consumer associations would have equal representation. Building up from these local communes would be an area, or regional, commune with similar organization, while at the national level the commune would be comprised of elected representatives of national guilds and national consumer groups. The political organization mirrored the industrial organization of the state, and both were democratic, both would maximize the potentialities and the powers of individuals which were denied realization in the contemporary economic structure and the political system which reflects it.

The other central work in this style is R. H. Tawney's (1880–1962) *The Acquisitive Society*, published in 1921, and to a lesser extent *Equality* (1931), a work which elaborates one aspect of the argument of the former work. In *The Acquisitive Society* Tawney, without explicitly committing himself to the guild socialist doctrine, provided both a critique and a remedy for the ills of industrial society which reflected a great deal of what was central to the guild socialist movement. Tawney shared the guildsman's abhorrence of the crippling psychological and social effects of industrial capitalism. Contemporary society was one in which the idea of purpose had been lost. There was no conception of the *ends* of human activity so the activity which was central to the achievement of ends, namely industry, was given the place of an end in itself. Only if people could become aware of the social purposes of industry could they see that industry was a means and not an end in itself. Without this true appreciation of the role of industry the whole of society was distorted and human nature was warped. At this point one naturally thinks of the character of Gerald in *Women in Love* by D. H. Lawrence:

Everything in the world has its function, and it is good or not in so far as it fulfils its function more or less perfectly. Was a miner a good miner?

then he was complete. Was a manager a good manager? that was enough. Gerald himself who was responsible for all this industry was he a good director? If he were he had fulfilled his life. The rest was byplay.[27]

Tawney himself traced the loss of purpose in contemporary society to the seventeenth century:

The rise of modern economic relations, which may be dated in England from the latter half of the seventeenth century, was coincident with the growth of political theory which replaced the conception of purpose by that of mechanism. During a great part of history men had found the significance of their social order in its relation to the universal purposes of religion.[28]

Man could no longer regard himself as part of the great chain of being, but only as a part of a machine designed to increase productivity more and more for no discernible purpose. In circumstances such as these men become mere cogs in a machine. This was a conception of society to which Eliot's vision of *The Waste Land* seems peculiarly appropriate.

To escape from the waste land of industrialism which perverted society and dehumanized man, it was necessary, in Tawney's view, to reintroduce the concept of purpose. This purpose can no longer be transcendent or religious, but rather immanent in the society itself. In his opinion the only way in which industry could be organized so as to be subordinate to a purpose rather than an end in itself, would be for industry to be turned into a profession. Industry as conventionally organized was designed to protect the economic rights of those within the activity. Organized as a profession, it would be concerned not so much with the accumulation of wealth as such, but rather with the social service which it performed. The other feature of contemporary society which distorted human relationships was inequality, and in his book *Equality* Tawney put the case for an egalitarian society. He pointed out that the case for equality does not depend on the acceptance of the doctrine that all men are in fact equal in capacity, character, ability, and attainment:

The equality which these thinkers emphasise is not equality of capacity or attainment, but of circumstances and institutions, and manner of life. The inequality which they deplore is not the inequality of personal gifts, but of social and economic environment . . . because men are men, social institutions . . . should be planned as far as is possible to emphasise and strengthen, not the class differences which divide, but the common humanity which unites them.[29]

The ways in which inequality in society was to be reduced were in Tawney's view through the extension of the social services to increase economic provisions for those whose circumstances were poor, progressive taxation to reduce inequalities in income, and the reorganization of industry on the lines which he had advocated in *The Acquisitive Society*. The reorganization of industry as a profession would involve all men in industrial decision-making and reduce inequalities of status, and industrial activity would be directed towards the production of socially useful goods and not towards the production of luxury goods for a privileged social class.

The Tragic Nature of Social Life: The Work of Freud

Sigmund Freud (1856–1939) revolutionized man's conception of himself, and in so doing changed his understanding of his social experience. In *Civilisation and Its Discontents* (1930), he formulated an interpretation of social life based upon the conception of man which he had developed in his central works on psychoanalysis. The basic point implicit in Freud's theory is that there can be no society, no civilization, and no culture which can fully express man's nature and fulfil his capacities, because the very existence of society as such depends upon the sublimation of certain instincts, or their total repression. Men are in a sense amphibious, in the Freudian view. They exist in two dimensions: the realm of the id dominated by the pleasure principle, and the super-ego, the social world dominated by the reality principle. Under the rule of the pleasure principle man is a creature of animal drives, particularly concerned with sexual gratification, seeking to maximize his own pleasure, and avoid painful experiences. But, as Hobbes pointed out before Freud, this seeking after pleasure and gratification is incompatible with the existence of society. In social life the full and painless gratification of human desires is impossible, because the individual is brought into contact with other like-minded individuals. The realization of this which happens with a particular individual in childhood, leads to a modification of the rule of the pleasure principle by the development of the ego and super-ego, and the dominance of the reality principle. The reality principle is embodied in the institutions, mores, and standards of a society within which an individual is reared as a child. The ascendancy of the reality principle over the pleasure principle alters the conception and the content of pleasure. Instinctual pleasures which are destructive of social life are either sublimated or totally repressed. Civilization and society have a value in that they provide for the higher psychical activities, but these activities are achieved only at great cost, namely the sublimation and repression of much more powerful id instincts in human beings. The kind of sublimation which Freud has in mind here is that of anal erotic desires into a group of socially acceptable and perhaps socially necessary character traits such as parsimony, a passion for order, and cleanliness. In place of the insecure temporary satisfactions of pleasure to be gained under the sway of the pleasure principle, adherence to the reality principle brings more certain gratification of socially accepted pleasures. This gratification is more restrained, it may not be so immediate, but it is more or less guaranteed.

This sublimation or repression of instinctual pleasures in Freud's view generates neurosis. For example the sexual life of man in a civilized community is severely impaired. Only heterosexual genital love has been saved from repression because such a form of sexuality is necessary for the continuance of civilization. Freud's views seem to be profoundly conservative in that repression and sublimation are endemic in any sort of society. There is always a tension between the one and the many, between the individual and society, because society demands repression as a condition of its own existence. Social problems cannot be solved by reforming society, or by revolution, but rather through therapy wherein the individual will become reconciled to his social reality, whatever that may be. Of course it might be argued that there are the germs of a critical theory of society in Freud, and these indications were seized upon in the 1950s by, among others, Eric Fromm in *The Sane Society* (1956), Herbert Marcuse in *Eros and Civilization* (1953), and by Lionel Trilling in *Freud and the Crisis of Our Culture* (1955). In the latter work Trilling points to a possible critical way of reading Freud:

Far from being a reactionary idea it is actually a liberating idea. It proposes to us that culture is not all powerful. It suggests that there is a residue of human quality beyond the reach of cultural control, and that residue, elemental as it may be, serves to bring culture itself under criticism and to keep it from being absolute.[30]

It must be stressed however that this was not Freud's view. Man is fundamentally alienated from society and all that can be expected is some kind of reasonable balance between individual drives and social claims.

The Death of Political Philosophy

It is one of the ironies of the period that at a time when political and social theories had such a close and in some cases disastrous effect upon the actual conduct of social and political life, academic philosophers declared that political philosophy as a meaningful discipline was dead. The main reason for this scepticism about what had traditionally been one of the central dimensions of a philosophical understanding of the world was undoubtedly the radical empiricism of the logical positivists, although other factors such as the rise of sociology and political science, and the 'sociology of knowledge' may have had a marginal effect. The statements which political theorists wish to make about political activity did not find a meaningful place, given the positivists' criterion of intelligibility. This criterion is considered elsewhere in this volume, but basically a distinction was drawn between analytic and synthetic statements, and these were regarded as being the only meaningful forms of discourse. Analytic statements are true in virtue of the meanings of the words, for example 'all bachelors are unmarried men'; synthetic statements are found to be true through public verification, or at least verification in principle. Analytic statements, because they make no claims upon the facts, are always true but not significant, at least to those who know the language in which the statements are made. Synthetic statements make claims upon facts and may therefore be true or false and which they are depends upon the relevant observations. Obviously a good deal of traditional philosophy does not pass this strict criterion of intelligibility and political philosophy is one such form. Political theories are not analytic; if they were everyone who understands the English language would agree with the statements made by theorists. But, notoriously, political theorists disagree even among themselves. If they think they are propounding analytic statements, then their statements, if true, would not be significant, and yet most political theorists want to draw attention to some new features of political life, or to change our conceptions of the political, and a set of analytic truths cannot serve this purpose. Nor can political theories be synthetic. If they were, their truth or falsity would depend on ordinary observation. It would imply, for example, that one could by observation test the truth of the Lockean notion of the state as based upon contract, and the falsity of the Hegelian conception that it is the actuality of the ethical will. To do this, however, is clearly impossible. Furthermore political philosophers do not seem on the whole to regard their theories as empirical, for they do not usually cite empirical evidence to support them. Political philosophy therefore seems to fall between the two stools of analytic insignificance and empirical non-confirmation. Because of this positivists concluded that the statements of the political philosopher were literally devoid of sense. As a consequence political theory was consigned, along with theology and ethics, to the prehistory of philosophy. This wholesale rejection of political theory as meaningless, not unnaturally led to a decline in interest in the subject by philosophers who were influenced by the ideas of the positivists. Indeed only during the last few years has there been anything like a revival in political philosophy, and even this approach seems somewhat apologetic. It is concerned with the piecemeal analysis of particular concepts, and it does not try either to come to terms with a whole tradition of political discourse or to recommend the adoption of particular characterizations of political experience.

The only approach to political and social life which positivism sanctioned was the scientific non-normative empirical study of particular social and political systems and people's behaviour and attitudes within those systems, and in fact positivism gave a theoretical boost to the development of a kind of behavioural social and political science, just as it did to behaviourism in psychology.

NOTES

[1] L. Woolf, *After the Deluge* (1931), 19.

[2] B. Mussolini, *The Doctrine of Fascism*, reprinted in M. Oakeshott, *The Social and Political Doctrines of Contemporary Europe* (Cambridge, 1939), 165.

[3] Mussolini, *Doctrine of Fascism*, 176.

[4] M. van den Bruck, *Das dritte Reich* (Hamburg, 1923).

[5] A. Rosenberg, *Das Mythus der 20. Jahrhunderts* (Munich, 1933), 525.

[6] Reich Citizenship Law, passed by the Reichstag on 15 September 1935.

[7] Quoted in W. McGovern, *From Luther to Hitler* (Boston, 1941), 665.

[8] V. I. Lenin, *Imperialism: The Highest Stage of Capitalism* (Moscow, 1967), 775.

[9] From 1927 onwards the Marx–Engels Institute in Moscow published the first 12 volumes of the *Marx–Engels Gesamtausgabe*. The most important writings published were *Kritik des Hegelschen Staatsrechts* (written 1843), *Ökonomische-Philosophische Manuskripte* (1844), *Excerpthefte* (1844–7), and *Die Deutsche Ideologie* (1845–6).

[10] K. Marx, *Preface to the Critique of Political Economy*, ed. K. Kautsky (Stuttgart, 1907).

[11] K. Mannheim, *Ideology and Utopia* (1957), 237.

[12] A. Koestler, *Arrow in the Blue* (1952).

[13] H. Gaitskell, 'At Oxford in the Twenties', in *Essays in Labour History*, ed. J. Saville and A. Briggs (1959), 6.

[14] S. Spender, *Poems 1933* (1933), 29.

[15] C. Day Lewis, *A Time to Dance and Other Poems* (1935), 62.

[16] J. Strachey, *The Theory and Practice of Socialism* (1936), 45.

[17] Republished in C. Caudwell, *The Concept of Freedom* (1965).

[18] Ibid. 25.

[19] B. Webb, *What I Believe* (1940), 34.

[20] For the influence of the contrary view that capitalism was on a fatal decline see D. Wright, 'The Prospects for Capitalism' in *A Survey of Contemporary Economics*, ed. H. S. Ellis (1948).

[21] See especially the work of J. Burnham, *The Managerial Revolution* (1941). For the contrary view that this does nothing to undermine the Marxian critique of capitalism cf. H. Marcuse, *One-Dimensional Man* (1964), 32.

[22] Republished in H. Marcuse, *Negations* (1968).

[23] 'The Challenge of Our Time' in *Two Cheers for Democracy* (1965), 66.

[24] W. H. Auden, *Poems* (1933), 76.

[25] *Immortale Dei*, Leo XIII in Oakeshott, *Social and Political Doctrines of Contemporary Europe*, 45–6.

[26] T. S. Eliot, *The Idea of a Christian Society* (1939), 64.

[27] D. H. Lawrence, *Women in Love* (ed. 1963), 251.

[28] R. H. Tawney, *The Acquisitive Society* (ed. 1961), 16.

[29] R. H. Tawney, *Equality* (1931), 50.

[30] L. Trilling, *Freud and the Crisis of Our Culture* (Boston, 1955), 48.

FOR FURTHER READING

There are few general works of interpretation on this period. Among the best of these is H. S. Hughes, *Consciousness and Society* (1967), but this book deals only with a part of the period, terminating its account in 1930. G. H. Sabine, *A History of Political Theory* (3rd ed., 1951) provides an accurate but unexciting conspectus of the major social and political doctrines of the period.

E. Nolte, *The Three Faces of Fascism* (1965) is a detailed, well-documented and deeply felt interpretation of the rise of Fascism in Italy, National Socialism in Germany, and Action Française. (The latter is discussed in volume I of *The Twentieth-Century Mind*.) An older work, but one which has stood the passage of time, is F. Neumann, *Behemoth* (Oxford, 1944). H. Finer, *Mussolini's Italy* (1935, reprinted 1964) is a standard work on the history of Italy under Fascist government, while the diplomatic papers of Ciano, edited by Malcolm Muggeridge (1948), shed, in many of their *obiter dicta*, a good deal of light on Fascist conceptions particularly in relation to the bourgeoisie. Schneider, *The Meaning of the Fascist State* (1928) was an early work of interpretation. The racialist background in German thought which the National Socialists both exploited and extended is well discussed in G. L. Mosse, *The Crisis of German Ideology* (1966). Houston Stewart Chamberlain, *The Foundation of the Nineteenth Century* (1910) was a seminal work systematizing a vague body of racialist ideas. Hitler's *Mein Kampf* has recently been republished in translation, ed. D. C. Watt (1969), and a selection has been made of Rosenberg's writings in *Alfred Rosenberg*, ed. R. Pois (1970). Diana Spearman, *Modern Dictatorship* (1939) is an interesting discussion of the rise of totalitarian governments in the 1930s. At a literary level,

Thomas Mann's *The Magic Mountain* (1924) involves allegorical comment on some central Fascist ideas.

General works dealing with left-wing social and political thought during the period are G. Lichtheim, *Marxism* (1961); C. W. Mills, *The Marxists* (1962); B. D. Wolfe, *Three Who Made a Revolution* (1956, a study of Lenin, Trotsky, and Stalin); and R. N. Carew-Hunt, *The Theory and Practice of Communism* (1950). General historical studies of the 1917 revolution are E. H. Carr, *The Bolshevik Revolution 1917–23*, 3 vols. (1954), and Christopher Hill,`Lenin and the Russian Revolution* (1963). At a more popular level, David Caute, *The Left in Europe* (1966) provides, with visual aids, a guide to left-wing thought and practice since 1789. The three major figures of the Russian revolution, Lenin, Trotsky, and Stalin, have all been extensively treated in biographies. The life of Lenin has been chronicled by David Shub in *Lenin* (1948); up to 1917 by E. Wilson in *To the Finland Station* (ed. 1960); and by a prominent British socialist in James Maxton, *Lenin* (1932). Isaac Deutscher did not live to complete his life of Lenin, but the first chapter, *Lenin's Childhood*, has been published (1970). On a different intellectual level, Georg Lukàcs's *Lenin* (1970) is a masterly attempt to establish the unity, the orthodoxy, and validity of Lenin's thinking. The life, thought, and work of Trotsky has been definitively recorded in Deutscher's masterly trilogy, *The Prophet Armed* (1954), *The Prophet Unarmed* (1959), and *The Prophet Outcast* (1963). Stalin also is the subject of Deutscher's analysis in *Stalin: A Political Biography* (1949). The standard life of Rosa Luxemburg is by P. Nettl, *Rosa Luxemburg* (1966). There is also an extended essay on this book by Hannah Arendt in *Men in Dark Times* (1970). The thought of Georg Lukàcs is discussed by G. Lichtheim in *Lukàcs* (1970) and in a volume of essays *Georg Lukàcs*, edited by G. H. R. Parkinson (1970). Interesting shorter pieces on Lukàcs are to be found in 'Marxism and the Literary Critic', 'Georg Lukàcs and his Devil's Pact', and 'An Aesthetic Manifesto', all essays by George Steiner published in *Language and Silence* (1967). For further discussion of the sociology of knowledge, the reader could consult the works of Werner Stark, particularly *The Sociology of Knowledge* (1958), and for a vigorous critique of the whole notion, chapter 23 of K. R. Popper, *The Open Society and Its Enemies* (1945).

An interesting interpretative essay on the problems facing British socialists during this period is R. H. S. Crossman, 'The Theory and Practice of British Freedom', originally published in *Political Thought, the European Tradition* (1938) and reprinted in *Planning for Freedom* (1965). *The God that Failed* (1950), edited by Crossman, includes interesting essays by disenchanted Marxists. Arthur Koestler's *Arrow in the Blue* (1952) encapsulates the experience of a Marxist in a European context, while *In the Thirties* (1962) by E. Upward constitutes a *Bildungsroman*, the growth and education of a Marxist in a British context. *The Mind in Chains* (1937), edited by C. Day Lewis, now the Poet Laureate, consists of a number of essays in cultural criticism by highly articulate Marxists. On the non-Marxist left, Ruth Adam and Kitty Muggeridge's *Beatrice Webb* (1967) provides a biography of a central figure of the period. S. Letwin's *The Pursuit of Certainty* (1965) also deals with the Webbs and their tradition of thought. Margaret Cole, *The Story of Fabian Socialism* (1961) deals with the history of the Fabian Society. *Downhill all the Way* (1967) and *The Journey not the Arrival Matters* (1969) by Leonard Woolf chronicle the thoughts and feelings of a prominent left-wing figure of the period. *The Political Quarterly in the '30s*, ed. W. A. Robson (1971), includes a selection of articles which represent typical views of the period on political matters. The introduction is particularly valuable. S. T. Glass, *The Responsible Society* (1966) is a useful work on guild socialism. There is a typically interesting discussion of Tawney in R. Williams, *Culture and Society* (1958). This book also has a chapter on T. S. Eliot's political and social thought.

Exposition, criticism, and developments of Freud's social thought may be found in P. Roazen, *Freud, Social and Political Thought* (New York, 1968); R. Wollheim, *Freud* (1971); E. Fromm, *The Sane Society* (1956); and H. Marcuse, *Eros and Civilization* (1969). Freudian analysis and Marxism were perhaps the two most important intellectual trends in the 1930s, and an interesting attempt to reconsider both is R. Osborn, *Marxism and Psycho-Analysis*, originally published in the 1930s and republished in 1965.

The decline of academic political philosophy dated from the rise of logical positivism during the late 1930s. The foremost British exponent of these views was A. J. Ayer in his book *Language, Truth and Logic* (1936). His mature reflections on politics are to be found in 'Philosophy and Politics', published in *Metaphysics and Commonsense* (1969). Although the implications for political philosophy were not made fully articulate at the time, they were drawn very forcefully in T. D. Weldon, *The Vocabulary of Politics* (1953). A discussion of the thesis that political philosophy is dead is to be found in Peter Laslett's introduction to *Philosophy, Politics and Society: Series I* (Oxford, 1956). A vigorous defence of the subject may be found in I. Berlin, 'Does Political Theory Still Exist?' in *Philosophy, Politics and Society: Series II*, ed. P. Laslett and W. G. Runciman (Oxford, 1962).

5

British Philosophy

R. F. ATKINSON

Twenty-five Years of Analysis

Analysis as opposed to speculation seems, from the viewpoint of today, to have been the dominant philosophical activity in Britain between the wars, although in fact the idealist metaphysicians Bradley and Bosanquet were both alive at the beginning of the period, and a number of major speculative works first appeared in the course of it. These include Alexander's *Space, Time and Deity* (1920), McTaggart's *Nature of Existence* (1927)—in which appears a celebrated 'demonstration' of the unreality of time—and Whitehead's *Process and Reality* (1929).* Most of Collingwood's works appeared in this period too, though he is perhaps distinguished more by lack of sympathy with anti-metaphysical contemporaries than by a propensity to engage in speculation himself. The really significant philosophers were, however, Russell, Moore, and Wittgenstein, in the front rank, with Ramsey (a man of great promise who died sadly young), Wisdom, Price, and Ayer greater or smaller distances behind. All were consciously engaged in the practice of analysis, though their conceptions of it varied a great deal. Moore thought of himself as analysing common-sense *beliefs* (not ordinary *language*, though he was to be seen as a forerunner by post-1945 'linguistic' philosophers)—beliefs whose truth, in opposition to the paradox-mongering idealists he and Russell had rebelled against, he did not question, but whose content needed to be made clear. Russell and the earlier Wittgenstein, however, were more concerned to find ways of re-expressing the statements of ordinary, careless, metaphysically misleading language in ways which brought out their relation to fact. They held that there were only a finite, and rather small, number of distinct types of elementary or atomic facts, and that everything that could intelligibly be said could be expressed in propositions which pictured atomic facts, or in compounds of such propositions. This logical atomism, critical though its proponents were

* In this chapter authors are referred to by surname only, regardless of whether they are alive or dead. Titles of books are sometimes abbreviated; in most cases the date given is that of *first* publication. Further detail will be found at p. 144, in the list of works referred to, and in the bibliography at p. 145.

of the more speculative sort of traditional metaphysics, was itself a metaphysical view in that it involved assertions about the nature of things that were not susceptible to empirical test. It accordingly went down before the logical positivist critique of metaphysics. But reductive analysis went on. Claims that minds and material objects were constructions out of perceptions or sense-data were replaced by claims that *statements* about minds and material objects could be translated into collections of sense-data *statements*. (Philosophy was transposed from the 'material' into the 'formal' mode—see p. 117 below for this distinction.) 'Clarifying' the short and simple statements of common sense by substituting for them long and complicated statements about mysterious entities became a major preoccupation of philosophers.

The analytical emphasis of the inter-war years does less to mark them out from other periods in the history of philosophy than is often supposed. There was, it is true, the sharpest possible contrast between the analysts and their immediate predecessors, the Hegel-inspired English idealists. The complaint of the many who feel that twentieth-century British philosophy has betrayed its nature, abdicated from the authority that belongs to the subject, is founded on the contrast between analysts and idealists. But in fact it is, if anyone, the idealists who are alien to the British philosophical tradition. The concerns of Russell, Moore, Ayer are continuous with those of Locke, Berkeley, Hume, Reid, and J. S. Mill. 'Cambridge analysis', logical atomism, and logical positivism were all offspring of a marriage between the new logic of Russell's and Whitehead's *Principia Mathematica* (1910–13) and the old empiricism. The endless talk about analysis symptomizes less a change in practice, though there was some, than a new anxiety about the nature of philosophy—an anxiety that derives from such facts as that some of the former concerns of philosophy had acquired independent scientific status (for example, psychology) and another (metaphysics) had come to be thought impossible.

In what follows I shall, first, sketch in the development that took place between the publication of Wittgenstein's *Tractatus Logico-Philosophicus* in 1922 and Ayer's *Language, Truth and Logic* in 1936. After that I shall consider logic and the philosophy of mathematics and science, theory of knowledge (mainly Moore, Russell, Price, and Ayer) and philosophy of mind (Broad and Ryle). Next will come ethics and political philosophy. The period was notoriously infertile in political philosophy, which needs the support of the Platonic illusion that pure reason can discover practical principles of great moment. Even the challenge to liberal democracy of European totalitarianism provoked no arguably great work in response before Popper's *Open Society* (1945). Ethics, on the other hand, had a more interesting record. The emotive theory was genuinely novel, even if not very plausible in its most original form, and proved a starting point for the fruitful post-1945 period of moral philosophizing. I shall conclude with an account of the highly untypical Collingwood, and a glance at the popular philosophy of the period.

There is, inevitably, some distortion in departmentalizing philosophy in this way. There are no fundamental differences between the sorts of thinking that go on in, say, ethics and epistemology. Indeed the main change in ethics between the wars—the decline of intuitionism—was more the result of developments in epistemology and philosophy of mathematics than of anything specific to ethics. Philosophy is one subject. I have followed conventional divisions more because comments on the works of the period have to be organized in *some* way than from any stronger belief in their significance.

The Tractatus *to* Language, Truth and Logic

Wittgenstein's *Tractatus Logico-Philosophicus* conforms closely to popular conceptions of a philosophical classic. It is aphoristic, in places technical, employs strange notations, makes vast claims, purveys clarification but does not denigrate the ineffable. It has had immense influence—positively in the development of logical positivism, negatively in provoking in its author (1880–1951) the radically counter-revolutionary ideas that were first officially published in the posthumous *Philosophical Investigations* (1953).

The *Tractatus* appeared in German in 1921, and in a bilingual German–English version, with a preface by Russell, in 1922. It expresses a metaphysical view of the nature of reality, discusses facts and propositions and the relation between them (rather beyond the point that a relation allegedly inexpressible in language can be discussed), the nature of logic, and the task of philosophy. The account of reality is close to that given by Russell in his lectures on logical atomism. It is perhaps best conceived as the attempt to say what reality would have to be like if it were to be describable in a language for which *Principia Mathematica* supplied the grammar.

The *Tractatus* begins: '1. The world is everything that is the case. 1.1 The world is the totality of facts, not of things.' Atomic, i.e. irreducibly simple facts (or, better, possible facts or states of affairs) are 'pictured' by elementary propositions. '2.1 We make to ourselves pictures of facts.' Elementary propositions consist of the names of the elements in atomic facts arranged in ways that reflect the structures of the facts. Complex or non-elementary propositions are logical compounds out of elementary propositions. Logic, in effect, is a set of rules for building up propositions of any order of complexity out of elementary, fact-picturing propositions. Thus the compound proposition, 'John takes the car and Mary the bicycle' (which can be symbolized as '$p \& q$'), is visibly made up of the simple propositions 'p' and 'q'. 'p' and 'q' have sense or meaning in virtue of their picturing possible facts in the world. If the facts obtain they are true, if not, false. But there are no complex facts. There is nothing additional to the facts pictured by 'p' and 'q' separately to be pictured by '$p \& q$'. Words like 'and', 'or', and 'not', the so-called logical constants, do not picture anything in reality. '4.0312 My fundamental thought is that the "logical constants" do not represent.' There are for Wittgenstein—Russell was at times more permissive—no conjunctive, disjunctive, or negative facts; though we can say in conjunctive ($p \& q$), disjunctive (p or q), or negative (not-p) propositions that two facts obtain together, that at least one of them does, or that one does not.

There is here the basis for a programme of reductive analysis. Apparently complex propositions need to be legitimized by being shown to be logical compounds of elementary ones. This programme, though some recent commentators deny that this was Wittgenstein's intention, can readily be aligned with the British empiricist project of reducing complex ideas to combinations of simple ones. How radical the reduction is depends on the variety of atomic facts recognized. Unlike Russell, the Wittgenstein of the *Tractatus* was very austere. He would have no truck with general facts, contending that quantifiers—words like 'all' and 'some' and their synonyms—refer to nothing, and consequently contending that *universal* propositions in the form 'All *A*s are *B*s' must be regarded as indefinite conjunctions, 'This *A* is *B and* that *A* is *B and* etc.,' and that *particular* propositions in the form 'Some *A*s are *B*s' must be indefinite disjunctions, 'This *A* is *B or* that *A* is *B or* etc.' These analyses are not, unhappily, very plausible. The quantifiers are replaceable, not by 'and' and 'or' alone, but by 'and' and 'or' plus 'etc.'. The problem of making sense of the quantifiers simply reappears as the problem of making sense of 'etc.', i.e. of the indefiniteness of the conjunctions and disjunctions in question. Nothing is thereby gained, and it appeared therefore to follow, within the terms in which the problem arose, that it was necessary *either* to admit the possibility of general facts *or* to deny the possibility of general propositions—and hence of science whose laws are general propositions. Russell, always fundamentally committed to science, was prepared to take the former line, Ramsey and Schlick favoured the latter, though they tried to 'save' science by construing natural laws as *rules* for making predictions rather than as general *statements* of fact.

Complex propositions were held to be *truth functional* compounds of elementary ones, i.e. compounds whose truth or falsity (truth value) is wholly determined by the truth values of their component propositions. Thus the truth value of 'p & q' is true if p is true and q is true, but false if either p or q is false or if they both are. Again 'p or q' is true so long as p and q are not both false. Wittgenstein devised a diagrammatic method for systematically surveying the possible combinations of the truth values of the constituent propositions of a complex—the American logician E. L. Post and the Pole J. Lukasiewicz did so independently at about the same time. This threw light on the nature of logical and, Wittgenstein thought, mathematical truth. Take any two propositions, p and q, each of which may be true or false. There are four possible ways in which their truth values may be combined: they can both be true, the first true and the second false, *vice versa*, or both false. For three propositions there are eight possibilities, for four sixteen, and so on. These possibilities can be represented in a *truth table*:

(A)	p	q		(B)	p	q	r
(1)	T	T		(1)	T	T	T
(2)	T	F		(2)	T	T	F
(3)	F	T		(3)	T	F	T
(4)	F	F		(4)	T	F	F
				(5)	F	T	T
				(6)	F	T	F
				(7)	F	F	T
				(8)	F	F	F

It is possible to work out for any compound proposition—say, 'p or q' or '(p & q) or r'—for which combinations of truth values (lines in the truth table) it is true, and for which false. 'p or q' is true in lines 1, 2, 3, of (A), false in 4. '(p & q) or r' is true in lines 1, 2, 3, 5, 7, false in lines 4, 6, 8 of (B). Most compound propositions are true on some lines and false on others and are accordingly said to be contingent. But some compounds are true in all lines and are called tautologies; others are false in all lines and are called contradictions. Thus 'p or not-p' is true on all lines and 'p and not-p' is false on all lines. Again 'If p then q, and p, therefore q' is true in all lines. This last example is a rule of propositional logic (or strictly a statement corresponding to such a rule). In fact the statements corresponding to all the rules of propositional logic are tautologies in Wittgenstein's sense—a conclusion he generalized, over-hastily but not unnaturally in the context in which he wrote, to the *whole* of logic and to mathematics too. The necessary truths of logic and mathematics are tautologies and hence 'without sense'; they do not picture reality, they are just part of the symbolism.

These seemingly, but not intentionally, derogatory remarks about logical and mathematical truth can be interpreted by reference to truth tables. A contingent (non-necessary) proposition, like '(p & q) or r', succeeds in saying something about reality because, though its truth is compatible with certain truth combinations of its constituents, it is incompatible with others. It is dependent upon reality in the sense that it is true if reality is represented by any of lines 1, 2, 3, 5, 7, of (B), false if not. It says that things are like this and not like that. A tautology, on the other hand, is true regardless of what reality is like, and so says nothing about it. Its necessity is based on this. It is because it says nothing about reality that no possible configuration of reality can falsify it. The price of necessity is informational emptiness. This is the proffered solution to the long-standing problem of the nature of logical and mathematical truth. Russell, whose philosophical inquiries were motivated by a Cartesian passion for necessary truth, confessed himself unhappy with the direction Wittgenstein's thought had taken. He would have liked logical and mathematical truth to be more than a by-product of the symbolism. Wittgenstein, on the other hand, felt he was simply exhibiting logic and mathematics free of all empirical dross.

Wittgenstein paid attention only to a fragment of logic. The *Principia Mathematica* programme of reducing mathematics to logic was not carried through. But a great many of the most influential philosophers of the inter-war years nevertheless felt on these bases that the problem of the nature of logical and mathematical truth had been solved, and solved in ways compatible with empiricism. The empiricist holds that all informational statements are empirical. J. S. Mill had tried to show that mathematical statements were like this, but it is impossible to credit that mathematical statements might be found to be false by observation or experiment. To hold them to be informational and non-empirical would, however, be to abandon empiricism. After the *Tractatus* the possibility of holding mathematical statements to *non-informational* and non-empirical afforded a way round the impasse.

The *Tractatus* purported to show how sense could be talked about the world, and how the propositions of logic and mathematics, though 'senseless', were not nonsensical. Metaphysics, however, was. It was not even part of the symbolism, but the result of *misusing* it. Metaphysical questions, questions about God, freedom, and immortality, and indeed ethical questions too, cannot even be formulated, let alone answered. This seems the farthest extreme of scepticism, and was so intended by some, but there is a sense in which it need not be. The sceptic proper is unable to see how to answer a formulated question, but if metaphysical questions cannot even be formulated how can there be doubt about how to answer them? This still perhaps sounds like a disingenuous form of scepticism, but it was not for Wittgenstein. He seems genuinely to have thought that there was the mystical, that of which one cannot speak and must therefore be silent (7). The dark references to God, ethics, the meaning of life echo something real in Wittgenstein's experience.

The *Tractatus* leaves us with two sorts of significant proposition, the tautologies of mathematics and logic on the one hand and the contingent statements of science on the other. But what about philosophy, the statements of the *Tractatus* itself? These seem to be neither tautological nor contingent. Wittgenstein had the hardihood to draw the only conclusion he had left himself. Strictly speaking the 'statements' of philosophy are nonsensical. They are not really statements at all, merely ways of getting us to see what cannot be said. When we have climbed the tree we may throw away the ladder (6.54). Philosophy is not a theory, not a body of statements, but an activity, in the practice of which what cannot be said is somehow shown—for instance, the relation between language and the world. Russell in his preface to the English version of the *Tractatus* commented mildly that a good deal of the unsayable appeared to get said, and suggested that, even if the relation between a language and reality could not be stated in *that* language, it might still be possible to talk about it in another, higher order or meta-language. Ramsey, more robustly, in a much-quoted phrase, remarked that what cannot be said cannot be whistled either.

The *Tractatus* is without doubt a great book: but not a very good one. It spreads darkness as well as light. Nor did it fulfil its author's high ambition and put an end to philosophy—though after it he abandoned philosophy for a while for schoolteaching. In the

Tractatus are expressed, at once succinctly and extravagantly, many of the most important philosophical themes of the inter-war years. It was a major influence on the logical positivism which is the topic of the remainder of this section.

Logical positivism had its immediate origin in the so-called Vienna Circle, a group of mathematicians and scientists, together with a few philosophers proper, which began to meet in Vienna after the first war. Logical positivism was not, however, in its inspiration a purely continental movement. Its root and branch opposition to speculative metaphysics was congenial to the British tradition, especially as exemplified by Hume. Vienna was a centre of science-oriented empiricism, and the chair to which Schlick, the leading *philosopher* of the circle, succeeded in 1922 had formerly been held by the great positivistic philosopher of science, Ernst Mach. Wittgenstein himself, having given up philosophy, was not a member of the circle. His *Tractatus* was nevertheless read with interest, and admired for its scientific rigour, its account of mathematical truth, and its dismissal of metaphysics. Wittgenstein, as we have noticed, felt the pull of metaphysical temptations even though he eschewed metaphysical propositions: but most of the Vienna Circle, with the exception of Waismann, did not. They wanted results in philosophy, not the elaboration of subtle difficulties. The prime philosophical task was to draw the line between sense and nonsense. So anxious were they to cut out nonsense that they were happy to risk letting go a little sense along with it. They were strangers to the humble assumption, common in post-Second War philosophy partly under the influence of the later Wittgenstein, that *every* type of utterance has its point.

For the empiricist all knowledge is founded on experience. Standing problems have been the existence of bodies of knowledge which seem independent of experience, notably mathematics, and the difficulty of explaining exactly how different categories of statement are dependent on experience. The logical positivists thought they had the solution to the former problem in Wittgenstein's account of mathematics and the key to the second in the shape of the celebrated *verification principle*—which also they claimed to find in Wittgenstein, although he is on record as saying that they had erected a suggestion into a dogma. The verification principle admits of a variety of formulations, but for the present it may be taken as stipulating that non-tautological propositions are significant only if they are empirically verifiable. The affinity between logical positivism and traditional empiricism is very plain. Hume had recognized

two sorts of significant proposition, namely those expressing relations of ideas (roughly, tautologies or analytic propositions in twentieth-century terminology) and those expressing matters of fact
(non-analytic or synthetic empirical propositions). Mathematics
came into the former class, science into the latter, and, apart from
some ambivalence about ethics, everything else was according to
Hume only sophistry and illusion. The logical positivists reached
very much the same *conclusions*, but their reasons were on an altogether higher level of sophistication. Their view of mathematics
was informed by the discoveries of Frege, Russell and Whitehead,
and Wittgenstein, and their conception of verification was an enormous improvement on the psychologistic doctrine of the old empiricism according to which every single element in a complex proposition had to be traceable to an origin in experience. The new
logic helped them at this point too. Russell's theory of descriptions
and conception of the incomplete symbol (i.e. a symbol which plays
a syntactical rather than a referential role and which consequently
can be eliminated when a sentence is paraphrased) liberated them
from the impossibly over-restrictive notion that significant propositions must be built up from elements every one of which refers to
experience. For the logical positivists propositions were units from
the point of view of verification.

It is an oddity of intellectual history that the relatively liberal
verification principle occasioned more scandal than traditional empiricism which in the twentieth century was felt to be completely
respectable. What provoked opposition was presumably the intellectual iconoclasm of the logical positivists and the ruthlessness
if not recklessness, with which they accepted the uncomfortable implications of their premises. Perhaps too its relation to traditional
empiricism helps to explain the awful plausibility of the verification
principle, the pull it seemed to exercise over proponents and critics
alike, a pull which goes some way to explain both the sometime
extravagant opposition to it and the continuing tendency to think as
if something of the sort must be correct, even though it is now
generally agreed that an acceptable formulation of the principle is
unattainable.

Ayer is much the best-known logical positivist (or ex-logical positivist) in Britain, but he is better approached by way of one or two
of the more influential continental figures. One of these was
Schlick (1882–1936), who has the doubtful, though among philosophers rare, distinction of having been murdered by an aggrieved
pupil. He agreed with Wittgenstein that philosophy was an activity

rather than a body of doctrine—for him it tended to be the activity of 'dissolving' as opposed to solving the traditional problems of philosophy. For instance, the supposed problem of free-will arises because there seems to be a contradiction between freedom and determinism, in both of which we nevertheless want to believe. 'Solutions', in the terms in which the problem is posed, have to be sought by trying to show that one of the conflicting theses is true and the other false. Schlick, however, argued that the problem was bogus in that it arose from confusing scientific laws, which determine but since they are purely descriptive do not restrict free-will, with juridical (prescriptive) laws, which do not in the same sense determine but which might, if the police were efficient, restrict free-will. Determinism, correctly understood, is fully compatible with freedom, properly understood. Similar treatment was meted out to the mind/body problem—the problem, stemming from Descartes, of explaining how body and mind, conceived as wholly different substances, can interact. The duality is held to lie between psychology and physiology, i.e. between two ways of *describing* phenomena, and not between two sorts of substance.

Such talk of dissolving problems often seemed to, and sometimes really did, reflect a fair contempt for the concerns of previous philosophers, and provoked attempts to rehabilitate the traditional problems, to show that they are not 'pseudo' but 'real'. But, of course, a dissolution is really a sort of solution, and there are parallels to Schlick's treatment of the free-will problem in, among others, Hume and Kant.

With regard to the status of the verification principle Schlick held that it was a truism or analytic statement, i.e. that our conception of meaning is such that it *follows* from it that a (non-analytic) proposition is meaningful only if it is empirically verifiable. (This, incidentally, is clearly false. Many locutions normally held to be meaningful are not verifiable. Conceived as a statement about meaning the verification principle is not a truism but a falsism. The best hope is to present it as a recommendation about, rather than an account of, the usage of 'meaningful'. Even then it would be necessary to find reasons for accepting it.) Schlick went on to rest some weight on a distinction between the verifiable in principle and the verifiable in practice. That there is an invisible, intangible, and otherwise undetectable ether through which all the heavenly bodies move and light waves are propagated is in principle unverifiable, it is logically impossible to verify it, and it is consequently a meaningless speculation. But to ask whether there is water vapour on Jupiter is perfectly meaningful because it is verifiable in principle although not yet in practice. (The stock example used to be the craters on the far side of the moon, but their presence has now been verified in practice.) A distinction between verifiability in principle and verifiability in practice seems indispensable if meaning is to be held to consist in verification, but setting up a firm distinction has proved to be harder than the examples given perhaps suggest.

Another essential distinction is between direct and indirect verification. Whatever statements are taken to be directly verifiable there will inevitably be others which are not. Logical positivists were not agreed which statements were directly and conclusively verifiable in a single experience. Popular candidates were singular material object statements like 'The cat is sitting on the mat', in which case direct verification would be a public affair, or sense-data statements like 'Red patch here now', when it would be private. Schlick considered verification to be a private affair and hence, rather oddly considering the characteristically secularist temper of logical positivism, held the statement that one would survive bodily death to be meaningful—if true it would be verified *post mortem*, though it would not of course be falsified if false. Carnap (1891–1970) too initially held verification to be private, the ultimate appeal being to memory or sensory data. His *Logische Aufbau der Welt* (1928) purports to show how statements about material objects can be translated into statements about sense-data. Later, however, he came to think that the public world of scientific knowledge cannot be constructed out of the private data of sense.

All possibly directly verifiable statements are singular, but the statements most characteristic of science, statements of natural law which logical positivism aimed to bring into the sphere of the meaningful, are universal. And many of them report the transactions of 'entities', if that is the word, such as perfect gases, bodies free from impressed forces, electrons, genes, the unconscious, that are not observable even in principle. Such universal statements can, however, be regarded as connected with experience to the extent that they may appear among the premises of arguments which yield directly verifiable statements as their conclusions, as when, for example, the laws of motion are employed in order to predict the path of a comet. This is, in outline, the doctrine of indirect verification expressed in such works as Carnap's *Logical Syntax of Language* (1935) and the second edition of Ayer's *Language, Truth and Logic* (1946). The verification principle had, in effect, been weakened order to accommodate statements that logical positivists could n bring themselves to dismiss as meaningless. It began as an offensive weapon, potent enough to determine once and for all which statements were meaningful and which not. It ends by being adapted to fit statements that are antecedently and independently held to be meaningful.

Carnap, who played a larger part in the history of logical positivism than it is possible to do justice to here, at first agreed with Wittgenstein that it is impossible to say anything about the relationship between signs and the world, a view which, as we have seen, leads to the frustrating conclusion that philosophy is the attempt to say what cannot be said. Carnap's opinions were, however, frequently changed. He went through an extreme conventionalist phase, for instance, in which it appeared that truth was to be ascertained by comparing statements one with another rather than with the world. (This was to revert to the coherence theory of truth, a central doctrine of the still despised idealism.) Later, however, Carnap conceded that it was possible to discuss the relationship between language and the world in a meta-language—this was to follow the suggestion made by Russell in his preface to the *Tractatus*—and came to the view that acceptable philosophical theses had to be considered as statements or recommendations about language. Philosophers frequently make statements apparently about objects (i.e. in the *material mode*), which are mysterious in that they seem both to be true and yet neither tautological nor empirically verifiable. It may, for example, be said that minds or numbers are not material, or worse that they are immaterial objects. What is true in such remarks can best be brought out by transposing them into the *formal mode*, i.e. making them explicitly remarks about language, to the effect, for example, that 'mind' and number words like 'one', 'two', 'three', etc., have a logical grammar very different from that of material object words like 'table', 'chair', etc. The pronouns in the questions 'Where is it?' and 'How big is it?' can be taken as standing in for material object words, but not for 'mind' or number words. More was sometimes claimed for the material/formal mode distinction than was reasonable—there is not enough difference between 'Minds are not material objects' and '"Mind" is not a material object word' for the latter to be significantly more perspicuous than the former, though there is illumination to be had when differences between the logical grammar of 'mind' and, say, 'table' are spelled out in detail. The material/formal mode distinction is not a philosophical panacea, nor, in view of the fact that no philosopher has managed to produce more than a few illustrative passages in the bewilderingly cumbersome formal mode, is inaptness for expression in the formal mode a decisive criticism of a philosophical utterance. Nevertheless it must be allowed to have proved to be up to a point a clarifying distinction, and the associated thesis that philosophy is about language has been profoundly influential. To give only one instance, in Ayer's hands phenomenalism becomes the linguistic thesis that material object statements can be replaced by sense-data statements, not the ontological thesis that material objects are made up of sense-data.

The importance of Ayer's *Language, Truth and Logic* (1st ed., 1936) is that it first made logical positivism widely known in Britain. Indeed, if Paton is to be believed, Ayer (b. 1910) succeeded in catching the attention of the large number of philosophers at Oxford, where Wittgenstein and Russell had failed to make an impact. The book is a brisk polemical work. The author employs an oddly imperious first person plural. The tone is of one who is sweeping away centuries of philosophical rubbish and inaugurating a new age. The matter is less novel than the manner—as we have already noted the significant thing about logical positivism was that it reminded British readers how radical their native empiricist tradition really was. Many present-day teachers of philosophy remember *Language, Truth and Logic* as a major excitement of their undergraduate days. Rereading it, however, one sometimes wonders why. It is a surprise to rediscover how dryly technical many passages are.

Ayer begins by disposing of metaphysics, employing for this purpose a fairly liberal version of the verification principle. He distinguishes between partial and complete verification—a universal statement is partially verified if there are confirming instances, but cannot be completely verified because there is no observing all the members of an open set. For a synthetic statement to be literally meaningful, a genuine as opposed to pseudo-statement, it is enough for some possible observation to be relevant to its truth or falsity. This would seem, incidentally, to be a weaker formulation than Ayer can have intended, for it would surely make 'God exists' literally meaningful, at any rate as understood by anyone who accepts the cosmological argument (the argument from the existence of 'contingent being' to the existence of God).

Mathematics is held to be analytic or tautological. There is some attempt to explain, compatibly with this, how mathematics is apparently informative and how discoveries can be made in it. The point is that analytic statements can be very complicated, and that when they are they will not be psychologically self-evident to limited intellects. An infinite intellect would see at once whether or not a theorem followed from an axiom set. But we cannot generally see this and consequently have need of procedures, i.e. proofs, for bringing to our attention what is implicit in the axioms. (Compare *Tractatus* 6.1262 'Proof in logic is only a mechanical expedient to facilitate the recognition of tautology, where it is complicated'.) Kant's contention that mathematical statements were not analytic derives from his failure to grasp that the *logically* analytic may not be psychologically self-evident.

A rather brusque view is taken of truth and falsity. There is no need for a theory of truth as distinct from a theory of verification. There is no longer any scope for grand theories of goodness, truth, and beauty once philosophy is thought to be about language. In response to jesting Pilate's question all that can be done is to define 'true' or otherwise explain its role in discourse. Ayer maintains that, since whatever verifies 'The cat is on the mat' also verifies 'It is true that the cat is on the mat', and since whatever falsifies 'The cat is on the mat' establishes 'It is false that the cat is on the mat', the words 'true' and 'false' have no meaning but simply function in language as marks of assertion and denial. This account of truth and falsity admirably illustrates the tendency, also evident in connection with the emotive theory of ethics, of inter-war philosophy to neglect or disparage all non-statement making uses of language. Certainly 'It is true that the cat is on the mat' does not *state* anything different about the whereabouts of the cat than does 'The cat is on the mat'— but it does not follow that 'true' has no meaning at all.

A paradoxical line was followed with regard to statements about the past, which cannot be directly verified. (Remembering might have been counted as direct verification by some, but we make many statements about past events that lie outside anybody's recollection.) Plainly we cannot see that the cat *was* on the mat in the way that we can see that it *is*, though of course we may conclude that it was on the basis of evidence, hairs, footprints, etc., that can be directly observed. Ayer is therefore led by his desire to explain meaning in terms of prospects of verification to interpret statements about the past as hypotheses about the occurrence in the present or future of the evidence that would verify them. Thus 'The cat was on the mat' has something of the force of 'If you were to examine the mat you would find black hairs, etc.'. There is a clear resemblance here with phenomenalistic analyses of material object statements, and it is just as doubtful whether the full content of categorical past tense statements can be rendered by conditionals about future evidence discovery, as it is whether categorical material object statements are replaceable by finite sets of sense-data statements. Reductive analysis, the attempt to reduce statements of one category to collections of statements of another, never works out. The repeated failures of such analyses in the thirties explains why reductionism became the bogy it did in post-Second War philosophy.

Language, Truth and Logic achieved most notoriety for its destructive criticism of ethics and theology—the philistine British appear to have taken less exception to the equally hostile treatment of aesthetics. The rejection of theology was a direct consequence of the operation of the verification principle; its chief importance, perhaps, that it aroused philosophical theologians from their dogmatic slumbers and provoked much useful work in philosophy of religion in the fifties and sixties. The critique of ethics was, as we shall see below, as much a result of Moore's anti-naturalism, which Ayer accepted, as of the verification principle. On naturalistic views ethical propositions are literally significant, and Schlick in fact took such a line. The logical positivist treatment of ethics has probably in the long run been most influential in stimulating explorations of non-statement-making uses of language.

Language, Truth and Logic was reissued in 1946 with a long new preface. Some concessions were made to critics—a notable one being that it is no longer held to be possible to rule out metaphysics in principle. Metaphysical arguments need to be criticized in detail. This is reversion to something like Kant's position, though Ayer does not give the impression of being able to feel the pull of metaphysics in the way Kant so clearly could.

Logical positivism was a strange interlude in British philosophy, alien less for its content than its tone and temper, its doctrinaire approach and contempt for detail. The so-called linguistic philosophy which succeeded it, though hailed as revolutionary in the fifties, was in most ways more congenial to the native tradition.

Logic and the Philosophy of Mathematics and Science

Principia Mathematica is on any showing a major landmark in the history of logic and the foundations of mathematics. Though anticipated by Frege on many important points, it was the first comprehensive system of logic to become widely known. It stimulated a great deal of technical innovation and development, most of which occurred outside Britain, but had a profound philosophical influence too. Russell (1872–1970), it may very well turn out, earns his high place in the history of thought mainly on the strength of his logic. Although he stands out as an intellectual giant among his contemporaries, some of them were better, if narrower, *philosophers*. Despite the fact that his pre-eminence is in logic, Russell clearly regarded himself as much or more a philosopher than a logician, and his work in logic was frequently motivated by philosophical concerns. The theory of descriptions—the paradigm of philosophy in Ramsey's phrase—was designed to solve a philosophical puzzle about how non-existent entities can be the topics of significant sentences, and the hierarchy of types, which he had to invent in order to avoid logical paradoxes, he clearly supposed to have some ontological or epistemological significance. Specifically, entities of the lowest type tended to be identified as sense-data. His logic, which makes possible the presentation of objects of higher types as constructions out of objects of lower types, becomes therefore a framework for the phenomenalist construction of material objects out of sense-data. The idea of 'logical constructions' and the idea, deriving from the theory of types, that a grammatical or well-formed statement might be meaningless, became influential among philosophers who had little interest in the formal logic where they first arose. Logical positivism made some aspects of the logic of *Principia Mathematica* widely known, but it did not initiate a logical renaissance in Britain. It is only very recently that a reasonable knowledge of contemporary formal logic has come to be thought a necessary part of a philosophical education. The post-Second War 'ordinary language' philosophy reacts to a formalism that had no strong local roots.

The Frege, Russell, Whitehead programme had been to present mathematics as derivable from a suitably extended logic. *Principia Mathematica*, however, had some serious defects. The theory of types seemed arbitrary—some way of excluding paradoxes was, of course, required, but the remedy involved fearful complications, which were then kept within bounds by the equally arbitrary axiom of reducibility. Also allegedly required was the so-called axiom of infinity (to the effect that there are an infinite number of entities in the universe) which hardly seems to be a truth of logic. Russell in his *Introduction to Mathematical Philosophy* (1919) wrote as if the *logistic* programme of *Principia Mathematica* was complete in all essentials, and challenged anyone who doubted whether mathematics could be derived from logic to say where, in his system, logic ended and mathematics began. But, as the Kneales have pointed out, developments in the theory of formal systems, which arose out of the alternative formalist approach to the foundations of mathematics, provide the basis for an answer to this challenge.

Hilbert's formalist programme was to establish foundations for mathematics, not by deriving it from something else, but by treating it purely formally, in abstraction from any interpretation, and proving its consistency and completeness by employing only elementary logical procedures. (A system is complete if every formula expressible in it can be proved or disproved from the axioms.) It turned out, however, that this programme could not be carried through. Gödel proved that any system of the level of complexity of arithmetic was incomplete. Propositional and lower predicate logic (roughly logic as traditionally conceived) are deductively complete, the higher reaches of logic and mathematics are not; there seems therefore to be a basis for denying that logic and mathematics are continuous. Gödel's result is fatal, not only to formalism, but to the logistic programme too. The relations of logic and mathematics are much more complex than the *Tractatus* led many to believe.

There also developed a third approach to the foundations of mathematics, that of the intuitionist school of Brouwer. This was a sort of puritanical attempt to restrict mathematicians to 'constructive' procedures, i.e. procedures which seemed acceptable to mathematical intuition. Intuitionists were particularly suspicious of indirect proofs in which a theorem is purportedly proved by disproving its contradictory. Many schoolboys must have marvelled at the way in which indirect proofs in geometry seem to have all the advantages of theft over honest toil. Intuitionists had to exercise great ingenuity in order to reach accepted mathematical conclusions by methods they considered respectable, but there were parts of mathematics that they had to reject altogether. They also, probably misguidedly, felt that they had to reject the hallowed logical principle of the excluded middle, namely, that a proposition is either true or false, no third possibility being allowed. This provides the basis for indirect proofs. One result of this was to encourage investigations into the possibility of three- and multi-valued logics, i.e. logics in which propositions were allowed other values as well as truth and falsity. Such possibilities were also explored by the very distinguished school of Polish logicians which flourished between the wars. The field of possibilities in logic opened up. In a period in which British philosophers were only slowly becoming aware of the great work of Russell and Whitehead, *Principia Mathematica* was losing its pre-eminence and becoming just one of many logical systems. The work of the American logician C. I. Lewis tended to the same conclusion. He was led by dissatisfaction with Russell's and Whitehead's careless claim that their 'hook sign'— ⊃ —represented implication, albeit *material* implication, to develop various systems of what he called 'strict implication'. These were systems in which the modalities, necessary, possible, impossible, are explicitly treated, as they are not in *Principia Mathematica*.

If we turn now from formal to inductive logic (the logic of empirical science) we may begin by recalling that Russell had briefly considered the Humean problem of justifying induction in his *Problems of Philosophy* (1912), still unsurpassed as a short introduction to philosophy. Hume's difficulty was how to justify inferences from particular observations to universal laws, inferences from 'some' to 'all'. Russell returns to the problem in his last substantial philosophical work, *Human Knowledge* (1948)—an under-admired work which, if it lacks the zest of some of the earlier books, is still a very solid, superbly professional production. Here it is contended that induction is possible, and science therefore respectable, only if certain rational principles are assumed, principles which cannot themselves be verified because they are assumed in the process of verification. Russell would have liked to be an empiricist of the Humean persuasion, but would rather deny empiricism than impugn the substantial validity of science. He sets himself the problem of formulating the minimum set of non-empirical principles that have to be assumed if science is to be possible. Russell the empiricist like Russell the logical atomist was always among the first to draw attention to the difficulties in his own position. A ground on which Russell may be criticized, however, is that he always addressed himself to the problem of induction as formulated by Hume. He does not sufficiently question the question. In this connection von Wright's *Logical Problem of Induction* (1941) rates a mention. It is remarkable for its careful discussion of the nature of the problem and its classification of the possible lines of solution. It is not characteristic of von Wright actually to propound solutions, but I think it can fairly be said of him that he was one of the first to advance discussion of the problem of induction beyond the point where Hume left it.

Popper (b. 1902), whose *Logik der Forschung* was published in 1934 (no English translation until 1959), is notable for denying that there is any place for induction in science. Observations cannot be the raw material out of which theories are made, the truth is rather that observations are made in the light of theories. The scientist hypothesizes a universal statement and then looks round for instances which might falsify it (or, if it is a high-level theory, he seeks to derive from it observation statements which might be falsified). If he fails, if that is to say the theory resists falsification, it is provisionally acceptable. If it is falsified one must try again. One proceeds, not by induction, but by conjecture and refutation. Popper in taking this line is motivated partly by logical considerations—the impossibility of formalizing inductive procedure and the superior force of a negative instance to a universal statement (there can be conclusive falsification, but not conclusive verification)—but partly also by the wish to do justice to the *creative* aspect of science. Science is not the passive accumulation of information, but a great adventure of the human spirit, a major cultural activity. But, while thus emphasizing the creative side of science, Popper still insists that its objective is truth. He will have no truck with pragmatist or instrumentalist views according to which scientific theories are mere intellectual devices for enabling people to predict.

Popper was never a member of the Vienna Circle and has been firm in insisting that resemblances between his views and logical positivism are superficial. He never accepted the verification principle as a criterion of meaning, but offered something like it as a principle of demarcation between science and metaphysics. To be scientific a statement must be falsifiable, it must assert that something logically conceivable is not so. This without doubt expresses something fundamental about science, even if it does not pin metaphysics down very tightly, but it is not any easier than it proved with the verification principle to give it an exact formulation.

Popper, despite his frequent concern with technical matters, is a philosopher on a larger scale than many contemporaries. He is also one of the few political *philosophers* of the period, in the sense that his political attitudes are to a high degree integrated with his general philosophical position. Russell did, of course, very frequently volunteer opinions on political matters but, by the integration criterion, is hardly a political philosopher at all.

Theory of Knowledge and Philosophy of Mind

Moore (1873–1958) had done his best to refute idealism in 1903, arguing that the distinction between the act of perceiving and what is perceived could be drawn as well with respect to inner as to outer perception. There was, therefore, no problem about getting outside the circle of our ideas and sensations. To have a sensation is already to be outside it in that it is to be aware *of* something, of an object distinct from our act of awareness. There is consequently no reason for supposing inner perception (introspection) to be more direct than outer nor, consequently, for thinking outer perception less reliable than inner. The idealist finds inner perception self-explanatory—Descartes's one initially indubitable proposition was an introspective report—and consequently feels that outer perception is problematic by contrast. In order to refute idealism it is necessary, therefore, either to argue that outer perception is as unproblematic as inner or, contrariwise, that inner is just as problematic as outer. Moore, like Kant before him, takes the latter line, although he does not follow Kant in contending that inner perception is actually dependent on outer—a line taken, though for different reasons, by the later Wittgenstein and his followers.

In his earlier writings on perception Moore held that we could be directly aware of material objects or at any rate the surfaces they present to our senses. Later, however, he came to think that there was a sense in which we were aware only of such objects as colours, sounds, textures, smells, i.e. of *sense-data*—a much-used phrase which Moore introduced in his lectures of 1910–11 (published in 1953 as *Some Main Problems of Philosophy*). He did not, however, give up the view that we have *knowledge* of physical objects, as witness his 'A Defence of Commonsense' (1925) and 'The Proof of an External World' (1939). He was left, therefore, with the problem of explaining the relation between sense-data and physical objects. In his painstaking, obtusely subtle way he explored many possible views, but, wholly characteristically, failed to find any completely satisfactory. Moore is clearly an important influence in the development of 'linguistic philosophy', for which problems about sense-data concern the relationship between two *terminologies*, but he never saw matters linguistically himself. It has, with reason, been doubted whether the phrase 'sense-datum' has a referent. Moore, however, always wrote as if he could focus his inner eye on these suspect entities (and upon the 'non-natural' properties of his value theory too) and, by some sort of non-visual observation, discover their nature and relations to other things.

Moore reconciled his common-sensical certainties and doubts about sense-data by saying that he was quite certain of the *truth* of many material object propositions, but highly uncertain about the correct analysis of them. He thus contributed to the widespread conviction between the wars that analysis was the proper business of philosophy, a conviction which co-existed with much disagreement about what was to be analysed into what and what the point of the exercise was. Logical atomists, as we have seen, conceived themselves to be analysing expressions that were rather remote from bedrock fact into others that were closer to it. But Moore never settled on any technical notion of analysis. Reflection upon much of his practice suggests that his attempted analyses were no more, or rather no less, than attempts to make clear, in a perfectly ordinary sense of 'make clear', what the very unclear, but putatively profound, statements of philosophers could possibly mean. There was something of the plain man about Moore, a Socratic capacity for sustained puzzlement that Russell, for instance, tended to lose in his later years.

Writers who tried to give accounts of the rationale of philosophical analysis included Susan Stebbing (1885–1943) and John Wisdom (b. 1904). Stebbing, author of a well-known early account of the new symbolic logic, moved from holding that analysis was a way of getting at the ultimate structure of propositions known to be true but imperfectly understood, to thinking that it was simply the 'same level' process of making obscure things clear. John Wisdom actually wrote an elementary textbook of philosophical analysis (*Problems of Mind and Matter*, 1934) in which, *inter alia*, statements ostensibly about minds were reduced to collections of statements about mental states and material object statements to sense-data statements. Later, in a series of articles, 'Logical Constructions' (*Mind*, 1931–3), in which alleged ambiguities of reference even in such words as 'this' and 'that' were removed by vowel variations, e.g. 'thet', 'thot', etc., Wisdom tried to explain the point of philosophical analysis. But he did not succeed, even in his own estimation. Subsequently he lost faith in the possibility of making exact statements in philosophy, preferring to appraise philosophical theses as illuminating or misleading rather than as true or false. A good example of his later style is to be found in the series of articles 'Other Minds'.

Russell's views about our knowledge of physical objects, as about other matters too, underwent a good deal of change during the period. He agreed with Moore that sense-data, not physical objects, are the objects of immediate awareness or 'acquaintance'. The material object, he at first held, is something we hypothesize in order causally to explain the occurrence and variation of sense-data. He came, however, in a Humean manner to doubt the propriety of inferences from sense-data to physical objects and, in accordance with the principle that wherever possible logical constructions are to be substituted for inferred entities, held that material objects were logical constructions out of sense-data, both actual and possible (*sensibilia* as well as *sensa*). A physical object is the series of actual sensa that are received as it is seen, touched, tasted, etc., from a point of view, *together with* all the series of possible sensa that would be received by anyone occupying other points of view. The worrying impression that this theory involves treating possible sense-data as somehow actual is mainly the effect of the material mode of speech— phenomenalism sounds better as a proposal for analysing material object *statements* than as an account of the constitution of material objects.

In *The Analysis of Mind* (1921) Russell took a similarly reductionist view of minds, and came close to the 'neutral monism' of William James, according to which both minds and material objects are equally constructions out of sense-data. Sense-data correlated according to the laws of psychology constitute minds, correlated according to the laws of physics they constitute material things. The analysis of minds has obvious affinities with Hume's account of the mind as a bundle of perceptions. Russell maintained this doctrine of the mind, but in his *Analysis of Matter* (1927) moved back in the direction of his original causal theory of perception. This was mainly in order to do justice to physics. Sense-data, it seems obvious to Russell, are brain dependent, indeed they are states of the percipient's brain, so that, as he weirdly puts it, the anatomist dissecting a brain is directly aware, not of the brain on the slab, but of a state of his own brain. But, although sensa are brain dependent, physical objects, unless physics is a sham, cannot be. This reversion to the much-refuted causal theory of perception excellently illustrates the relative strengths of Russell's commitments to empiricism and (the substantial correctness of) science. He genuinely has the robust sense of reality that he believes to be indispensable in philosophy inasmuch as his commitment to science is so much the stronger that he will even risk inconsistency in its service. He is more of a Locke than an (early) Berkeley. There is in Russell's theoretical philosophizing a massive reasonableness that was, unhappily, less evident in his practical concerns.

Oxford philosophers were slow to learn from Cambridge, but Price (b. 1899), whose very influential *Perception* appeared in 1932, was one of those who did. He follows Russell, and indeed Locke, in holding that sensing is a form of knowing of which the immediate object is a sense-datum, and thinks that the central task of epistemology is that of explaining how sense-data are related to physical objects. He denies that sense-data are causally produced by material objects on the Humean ground that causal inferences, being founded on *observed* conjunctions between types of events and entities, can never justify a belief in unobservable entities. Moreover, he maintains, we do not come by our belief in material objects by causal reasoning. (This last is surely a psychological point of doubtful epistemological significance, but highly characteristic of the British empiricist tradition.) The correct account of the relation between sense-data and material objects is, in Price's view, complicated. A sense-datum is typically a member of a 'family' of associated sense-data. Sense-data obtained at various points of view fit together and, so to say, converge on the 'standard solid', i.e. the sense-data we obtain when we are, as would ordinarily be said, seeing the thing as it really is—for example, seeing a penny from above as round and not, as it looks from one side, as elliptical. A family of sense-data consists of the standard solid together with the various series of sense-data that converge on it. Any one person's series of sense-data will, of course, contain gaps (the 'gappiness' of perception is emphasized in Price's *Hume's Theory of the External World*, 1940)—a family of sense-data includes obtainable or possible sense-data (*sensibilia*) as well as actual ones.

Price is very nearly a phenomenalist but, he hopes, not quite, in that he provides for a distinction between a family of sense-data and a physical object. Physical objects are characterized as occupying physical as opposed to perceptual space and as operating causally. They exist as particular entities in a way that families of sense-data do not. These are all grammatically correct elucidations of the phrase 'physical object' but the real problem, as Price conceives it, is whether there is anything for the phrase to refer to. He admits that there is nothing to be said about physical objects beyond the fact that they have certain powers. Their intrinsic qualities are wholly unknown.

It remains to place in relation to physical objects and families of sense-data the familiar things of everyday speech. According to Price they are to be identified as *both* the family of sense-data *and* the physical object taken together. Locke made things mysterious by identifying them with physical objects by themselves, phenomenalists make them unsubstantial by identifying them with families of sense-data alone. Price would prefer to avoid phenomenalism, but of the two errors it is the one he dislikes less.

In Ayer's *Foundations of Empirical Knowledge* (1940), apparently completed in the Brigade of Guards Depot at Caterham but showing no other signs of the impact of war, British empiricism as transmitted by Price is united with a somewhat muted logical positivism. Ayer points out that no possible observations could settle the dis-

pute between realists and sense-datum theorists. The issue between them is, therefore, not scientific but either metaphysical, in
the pejorative sense, or simply linguistic, a dispute as to which of
two languages is the more 'convenient' in the sense of being the less
'misleading'. (In view of the fact that one of the two languages is
perfectly plain English, surely the paradigm of unmisleadingness,
Ayer is perhaps less innocent of metaphysical mystery-mongering
than he thought.) Ayer favours the sense-datum language, mainly
on the ground that 'sense-datum', as a term of art, has no connotations apart from those it was explicitly assigned when it was added
to the vocabulary of philosophy. In this Ayer was, alas, over-
optimistic. The burden of Austin's criticism in *Sense and Sensibilia* (lectures published posthumously in 1962 but given much
earlier) is precisely that the term 'sense-datum' is not adequately
specified and that it helps to obscure important distinctions plainly
made in common speech.

Phenomenalism in Ayer's linguistic guise is the view that every
statement about material objects can be translated into a set of
statements referring exclusively to sense-data. Thus, 'There is a
table in the next room' has to be replaced by a set of statements of
the form 'If one were to go into the next room one would have such
and such sense-data'. It is, unfortunately, much easier to say what
has to be done than to do it. In the sense-data statement form illustrated reference to material objects is not completely eliminated—
'next room' is a material object expression. It seems impossible to
find any *finite* set of sense-data statements that is equivalent to a
material object statement and, moreover, any *large*, let alone infinite,
collection of sense-data statements contains a complexity that is
lacking in the material object statement analysed. So great is the
complexity involved that Ayer was forced to revert to the material
mode of speech in order to state his view with reasonable clarity and
brevity. He concedes, even in *Foundations of Empirical Knowledge*,
that a material object cannot be completely specified in terms of
sense-data, but insists that there is no need to refer to anything
other than sense-data in order to specify it. And in his later writings,
the second edition of *Language, Truth and Logic* (1946) and *The
Problem of Knowledge* (1956), though he continues to defend
phenomenalism, it is with greater circumspection and reduced
claims. What seems to me to stand out from the many years of discussion of phenomenalism is that the only really important objec-
tions to it are fundamental—if, but only if, the sense-datum language can be made coherent and self-sufficient then the remaining

difficulties might be overcome. But, of course, it is very doubtful whether the sense-datum language can be defended. Apart from the Austinian criticism of its inadequacy mentioned above, there is, in the later Wittgenstein's destructive criticism of the idea of a logically private language, a ground for thinking that the sense-datum language, being private, is actually less fundamental than public, material object language. It is no doubt significant that Ayer has opposed Wittgenstein's rejection of the possibility of a private language.

So much for the problem of the external world. As we turn or, remembering Russell's *Analysis of Mind*, return to the philosophy of mind C. D. Broad (1887–1971) is the first writer who needs to be discussed. He was a Cambridge philosopher whose main works were published between the wars. His claim to a place in the history of philosophy rests, not on his originality, but more remarkably on his capacity to produce enlightening critical discussions of the views of others—views which he was dauntingly often capable of restating with greater force and clarity than their original proponents had achieved. His practice was analytical, but he had no special theory about analysis, only the ambition to make obscure things clear. In *Scientific Thought* (1923) he attempted to explain some of the concepts of natural science, and in *Mind and Its Place in Nature* (1925)—a book notorious for distinguishing no fewer than seventeen possible theories of the mind-body relation—he turned his attention to psychological concepts. Though as sober-minded a critical philosopher as ever was, he had never been opposed to speculation in principle, and devoted a major work to the criticism of McTaggart's metaphysics (*An Examination of McTaggart's Philosophy*, 1933–8). He is, moreover, notable, along with Price, for taking a serious interest in allegedly paranormal psychical phenomena.

Broad's work in philosophy of mind was conducted within the framework of Cartesian dualism. Later work in the field shows signs of the drastic reorientations brought about by the oral teaching of the post-*Tractatus* Wittgenstein, notes of which were circulated semi-privately between the wars, but which was not formally published until after his death in 1951. Wittgenstein continues to analyse usage, but casts his net much wider than formerly, and has no longer a preconceived notion of what the outcome of analysis should be. Unlike some Oxford philosophy analysis is not conducted for its own sake, but rather in order to track philosophical worries back to their source. Philosophers are still held to be misled by language, but the idea of a perfect or ideal language in one–one correspondence with reality is abandoned, and very full account is taken of contextual and even extra-linguistic matters. Language, languages, it is claimed, can be understood only in relation to the forms of life in which they figure. Gone too is the old tendency towards solipsism. Language is seen as essentially a public affair. There cannot be a *logically* private language, as distinct from a logically public language *de facto* spoken by a single person—as may well have been the case with Cornish just before it died out. Without the possibility of public (inter-personal) reference there can be no criterion of correct or incorrect use, i.e. no rules of use, and hence no reason for saying one thing rather than another, and hence no language. Wittgenstein is not, of course, denying that there can be talk about private experiences, only insisting that such talk is dependent upon the possibility of interpersonal talk about public objects. Phenomenalism is thus, as already noted, undermined; and the mind-body problem is trans-formed. The sceptic about other minds, the solipsist, thinks he understands what it means to say that he himself is, for example, in pain. The difficulty is to discover whether anybody else is. But, if Wittgenstein is right about private languages, there is no possibility of understanding such utterances as 'He is in pain' unless there are public criteria for their application, whence it follows that, if we have any knowledge of what goes on in minds at all (even in our own), we may perfectly well have knowledge of what goes on in other people's.

The influence of the later Wittgenstein is apparent in the work of John Wisdom, whose *Other Minds* was referred to above.

Ryle (b. 1900), whose major book *The Concept of Mind* (1949) falls just outside our period, shows signs of the influence of the later Wittgenstein, although his response stops well short of disciple-ship. He is also deeply rooted in the Oxford tradition, though re-sponsive to continental influence from Husserl and the Vienna Circle. Ryle begins, in 'Systematically Misleading Expressions' (1931), as a proponent of Cambridge type analysis concerned to re-express locutions in a form which makes their logical structure clear. He went on, in 'Categories' (1937) and 'Philosophical Argu-ments' (1945), to think that philosophical error consisted in 'cate-gory mistakes'—typically a matter of supposing that two terms belong to the same category when they do not. To ask for the where-abouts of the University after one has been shown the Oxford colleges, laboratories, examination schools, etc., is to make the (trivial) category mistake of supposing that the University is an entity of the same order as the colleges, etc., which make it up. To think of the mind as a spiritual *substance* is to make an important category mistake. Category mistakes can be exposed by *reductio ad absurdum* arguments. For instance, the intellectualist error of supposing that every piece of intelligent action must be preceded by some explicit mental theorizing leads, since theorizing is itself a species of intelligent action, to an infinite regress of theorizing before theorizing before theorizing. . . . Ryle denies that he is concerned with philology, language as such, but he frequently tries to bring potential absurdities to light by reminding his readers, in the Aristotelian manner, of what they would or would not say.

The Concept of Mind is a set-piece attack on a major category mistake, the 'myth' of Cartesian dualism. This is the view that psychological terms refer to a mental entity (the 'ghost in the machine'), and to its various acts and states; that people are compounded out of two sorts of substance, the physical and the mental, whose relations have set epistemologists insoluble problems for the last three centuries. In fact the function of psychological terms is to describe human *behaviour*. Typically such terms are dispositional. To say that someone acted intelligently is not to say that he first thought (a mental act) and then performed (a physical act), it is rather to commit oneself to an indefinite number of unfulfilled hypothetical statements to the effect that *if* the situation had been different in certain ways the deed *would have been* modified appropriately. To be intelligent is not to perform mental acts before physical ones, it is rather to be disposed to modify one's behaviour in ways that will lead to the accomplishment of one's purposes in changing situations.

The Concept of Mind is by any standard an important book which succeeds in expressing a distinctive point of view with both argumentative and literary power. It is possible to misunderstand the book as advocating metaphysical behaviourism, i.e. as denying the reality of mental phenomena or as 'reducing' them to the physical. But this is not the author's intention, although his employment of the material mode may tend to obscure this. He has no wish to dispute the truth of anything that would ordinarily be said about minds and their activities, he aims simply to rectify the 'logical geography' of psychological concepts, to provide better aids to logical navigation than the still popular Cartesian charts. He does not deny, indeed he asserts, that most of us most of the time succeed in talking sense *with* psychological concepts. His only point is that philosophers have frequently failed to talk sense *about* them. The root trouble with the 'official' (Cartesian) doctrine is that it fails to make sense of ordinary, intelligible, and successful usage.

Ethics and Political Philosophy

In ethics or moral philosophy our period was dominated by writers of the intuitionist persuasion, though towards the end the emotive theory began to win adherents. The intuitionists have been much criticized for the sterility of their views but, while it is true that they failed to say much that was positively illuminating about the logical status of moral judgements, they were not as *moral* philosophers (i.e. in their account of the 'moral consciousness'—our moral talk and thought) significantly inferior to many of their successors and notably superior to most of the emotivists. Philosophical interest, both between the wars and subsequently, centred on the nature of moral judgements as such, on what distinguished them, if anything did, from judgements and statements in other fields. Less attention was paid to differences *within* the moral field. Moral philosophy seemed to grow remote from moral practice, a tendency reinforced by, or part of, the general trend towards thinking of philosophy as a second order analytical activity. In spite of this, or perhaps because it was misunderstood, there were frequent head-shakings over the allegedly dire practical consequences of accepting certain ethical views. The emotive theory was apt to be attacked as *immoral* (not, more relevantly, as a mistake *about* morality) and, in retaliation, intuitionism was sometimes condemned as a recipe for intolerance.

In the early years of the century Moore and Prichard had, in their different ways, tried to correct the errors of, as they thought, virtually all previous moral philosophers. The most substantial writer of our period is Ross (1877–1971), whose *The Right and the Good* appeared in 1930, and the larger *The Foundation of Ethics* in 1939. Ross agreed with Moore about the distinctiveness of moral concepts, but disagreed about the primacy of good and hence with Moore's consequentialism. (He diverged from Moore in the Prichardian direction.) We can according to Ross determine what is right or obligatory without finding out which of the possible courses of action open to us will produce the best results. An action can, moreover, be right or obligatory even though its consequences are foreseeably worse than those of another action. (So far Ross is at one with Prichard, and both, for what it is worth, probably closer to the moral consciousness than Moore. Moore had in fact made some moves in their direction in his second work in moral philosophy, *Ethics*, 1912.) Where Ross disagrees with Prichard is about the status of moral principles. According to Prichard one intuits a duty in a particular, concrete situation—one might, for instance, 'see' that one had a duty to do something one had promised to do. But one does not intuit the universal principle, 'Promises ought to be kept', though it might be possible to arrive at generalizations about duty by induction from judgements in particular cases. Such generalizations would, however, never have authority over judgements made in particular cases. For Ross, on the other hand, universal principles are intuited. These alone are self-evidently true, while it may be very uncertain what one's duty is in particular cases. Duty in particular cases has to be worked out by balancing the, possibly conflicting, moral principles bearing on the case against one another.

Both Ross and Prichard see an analogy between moral judgements and mathematical propositions—a result, presumably, of their being determined to avoid the offence of naturalism by stressing the differences between moral judgements and statements of empirical fact. In this regard Ross's view is more coherent than Prichard's— the geometrical propositions with which they compare moral judgements are universal not singular. But this is a rather minor merit, since moral judgements are not very like mathematical propositions of any sort. It is significant that Ross, Prichard, and the intuitionists generally held mathematical propositions to be synthetic *a priori*, i.e. necessary truths of substance. When, under the influence of *Principia Mathematica* and logical positivism, this view of mathematics was abandoned, it ceased to be plausible to claim an analogy between mathematics and morals. Moral intuitionism foundered on developments in the philosophy of mathematics rather than on anything specific to moral philosophy.

Ross's principal innovation was explicitly to represent moral principles as rules of *prima facie* as opposed to strict obligation. For him the promise-keeping principle stipulates that promise-keeping *tends to be* a duty, provided that keeping a promise in a particular case would not bring one into conflict with some other rule of *prima facie* duty, for instance, the rule that one should, other things being equal, show gratitude to benefactors or refrain from harming other people. There are two advantages that may be claimed for Ross's proposal. The first is that it is probably in line with the moral consciousness, i.e. that reflects the way in which moral principles usually are regarded. Secondly it offers a way round the difficulty that the conflict of moral principles presents for intuitionism. If moral principles can conflict they can hardly all be quasi-mathematically necessary principles of *strict* duty. It may, of course, be thought that the price of saving intuitionism is too high. It involves admitting that the necessary moral knowledge we allegedly enjoy is insufficient to determine in cases of conflict of principles what actually ought to be done. Ross goes to the length of denying that it is possible to arrange the various principles of *prima facie* duty in a standing order of relative stringency, and admits that judgements of relative stringency in particular cases may be very uncertain indeed. So they very obviously are, but Ross's recognition of this is more creditable to him than to intuitionism. The fact that, despite all the brave talk of self-evidence and necessary truth, the theory has to come to terms with the uncertainties of practical life shows how little the *distinctive* features of the theory illuminate moral judgements.

Moore, as has been noticed, made good the primary ethical concept, defining (in *Principia Ethica* at least) the right and the ought in terms of it. Ross, like Prichard, accorded a greater measure of independence to right and ought. Most of the other intuitionists—Broad, Carritt, Ewing—follow with minor deviations the Prichard–Ross line. They are, that is to say, deontologists as opposed to teleologists or consequentialists. In another respect too they differed from Moore. Despite his faintly self-righteous attempt to introduce theoretical rigour into ethics, Moore still maintained that the subject had practical reference—casuistry, the attempt to work out what should be done in particular circumstances, fell within its scope. Later intuitionists, however, tended to stress the purely theoretical nature of the subject. They took the considered judgement of the ordinary reflective moral man as *data*, which they sought theoretically to account for but not to improve upon. Broad gave rather extreme expression to this point of view when he held (*Five Types of Ethical Theory*, 1930) that moral philosophy has as little relevance to the problems of the moral life as has the physical theory of projectiles to the practice of golf. (It should perhaps be noted, however, that in a later essay on pacifism he held that the theoretical issue between deontologists and teleologists had a bearing on the morality of conscientious objection.) The emotive theory of ethics and subsequent 'linguistic' ethics have often been criticized as lacking the practical concern that alone gives moral philosophy its point. But even if this was a fair criticism, which it is not, it would apply to intuitionism too. The formal resemblance between emotivism and the intuitionism it succeeded is in fact very close. To a great extent emotivism is intuitionism purged of what logical positivists held to be nonsense.

This comes out very clearly in chapter 6 of Ayer's *Language, Truth and Logic*, which first made the emotive theory widely known. Ayer explicitly follows the intuitionist criticism of naturalistic ethical theories, subjectivism and utilitarianism, but the verification principle prevents his accepting the positive intuitionist view that some moral terms stand for 'non-natural' (i.e. non-empirical) properties. Instead he maintains that they stand for nothing at all, but are simply linguistic devices for the expression and evocation of emotion. Moore, interestingly, had in *Principia Ethica* ruled out such a view as self-evidently false. He clearly could not see how a word could be meaningful without standing for something—a mistake to which the earlier Wittgenstein too fell victim, but which the late one did more than anyone to expose. That Ayer was prepared to embrace the emotive theory shows that he was partly emancipated from the naming or referential theory of meaning —though only partly, for he writes as if he thought that emotive meaning was an inferior species, and stigmatizes words that are purely emotive as expressing 'pseudo-concepts'. It has sometimes been suggested that the emotive theory is a fundamentally inadequate view of moral judgements that Ayer was simply forced into by his acceptance of the verification principle. No doubt the briskness of the critique of ethics and theology in *Language, Truth and Logic* lends colour to this assessment. But the emotive theory proved capable of subtle development in the hands of Stevenson (*Ethics and Language*, 1944), and it is in fact, as Ayer himself pointed out, not the only ethical theory that is compatible with the verification principle. Schlick, for instance, in his *Problems of Ethics* (1930), with perfect consistency adopts a naturalistic theory that would have been congenial to any eighteenth-century empiricist. Ayer became an emotivist, not only because he accepted the verification principle, but at least as importantly because he agreed with Moore about the naturalistic fallacy.

An earlier source in the inter-war period for the emotive theory is Ogden's and Richards's *The Meaning of Meaning* (1923). There are, moreover, anticipatory passages in Berkeley, and Hume could have made his ethical theory more consistent by adopting emotivism but, apart from a few uncertain passages, it seems that he did not recognize it as a possibility.

It will have become apparent that philosophical ethics in the period we are concerned with was very rigidly philosophical, a matter of philosophers dealing with philosophical questions. No major philosophical work of the period so far as I am aware makes any very determined attempt to come to terms with the new psycho-analysis and anthropology, as Ginsberg, MacBeath, and others did after the Second War. The 'acids of modernism' corroding the old certainties, which feature so prominently in the layman Walter Lippmann's *Preface to Morals* (1929), pass unremarked in academic moral philosophy. The only possible exceptions are Macmurray's *Reason and Emotion* (1935), and the popularizing moral and political writings of Joad. Russell, of course, frequently wrote on moral and political topics, but more as a man with practical concerns than as a philosopher. The same high intelligence informs both his philosophical and practical works, but there is no other close connection between them. He is a philosopher and a moralist, but hardly a moral philosopher.

In political philosophy the inter-war period was notoriously barren. A number of respectable works were produced, but little new ground was broken. Liberal democratic values continued to be defended. There were few signs of Marxist influence, though some of Hegel's as transmitted by the English idealists, and rather little reaction to Communist and Fascist totalitarianism (Collingwood and Popper are exceptions here). Of all branches of the subject one would expect political philosophy to be most relevant to the concerns of the day, but this can hardly be said of it between the wars. Part of the explanation of this is that political *philosophy* nowadays constitutes a small proportion only of social and political theorizing. The social sciences, politics (or political science), economics, sociology have acquired independent status, and deal with much of the traditional subject-matter of political philosophy. A great deal of the liveliest and most relevant social thinking of the twenties and thirties (Keynes's *General Theory*, for instance) is not philosophy at all in the modern narrow sense. The political philosophy that there was was not markedly innovatory, and, until the end of the Second War, showed few effects of the winds of change that had blown through philosophy generally. Logic and epistemology are the heartlands of philosophy. It is there that philosophical revolutionaries seize power. It takes time for them to extend their influence to the provinces of ethics, political philosophy, and aesthetics.

For the remainder of this section I shall concentrate on narrowly philosophical works. This involves ignoring a body of Marxist writings, and Tawney's very influential criticism of capitalist attitudes. These are discussed in the chapter on Social Thought.

Bosanquet's Rousseau- and Hegel-inspired *Philosophical Theory of the State* reached its fourth edition in 1923. It had been sharply attacked, not without some anti-German animus, in Hobhouse's *Metaphysical Theory of the State* (1918). Its monistic conception of the state came under attack by such pluralists as Cole and Laski. The monistic/pluralistic controversy is a tangled one in which socio-logical questions about the independent origin and empirical via-bility of non-state groups are mixed up with value questions about the most desirable form of political organization, and both mixed up with metaphysical questions about the relative 'reality' of groups and individuals. It is the latter connection, or confusion, that gives the controversy its philosophical interest—it will be remembered that the philosophical rebels at the turn of the century had been moved to attack Hegelian monism in other fields.

Sabine's influential *History of Political Theory* appeared in 1937. Partly because of its merits as a history it tended to encourage the notion that the subject had no future. It leaves one feeling that the political thought of a period is an aspect of its life, relatable to other aspects, interesting as an episode in human experience, but presenting no intellectual challenge. Much traditional political philosophy was indeed profoundly unhistorical. One was supposed to argue with Plato, Hobbes, Rousseau, Marx, as though they could sensibly be regarded as offering competing solutions to *our* questions. This was manifestly absurd, and Sabine was a splendid corrective, but the reaction against it arguably went too far. Professional philosophers were mostly interested in other areas of their subject and tended to discharge their obligation to teach some political philosophy by telling their pupils to read it up in Sabine for them-selves. Despite the publication of Popper's *Open Society and Its Enemies* in 1945 there was no general revival of political philosophy until the sixties.

Popper's book is superficially most remarkable for the intemper-ance of its attacks on the totalitarianism of Plato and Hegel (the attack on Plato was anticipated in Crossman's lively *Plato Today*, 1937), but its more serious claim to fame rests on the way the author tries to get at the philosophical roots of the political ten-dencies he had good cause to deplore. The most important of these are Plato's *essentialism*, the view that conclusions of political sub-stance can be extracted from definitions, and Hegel's and Marx's *historicism*, the view that history runs according to some humanly discernible plan. Both views encourage the idea that there is an ideal or inevitable form of social order in the service of which individuals may legitimately be coerced. Popper is wholly guiltless of that avoid-ance of positive assertion and categorical commitment that many find so tiresome in philosophy. He is full of moral and political passion, but he always *argues*, always states his reasons with sufficient clarity for them to be checkable by others. His partisanship has most probably led him into serious errors in the interpretation of Plato and Hegel, and his conclusions seem sometimes to go beyond his premises, but he deserves great credit, whether one likes the conclusions or not, for bringing clear argument to bear on matters of great practical importance.

Idealists and Metaphysicians

It was remarked at the beginning of this chapter that a considerable number of bulky metaphysical works were published in our period. These include writings by McTaggart, Alexander (about whom a little was said in the previous volume), Whitehead, Stout, the American Blanshard, and Collingwood too if he is to be accounted a metaphysician. He certainly looked like one in his *Speculum Mentis* and *Essay on Philosophical Method*, but in the *Essay on Metaphysics* he is no longer defending any form of metaphysics that a logical positivist would be obliged to take exception to. None of the writers mentioned really lends himself to brief discussion. Nor has it yet appeared that the historical importance of any of them is very great. None has made much impression on British philosophy, though Whitehead has some exegetes and followers and his influence may grow. In this situation the best I think I can do is to write a very few lines about Whitehead, more about Collingwood, and ignore the rest.

Whitehead (1861–1947), after his immensely fruitful period of collaboration with Russell, set himself the idealist aim of giving a unified picture of reality in which knowledge, feeling, and emotion all had due place. Not for him the piecemeal, one-problem-at-a-time approach characteristic of mainstream British philosophy in this century. Some of his earlier works on the new physics were mentioned in the previous volume. His major metaphysical works are *Science and the Modern World* (1925), *Adventures of Ideas* (1933), *Process and Reality* (1929)—the last, very difficult work being the most complete statement of his views. There he attempts to bring out the inter-relatedness of all forms of human inquiry and experience, and in particular to bridge or close the gulf between nature and man, fact and value. He makes use of biological concepts and thinks of himself as producing a philosophy of organism. The difficulty of his writing, whether deriving from unclarity of thought or complexity of subject-matter, is such that a vast expenditure of time is needed in order to come to terms with his system. His opponents therefore ignore him instead of criticizing him in detail. Some at least of his admirers praise him more for his insights than for his success in welding them into a whole, thinking better of him as a source of possibly fruitful ideas than a systematic philosopher.

Collingwood (1889–1943) is a wholly different proposition. He always writes with *literary* clarity, in the sense that, although his ideas may be at times unclear, one never feels that they are obscured by being badly expressed. He grew up philosophically (as he explains in his possibly hindsightful *Autobiography*, 1939) in the last stages of English idealism and, though he did not profess much positive idealist doctrine, he retained the idealist interest in humane as opposed to scientific studies, and remained convinced that the realist doctrine that knowing makes no difference to what is known (that knowing is a sort of contemplation) was a fountainhead of philosophical error. Knowledge is not the passive absorption of *data*, it is the fruit of strenuous inquiry. Propositions make no sense outside the context of question and answer—an important half-truth that lies at the root of the idealist and pragmatist disregard of formal logic. For the logic of propositions he proposed to substitute a logic of question and answer. He did not, however, produce anything substantial along these lines, though his emphasis on contextual matters parallels emphases of the later Wittgenstein, and his conception of propositions presupposing questions was important in his account of historical inquiry.

Collingwood was a distinguished ancient historian and thought it worthwhile to devote to historical method the level of attention his more fashionable contemporaries paid to the method of science. In part the outcome of this was a wholly salutary stress upon the place of thought in historical investigation, upon the need to formulate clear hypotheses and to subject them to systematic test. There was also the much more dubious contention that history, since its subject matter is human action, is a radically different study from science, of which the subject matter is inanimate. We can understand what happened in history because, it is claimed, we can get on the 'inside' of historical events and rethink the thoughts of historical figures, which we cannot of course do with atoms or planets. Despite appearances there are no implications for historical method—Collingwood is emphatically not advocating that historians should use their intuition and neglect the evidence.

A somewhat similar idea infects Collingwood's theory of art (*Principles of Art*, 1938). Art is held to be the expression of emotion and appreciation to consist in re-experiencing the artist's emotion. It is not made clear how one is to know when it has been re-experienced aright. Both the philosophy of history and the aesthetics are more impressive for their denials than their assertions. Collingwood is splendidly trenchant in repudiating what art and history have often been thought to be but are not. His positive views, however, tend to fluctuate between paradox and vacuity. They are, moreover, very heavily influenced by Croce, but in ways that Collingwood does little to make clear, possibly because he thought that he and Croce were equal labourers in the same vineyard, or possibly because he felt he had no time. His later works were written hastily because of illness and approaching death. For this reason he felt entitled to disregard the concerns of his British philosophical contemporaries. There is indubitably a question about Collingwood's originality if one takes a wider view, but in Britain he was unique. More remarkable than the substance of what he had to say is the simple fact that, in the age of analysis and logical positivism, he produced a major work on aesthetics and left materials for a post-humous volume on the philosophy of history (*The Idea of History*, 1946).

The last important philosophical work of Collingwood's to appear in his lifetime, unless the very singular *New Leviathan* (1940) is to be accounted a major work, is the *Essay on Metaphysics* (1940). His views about philosophy had by then changed a good deal. In *Speculum Mentis* (1924) philosophy is a critical review of the main forms of human experience—science, morality, art, religion—but it has no authority over them and is without a first-order subject matter of its own. The *Essay on Philosophical Method* (1933), however, conceives philosophy as a specific inquiry with a method of its own. In the *Essay on Metaphysics* philosophical method is conceived as analytic and historical. Statements are relative to questions, questions have presuppositions—for instance, questions about causes presuppose that there are causes to be found. The causal principle, however, is a possibly ultimate presupposition. There is no question of justifying ultimate presuppositions, nor are they true or false, but they have a history and change through time. Metaphysics should be, and, though misunderstood by its practitioners, often has been, the history of absolute presuppositions. Aristotle set out the presuppositions of Greek science, Kant those of Newtonian science. Some of Whitehead's writings might be regarded as attempts to formulate the presuppositions of Einsteinian science. Collingwood's posthumous *Idea of Nature* (1945) dealt with Greek science. It is perhaps not always sufficiently noticed how radically relativistic Collingwood's final view is. It is a serious error to suppose that he had even attempted a rehabilitation of the traditional metaphysics.

Popular Philosophy

The philosophy surveyed above is academic in the sense of being written and in the main read by professionals. It had comparatively little impact on general literature. Moore, it is true, had some influence on members of the Bloomsbury Group, Russell rated a poem by Eliot ('Mr. Appollinax'), and *Language, Truth and Logic* created a mild disturbance—but Freud and Marx were more influential in the twenties and thirties than any philosopher. There was nothing comparable to the influence of Sartrean existentialism after the Second War. Russell's educational and moral writings, *On Education* (1926) and *Marriage and Morals* (1929), attracted a certain amount of notice but, unlike Sartre, who is very much the literary sage and the worse as a philosopher for it, Russell was a highly professional philosopher who from time to time set up as a sage. He apparently conceived the lucid, but by no means easy, *Human Knowledge* as a work of high-grade popularization, and was genuinely astonished that reviewers failed to understand it. Hence the impatient title, *Unpopular Essays*, for a later work. The eclectic Joad was perhaps the nearest to a respectable professional philosopher to achieve much general notice, and this was, I think, due more to his wartime B.B.C. 'Brains Trust' broadcasting than his voluminous writings. Though radical in political and moral matters, except at the end of his life when he returned to the Church of England, Joad was a conservative in philosophy, as his *Critique of Logical Positivism* makes all too clear.

Some semi-philosophical writings on the new physics and astronomy, notably by Jeans and Eddington, were widely read. Eddington exploited atomic theory in order to cast doubt on the reality and solidity of material objects—tables, for instance, despite appearance were 'really' practically empty volumes thinly populated by occasional atoms. His principal works were *Space, Time and Gravitation* (1920), *The Nature of the Physical World* (1928), and *The Philosophy of Physical Science* (1939). It is to be feared, however, that Eddington brings idealism to physics rather than, as he thought, finding it there. His philosophical naïveté was ably exposed by Stebbing in *Philosophy and the Physicists* (1937)—still a fresh and lively book. Despite the failure of his more ambitious philosophical enterprises it should be allowed that Eddington usefully emphasized the constructive as opposed to the merely descriptive aspects of science.

Retrospect and Prospect

British philosophy in the inter-war period was an insular pheno-menon, open to a few continental influences, but mainly pursuing a path of its own. The early Moore and Russell were influenced by Hegel to the extent that they reacted against him. They then re-verted to the British tradition. Wittgenstein was, of course, an Austrian, but, although his influence on British philosophy has been enormous, it cannot without qualification be said to be an influence from outside. He went to Cambridge because his interests at that time were the same as Russell's. Much the same is true of the effect of logical positivism. It started in Vienna and its proponents came to British, and American, shores largely for extraneous political reasons, but they found there an established native tradition which could accommodate them without undue strain.

Bochenski, in his *Contemporary European Philosophy* (2nd Ger-man ed. 1951, English trans. 1957), held that the two most powerful contemporary influences in philosophy were Bergson and Husserl. This is something no one could have guessed from a study of British philosophy, though there was in fact some Husserlian influence on Ryle and Bergson figures' in the eclectic philosophy of Joad. Exis-tentialist writers too make no impression, except that choice speci-mens of metaphysical nonsense culled from Heidegger are some-times quoted in logical positivist writings. Neo-Thomism and Marxism make no impression at all.

I have in this chapter emphasized the line of development that runs from Cambridge analysis, through the dogmatic interludes of logical atomism and logical positivism, to the linguistic philosophy (Oxford Aristotelian, Cambridge Wittgensteinian) of the postwar years. Judgements of historical importance are, of course, histori-cally relative, and I am very conscious that philosophers writing at another point in time may see the British inter-war period very differently, as those in other places already do. One thing certainly, that seemed to be very much a feature of inter-war philosophy, has proved to be a temporary phenomenon. I mean the growing intel-lectual illiberality of the more influential philosophers, their ten-dency to dismiss as nonsense whole areas of human concern—morality, aesthetics, religion. Philosophical attention shifted from things to words, from truth to meaning, and restrictive criteria of meaning were formulated. But, when attention is firmly fixed on language, it becomes apparent that there are many different sorts of language, and no reason to expect them all to conform to a single criterion of significance. Once this came to be understood post-Second War linguistic philosophy ceased to be logical positivism in linguistic disguise (though the two movements still tend to be identified in the public mind). The linguistic approach to philosophy came to be seen as metaphysically neutral, and areas of philosophical study neglected or disregarded between the wars were opened up again.

WORKS REFERRED TO IN THE TEXT

Unless otherwise stated the date given is that of first publication.

S. Alexander, *Space, Time and Deity* (1920). J. L. Austin, *Sense and Sensibilia* (1962). A. J. Ayer, *Language, Truth and Logic* (1936; 2nd ed. 1946); *Foundations of Empirical Knowledge* (1940); *The Problem of Knowledge* (1956).

I. M. Bochenski, *Contemporary European Philosophy* (2nd German ed. 1951; English trans. 1957). B. Bosanquet, *The Philosophical Theory of the State* (4th ed. 1923). C. D. Broad, *Scientific Thought* (1923); *Mind and Its Place in Nature* (1925); *Five Types of Ethical Theory* (1930); *An Examination of McTaggart's Philosophy* (1933–8).

R. Carnap, *Logical Construction of the World* (1928 in German, English trans. 1967); *Logical Syntax of Language* (1935). R. G. Collingwood, *Speculum Mentis* (1924); *Essay on Philosophical Method* (1933); *Principles of Art* (1938); *Auto-biography* (1939); *Essay on Metaphysics* (1940); *The New Leviathan* (1940); *The Idea of Nature* (1945); *The Idea of History* (1946). R. H. S. Crossman, *Plato Today* (1937).

A. S. Eddington, *Space, Time and Gravitation* (1920); *The Nature of the Physical World* (1928); *The Philosophy of Physical Science* (1939).

L. T. Hobhouse, *The Metaphysical Theory of the State* (1918).

C. E. M. Joad, *Critique of Logical Positivism* (1950).

J. M. Keynes, *General Theory of Employment, Interest and Money* (1936).

W. Lippmann, *Preface to Morals* (1929). J. Macmurray, *Reason and Emotion* (1935). J. E. M. McTaggart, *The Nature of Existence* (1927). G. E. Moore, *Principia Ethica* (1903); *Ethics* (1912); 'A Defence of Commonsense' (1925) and 'The Proof of an External World' (1939), both in *Philosophical Papers* (1959); *Some Main Problems of Philosophy* (1953).

C. K. Ogden and I. A. Richards, *The Meaning of Meaning* (1923). K. R. Popper, *The Logic of Scientific Discovery* (1934 in German, English trans. 1959); *The Open Society and its Enemies* (1945). H. H. Price, *Perception* (1932); *Hume's Theory of the External World* (1940).

W. D. Ross, *The Right and the Good* (1930); *The Foundations of Ethics* (1939). B. Russell and A. N. Whitehead, *Principia Mathematica* (1910–13). B. Russell, *The Problems of Philosophy* (1912); *Introduction to Mathematical Philosophy*

(1919); *The Analysis of Mind* (1921); *On Education* (1926); *An Analysis of Matter* (1927); *Marriage and Morals* (1929); *Human Knowledge, Its Scope and Limits* (1948); *Unpopular Essays* (1950). G. Ryle, 'Systematically Misleading Expressions' (1931), and 'Categories' (1937), *Proceedings of the Aristotelian Society*; *Philosophical Arguments* (1945); *The Concept of Mind* (1949).

G. H. Sabine, *A History of Political Theory* (1937). M. Schlick, *Problems of Ethics* (1930). S. Stebbing, *Philosophy and the Physicists* (1937). C. L. Stevenson, *Ethics and Language* (1944).

A. N. Whitehead, *Science and the Modern World* (1925); *Process and Reality* (1929); *Adventures of Ideas* (1933). J. Wisdom, *Problems of Mind and Matter* (1934); 'Logical Constructions' (1931–3) in *Mind*; *Other Minds* (1952). L. Wittgenstein, *Tractatus Logico-Philosophicus* (1921 in German, English trans. 1922); *Philosophical Investigations* (1953). G. H. von Wright, *The Logical Problem of Induction* (1941).

FOR FURTHER READING

John Passmore's *A Hundred Years of Philosophy* (1957) is unquestionably the most useful book covering the period as a whole for logic, epistemology, and metaphysics. It includes ample bibliographies. Other varyingly useful general works include the following: F. Copleston, *A History of Philosophy*, vol. VIII (1966); G. J. Warnock, *English Philosophy since 1900* (1958); I. M. Bochenski, *Contemporary European Philosophy* (2nd German ed. 1951, English trans. 1957) —cited above; J. O. Urmson, *Philosophical Analysis* (Oxford, 1956); and *A Critical History of Western Philosophy*, ed. D. J. O'Connor (1964).

The following collections contain interesting material: *Contemporary British Philosophy*, ed. J. H. Muirhead (1st Ser. 1924/5, 2nd Ser. 1929); *Contemporary British Philosophy*, ed. H. D. Lewis (3rd Ser., 2nd ed., 1961); and *British Philosophy in Mid-Century*, ed. C. A. Mace (1957). For particular aspects of the period the following may be useful:

(a) *Tractatus* etc.: N. Malcolm, *Ludwig Wittgenstein: A Memoir* (1958); G. E. M. Anscombe, *An Introduction to Wittgenstein's Tractatus* (1959); M. Black, *Companion and Critique of Wittgenstein's Tractatus* (Cambridge, 1964); V. Kraft, *The Vienna Circle* (1950 in German, English trans. New York 1953); and *Logical Positivism*, ed. A. J. Ayer (Glencoe, Ill., 1959).

(b) *Logic* etc.: W. M. and M. Kneale, *The Development of Logic* (1962); and S. Körner, *The Philosophy of Mathematics* (1960).

(c) *Theory of Knowledge* etc.: *The Philosophy of Bertrand Russell* (1944) and *The Philosophy of G. E. Moore* (1942), both ed. P. A. Schilpp; and B. Russell, *My Philosophical Development* (1959).

(d) *Ethics* etc.: M. Warnock, *Ethics Since 1900* (1960); G. J. Warnock, *Contemporary Moral Philosophy* (1967); and A. MacIntyre, *A Short History of Ethics* (1967).

(e) *Idealists* etc.: A. Donagan, *The Later Philosophy of R. G. Collingwood* (Oxford, 1962).

6

Theology

S. W. SYKES

The Controversy over Liberalism

The period 1918–45 was one in which the meaning of liberalism for Christian theology was re-examined. Liberalism is, as has been frequently pointed out, a negative virtue.[1] In theology it consists of the temper of mind that is prepared to allow something (either from science, from reason, or merely from personal or moral experience) to count *against* the authority of the traditional Christian account of the world. Frequently it manifests itself in the attempt to make a synthesis out of elements of traditional belief and the discoveries of science, reason, or experience. It regards itself, and is widely regarded, as 'progressive', 'contemporary', or 'modern'.

The theological liberalism of the pre-war era had the considerable advantage of being able, tacitly, to appeal to the common feeling that real progress was being made on all sides by human society. The postwar churches were not so certain; and uncertainty added a measure of anxiety to the question traditionally posed of all forms of liberalism: Are these 'new' developments truly advances, or are they a sell-out?

Because theological liberalism seeks change and rethinking, it is always open to the charge that it is dissolving the absoluteness of Christianity. In order to defend itself against this charge it produced the distinction between the unchanging essence of the faith, and the changing and relative inessentials. The trouble was, however, that the content of this distinction itself proved to be a highly variable one, corresponding closely to the author's own ethical and metaphysical predilections. The discovery of this fact greatly, if temporarily, strengthened the hand of the traditionalists; but their negative verdict on the whole enterprise is by no means the last word on the significance of liberalism for theology.[2]

There are certain stock characters in this period. The most obvious is the Liberal, continually 'purifying' the tradition of spurious elements, or outlining possible syntheses of Christian truth and modern knowledge. There is also the Traditionalist, urging, sometimes with polemical passion, sometimes with constructive restraint, the real advantages of a frequently misunderstood orthodoxy. There is also the Academic, often a Biblical scholar of traditional enough piety, whose commitment to the disinterested quest for knowledge in his own field makes him suspicious of the too-hasty drawing of conclusions, or the use of his research for polemical purposes. And there is, on the side lines, the Conservative Sceptic, ever ready to form an alliance with the Traditionalist against the Liberal, infinitely preferring the traditional assertions he knows he cannot believe to the innovations which may force him to reconsider. The verdict of history upon their controversies is ambiguous. Frequently enough a change in the prevailing fashion of historical and philosophical inquiry has shown that the orthodox had good grounds for not yielding under the pressure of allegedly progressive, but nevertheless culturally conditioned, programmes of criticism. At the same time the exploratory function of the liberals, who constantly tested the compatibility of new ideas with traditionalism, was irreplaceable. An admirable illustration of the position in theology at the start of our period is the famous Girton Conference (1921) of the Modern Churchman's Union. The subject of the morning sessions of this conference was the Person of Christ and the readers of papers were the leaders of the Modernist movement in the Church of England.[3] The storm it raised was immense. It was widely reported in the ecclesiastical and secular press that this group of churchmen had denied the divinity of Christ. A petition was presented to the Bishops to declare the doctrines asserted there contrary to the teaching of the Bible and the Church. Particular exception was taken to the contribution of Hastings Rashdall (1858–1924), Dean of Carlisle. One newspaper was successfully accused by him of libel, and paid damages out of court.

The irony of the situation is that some of the speakers regarded themselves as defenders of the faith against a form of modernism that was held to be pernicious and debilitating. This offence was offered by the first volume of the *Beginnings of Christianity* (5 vols., 1920–33) by Professor E. J. Foakes-Jackson and Professor K. Lake, and also by Professor Lake's shorter and more popular *Landmarks in the History of Early Christianity* (1920). Of these works one of the speakers said, 'the fundamental criticism on these books is that they fail historically because they make Jesus unimportant and uninteresting. Such a view explains neither the figure of Jesus as given us in the Gospels, nor the impact of Jesus in His age.'[4] In view of this explicit criticism Professor Foakes-Jackson (1855–1941) was invited to make a defence of his position. His counter-charge against the Modern Churchmen was equally clear,

They are really preaching an entirely new religion, and concealing the fact even from themselves by disguising it in the phraseology of the old, which as employed by them is sometimes without meaning.

These are the people who look for help from us, who are labouring in the obscure field of primitive Christianity. They ask us to give them Christ as they want Him to be, and when we lay the facts before them, they declare them to be stones presented to hungry folk who are clamouring for bread.[5]

This was the same charge as that levelled by Albert Schweitzer (1875–1965) against the nineteenth-century liberals in his epoch-making work *The Quest of the Historical Jesus* (1906, trans. 1910). The attempt made both by these early liberal Protestants and by the Modern Churchmen (who wished to distinguish themselves from the former) was to find a basis in historical study of the New Testament for the kind of thing they wished to say about Christ. And what they wished to say about Christ rested upon their mistrust of the supernaturalism of the New Testament and Patristic world-view. Professor Bethune-Baker (1861–1951), another of the speakers, bluntly stated, 'To clear the ground I would start with two or three premisses, and the first of them is that "orthodoxy", in beginning with God, began at the wrong end.'[6] Hence other excellences than supernatural ones had to be found by which the teaching of the divinity of Christ could be substantiated. These naturally tended to be moral ones. Of the Godhead of Christ Bethune-Baker writes,

So far as I can make His ideals and His values of life my own, I am sure I am doing the will of God. God stands to me for the highest values in life, and because I believe those values were actualized in the person and life of Jesus, I must use the title 'God' of Him.[7]

On the historical and critical side this meant that the 'values' expressed in the Gospels were given a special prominence, and a determined effort was made to ground them as securely as possible in the life and teaching of the historical Jesus. Along with this went the tendency to draw attention to the supernaturalism only when it could be plausibly shown to be later teaching.

But this procedure satisfied no one, particularly not the conservative churchmen, who were led by Bishop Charles Gore (1853–1932). The Archbishop of Canterbury, Randall Davidson (1848–1930), contrived to take the heat out of the debate by seeing through the Upper House of Canterbury Convocation an ambiguous blanket resolution. The real debate in the Church of England concerned not the theological point so much as the question of ecclesiastical discipline. Gore, who understood the theology perfectly well, wrote that it seemed to him that if the Bishops did not act to reaffirm 'the basis on which the Church of England stands and the message which the ministers of the Church are commissioned to deliver, it will have assented to the idea that Major and Rashdall's teaching is legitimate—a "school of thought" within the Church of England.'[8] Without a doubt Gore was right. The failure of the Church to discipline the Modernists was an ecclesiastical victory for them—a victory fully confirmed by subsequent developments, especially the Commission on Doctrine in the Church of England.[9]

But the fact that liberal theologians had established a clear position for themselves within the Church of England by 1922 could only be regarded as a matter of great significance by one whose eyes were narrowly focused on the English scene. By that year developments were already on foot in the Continent which were to sweep aside the old terms of the debate. In 1921 Karl Barth (1886–1968) published the second fully revised edition of his *Commentary on Romans* (trans. 1933); the same year marked the publication of Rudolf Bultmann's (b. 1884) *History of the Synoptic Tradition* (trans. 1963).

The work of these two men inaugurates an era in which the terms of the controversy between the liberal and conservative sections of the Church of England begin to look distinctly old-fashioned. Both these men, as we shall see, were strongly influenced by their background in liberalism, and in different ways sought to ward off the threat of the dissolution of the faith in something less than itself.

The precise nature of this threat, as it presented itself to both, can be shown in the career and writings of the philosopher Ernst Troeltsch (1865–1923). Having taught as a theologian in several universities from 1891, in 1915 he became Professor of Philosophy at Berlin, lecturing in the philosophy of religion, the philosophy of general civilization, and the philosophy of history.[10] The change was in itself significant. Troeltsch all his life had been engaged in the problem set by the liberalism of the eighteenth and nineteenth centuries, as his early work *Die Absolutheit des Christentums und die Religionsgeschichte* (The Absoluteness of Christianity and the History of Religions, 1902, trans. 1972) shows. Invited to Oxford to lecture in 1923, his projected address, entitled 'The Place of Christianity among the World Religions', summarized his former views, but indicated that he had become more radical. His close study of the history of Christianity, and in particular of the social groups of Western Christendom,[11] as well as the history of other religions, had convinced him that the Christian's simple claim for the supreme validity of his religion had to give way to something less sweeping.

In claiming to know the truth, the theologian must be careful to add, the truth *for me*. It is only final and unconditional in the sense that he has nothing else. 'But this does not preclude the possibility that other racial groups, living under entirely different cultural conditions, may experience their contact with the Divine Life in quite a different way.'[12] The work of Troeltsch was influential, though rather more in Germany than in England. It raised explicitly the problem of the absoluteness of Christianity when examined from the standpoint of the history of religion in Western society, and it was one of the main challenges goading both Barth and Bultmann in their search for alternative accounts of Christian faith.

Biblical Research

Our period is notable for an important shift of emphasis in Biblical research. The main method by which the Biblical documents were handled by critics in the nineteenth century and the early years of the twentieth was that of source analysis. Scholars felt that many of the narrative books in the Bible, for example the Pentateuch and the Synoptic Gospels, showed clear signs of having been compiled from earlier independent strands. These strands could be separated, analysed as sources, and fitted into an overall picture of the religious development of Israel or the Early Church. By the opening years of our period, this understanding of the Biblical documents had produced what was very nearly a critical consensus of opinion. A. S. Peake, in a review of recent developments in Old Testament criticism, wrote in 1928, 'The net result of the recent critical movement, it seems to me, is that we are left, in the main, where we were a quarter of a century ago.'[13] The monument of New Testament literary criticism was B. H. Streeter's (1874–1937) *The Four Gospels* (1924), which argued for the existence of four basic written sources behind the Gospels as we know them. This study remained fundamental for the examination of sources up to quite recent times.

The new development in Biblical research arose out of dissatisfaction with the narrowly literary approach of source criticism when applied to the Old Testament. Hermann Gunkel (1862–1932), in his work on Genesis and on the Psalms, insisted that the literature must be studied in relation to the *Sitz im Leben* (situation in life) of the community in which it was handed on.[14] This involved extensive study of the literary and religious parallels to the Biblical documents from other civilizations of the Near East. In this way one could establish a *Formgeschichte* (a history of forms), which would place the various elements of the literature in historical relation to the cultural and religious background out of which they arose.

The method of form criticism, as *Formgeschichte* came to be called in England, was applied to the New Testament in order to solve a particular problem in the understanding of the Gospels. Earlier research in Germany, notably by W. Wrede (1859–1906), had shown the extent to which Mark, in the earliest Gospel, far from recounting the bare history of Jesus, was conditioned by his own theological viewpoint.[15] How had this viewpoint been arrived at, and what was the history of the Gospel stories up to the time they were incorporated into the earliest written document? To trace the history of these stories was the new task of form criticism, undertaken by K. L. Schmidt, M. Dibelius, and R. Bultmann. These scholars offered not merely to establish and categorize the individual units of the Gospel narrative, and distinguish them from editorial additions, but also to comment on the probable extent of adaptation of each to the needs of the early community. The new method of studying the Gospels naturally raised the question of whether the stories, in the course of being handed down, had not been considerably modified by the beliefs and practices of the first-century world. Knowledge of this world greatly increased and many authors concerned themselves with the extent of borrowings and influence from Hellenistic and Rabbinic Judaism, the Hellenistic mystery religions, and early Gnosticism.[16]

An early, and still considerable, attempt to make a simple account of the period is found in an essay in *Essays on the Trinity and the Incarnation* (1928), edited by A. E. J. Rawlinson, entitled 'Early Gentile Christianity and its Hellenistic Background'. The young author of this work, A. D. Nock (1902–1963), refused to be moved by appeals to alleged Hellenistic borrowings, pointing rather to Septuagintal and Judaistic origins.

The problems of dating much of this material are crucial to the attempt to establish lines of influence. It would not be unfair to say that much of it has not yet been adequately assimilated. Certainly its bewildering variety appeared, and still appears, to allow a be-wildering variety of interpretations of New Testament texts. Under the weight of possible constructions placed upon apparently simple statements, a reasonable view of the character and deeds of the historic person, Jesus of Nazareth, seemed to become impossible. Many of the form-critics, true to the disinterested principles of the *religionsgeschichtliche Schule*, gave up the quest for historical certainty. Even R. H. Lightfoot (1883–1953), the first Anglican scholar of real repute to avow the principles and many of the conclusions of the early German form-critics, concluded in his Bampton Lectures for 1934 with a negative-sounding verdict.

> It seems, then, that the form of the earthly no less than of the heavenly Christ is for the most part hidden from us. For all the inestimable value of the gospels, they yield us little more than a whisper of his voice; we trace in them but the outskirts of his ways.[17]

Others were not so daunted. Sir Edwyn Hoskyns (1884–1937) believed that much more confidence could be placed in the Gospels as a whole, arguing that the distinction between the early natural Jesus of history and the later theological Christ of faith was not borne out by the evidence, and that the only satisfactory way to explain the theological estimate of Christ was to suppose that it came from Jesus' own teaching.[18] Rudolf Otto (1869–1937), employing his own variation of source criticism, offered a strong portrait of Jesus as Messianic healer and preacher of a supernatural kingdom.[19] This was quickly followed by an English work, *The Parables of the Kingdom* (1935), in which C. H. Dodd (b. 1884), argued that the proper interpretation of the parables showed that Jesus himself regarded the Kingdom as having come with his own person. This book and *The Apostolic Preaching and Its Development* (1936) developed with great clarity and brevity a most influential perspective on the whole of the New Testament, the scholarship of which is at once independent and conservative.

The point of divergence between the conservative and the radical treatments arose over history. Scholars of both camps mention with approval the new form-critical techniques, in so far as they had made possible the examination of the pre-literary period of the Gospel traditions. They were agreed that the presentation of Christ in the New Testament was thoroughly supernatural and eschatological. And yet they disagreed radically with regard to the degree of confidence they felt could be placed in the historicity of these narratives. In this disagreement there was undoubtedly a genuine difference of opinion about the process of development in the crucial years between the crucifixion of Christ and the writing of

Mark, namely about the extent of the intrusion of adaptations or in-authentic material into the narrative. But there were also undoubtedly theological and philosophical factors involved. With the claims made by the narratives for themselves it could hardly be otherwise.

It was the recognition of this fact which has opened out a line of theological development, of which Rudolf Bultmann was the originator and which is only now reaching its end. In 1926 Bultmann published his study of Jesus (translated as *Jesus and the Word*, 1935), in which he set himself the task, not of picking up the remains from his radical programme of form criticism, but of finding out the purpose or intention of Jesus' teaching. There can be no question of an historical description of his deeds and words, nor of any psychological account of his personality. The important thing is to be free of history in order to concentrate on the understanding of man's existence in history. In his own words, one must attend to 'what he (Jesus) *purposed*, and hence to what in his purpose as a part of history makes a present demand on us.' Characteristically Sir Edwyn Hoskyns's review of the work omits all mention of the orientation of this book, confining its criticism to the conclusions reached in Bultmann's earlier critical work. He comments: 'Professor Bultmann has in fact abstracted the will of God from the concrete occasion of its expression to which the Synoptic Gospels direct especial attention.'[20] This was the opening shot in a battle the sounds of which have not yet died away. From 1927 onwards the existentialist philosophy of Martin Heidegger (b. 1889) increasingly coloured the theological outlook of Bultmann, and the emphasis on the attitude of the reader to the text has received increasingly greater attention. English scholars on the other hand, untouched by the existentialism of continental philosophy, pursued their traditional course, believing in the possibility and importance of establishing historical probabilities on the basis of the available evidence.

Philosophical Developments

Very many developments belonging properly to a description of the history of philosophy are influential also in theology. Frequently behind the positive work of a theologian lies an explicit inheritance from the philosophical study of the period, though not necessarily that of his contemporaries.

This general observation is true also of the influence on theology of studies in psychology, particularly in view of the fact that from the time of F. D. E. Schleiermacher so much emphasis had been placed upon the self-validating authority of religious experience.

The influence of these studies was not invariably direct. Although Freud continued to write works in which religion was reduced to neurosis, especially *The Future of an Illusion* (1927, trans. 1928), the direct onslaught was not in the long run the most damaging to theology. As J. K. Mozley rightly pointed out, the real danger lay 'in the impression of insecurity in the foundations of religion which has been conveyed through psychological teaching and writing'.[21] Faith appears to offer various assurances, for example, of forgiveness of sin or of future bliss, which when studied psychologically as states of feeling, lose their compulsive attractiveness. Fully involved in the consequences of this as we are, we are not yet able to take a detached or historical view of the matter. But it is certain that any future historical account of the theology of this period will need to devote considerable attention to the impression of insecurity which popularized psychological knowledge brought.

Theologians also continued studies in the phenomenology of religious experience. Rudolf Otto's *The Idea of the Holy* (1917, trans. 1923) was an attempt to establish the autonomy and uniqueness of the 'holy' as a religious experience, for which the author coined the term 'numinous'. This was an unfamiliar concept for English readers, and the translator felt obliged to provide an appendix giving examples of what was meant from Coleridge, Blake, and Wordsworth. Otto defined numinous as the non-rational mystery behind religion, which is both awesome and fascinating. It is, he asserted, the permanent and essential feature of all religion, including Christianity. An independent critic of Otto was the Scottish-born theologian, John Oman (1860–1939), who lived in Cambridge from 1907. In his account of the phenomenon of religion he emphasized the element of the sacred, that is, of something of absolute worth, as an experience inextricably intertwined with the holy in all religious feeling.[22]

But Oman was primarily a theologian rather than a student of the phenomenon of religion. His two greatest works, *Grace and Personality* (1st ed. 1917, 3rd ed. 1925) and *The Natural and the Supernatural* (1931), set out a whole method in theology and included an epistemology, metaphysics, and a classification of religions. The principle which he espoused was that, in religion, inquiry must refer first and foremost to the experience of the religious man. Hence in the earlier of the two works he asks initially what is meant by a moral personality, before discussing the meaning of God's grace, and in the latter, the inquiry begins with the problems of knowing and being rather than with alleged facts about the supernatural or the natural. Oman's work has never received from English philosophers and theologians the attention it deserves. Though widely respected, it was often regarded as obscure. Also its climax came at a time when the centre of interest in theology had shifted away from such painstaking prolegomena. What can justifiably be said of it is that it kept alive a tradition of theological activity, until such time as the fashion changed.

Another neglected writer, who was deeply indebted to the philosophy and psychology of his day, was F. R. Tennant (1866–1957). Educated in the natural sciences, he believed that only a theology which carefully explained its relation to natural knowledge about the self, mankind, and the world would command any intellectual respect. The first volume of his *Philosophical Theology* (1928; vol. II, 1930) relied heavily upon the work of the Cambridge psychologist, James Ward, and attempted an account of the soul and its faculties as the essential prolegomena for the natural theology of the second volume.

The neglect of Tennant and Oman is in particular ascribable to the interest, stimulated by existentialism on the Continent, in an apparently new way of approaching the whole question of rational, philosophical inquiry and religious belief. Religion, as Oman himself pointed out, has generally, since Kant, been ascribed to a department of the mind which is to a large degree susceptible to a rational philosophical discussion.[23] Kant placed it in the will, Schleiermacher in the feelings, and Hegel in the reason. It is always open to a hostile critic to say that when religion is so ascribed to a department of the mind, it becomes *subordinate* to that department. In the history of theology there have not been lacking those who say that Kant 'reduced' Christianity to ethics, Schleiermacher to aesthetics, and Hegel to a logical system. Existentialism in its Christian form appeared to resolve this dilemma by denying that Christian faith had anything whatever to do with philosophical inquiry.

There are many reasons why existentialism gained such a following on the Continent, and many reasons why it has subsequently proved so attractive in postwar Christian theology. But the original reason is implicit in the work of Sören Kierkegaard, its Danish founder.[24] Kierkegaard had taught against Hegel that the basic viewpoint of theology was not arrived at by complex mental analysis, but by a leap of faith. Faith had no need of a favourable verdict from reason; it had its own methods and criteria. Theology need no longer sit rouged at the window, courting philosophy's favour and offering to sell it her charms.[25] Kierkegaard's way of arguing was seen, for example by Karl Barth, as a way of shedding the liberalism of Harnack and Troeltsch, and of asserting the autonomy of theology and its irreducibility to other categories.

The thought of Kierkegaard had quite different attractions for others, many of whom were not Christians. His emphasis on the subjective experience of the individual, on his uniqueness, and on his freedom was developed in often divergent directions, notably by Martin Heidegger, Gabriel Marcel (b. 1889), Jean-Paul Sartre (b. 1905), and Karl Jaspers (1883–1969). But their common interest in the human situation, and in particular, following Kierkegaard's example, in its black or negative side and in the difficulty of real exchange between persons, resulted in an important change of direction for European culture. The strong vein of optimism and confidence which had characterized much European thought was challenged to a re-examination of its own basis. That this also occurred during a period of profound social unrest makes it impossible to establish cause and effect.

One of the individuals who, in his own words, grew up 'out of Dostoevsky, Nietzsche, Ibsen and Kierkegaard', was the Russian thinker, Nicolas Berdyaev (1874–1948). Although formerly a Marxist, his ideology was unacceptable in the revolution, and greatly against his own wishes he was banished from Russia in 1922, finding refuge eventually in Paris. From here stemmed his large output of prophetic writings which enjoyed a great vogue in the 1930s.

The essential emphasis of Berdyaev was that only the world of the eternal was real; that this world is characterized by an estrangement and dislocation which must be transcended. Such transcending is achieved by the one who recognizes mystery beyond and beneath this world. 'If the experience of flatness and insipidity were not relieved by an awareness of mystery, depth and infinitude, life would no longer be livable.'[26] The mystery of man is that his humanity consists in both humanity and divinity. It is through the divinity of man, his having been created in the divine image, that man achieves his freedom. Much of Berdyaev is obscure and paradoxical. His emphasis on freedom led him to an extreme form of subjectivism, and his writings are frequently aphoristic in the style of Nietzsche. But his breadth of interest and his attempt at a liberal synthesis attracted wide attention, particularly among students.

Two further thinkers strongly influenced by the rediscovery of Kierkegaard in this period, and themselves stamping their own influence upon the thought of their times, were Martin Buber

(1878–1965) and Gabriel Marcel. The former, a Jewish philosopher and interpreter of Hasidism, developed in an influential short work, *I and Thou* (1923, trans. 1937), a distinction between knowledge derived from experience of the world on an I–it basis, and that derived from relation with a fellow-being on an I–Thou basis. This latter he describes as a direct relation; 'no system of ideas, no foreknowledge, and no fancy intervene between *I* and *Thou*.'[27] Such relation is fundamental to true humanity. 'All real living is meeting.'[28] Further, it is through all particular *I–Thou* relationships that the eternal Thou is glimpsed. But God may not be objectified as an *It*, either as distinct from the world or immanent in it. 'To eliminate or leave behind nothing at all, to include the whole world in the *Thou*, to give the world its due and its truth, to include nothing beside God but everything in Him—this is full and complete relation.'[29]

Gabriel Marcel arrived at a similar *I–Thou* philosophy independently of Buber, in particular in his *Metaphysical Journal* (1927, trans. 1952). Marcel was received into the Roman Church in 1929, though this affiliation did not alter the direction of or content of his philosophical effort. In *Being and Having* (1935; trans. 1949) he lays bare the dynamics of the spirit of abstraction, whereby by subtle reversal of roles what we claim to *have*, whether knowledge or object, gains control over us and destroys us. Marcel's protest against the habit of objectification is identical with Buber's warning against the I–it relationship; and he shares with him the aim of wanting to provide as an agreed basis for theology an understanding of human nature and the human situation which preserves the mysterious character of being.

The movement of existentialism had a profound effect upon the theologians of this period in two particular ways. In the first instance, as we noted, it appeared to offer escape from the threat of a reduction of Christian belief to non-religious categories, by offering an account of the faith-relation as a direct and immediate relation with God. Secondly, it provided considerable ammunition for the further criticism of much earlier dogmatic theology, by pointing to its tendency to objectify God and what is said to be known of him in propositional form. But by itself existentialism does not necessarily lead either to a renewal of orthodoxy, or to the further liberalization of theology. Its epistemology is compatible with the Catholicism of Marcel, or the Lutheranism of Friedrich Gogarten (1887–1968), as with the Evangelicalism of Karl Heim (1874–1958) or the liberalism of Paul Tillich (1886–1965). If it appeared to give

shelter from the blasts of relativism, it also allowed further concentration upon the description of the human condition. The one
tendency might lead to dogmatism, the other to a more thoroughgoing anthropocentrism. The effects of this alternative are still
with us today, although they have no longer the aspect of an either/
or, without mediating positions.

Two further developments in the realm of metaphysics, influential on theology in our period, are to be remarked upon: namely,
what is now called 'process' metaphysics, and a revival of interest
in Thomism. The renewal of the metaphysical enterprise is itself
remarkable. It can be seen as yet another reaction to the tendency
of liberalism to issue in anti-metaphysical and reductive accounts
of faith, but its importance lies in the fact that it provides a stable
alternative to existentialism.[30]

The former movement of process metaphysics is notably associated with A. N. Whitehead (1861–1947), though it has its roots in
the earlier works of C. L. Morgan (1852–1936) and S. Alexander
(1859–1938). Taking up a typically Anglo-Saxon preoccupation
with the problem of the relations of religion and science, Morgan, a
zoologist and Fellow of the Royal Society as well as a philosopher,
proposed in his Gifford Lectures *Emergent Evolution* (1923) and
Life, Mind and Spirit (1926) a metaphysical theory of the activity
of God within the evolutionary process. In a collective work on
Evolution in the Light of Modern Knowledge (1925) he wrote, 'Many
of those who attribute, as I do, the whole sweep of evolutionary
advance to Spiritual Agency conceive the Divine Purpose, thus
manifested, as itself timeless and omnipresent, and therefore not
susceptible of treatment in temporal or spatial terms.'[31] Samuel
Alexander had already extended the philosophical basis of this thesis
more systematically and comprehensively in his two-volume work
Space, Time and Deity (1920), but by contrast with Morgan he draws
the doctrine of God into still closer connection with the process of
evolution. Deity, for Alexander, is that towards which the whole
created order is evolving.

The tendency in these metaphysics to offer a new account of the
doctrine of God becomes fully explicit in Whitehead. In three
works of metaphysics, *Science and the Modern World* (1926),
Process and Reality (1929), and *Adventures of Ideas* (1933), published
at the end of a distinguished career in mathematical logic and the
philosophy of physics, Whitehead outlined a metaphysical basis
for the Christian religion which was explicitly revolutionary. He
felt that in its doctrine of God as the absolute despot, orthodox

philosophical theology had itself erected a barrier to its further progress and failed in its task of providing a rational account of the world. Liberal theology, in the other hand, 'has confined itself to the suggestion of minor, vapid reasons why people should continue to go to church in the traditional fashion'.[32] He substitutes a bold, speculative doctrine of God which brings him into the closest possible relationship with the physical universe. There are two poles, or two natures in God; one, 'primordial' and complete, is conceptual and limited by no actuality: the second is 'consequent', originates with the physical experience derived from the temporal world, and is incomplete and limited. Only the two together comprise a complete account of the nature of God, and of his relations with the world. For it is of the essence of his nature, in particular, of his patience to be saving the world (i.e. drawing it towards ultimate unity) by the completion of his own nature.[33]

The second development of importance for theology was a revival of interest in Thomism and the appearance of neo-Thomist metaphysics. This also was by way of reaction from earlier liberalism, and in particular, from the criticisms of Thomism levelled by the Catholic Modernists. It was by no means an obscurantist return to a pre-Copernican world-view. The neo-Thomists were interested both in presenting a thoroughly realist account of modern scientific discovery, and also in relating Thomism to the modern emphases of existentialism. This is particularly evident in the work of Jacques Maritain (b. 1882), who after being brought up in French liberal Protestant circles was received into the Roman Church in 1906 and taught in the Institut Catholique de Paris from 1914. His writings include works on ethics, art, and politics, as well as on specifically philosophical and metaphysical topics. Of the latter particularly important is his *The Degrees of Knowledge* (1932; trans. 1937), in which he distinguishes between scientific knowledge, metaphysical knowledge, and the supra-rational knowledge of mystical experience. Maritain defends himself against the charge of objectifying God, by insisting that such rational knowledge of God as exists in metaphysical inquiry is itself natural adoration, rather than mere intellectual manipulation. The third degree of knowledge includes both theology of divine revelation and mystical experience, bringing the individual into close communion with God.

The renewal of the Thomist interpretation of the world was carried on with great energy within the Roman Church, but has not been widely taken up outside it. An exception to this at the close of our period is the early work of the Anglican philosophical theologians

E. L. Mascall (b. 1905) and Austin Farrer (1904–1968), the latter particularly in his *Finite and Infinite* (1943). Although at one time it seemed that there was to be a revival of a more fully Catholic dogmatic theology in the Church of England, the Anglo-Catholic tradition followed in the main the leads of liberal Catholicism, and concentrated on historical, scriptural, and sacramental issues, rather than upon philosophical theology.[34]

Finally mention must be made of the impact of studies in the philosophy of history. The common estimate of the credibility of the Christian world view is in Western Europe inseparably bound up with the viability of the concept of Christendom, that is, of a culture dominated by Christian ideals and institutions. The postwar suggestion that Christendom, far from being the centre and goal of the harmonious development of mankind, was a moribund and totally relative historical phenomenon is therefore of considerable importance. Made by the German philosopher, Oswald Spengler (1880–1936), in volume I of his celebrated *The Decline of the West* (1918; trans. 1926), it offered historical support to the pessimistic view that the First World War had dealt the Christian faith a death blow.

Spengler's thesis that cultures rise and fall in fixed cycles bears some resemblance to the less pessimistic philosophy of A. J. Toynbee (b. 1889). In his ten volumes of *The Study of History* (1934–54) Toynbee traces the history of twenty-six civilizations as separable entities. He attaches far greater importance to religion as a continuing element in the changes of civilization, but the effect of his study is to minimize the dogmatic differences between religions in a theory of their essential unity.

The third philosopher of history of importance for the theology of this period is R. G. Collingwood (1889–1943).* Starting as a realist, Collingwood worked himself through the study of Hegel to a broadly idealist position. He came to believe that philosophy as a study could be reduced to the study of history. History is not the description of successive events or changes; fundamentally history is 'the knowledge of what mind has done in the past, and at the same time it is the redoing of this, the perpetuation of past acts in the present.'[35] History is studied in order to achieve self-knowledge, which is attained by reflection. The history of religion is thus of the very greatest significance, because 'in religion the life of reflection is concentrated in its intensest form'.[36]

Collingwood's work suggested ways in which an influential

* See also the discussion of Collingwood in Chapter 5, pp. 140–2.

Christian faith might be retained out of the ashes of postwar 'Christian' Europe. The extraction of faith from the relativities of history by a still more far-reaching commitment to history was carried out by Rudolf Bultmann. According to him Christian faith, by falling back upon the reflective analysis of man by himself, can clarify its own conceptual basis. If the Christian faith is a revelation occurring in an historical event, then speaking about that revelation (the task of theology), far from meaning a relegation of the event to the relativities of past history, involves the redoing of the event in the present, and issues in a deeper and more critical self-understanding.[37]

Apologetic and Doctrinal Theology

The picture is emerging of a period of considerable vitality in theology, and this is indeed justified as we look back on it from the vantage point of the present. It would be wrong however to give the impression that the churches were holding the allegiance of the people. One church historian of the period speaks of 'the Waste Land after the War';[38] another of 'the great blight'.[39] Despite the remarkable work in literature and apologetics of T. S. Eliot (1888–1965), whose *Murder in the Cathedral* appeared in 1935, Dorothy Sayers (1893–1957), C. S. Lewis (1898–1963), and Charles Williams (1886–1945), the churches broadly speaking failed to capture the imagination. In order to account for this one is obliged to distinguish between the theological and the ecclesiastical situation. Theologically, the inter-war years were a period of exciting and important activity, the tone of which was largely that of critical reaction from the superficialities of much earlier popular liberalism. Ecclesiastically, however, the picture is different. Many clergy had discovered in the trenches the extent to which the industrial masses had become separated from the Church. This was noticed by many observers, among them the young poet Wilfred Owen (1893–1918). At one time Owen might have taken Holy Orders, but during wartime he became convinced that the teachings of the state churches bore no relation to those of Christ. 'So the church Christ was hit and buried/Under its rubbish and its rubble.'[40] Many returned determined that something should be urgently done to reform the institution. But with the power resting with those spheres of influence established in Victorian days, the Church of England at least proved incapable of meeting with sufficient urgency the demands of a restless and disillusioned public. The commonly expressed criticism of liberalism was widely interpreted by the clergy as a retrenchment in old positions. The social failure of the Church was pursued by its failure to grasp real problems in its pulpits.[41]

In the universities, however, important work was being undertaken in two distinguishable but converging disciplines. On the one hand much effort continued to be poured into the task of apologetics, or the justification of Christian faith, both in the historical study of the New Testament (as mentioned above) and also in philosophical theology. On the other hand, we find a few individual attempts at constructive doctrinal theology, or the systematic statement of the distinctive content of the Christian creed.

In apologetics, British theologians continued to pay close attention to the realm of science and religion. In an important collection of essays entitled *Science, Religion and Reality* (1925), edited by Joseph Needham, Lord Balfour observed in the introduction that the relations of science and religion were more satisfactory than fifty years previously, when the western world appeared to be on the edge of a catastrophic intellectual revolution, which would totally unseat religion. Christian writers competent in scientific fields such as E. W. Barnes (1874–1953), mathematician and Fellow of the Royal Society as well as Bishop of Birmingham from 1924 to 1952, and C. E. Raven (1885–1964), biographer of the scientist John Ray and Regius Professor of Divinity in Cambridge, combined with scientists sympathetic to religion, such as A. S. Eddington (1882–1944) and Joseph Needham (b. 1900), to create a climate of opinion in scientific circles which was far more tolerant of religion. Theologians, in particular B. H. Streeter in *Reality* (1926) and F. R. Tennant in *Philosophical Theology* (1928–30), paid careful attention to what might be reasonably asserted about the way things are in the world on the basis of rigorous scientific statement.

Other apologists used philosophical theory as a springboard for the justification of religion. In particular, the idealist C. C. J. Webb (1865–1954) in his Gifford Lectures, *God and Personality* (1915) and *Divine Personality and Human Life* (1920), explored the sphere of religious experience with the aid of the category of personality, seeking within a broadly immanentist doctrine of God to bring in divine transcendence by speaking of the personality of God. A. E. Taylor (1869–1945), in his article 'The Vindication of Religion' for the Anglican volume, *Essays Catholic and Critical* (1926), offered a threefold basis for the rationality of belief, in argument from nature, morality, and religious experience. His Gifford Lectures, *The Faith of a Moralist* (1930), pursue further the argument from the moral life.

The converging lines of apologetic prolegomena and constructive statement meet principally in the works of W. Temple (1881–1944), W. R. Matthews (b. 1881), and O. C. Quick (1885–1944). All three show a considerable sensitivity towards the philosophical climate of opinion and combine gifts of lucid exposition with critical acumen. It is no discourtesy to the latter two that in this place particular emphasis is laid upon the work of Temple, for in his life and achievements is summed up in a curiously complete manner the movements of the theology of the period, both in its greatness and its failures. His interests and concerns, for the reform of church administration, for the ecumenical movement, and for the cause of social justice, were the interests and concerns of the whole Church. His weaknesses, a naïveté about the problems of Scripture, a deep assumption of the rationality of believing, and a somewhat patrician involvement with working-class ambitions, are among the distinctive failures of the Church. But tragically deprived of his leadership in 1944, the Church quickly lost those vestiges of initiative in national life which Temple had acquired for it.

More significantly for our purposes, Temple's intellectual development is in many respects the history of the development of apologetic and doctrinal theology in the period. In *The Faith and Modern Thought* (1910) appeared the theme which reoccurs throughout his work, the relations of reason and revelation in the construction of the Christian view of God, the world, and man. His three successive major works, *Mens Creatrix* (1917), *Christus Veritas* (1924), and his Gifford Lectures, *Nature, Man and God* (1934), show Temple struggling to free himself from his early idealism to a view which he entitled (in deliberate opposition to Marxism) 'dialectical realism'. In 1942 he was further criticizing even this viewpoint as giving the impression that a Christian philosophy could rationally defend a systematically constructed view of the world. 'The world as we see it is strictly unintelligible. We can only have faith that it will become intelligible when the divine purpose, which is the explanation of it, is accomplished.'[42]

Temple's development from broadly idealist metaphysics to this position is only explicable in the light of the strong influences from continental, predominantly German, theology during the inter-war years. This new influence begins in 1921 with the publication of the second edition of Karl Barth's famous commentary upon Romans. With this work, Barth declared war upon all liberal theology, whose tendency, he claimed, was to domesticate God and exalt human criteria of judgement to a position of supremacy. Strongly influenced by his reading of Kierkegaard, Barth deliberately set out to shock and provoke his readers into once again taking seriously the 'wholly other' God of the Bible. Expressing the hope that his views would not be interpreted as a recall to Biblical literalism, he urged scholars to concentrate their attention less on the human, historical, and psychological aspects of the Bible, a document like other documents, than on 'the special *content* of this human document, and remarkable *something* with which the writers of these stories and those who stood behind them were concerned, the Biblical *object*'.[43]

The essential point which Barth was seeking to make was the sovereignty of God's revelation of Himself over all forms of human response. His contentions met with a ready response on the Continent. In 1922 he and a group of like-minded theologians founded a new periodical, *Zwischen den Zeiten* (Between the Times), in which the so-called 'dialectical theology' could be proclaimed. In 1924 Emil Brunner (b. 1889) published *Die Mystik und das Wort* (Mysticism and the Word), a far-reaching attack upon the supposed subjectivism of all theology which emphasized religious experience. Bultmann was also a member of the movement, and, though long ago disowned and denounced by Barth, still today understands himself to be faithful to it. The original founders did not, however, stay together. In 1933 Barth ceased to contribute to the periodical, which shortly afterwards came to an end; in 1934 a sharp controversy with Brunner resulted in a parting of the ways.

Barth's reasons for parting from his former collaborators lie at the very heart of his theology. Initially strongly influenced by Kierkegaard, he came to doubt whether the growing tide of interest in existentialism was in reality a help in theology. In particular, its tendency to devote attention to the human predicament was leading, he thought, to the use of analyses of man as regulative criteria in theology. He claimed this to be the case in Bultmann's increasing dependence upon Heidegger. He himself in what he calls 'my self-known false start', the *Christliche Dogmatik im Entwurf* (Christian Dogmatics in Outline, 1927), had placed considerable emphasis on the human recipient of the divine revelation; 'The Word of God is a concept which is only accessible to an existentialist thinking.'[44] By contrast in his later *Church Dogmatics*, started in 1932 and not completed, Barth taught that we only know about man by what we know about the Man, Jesus Christ. The doctrine of the person of Christ is the focus of the whole of what needs to be said in a Church Theology. The only hope of abandoning once and for all

the human point of view is to adopt the point of view of God's
concrete act of grace in Jesus Christ. From this principle followed
Barth's spirited rejection of Brunner's attempt to allow limited
validity for the traditional discipline of natural theology, a discipline
leading to information about God, the world, and man. [45]

It will be clear that Barth's theological enterprise is fundamentally at variance with the whole tradition of solid metaphysical
inquiry and apologetic writing which is characteristic of English
theology. For this reason he did not find, and has not found, a ready
audience in this country. However, commentary upon, and English
translations of the literature of dialectical theology began in the
1930s. Sir Edwyn Hoskyns's translation of Barth's commentary on
Romans appeared in 1933, followed in the next year by E. Brunner's
major work of Christology, *The Mediator* (published in German in
1927). The first volume of Barth's *Church Dogmatics* was available
in English in 1936.

Not all the effects of this new influence were entirely happy. The
innate tendency of British Biblical scholarship towards conservatism
was somewhat strengthened in the direction of biblicism; certain
quarters interpreted Barth's defence of the autonomy of faith as a
heaven-sent opportunity to return to unreflective dogmatism; the
sniffers of the theological atmosphere might be heard to say that
liberalism was 'out of date'. But overall the main effect was a valuable
stimulus to theological activity. As John Baillie (1889–1960) remarked of Barth in his book, *Our Knowledge of God* (1939),
'nobody seems to be able to talk theology these days without
mentioning him'.[46] Barthianism became one of the points of reference in theological chart-making.

One work showing a conscious movement of standpoint on behalf
of the author was L. S. Thornton's (1884–1960) *The Common Life
in the Body of Christ* (1942). Whereas in his earlier work *The In-
carnate Lord* (1928) he had extensively employed the philosophy of
emergent evolution of Lloyd Morgan and S. Alexander, in the
later book he asks, 'What if the Gospel becomes obscured by our
presuppositions and preoccupations, so that we neither see the scope
of its application nor suffer it to speak for itself?'[47] In accordance
with that principle the later work is largely governed by New
Testament exegesis.

There is a pronounced tendency for the effect of dialectical
theology to be felt as a turning in of theology upon itself. The
strengthening of confidence in the constructive purpose of theological
activity was sometimes matched by a withdrawal from engagement

with social and political realities. Slowest of all to respond con-
structively to Barthianism was the United States, whose theology
since the turn of the century had been so largely dominated
by social concerns.[48] But to this generalization, one must add a
most important qualification. In the work of Reinhold Niebuhr
(1892–1971) we meet a theologian who is both influenced by Karl
Barth and critical of liberal optimism, and yet who retains throughout his work a deep appreciation of the need and purpose of the
Christian presence in social and political structures. From this
concern springs Niebuhr's preoccupation with the Christian doctrine of man, of which his Gifford Lectures, *The Nature and Destiny
of Man* (1941–3) are the fullest expression. Although he invariably
mentions Barth in order to refute him, his return to the traditional
doctrines of the fall and of original sin and his criticism of all forms
of optimistic idealism place him firmly within the movement of
return to Biblical categories. Quoting Luther, he observes that the
final sin of man is his unwillingness to concede that he is a sinner.
But he will have nothing to do with the Barthian doctrine that there
is no point of contact in man to which divine grace can appeal,
and insists on equal emphasis upon both sides of the paradox of
human freedom and divine grace. In the final sections of the lectures, Niebuhr turns to his favourite theme, the working out of
human destiny under God in the practical spheres of politics.
Only the Christian doctrine of the Atonement, with its talk of the
judgement and the mercy of God, 'contains symbolically all that the
Christian faith maintains about what man ought to do and what he
cannot do, about his obligations and final incapacity to fulfil them,
about the importance of decisions and achievements in history and
about their final insignificance'.[49]

Temple had himself felt the importance of the new direction in
Christian theology. He summed it up as it impinged on his own
theological position, shared so widely in the Anglican Church by
his contemporaries, in an introduction to the report on *Doctrine in
the Church of England* (1938). The commission set up to produce the
report started its work in 1922, when the centre of interest was
largely that of constructing a metaphysic in which the doctrine of
the Incarnation could be seen to be central (cf. his own *Christus
Veritas*). In the course of the inter-war years, and in particular
in the shadow of the threat of Nazism, a more prophetic theology emerged, essentially based on man's awareness of the
irrationality and unintelligibility of much of his world. 'We have
been learning again how impotent man is to save himself, how deep

and pervasive is that corruption which theologians call Original Sin.'[50]

Despite the impression of a return to old fundamental doctrines which Temple's assessment gives, the truth is more disturbing and more complex. The period 1918–45 was too rich in new methods, new ideas, and new experiences in theology for anything like a simple, orderly pattern of development to emerge. As a discipline theology requires, as part of its verification procedures, a large measure of public experimental testing in the churches. In this period far too much had been thrown into the melting pot. The speed of change, both in a basically and necessarily conservative discipline and in the churches as a whole, proved too great for any sense of consensus to emerge. It was a scarcely surprising result that many German Christians entered a period of totalitarianism unsure whether their leader was saviour or devil.

Who was to blame for this? 'The logical end of Adolf Harnack and his social gospel is Adolf Hitler and his Nazism'; so a British convert to Barthianism.[51] The cry that liberalism, meaning compromise, in theology was responsible for the capitulation of Germans under Nazi *Machtergreifung* was heard on all sides. But this, too, emerges as a massive oversimplification once both anti-German sentiment and the histories written by the *Bekennende Kirche* rivals of the *Deutsche Christen* have been properly evaluated.[52] Liberal theologians, more credibly it seems today, blamed 'the inability of mankind to make sense of his world, to agree upon the significance of existence, and to co-operate for its welfare; [and] . . . the consequent appearance of incompatible, indeed of violently contrasted, ideologies'.[53] The suggestion that the western world lacked a soundly based interpretation of life is indeed borne out by this study. And the challenge taken up in the post-World War years was that of a still more restless and invigorating quest for new solutions.

NOTES

[1] E.g. by T. S. Eliot in *The Idea of a Christian Society* (1939), 16–17.

[2] Roger Lloyd's *The Church of England in the Twentieth Century*, vol. II (1950) poke in one hasty chapter of the '"Liberal" heresy', 'the Decline and Fall of Modernism', and 'the Eclipse of Liberalism' (26–57). In the revision of the book s *The Church of England 1900–1965* (1966) the chapter remained substantially unaltered; but oddly enough the 'radical' theology of the 1960s was said to

'offer a new hope' (606). For other reading on this period, see the appended bibliography.

[3] *The Modern Churchman*, XI (1921), 201–348.

[4] C. W. Emmet, ibid. 216.

[5] Ibid. 231.

[6] Ibid. 287.

[7] Ibid. 300.

[8] Quoted in G. K. A. Bell, *Randall Davidson* (3rd ed., 1952), 1141.

[9] *Doctrine in the Church of England*, the Report of the Commission on Christian Doctrine appointed by the Archbishops of Canterbury and York in 1922 (1938). Cf. especially the section 'On Assent', 38f.

[10] See the account of his life by Baron von Hügel in E. Troeltsch, *Christian Thought* (1923).

[11] In E. Troeltsch, *Die Soziallehren der christlichen Kirchen und Gruppen* (Tübingen, 1912), translated as *The Social Teaching of the Christian Churches* (1931).

[12] Troeltsch, *Christian Thought*, 26.

[13] *Bulletin of the John Rylands Library*, XII (1928), 72.

[14] Cf. his contributions to the Göttinger Handkommentar zum Alten Testament, *Genesis* (Göttingen, 1901) and *Die Psalmen* (Göttingen, 1926).

[15] Cf. esp. W. Wrede, *Das Messiasgeheimnis in den Evangelien* (Göttingen, 1901).

[16] Cf. especially H. L. Strack and F. Billerbeck, *Kommentar zum Neuen Testament aus Talmud und Midrash* (4 vols., München, 1922–8), which gathered the Rabbinic parallels to Gospel material. A Harvard scholar, G. F. Moore (1851–1931), completed a monumental study of *Judaism in the First Centuries of the Christian Era* (Cambridge, Mass., 1927–30), and English translations appeared of the Mishnah (1933), the Babylonian Talmud (1935–52), and the Midrash Rabbah (1939). On the Hellenistic environment of the early church, following on R. Reitzenstein's *Die hellenistischen Mysterienreligionen* (Leipzig, 1910) and his studies of Iranian redemption myths, there appeared F. C. Burkitt's *The Church and Gnosis* (Cambridge, 1932) and C. H. Dodd's *The Bible and the Greeks* (1935).

[17] R. H. Lightfoot, *History and Interpretation in the Gospels* (1935), 225. On Lightfoot, see D. E. Nineham's 'Introductory Memoir' in *Studies in the Gospels*, ed. Nineham (Oxford, 1955), esp. ix–x. Lightfoot only learnt German in 1931

[18] In 'The Christ of the Synoptic Gospels', *Essays Catholic and Critical*, ed. E. G. Selwyn (1926), 151ff., and 'Jesus, the Messiah', *Mysterium Christi*, ed. G. K. A. Bell and A. Deissmann (1930), 67ff.

[19] R. Otto, *Das Reich Gottes und Menschensohn* (München, 1934), translated as *The Kingdom of God and the Son of Man* (1938).

[20] *Journal of Theological Studies*, XXVIII (1927), 169.

[21] J. K. Mozley, *Some Tendencies in British Theology* (1952), 93.

[22] In 'The Sphere of Religion', *Science, Religion and Reality*, ed. J. Needham (1925), 259–99.

[23] J. Oman, *The Natural and the Supernatural* (Cambridge, 1931), 29f.

[24] Interest in Kierkegaard was stimulated in Germany by the publication of a translation into German of his collected works, published 1909–12. In Britain and America, although we find isolated instances of interest (e.g. in P. T. Forsyth's *Work of Christ* (1910)), it was not until after the Barthian movement had become known, that notice was paid to its partial origins in Kierkegaard

philosophy. E. L. Allen claims to be the first to have made Kierkegaard known in Britain by his *Kierkegaard, His Life and Thought* (1935) (cf. in *Religion in Britain since 1900*, ed. G. S. Spinks (1952), 'British Theology and the Great Blight', p. 182); though an earlier privately printed pamphlet by F. W. Fulford, 'Sören Aabye Kierkegaard. A Study' (1911), had the same aim. See the exhaustive bibliography of *Søren Kierkegaard*, International Bibliography, ed. J. Himmelstrup (Copenhagen, 1962).

[25] S. Kierkegaard, *Fear and Trembling* (Princeton, 1941), 42.

[26] N. Berdyaev, *Dream and Reality* (1950), 310.

[27] M. Buber, *I and Thou* (1937), 11.

[28] Ibid.

[29] Ibid. 79.

[30] This must be said, although there are important points of contact between existentialism and process philosophy, as indicated by Charles Hartshorne's comparison of Berdyaev and Whitehead in *The Journal of Religion*, xxxvii (1957), 71–84.

[31] *Evolution in the Light of Modern Knowledge* (1925), 162.

[32] A. N. Whitehead, *Adventures of Ideas* (Cambridge, 1933), 218.

[33] A. N. Whitehead, *Process and Reality* (Cambridge, 1929), 484ff.

[34] The hopes expressed by E. L. Mascall, in 'The Future of Anglican Theology', *Theology*, xxxix (1939), 406–12, were not realized.

[35] R. G. Collingwood, *The Idea of History* (1946), 218. This work was published posthumously.

[36] Ibid. 315.

[37] Cf. Bultmann's article, 'The Historicity of Man and Faith', published in German in 1930; translated in *Existence and Faith*, ed. S. M. Ogden (1961).

[38] R. Lloyd, *The Church of England 1900–1965* (1966), ch. 11.

[39] E. L. Allen in *Religion in Britain since 1900*, ch. 10.

[40] From 'Le Christianisme', in *The Collected Poems of Wilfred Owen*, ed. C. Day Lewis (1963), 83.

[41] A preacher who realized the needs and missed opportunities of the moment was G. A. Studdert-Kennedy (1883–1929), who won the deep affection of the trench soldiers in the First World War. See his popular sermons, *Food for the Fed-up* (1921).

[42] W. Temple in a letter to Dorothy Emmet, 16 July 1942, quoted by Prof. Emmet in F. A. Iremonger, *William Temple* (1948), 538.

[43] K. Barth, *The Word of God and the Word of Man* (English trans., 1928), 61.

[44] K. Barth, *Christliche Dogmatik im Entwurf* (München, 1927), 111.

[45] In *Natural Theology* (1946).

[46] J. Baillie, *Our Knowledge of God* (1939), 17.

[47] L. S. Thornton, *The Common Life in the Body of Christ* (1942), vii.

[48] Cf. the work of Shailer Matthews (1863–1941), who interpreted the message of Jesus almost entirely in social terms in his *The Social Teaching of Jesus* (New York, 1897). Cf. H. J. Cadbury's powerful reply in *The Peril of Modernizing Jesus* (New York, 1937).

[49] R. Niebuhr, *The Nature and Destiny of Man* (1941–3), ii. 220.

[50] *Doctrine in the Church of England* (1938), 17.

[51] D. R. Davies, *On to Orthodoxy* (1939), 17.

[52] Cf. J. S. Conway, *The Nazi Persecution of the Churches 1933–45* (1968).

[53] C. E. Raven, *Science, Religion and the Future* (Cambridge, 1943), ix.

FOR FURTHER READING

W. M. Horton, *Contemporary English Theology* (1936) is a sound, moderate statement by a visiting American. Also useful is W. M. Horton, *Contemporary Continental Theology* (New York, 1938). For German theology H. Zahrnt, *The Question of God, Protestant Theology in the Twentieth Century* (1969) and W. Nicholls, *Systematic and Philosophical Theology, The Pelican Guide to Modern Theology*, vol. 1 (1969) are useful introductions. *The Beginnings of Dialectical Theology*, vol. I, ed. J. M. Robinson (Richmond, Va., 1968) offers extracts from the early literature of the movement. *Twentieth Century Theology in the Making*, vols. I–III, ed. J. Pelikan (1969–70) provides an exceptionally interesting selection of articles from the second edition of the authoritative encyclopaedia, *Die Religion in Geschichte und Gegenwart* (Tübingen, 1927–32), which illustrate the state of research on basic questions of theology in the inter-war years. *Religion in Britain since 1900*, ed. G. Stephen Spinks (1952) includes 13 essays on various aspects of religion, and provides a competent survey. J. K. Mozley, *Some Tendencies in British Theology: From the publication of* Lux Mundi [1889] *to the present day* (1952), is sound and judicious. This is an uncompleted, posthumous work reviewing theology up to 1939. Probably the best available brief review is D. D. Williams, *What Present-day Theologians are Thinking* (New York, 1967), a revised edition of the author's earlier report, *Interpreting Theology, 1918–1952* (1953). A.M. Ramsey, *From Gore to Temple* (1960) provides an important account of Anglican theology, 1889–1939, from the liberal Catholic viewpoint. Roger Lloyd, *The Church of England 1900–1965* (1966) is a personal meditation, full but often partisan on theological questions. The most inclusive attempt at description of the actual life of the churches in this century is Horton Davies, *Worship and Theology in England: V, The Ecumenical Century, 1900–1965* (Princeton, 1966): a valuable book, sometimes wrong in details. D. L. Edwards, *Religion and Change* (1969) makes an ambitious attempt to set the developments in religion in this century against their sociological and psychological background and to account for the 'downfall' of Christian dogmatism, from a liberal standpoint.

The standard biography, F. A. Iremonger, *William Temple* (1948), contains a valuable essay by Dorothy Emmet on Temple's philosophy. The book is less strong on the theological side. C. W. Kegley and R. W. Bretall, *Reinhold Niebuhr: His Religious, Social and Political Thought* (New York, 1956) offers an uneven collection of essays, with replies from Niebuhr. D. A. Lowrie, *Rebellious Prophet, a Life of Nicolai Berdyaev* (1960) is the standard biography. A reliable guide to the formative years of Barth's development can be found in T. F. Torrance, *Karl Barth, an Introduction to his Early Theology, 1910–1931* (1962). Five sound and readable introductions by acknowledged experts in the 'Makers of Contemporary Theology' series are Ian Henderson, *Rudolf Bultmann* (1965); Ronald Gregor Smith, *Martin Buber* (1966); Sam Keen, *Gabriel Marcel* (1966); John Macquarrie, *Martin Heidegger* (1968); and Norman Pittenger, *A. N. Whitehead* (1969). Finally, Walter Schmithals, *An Introduction to the Theology of Rudolf Bultmann* (1968) is a most readable and sympathetic exposition by one of Bultmann's pupils, and a valuable corrective to much uninformed criticism

7

Psychology

O. L. ZANGWILL

I. INTRODUCTORY

'By 1918, most of the new trends and schools of thought which were to re-make psychology had emerged into the daylight. What had not emerged was any agreed conceptual framework or body of theory. Psychologists spoke not with one voice but with several conflicting voices.' In these words, Professor Hearnshaw sums up the position towards the end of his contribution to the first volume of this series. It would be hard to envisage a more fitting opening to the present chapter.

As the postwar years ran their course, psychology's 'conflicting voices' spoke with ever-increasing vehemence. For this was the period of the 'schools', when psychology was torn asunder by internecine warfare. Although the schools waned in influence towards the end of the thirties and virtually evaporated under the stress of war, there can be no doubt as to the significance they held for all who—like the present writer—came into the subject between the wars. For us, schism was endemic in psychology and the possibility of unification too remote for serious consideration.

What is a 'school'? According to the late Professor Woodworth, it is '. . . a group of psychologists who put forward a certain system of ideas designed to point the way that all must follow if Psychology is ever to be made a genuine productive science of both theoretical and practical value'.[1] Among the schools Woodworth lists are:

(1) *Structural psychology*. This was the traditional German psychology of 'conscious elements and processes' born in Wundt's laboratory at Leipzig (established in 1879) and represented in America chiefly by E. B. Titchener (1867–1927), an Oxford man who for long held the Chair of Psychology at Cornell University. Structural psychology was essentially a psychology of introspection, its aim being to define and classify conscious states and to elucidate their modes of combination. It is sometimes referred to as the 'Existential School', though this term is nowadays used almost exclusively to denote a well-known brand of continental philosophy.

(2) *Functional psychology*. Broadly, this school placed emphasis

upon the biological utility of consciousness and upon behaviour as
envisaged in terms of adaptation to the environment. Although
functionalism originated in the post-Darwinian climate of late
Victorian England with the work of such men as G. J. Romanes and
C. Lloyd Morgan, as a school of psychology it developed principally
in the United States, owing much to the influence of William James
(1842–1910) and G. T. Ladd (1842–1921). Its main stronghold was
in the University of Chicago, where J. R. Angell (1869–1949) did
much to inject a biological attitude towards psychological issues.
But in view of its lack of a formal system or of any real coherence
of outlook, functionalism is perhaps better described not as a
school but as a loose grouping of psychologists who agreed only
that psychology should be envisaged as a biological science and
with emphasis upon the nervous system as the instrument of
behaviour.

(3) *Behaviourism*. As Professor Hearnshaw has pointed out, the
origins of behaviourism go back at least to 1913, when John B.
Watson first explicitly promulgated the behaviourist programme.[2]
Watson, whose antecedents lay in American functionalism, called
for complete objectivity in method and repudiation of consciousness
as the distinctive subject-matter of psychological inquiry. In the
twenties, behaviourism virtually took over American psychology,
though gradually losing much of its didactic and crusading character. From behaviourism arose the 'behavioural sciences' as we know
them today.

(4) *Gestalt psychology*. This essentially German movement was at
the same time a continuation of and a revolt against structuralism
In its heyday—roughly from 1918 to 1935—Gestalt psychology had
a considerable following in the German-speaking countries and was
not without influence in Britain and America. But it never took firm
root outside Germany, in spite of the fact that many of its leading
exponents were driven out by Hitler and settled in the United
States.

(5) *Psychoanalysis*. Alone among the schools, psychoanalysis was
born outside the universities and its connection with academic
psychology has never been close. It should also be borne in mind
that what is often loosely called 'psychoanalysis' is in fact a con-
geries of schools, which have in common only a belief in unconscious
mental events and in the virtues of psychotherapy. Alfred Adler
(1870–1937), the first of the secessionists (although in fact he had
never been a strict Freudian), established his own school of individual psychology, stressing the ubiquity of aggression and the need

for its social control. This school had some influence in the twenties and thirties, not least in England, where to many the theories of Adler seemed less fanciful than those of Freud. C. G. Jung (1875–1962), who finally broke with Freud in 1913, described his own system as 'analytical psychology', much emphasis being placed on the diversity of human types and the importance of so-called universal symbols ('archetypes'). Jung's ideas had a good deal of influence in cultural circles though their empirical foundations remained distinctly insecure.

It is virtually impossible to understand the origin, growth, and ultimate decline of the twentieth-century schools of psychology without considerable reference to historical factors and to differences in national tradition. As we have seen, structuralist psychology grew up in Germany within the tradition of Fechner and Wundt and for the most part only those who had studied in the early German psychological laboratories subscribed to its tenets. The dissident heir to structuralism, Gestalt psychology, likewise reflected a traditionally German mode of thought distinctly foreign to the Anglo-Saxon mind. Neither structuralism nor Gestalt psychology found congenial soil in the United States; functionalism, on the other hand, fitted well with the practical, competitive American outlook and perhaps for the same reason its radical offshoot—behaviourism—soon came to dominate the American psychological scene. At the same time, it is interesting to note that behaviourism, in spite of its enormous reliance on Pavlov's work, never found acceptance in Russia and was stoutly opposed by Pavlov himself.

In the present survey, we shall have little to say about the first two of Woodworth's schools, whose interest is now almost wholly historical. By 1918, the year in which our period begins, structuralist psychology was already on the decline and by the time of Titchener's death in 1927 was itself moribund. Functionalism, too, had ceased to exist as a self-conscious school—if indeed it ever had—and its younger adherents were already beginning to rally to the behaviourist cause. In so far, therefore, as psychology between the wars was dominated by the schools, it is to behaviourism, Gestalt psychology, and psychoanalysis that we must turn. These were undoubtedly the major intellectual movements in Western psychology during the first half of the twentieth century.

II. BEHAVIOURISM

Let us look first at behaviourism. In spite of its brashness and philosophical naïveté, behaviourism has probably had more to do with the foundation of modern psychology than any other movement of our time. It is therefore of some importance to examine its origins and development, even if this may mean going slightly outside the period allocated to this volume.

J. B. Watson (1878–1958), the self-styled founder of behaviourism, began his professional life as an instructor in psychology at the University of Chicago, where he had himself completed his graduate studies. His interests had lain almost wholly in animal behaviour, and while at Chicago he published at least one important study on maze learning in rats and its sensory control. Later he was appointed to a senior post at Johns Hopkins University, where he was joined by K. S. Lashley, with whom he published several papers on bird behaviour. It is important to note that Lashley identified himself from the start with the behaviourist movement, which was indeed very largely created by these two men. What led them to take this fateful step?

As in all revolutions, protest against current convention was undoubtedly an important element. While still at Chicago, Watson had been much troubled by the psychophysical mould in which instruction in experimental psychology was still cast and even more, by the conflicting results reported from different laboratories. His dissatisfaction evidently came to a head with the long and fruitless controversy over the existence (or otherwise) of 'imageless thought', i.e. thought processes lacking specific sensory or imaginal content. By 1913, Watson clearly felt that the time had come publicly to castigate experimental psychologists for their almost exclusive reliance on introspective method and the analysis of conscious states. 'The time seems to have come', he proclaimed, 'when psychology must discard all reference to consciousness; when it need no longer delude itself that it is making mental states the object of observation.' More generally, 'Psychology, as the behaviourist views it, is a purely objective, experimental branch of natural science. Its theoretical goal is the prediction and control of behaviour. Introspection forms no essential part of its method; nor is the scientific value of its data dependent upon the readiness with which they lend themselves to interpretation in terms of consciousness.'[3]

At the same time, Watson's revolution undoubtedly embodied a constructive element. In his work on animal behaviour he had inevitably been obliged to devise objective methods of study. If psychology were to become a truly comparative science, it would seem essential to develop methods of studying human behaviour directly comparable to those used in animal experiment. As Watson himself wrote: 'The behaviourist in his effort to gain a general understanding of behaviour recognises no dividing line between animals and man. Human behaviour, with all its refinement and complexity, forms only a part of the behaviourist's total sphere of investigation.'

Although behaviourism is often thought of as virtually synonymous with 'conditioned reflexes', in fact Watson's early proclamations contain no mention of Pavlov or his work. This is surprising when it is borne in mind that Pavlov's work was already well known in the West: he had given the Huxley Lecture in London in 1906 and an account of his work had been published by Yerkes and Morgulis in an American psychological periodical as early as 1909. Indeed Watson's first reference to Pavlov seems to have been in his Presidential Address to the American Psychological Association in 1916, when he urged the adoption of Pavlov's method of 'conditioned differentiation' in studying sensory capacity in animals as 'a method which we might *begin* to use in place of introspection'.[4] At the same time, there can be no doubt that Watson's views were influenced by the writings of another—and altogether less distinguished—Russian scientist, V. Bechterev, who as early as 1886 had carried out experiments on what is nowadays called 'avoidance training', e.g. the withdrawal of a hand or foot to avoid electric shock paired with a warning signal. This type of conditioned response was seen by both Watson and Lashley as having much more in common with human behaviour than Pavlov's glandular reflexes and has had great importance for modern learning theory.

The first systematic text embodying the new viewpoint is Watson's *Psychology from the Standpoint of a Behaviourist* (1st ed., 1919). Here the subject is defined as 'the attempt to formulate, through systematic observation and experiment, the generalizations, laws and principles which govern man's behaviour'. Note the emphasis on *man*: no longer is behaviourism limited to the special problems of studying animal behaviour. Watson is making a take-over bid for the whole of traditional psychology. But Watson's aims and methods are entirely different from those of his predecessors. No longer is the behaviour studied limited to 'those responses which directly or indirectly throw light on the analysis and course of consciousness' (as C. S. Myers defined the scope of experimental psychology in 1911), since consciousness is no longer accepted as a valid datum for natural science. Instead we are invited to correlate stimulus with response and response with stimulus, such that—at all events ultimately—knowledge of response will permit prediction of the probable situation and knowledge of situation will permit prediction of probable response. Thus was born the celebrated 'stimulus–response' (S–R) conception of human behaviour which dominated American psychology for the next twenty years.

We cannot go into the details of Watson's psychology, in particular his views on emotion and on the relative importance of heredity and environment, which have been much misunderstood. While he certainly made brash statements about the power of environment to shape and mould individual personality, it is none the less true that he put great emphasis on inborn behaviour patterns. Behaviourism, it should be remembered, produced not only learning theory but also the concept of maturation, and thereby set the stage for the development of behaviour genetics in the second half of this century.

Although Watson passed from the psychological scene in the early twenties (though himself surviving until 1958), the movement he and Lashley had launched rapidly gathered momentum. William McDougall, to whom Professor Hearnshaw has devoted such sympathetic consideration in an earlier volume, put up a spirited rear-guard action. Yet in his polemics McDougall appeared to forget that he had himself advocated a form of behaviourism many years before Watson.[5] This behaviourism was likewise to exclude hypothetical mental entities—'Neither life, nor mind nor soul'— but it cannot be said that McDougall stuck to his guns. Indeed 'mental entities' feature largely in his later psychological writings and he ended a convinced opponent of behaviourism in all its forms. Apart from McDougall, only Titchener and his small band of structuralists held out for a time against the behaviourist onslaught. Quite possibly, they regarded behaviourism as too contemptible to merit serious academic consideration.[6]

Behaviourism between the wars evolved in three principal directions. First, it led to fresh interest among experimental psychologists in the physiological foundations of behaviour and in the brain conceived as the instrument of behaviour. (This interest had of course long been latent in American functionalism.) Secondly it stimulated important work on the early development of behaviour in animals and man and its dependence upon inborn no less than acquired factors. And, thirdly, it created an almost compulsive interest in the nature of learning and its relation to Pavlovian conditioning. It was this aspect of behaviourism that created the stereotype of the 'rat psychologist', obsessed with his mazes and oblivious of all other aspects of animal behaviour.

The first line of growth will always be associated with the name of Karl S. Lashley (1890–1958), co-founder of behaviourism and a leading experimentalist for over thirty years.[7] Although by no means the first to ask the question of how the brain controls behaviour, Lashley devised many of the techniques that enable us to begin to answer it. What he did, essentially, was to combine the physiologist's method of excising different areas and amounts of brain tissue with the psychologist's methods of studying animal learning using mazes, discrimination boxes, and similar methods which enable performance to be assessed in quantitative terms. He was also the first in this field to apply statistical method to the analysis of his results.

Lashley's experimental work was built around two main themes: the first was concerned with the central mechanisms of vision and the second with brain function and learning. In so far as the latter is concerned, it is noteworthy that Lashley's results led him far from the relatively simple model of the nervous system in terms of reflexes and conditioned reflexes from which his work had taken its departure. As early as 1923, he wrote that the behaviourist must no longer be content to limit his accounts of behaviour to the simple reflex hypothesis. He also came increasingly to distrust conceptions of learning based on the conditioned reflex model. Although 'reflexology' is not of course synonymous with behaviourism, Lashley's rejection of the 'S–R' model undoubtedly helped to undermine the theoretical basis of Watson's revolution.

The one positive contribution which we owe to Lashley is his discovery of an important relation between brain mass and intelligence. Roughly speaking, the more extensive a brain lesion the greater its detrimental effect upon learning and performance, irrespective of its location. This relation is usually formulated as the Principle of Mass Action. It suggests that the brain cortex in some sense acts as a unit in the control of complex behaviour and that no one part of it is more specialized than another for particular activities. While the application of this principle is now known to be a good deal more limited than Lashley supposed, it had great value in directing attention away from oversimplified conceptions of brain localization towards a broader understanding of the organization of behaviour.

The second line of interest was expressed in careful developmental studies in both animals and man. Interest centred mainly on behaviour patterns which emerged in fixed sequence in the course of early development and which appeared to be largely independent of environment. This type of 'longitudinal study' had been much neglected and brought a new realism into psychological inquiry which hitherto had been almost exclusively preoccupied with what E. G. Boring has called 'the generalized adult normal mind'. It opened the way to fresh studies of infancy and childhood, of maturation and learning, and of the relations between physical growth and the development of behaviour. One of its most celebrated protagonists was Arnold Gesell, whose 'norms' of infant behaviour had a considerable vogue, any deviation from them creating consternation in many a psychology-minded American home.[8]

The third and most influential effect of behaviourism was undoubtedly in the field of learning. As early as 1899, E. L. Thorndike (1874–1949) had begun experiments on animal learning, seeking its explanation in terms of the quasi-automatic effects of reward and punishment upon the connections between situation and response. Such learning, he thought, was explicable without recourse to higher mental processes. With the advent of behaviourism, many attempts were made to re-state Thorndike's essential findings in terms of conditioned reflex principles, but it soon became clear that the problem was a good deal more difficult than Watson, at all events, had anticipated. It seemed essential to develop broader theories of learning, able to comprehend both Thorndike's and Pavlov's findings, and to specify more stringently than either had done the relations between motivation, reinforcement, and performance.[9]

Clark L. Hull (1884–1952) began as a hard-headed experimentalist—he wrote a debunking book on hypnosis—but gradually became obsessed with the need to build a theory of learning constructed along the lines of a truly deductive system. In this task, he seems to have been considerably influenced by J. H. Woodger, the British philosopher of science. Hull's work, which began to appear in periodical form in the early thirties, reached its climax in his *Principles of Behaviour*, published in 1943. In this remarkable book Hull formulated sixteen basic postulates from which numerous theorems embodying specific predictions were derived. Some of these were verified by his own experiments or those of others others not so verified were modified or discarded. Unlike Pavlov whose concept of motivation was primitive in the extreme, Hull devoted a great deal of attention to reinforcement, which he defined in terms of reduction in the level of biological need (e.g. hunger, thirst, or fear). He further tried to quantify the major variables in the learning situation in terms of habit strength, generalization, motivation, and inhibition, these terms being defined in a strictly operational manner.

Hull's system attracted great interest and to some it seemed that the Newton of psychology had indeed arrived. Alas, this was not to be. Apart from special difficulties encountered by the theory in explaining particular facts of animal learning, e.g. the existence of 'latent learning' or the 'exploratory drive', the theory proved to lack true generality. None the less, Hull's work did much to combat looseness in psychological thinking and to stress the need for logical no less than experimental precision. He is remembered not so much for his theory as for his example.

Another theorist of the period was E. C. Tolman (1886–1959), who considered himself a behaviourist though his outlook seemed to some tainted by 'mentalism'. This is no doubt because Tolman used terms such as 'expectation' which were no longer thought respectable. His system, which placed emphasis on the 'map-making' element in maze learning in the rat, had the virtue of drawing attention to many features of learning which could be fitted with difficulty, if at all, into a Hullian framework. Tolman was also one of the very few behaviourists whose ideas showed some influence of Gestalt theory.[10]

Finally, mention should be made of B. F. Skinner, who began his work in the thirties though it did not become widely known until after the Second World War. Like Lashley (though this is perhaps the only thing the two men had in common), Skinner was from the start sceptical of the reflex theory and drew a sharp distinction between 'respondent' (i.e. reflex) and 'operant' (i.e. self-generated) behaviour. Whereas conditioning of the 'respondent' type of behaviour follows an essentially Pavlovian course, that of 'operant' behaviour is very different. In particular, the relation between reinforcement and learning is a good deal more complex than had previously been supposed—even by Hull—and much that is best in Skinner's work is concerned with just this particular problem and the experimental techniques ('schedules of reinforcement') that he designed to study it. After the war, Skinner became widely known for the application of his work to the design of teaching machines and for his writings on language and its acquisition.

Behaviourism, according to J. B. Watson, was a purely American production. This is not of course strictly true. As Professor Hearn-shaw has pointed out, somewhat similar proposals to exclude subjective observation from psychology had been made by Comte in France, by Maudsley in England, and by Sechenov—Pavlov's teacher—in Russia. As we have seen, too, Bechterev's ideas were not unimportant. Nevertheless, Watson's statement is broadly true and it is inconceivable that behaviourism could have established itself with comparable speed and permanence in any other country. To understand this fully would demand a far greater acquaintance with American social history than is within the competence of the present writer.

Outside America, behaviourism made little impact. In England, it received qualified approval from Bertrand Russell and, much later, appears to have influenced another celebrated philosopher, Professor Gilbert Ryle. Among psychologists, on the other hand, it had a decidedly cool reception. Professor (later Sir) Cyril Burt was a consistent opponent from the start, often seeming to rival McDougall in his denunciation of any psychology that would appear to de-throne consciousness. Another strong opponent was C. W. Valen-tine, for long Professor of Education at Birmingham. Valentine took issue particularly with Watson in his analysis of emotion along conditioned reflex lines. Professor (later Sir) Frederic Bartlett took over from behaviourism its biological outlook but saw little virtue in conditioned reflexes or the taboo on consciousness. Yet in his own department at Cambridge one of the first studies of conditioning and learning in the guinea pig was carried out in 1931 by G. C. Grindley. One should also mention that George Humphrey, who was later to become Oxford's first Professor of Psychology, pub-lished in 1933 a most important critical discussion of the conditioned reflex and its place in the theory of learning.[11] It cannot therefore be said that behaviourism was wholly without influence on psycho-logical thought in Britain.

One of the more surprising features of psychological history is that no behaviourist movement emerged in Russia, where both the scientific and philosophical climates might be thought extremely favourable to such an outlook. There are several reasons for this. First, Pavlov himself was bitterly hostile to psychology (which he persisted in regarding as concerned solely with conscious experience and thoroughly disliked attempts by American behaviourists to erect theories of learning on the basis of the conditioned reflex. Secondly, psychology in Russia had been traditionally concerned with man and took little account either of animal behaviour or physiological issues. In the inter-war period, the outstanding figure in Soviet psychology was undoubtedly L. Vygotski (1896–1934), a perceptive and dedicated man, whose approach had much more in common with that of Piaget than of Pavlov. He was interested principally in the growth of language in children and its relation to thought.[12] It should be said, too, that whereas American behaviourists have tended to view the conditioned reflex as the paradigm of learning in general, Soviet psychologists have always accepted Pavlov's tenet that, because of the evolution of speech, conditioning is quite different in animals and man. In consequence, it is the differences rather than the resemblances between man and animals upon which they have placed the major stress.

III. Gestalt Psychology

In Germany, behaviourism had no influence whatsoever. Although experimental psychology had flourished for many years in the German universities, its character in 1918 still remained strongly 'philosophical' and, as in Russia, almost wholly restricted to the study of man. True, a group of German biologists at the turn of the century had tried to interpret animal behaviour without reference to mental events, which led them rigorously to exclude all terms that might appear to imply subjective experience, e.g. 'photoreception' was substituted for 'vision'. This movement seems however to have come to very little, and when indeed animal behaviour studies (later christened 'ethology') began seriously in Germany some decades later, unduly free use was made of terms such as 'appetite' or 'mood' which might appear to have unmistakable subjective connotations. In any case ethology had virtually no contact with experimental psychology and it was only in the early fifties that links between them were gradually forged.

Of the 'new trends and schools of thought' that had 'emerged into the daylight' by 1918, Gestalt psychology occupies an important place. But it is far from easy to say exactly what constituted Gestalt psychology. Like functionalism, it embodied quite a range of opinion among German psychologists, who seemed agreed only that 'psychological atomism' had outlived its usefulness and should give place to a psychology doing fuller justice to the essential indivisibility of mind. Felix Krueger established something of a school at Leipzig in which such views were proclaimed. But these were in general too vague and remote from experiment to gain currency elsewhere. Only the so-called Berlin School, comprising

Max Wertheimer (1886–1943), Wolfgang Köhler (1887–1967), Kurt Koffka (1886–1941), and Kurt Lewin (1890–1947), became really influential and it is to the work of this group alone that the term Gestalt psychology is generally applied.

How did Gestalt psychology begin? It is usually held to date from the publication, in 1912, of an important paper by Wertheimer on apparent visual motion.[13] The origin of any new movement, however, can seldom be traced to a single event, no matter how portentous. If we are to understand Gestalt theory, it is important to consider not only Wertheimer's work itself but also its place in the context of German experimental psychology, particularly in the field of sensation and perception. We may therefore be forgiven for stepping outside our period and seeking the origins of Gestalt theory in the decades preceding Wertheimer's classical study.

Ernst Mach's *Analysis of Sensations* had appeared in 1886. In this lively and provocative little book, Mach showed himself entirely willing to denote as 'sensation' not only elementary experiences such as brightness, colour, or pitch (which could for the most part be correlated with the activities of specific receptor units), but also what might appear highly complex experiences, such as the perception of a tree or a melody. In such cases, he urged, the content of perception may be directly 'sensed' without the intervention of higher mental processes such as association and inference. Mach's ideas were eagerly seized upon by the Austrian philosopher, C. von Ehrenfels, who in 1890 introduced the term *Gestalt quality* to denote these more complex attributes of perception.[14] In his view, Gestalt qualities (e.g. visual form, melody) while based upon more elementary sensory units, are in no sense compounded of them. They might perhaps be regarded as emergent properties of perceptual integration.

A point on which Ehrenfels placed particular importance—and which later became cardinal in Gestalt theory—is that of *transposition*. A melody can still be recognized when played in a different key and visual forms can be varied in size or orientation without loss of their specific identity. A Gestalt quality may, then, be largely independent of the specific complex of sensory events upon which its existence depends.

It cannot be said that Ehrenfels attempted much in the way of explanation of Gestalt qualities, though it is clear that he regarded them as directly experienced and not as the outcome of comparison and judgement. He even suggested that their origin is ultimately physiological, sensory excitations in close spatial or temporal proximity interacting in such a manner as to generate new dimensions of perceptual experience. We see here an anticipation of Wertheimer's principle of isomorphism, about which more will be said later. However, his views had considerable influence, not least on the British philosopher and psychologist G. F. Stout, whose *Analytical Psychology* appeared in 1896. One may note in passing that Stout was one of the very few British psychologists to see merit in the later developments of Gestalt theory.

Let us now turn to Wertheimer, whose studies of apparent visual motion initiated the Gestalt theory proper. Not, of course, that Wertheimer was the first in the field. Apparent motion (i.e. seen movement in the absence of an object in actual motion) had intrigued scientists ever since the invention of the stroboscope a hundred years before and had long been a favourite topic for study by the early experimental psychologists. What was original about Wertheimer's work was not the discovery of apparent motion but the explanation which he gave of it.

In principle, Wertheimer's set-up for the study of apparent visual motion was very simple: Two lines were exposed in close succession with a brief, though variable, interval between them. The lines were as a rule parallel and about 2 cm apart, though in some of the experiments they formed a right angle. Under these conditions, what is seen depends very largely on the interval between the two exposures. Where it was less than about 30 milliseconds, Wertheimer's subjects for the most part reported that both lines were seen together and, where it was more than about 200 milliseconds, that they appeared in succession. Where, however, the interval was approximately 60 milliseconds, what the subjects reported was apparent motion of a single line from the first position to the second. This later came to be called beta movement.

Although it might be tempting to ascribe beta motion to an apparent change in the position of a single object, Wertheimer was adamant that visual motion is an experience in its own right— 'what lies in the interspace'—and can be dissociated from the perception of the successively presented objects. He used the term *phi-phenomenon* to denote this unitary impression of 'movingness' and claimed that there were even circumstances in which it could occur without perception of any object whatsoever ('pure phi'). He insisted that the phi phenomenon was determined purely by the spatio-temporal conditions of visual stimulation and could not be explained away as a carry-over from past experience or as the result of 'unconscious inference'. It was, he suggested, a Gestalt quality evoked by successive perception of two stimuli in appropriate spatio-temporal relationship.

Wertheimer's theory of motion perception was formulated in quasi-physiological terms. If, he suggested, we have two successive stimuli a and b, these will give rise to central excitatory processes a' and b' located at discrete points in the visual cortex. Each of these processes may be supposed to 'irradiate' over the cortex and, if the interval between a and b is neither too long nor too short, to enter into dynamic relationship with one another ('short-circuit reaction'), thereby generating a new psychophysiological event, viz. movement. Wertheimer's theory embraced real no less than apparent movement, the former being regarded as a limiting case of the latter. Thus movement experience in general was ascribed to dynamic interaction between contiguous foci of excitation in the visual cortex. Wertheimer was however careful to point out—which few of his critics seem to have noticed—that the kind of central interaction he had in mind need not necessarily be envisaged in spatial terms.

Even in his 1912 study, Wertheimer was quick to see that processes of organization of the kind he believed to underlie motion perception might likewise explain Gestalt qualities of other kinds, e.g. form and grouping. For instance, apparent motion often seems to follow a 'preferred' path in spite of the fact that quite other directions of motion would appear equally possible. Even stationary configurations, moreover, may show characteristic Gestalt qualities, implying underlying cortical 'forces of organization'. These problems were discussed more fully in a later paper on 'Laws of Organization in Perceptual Forms' (1923)[15] in which Wertheimer demonstrated the ways in which proximity, similarity, 'good continuity', and other simple principles govern the perception of form and the grouping of discrete items—essentially the problem of 'why the stars are seen in constellations'. From this study arose the Gestalt principle of *Prägnanz*, according to which configurations appear as simple, regular, and symmetrical as the prevailing conditions permit.

In Wertheimer's theory of motion perception is embedded the germ from which all later Gestalt theory has sprung. His view was essentially that Gestalt qualities result from integrative processes at the physiological level—as indeed was hinted by Ehrenfels many years earlier—and that there is a certain parallel between the structure of these processes and that of the psychological events which they condition. This supposed parallelism came to be called isomorphism, although it is not clear whether Wertheimer himself introduced the term or how essential he considered it to be in psychological explanation generally.

Wertheimer's highly original—if admittedly nebulous—ideas were developed very considerably by his colleagues W. Köhler and Kurt Koffka, both of whom had been contemporary with him at Frankfurt and had acted as subjects for his famous experiments on apparent movement. Köhler's first main contribution was an impressive endeavour to habilitate the Gestalt idea in scientific thinking.[16] If, he argued, it can be shown that properties analogous to Gestalt qualities are possessed by physical and neurological systems, the case for psychological isomorphism would be immeasurably strengthened. These properties he claimed to discover, though it cannot be said that his arguments have ever found general acceptance. None the less, Köhler's early work did give a certain scientific respectability to the Gestalt idea.

In spite of its imprecision, Gestalt theory was of distinct value in stimulating fresh experiment. Throughout the twenties and early thirties, a whole series of experiments inspired by the Gestalt theory were reported in the pages of the *Psychologische Forschung*, a journal founded in 1921 to represent the new movement. Many of these experiments owed their origin directly to Kurt Koffka, himself a good experimentalist and a most able expositor of the Gestalt philosophy. Broadly, his interests lay in application of Gestalt theory to many traditional problems in visual perception, among them brightness and colour constancy, spatial organization and the stability of the visual world. These various phenomena were largely re-interpreted in terms of Gestalt theory, special emphasis being placed on supposedly inborn 'forces of organization' which interact with sensory input and thereby impose upon the visual environment its characteristic invariance and stability. In 1935, Koffka brought much of this work together in his persuasive, though difficult, *Principles of Gestalt Psychology*.

While perception (especially visual) was always the main focus of Gestalt interest, it was by no means the only one. An inquiry of particular relevance to the whole Gestalt movement was Köhler's brilliant study of the mentality of chimpanzees, which appeared in English translation in 1925.[17] In this study, Köhler asserted flatly that the kind of problem-solving that he had observed and documented could not find explanation in terms of associationist theories of learning. It seemed necessary to postulate a measure of *insight*, i.e. an intelligent grasp of the pertinent relationships within the problem situation as a whole. Insight, Köhler contended, as a rule appears suddenly and involves a certain 're-structuration' of the perceptual field, such that objects or their functions are seen 'in a new light', e.g. a stick is no longer seen merely as a stick but as a tool with which food placed out of reach may be obtained. The outcome is a novel, intelligent, and truly adaptive act.

Although the idea of insight was widely—and not unjustly—criticized as lacking in explanatory value, there is no doubt that Köhler's work did much to revive interest in the productive aspects of thinking. These have always given difficulty to associationists and Gestalt theory at least offered the hope of a more constructive solution. The ingenious experiments by K. Duncker, published in 1935, took Köhler's ideas further with particular regard to problem-solving in man. Later, Wertheimer himself took a hand in the application of Gestalt ideas to thinking and the results appeared in a posthumous book.[18] It should also be said that Köhler's ideas about the perceptual field and its structure had a strong influence on the thinking of K. Lewin, whose 'field theory' was later to inspire a whole generation of social psychologists in the United States.[19]

The later stages of Gestalt theory can be more briefly charted. Koffka emigrated to the United States in the late twenties, to be followed within a few years by Wertheimer, Köhler, and Lewin. With the exception of Lewin, who alone seemed able to develop his ideas further, the Gestalt psychologists clearly found difficulty in coming to terms with behaviourist America. Yet all continued with work along the lines already well established before leaving Germany. Koffka, for example, continued to publish ingenious experiments on perception and some of his work undoubtedly impressed J. J. Gibson, who was himself later to publish an outstanding book on *The Perception of the Visual World* (1950). Although Gibson rejected the Gestalt principles of organization, he made important use of several Gestalt concepts, especially that of invariance. Köhler drew attention to an important class of after-effects of visual stimulation ('figural after-effects') which he attempted—not very successfully—to explain in terms of an electrical field theory of brain action.[20] He also devoted some attention to memory as envisaged from the Gestalt standpoint. Although publishing little, Wertheimer continued to occupy himself with Gestalt problems, more especially in the sphere of thinking. Yet none of these men, highly respected as they were, made many converts to Gestalt theory or signally changed the course of American psychology.

Although the account which has been given of Gestalt psychology is summary in the extreme, it is at least clear that to understand it fully would demand a major exercise in the history of ideas. Its roots are deeply buried in nineteenth-century German *Natur-philosophie* and the theory, such as it is, embodies many traditional themes. For example, considerations of wholeness and form, of order and significance, are deeply embedded in Gestalt thinking. Even Köhler's *Gestalt Psychology* (1931), written for an un-sophisticated American public, clearly betrays its philosophical ancestry. It is hardly surprising, therefore, that Gestalt psychology had much more influence on the Continent, where experimental psychologists still looked to Germany for leadership, than in Britain or America, where psychology had already achieved a much larger measure of emancipation from philosophy.[21] It should also be said that the nativism of Gestalt psychology and its strongly anti-analytical posture were hardly likely to commend it to the empirical Anglo-Saxon mind.

While it is tempting to explain both the rise and ultimate decline of Gestalt psychology in terms of history and culture, such an explanation would be far from adequate. Even had Hitler never existed and the Gestalt psychologists remained free to pursue their inquiries in an intellectual atmosphere more congenial to them than that of America, it seems unlikely that the Gestalt theory would be with us today. By modern standards, Gestalt theory is bad theory. Its terms are ill-defined, its principles cloudy, and few of its hypotheses open to precise experimental verification. Like psycho-analysis, too, it was tainted by the zeal of its prophets, who imposed a sectarian character upon it. In short, Gestalt psychology was not murdered; it died of its own inherent shortcomings.

IV. PSYCHOANALYSIS

Unlike behaviourism and Gestalt psychology, psychoanalysis evolved outside the universities and its relations with academic psychology have always been distant. By and large, academic psychologists have seen in psychoanalysis a strange and esoteric system, possibly of some value in psychological medicine but having little to offer to the systematic study of normal human behaviour. Psychoanalysts, on their side, have seen academic psychology as superficial, trivial, and divorced from the realities of human conduct. They protest that few academic psychologists have really under-stood what Freud was trying to say and that even fewer have them-selves undergone training in the psychoanalytical technique. Not surprisingly, therefore, little contact has been achieved.

It also seems to be the case that psychoanalysis has been more of a 'school' in the strict sense than either behaviourism or Gestalt psychology, both of which constituted attitudes of mind rather than formal bodies of doctrine. Although there were of course many people who were influenced by psychoanalysis without necessarily subscribing to all its theories, it cannot be denied that there was a strong sectarian element in the movement. This was perhaps less true of psychoanalysis in Britain than elsewhere, partly due, no doubt, to the diplomacy and finesse exercised over many years by the dean of British Freudians, Ernest Jones. There was also greater tolerance for the deviants and eclectics, provided that they sub-scribed to the general idea of *psychogenesis*—i.e. the belief that neurosis has a psychological rather than a physical cause.

The earlier stages in the development of psychoanalytical theory have been well summarized by Professor Hearnshaw in the previous volume. We shall therefore confine ourselves to a brief outline of the main developments that took place between the end of the First and that of the Second World War. First, there was a gradual shift of interest from unconscious and instinctual processes to problems of character development and relations within the family. This shift was clearly foreshadowed in—if not initiated by—Freud's *Ego and the Id* (English trans., 1927) and given more systematic expression by his daughter Anna Freud, in her book on *The Ego and the Mechanisms of Defence* (1937). Freud's new (though in a sense very old) ideas about the structure of the mind inaugurated what might be called the modern era of 'character analysis'.

Secondly, psychoanalysis made a decided irruption into child psychology. Whereas Freud himself had based his theory of human development (particularly in its psychosexual aspects) largely on data obtained from the analysis of adults, the new tendency was to go directly to children to seek more direct evidence of the truth of his teaching. The work of this new generation of child analysts, in particular that of Melanie Klein (1882–1960), gave rise to important revisions of the Freudian theory, many of which became in time assimilated to the 'orthodox' position.[22]

Thirdly, there was throughout the twenties and thirties an in-creasing awareness of the part played by social factors in individual development which led to a more optimistic reappraisal of the relations between the individual and society. Freud's outlook had always been tinged with an underlying pessimism: As he saw it, the individual was and always would be in conflict with society, which by its very nature frustrates him in his search for instinctual satisfaction. Adler, it is true, had preached a more optimistic social philosophy but his views carried little weight, largely because they were so superficial. It remained for the anthropologists and sociologists to seek to bring psychoanalysis within the framework of the cultural rather than the biological sciences, which was achieved to a large extent during and after the Second World War, when many analytically-minded psychiatrists had to face for the first time the claims of organizations (in particular the Armed Services) no less than those of their individual patients.[23] The development of methods of group therapy also sought to explore more realistically the relations between man and his fellow-men and brought what one might call a new social dimension into psychoanalytical thought.

As has been said, psychoanalysis made little impact on academic psychologists, at all events in Britain, though there were of course some notable exceptions. W. H. R. Rivers, who had had much to do with the beginnings of experimental psychology in Cambridge, came to accept much of the Freudian system, though always seeking to integrate it with broader biological principles.[24] Nor was his successor C. S. Myers unsympathetic. Indeed it was largely through Myers that J. T. McCurdy was brought to Cambridge to foster instruction in psychological medicine. McCurdy wrote a major work on emotion from the psychoanalytical standpoint which had considerable influence in its day. Another convert was J. C. Flugel, for long a lecturer in Psychology at University College, London, and one of the very few academics of his time who was also a qualified psychoanalyst. But these men were exceptional. For the most part, the Freudian revolution passed the universities by.

Yet the impact of psychoanalysis on the general climate of Western thought has of course been immense—and some would say out of all proportion to its scientific standing. After all, it was to Freud and not to Pavlov that Einstein addressed his famous query, *Why War?* (1933). It was psychoanalysis, not behaviourism, that the botanist Sir Arthur Tansley dubbed the 'new' psychology.[25] In spite of the very real limitations of psychoanalysis as science, its success in opening up a whole new view of human behaviour will ensure its place in twentieth-century history.

V. THE MIDDLE OF THE ROAD

'So if you ask me what school to choose for your own,' wrote Woodworth, 'I should be inclined to advise you to stay in the middle of the road.'[26] Although some may regard the middle of the road as a dangerous place, Woodworth's advice is in many ways sound. In psychology, as in so much else, the middle of the road has always commended itself to the English mind and in the era of the schools British psychologists were only faintly stirred by the winds of doctrine. Neither behaviourism nor Gestalt psychology made British converts and convinced Freudians were the exception rather than the rule. What ideas, then, animated British psychologists in the years between the wars? To what extent, indeed, was there a characteristic British psychology?

In 1918, psychology in Britain was in transition. The older philosophers of mind—men such as James Ward, G. F. Stout, and G. Dawes Hicks—though still active and accorded high respect were becoming increasingly remote from the newer tendencies in the subject. William McDougall continued to exercise some influence, though his writings were prolific rather than profound. He had in any case long withdrawn from the British psychological scene. On the other hand, experimental psychology was still struggling for recognition and did not become established on any scale in the universities until after the end of the Second World War. In brief, the position was that while 'armchair' psychology was in decline, 'experimental' psychology lacked both the strength and opportunity wholly to replace it. Further, psychoanalysis and its derivatives were becoming widely known in Britain and to a large extent supplanting traditional psychology in the popular interest.

A senior figure whose theoretical outlook had been largely formed before the First War was Charles Spearman (1863–1945), who for some years held the Grote Professorship of Philosophy of Mind at University College, London. Spearman's contribution to the theory of intelligence and its measurement has already been outlined by Professor Hearnshaw and it is unnecessary to repeat it here. It should however be said that during his tenure of this Chair, Spearman consolidated his ideas about human ability in two once well-known books[27] and established the nearest thing to a school ever known in British psychology. Its members, whether or not they believed strictly in Spearman's two-factor theory of intelligence, were at all events agreed that factorial analysis constitutes a powerful tool in the analysis of human ability. Among their number were Cyril Burt, who succeeded Spearman as Professor of Psychology at University College, London,[28] William Stephenson, later Director of the Institute of Experimental Psychology at Oxford, and R. B. Cattell, one of the first to extend the methods of factorial analysis to the study of personality.

The work of Spearman and his pupils was mainly concerned with the measurement of individual differences in the tradition of Sir Francis Galton. It owed little to experimental psychology as it had evolved in Germany and had virtually no links with the biological sciences. Psychology at Cambridge was very different. Here, a psychological laboratory had been established in 1913, largely through the efforts of C. S. Myers (1873–1946), who became its first Director. Myers had written a textbook of experimental psychology in 1911 and, together with W. H. R. Rivers, instituted the first courses in the subject ever to be taught in a British university. On the whole, their instruction was in the German psychophysical tradition, though with powerful emphasis on the physiology of the senses. When, in 1921, Myers left Cambridge for London to found the National Institute of Industrial Psychology, he was succeeded by F. C. Bartlett (1886–1969), who soon became the dominant figure in British psychology in the period covered by this survey.

Bartlett's work falls into two main phases. The earlier was concerned principally with the higher mental processes, in particular memory. In his book on *Remembering*, published in 1932, Bartlett provided a convincing illustration of the ways in which simple and flexible experimental procedures can be used to exemplify the working of memory and the social factors which affect its accuracy. He was also led to advance a theory of memory based in part on the work of the neurologist, Henry Head, on sensation and the cerebral cortex. To account for the disturbances in sensation following cerebral lesions, Head had postulated the existence of cumulative dispositions or 'schemata', which record the position of the limbs in space and thereby make possible prompt and accurate motor response. Bartlett extended the concept of 'schema' with some success to account for perceptual recognition and the execution of motor skills, though his attempt to explain remembering itself was less happy. At the same time, his theory represents well the thinking of the period, combining as it does both neurological and psychological considerations and making due allowance for social factors in governing individual performance.[29]

The second phase of Bartlett's work was ushered in by the outbreak of war. From 1939 to 1945, the Cambridge Laboratory was engaged almost exclusively in research work relevant to the war effort, much of it concerned with the analysis of human skill as it is built up and deployed in such tasks as gunnery or aircraft navigation. Bartlett laid particular stress on the need to study not only the final level of performance of any skill but also the timing, grouping, and stability of its component elements. Only in this way, he believed, was it possible to understand the nature of fatigue or to discover a genuine rationale for training methods.[30] This work owed much to the singular genius of Bartlett's pupil, K. J. W. Craik, whose premature death in 1945 cut short a brilliant scientific career.[31] A fuller account of the Cambridge work on skill and its postwar development is given by Professor Hunter in his contribution to volume III of this series.

It must not be thought that Cambridge was the sole university in Britain to make provision for experimental psychology. In the twenties, psychological laboratories were set up in Manchester, Edinburgh, and Glasgow, but staff were few and resources limited. An Institute of Experimental Psychology was established in Oxford in 1937 but did not get fully into its stride until after the war. None the less, the active interest in experimental psychology that grew up in Cambridge and elsewhere between the wars provided an essential nucleus for postwar developments. At the present time, psychology as taught in our universities is almost without exception experimental psychology, though it is nowadays governed by theoretical considerations very different from those of thirty years ago. Information theory, decision theory, mathematical models—these are the current preoccupations of experimental psychology today.

VI. Conclusions

Is it possible to assess the contribution of the 'schools' to the development of psychology as a whole? Perhaps we still stand too near them for such an exercise to be viable, but in so far as it is possible at all the following tentative conclusions can be drawn:

(1) Although behaviourism was in many respects a crude and philistine psychology, it has left a lasting imprint on the subject in its modern form. By and large, psychology is nowadays accepted as a largely biological science whose main object is the systematic study of behaviour, both animal and human. It employs wherever possible objective and experimental methods and makes little use of introspection, at all events in the pseudo-precise way in which it was formerly practised. Further, behaviourism has resulted in a sharp improvement in the standards of psychological theory and in the development of a more rigorous methodology in what are nowadays called the behavioural sciences.

(2) Gestalt psychology, in spite of its freshness and fascination, remains as little more than a reminder of the great days of German experimental psychology. While it served a valuable purpose in helping to break down the naïve psychological atomism of Wundt and in making evident the limitations of association theory, Gestalt psychology failed to develop sufficient rigour and predictive power to compete successfully with behaviourism and its derivatives. None the less, the Gestalt psychologists discovered a number of really important phenomena, especially in the field of visual perception, which even now elude satisfactory explanation. The view is not uncommonly advanced that some of the Gestalt principles may well be resurrected (though no doubt in much modified form) as our knowledge of brain/behaviour relations slowly advances.

(3) Psychoanalysis, which has now been in existence for eighty years, has made very important (if not always fully substantiated) contributions to our understanding of early development and the origin of certain forms of nervous disorder. Certain of these contributions, e.g. the Freudian theory of dreams, are now securely embodied in general psychological thought. It is also agreed that the technique of psychoanalysis has made possible a degree of insight into human motives unsurpassed in human history. Yet doubt attaches both to the scientific status of psychoanalysis and its therapeutic efficiency. In spite of the widespread dissemination of psychoanalytical ideas, it still retains something of the nature of a cult.

(4) The general development of experimental psychology geared to a 'middle of the road' approach to psychological issues has virtually rendered the schools redundant. There are hopeful signs of a *rapprochement* between experimental and clinical psychologists, and between fundamental and applied interests. These trends, forged under the stress of war, will be delineated more fully in the final volume.

NOTES

[1] R. S. Woodworth, *Contemporary Schools of Psychology* (8th ed. rev., 1949). The first edition, which was published in 1931, captures the spirit of the times much more vividly.

[2] L. S. Hearnshaw, ch. 7, *The Twentieth-Century Mind*, I (1971), 233.

[3] J. B. Watson, 'Psychology as the Behaviorist Views it', *Psychological Review*, x (1913), No. 2, 158–77.

[4] J. B. Watson, 'The Place of the Conditioned-Reflex in Psychology', *Psychological Review*, XXIII (1916), No. 2, 89–116.

[5] W. McDougall, *Psychology, the Study of Behaviour* (1912).

[6] It is true that Titchener did devote quite serious consideration to Watson's article on 'Psychology as the Behaviorist Views it', but the gist of his critique may be summed up in the statement that, '. . . logically, so far as I can see, behaviorism is irrelevant to introspective psychology.' At the same time, Titchener did believe that psychology would ultimately be furthered by increased knowledge of the bodily mechanisms correlated with conscious phenomena, and to this extent wished the new movement 'all success'. See E. B. Titchener, 'On Psychology as the Behaviorist Views it', *Proceedings of the American Philosophical Society*, LIII, No. 213 (April 1914).

[7] For Lashley's defence of behaviourism, see his articles on 'The Behaviorist's Interpretation of Consciousness', *Psychological Review*, XXX (1923), No. 4, 237–72, and No. 5, 329–53. For his experimental studies, see *Brain Mechanisms and Intelligence: A Quantitative Study of Injuries to the Brain* (1929), and *The Neuropsychology of Lashley*, ed. F. A. Beach, D. O. Hebb, C. T. Morgan, and H. W. Nissen (1960). For mass action, see O. L. Zangwill, 'Lashley's Concept of Cerebral Mass Action', in *Current Problems in Animal Behaviour*, ed. W. H. Thorpe and O. L. Zangwill (1961), 59–86.

[8] For a useful review and discussion of developmental studies during the period covered by this survey, see *Manual of Child Psychology*, ed. L. Carmichael (1946). Gesell contributes a chapter on 'The Ontogenesis of Infant Behavior'.

[9] The extent to which Pavlovian principles are or are not applicable to learning in general has been well discussed by E. R. Hilgard and D. G. Marquis, *Conditioning and Learning* (1940). This was one of the best studies of the time on the general relations between conditioning and learning and still merits attention.

[10] Tolman's best-known work is *Purposive Behaviour in Animals and Man* (1932).

[11] G. Humphrey, *The Nature of Learning* (1933).

[12] L. S. Vygotski, *Thought and Language*, ed. and trans. E. Hanfman and G. Vakov (1962).

[13] M. Wertheimer, 'Experimentelle Studien über das Sehen von Bewegung', *Zeitschrift für Psychologie*, LXI, 161–265; reprinted in *Drei Abhandlungen zur Gestalttheorie* (Erlangen, 1925).

[14] M. von Ehrenfels, 'Über Gestaltqualitäten', *Vierteljahrschrift für wissenschaftliche Philosophie*, XIV (1890), No. 3, 249–92.

[15] M. Wertheimer, 'Untersuchungen zur Lehre der Gestalt II', *Psychologische Forschung*, IV (1923), 301–50. An abstract of this paper was published as 'Laws of Organization in Perceptual Forms' in *A Sourcebook of Gestalt Psychology*, ed. W. D. Ellis (1938).

[16] W. Köhler, *Die Physischen Gestalten in Ruhe und im Stationären Zustand* (Braunschweig, 1920).

[17] W. Köhler, *The Mentality of Apes*, trans. E. Winter (1925).

[18] M. Wertheimer, *Productive Thinking* (1945).

[19] Lewin's best-known works are *A Dynamic Theory of Personality: Selected Papers*, trans. D. K. Adams and K. E. Zener (1935); *Principles of Topological Psychology*, trans. F. and G. M. Heider (1936); and *Field Theory in Social Science: Selected Theoretical Papers*, ed. D. Cartwright (1952).

[20] W. Köhler, *Dynamics in Psychology* (1942); W. Köhler and M. Wallach *Proceedings of the American Philosophical Society*, LXXXVIII (1944), 269–357.

[21] European psychologists influenced in greater or less degree by Gestalt theory included David Katz, whose *World of Colour* appeared in English translation in 1935 and *Gestalt Psychology* in 1951; Wolfgang Metzger (*Gesetze des Sehens*, Frankfurt, 1953); and A. Michotte, whose important work on phenomenal causation (a classic example of a Gestalt quality) appeared just after the end of the Second War (*La Perception de la causalité*, Louvain, 1946; *The Perception of Causality*, English trans. by J. R. and Elaine Miles, 1963).

[22] For Melanie Klein, see *The Psychoanalysis of Children* (1932) and *Contributions to Psycho-Analysis, 1921–1945* (1948).

[23] See, e.g. A. Kardiner, *The Psychological Frontiers of Society* (1945).

[24] W. H. R. Rivers, *Instinct and the Unconscious* (1920).

[25] A. G. Tansley, *The New Psychology and its Relation to Life* (1920).

[26] R. S. Woodworth, *Contemporary Schools of Psychology* (1931), 229.

[27] C. E. Spearman, *The Nature of 'Intelligence' and the Principles of Cognition* (1923) and *The Abilities of Man* (1927).

[28] Sir Cyril Burt, *The Factors of the Mind* (1940). For a good review of 'factor' psychology, with special reference to work done between 1935 and 1949, see P. E. Vernon, *The Structure of Human Abilities* (1950; 2nd ed., 1961).

[29] For an exposition and critique of the views of Head and Bartlett, see R. C. Oldfield and O. L. Zangwill, 'Head's Concept of the Schema and its Application in Contemporary British Psychology', *British Journal of Psychology*, XXII, Part 1 (1942), 267–86; XXIII, Part 2 (1942), 58–64; ibid., Part 3 (1942), 113–29; ibid., Part 4 (1942), 143–9.

[30] See F. C. Bartlett, 'Fatigue following Highly Skilled Work', *Proceedings of the Royal Society of London, Series B*, CXXXI (1943), 247–57, and 'The Measurement of Human Skill', *British Medical Journal*, 1 (1947), 835 and 877.

[31] Something of the quality of Craik's thought can be surmised from his little book on *The Nature of Explanation* (1943) and from the selection of previously unpublished papers, essays, and notes compiled by S. L. Sherwood (K. J. W. Craik, *The Nature of Psychology*, 1966).

FOR FURTHER READING

A number of the books recommended by Professor L. S. Hearnshaw in his chapter in volume I of *The Twentieth-Century Mind* are equally relevant to the present chapter. I would particularly recommend E. G. Boring, *A History of Experimental Psychology* (New York, 1950), L. S. Hearnshaw, *A Short History of British Psychology* (1964), and R. S. Woodworth and Mary Sheehan, *Contemporary Schools of Psychology* (1965).

Other works relevant to the period covered by this chapter are: F. C. Bartlett, *Remembering* (1932); K. J. W. Craik, *The Nature of Explanation* (1943) and *The Nature of Psychology*, ed. S. Sherwood (Cambridge, 1966); J. J. Gibson, *The Perception of the Visual World* (1950); C. L. Hull, *Principles of Behavior* (New York, 1943); M. Klein, *The Psychoanalysis of Children* (1932) and *Contributions to Psycho-analysis, 1921–1945* (1948); W. Köhler, *Gestalt Psychology* (New York, 1947) and *The Task of Gestalt Psychology* (Princeton, 1969); G. Ryle, *The Concept of Mind* (1949); B. F. Skinner, *The Behavior of Organisms* (New York, 1938); R. S. Woodworth, *Experimental Psychology* (1939).

8

Physics

G. H. A. COLE

Science aims at constructing a world which shall be symbolic of
the world of commonplace experience.

Sir Arthur Eddington

Introduction

For physics, the twenties and thirties were a period of great
adventure and enormous excitement. The decisive break with the
Newtonian world had been made already with the development of
relativity theory by Einstein and of the quantum concept by Planck,
as discussed in chapter 8 of volume I of this series.* The concepts
of absolute space and absolute time, which had stood the test of
experience over thousands of years, proved unsuited to generalizations involving higher speeds. The new theories of relativity give
each observer his own personal combination of space–time, the
exact details of which depend on the motion of the one observer
relative to others. Expressed in everyday terms, where the observers
are to be identified with people (i.e. with you and me), according to
Einstein's theories each person has his unique space–time world to
explore. But in everyday terms, the relative motion between people
is so extremely small that the differences between the space–times
of different people are entirely negligible. There is the appearance
of everyone having the same space–time, which can be separated into
a space and a time independently: this is the common space and
time of the Newtonian world, called absolute because it appears
unique. Higher speeds and greater separations between observers
make it imperative to appeal to the more general space–time concept.
These wider aspects were discussed during the period that concerns
us now. New observational knowledge of the universe became
available during this period, due very largely to the erection of the
100-inch optical telescope on Mount Wilson, California. Galaxies
became the object of detailed study and the scale of the universe
known to us was increased correspondingly. The theory of general
relativity gave important guidance in the use of the new telescope
for surveying the galaxies, and astonishing results became confirmed.
But more than this; the stars themselves, both in our own environ-

* See *The Twentieth-Century Mind*, vol. I (1971), pp. 267ff., 293ff.

ment and in the other galaxies, came under quantitative study for the first time and it was found that the key to the understanding of stellar behaviour and structure lies in the properties of atoms of which all matter is composed.

The newly conceived quantum theory for the first time brought atomic and molecular phenomena within the sphere of informed numerical study. The original ideas of Planck were soon found to be too naïve for the extensive study of all atomic systems, but did, nevertheless, provide a base upon which the more refined and powerful quantum theory could be developed. At first the theory did not take account of relativity but, once the non-relativistic ideas became firmly established, the generalization to a fully relativistic theory was begun. The two great developments of twentieth-century physics were welded together.

The jazz and charleston ages were dominated in physics by these various developments in relativity and quantum mechanics. Other developments in physics were very largely off-shoots of these two studies. There is not space here to include the derivative work, important as it might have been in technological or other terms, and the reader is referred to the general literature for details. In following through the story of this unprecedented period of development in physics we shall see how the seemingly quiet and limited environment of earlier physical theory was replaced by a dynamic universe of almost limitless extent and of unimaginable depth and complexity. This was a momentous period, comparable in importance to the earlier periods when Archimedes, Copernicus, and Galileo in turn fundamentally changed our understanding of the universe. It involved a complete reassessment of our universe and man's place in it. But more than this, our new knowledge allows us to approach the question of the origin of the universe in scientific terms involving physical concepts of tested validity, although admittedly tested in more restrictive circumstances. A natural extension is an estimate of the possible future evolution of the cosmos. We cannot expect to achieve a full solution to the problem of the cosmogonical nature of the universe, but it is an impressive achievement to have reached a stage where we can at least begin to survey the problems involved in quantitative terms.

I. QUANTUM MECHANICS

Further Developments of the Bohr Theory

The success of the Bohr hypotheses was seen to provide an astonishingly accurate description of the more prominent features of the spectrum associated with the hydrogen atom. In volume I (p. 306)* we saw that the frequencies of the Balmer, Paschen, and Brackett spectral series are predicted almost perfectly on the model of the Rutherford atom but with the energy and angular momentum of the planetary electron quantized according to the rule of Planck. But the theory could not predict every aspect of observation. One immediately obvious shortcoming is its inability, without further hypothesis, to account for the intensity (i.e. strength) of the emitted radiation, and the polarization (i.e. directional) properties of its vibrations. Indeed, we saw at I. 308 that Bohr had to propose his correspondence principle to remedy this deficiency, according to which certain important parts of the quantum calculation are made on the basis of classical theory. Clearly the model needed to be explored further to see whether it was capable of appropriate development or whether it must be abandoned. This work was pursued around 1920.

To begin with, the electron orbit had been supposed circular, but it was soon realized that specific elliptic orbits can have the same energy as a particular circular orbit. This opens a new possibility; the electron will not travel an elliptical orbit with constant speed because the angular momentum of the orbiting electron must be conserved: the speed of the electron will be greatest at the point where the orbit is nearest to the nucleus (which is the perihelion in terms of celestial mechanics). The theory of special relativity will lead us to assign a higher mass to the electron at this point than at other points on the orbit. The acceleration of the electron moving in its orbit under the action of the electric attraction between the negatively-charged electron and the positively-charged nucleus will vary periodically and the stable closed orbit will be disturbed. The orbit will not be closed with the electron exactly retracing the same path on successive tracings; rather, it will advance, forming the pattern of a rosette, and such an orbit is described as open. The open orbit has slightly more energy than the closed one, and each of the possible open elliptical orbits is then distinguished by an energy which differs slightly from the others. Because the observed spectral lines have energies associated with the difference of the energies between independent orbits, the arguments that we have outlined will predict a spectral line to be a complicated thing with a number of components of slightly differing frequency. This fine-structure is observed in practice and A. Sommerfeld (b. 1868) was able

* Page references to chapter 8 in volume I of this series will be given hereafter as follows: I. 306.

to show that the theory accounts for the numerical details very accurately. In particular, Sommerfeld isolated a fine-structure constant to characterize the effect; this was the electron speed in the first circular Bohr orbit given as a fraction of the speed of light.* Inserting the appropriate numbers into the expression for the fine-structure constant it is found that the numerical value of the constant is very nearly the inverse of the number 137—not exactly but not more than two-tenths of a per cent away from it. The number 1/137 will appear again in a later section involving certain cosmological arguments.

The recognition of fine-structure might appear a further triumph for the theory but in fact this is not so. To begin with, the argument we have developed is not legitimate. The electron is supposed to be moving under the action of an instantaneous, central electric attraction to the nucleus and at the same time to show a relativistic mass variation. Instantaneous action at distance is foreign to the whole basis of relativity; we have an electron linked to the nucleus in a way that is denied by the remainder of the calculation. Just as an isolated experimental result is impossible to assess in the absence of other data, so the calculation of one effect is not meaningful in the absence of the full background of theory. But even forgetting the theoretical inconsistencies in our argument, further developments are needed. For it is found that the theory developed so far is not able to account adequately for the behaviour of the atom in a magnetic field (Zeeman effect (1896) if the field is uniform, or the Stern–Gerlach effect (1921) if the field is non-uniform, or in an electric field (Stark effect (1913)). The effect of applying a field of external origin to the atoms is observed to be the splitting of the spectral lines still further. This effect requires that the individual electron orbits shall not be oriented at random in space but that their possible orientation relative to the direction of an applied field shall be quantized to have only integral multiples of a definite total elementary angular momentum in the direction of the field.† But closer analysis of the behaviour of the electron in a non-uniform magnetic field (the Stern–Gerlach effect) shows that even this is not

* Explicitly, the fine-structure constant is equal to twice the number $\pi = 3.14159 \ldots$ multiplied by the square of the electronic charge, and divided by the product of Planck's constant and the speed of light *in vacuo*. The number π is the ratio of the circumference of any circle to its diameter, which is the same for all circles. This number arises widely in physics, indeed whenever we are concerned with any complete cyclic process.

† The elementary angular momentum is found empirically to be Planck's constant divided by the number 2π (i.e. $6.2832 \ldots$).

enough; experiment requires the addition of a further angular momentum equal to one half the elementary one associated with the orbit. This new angular momentum is presumably not explicitly a property of the orbit and Uhlenbeck and Goudsmit (1925) assigned it to the electron itself. They did this by supposing the electron to spin about an axis with the required fixed amount of angular momentum. It is interesting to notice that Stark had earlier believed such a spin necessary in order to explain certain results due to the application of an electric field.

The theory is complicated even for the simplest case of the hydrogen atom, but it becomes the more so when larger atoms, such as the alkali-metal halides, are treated. The angular momentum of the spinning electron is vital now (as it was really in accounting for the doublet structure of spectral lines in the case for which Uhlenbeck and Goudsmit first proposed the notion of the spinning electron) and must be added vectorially to the angular momentum of the electron in its orbit (remember that an electron moving in its orbit is equivalent to a circulatory electric current). And even when the extreme complication is accounted for, the theory does not predict all the observed properties of spectra without additional hypotheses (dignified then by being called rules). Complication is bad at any time, but when it even gives the wrong answers as judged by experiment it is intolerable: the Bohr theory is too limited in scope. It remains even now a useful qualitative picture of something deeper, but no more.

One important way in which the Bohr theory proved inadequate was that it did not account for the experimental fact that atoms are not flat but are three-dimensional objects.

Corpuscles and Waves

The Bohr theory is a corpuscular theory, the nucleus and the electron being regarded as particles in interaction through electric forces. There is no doubt that the replacement of the classical theory by the theory based on Planck's quantum hypothesis is basically correct even though the resulting theory is not complete. It is not clear how the Bohr theory itself can be improved further; we must salvage from it what is important and graft it on to an alternative development of quantum theory capable of more fruitful development. The problem is, of course, to find a replacement of the Bohr theory.

In generalizing our previous arguments it is important to remember that we are concerned principally with the transference of energy from one physical system (e.g. an atom) to another (e.g. the surrounding space), and that classical theory recognized two separate mechanisms: the transference of mass as a projectile with a trajectory that can be calculated and wave motion (involving no net rearrangement of mass). But then Einstein showed (see 1. 298) that radiation has a particle aspect as well as a wave aspect.

Having accepted this, we come to a wider question. Relativity theory itself is more general than Newtonian principles, and follows from the Maxwellian picture. Is the particle structure of matter inevitable or are there circumstances under which matter itself can show unambiguous wave-like behaviour? We must say at once that, because wave characteristics for matter had not been observed before this time, we might expect the physical circumstances under which they could occur to be unusual from an everyday, commonplace point of view. As a corollary, the physical nature of these matter waves, as we might call them, can be expected to be difficult to comprehend, at least at first. But nevertheless, the simplicity and unity of our description of the world would make it reasonable to suppose that if radiation (normally accepted as wave-like) can have particle-like properties under suitable circumstances, then particles themselves might have wave-like properties under other special circumstances. After all, radiation is a manifestation of energy, and special relativity tells us that energy and mass are equivalent things. If energy can have a dual wave–particle form in one context, why not in another?

These questions are of little meaning as they stand since nothing has been said yet about the precise conditions under which they might be unambiguously identified. It is necessary to put the associated ideas into quantitative form, and then to test them experimentally. This is the programme that workers in the field set themselves during the twenties and thirties.

Waves and Integers

Integers are known to play a prominent role in the classical theory of waves. Young discovered that under certain circumstances two beams of light can combine one with the other so that the resulting intensity of the combination is weaker than would follow from the simple superposition of the two waves separately. This pheno- menon is known as interference, the enfeebling effect being called destructive interference. Other circumstances provide constructive interference, where the combined intensity is greater than the average. Interference effects are not restricted to light but are a general property of wave-motions, whether transverse (e.g. electro-magnetic) or longitudinal (e.g. sound waves).

If two wave-motions are superimposed one upon the other they will reinforce each other at those points where the wave crests coincide (constructive interference), but will weaken each other (destructive interference) at other points where the crest of one wave coincides with the trough of the other. If the two wave-motions have the same amplitude, then the contrast between reinforcement and enfeeblement is at the most extreme; the range of intensity is between a maximum and complete extinction. This pattern of light and dark is stable if the spatial location of the interference does not change with time. Such a steady distribution of intensity is possible if the wave motions remain always 'in step'; such wave-motions are said to be coherent. The condition for interference is readily isolated and is easily seen to involve integers. For two wave-motions of the same wave-length to reinforce each other at any point in space it is necessary that both waves shall have a crest at that point, or that both waves shall have a trough. Clearly, the difference in the distance between the source of each wave-motion and the point where interference is to be observed must be an integral number of wave-lengths: the numerical expression of the condition of constructive interference apparently involves integers. On the other hand, for destructive interference the trough of one wave train must fall on the crest of the other, that is the two wave trains must be displaced by half a wave-length. It is seen that the distribution of the interference regions (called collectively the interference pattern) depends upon the wave-length of the radiation, and also involves either an integer (constructive interference) or an integer *plus* one half of a wave-length. If neither of these conditions apply, neither a full reinforcement nor a complete depletion of the wave amplitude will result. The wave field will show only partial interference effects. If the two wave-motions are not steady, but change with time, the interference effects will change with time in a corresponding manner. If the changes are very rapid, the eye alone may not be able to detect the presence of interference effects at all, and the wave field will then show a uniform intensity of average value, somewhere between the local maximum and minimum values. These effects can be seen easily for water waves due to vibrating coherent sources.

A stable wave-pattern of the type we have been discussing can be set up in a closed volume by the reflection of the waves at the walls.

For this purpose it is necessary that at the walls, presumed rigid and fixed, there shall be no wave-motion: this point of zero wave-displacement is called a node. The volume of given size cannot then maintain waves of any wave-length, but only those with nodes at the walls. This implies that the length of the container in any direction is to be an integral number of *half* wave-lengths of the contained radiation. It might be very properly objected that we have been dealing with a very much idealized situation in that the boundary wall, being composed of atoms and molecules, will not be exactly definable and rigid, and so will not continuously coincide exactly with radiation nodes. This objection is not a trivial one and displays an important facet of physics. The wall is supposed 'perfect' at first, with a continuous structure, the discrete atomic structure of the fine-scale description being overlooked. With the solution having been found for the 'perfect' boundary situation, it must then be demonstrated that this solution can be maintained when the fine detail of the wall is accounted for. In this way, the idealized discussion is made applicable to real situations.

The interference effects considered so far are applicable to more complicated situations when many waves interfere. The phenomenon is now often called diffraction, and was met with before at I. 288 in connection with the experimental determination of the ordering of molecules in space using X-radiation. The phenomenon is easily pictured using the virtual secondary sources of spherical waves as suggested by Huygens (apart from his work in wave optics, Huygens discovered Saturn's rings, and invented the pendulum clock). Each point of the front of a wave in space is supposed to be the source of a spherical wave, spreading out in all directions. The resulting wave-pattern arises from the superposition of all the multitude of such sources. This construction allows us to investigate the effect of boundary surfaces on a wave-field, where the dimensions of the surfaces are comparable to the length of the wave. Diffraction patterns arise and are characteristic of the geometry of the boundary. Thus, an interference pattern arises when a wave meets a corner, well-known in optics and of crucial importance (through the work of Young and Fresnel particularly) in establishing the apparent wave-nature of light. Light can 'go round corners' even though the effect is very small and needs very refined instrumentation for its practical demonstration: waves can do this, but a collection of corpuscles (such as were proposed by Newton) could not unless the boundary is presumed to possess undemonstrable, and so unbelievable, powers of attraction on the corpuscles. On passing the waves through one slit, or many slits, or through a molecular 'forest' (array of molecules in a solid) of carefully spaced 'trees' (i.e. molecules), we get diffraction effects that are characteristic of both the size of the obstruction and of the wave-length of the waves. For extensive collective diffraction effects to occur, the size of the obstruction must be comparable to the length of the waves. This fact has been used in many ways as a means of determining the length of given waves (in optics, for instance, there is the ruled grating, the echelon grating, the Fabry–Perot plate, and the Lummer–Gehrke plate among others for this purpose, while for X-rays there are naturally-occurring crystals). It is well known in optics how white light can be separated into its constituent (rainbow) colours by these means, and a general wave-field rearranged so that waves of virtually (though, of course, not exactly) a single wave-length are separated from the remainder.

All that has been said so far is applicable to classical theory without invoking the Planck quantum hypothesis (see I. 293ff.). In particular we see that, through wave-motion, classical theory involves integral numbers as a central feature of the description of certain physical situations.* The point is important because it is often said rather loosely that quantum theory is involved with discontinuous processes in matter, whereas classical theory is not. This is true so far as the transference of energy between matter and radiation is concerned, but not in other ways: in all other ways, classical and quantum physics are each equally, in their separate ways, concerned with discontinuous and continuous processes.

The Waves Proposed by de Broglie

Physical systems involving wave-motion are described mathematically in terms of integral numbers; the Rutherford–Bohr theory of the atom relates measured spectral lines to certain integers. In 1923, L. de Broglie (b. 1892) raised the exciting, though rather astonishing, possibility of relating the empirical quantum conditions associated with atoms and molecules to the interference effects between matter waves associated with particles (particularly electrons) in the atom or molecule. For this purpose, de Broglie

* We have considered electromagnetic waves and acoustic waves in fluids particularly so far but there are other situations where integers also appear, such as waves in strings and the vibrations of membranes. This wide study of wave-motion and vibrations is of absolutely central importance for physics but is far too extensive to treat here in any balanced way.

asserted that each particle of matter has an associated wave-structure with a length dependent on the motion of the particle. What an astonishing proposition! A particle, characterized by a firm and restricted location in space, is (under special circumstances presumably) to be described by a wave, characterized by the very lack of a precise location in space.

Consider an electron in a closed circular orbit according to the Rutherford–Bohr picture (I. 306). If the electron in the orbit has a wave associated with it, constructive interference will occur in the wave (parts of the wave will 'overlap' with each circuit the electron makes) only if the length of the orbit (i.e. the circumference of the orbit) is an integral number of wave-lengths. An electron in a given motion will be associated with a specific wave-length and in this way the possible size of the stable orbit, where the matter waves do not destructively interfere, is automatically fixed. The appearance of particular electron orbits is accounted for (in contrast to the solar system where no such restriction is relevant); the quantum conditions of Bohr are described in terms of interference effects. The waves associated with material particles will be called de Broglie waves.

In order to consider this idea further it is necessary to relate mathematically the length of the waves to the details of the motion of the electron, or more generally to the particular particle in question if the notion is to be generalized beyond the case of an orbiting electron in an atom. For this we consider the descriptions of a chosen particle, made by two observers each at rest with respect to a specific inertial reference frame (see I. 258, 270). These descriptions, involving the space and time characteristics of the particle, will be linked mathematically by the transformation rules of Lorentz and Einstein. Space and time are not independent in relativity theory and it is here that special effects arise that are of interest to us now. If a particle in motion has a wave associated with it, and if the special theory of relativity is to apply, it is found mathematically that the length of the matter-waves must be related to the momentum of the particle (i.e. its mass multiplied by its velocity) in a specific way. Explicitly, the length of the *matter-waves* must be equal to the Planck constant of quantum theory divided by the momentum of the *particle*. This relationship is now called the de Broglie relationship and the predicted length of the matter-waves the de Broglie wavelength. This is an entirely new relationship, which can be said to typify quantum theory; it is quite without meaning in classical physics where Planck's constant does not occur.

This daring hypothesis had to be subjected to the most searching experimental tests. The first test comes from a study of electromagnetic theory. In this case the energy (of the photon in fact) is to be equated to the product of Planck's constant and the frequency of the (wave) radiation: the momentum of the photon is equal to the photon energy divided by the speed of light. Inserting these expressions into the de Broglie relationship provides immediately the result that the wave-length is equal to the speed of light divided by the frequency of the radiation, which is the normal definition of the wave-length of the radiation. Certainly the de Broglie hypothesis and relationship apply to electromagnetic radiation: historically, it was just this consideration that led de Broglie to his hypothesis. The radiation emitted from an atom (naturally under the appropriate conditions of stimulation) is, according to the Rutherford–Bohr theory, to arise from the jump of an electron between two orbits of different energy. The de Broglie relationship for the wave-length of matter waves leads to exactly the Bohr quantization condition for angular momentum in an orbit. It appears that the de Broglie hypothesis of the existence of matter-waves can be viewed as an alternative statement of the Bohr conditions for quantization.

With this successful application to ordinary radiation, what is likely to be the magnitude of the wave-length of matter-waves for ordinary matter? We can look at one or two examples. First, suppose a particle of matter has a mass of 1 gram and moves with a speed of 1 cm per second; this is a small macroscopic mass moving quite slowly. The de Broglie relationship predicts a wave-length for matter waves of about 6×10^{-27} cm, an incredibly small length. As the particle speed increases so the wave-length will become even smaller; but as the speed decreases so the wave-length will increase, becoming indefinitely large when the particle is at rest. The wave-length also decreases as the mass increases: for a mass the size of the earth moving in its orbit round the sun the associated wave-length is all but zero, and wave properties have virtually no relevance to the discussion of the motion. We might, on the other hand, inquire about the wave-length for a very small mass, like an electron. In this case the electron can be caused to move by setting up an electric potential-difference around it, the de Broglie wave-length being proportional inversely to the square root of the electric potential difference. We find that an accelerating electric potential of about 100,000 volts will produce electrons moving with a de Broglie wave-length of about one-tenth of an Ångstrom (i.e. of length about one-thousand-millionth of a centimetre). This is the same wave-length as for hard X-rays.

The question must be faced of the possible physical nature of the matter-waves. As a preliminary to answering such a question we must refer again to the general theory of waves. Two wave velocities must be recognized. One is the speed of the individual waves themselves (called the phase velocity), and is intuitively clear. Unfortunately, although the phase velocity is apparently immediately visualized, in fact it is a purely formal, fictitious concept in that it cannot be determined experimentally. It refers to a wave of infinite extent, and if the velocity of such a wave is to be determined, it is necessary to mark some part of the wave and observe its motion in time. But you cannot mark a wave with a pencil; the only way of marking the wave is to superpose other wave motions upon it, creating a hump on the original wave. The hump is composed of a group of waves; the velocity of the hump is called the group velocity. The passage of energy in wave-motion proceeds with the group velocity; the phase velocity is not linked directly with any physical signal-process. In the mathematical theory of wave-motion it is known that in some cases the group and phase velocities are equal, whereas in others they are not. For the case of an electromagnetic wave in free space, the two speeds are equal to each other, and to the speed of light; the product of the phase and group speeds is equal to the square of the speed of light. This last result is a general result which applies to the case of matter-waves, but the phase and group speeds are not equal. The group velocity is to be identified with the velocity of the real particle (which special relativity theory requires to be less than the speed of light in free space); accordingly, the phase velocity is *greater* than that of light. This does not contradict the principle of special relativity, that energy cannot be transported faster than the speed of light *in vacuo*, because the phase speed of the wave is not associated with the energy transport involved in the movement of matter. We draw the conclusion that matter-waves, if they exist, do not have an immediate physical reality. The reconciliation between the corpuscular and undulatory features of real matter must be considered further, and this topic will concern us later at p. 223. One thing we can say is that, however tempting it may be, we cannot associate a material particle directly with a group of matter-waves (sometimes called a wave-packet). Such a wave-packet can be shown mathematically to be very unstable, undergoing very rapid dissipation.

Some Early Evidence from Experiments

The account of matter-waves given in the last section does no more than develop a hypothesis and show that, while it raises important difficulties, it also provides exciting new possible experimental and theoretical situations. The next step in the development of the physical theory of matter-waves should be to put the whole thing on a firm basis by the development of a wave mechanics in three dimensions, and this was historically what happened. But we are, rather fortunately, not attempting a strictly accurate chronological development of physics here; rather we are concerned with the movement and evolution of the ideas behind our subject and our understanding of it. It is, then, acceptable for us to mention some early experimental studies of matter-waves, even though in reality these studies came after many of the developments that will concern us in the next sections.

In the preceding section we saw that the length of matter-waves for electrons can easily be arranged (of course, if they do in fact exist) to be comparable to X-radiation. And we saw at 1. 288 that real crystals diffract X-rays in a way dictated by the molecular structure of the crystal. The obvious experimental arrangement for the demonstration of the general occurrence of matter-waves is that involving the diffraction of electrons by crystals; such an arrangement was used by the early experimenters for this purpose.

The first unambiguous demonstration of the reality of an undulatory aspect of electrons was made by Davisson and Germer in 1927.* A beam of electrons was reflected from selected surfaces of a single crystal of nickel, and of other metals. They found that reflection occurred not according to classical theory, which considers the electrons as corpuscles, but in a way consistent with an undulatory process. Selective reflection was observed, more electrons being reflected in certain directions than in others. But more than this, the reflection was essentially that to be expected of X-rays of the same wave-length. By varying the speed of the incoming

---

* Actually, Davisson and Kunsman in 1923 obtained some strange experimental results when bombarding crystalline material with fast electrons. The results could not be understood at the time, but Elsasser suggested a possible interpretation in terms of matter-waves in 1925, in the light of de Broglie's hypothesis. This is yet one more example of the general fact that isolated experimental information is meaningless unless it can be interpreted by being related to the generally accepted corpus of physical knowledge. Experimental information can only be accepted as meaningful after it has been given an acceptable theoretical interpretation.

electrons, the wave-length is changed; Davisson and Germer found the observed reflection patterns to be entirely consistent with the de Broglie relationship (see p. 205), within the errors of the experiments.

These reflection experiments of Davisson and Germer in the United States were quickly followed by other experiments by other workers. Sir George Thomson (b. 1892) in 1927 in Great Britain and Rupp in 1928 in Germany shot high-energy electrons through thin metal foils (only some one ten-millionth of an inch thick). One of the central features of the experiments was the development of practical techniques able to provide such thin foils of metal. The effect of the thin foil on the electrons was to induce diffraction effects entirely equivalent to those known from replacing the electrons by X-radiation. Using the de Broglie relationship, the electron diffraction pattern can be used to infer the mean spacing between the atoms of the foil; the result derived in this way is in complete agreement with the results of other independent measurements. The similarity in these experiments between the diffraction patterns for electrons and for X-rays raises the possibility that the pattern apparently caused by the electrons is, in fact, due to X-rays produced in some way as the electrons pass through the foil. To eliminate this possibility it is necessary to subject the diffraction pattern to the action of some single influence which will affect each of the two cases differently. Moving electrons are affected by the presence of electric and magnetic fields (because they are charged particles) whereas X-rays, being pure radiation, are not. Putting the foil in an electric field transverse to the axis of the electron beam, or alternatively in a magnetic field along the axis, distorts the diffraction pattern for the electrons but leaves the X-rays unaffected. This test is unambiguous and the results conclusive; fast electrons do behave like waves in passing through thin foils. Slow electrons or thicker foils do not provide diffraction patterns of the same type. This fact is not to be interpreted as showing that only fast electrons actually have associated undulatory properties in connection with thin foils. For more general circumstances, the lattice fields of the diffracting crystal have a strong influence on the electrons and destroy any simple diffraction effect. It appears that all electrons in experimental conditions are associated with waves even though this is not always immediately apparent: once again we see that the immediate results of limited experiments cannot be assessed and interpreted without an appeal to the full body of physics.

Other experiments on matter-waves quickly followed. Thus in

1930, Mark and Wierl showed the wave-nature of electrons passing through a stream of gas. In this way they repeated for electrons the experiment performed first in 1927 by Debye for X-rays. Then electrons were replaced by protons (the stable unit positive-charge; see 1. 304) in the experiments of Rupp (1932): protons shot through thin gold foil show the wave-like diffraction pattern fully consistent with the de Broglie relationship. More than this, Ellett and Olson (1928) and Estermann and Stern (1930) showed that the earlier experimental arrangements of Davison and Germer, where now beams of cadmium atoms or of mercury atoms (instead of electrons) are reflected from rock salt (instead of a single metal crystal such as nickel), can be used to support the validity of the de Broglie relationship of matter-waves for atomic particles and not just for electrons. Many further experiments, even using molecules of hydrogen or helium atoms, have fully supported the conclusion that all particles have associated matter-waves, and the general existence of matter-waves is now an established fact. We can notice here in passing that the association of wave properties with an atom or a molecule as a unit raises interesting implications, for such a unit is a composite body (composed of nuclei and electrons) and not a single particle. Apparently the centroid of the constituent particles obeys the same undulatory laws as does an individual electron—but the centroid of an atom or molecule is an abstract point not associated with any specific particle. The physical nature of matter-waves must surely be complicated.

But matter-waves do exist, so much so in fact that they are now widely used in technology. They have one advantage of not being as penetrating as X-rays, and therefore present no medical hazard to the human operator. And again, their wave-length can be very readily changed. One well-known application of matter-waves is in the electron microscope. Electric and magnetic fields of carefully chosen strength and spatial distribution affect the motion of an electron beam, and so also the distribution in space of the associated matter-waves. Expressed another way, the electric and magnetic fields can be made to affect the electron matter-waves in precisely the same way as a glass lens affects a beam of light.* The wave length of electron matter-waves (let us agree to call them electron waves from now onwards) can be made very small in comparison with optical wave-lengths (perhaps 10,000 times smaller or even

* The importance of focusing of electronic beams by condensers and magnetic coils was stressed early by Busch (1927): no method is known even now of constructing lenses for X-rays.

more) so that they are more able to show the fine detail of an obstruction than are optical wave-lengths. The electron microscope is an important modern tool with applications to a wide range of problems, from medicine to mechanical engineering.

Measured Quantities and Generalized Numbers

Physics advances by the generalization of established physical concepts on the basis of new, wider experimental information, but it is vital not to let imagination run away with us in the process. New, and consequently strange, physical concepts are constructed and tested under various practical circumstances. We are now developing new quantum concepts, but it may seem that we are being stretched to the limits of our credulity in the process. It is necessary to make sure that these new constructions are actually valuable practical tools.

The physical concepts to be used in the theoretical description of the real world are safely practical if they relate directly to experiment, but there can be ambiguity as to what is meant by a direct relation to experiment. The most extreme requirement, and at first sight the safest, is for any theoretical description of the world to involve only quantities that can be measured directly. The importance of such an operational approach to physics had been made very clear by Einstein in his development of special relativity. This theory (see I. 270f.) involves observers with measuring rods and clocks, and is based explicitly on operations that can be envisaged as occurring in practice. In the event it proved necessary to compromise and to accept operations which can be at least defined in principle even though they may not be useful for actual measurements. Quantities which cannot even be envisaged in principle are to find no place in the discussion.

We might ask whether the same criterion of practicality can be imposed on quantum arguments. Certainly our discussion in the earlier sections has involved very strange notions. The idea of an electron in an orbit is an immediate consequence of the familiar planetary form of the solar system, but it must be recognized at once that there is no direct evidence for the reality of such an entity in the case of an atom. No one has ever seen an electron orbiting in an atom and there is no reason to suppose that anyone ever will. The only measurements actually made refer to the frequencies of spectral lines, and to the stability of these lines against various processes, including collisions between atoms. But spectral lines are complicated things, and become more complicated the more finely they are viewed. To account for these additional features such concepts as the space-quantization of the orbits and the spinning electron are introduced, which are further properties that are incapable of immediate and direct experimental demonstration. Perhaps the most extraordinary development is that of matter-waves, even though they apparently have experimental validity. From the theoretical point of view, the de Broglie relation referred to at p. 205 defines the wave-length *only* where the momentum of the particle is itself defined. Since the momentum of the particle is defined only within the boundaries of the particle, this means that a wave-length is defined only *at* the particle itself. The extension of the wave-structure beyond the particle, through all space, is a further hypothesis. In these terms the achievement of linking particle and wave concepts together becomes the less impressive and even more questionable. Surely it is time to review the whole story from the strictly operational point of view.

This whole matter was investigated by Werner Heisenberg (b. 1901) who, starting in 1925 and joined by Born and Jordan, attempted to provide a mathematical account of the observed spectral characteristics which do not appeal to any pictorial description of what the inside of an atom 'looks' like. The whole purely mechanical picture was abandoned because it attempted to describe too much detail; we are not concerned with drawing pictures of atoms as such but only with accounting for them as working units through their measured properties.

Let us set out the evidence that we have to work on. This is of two kinds. First, there are the measured spectral lines, each specified by two numbers, one referring to the frequency of the line and the other to the intensity. Second, there is the Bohr correspondence principle that can be expressed in the general form that the quantum statements must reduce to the corresponding classical form for large (i.e. essentially macroscopic) systems. This is what we have and it must be enough. Consider these two kinds of evidence in turn.

The problem of displaying clearly the extensive measurements of the frequency and intensity of spectral lines was recognized before the advent of quantum theory. A very important service that the experimentalist must perform is that of arranging his measured results into as compact and as clear a form as possible. For spectroscopy, this has come to involve the theoretical concept of the transition probability for an electron in an atom moving from one orbit to another; this is expressed by employing certain two-dimensional arrays of numbers composed of rows and columns. The empirical relations between these arrays, derived from observation, were found in the event to fall into a special mathematical pattern: the arrays need to be combined (if experimental results are to be reproduced faithfully) in precisely the same way as mathematical entities called matrices. In fact, the two-dimensional arrays can be identified themselves as matrices.

Matrices and the mathematics associated with their manipulation (usually called matrix algebra) have been studied abstractly and systematically since the subject was devised by Cayley in 1858. The invention was not made in connection with a physical system; in his original memoir, Cayley was concerned with the study of the combination of transformations in the theory of algebraic invariants (a mathematical study developed originally by Cayley and by Sylvester). This is the theory of certain linear transformations that, during the nineteenth century, were studied as pure mathematics. The analysis became of interest to physicists during the present century when the importance of the relation between the descriptions of a chosen physical situation by two different inertial observers became of central importance.* This is an example of the mathematical analysis necessary for the expression of a new physical development being already available in a rather advanced form due to the previous work of mathematicians. Logical developments made on the basis of experimental measurements have been recognized long before, and independently, within the abstract realm of pure mathematics. Tensor calculus is another case, devised during the last century without immediate application to the physical world, which was available to act as a language for the expression of the new ideas of relativity when they were devised. Because both matrices and tensors are concerned with the transformation of co-ordinates, it is not surprising that these two entities are closely related to each other.

The theory of atomic phenomena is now to involve the manipulation of matrices. Any characteristic features of matrix algebra are to be interpreted in quantum terms, and in particular are to be arranged to involve the Planck constant of action. Only physical

---

* The reader may be reminded of the theory of special relativity, and will not be surprised to learn that the Lorentz–Einstein transformation can be expressed in terms of a matrix. The transformation involves both position-co-ordinates and time, and the transformation matrix is found to describe a rotation in four dimensions. The rotation angle is not, however, a simple angle that can be expressed in the normal language of real, three-dimensional space.

measurements are to be involved in the theory and it is natural to assert that each physical magnitude is represented in the theory by a matrix. Once this is asserted, the form of the relationships between the physical quantities is automatically also laid down. Our theory is now based on a range of matrices, some related to the position-co-ordinates, some to the momentum-co-ordinates, some to the energy values available to the physical system, and so on. The matrices referring to physical variables such as position and momentum will depend upon time. Derived matrices, such as the energy matrix, will not depend upon time if the corresponding physical system is itself unchanging and so steady in time. A matrix can be regarded in some ways as a generalization of an ordinary number; it is not inappropriate for a measured quantity to be expressed as a number of some form. Once the physical variables are defined, calculations involving them can be made in virtually the same way as in classical mechanics.

Matrix algebra differs from the algebra of ordinary numbers in two very important ways. To begin with, the generalized numbers (matrices) have many components; in fact, it is found that atomic phenomena can only be accounted for if each matrix has an in-definitely large number of components (i.e. we are dealing with an infinite matrix). This is certainly a complication not met with in ordinary algebra. The second difference involves multiplication. In ordinary algebra, if two numbers are multiplied together the answer does not depend upon the ordering of the numbers; three multiplied by four is the same as four multiplied by three. This property of ordinary numbers is called the commutativity rule; ordinary numbers commute with each other so that ordinary algebra is commutative. The generalized form of numbers that we call matrices generally do not satisfy this rule. This leads to the character-istic result that the multiplication of certain matrices together may give zero (strictly speaking a zero matrix, which is one in which every component is zero) even when the individual matrices are not zero. Expressed in technical terms, matrix algebra does not necessarily show the commutative property. Certain matrices do commute, but generally speaking they do not. This non-commutativity is the key to the detailed development of quantum theory in terms of matrices.

Classical mechanics is particularly concerned with the position and momentum of each particle. The product of these two variables for each particle gives its phase; the dimensions of this product are precisely the dimensions of Planck's constant of action. This is the hint we have been seeking: the position and momentum of each particle should be linked directly to the Planck constant. Born and Jordan (1925) proposed how this should be done. In classical physics, the product of the momentum and the position for a representative particle is equal precisely to the product of the position and the momentum (commutative property). But this is not true for matrices; the product of the matrices representing the momentum and the position of the same particle is *not* equal to the product of the matrices for the position and the momentum, in that order. The difference between these two products is not zero, and Born and Jordan postulated that this difference should be equal to the Planck constant of action, apart from a constant matrix. The numerical constant is a scale-factor and is to be chosen * on the basis of experiment. This non-commutativity postulate is about the simplest that can be made, and this was the reason for its original choice by Born and Jordan: we are groping towards a new theory and must make every attempt to keep the discussion as simple mathematically as is possible. If this rather extraordinary non-commutativity hypothesis is accepted, various atomic properties can be calculated to a high degree of accuracy. On the other hand, the non-commutative rule is not to apply for the product of the position of one particle with the momentum of another different particle. The momentum and position variables referring to one and the same particle are said to be canonical variables. Otherwise, if more than one particle is involved, the variables are said to be non-canonical. This nomenclature is carried over from classical physics.

Using the theory constructed this way, Heisenberg, Born, Jordan, Dirac, and others were able to show that the properties of atoms can be calculated as satisfactorily as by using the Bohr theory. Indeed, the non-commutative rule of Born and Jordan takes the place in this new theory of the quantum conditions in the Bohr theory (see I. 306). If the new theory did no more than the older Bohr theory nothing would really have been gained, but in fact something new was discovered: it was found that each calculated energy is larger than the corresponding energy from the Bohr theory by one-half a quantum of energy. This makes no difference to many properties, like the frequency of spectral lines, which are calculated from the difference between two energies. The zero-level of the energy has been moved slightly. Generally this is unimportant, but it has an important consequence when applied to simple harmonic motion. Here the Bohr theory shows that the oscillator may have

---

* Explicitly it needs to be one divided by the number two times π multiplied by the square root of minus one.

no energy; the matrix theory predicts instead that the lowest energy available to the oscillator is not actually zero, but is one-half a quantum of energy. This lowest state of the oscillator is called the zero-point energy and will be found in volume III of this series to exist and to be important.

The matrix theory is of value in showing that it is possible to construct a theory, of at least restricted scope, where only measurable quantities are involved. But two difficulties mar its general use and development. First, it has been found necessary to express each measurable physical variable by a matrix. It is by no means immediately clear how this is to be done for complicated variables; the problem of finding the matrices to be used in the theory can be a formidable one. Second, the analysis does not as it stands satisfy the requirements of special relativity, and is not readily rearranged to satisfy these requirements.

The matrix methods avoid any picture of the atom, and treat such concepts as electron orbits, or spinning electrons, as meaningless. There is no doubt that a theory is not required to provide a comfortable pictorial representation of the physical system that it represents, and must do no more (and also no less) than lead to calculated values which compare favourably with measured data of appropriate accuracy. Children look at pictures and adults read words, or so the Victorians said. It may be that the adult stage in physics is achieved when pictorially-associated physical concepts are unnecessary. However, pictorial representations may be useful in the process of further generalization. The Heisenberg approach to quantum problems has been a success over a useful range of experimental conditions, and is still used in calculations even though the explicit application of the theory is often difficult in the extreme

Wave Mechanics: Intuitive Approach

The non-pictorial matrix theory of Heisenberg does not concern itself with the explicit appearance of matter-waves. Historically it pre-dated by some two years the first of the experimental studies of matter-waves referred to at p. 208, and when the matrix theory was first developed, the wave aspects to be associated with particle were not suspected. But the concept of matter-waves, proposed by de Broglie at about the same time that Heisenberg was beginning to expound his theory, was too exciting a thing to leave in rudimentary form. Not every physicist felt impelled to talk only of things that can be measured but not pictured. In particular, Erwin Schrödinger

(b. 1887) set himself the task of putting the hypothesis of matter-waves on a firm theoretical footing. He was able to do this successfully and in the process developed the wave mechanics of matter, which has proved to be one of the great developments in physics over recent years. Because we are not attempting a strictly historical account of our subject we can call on hindsight as an aid in presenting the conceptual development of physical ideas more clearly and logically. Had the experimental results been available in 1926, the development of wave mechanics by Schrödinger would almost certainly have been different. It might even have taken something of the form that we will expound now. In order to keep the record straight, however, we will support the largely intuitive arguments of the present section by more formal arguments collected together below, at p. 227, where an attempt will also be made to relate Schrödinger's theory to the earlier directly relevant arguments of the classical theory. That we can approach our subject this way shows that physics (and indeed all science) is not the infallible, consistent, logically developed subject that it is often thought to be. One development does not follow inevitably from the one before. Generalization often involves irrational imaginative leaps. Experimental studies are not always in step with the theory, partly for conceptual reasons but also often because the appropriate technology has not been developed, and work in the laboratory often provides results which are totally unexpected. There have been examples of this before and there will certainly continue to be more examples in the future.

In accounting for the properties of atoms and molecules in terms of waves we must consider the interference effects for waves associated with matter, where the wave-length multiplied by the momentum of the associated particle is to equal the Planck universal constant of action (this is the de Broglie relation). We saw at p. 202 that the theory of general wave-motions is well understood. Whether the waves are longitudinal or transverse, the waves in real matter arise from a balance between a restoring force (which acts to restore the deformable body to an equilibrium configuration) and an inertia force (which is the rate of change with time of a momentum). The inertia of the material tends to maintain the movement of the matter while the restoring force acts to stop the motion. The restoring force brings the system to the equilibrium configuration, but the inertia force causes the system to overshoot. The restoring force is consequently brought into action again but this time in a reverse sense, tending to achieve equilibrium again but from the other side, as it were. If energy is not dissipated in other ways through the action of viscosity for a fluid, or through the various elastic moduli for an elastic solid, this wave-motion will continue with fixed amplitude and frequency, indefinitely. Alternatively, if energy is dissipated, the wave motion is damped out. The mechanics of this wave mechanism was put into a mathematical form long ago, and the equation describing the motion is called the wave-equation. The rate of change with position of the rate of change with position of the wave amplitude is equal to the time rate of change of the rate of change with time of the wave amplitude, divided by the square of the speed of the wave. If there are no dissipative effects, this is the form of the wave-equation; if dissipative effects are present then they must be accounted for by the appearance of appropriate mathematical terms in the wave-equation. Maxwell's theory shows that the very same wave-equation applies to the propagation of waves in free space; the appearance of wave-motion is now a consequence of the mathematical expression of a physical system in terms of a wave-equation. The wave theory is removed from a dependence on the vibration of a material medium. This is a well-established result and can be applied quite generally. For matter-waves we have already noticed that the associated wave-motion is likely to have a complicated physical interpretation and is unlikely to be associated with the motion of any real medium, either material or energetic. But nevertheless it is safe to apply the standard wave-equation in this case if we do not attempt any physical interpretation of the waves at this stage.

For these purposes we disregard any dissipative effects and consider a material system that is in a steady state, by which we refer to a physical state of the system which does not change with time.

In constructing a wave-equation we must remember the de Broglie relationship linking the wave-length to the momentum of the particle. Because the wave-length is equal to the speed of wave divided by the frequency of the wave, the de Broglie relationship also links the wave frequency to the particle momentum. But we can rearrange the expression further to include the energy of the particle. The momentum of the particle is equal to its mass multiplied by its velocity: the kinetic energy of the particle is equal to one-half the mass multiplied by the square of the velocity. Consequently, the momentum can be equated to the square root of twice the mass multiplied by the kinetic energy. For a physical system of the type that concerns us now, a force acting on the particle is derivable from a potential energy and the total energy of the particle is to be equated to the sum of the kinetic energy of the particle and the potential energy of the force acting on it. This means that the kinetic energy is equal numerically to the difference between the total and the potential energies. This line of argument allows the frequency of the wave to be related directly to the difference between the total and potential energies. This rearrangement is of great formal importance. The momentum is associated with a restricted location (that is, the body of the particle itself) and is a directed quantity. The total and potential energies are scalar quantities, by which we mean they have magnitude but no directional properties; and they are not entirely localized quantities. It is the non-local feature which is characteristic of wave-motion. In this way the original de Broglie relationship is rearranged into a form more suitable for inclusion in a wave theory. This is an essential part of any theoretical discussion: not only must the physical information be available (in this case the de Broglie relationship and the energy principle) but it must also be expressed in an appropriate form (in this case to involve the energy rather than the momentum). The standard theory of wave-motion can now be applied to obtain a mathematical equation that must be satisfied by the amplitude of the matter-waves, in terms of the total energy of the particle and the potential energy of any force acting on it, and also involving Planck's constant (because the de Broglie relation is invoked). The appearance of Planck's constant is an essential feature of this equation describing a quantum phenomena. The wave-equation we have been discussing was derived by Schrödinger in 1926, though by a quite different method (but see p. 228). It is the basic equation * of the theory and has proved of enormous value in the elucidation of a wide range of atomic problems. It has the important restriction, however, of applying only to non-relativistic situations. While this is of little consequence in many physical circumstances, it does prevent the equation from being of use in the investigation of processes involving emission and absorption of radiation by matter. For this a relativistic theory is necessary.

Not just any solution of the wave equation of Schrödinger has physical relevance, but only those special solutions which satisfy certain conditions at any boundary containing the physical system. This restriction is not peculiar to quantum physics, but is the

---

* From the purely technical mathematical point of view, the equation is a second-order differential equation involving the position and so is in the same class as the celebrated equations of Lagrange–Euler, Laplace, and Poisson in classical physics. They are all essentially expressions of continuity.

standard appendage for any equation used in physics. Two conditions are necessary because of the detailed mathematical form of the Schrödinger equation. The conditions imposed are that the wave function must vanish at an impenetrable boundary (because by the definition of such a containing boundary the physical system that it contains will not have a portion outside) and also that the change of the wave amplitude with position will be zero at the boundary, because the physical system by definition cannot penetrate it. These conditions are analogous to the requirement that the wave pattern shall have a node at the boundary wall (see pp. 203, 207). It turns out in application of the equation to specific physical systems that these boundary requirements impose restrictions on the solutions of the wave equation that can be interpreted physically as being precisely the quantum conditions recognized by Bohr.

The first application of the theory by Schrödinger to the discussion of the hydrogen atom gave its first triumph. The theory is able to account for the observed spectral series, as is the Bohr theory in its extended form including elliptical orbits, but the Schrödinger equation does not refer to mechanical orbits. Instead, the electronic state of the atom is described in terms of the various possible modes of vibration of the atom. And, very important, the analysis provides a full three-dimensional atom. This is an advance over the Bohr-type model. The discussion can proceed to discuss the helium atom and the more complicated atoms and even molecules. Such an extension of the calculations provides many technical complications of mathematics of a severe kind, which are still being actively studied today. The theory is able to account satisfactorily for the Zeeman and Stark effects. New theories should provide new insight into physical processes and the theory developed by Schrödinger has done that in several ways. One of these concerns the atomic nucleus.

The interpretation of the scattering experiments of Rutherford (see f. 304) in terms of a central atomic nucleus (with a diameter of about 10^{-11} cm) and a surrounding 'planetary' electronic structure implies certain properties of the nucleus. The nucleus repels another positive particle (which is the cause of the large deflections observed by Rutherford) and yet remains as a stable entity, even though it may contain protons within its own structure. It follows that the structure of the nucleus is almost certain to be highly complicated in its detail, but that in a broad way it can be looked upon as a kind of barrier which keeps the internal constituent inside, and keeps other independent atoms outside. The barrier i the seat of energy, not active but potentially there to maintain th *status quo*, and it is natural to refer to the barrier as a potential barrier. In order for an external particle to penetrate into the nucleus, or a particle inside the nucleus to pass outside, it is necessary in each case for the particle to have sufficient energy to pass over the barrier. The classical picture is acceptable until experimental information is taken into account. The experimental evidence involves on the one hand the bombardment of a nucleus by protons from outside (Rutherford, Rauch von Traubenberg), and on the other hand the study of the particles of radioactive decay (Rutherford). In each case it is found experimentally that particles are involved whose energy is much less than that associated with the potential barrier which the particles must overcome. Thus, if a range of nuclei are bombarded by protons it is found that low-energy protons can, on occasion, penetrate the potential barrier, even though the energy of the protons may be only one-hundredth that required to pass over the potential barrier on the basis of classical physics. On the other hand, in radioactive decay an analogous situation occurs. For example, when uranium disintegrates, each nucleus gives off an alpha-particle (a helium nucleus): the energy associated with the α-particle is only one-half that needed to penetrate the encompassing potential barrier, on the basis of classical theory. Clearly, once again classical theory is inadequate. The Bohr theory is unable to offer an explanation of the effect that is in any way convincing, but the wave mechanics of Schrödinger offers a natural explanation without further troubles. Whereas the potential barrier can act as a true barrier in purely mechanical terms as far as the mechanical (particle) aspects of the proton or α-particle are concerned, it is not able to exclude the matter-waves. These seep through the barrier, either from the inside outwards, or from the outside inwards, and ultimately so many have seeped through that the particle finds that it too has passed through the barrier! This is an entirely quantum effect with no counterpart whatever in the classical theory. The full interpretation of this effect will become clear below when the matter-waves will be interpreted in terms of a probability. Apparently it is possible for material particles under quantum conditions to pass through a physical volume which would be denied to them classically.* It is almost as if there were a subtle

---

* From the technical point of view, the kinetic energy of each particle would be negative when measured against the potential energy of the force in the volume. Classical theory does not regard a negative kinetic energy as physically meaningful, but quantum theory does accept it as having a genuine, though very closely defined, physical reality.

mechanism by which a person in particular circumstances could pass from the earth to the moon without the aid of a rocket or other mechanical means. This is a most remarkable affair and is indicative of the severe limitations that must apply to any extension of commonplace concepts and ideas to the atomic world.

One thing is lost by this more general theory and that is the splitting of the spectral lines due to electron spin. Because the electron is not localized it cannot be pictured in a simple way as spinning about an axis like a particle. This often happens in the processes of generalization: a simple pictorial extension of an initial model has no immediate counterpart in the more rigorous and polished discussion that supersedes it. A further generalization is often required to retrieve the refinement so easily won initially. In the case of the fine-structure effect of the spectral lines, the generalization is made by realizing that the Schrödinger equation refers to non-relativistic physical systems. The theory must be replaced by a relativistic form—this will be considered in a later section.

The wave theory of Schrödinger had other successes. Thus, it accounts properly for the quantized form of the harmonic oscillator, including the one-half quantum number given by the Heisenberg theory and referred to at p. 216. Indeed, the physical results to which it leads are entirely equivalent to those provided by the Heisenberg approach. This is no accident, for Schrödinger was able to show that his theory and that of Heisenberg are mathematically equivalent, and corresponding steps in the two approaches can be recognized in applications to a given physical problem. The difference between the work of Heisenberg and that of Schrödinger is simply one of mathematical formalism. Whereas Heisenberg retained the classical form of the equations of motion by introducing a generalized number (the matrix) as an expression of physical observables, Schrödinger retained the classical wave picture by replacing the classical equations of motion by more general rules. This shows that there need be no unique mathematical description of a given physical system: there is generally a choice of description, the choice being taken purely on the grounds of convenience of calculation in any specific case.

Uncertainty in Physics

In the previous sections we have built up an interpretation of the experimental study of atomic phenomena using the concept of wave-motion. Electrons and protons, which are so unmistakably particulate in some circumstances, are equally unmistakably wave-like in others. It is necessary to reconcile the mechanical (particulate) properties of matter with the undulatory (non-mechanical) description. Clearly it is not possible for both a mechanical *and* a non-mechanical description to apply exactly and simultaneously. Physics is in essence concerned with the acceptance of reality and it is necessary now to face squarely the reality of the surprising particle–wave duality. This is done by accepting an uncertainty in our knowledge of the physical world summarized by Heisenberg in 1927, and now well-established as a central part of the structure of physics.

To understand the nature of this uncertainty let us attempt to make a classical specification of an electron; that is, let us see how we might determine experimentally the momentum of the electron at a definite location. This means that we wish to determine simultaneously the momentum and position of the electron, which is a very respectable thing to want to do. The electron is very small, and in order to find out precisely where it is we would use a narrow beam of light. We would then observe the electron so illuminated through a microscope to obtain great precision in locating it. The limitation on locating an object is fixed entirely by the wave-length of the light used to illuminate it. The object illuminated sets up a surrounding diffraction pattern whose characteristic size is the length of the waves of the radiation used for the illumination. This gives the scale of the details that can be observed. To observe finer details, it is necessary to reduce the length of the waves, and this can be achieved by passing to waves of very short length (so-called γ-rays) which are far too small to be in the optical region of the electromagnetic spectrum. But the position can, so we might suppose, be observed by using a suitable microscope (a fictional 'γ-ray microscope') and no difficulty would be encountered in the process. But to say this is to forget that the radiation must be treated as corpuscular in its interaction with the electron, the energy of the γ-ray photon being proportional to the frequency of the γ-radiation. The smaller the wave-length (necessary to ensure the greatest precision in locating the electron), the greater the frequency of the γ-radiation and so the greater the energy associated with each photon. The collision between a γ-ray photon and a free electron is precisely the effect discussed by Compton (see 1. 300) using X-rays. The greater the energy of the photon, the greater the effect it has on the electron when it collides with it. By locating the electron even more accurately, we introduce a progressively greater inaccuracy into the motion of the electron (i.e. into the observed momentum). It would seem from this example that the γ-ray microscope does not allow both the position of the electron *and* its momentum to be ascertained to a high degree of accuracy. Of course, we can locate the electron more and more accurately if we are not concerned with the momentum at all, and vice versa: but we cannot do the two things together.

Other experimental arrangements are no more helpful. Suppose, instead of employing a γ-ray microscope, we send electrons of given energy through a narrow slit. Then, surely, the electron-energy (and so its momentum) can be very closely controlled (such as by accelerating it through an electrical potential-difference of known magnitude), and the slit can be very narrow. We cannot, of course, observe a single electron here—we must experiment with a beam containing many electrons. But this is not critical, for the idea is the same however many electrons there are. The idea would be good if the electron had no wave properties, but in practice it is found that the electron beam is diffracted by the narrow slit (see p. 210), the spreading effect being the greater the narrower the slit. Of course, if the slit were of width less than the diameter of an electron (assuming an electron to have a diameter) then no electrons would pass through anyway. Apparently our conclusions are the same as before even though our methods are different. We still have not found a method of determining simultaneously the position and momentum of the electron.

These two experiments, and others that are equivalent, can be analysed mathematically in great detail and a relationship deduced between the error involved in measuring the momentum and the corresponding error involved in measuring the position. This analysis was first conducted by Heisenberg (1927); the subsequent analyses of equivalent physical situations have always led to the same conclusion, viz. that the uncertainty in the value of the momentum of the electron multiplied by the uncertainty in the location of the electron is of the same order of magnitude as the Planck constant of action. Certainly Planck's constant has a very small value, but it is not zero. Absolutely precise information about either the momentum or the location must be accompanied by complete ignorance of the corresponding location or momentum. If you wish to have simultaneous information about location and motion, each must be open to some uncertainty which is inherent in the situation and has nothing whatever to do with any experimental errors that may be present because of the fallibility of man, the experimenter

This relation between the uncertainties of the simultaneous position and momentum of the electron is one example of the uncertainty relation of Heisenberg.

We might notice in passing that if Planck's constant were equal to zero then both the momentum and the location of the electron can be specified to arbitrary accuracy because each uncertainty can then be zero. This is the classical case; once again, classical results re-emerge when Planck's constant is set equal to zero.

We have so far not thought about the energy, nor have we considered the time taken for an event to occur. Let us consider the problem of measuring the time of some event, say the passage of a wave of known wave-length past a chosen point in space. Because the wave is supposed to be of a single wave-length, the total wave-train must be of indefinite length, containing an infinite number of wave-lengths. We can only view the wave by superimposing another wave-train on to it (e.g. see p. 202) and this destroys the single wave-length property of the wave-train. The observation of the passage of the superimposed marking wave can be made by using some shutter mechanism: the shutter time can be made smaller only by sharpening the marker. But the marker can be made sharper only by combining more wave-lengths together, which means increasing the frequency spread. Now, the energy of the photons is proportional to the frequency, and it follows that the more precisely we know the time that an event occurred the less we know about the energy involved. Other equivalent analyses lead us to the conclusion, entirely analogous to the case when the location and momentum are involved, that the uncertainty in the energy involved in some process multiplied by the uncertainty in the time which the process lasts is of the same order of magnitude as the Planck constant of action. This is another example of the Heisenberg uncertainty relation.

We are familiar with such pairs of variables quite independently in classical theory where they are called conjugate quantities. We can, then, follow Heisenberg and enunciate a general principle of indeterminacy or uncertainty by asserting that the maximum-possible accuracy attainable in the description of any physical process is such that the product of the uncertainties in the measured values of two observed conjugate quantities necessary to describe the action for the process is of the same numerical order of magnitude as Planck's constant (i.e. 6.55×10^{-27} erg sec.). This empirical deduction from many experiments is an expression of the limitation that is inherently imposed on our ability to describe microscopic (molecular, atomic, and sub-atomic) processes. We will refer to it as Heisenberg's uncertainty principle.

Before making general deductions from this principle, it is important to be clear what it does and does not say. To begin with, it is not concerned with accidental errors of measurement that might be progressively eliminated by improving the measuring techniques themselves or improving the skill of the observer. What is referred to is an indeterminacy of principle which cannot be eliminated whatever we try to do. The reconciliation between the particle and wave aspects of matter and radiation can be effected only by not being allowed exact information about both at once: perfect information about the particle aspect precludes any information about the wave aspect, while perfect information about the wave aspect precludes a knowledge of the particle aspects.

The indeterminacy refers only to the one system under consideration and does not apply outside this. For instance, the uncertainty in the knowledge of the momentum of one particle is not related to the uncertainty in the knowledge of the location of a second, independent particle. The uncertainty statement is only to apply to conjugate variables; independent systems remain independent in the theoretical description. This statement, incidentally, already has an expression in the Heisenberg matrix approach outlined in the last section. Only conjugate variables, referring to one single aspect of the particle, satisfy the non-commutativity rule: otherwise the variables commute as in classical theory. As an example, consider the components of the momentum and location of a particle in a particular direction, say along the x-direction. The product of the component of the momentum and the corresponding component of the position of the particle, measured from some standard reference point, is not equal to the product of the position and the momentum in that order, that is the reverse order. These two variables therefore do not commute and their difference is essentially equal to the Planck constant of action. But the product of the component of the momentum in the x-direction multiplied by the component of the location in another direction, say the y-direction, is independent of the ordering of the momentum and position: one component of the momentum *does* commute with *another* component of the position. Classical arguments apply when the products commute, but quantum arguments apply when the products do not commute. In this way, the wave and particle aspects of matter and radiation are reconciled in a natural way. It is not necessary now to restrict the use of quantum theory to Monday, Wednesday, and Friday, and classical theory to the other days. Through the use of the uncertainty principle these two aspects are blended into a unity which applies all the time.

Formal Developments and Interpretations

The wave mechanics of Schrödinger, and the equivalent matrix theory of Heisenberg, can account for a wide range of atomic and molecular phenomena in direct, quantitative terms. The pictorial description of matter-waves associated with the Schrödinger representation in particular calls for a firm physical interpretation of the waves. There was much discussion at first about the physical association to be assigned to these waves but the interpretation that is now universally adopted was first proposed by Born. According to this, the matter-waves have no physical existence, but the square of the amplitude of the wave at any point (called the wave intensity at the point) is a measure of the probability of finding the associated particle at the point in question. Apparently there is to be no absolute certainty of finding a material atomic particle at a chosen position in a volume available to it, but only a greater or smaller probability for doing so. The certainty characteristic of classical theory has been replaced by a controlled uncertainty summarized in the Heisenberg indeterminacy principle set down in the last section.

This circumstance allows us to make a much more acceptable description of various physical processes using quantum theory than has been possible so far. Let us give three examples that we have discussed in previous sections. In the discussion of the Bohr theory of the atom and its generalization (see I. 306 and also p. 198 above) we saw that the spectral lines observed in practice are envisaged as arising from the spontaneous jump of an electron from one allowed orbit to another of lower energy; the energy excess is radiated with the frequency of the spectral line. We raised the question of the exact nature of the jump between the energy states. Using wave mechanics and the uncertainty principle of Heisenberg the question receives a definite, if rather complicated, answer. To begin with the stable orbits of the electrons are not a type of railway line for the electron to run on but are instead a three-dimensional shell of probability. An electron (now not treated as a simple particle) is everywhere within the atom at once, but with a much higher probability of being in one region of space than another. The exact details of this probability distribution depend on the external circumstances. Exciting stimuli from outside (such as an inter-action with another atom through a collision, or with a photon of energy) can cause a redistribution of the probability distribution within the atom and a consequent rearrangement of the energy. But Heisenberg's uncertainty principle holds good and it is not possible to pin-point a time-sequence of events in the classical, everyday manner. The correspondence between this interpretation and that to be expected from the Heisenberg (matrix) representation is quite clear. The questions raised by making an entirely literal mechanical study of the Bohr theory of the atom disappear because we can claim now that such a study is meaningless!

At p. 221 we met the extraordinary result that a proton, or an alpha-particle, with a particular energy can, under appropriate circumstances, pass through a region from which it would be excluded on classical arguments because it did not have enough energy. We talked of the seeping of the matter-waves through the excluded region, and that sort of language hardly sounds scientific. Things appear better, however, when interpreted in terms of a probability. For it turns out on the basis of the mathematics associated with the Schrödinger equation that the wave amplitude is strong in those regions which would be available to the particle anyway on the basis of classical theory, but is not zero in classically-excluded regions. To be sure, the amplitude is strongly damped, but it does not vanish abruptly. This means that, interpreting the matter-wave in terms of a probability, there is a definite probability, small perhaps but not zero, of the 'particle' penetrating into a region from which it would be entirely excluded classically. If the thickness of the excluded region is not too great, the wave amplitude may not actually decay to zero across it: the amplitude emerges at the other side and is then onwards undamped, as it always is in a region from which the 'particle' is not classically excluded. In terms of the probability interpretation of matter-waves, the 'particle' has a probability 'tunnel' through the excluded region, and it is possible for the particle to pass through this region. We must not ask questions about the physical circumstances of the particle inside the excluded region; we can only accept that the particle can pass through. It is on this basis that the emission of an alpha-particle in the radioactive disintegration of uranium, and the selective absorption by the nucleus of the low-energy proton, can find a place in our discussion.

The interpretation of matter-waves as probability distributions in space or in momentum has a number of very strange consequences.

In particular, it has a very profound effect on our views of causation. The ideas of cause and effect are very basic indeed, arising from firm experience in everyday life. Hit a golf ball properly with the appropriate golf club and the ball will move according to a predictable trajectory, and so on. We know as a part of our experience that cause and effect are linked indissolubly together. Nothing occurs without a cause. Classical theory is quite firm in linking cause and effect. Thus, according to the second law of particle motion (see I. 258), the application of a force on a body will provide a change in the momentum of the body which is unambiguously calculable. It is a further assertion in the classical theory that any physical system can be specified exactly in terms of the location of the elements of the system, and their speed at each instant of time. When once a given system is set into motion, under the action of a set of forces that is fully prescribed initially, the future behaviour of the system can be calculated to any desired degree of accuracy by applying the established laws of particle motion. Nothing here is left to chance; everything is pre-ordained in the initial specification. We have used rather emotive words purposely because the arguments of classical physics have been applied by some writers in the past to the wider content of human behaviour to suggest that the full behaviour of a person could, in principle at least, be reduced to such a calculation. More than this, the idea has been applied to the whole evolution of the world from which the conclusion is snatched that, according to the classical arguments of physics, the whole evolution of the universe was determined by God in the very process of creation. While this may be comforting to the sinner who is happy as he is, this whole argument proved embarrassing to religious apologists who insisted on the existence and value of free will. It is important to notice this apparent contradiction between the material determinism of classical physics and the Christian doctrine of free will. Of course, we saw at I. 280 that the uncompromising determinism of classical physics could not be given practical expression for complicated systems: if it were true that the future behaviour of a real gas is fixed when the location and velocity of each constituent molecule is specified at some initial time, there would still be so many molecules to specify that the whole process is outside the realms of the possible. This was, indeed, the very reason why statistical arguments were developed in classical physics. But nevertheless, as a matter of principle, classical physics is remorseless in its full determinism, even though it is not possible to be certain that every relevant influence (i.e. cause) on the physical system has been adequately accounted for. If the cause is perhaps only ill-defined, strict causality becomes no more than a postulated ideal.

Not so quantum theory. The uncertainty principle of Heisenberg, and the whole conception of quantum physics, asserts from the very beginning that no physical situation can be specified exactly even in principle. The universe has an element of uncertainty built in; it is not possible to focus on all things at the same time. This has nothing whatever to do with human errors of measurement—we look at the world through a lens that has a restricted depth of focus. If we wish to enter metaphysics we might argue that quantum physics is fully compatible with at least a limited amount of free will. This may be interesting as a comment in passing which could possibly have implications outside physics, but (more important for our present purposes) it has serious implications for physics itself. Because every physical system is indeterminate to at least a limited degree, it is never possible, on the basis of quantum arguments, to make a deterministic calculation of the classical type. There will always be some uncertainty in both the effect and the cause; the invariable relation between these two aspects of a process is blurred. Of course, quantum physics will never provide the nonsensical result that the effect precedes the cause, but it will not associate every aspect of an effect with a closed, well-specified cause. Probability has entered, and a cause will have at best most-probable, but not certain, effects. The probability of a particular effect may be very high, so high indeed as to amount to a virtual certainty, but the certainty will never be complete. The classical idea of cause and effect must be modified, and this means that the description of the motion of a quantum system must involve statements about average behaviour and the probability of one outcome in comparison with another one that is possible though perhaps unlikely. The quantum world is at root a statistical world: nothing is certain, but only more or less likely.

The state of a physical system at a chosen time can be calculated in terms of a probability function (for example, the wave function of the Schrödinger theory). This function can be expressed in terms of the position-co-ordinates of all the components of the system, or alternatively the momentum-co-ordinates, although a mixed position/momentum specification is barred. The evolution of the physical system in time is calculated from an equation involving time. It has the form of a relation between the state of the system at one time and the change of the state with the time. For the Heisenberg theory this equation is essentially the same as the classical equation of motion, except that the physical variables are expressed in matrix terms. For the Schrödinger theory, the equation is the wave equation involving time. But in each case, the rate of change of the physical variable is involved, and not a second or higher rate of change. The equation is closely similar to the diffusion equation of classical theory and both are continuity equations.

Because the present state of the physical system is expressed in terms of a probability, and the future state of the system depends upon the present state, the uncertainty about the system in a very real sense increases with the time. When we conduct an experiment on the macroscopic system to determine its state the apparatus used by the observer is a macroscopic structure which is supposed to be a classical structure. The state of the system is polarized by such a measurement, and can be fully specified according to the quantum conditions and concepts. The state of the system at a later time can be calculated in terms of a probability, interpreted as the relative likelihood of that particular state being observed in a later experiment if one is made. The elaboration of the details of the development of quantum theory is entirely beyond the scope of this chapter. Suffice it to say that the 1930s were a period of great theoretical activity when the subtle implications of the theory were worked through by physicists and mathematicians of great, and sometimes of outstanding, ability. Particularly we must mention the work of P. A. M. Dirac (b. 1902) and J. von Neumann: these two men transformed the theory by their work, the full implications of which may not have been fully utilized even today.

Of special importance is the generalization of the theory to include relativistic effects. Again, this is unfortunately beyond our present scope to discuss in any detail. The essential development was the relativistic theory of the electron, developed by Dirac, although an earlier attempt at the problem had been made by Klein and Gordon. Dirac found that the appropriate mathematical form of the theory was that involving matrices (see p. 213). The relativistic theory provides the fine-structure of the spectral lines which was earlier ascribed to electron spin. But more than this, the theory predicts a dual particle to the electron, the same in every degree such as mass and strength of electric charge, except that it carries a positive electric charge instead of the negative charge of the electron. The new particle is the positron, known also experimentally. In fact experiment shows that the positron differs from the electron in that it has a great affinity to react with a negative electron, and so to disappear. The electron is a stable particle, whereas the positron is not. The disappearance act is highly interesting. The positron and electron combine with some violence and become converted into a photon of radiation with energy equal to the sum of the rest-masses of the electrons. The original particles are annihilated. This annihilation process satisfies the conservation requirements of energy (including mass on the relativistic theory) and of momentum. It may be necessary for a third body (for example, the nucleus of an atom) to be present to allow these conservation requirements to be met. This will certainly be true in the reverse process of creation, where a photon of sufficient energy can, under the appropriate circumstances, convert into an electron and a positron (a so-called electron-pair). The interconvertibility between matter and energy is now demonstrated completely.

In the Laboratory

Physics is an experimental science, and while it might be expected that theory and experiment will keep very close contact, the theoretical aspects at any time being reflected in the experiments being performed and the experiments being reflected in the theory being pursued at that time, this is true to only a limited extent. Experiment and theory each have an individual and characteristic coherence which can make each aspect of physics in some ways self-contained. Provided that this self-containment does not go too far, it is healthy that each aspect shall not become the handmaiden of the other. An investigation, whether experimental or theoretical, should develop as an organic whole and not be restricted excessively by outside criteria. Of course, it must be tied within the general area of the subject; theoretical discussion can only proceed on the basis of firm and reliable experimental data, and experimental data can only be interpreted within the range of established theory. The independence of theory and experiment has provided rich dividends in the past. The wave aspects of matter were first explored theoretically and experiment has consistently turned up new and quite unexpected phenomena to delight all physicists. Such an unexpected harvest came about in the period under discussion with the experimental discovery of three new particles.

Radioactivity was discovered experimentally by Becquerel (1896) and studied by P. and M. Curie (1898), Rutherford and Soddy (1902), and many other workers. This is a situation whereby the atoms of certain radioactive substances (such as radium) spontaneously change into different atoms. These also may be unstable a sequence of changes resulting. The end product of these changes is lead. This spontaneous change is quite random in its character. The decay process is described in terms of the half-life of an atom, which is the time needed for the atom to have a 50–50 chance of having decayed or not. This time varies from one species of radioactive atom to another and the known life-times range between a milli-second and thousands of years. The rate of radioactive decay found in nature cannot be accelerated or retarded by any known means; it does not, for instance, depend upon the temperature of the radioactive material nor does the external pressure have any effect. The decay process is, so it seems, entirely random. Irrespective of age or any other variable, one atom out of the multitude decays for no obvious reason: a nucleus that may have been stable for millions of years disintegrates quite spontaneously. And this is done according to the rules of pure chance. The effect is quite distinctive and the loss of atoms obeys precisely the same rules that would describe the mortality rate of soldiers on a battlefield if bullets were sent completely aimlessly among them. It is difficult to avoid thinking that fate itself controls the process of radioactive decay, which is another way of saying that, for the present at least, we know nothing of the nuclear rules that control it.

The radioactive decay of an atom can be accompanied by the emission of an α-particle (a helium nucleus), a β-ray (which is a fast-moving electron), or a γ-ray (electromagnetic radiation of extremely high frequency, higher than for an X-ray), or in some cases a combination of these three entities. These rays were useful in the 1920s as projectiles for the investigation of other atoms, because at that time artificial methods were not available to provide such a source of energetic, penetrating particles. These particles will cause the disintegration of other nuclei that they might strike and, by studying the products of such a disintegration, valuable information can be inferred about the structure of the target nucleus. Experiments of this type formed the basis of investigations of nuclear structure during this period. For example, Bothe and Becker in 1930 discovered that both lithium and beryllium atoms give off γ-rays when they are bombarded by α-particles. I. Joliot-Curie and F. Joliot discovered, in 1932, rays produced by bombarding beryllium with α-particles with the property that, if these rays fall on a substance containing hydrogen (for example, paraffin), the substance gives off fast protons (with a speed as high as one-tenth the speed of light). Chadwick slightly earlier (1931) had found related effects experimentally. The fast protons could not have been produced by γ-rays, a conclusion that follows from unsuccessful attempts to understand such processes on the basis of the conservation of energy and the conservation of momentum.

Chadwick (1932) interpreted these experimental data by asserting that the new radiation emanating from beryllium bombarded by α-particles consists of heavy particles which do not carry an electric charge. N. Feather in the same year confirmed this interpretation using the Wilson cloud chamber (see I. 303). The ionization characteristics are those of a neutral particle with a mass very similar to that of a proton; this particle is called a neutron. The neutron is now a well-established particle of physics, as a result of a detailed experimental study of its properties. Particularly important is the very large penetrating power of the neutrons (the neutron is affected by the atomic nucleus but not by the outer electrons), and the dependence of the neutron absorption on the number of nuclei per unit volume instead of on the nuclear mass as for charged particles and for radiation.

Further experiments with neutrons led to new discoveries. For instance, it was found that neutrons of appropriate energy could penetrate certain nuclei, causing them to explode with the expulsion of a range of particles (Feather (1932), Harkins (1932), Fermi and collaborators (1934)). In many cases the neutron is absorbed into the nucleus to form an unstable structure which then, a very short time later, disintegrates. This artificial radioactivity brought about by neutron bombardment is comparable to the disintegration brought about by α-particles (Rutherford (1919)), protons (Cockcroft and Walton (1932)), and γ-rays (Chadwick and Goldhaber (1934)). An important feature of this work is the introduction and development of the technology of producing a copious stream of the various particles necessary for the bombardment processes. The whole development followed the pioneer work by Cockcroft and Walton who, in 1932, constructed an electrical device for the production of fast protons (for proton energies of about one-quarter the energy associated with the electron rest-mass: this is some sixty times smaller an energy than is possessed by naturally-occurring α-particles). This development was followed by the invention of the cyclotron by Lawrence in 1934 for the production of a beam of fast ions, and the betatron, by Kerst and Serber in 1941, for the production of a beam of electrons. More recently (post-1945), the nuclear pile has provided a strong source of neutrons.

These various devices, and the experiments that they permitted, led to the detailed study of the nucleus of the atom, and the development of nuclear physics as a major branch of physics. The recognition of the strength of the interaction between a neutron and an atomic nucleus soon led to the acceptance of the neutron as a basic constituent of the nucleus. The neutron is not a stable particle but decays to a proton and an electron; the mean life-time of a neutron is a little under twenty minutes. This decay process is the source of electrons for emission as β-particles. The chemical properties of atoms are determined to a large measure by the positive charge on the nucleus, which is balanced by an equal number of extra-nuclear electrons. But the same nuclear charge can be associated with nuclei having the same number of protons but different numbers of neutrons. Such nuclei are called isotopes; virtually all elements have isotopes, first recognized by Aston (1919) using his newly-developed mass spectrograph. As one example, the chemical atomic-weight of naturally-occurring chlorine is measured to be 35·4, on a scale for which the atomic mass of oxygen is 16·00. The mass spectrograph showed that naturally-occurring chlorine is in fact composed of a mixture of two isotopes of chlorine, one with a mass of 35 and another of mass 37. Neon, with an atomic weight of 20·2, has two constituents, of mass 20 and 22 respectively. Isotopic structures can be more complicated than this: xenon has no fewer than nine component isotopes with masses ranging between 124 and 136. Detailed treatment of these matters is perhaps more appropriate to chemistry than physics; but we should notice the isotopic structure of the element uranium.

Uranium has been studied for a long time. As early as 1900, Sir William Crookes was able to show that the element is radioactive. It has an isotopic structure and the isotopes of mass 235 and 238 are particularly important. In 1934, Fermi found that thorium and uranium are each excited into β-ray activity by bombardment with neutrons. Fermi came to the surprising conclusion that in this process one or more substances are formed which are entirely new and extend the periodic table beyond what occurs naturally. This is known to be so today but was entirely unexpected then. Considerable experimental effort went into exploring this new field which culminated in experiments on uranium in 1939 by Hahn and Strassman. These workers found that neutrons cause uranium to break up into two or three large fragments, each fragment being a moderately sized atom. This was a new type of disintegration and was termed fission by Meitner and Frisch. The effect is different for the uranium isotope 235 from that for 238. For, while 238 is disintegrated only by fast neutrons, the isotope 235 is only affected by neutrons having thermal energy. More than this, thermal neutrons themselves are among the fission products, and so are available for the further disintegration of other 235 isotope atoms that might be present. It was found that each uranium atom provides two or three neutrons upon fission. But the relative abundance of the 235 isotope compared with the 238 isotope is very low so that the chance of fission neutrons causing the disintegration of further atoms of the 235 isotope is also low. A chain reaction could occur if the concentration of the 235 component were increased by chemical means, or otherwise. Such a chain reaction has important techno-logical implications because it was found that enormous quantities of energy are released during a fission process. It is well known how these simple experiments were developed, by further experiments and theoretical discussion, into a vast modern technology able to provide on the one hand the unbelievable explosive power of the atomic bomb (where the energy is released over an incredibly small fraction of a second), and on the other hand the controlled release of energy in the industrial nuclear reactor. It is interesting to reflect on the virility of experiment only moderately backed by fundamental theoretical knowledge.

But this is not always the case. For instance, the study of the β-decay of nuclei meets a number of difficulties when the conserva-tion law of energy is applied to it. The measured energy distribution of the emitted β-particles varies greatly from one atom to another of a different kind and there is little systematic progression in the observations. The variations are so large that Bohr was even led to the suggestion that the law of energy conservation does not apply to β-decay processes. Such is our belief in the conservation law that we are loath to abandon it, perhaps the more so for just one physical process. In order to retain the law, Fermi (1934) proposed the hypothesis that a new particle is also ejected in the process of β-decay, which carries no charge (because all the charges can be accounted for) and which has at most only a very small mass (there is no difficulty over the mass balance). This new particle, called the neutrino, carries a large amount of energy with it, indeed enough to balance the deficit in the energy conservation balance. With no charge and virtually no mass (certainly no more than an electron), such a particle could penetrate miles of matter entirely unhindered and would be virtually impossible to detect experimentally. The neutrino is now an established and respectable particle of physics and we shall have more to say about it in volume III. From our present point of view it is interesting to notice the devious method of experiment—a new particle has been discovered experimentally even though we might seem to be stretching our credulity in the process. Actually, things are not as vague as this. The ejection of a neutrino from a nucleus is somewhat like the ejection of a shell from a gun: the ejection of the shell causes the gun to recoil, and the ejection of a neutrino from a nucleus will cause the nucleus to recoil. Measurements of the nuclear recoil can be used to determine the presence of the neutrino. This approach was put to the experimental test by Leipunski (1936) and Crane and Halpern (1938, 1939) using heavy nuclei; evidence in favour of the existence of the neutrino was obtained by these means. A particularly favourable element for this experiment is the radioactive isotope of beryllium, with a mass of only 7 units. For here a rather special decay process occurs in which only the neutrino is expelled. This was realized by Allen, who performed the experiment in 1942. From experiments such as these the existence of the neutrino has now been fully substantiated.

Let us turn to another topic where experiment provided an unexpected, new particle. This is the positron already referred to at p. 231 in connection with Dirac's relativistic theory of the electron. Actually the positron was first found experimentally; the Dirac theory refers to a particle which is a stable counterpart of the electron, but the positron is very unstable. The positron was discovered by Anderson in 1933 during studies of certain aspects of cosmic radiation. This is very energetic radiation composed of atomic particles which enter the earth's atmosphere from outside. The study of cosmic radiation has been a major branch of physics in the past and even today the origin of the cosmic radiation is still not quantitatively understood. The radiation causes atomic disintegration of some of the atoms in the earth's atmosphere, and the products of these disintegrations reach the surface of the earth. Anderson was studying such products using a Wilson cloud chamber, and noticed a particle which gave the same ionization track as an electron, but which curved in the opposite direction when passed through a magnetic field maintained from outside the chamber. Further study of this particle has established it as a true particle of physics.

Mesons: The First of the New Particles

We have seen how experiments involving cosmic rays led to the discovery of positrons. Further studies also led to recognition of a new species of particles, destined to be of key importance in the post-1945 development of physics. Although it was not fully recognized at the time, these further studies were to be a prelude to the discovery of a new world of physics, the world of sub-atomic 'elementary' particles.

The new species of particles was discovered from the careful study of ionization tracks in a Wilson cloud chamber, caused by the passage of atomic fragments resulting from the interaction of cosmic rays with atmospheric nuclei. The most characteristic property of the new particles leaving these tracks is their very great penetrating power when compared to that of electrons. They are also unstable, being found subsequently to have a mean lifetime of only a few millionths of a second. This is certainly a very short time on the scale of everyday affairs, but it soon came to be recognized as long on the time-scale to be associated with elementary particles (which is some million million million times smaller—but more of this in volume III). The new particles were found to carry an electric charge, which could be either positive or negative. This presumably implies two types of complementary particles, with the possibility of a third type which does not carry an electric charge. Great penetrating power implies a large mass; it was at first thought that protons were being observed, but protons carry only a positive charge and experiments on the new particles showed negative charges as well. In fact, Williams and Pickup showed in 1938 that the mass of each of the new particles was about one-tenth that of a proton, which is about two hundred times that of an electron. Because the new particles are intermediate in mass between that of the proton and that of the electron, they were called mesons, from the Greek for 'middle'.

Actually, the existence of a particle like the meson had been predicted theoretically by the Japanese theoretical physicist Yukawa (b. 1907) in 1935, three years before such a particle was observed experimentally. Yukawa was led to his prediction by the general study of the interaction between a proton and a neutron. Neutrons and protons are the primary constituents of all nuclei, and occur in approximately equal numbers. The simplest compound nucleus is that of helium, which consists of two neutron–proton pairs (two rather than one because of the two possible spin-orientations of the pair which may be either exactly parallel or exactly anti-parallel). The helium nucleus (i.e. the α-particle) is particularly stable. Again, deuterium is a heavy isotope of hydrogen, having a nucleus of a proton–neutron pair (this isotope is heavier than the more common hydrogen with a single proton for a nucleus, thus accounting for the heaviness of heavy water). The distance between a proton and a neutron in a nucleus is about 10^{-13} centimetres, which is a half or a third the nuclear diameter. Protons and neutrons are attracted together by some special force, and Yukawa set out to discover its nature.

Because the proton is electrically charged but the neutron is not, the attractive nuclear force cannot have a simple electric origin. Using hindsight, we will call this force the meson force, although the use of the word 'force' in this connection is not entirely a happy one. To progress further we must use analogy. We can specify the characteristics of the electric force, and we will use this knowledge by supposing that both the proton and neutron carry a new type of charge, called now the mesonic charge. It differs from the ordinary electric charge, so we will now assert, by having an effective range comparable to the size of a representative nucleus (something like 10^{-13} centimetres) rather than a range comparable to the size of an atom (which characterizes electric forces between protons and electrons). The mesonic force is thus very short-ranged, having something like one ten-thousandth the effective range of the electric force.

The fact that a neutron and a proton form a stable doublet unit reminds us of the stability of certain molecules, thinking now on the much larger molecular scale. The cohesive force for molecules was shown, on the basis of the application of quantum mechanics to the chemistry of molecules, to be due to exchange forces, according to which one or more electrons are the common property of each constituent atom. The wave-structure of the electron forms a sort of cocoon around the constituents, providing the observed chemical saturation properties of the molecules. Heisenberg in 1932 proposed the same exchange mechanism as the origin of the peculiar affinity between protons and neutrons. More specifically, it was proposed that the meson field is able to act as a vehicle for the transfer of the electric charge between the proton and the neutron. In rather crude terms, the proton is regarded as being a neutron with a positive charge, and the binding mechanism is the transference of this charge between the two particles of the doublet. In this way a proton–neutron pair becomes a neutron–proton pair, and then a proton–neutron pair again. It is like a game of touch in which neither particle wishes to be caught with the charge. Of course we could instead picture each particle of the pair wishing to possess the charge. The pair can be disrupted by collision with another particle and the meson field excited. Meson waves will be produced and they will be electrically charged. According to the quantum arguments developed earlier (see p. 201), the meson waves will have a particulate structure so that charged meson particles can be expected to be found as the result of such a process.

We have painted a crude semi-classical picture but the concepts developed here can be formulated mathematically within the requirements of special relativity theory. Yukawa carried through the analysis and came to the conclusion that charged meson particles could exist with a mass between 130 and 200 electron masses. The mesons found in cosmic ray studies have just this sort of mass and the identification of these observed particles with those pictured by Yukawa seems quite natural.

Yukawa was led to the conclusion that the mesons will be unstable, as the cosmic ray mesons have been shown to be. In isolation from other particles a meson decays into an electron and a neutrino. Such a decay process was observed in 1940, when photographs were obtained from a Wilson cloud chamber showing a meson track stopping abruptly, with an electron track emerging from the end proceeding in an apparently random direction; the random element is taken away by considering the neutrino. It became clear, however, that the observed particle is not in fact the Yukawa particle, even though the concept of a meson particle has experimental support. The whole story of these elementary particles will concern us in volume III, where we will see that, even though the first-discovered particle of intermediate mass was not the particle predicted by Yukawa, such a particle does indeed exist and is associated with the interaction between the nucleons (nuclear particles).

Quantum-statistical Physics

The probabilistic aspect of quantum physics has become abundantly clear in our arguments so far, as a matter of principle, but we became used to this idea in volume I (part IV of the chapter) as a matter of practical necessity. All that was said there in general physical terms will apply in quantum physics except in the prescriptions allowable for counting the possible states of any given physical system. The Heisenberg uncertainty principle controls the counting process together with the problems of identifying individual atoms and molecules. Individual atoms can be observed, e.g. in a Wilson cloud chamber (where the thickness and length of the ionization track is a measure of the uncertainty of location of the ionizing particle and the mean speed throughout the track measures the uncertainty in the speed), but specifically-chosen particles cannot be observed. The properties of the particles of physics are only defined on the average and particular features are deduced from the collective properties of an astronomically large number of particles. Quantum statistics recognizes this situation explicitly. All the atoms and molecules of a chemically pure substance must be taken as being identical one with another. Consider the description of a physical system using wave mechanics, with each physical state represented by a wave function.

For reasons of mathematical expediency, it is necessary at the present time to represent the wave-function for a total system as being the product of the wave-functions for each separate component particle. The probability of the occurrence of a given state is to be expressed by the square of the appropriate total wave-function (see p. 228). Now, if all the particles composing a chemically pure substance are to be identical then the physical probability will not be affected by an interchange of any two particles. Although the square of the wave-function remains unaffected, we cannot be sure about the wave-function itself (which is not open to measurement) and two possibilities arise. The first is that the interchange of particles does not affect the wave-function in any way: such wave-functions are said to be symmetric. The second is that the interchange simply changes the sign of the wave-function: such wave-functions are said to be antisymmetric. For a particle with an antisymmetric wave-function, interchange of two particles is recognizable in the wave-function; for particles with a symmetric wave-function, interchange of particles leaves the wave-function unaffected. These two possibilities lead to a bifurcation of the statistics of quantum mechanics that affects the development of the theory in a fundamental way.

It is a mathematical consequence of the antisymmetry property that no two particles having such wave-functions can occupy the same quantum state. This situation had earlier been deduced by L. Pauli as applying to planetary electrons in atomic orbits to account for the ordered sequence of different atoms in the periodic table. In its original form (1925) the Pauli exclusion principle expresses the fact that two different electrons cannot occupy the same quantum state and so cannot have the same set of quantum numbers assigned to them. Although deduced for extra-nuclear atomic electrons, the principle applies to electrons everywhere. The present arguments have generalized the expression of the principle, first to the statement that an electron is to be assigned an antisymmetric wave-function, and then to the proposition that all particles having an antisymmetric wave-function will obey the Pauli principle. This is how the generalization comes about in physics. Other particles that are known experimentally to obey the Pauli exclusion principle are protons and neutrons, and indeed all particles with a half odd-integral spin. Particles with an odd-integral spin (being two half odd spins) have a symmetric wave-function and do not obey the Pauli principle; an example already met with is a photon.

The statistics for the two symmetry-possibilities have characteristic features which make them totally different. The antisymmetric system was expressed mathematically, independently, by Fermi and by Dirac in 1926. The characteristic feature is the expression of the Pauli principle in the form that any element of phase space can contain only one representative point, and the resulting statistics are called the Fermi–Dirac statistics. These statistics have very wide applicability including the properties of electrons in metals, the theory of white-dwarf stars, diamagnetism, and paramagnetism. The alternative statistics, referring to symmetric systems not obeying the Pauli principle, were developed by the Indian physicist Bose (1924) and applied to gases by Einstein (1924, 1925). Here more than one particle can be contained within the same element of phase space. These Bose–Einstein statistics have also been applied widely. One extraordinary application is to electromagnetic radiation, treated from the point of view of photons. The laws of particle statistical-mechanics are applied, but without the condition that photons are conserved in number since they clearly are not; the radiation laws result. Another application is to the collective vibrational motion of ions in a crystal, the quantized particles in this case being the phonons. A third application rests on a peculiar condensation property of Bose–Einstein particles where many members of a large collection can congregate in the zero-energy state, a possibility denied to Fermi–Dirac particles. A practical application is to the transition of liquid helium 4 from phase I to phase II as its temperature falls through the temperature $4 \cdot 2°$K, on the absolute temperature scale. Superconductivity (no ohmic resistance in a very cold conductor of electricity) can also be understood in these terms.

The statistical structure of the physical world plays a major role in modern physics and in a sense all applications of atomic physics rest on statistical arguments. At sufficiently high temperatures both Fermi–Dirac and Bose–Einstein statistics degenerate into the common Boltzmann–Maxwell statistics of the classical theory. The usual link between classical and quantum physics is maintained.

II. The Realm of Stars and Galaxies

In our study of atomic phenomena we have resorted continually to concepts and interpretations derived from the large-scale macroscopic world. This is the world we can see and it is natural for us to extend our quantitative study of it as and when we can. The present century has seen an enormous increase in our numerical awareness of the universe.

Some Background Information

At the beginning of the present century our knowledge of the stars was meagre. It was supposed that they were spread randomly throughout space in a broadly static arrangement. The overall picture was one of a static backcloth unlikely to provide any particular surprises. Our present views of the structure of the universe are very largely the product of the present century—indeed the product of the last forty years. The reader will be aware that our sun is one rather ordinary star in a collection of some thousand million which form the galaxy. He will be aware that, if looked at from afar, the galaxy will look not unlike a flat catherine wheel with spiral arms linked through a central concentration of stellar material. He will also know that our galaxy is one of an enormous number of galaxies, like islands, separated from each other by vast oceans of virtually empty space. But he may not know how this picture came to be constructed, and so we will sketch in the outlines of the story now as an example of the way scientific thought develops. The problem is one of locating various objects in distant space and of assigning a time-scale for their motion; the story is a subtle interplay between observation and theoretical interpretation.

In 1543, Copernicus proposed that the earth should not be thought to be at the centre of the universe. His arguments were based not on new observational data, but on considerations of rationality and simplicity in the reinterpretation of already existing data. The ages-old cosmology of antiquity was now to be abolished, and the way was opened for new discoveries. Still using the authority of rationality and simplicity, Thomas Digges and independently Giordano Bruno conceived the notion, about the year 1576, that each star seen in the sky is very much like our sun. Accepting the new ideas of Copernicus, there arose the problem of distributing the stars in space. In 1750, Thomas Wright suggested that the stars were collected together in a series of conglomerations of many stars, the separate stellar concentrations being scattered throughout space. This idea of island universes of stars, very largely independent of one another, was clarified by Immanuel Kant around 1755, when the general proposition of uniformity was enunciated, it being asserted that any one observer located at one place in the universe will see the same general picture (disregarding accidental local features) as any other observer located anywhere else. This principle of uniformity still plays a vital part today in our understanding of the universe. The first observational support for these ideas came from the work of Sir William Herschel. It was already known that, apart from stars, there are localized nebulosities in space, and in 1735 Herschel was able to resolve some of these into stars. At about the same time Messier was able to list over one hundred such objects and his numbering is still in use today (for example, the nebula in the constellation of Andromeda is referred to as M31, and so on).

The beautiful spiral structure of many galaxies was first seen in 1845 by Lord Rosse who was using his 6-foot-diameter reflecting telescope almost for the first time: he was observing the nebula M51 in the 'handle' of the constellation The Plough. Lord Rosse was able to list fourteen such nebulae eventually, but, because of the faintness of most of these objects, it was only with the advent of the large modern telescopes and photographic methods that the systematic study of the nebulae (or as they are now more usually called, 'galaxies') became feasible. This work in the 1930s was dominated by the data collected by the 100-inch telescope at Mount Wilson observatory; for about 21 years after its completion in 1924 it remained the world's largest telescope. This title has now passed to the 200-inch telescope at Mount Palomar, although several telescopes of this general class are now in use at various observatories and more are planned.

The realization that nebulae are composed of stars is interesting but the major issue is that of setting up a scale of distance. This problem was the cause of great controversies for more than a hundred years, and was only finally solved in 1917. (The reader might notice that the difficulty is still met with today in connection with quasars—but this will concern us in volume III.) The problem of assigning a length-scale to a system is met with throughout physics. It is no more possible to measure *directly* a length of 1,000 million miles than to measure a length of one-millionth of centimetre. In each case we must use indirect arguments based very firmly on theory.

It is clearly not possible to lay out rulers between the stars, nor is it possible (outside the solar system at least) to use any form of radar technique. For stars relatively near to the sun it is possible to measure distances directly by parallax. This is the apparent shift of the star as seen on earth relative to the background of more distant stars; it is due to the movement of the earth in its orbit. Edmund Halley realized the potentialities of this method, using as baseline the diameter of the orbit of the earth (some 180 million miles). But it was Friedrich Bessel who first used the method (in 1838) to obtain a reliable estimate of the distance of a star, 61 Cygni. He obtained a distance of some 66,000,000 million miles, or about one half a million times the distance of the earth from the sun. A month or so later Thomas Henderson showed that Alpha Centauri is about 24,000,000 million miles away—this is, in fact, the nearest star to our sun. These enormous distances are too vast to comprehend, although they become more meaningful when expressed in terms of the time it takes the light to travel from the star to us. Light travels in a vacuum at about 186,000 miles per second, so that in one year it travels 6,000,000 million miles. Thus, the light from 61 Cygni has taken about eleven years to reach us, and that from Alpha Centauri about four years. An alternative unit to the light-year is often used, based on a specific parallax which we cannot go into now; this is the parsec, which is 3·26 light years. Actually the stellar distances found by Bessel and Henderson were not entirely unexpected, for much earlier Newton and Huygens had estimated (on grounds of luminosity) that other stars may be millions of miles away, although they grossly underestimated the distances. The method of parallax is limited in its application to the nearer stars, and in fact the distances of only about 200 stars can be measured this way. Other stars must be treated differently.

The apparent brightness of the stars whose parallax can be measured can be converted to the actual brightness of the star. It is known that the intensity of a light-source decreases with the observer's distance from it, in proportion to the inverse square of the distance. It was found that the actual brightness of these stars (the absolute magnitude) is very much the same for all the stars. If this is taken to be the case universally, then the distances of other stars can be inferred from the measurement of their absolute brightness. (Actually, Newton and Huygens had used this idea before, but they calculated grossly wrong distances because they had no star of known distance to act as a datum.) The distance at which the star would need to be placed in order to show the measured (apparent) luminosity is taken to be the actual distance of the star, in the absence of any obscuring material between the star and the observer. Using this method, with statistical refinements, the galaxy was plotted and its broad outline ascertained: but a new distance beacon was urgently needed. This was provided in 1912, from work by Miss Leavitt, by the Cepheid variable stars, named after Delta Cephei, the prototype of this type of star. It was known that the brightness of certain stars changed periodically in a characteristic way. Miss Leavitt found empirically that a relation exists between the actual brightness of the star and the period of intensity: explicitly, the fluctuation is less rapid the brighter the star. The distance of a few of the near Cepheid variables can be measured by methods of parallax, so here was an absolute distance scale. One of the consequences of having such a scale available was to allow us to be sure that our sun is not anywhere near the centre of our galaxy.

The nebulae remained a difficulty, however, because it was not clear whether they are faint because the stars in them are faint, or because they are a long way away. These two possibilities were hotly debated until 1924, when Edwin Hubble (1889–1953), using the newly-completed 100-inch Mount Wilson telescope, identified Cepheid variables in one or two of the nearer nebulae.* This was accepted as conclusive evidence that the nebulae are separate islands of stars, outside our galaxy and separated from it by enormous distances. As an indication of the general size of a galaxy, they may have a diameter of between 3,000 and 200,000 light-years: the distance between galaxies is generally rather more than a million light-years, i.e. about ten times a galactic diameter. These distances are almost meaningless, for the mind cannot grasp such an enormous distance-scale. We might notice in passing only that the galaxies themselves are not all of spiral structure, but have a wide range of forms.

The Red-Shift

We observe the galaxies by the radiation they emit. In the period under discussion, the optical frequencies were the only ones open to study. Nowadays the radio frequencies are studied in radio

---

* Actually G. W. Ritchey had located an exploding 'nova' star in a nearby nebula and this had indicated that it is outside our galaxy, but this was not accepted as entirely conclusive evidence.

astronomy, and the possibility of removing telescopes into space beyond the absorbing and blanketing effect of the earth's atmosphere promises enormous things for the future because the full range of electromagnetic frequencies will then be available to us. But for the period that concerns us now, only optical properties are relevant. The light received from any galaxy is composed of a spread of different wave-lengths (i.e. colours) and the study of the colours in any particular case (which is the object of spectrometry) can be used to determine a great deal about the physical conditions of the source of the light.

In 1912, the American astronomer Slipher obtained the spectrum of the nebula in Andromeda, which is the nearest galaxy to our own (neglecting the Magellanic clouds). He was able to identify lines in the Andromeda spectrum with corresponding lines known from laboratory studies * and found the surprising result that the spectrum of Andromeda is shifted *en bloc* towards the blue end of the spectrum. By 1917, Slipher had photographed and analysed the spectra of fifteen of the brighter spiral nebulae and found that for thirteen of them the spectrum showed a systematic shift to the red end of the spectrum. Apparently the Andromeda result was the odd man out. The shift of the spectrum to the red in virtually every case was a surprising result, and led to the investigation of the fainter galaxies. These were studied by Humason and Hubble in the late twenties and thirties, and it was observed that all galaxies without exception show a shift of the spectrum to the red end. More than this, Hubble in 1929 proposed the conclusion that the relative shift of each part of the spectrum towards the red is greater the more faint the galaxy in question: apparently there is an inverse dependence of the measure of the red-shift of the spectrum on the measure of the brightness of the galaxy (the apparent brightness). Hubble had already estimated the distance of the nearer galaxies using the Cepheid variables as beacons (see p. 246), and had noticed that each of the galaxies involved in the study had similar intrinsic brightness. If we suppose that all galaxies are essentially comparable in energy output, and so have a comparable intrinsic brightness, then the distance scale of the universe can be extended to include distant galaxies where Cepheid variable stars cannot be resolved or identified. If there is essentially

* The study of the composition of the stars (including the sun) from the detailed study of the spectral lines of the emitted spectra dates from 1814 when J. von Fraunhofer pioneered the technique. Since then it has been continually refined and is now a standard powerful astronomical tool.

no screening gas or obscuring material between the galaxies, then the assumption of equal brightness of all galaxies will allow us to interpret the faintness of any particular galaxy as a measure of its distance from us. Accepting all this, Hubble was able to interpret the observational data by the general conclusion that the relative red-shift of the spectral lines for a galaxy is directly proportional to the distance of the galaxy from us. This is the law of the red-shift, sometimes called Hubble's law. If this relationship is accepted it may then itself be used as a scale of distance: measure the red-shift of a galaxy and use the Hubble law to infer the corresponding distance. Of course, the linear relationship is open to large observational error (10 per cent or more) so that such a length-scale must be statistical. On this basis, galaxies have been observed as much as 7,000 million light-years away. This example shows the difficulty of extending everyday measurements to the universe at large.

Interpretation of the Red-Shift

The Hubble law is presumably the result of some widespread physical process involving the galaxies and the passage of light between them. The immediate interpretation of the law was that based on the Doppler effect. In 1842, J. C. Doppler showed that the actual colour of a light-source as measured by an observer depends upon the relative 'line of sight' motion between the source and the observer. If the source is moving towards the observer, the light is made more blue than it actually is, while conversely if the source is moving away from the observer it appears more red than it should do. This effect is also found with sound waves; the reader will be familiar with the pitch of the whistle from a fast train which becomes steadily higher when the train is approaching and then lower when it is moving away. The effect is common to all waves; the emitted waves are 'compressed' by the approaching source, but 'extended' by the receding source. This effect was applied, in 1868, to the study of the radial velocity of celestial bodies by Sir William Higgins. He was able to show by this means that Sirius is receding from our solar system with a speed of several tens of miles per second. The effect is now well-established: more recently, it has been used to observe the details of the soft landing of an automatic lunar vehicle on the moon.

Suppose the red-shift of the Hubble law is interpreted using the Doppler effect. We then draw the astonishing conclusion that the galaxies are all receding from us.* But the conclusion is the more strange when the speeds are determined. Each million light-years of distance adds about a hundred miles per second to the recessional speed, so that speeds of recession of tens of thousands of miles per second were 'measured' by Humason. At these speeds one could travel to our sun from the earth in about one hour! The furthest galaxy isolated so far using Hubble's law (about 7,000 million light-years away) would have a recessional speed of about two-fifths of the speed of light. These are enormous speeds.

Such a general recession is not to be interpreted as implying that our own galaxy is at the stationary centre of the universe. Any part of the universe is to be statistically the same as every other part, and so we must assert that the same recessional characteristics are to be applied everywhere. The universe, on the basis of Hubble's law and the Doppler effect, is expanding everywhere: we have an expanding universe moving to continually greater dilution. Ultimately each galaxy will be isolated from every other one by untold distances —in the end every galaxy will be alone.

If the galaxies are moving apart today, they were presumably that much nearer together yesterday, and at some time in the past, if the recession had the same characteristics then as today, all the galaxies must have been very close together. This situation of dense packing has been interpreted as the beginning state of the universe, and on present recessional speeds, this would have occurred some 100,000 million years ago: this, on the present interpretation, is the age of the universe. What an extraordinary and exciting conclusion to reach on the basis of careful measurement and scientific analysis; it was even more astonishing in the 1930s because before this the universe had been regarded as essentially static. According to this theory, often referred to as the big-bang theory, all the matter in the universe was originally tightly packed together, but broke up and moved apart with enormous force. Some parts moved off faster than other parts, and so led to the present distribution over distance, and consequently to a linear distance–velocity law.

The concept of the expanding universe depends entirely on the interpretation of the red-shift as a Doppler effect, but this,

* The Andromeda nebula, with a blue-shift, is the one exception. On this basis it is approaching us with a speed of about 125 miles per second: if it continues at this speed it presumably will collide with us in about three hundred million years' time. But our galaxy is known now to be a member of a local group of about seventeen assorted galactic types, and in consequence the Andromeda result can be disregarded as not typical.

presumably, need not be the case. It is possible to suppose the galaxies to be stationary in space with the red-shift arising from some as yet unknown effect of the light as it travels to us over enormous intervals of space, and so of time. As attractive as such an explanation might be, there is no physical process that can be used to account for the observed red-shift without introducing subsidiary effects that are not observed. If the interpretation of observational data is to be made without invoking the Doppler effect, it seems that a new physical principle will need to be isolated. We face a crossroads. The expanding universe is a finite universe, with a beginning and consequently a finite amount of matter, and energy. There is dynamic motion everywhere but it ultimately becomes indefinitely diffuse. The main features of the evolution of such a universe can be envisaged within existing physical theory. On the other hand, if we reject the interpretation of the red-shift as a Doppler effect, we can have an infinite universe without beginning and without end, and containing very little galactic motion. We have to make a choice; a dynamic restricted universe within presently-known physical theory, or an unlimited static universe plus a new physical principle. We might be reminded of Copernicus: he replaced a limited universe (as attributed to Aristotle) by an essentially limitless universe plus a new physical principle (gravitation) although it took a hundred and fifty years or more after his work to isolate the principle. The reader might be excused if he wonders whether the advances in cosmology made between 1543 and 1939 might be of complication but not of principle. This was the observational situation which faced cosmologists in 1939; the story will be continued in volume III. There we will see that a new possibility was raised in 1948, the steady-state universe in which there is a continual creation of matter; this provides the possibility of a dynamic universe of unlimited extent plus the new mysterious physical principle of the continuous creation of matter.

Actually, the ambiguity of interpretation of observation seen above had been foreshadowed long before by Olbers (1826) who asked the simple question: 'Why is the night sky so dark?' Questions that seem to be trivial often lead to fundamental issues, and this is one such. By applying the known laws of physics to a uniform steady distribution of stars virtually at rest in a Euclidean space, Olbers reached the conclusion that an observer inside the system but away from a star should receive a flux of radiation comparable to that at the surface of a star. Put another way, the night sky (where there is no direct light from the sun) should be of enormous brightness because of the accumulated energy radiated from all the stars. Olbers's paradox can be resolved by relaxing certain of his initial premises (for example by introducing new physical principles, but we disregard this possibility now): in effect, this amounts to accepting that the universe has not reached an equilibrium state. This might be because the stars are young (no older than 10^{10} years) or because the stars are in rapid motion. The concept of the expanding universe will satisfy the second possibility; the first possibility raises extreme difficulties of time-scale because this upper limit to be put on the age of the universe is barely larger than the age of the earth itself, estimated by various means to be some 4,000 million years.

The universe is clearly far from the condition of thermodynamic equilibrium. For such equilibrium, the energy radiated by an object should just balance the energy absorbed by it. The presence of stars in a dark sky shows that this is far from the case in practice, the conversion of energy into radiation (which is the action of a star) far exceeding the energy absorbed by matter. Radiant energy must be absorbed by a 'sink'. The red-shift implies a loss of energy because the frequency of the light is decreasing. An expanding universe would provide a sink of energy automatically since work must be done in the expansion against gravitational forces. If the red-shift is not an expansion an alternative energy sink must be sought. Thermodynamic arguments have a wide range of validity.

Cosmology: Model Universes

The interpretation of the red-shift as a velocity of recession implies that the portion of the universe that can be explored by present telescopes is a significant fraction of the whole. On the other hand, if the galaxies are not accepted as receding from us, the sample of the universe that falls within our gaze will not necessarily be a representative sample because the universe may be of infinite extent. The distribution of the galaxies should be different in each of the two cases, and considerable efforts were made in the 1930s to distinguish between the two possible interpretations on the basis of the counting of galaxies in space. But the attempts failed to provide any conclusive answer primarily because the observations could not then be made with sufficient accuracy. It was found, however, that galaxies have a tendency to form limited local groups and this tendency to congregate together in small numbers has more recently been confirmed with modern observational techniques. (Actually, measurement of the distribution of galaxies in space has now been made using radio astronomy, but this is postwar and will have to wait for volume III.) We need to appeal to theory for guidance if the observations are to be interpreted unambiguously.

Historically, cosmology as a numerate study began to be developed in 1917 as a direct consequence of Einstein's theory of general relativity. The theory had been used, it will be remembered, to construct the three 'crucial tests' (see I. 276f.) and its authority at that time was immense. The question naturally arose as to what it had to say about the universe as a whole: modern cosmology was born. Cosmology became an off-shoot of general relativity, but this was unfortunate, for it should be regarded as a study in its own right. Indeed, this became very clear in 1934 when W. H. McCrea and E. A. Milne showed that a consistent cosmology can be built up on the basis of Newtonian theory, and later Sir Arthur Eddington developed a cosmology which need not depend upon general relativity at all. This is consistent with the fact that the three crucial tests refer only to the solar system, and even if they are accepted as true the application of the mathematical equations of general relativity to the regions beyond the solar system must be treated as an assumption whose validity can only be judged by the usefulness of the conclusions to which it leads.

In 1917, when these studies began, the accepted universe was vastly different from that accepted even ten years later. Galaxies had still not really entered into the discussion and the whole concept of the expanding universe was unknown. The stars on the average were thought to have a very small motion, and a static universe was a good first-approximation as a model of what was observed. The universe was regarded as being rather young (no older than a few tens of millions of years): indeed, even later, one of the difficulties of interpreting the red-shift as a recessional speed was that this led to an expansion period considerably shorter than the age of the earth, based on alternative evidence. The difficulty was only resolved after 1945 with the advent of the 200-inch telescope, and the help of radio astronomy.

The application of general relativity (or any other principle for that matter) to cosmology must involve certain simplifying assumptions. To begin with it is logical to accept the validity of the general principle that the appearance of the universe is the same for all observers everywhere. Expressed another way, the universe is homogeneous, all regions being similar to that actually under surveyance. This expresses the necessary criterion that the volume of the world under discussion is a significant sample of the whole universe. This is to be true for all times even though the universe is evolving. Specific account is not to be attempted for the motion of individual galaxies. Rather, the galaxies are to be treated as points without structure moving in response to the motion of a continuous substratum. The actual discrete universe is in this way represented as a type of continuum, and calculations are made on the possible behaviour of the continuum. Finally, interest is focused on the full range of motions allowed by the accepted equations of motion so that we are concerned with a wide range of possible models for the universe. Although the attempt is made to understand the universe in which we find ourselves this is done by comparing it with other possible structures which could have existed but apparently do not, rather than directly treating it as the unique thing that it undoubtedly is. Put in a more mathematical way, interest is focused on the general solution of the equations of motion and observational data are to be used to select that particular solution most applicable to the universe we seem to inhabit.

The first analysis was by Einstein who reached the conclusion (in 1917) that general relativity is compatible with a static universe of finite radius. But the radius is in the four-dimensional space–time of general relativity (see I. 276) so that we have the strange description of a finite universe in space–time but being curved and so having no boundaries in three-dimensional space. We are, in fact, used to this situation in ordinary life: the surface of a sphere (such as the earth) has an area of 12·57 multiplied by the square of the radius of the sphere and so is finite. But in travelling over the surface no boundary bars movement and, provided we accept the geometry of the surface, the 'space' available to us is unlimited. Although we cannot picture four-dimensional space, this three-dimensional analogue is useful as a guide in the interpretation of the mathematical formulae involved. Real material with a positive non-zero density is associated with a positive non-zero pressure and the radius of space–time curvature for the model is real and positive. This would suggest that this static model is physically possible and is unlikely to transgress thermodynamic requirements. Actually Sir Arthur Eddington (1882–1944) showed in 1930 that this Einstein universe involving matter but not motion is not stable. Any accidental condensation of radiation into matter will cause it to expand, while any transference of matter into radiation will cause it to contract. The importance of this work is not in its detailed numerical predictions but in the conclusion that the universe looked at in these terms does not naturally contain a state of truly static equilibrium.

Mach had earlier and independently proposed the view that the property of inertia of a particular element of matter is to be regarded as the result of the interaction between the element and the surrounding matter. Einstein generalized this to become what he termed Mach's principle, according to which the metrical field is determined by the distribution of matter and energy in the universe. This relationship can be formalized by the introduction of a cosmological constant; the constant would have a positive value for an expansion but a negative value for a contraction.

The Einstein universe of matter without motion satisfies Mach's principle but other models proved possible. The first generalization was proposed by de Sitter in 1917 simultaneously with Einstein's work. De Sitter showed that a space–time metric exists which satisfies the field equations of general relativity and yet which is associated with zero density and pressure for matter and radiation. The de Sitter universe is one of motion without matter and so is the diametrically-opposite limit to the Einstein case. In fact the de Sitter universe is the limiting case approached by all models which show a continuous expansion in time.

With the Einstein and de Sitter universes known, more alternatives became recognized due particularly to the work of Lemaitre, Robertson, Weyl, Lanczos, Tolman, Eddington, and others. A wide range of characteristics came to light and by the mid-thirties it was realized that the existing laws of physics do not of themselves hint at a unique evolutionary development for the universe. Present notions are consistent with either a universe that is expanding indefinitely from a restricted high-density core (ultimately becoming indefinitely dilute), the core either resting in equilibrium for some time and expanding as the result of an instability, or expanding on formation; or a universe that is contracting from an initial state of great dilution; or an oscillating universe expanding for one time-interval and contracting in the next. And if a new principle of physics is suitably constructed, a static universe can be constructed where there is plenty of matter but no motion. The matter and radiation in these models is supposed constant overall, but in 1948 Bondi, Gold, and Hoyle extended the analysis by proposing the possibility of the constancy of mass (and so of energy) more locally by the continuous creation of matter throughout the universe. In this way the conservation principles for matter and radiation can be preserved locally for all time; otherwise, they will have only ephemeral value although this would not be detectable in our laboratories now because the time-scale for change would need to be measured in hundreds, if not thousands, of millions of years. It will be realized that these various cosmological models are associated with ambiguity over the time-element in the universe; theory can accept a universe with a finite past and an infinite future, or an infinite past and an infinite future. It offers no reason why the universe (as opposed to the solar system, see below, p. 260) should end, and can only account for a beginning by accepting an irrational situation at some finite time in the past, which cannot be discussed quantitatively because conditions then would be outside the scope of our present physical laws.

These cosmological studies lead to a wide range of possible model universes, characterized by three variables: one is the distribution of the galaxies in space which determines the density of matter in space; another is the curvature of the metric; and the third is the cosmological constant. The particular model that best fits the observed universe can only be ascertained by direct observation. And the interpretation of the observations themselves must depend upon a decision as to whether the red-shift is associated with an expansion or not. The reason is clear; in assessing the distribution of galaxies in space, as a first step in obtaining a smeared-out density for use in the cosmological model, it is necessary to relate all information to the same time-instant and this can be done only if we can assign particular motion to the individual galaxies. This whole problem of interpretation is both interesting and important and it is unfortunate that we have no space to consider it now. Suffice it to say that the best observational data available in the late thirties favoured (though did not uniquely isolate) an expanding universe of positive radius of curvature of 470 million light-years, a smeared-out mean positive density of a little less than 10^{-26} grammes per cubic centimetre, and a positive cosmological constant (interpreted by Eddington as representing the large-scale cosmical repulsion exemplified in the expanding galaxies) of value $4 \cdot 5 \times 10^{-18}$ (years)$^{-2}$. The universe is therefore of finite volume and is relatively small. Indeed, the 100-inch telescope can penetrate to a distance of about 100 million light-years, which is almost a quarter of the radius of curvature. We are, therefore, observing a very representative sample of the whole universe. If the red-shift is not a Doppler shift, theory can also account for the observational data in terms of a static universe of infinite extent, but with the spatial curvature adjusted suitably. One difficulty in accepting the expanding-universe model at this time, which we have referred to already, was the time-scale. The age of the universe (measured since expansion started) could not be much in excess of 500 million years, which is less than the age of the earth and which is hardly large enough to allow the known evolutionary features of the universe to occur. This is the dilemma that faced cosmologists in the late thirties; an expanding universe involving the established laws of physics but with far too short a life-span since expansion started, or a universe not expanding but which can only be understood if a new principle of physics is isolated to allow the red-shift to be interpreted without invoking the Doppler effect.

Other Approaches to Cosmology

The difficulties outlined in the last section make it profitable to explore alternative descriptions of the universe at large. A central feature of these various arguments is the assertion that the laws of physics cannot be separated from the universe at large because there could be no laws without the universe and no recognizable universe without the laws. As a corollary it follows that the behaviour of atomic processes must be linked to that of the universe as a totality.

Eddington (1936, 1946) developed arguments linking the constants of nature through a series of extraordinarily complex mathematical steps which even today have not been adequately assessed. According to these arguments, the universe is finite and the number of particles in the universe turns out to be a few times 10^{79}. This huge number, or its square root which is of the order of 10^{39}, is linked to atomic phenomena. The ratio of the radius of a closed Einstein universe to the radius of an electron is also of the general order 10^{39} and Eddington links these entities together. The theory also gives an invariable relation between the ratio of the mass of the universe as a whole to the mass of a proton, which must, as to general order of magnitude, be the number of particles in the universe. The arguments provide also numbers like 136 and 137 which are closely related numerically to the inverse of the fine-structure constant (see p. 199). The theory has provided no data not known already although it has derived it in a highly original way. It is too early to say whether the work is a *tour de force* or just a mirage: we might know this fifty years from now.

A different approach was explored by E. A. Milne (1935, 1948) who aimed to understand as much about the universe as possible on the basis of the cosmological principle and the basic definitions of space and time. The behaviour of particles (i.e. the laws of particle motion) were to be derived in these terms and not postulated as is the more usual approach. The theory came under very great criticism when it was first proposed and is still not generally accepted—but it has led to a greatly increased understanding of our concepts of space and time.

Alternative approaches have also been explored by Dirac (1937) and Jordan (1947). They call attention to the large magnitudes (which have already been mentioned above in connection with Eddington's work) and suggest that the appearance of various ratios having the same enormous magnitude is hardly to be ascribed to chance. The suggestion is that these numbers are linked mathematically and that they will maintain their numerical values and relations permanently. There is a certain appeal to the emotive assertion that we do not live in a preferred region of the universe, nor at some preferred time. These arguments lead to strong conclusions, such as that the 'constant of universal gravitation' in fact changes with time, though on a much longer time-scale than that associated with the human life-span. These various theories are speculative in the extreme and cannot be pursued here. But they do show that late in the thirties we had begun to explore some of the greatest problems that have yet been envisaged and that the exploration was in strictly numerical terms.

Structure of the Stars

Apart from studying the universe as a whole, the stars themselves were being explored in terms of physical principles familiar in the laboratory. Here a genuine link with atomic physics arose through the problem of explaining how a star could continue to radiate the enormous amount of energy it is known to do for thousands of millions of years. Conventional energy sources (fossil and chemical) are clearly totally inadequate for these purposes, but the new ideas about the structure of the atom gave a source of power of the enormous strength required to understand stellar properties. More particularly, the fusion of hydrogen atoms to form helium atoms (the so-called carbon-nitrogen cycle because carbon and nitrogen were found theoretically to be necessary catalysts for the fusion process) became recognized as the most likely source of energy for the ordinary star. The validity of such a fusion process was tragically confirmed later since it forms the basis of the hydrogen bomb. The recognition of nuclear reactions in physics allowed the theory of stellar structure to develop as an ordered study: indeed, Eddington was led to say that even if nuclear physics had not evolved in the way it did, it would have followed as a necessity from the study of the stars.

The detailed mathematical studies of the stars that were initiated during the 1930s laid the foundations for the subsequent quantitative understanding of stellar behaviour and evolution. The work of Eddington was of singular importance in this connection, but many other people made basic contributions and we should mention in this connection the work of E. A. Milne, S. Chandrasekhar, H. N. Russell, V. R. Emden, D. Hilbert, S. Rosseland, K. Schwartzschild, E. Hertzsprung, and G. P. Kuiper, among many others. As the result of this work, the interplay among the various physical factors which can lead to an equilibrium stellar configuration was recognized. It became established that stars fall into five broad categories: the main sequence of standard stars (of which the sun is a broadly typical member); the red-giant stars, which are extremely large for their brightness (Betelgeuse is typical here); the white-dwarf stars (such as Sirius B) which are extremely small (perhaps only one-fiftieth of the solar radius even though they are about the same mass as the sun) and not very luminous; the variable stars, such as the Cepheid variables, along with other stars of differing variability characteristics; stars showing specific peculiarities, like the nova (where a star 'explodes' and ejects matter in order that a new equilibrium condition may be set up: the Crab nebula is one such example, from the supernova of 1057); stars showing unaccountable spectral features; and so on. Apart from noticing in passing that the white-dwarf is an example of a quantum structure obeying the Fermi statistics (see p. 242), we can say only a little here about the main-sequence stars to show the general way in which stellar behaviour began to be understood in this period. Understanding the main-sequence stars is a great step forward because this category contains most stars; the other stars were interesting, of course, simply because they were different and unexplained.

It was found that the behaviour of the main-sequence stars can be understood as a consequence of six basic premises. These can be listed as follows: (i) the star is in a state of mechanical equilibrium under gravity, the weight of the material above any layer being supported by the pressure in the star at that level; (ii) the pressure due to radiation (see I. 298f.) is small in comparison with the pressure in the material everywhere in the star; (iii) the transport of energy in the star is entirely by radiation (expressed by saying the star is in radiative equilibrium), the effects of material convection being negligible; (iv) the material of the star behaves as if it were an ideal gas; (v) the star is opaque because photons cause changes in the electronic configurations within the atoms (the so-called photo-electric opacity, described by Kramer's law of quantum-mechanical origin); and (vi) the energy generation is of thermonuclear origin involving the build-up of elements from hydrogen (and particularly helium) in the central regions of the star. The premises (iv), (v), and (vi) involve particularly the properties of the material of the star, including the temperature; more particularly, the opacity is taken to be inversely proportional to the temperature raised to the $7/2$ power, while the rate of energy generation is supposed to be directly proportional to the temperature raised to the 18th power (Bethe's rule). These six axioms lead to the most astonishing and far-reaching conclusions. Thus it follows that, for a given chemical composition, the radius of the star is proportional to (mass of star)$^{3/4}$, in agreement with the observed mass–radius relation. Again, the luminosity of the star is proportional to the fifth power of its mass, to the seventh power of its radius, to the $5/2$ power of the effective temperature. The fourth power of the effective temperature itself is also pro-portional to the mass of the star. The relation between luminosity and effective temperature mentioned just above is particularly interesting because it agrees well with the diagram constructed beforehand by Hertzsprung and Russell on empirical grounds. These results were rather startling when they were first isolated because they showed that the stars can be treated in broad quantitative terms from rather simple means. We cannot delve further into this now but the analyses show also the relative unimportance of chemical composition for the average star, and also (very important for the time-scale discussion) they show the relative unimportance of the exact strength of the thermonuclear energy source. Such general conclusions are always of the greatest importance in science for they give an indication of the variables that cannot be easily investigated by observation alone due to their relative ineffectiveness in controlling the overall situation. Apart from these variables not being accurately accessible to observation, it is always best to test predictions of theories using variables that control the overall physical conditions critically, since then the test can be decisive.

Among the most exciting studies are those involving the nearer galaxies. We saw earlier that Cepheid variable stars can be isolated in the nearer galaxies and provide a means of distance determination. It has also been found that the relationships between stellar variables quoted above also apply to these galaxies. Other galaxies really are like our galaxy in detail, and the rules of physics deduced in our immediate environment do seem to have universal detailed validity.

The details of a possible evolutionary sequence for a star from birth to death will concern us in volume III, but we might notice here that a star has only a finite lifetime. When its store of thermo-nuclear combustible material is used up it will cease to radiate energy; it may pass through some nova stage involving explosive convulsions, or it may quickly cease to radiate. These arguments could apply to the sun: indeed, the earth itself might well cease to exist if our sun were to undergo any explosive rearrangement. It need hardly be said that such a situation is most unlikely to arise for another hundred million years from now, or even more.

Solar and Terrestrial Studies

Our sun and earth began to be studied in detail as physical entities during the period under discussion. We mention this work briefly now primarily for completeness; it does not introduce any new principles of physics, but it does show the wide range of applicability outside the laboratory of the new physics that was emerging.

Devastation of areas of the earth by earthquakes has been met with from time immemorial but it was after the Lisbon earthquake of 1 November 1755 that the effects of such disturbances began to be studied and catalogued. It was only at the end of the last century that seismic laboratories were set up on a global basis. It was during the present century that it has been realized that seismology can be used to explore the inner structure of the earth. This is perhaps surprising when we see that it was in 1760 that John Michell realized that it is the elastic waves set up in the earth by earthquakes that are observed at the surface.

The presence of both transverse and longitudinal wave-fields were recognized in the main body of the earth, particularly as a result of the general mathematical work of Lord Rayleigh, H. Lamb, A. E. H. Love, and Sir Harold Jeffreys. Jeffreys, K. E. Bullen, and B. Gutenberg particularly are associated with the construction of travel-time charts showing the paths of seismic waves within the earth. These studies show that the central half of the earth is of the nature of a liquid (more precisely, of material without rigidity) encased in an outer half which is solid. Models of the earth (consistent with the known mass and moment of inertia) began to be constructed, guided by the work of L. H. Adams and E. O.

Williamson—a prototype for later studies—who reported in 1923 a computed distribution of density within the earth.

The earth's atmosphere could be studied using the new developments in quantum physics. In particular Sir Harrie Massey showed, in the late twenties and early thirties, how the properties of the terrestrial, and also of general planetary, atmospheres can be understood in detail on the basis of atomic collision processes obeying the then-new quantum mechanics. This work, together with the seismic studies for the structure of the condensed earth, allow for the foundation of planetary structures with the observed structure being but one example of a range of possible models that might have been.

Electric properties of the atmosphere were recognized and studied between the wars. Wireless communication between Cornwall and Newfoundland had been established by Marconi in 1902, the associated electromagnetic waves having to be bent round the curved surface of the earth for such a process to be possible. A. E. Kennelly and O. Heaviside independently showed that this can only occur if the upper regions of the earth's atmosphere are able to conduct electricity. Further work, particularly by Sir Edward Appleton and his co-workers, isolated the E-layer (about 60 miles up) and the F-layer above this: the E-layer is that recognized by Kennelly and Heaviside.

The physical conditions in the conducting atmosphere were explored, particularly by Sir Sydney Chapman. It was realized that there is a close link between the electrical properties of the atmosphere and the spectacularly colourful auroral activities often present at the poles. Further, it soon became clear that all these phenomena are closely related to magnetic processes on the solar surface, and particularly to sun-spot activity. The time-scale of observed events showed the link between the earth and sun to be through the emission of fast charged particles by the sun (mainly protons, it seemed) and not primarily through the emission of electromagnetic radiation.

Summary and Thoughts in Retrospect

In this and the chapter in volume I we have spanned the first four decades of this century and have witnessed nothing less than a revolution in physics. As in all revolutions the outcome is a condition apparently unrelated to that pertaining initially, but on closer scrutiny the discontinuity is not as complete as appears at first sight. A potential for generalization, initially present but out of the mainstream of development, is thrust forward and fostered.

Before the year 1900 the physical world was generally treated in strictly mechanical terms, as if the universe were a vast machine. The description of experiments and observations were made on the implicit assumption that all natural phenomena can be given a mechanical explanation, involving the twin concepts of force and acceleration. This was started by Galileo and Newton, and reached its high point at the middle of the last century when Helmholtz proclaimed that 'the final aim of all natural science is to resolve itself into mechanics'. At the same time, Lord Kelvin admitted that he could understand nothing of which he could not make a mechanical model. The second law of thermodynamics showed that the machinery may be far from perfect, as if the various components show backlash of some unusual sort, but there was no fear that the ponderous, shining components would wear out or fail to function. Indeed, it might even be found eventually that the backlash itself was the result of the action of other smaller coupling machines; it could well appear in the end that all was in fact perfection and exact precision. The physical world could then be described in one way in terms of an all-embracing master plan, setting out the details of, and relation between, all components once for all, or in another way in terms of a vast time-table laying out the absolute time of arrival of each particle of the world at each unique point where an observer can be located (one suspects seated comfortably in a leather armchair with a hamper). Matter was the material composing the universal machine, and its movement was recognized as energy. Each particle of matter was to act as a container for energy much as a bottle is a container for wine, and the transference of energy from one piece of matter to another was to be a simple operation that leaves the matter unaffected as to its structure, affecting only its motion. There was no reason (other than human frailty) why the whole structure of the universe should not ultimately be described with limitless accuracy: practical limits to measurement arising from our clumsiness could be reduced by a polish of skills, and by the introduction of automotive devices. All the physical principles necessary for the description of physical phenomena were apparently available, summarized succinctly in the conservation rules of mass, momentum, and energy, and the laws of particle mechanics. Future work seemed aimed towards improving our accuracy of calculation from principles already established and essentially complete.

This classical world-picture, based on the superiority of matter over energy, was derived directly from a study of the macroscopic world of everyday affairs. But a more subtle interpretation was already being explored. Thus, Carathéodory (1909) was able to base thermodynamics on an analytic discussion that does not involve the hypothetical heavy engineering proposed by Carnot. Much earlier, Maxwell had shown that Newtonian mechanics is not capable of being applied to electromagnetic processes, where instantaneous action at a distance has no place. Other work turned out to be prophetic. Hamilton had shown (1834) the final advantage of describing mechanical events in terms of the scalar kinetic and potential energies instead of appealing to the acceleration and the force vectors and Jacobi had realized the enormous power of Hamilton's methods (which Jacobi was forced to term canonical because of their all-embracing beauty). Further than this, the value of the variation principle had been recognized (particularly by Euler and Lagrange) as a method of deriving certain basic mathematical equations of physics and Jacobi (1850) had realized by this method that classical theory takes on a special mathematical symmetry if the time is treated as a dependent rather than an independent variable—this puts space and time on an equal footing, later to form an essential feature of relativity theory. Hamilton also developed a wave theory (1827) able to account for the mechanical trajectories of particles. (About a hundred years later, the wave-equation of quantum physics was derived by Schrödinger using a variation principle and the equation of Hamilton–Jacobi.) This work, along with other discussions, showed the purely mechanical picture of the world not to be unique, and that a non-mechanical theory was possible. The reason why these analyses could do no more than be a silent portent of the future was the lack of any experimental authority to establish their validity in the real world. They were interesting mathematical curiosities but no more at that time.

The experimental authority which gave these apparent curiosities life and power came with the study of atomic processes and with a closer scrutiny of the macroscopic concepts of space and time. These new experimental and theoretical studies caused a revolution in thought because they showed the barrenness of thinking of the universe in purely mechanical absolute terms. Matter and energy are one thing, and all is waves. Matter crumbled and was found to be a wave all the time. What was initially complete order and precision at the macroscopic level became diffuse and somewhat disordered at the microscopic level. Physics was recognized for the first time as a hierarchical subject in which at least three layers could be discerned: one has a useful characteristic length-scale of the mile—this is the commonplace world; another a length-scale one-million-millionth this size—which is the atomic world; and the third has a length-scale measured in millions of light-years—this is the galactic world. The material piston and the crankshaft swathed in asbestos had given place to the abstract study of invariance and covariance. From being in 1900 on the threshold of all knowledge of the physical world, forty years later we were admitting incomprehension and even incredulity when viewing the universe of our experience. From inhabiting a comfortable, restricted, and essentially friendly universe we turned to realize that we have an insecure foothold on a rather insignificant, minute planet in an enormous expanding universe which appears basically hostile to life. Instead of stooping to pick up the key to the universe, some physicists were even wondering whether the very order we call science is not itself no more than a useful construct of our own imaginations. Instead of reaching the summit of knowledge we had done no more than spy out the land in preparation for establishing a base camp. Such was the position in 1939 when we were brought to a narrower and more immediate reality by the advent of war.

FOR FURTHER READING

See p. 305

9

Chemistry*

JOHN WREN-LEWIS

I. DEVELOPMENTS AFTER 1918

The 1914–18 War brought many blows to Western man's self-confidence, and not the least of them was a considerable amount of disappointment about the 'miracle of chemistry' which at the beginning of the century had inspired many people to feel that the Biblical promise of dominion over nature was within sight of achievement. The war had brought chemistry to the notice of a far wider section of the general public than ever before, but with unpleasant associations overriding the pleasant ones. The memory of poison gas for most people overshadowed that of new antiseptics.

---

* For readers generally acquainted with the language and basic ideas of chemistry, this chapter should be completely self-contained and does not presuppose prior reading of the corresponding chapter (pp. 311–41) in vol. I of *The Twentieth-Century Mind* (1971). Only the most fundamental notions—the idea of elementary substances and their compounds, and the basic principle of writing formulae to represent compounds and equations to represent chemical reactions—have been presupposed in what follows: all the other major concepts with which chemical science was equipped by the end of the First World War are explained as they are introduced, even though this has involved repeating, in summary form, some of the material expounded in the earlier chapter.

A reader with no knowledge of chemistry at all, on the other hand, is recommended to read the earlier chapter before tackling the present one. He will find there a complete elementary exposition of the development of chemical science up to 1918, including such basic topics as the idea of the atom and the molecule; the use of symbols to represent chemical elements; the construction of chemical formulae; the special language needed to deal with the very complicated chemistry of carbon compounds (which is known as organic chemistry because it underlies the subtle complexities of living materials and processes); the classification of the chemical elements into broad groups and the relationship of this classification to modern ideas about the internal structure of atoms; and the intimate relationship between the development of chemical theory and the growth of chemical technology.

New colours brought into daily life by synthetic dyes were now clouded by the spectre of their use in military uniforms. The ability to make use of the vast reservoirs of nitrogen in the atmosphere was associated more with high explosive manufacture than with the new fertilizers that gave the world more food, while the production of margarine by hydrogenation of vegetable oils led many people to think of chemistry primarily as a matter of making cheap and nasty substitutes for the good things of life. And over and above all this was the fact that in one very important field the chemists had notably fallen short of their reputation as miracle-men. Their efforts to provide the embattled nations with synthetic materials to remedy the shortage of rubber, wood, and metals had failed dismally.

Expectations had been high in this area when the war began. For nearly fifty years business had been booming in new materials made by chemical processing of cheap vegetable tissues such as wood pulp or cotton waste—celluloid (used in combs, spectacle frames, and golf balls), cellophane, cellulosic photographic films, and various 'artificial silks'. From the end of the nineteenth century there had also been buttons and other articles made from 'casein plastics', produced by treating skimmed milk with the simple chemical formaldehyde (which could be produced on an industrial scale by reacting coke with steam). Most encouraging of all, there was the wholly synthetic plastic known as Bakelite, taking its name from the Belgian-American, Leo Baekeland (1863–1944), who in the early years of the twentieth century had developed an industrial process for making a moulding material from the 'p.f. resin' that forms when formaldehyde reacts with phenol (the coal-tar product commonly known as 'carbolic').

But when chemists in their wartime laboratories tried to make new synthetics, the results were very disappointing, and behind the practical disappointment lay a nagging awareness that no one really understood the basic principles of making a new material of this kind. The discoveries so far made had been largely accidental, and the precise chemical character both of new materials and of their natural precursors like rubber, gutta-percha, wool, and wood pulp, remained curiously elusive in spite of the best efforts of chemical analysts.

It was out of this frustrating situation that the science of chemistry made a completely unexpected breakthrough in the inter-war years, opening up a whole new area of chemical understanding and bringing in sight practical miracles which only the wildest optimists had hitherto dreamt of. The breakthrough was the discarding of a prejudice, and provides a good illustration of a very common feature of scientific progress, namely that the revolutionary insights of one age can become the limitations of another that have to be discarded, not without intellectual turmoil, before major new advances can be made.

The seemingly miraculous advances of chemistry during the previous century had been made possible because the great pioneers of modern science in the eighteenth century had refused to be satisfied with the semi-mystical notions of earlier alchemists and 'natural philosophers' about how substances might be transformed into other substances. The whole subject had been opened up by the great scientific pioneers insisting that every substance, however apparently complex, should be rigorously analysed down into definite combinations of chemical elements. The messy mixtures of ordinary experience were separated out into definite chemical entities, each of which was allocated a definite formula like H_2O (water) or H_2SO_4 (sulphuric acid) or $C_{12}H_{22}O_{11}$ (cane sugar) or $C_{55}H_{72}O_5N_4Mg$ (chlorophyll). Substances like rubber, starch, wool, celluloid, or p.f. resin simply will not yield to this procedure, however, and chemists could find no way of coming to terms with this fact without going back on what seemed to be the very basic principles of their science, which had been established only after considerable struggle against the vagueness of pre-scientific ways of thinking.

Formulae like H_2O or H_2SO_4 imply that each tiny particle or 'molecule' of the substance in question is a definite structure of atoms of specified component elements. In the early years of the twentieth century scientists had learned to envisage atoms as concentrations of electrical force gripping each other by electrical attraction, the distances between one atomic centre and another in an average molecule being measured in billionths of a centimetre. They had also become accustomed to the notion that substances involving the element carbon often have very complicated molecules, with dozens of atoms held together in elaborate structures that need to be drawn out—sometimes in 3D—to make sense in terms of the standard laws of chemical combination between atoms. For example, it was known that many of the essences found in the leaves, stems, or flowers of plants have molecules containing ten carbon atoms and sixteen hydrogen atoms, although there are many different essence, with considerable (though sometimes subtle) differences in smell and other properties: they can be understood as distinct chemical entities only when their formulae are drawn out diagrammatically, like this:

Limonene (from bitter
orange oil)

α-pinene (from oil of
turpentine)

When these formulae are drawn out it becomes evident that both substances are related in their chemical structure to a simpler material, the gaseous substance called isoprene which is distilled off when rubber is heated gently. Isoprene has molecules with five carbon atoms and eight hydrogen atoms linked in the structure

$$\underset{\displaystyle CH_2{=}\underset{\textstyle |}{C}{-}CH{=}CH_2}{\overset{\textstyle CH_3}{}}$$

In fact so many natural oils have structures that look like two isoprene molecules joined together in various ways that it was evident to chemists well before the end of the nineteenth century that nature uses the isoprene grouping as a basic building-unit for more complex structures. This is a general principle quite often found in the chemistry of carbon compounds, to which had been given the technical term 'polymerism', coined originally by one of the greatest of the early pioneers of chemistry, Jöns Jacob Berzelius of Sweden. Isoprene, C_5H_8, is said to be a 'monomer' of which limonene, α-pinene, and a great many other plant-oil chemicals are different 'dimers', all with the formula $C_{10}H_{16}$, while other natural substances with formulae $C_{15}H_{24}$ are 'trimers' of isoprene, and yet others, with formulae $C_{20}H_{32}$, are 'tetramers'. In the same way the sleeping drug paraldehyde, $C_6H_{12}O_3$, is said to be a polymer—specifically, a trimer—of the simpler chemical acetaldehyde, C_2H_4O, and in this case the more complex material can actually be made directly from the simpler one under certain conditions, the molecules of acetaldehyde intercombining with one another in threes in a way which is best shown by an equation with drawn-out formulae thus:

$$H_3C \cdot CH = O$$
$$+$$
$$H_3C \cdot CH = O \quad \longrightarrow$$
$$+$$
$$H_3C \cdot CH = O$$

| Three molecules of acetaldehyde | combine to form | one molecule of paraldehyde |

Now rubber can be completely converted into isoprene, if distilled for long enough with heat sufficiently gentle to avoid charring or burning, so it seemed clear—again, before the end of the nineteenth century—that rubber itself was almost certainly some kind of polymer of isoprene, although it is nothing like the plant-oil substances with formulae $C_{10}H_{16}$ or $C_{15}H_{24}$ or $C_{20}H_{32}$, known collectively as 'terpenes'. When efforts were made to find out just how many isoprene units went to make up a rubber molecule, however, the results were baffling. In so far as they suggested anything they seemed to imply enormous molecules containing hundreds or even thousands of atoms, a concept which was itself somewhat alarming to chemists accustomed to regarding chlorophyll, with a few dozen atoms per molecule, as extremely complicated. But far more alarming was the fact that different specimens of rubber gave different results, with no apparent underlying consistency apart from the basic polymerism with isoprene. It was as if rubber were a messy mixture which totally defied resolution into component substances with definite formulae—and the same applied to other 'structural materials', both natural and artificial. For example, chemical analysis of the material common to bulky plant tissues, from cotton to wood, shows a composition involving carbon, hydrogen, and oxygen in the proportions 6:10:5, but chemists had no success at all in trying to determine whether its formula should be $C_{24}H_{40}O_{20}$ or $C_{36}H_{60}O_{30}$ or $C_{48}H_{80}O_{40}$ or any other polymer of $C_6H_{10}O_5$. (In this case the basic monomer unit $C_6H_{10}O_5$ was moreover not found to correspond to any actual substance that could be compared to the isoprene into which rubber breaks down.)

The suggestion most commonly made to try to solve the problem in the first quarter of the twentieth century was that materials of this sort had molecules which agglomerated into large clusters of various sizes, the clusters being held together by electrical attractions which 'overflowed', as it were, from the forces holding the atoms together within the molecules themselves. This was by no means an implausible notion, even though it presented some difficulties: the main objection to it was that it was sterile, inasmuch as it gave no clues about what might make some substances agglomerate and others not. It also, incidentally, offered no explanation of why efforts to persuade isoprene to turn back into rubber in the laboratory led at best only to resinous messes with few rubbery characteristics. During the war years German chemists trying to beat the blockade on imported rubber tried in some desperation to see what they could do with chemicals closely related to isoprene, and scored some success with dimethylbutadiene, whose drawn-out formula is:

$$H_2C=C\!\!-\!\!\!-C=CH_2$$
$$\underset{\displaystyle CH_3\ \ CH_3}{|\qquad\ |}$$

The resulting *ersatz* rubber (known technically as methyl rubber because dimethylbutadiene is like isoprene with one of the hydrogen atoms in each molecule replaced by the group CH_3, which is known as the methyl radical) was far from satisfactory, however, and there was still no hint of just what kind of polymer was being formed.

This work nevertheless must have played its part in inspiring the man who, more than any other, broke through the intellectual impasse to lay the foundations for a proper understanding of structural substances, and in so doing opened up what is now virtually a whole new branch of chemical science as well as a major field of technology. This was Hermann Staudinger (1881–1965), who since 1912 had been establishing a growing reputation both as a scientist and as a teacher in the German Chemical Laboratory at the Swiss Federal Institute of Technology in Zürich. His own war-work for Germany had been in quite different fields—he had done research on synthetic medicinals and on synthetic flavouring materials—but before the war he had been considerably interested in the chemistry of isoprene, even to the extent of inventing an industrial-scale process for manufacturing it, and after the war he became more and more dedicated to solving the problem of the puzzling nature of 'structural materials'. He was one of those great scientists who have a clear, unwavering vision of the social importance of their subject; he saw it as an essential part of his duty as a teacher to imbue his pupils with awareness of the power both for good and ill that chemistry could offer mankind, and in the decade after the war he became more and more convinced that a proper understanding of the nature of structural substances would provide the key to imitating, and perhaps even outdoing, some of nature's most fundamental processes, including possibly the process of life itself.

Having carried out extensive measurements of his own to try to determine the size of rubber and cellulose molecules, and come up consistently with the same awkward results that had perplexed earlier workers, he decided to grasp the nettle. He took up the hypothesis—already under discussion to some extent, but at that stage only as a hesitant speculation—that structural substances *do* have enormous molecules containing thousands or tens of thousands of atoms; rubber, for example, he envisaged as a polymer involving not dozens but hundreds or thousands of isoprene units strung together in long chains which might be diagrammatically represented (albeit with some over-simplification) something like this:

$$\ldots -CH_2-\underset{\underset{CH_3}{|}}{C}=CH-CH_2-CH_2-\underset{\underset{CH_3}{|}}{C}=CH-CH_2-CH_2-\underset{\underset{CH_3}{|}}{C}=CH-CH_2- \ldots$$

On this basis any particular specimen of rubber would indeed be a 'messy mixture' defying resolution into definite substances with definite formulae, for it would be a mixture, not of four or five or a dozen or a score or even a hundred substances, but of millions of individual giant chain-molecules, each of which would differ from the next by a few isoprene units—or perhaps a few dozen or even a few hundred such units.

This was a new kind of chemical thinking, which most chemists in the early 1920s resisted strongly. It seemed like opening the floodgates to chaos, perhaps even to the mystical vagueness of pre-scientific days. Staudinger had to persist with building up evidence for his views in the face of criticism that often amounted almost to ridicule: some of the most distinguished chemists of the day told him he was indulging in a vast theoretical fantasy which would collapse if only he would take more trouble to clean up his materials before analysing them. But as the decade wore on, and particularly after he moved to the University of Freiburg in 1926, the weight of the evidence he had assembled began to tell. The theory of 'macromolecules', as Staudinger called them, not only made sense of the facts already known: it also made possible a prescription for synthesizing substances of this kind, and as the prescription was shown to work for more and more substances, the theory gradually gained universal acceptance.

The prescription for synthesizing 'structural substances' is one of those major scientific notions which has only to be stated to seem simple to the point of obviousness. It is to find ordinary chemicals whose molecules have some feature which enables them to react with one another when energy is applied to the material, and moreover to go on inter-reacting so that dozens or hundreds of them become linked together in some form of chain-structure. The most obvious class of chemicals for which this is true, to which both isoprene and methylisoprene belong, are those whose molecules contain what is commonly called a 'double bond' between two of the carbon atoms— that is to say, where two (at least) of the carbon atoms in each molecule are holding on to each other with more than one of their four electronic valency-links, as represented diagrammatically by the device —C=C— in such formulae as

$$H_2C=CH_2 \qquad H_2C=C \underset{Cl}{\overset{H}{<}} \qquad H_2C=CH \hexagon$$

Ethylene	*Vinyl Chloride*	*Styrene (or Vinylbenzene)*[*]
(a component of coal gas and oil refinery gas)	(made by reacting acetylene with hydrogen chloride: the name derives from the fact that the group $CH_2=CH-$ occurs in the flavour-components of wines)	(prepared by synthesis, but also a component of coal tar, and a product of the distillation of the gum Storax)

[*] In this chapter the skeleton formula (a) is used for benzene, and (b) for the phenyl group (benzene minus one hydrogen atom). More detailed representations are the Kekulé formula (c) (see vol. I), and one of the forms mostly used now (d). Corresponding diagrams can be used for pyridine (e) and related structures.

(a)   (b)   (c)   (d)   (e)

Formulae of type (a) are now generally used for more fully hydrogenated compounds, but in this chapter formula for such compounds are more specifically represented by giving the C and H symbols (see p. 268).

This 'double-bonding' of the carbon atoms indicates not extra strength but rather the reverse. The build-up of electron density between the two carbon atoms makes the molecule quite susceptible to attack by electron-seeking reagents; ethylene, for example, will react with chlorine, or with water under certain conditions:

$$CH_2{=}CH_2 + Cl_2 \longrightarrow \underset{\underset{Cl}{|}}{CH_2}{-}\underset{\underset{Cl}{|}}{CH_2}$$

(ethylene dichloride)

$$CH_2{=}CH_2 + H_2O \xrightarrow[H_2SO_4]{} CH_3CH_2OH$$

(ethyl alcohol)

Staudinger reasoned that if substances with double-bonded molecules are energized, *the molecules can react with one another—and moreover can do so in such a way as to give a new material capable of further reaction of the same kind.* For example, with vinyl chloride, energy might be envisaged as causing one molecule here and there to convert into a new form wherein the double bond is exchanged for an ordinary single bond and the carbon atoms acquire free, unattached valencies. In practice, this new 'active' form of the monomer comes into existence as a result of the action of an initiator; molecules such as vinyl chloride readily absorb oxygen from the atmosphere to form peroxides and, under suitable conditions, these peroxides can act as initiators thus:

$$CH_2{=}CH{-}Cl \xrightarrow[\text{Initiator } I^\star]{} I{-}\underset{\underset{Cl}{|}}{CH_2}{-}CH^\star$$

ordinary vinyl   'active' form of
chloride   vinyl chloride

These activated molecules promptly attack neighbouring ordinary molecules to give dimers which still have 'free' valencies:

$$CH_2=CH-Cl + I-CH_2-\underset{\underset{Cl}{|}}{CH}\star$$

$$\downarrow$$

$$I-CH_2-\underset{\underset{Cl}{|}}{CH}-CH_2-\underset{\underset{Cl}{|}}{CH}\star$$

The dimers attack further ordinary vinyl chloride molecules to give still larger active polymeric molecules, and so on almost *ad infinitum*—except that eventually some accident occurs to stop the growth of the chains, as, for example, collision of two growing chains to give one massive chain:

$$I-(\text{long chain of } CH_2CHCl)-CH_2\underset{\underset{Cl}{|}}{CH}\star$$

$$+$$

$$\star\underset{\underset{Cl}{|}}{CH}CH_2-(\text{chain})-I$$

$$\downarrow$$

$$I-(\text{chain})-CH_2\underset{\underset{Cl}{|}}{CH}\cdot\underset{\underset{Cl}{|}}{CH}CH_2-(\text{chain})-I$$

polymer

Along these lines Staudinger was able not only to explain the long-known facts that both vinyl chloride and styrene form resinous deposits when exposed to light, but also (and much more important) to predict that different ways of applying energy to these and similar starting-materials would lead to polymerization reactions proceeding for different lengths of time, and so would yield a wide range of varieties of product corresponding to mixtures of macromolecules of different size-ranges. At Freiburg Staudinger embarked on a massive programme of research on different ways of polymerizing styrene under different conditions, and so laid the foundations for the first truly scientific manufacture of synthetic structural materials.

In the following decade polystyrene became (what it still is today) an important material capable of taking many different forms, from a light white solid suitable for use in building or packaging, to a clear transparent plastic which opened up the possibility of 'unbreakable' windows. At the same time research workers all over the world were inspired to follow up Staudinger's lead by applying his ideas, results, and techniques to other simple chemicals with double-bonded molecules. Vinyl chloride, which had been the subject of unsuccessful speculation and experimentation in the chemical industry for many years, now became the starting-point for a very wide range indeed of new plastic materials, as chemists developed repertoires of tricks for starting and stopping polymerization reactions so as to produce different kinds of macromolecular product (i.e. different mixtures of macromolecular chain length): the resulting product, *polyvinyl chloride*, became known by its initials, P.V.C. In a similar way, research on derivatives of acrylic acid, CH_2=$CH\cdot COOH$, several of which had been known since the beginning of the century to form rubberlike polymers of some minor value, took on a new lease of life with the new understanding that had come out of Staudinger's work, and in the 1930s led to the industrial production of *polymethyl methacrylate*, the high-quality, tough, transparent plastic known variously under the trade names 'Perspex', 'Lucite', and 'Plexiglas'. This is based on the starting-material methyl methacrylate, which has the formula

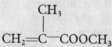

and in the early 1930s British chemists working for Imperial Chemical Industries Ltd. developed a process for making methyl methacrylate cheaply from very simple starting-materials. And from another division of the same firm came what was perhaps the most notable of all the discoveries to follow from Staudinger's research, the discovery—in the first place by accident—of the trick of producing a useful macromolecular material from the simplest of all substances with double-bonded molecules, ethylene. The trick consisted of using high pressure as an energizing agent, in the presence of a tiny amount of oxygen to help start the process of forming molecules with 'free valencies', and the discovery was made when ethylene was used as a gaseous filler for pressure-vessels in the course of experiments that had nothing to do with polymerization. When the pressure-vessels were opened it was found that the experiment the research workers had been trying to do had failed, but it was also noted that the ethylene had largely vanished, to be replaced by a white waxy solid—the substance which is now known as polyethylene or polythene.

In all this welter of new discovery, one somewhat galling problem remained unsolved—that of making synthetic rubber from isoprene. This had to await a new fundamental development in the theory of macromolecular materials which did not take place until the 1950s, namely, the recognition that where long-chain molecules have groups sticking out from the chain like knobs (see the formula for rubber on p. 271), there can be crucial differences in properties between those varieties in which the knobs in each molecule all stick out in random directions, and those in which the knobs in each molecule all lie parallel to each other in the same plane. In the 1930s some research workers may have suspected this possibility of the need to consider macromolecules in three dimensions rather than just two (or 'stereochemically', to use the technical term), but it remained no more than a suspicion, and at that stage no one could have made any practical use of the idea, since hardly anything was known about the art of making molecules join on to one another systematically (or 'stereospecifically') rather than just randomly. As far as isoprene polymerization was concerned, stereospecific polymerization to rubber remained the rubber tree's secret at that stage, and there were still not a few scholars around who thought there might be something inherently 'vital' about the structural materials of the living world—not perhaps anything ultimately magical or mystical, but at least a degree of complexity which might for ever defy laboratory imitation. It was partly this challenge that stimulated one brilliant young American chemist Wallace H. Carothers (1896–1937) of Harvard, to launch into a programme of research to follow up Staudinger's ideas of synthe sizing 'giant molecules of known structure by strictly rational methods'.

Carothers's ideas attracted the attention of the Du Pont company to such an extent that in 1928 they offered him a free hand to work in their laboratories at the head of a research team, in the faith that whatever the team did in this new field would ultimately yield something of commercial interest. Before ten years were out that faith had been amply vindicated. Although Carothers never lived to see the revelation of the rubber tree's secret, he succeeded, in 1931, in inventing the first really successful substitute for rubber, 'Neoprene', based on the polymerization of a close relative of isoprene known as chloroprene, which has the formula

$$CH_2{=}CCl{-}CH{=}CH_2$$

Even more important, however, was the fact that Carothers worked on an entirely different approach to making macromolecular materials which was suggested to him by Staudinger's theory, and in the course of doing so invented the material which was to do more than any other to overcome the widespread notion of synthetics as cheap and nasty—namely, nylon.

Behind Carothers's work here lay the brilliant researches done in the early years of the century by the German chemist Emil Fischer (1852–1919) on the chemical structure of nature's most important living structural materials, the proteins. Fischer had shown that proteins could be broken down with water into complicated mixtures of *amino-acids*, substances whose formulae have in common the chemical groups $-NH_2$ (amino) and $-COOH$ (carboxyl, the common constituent of almost all organic acids). Some common amino-acids are:

Glycine $H_2N{\cdot}CH_2{\cdot}COOH$

Methionine (containing sulphur)

$$H_2N{\cdot}CH{\cdot}COOH$$
$$|$$
$$CH_2$$
$$|$$
$$CH_2$$
$$|$$
$$S$$
$$|$$
$$CH_3$$

Phenylalanine $H_2N{\cdot}CH{\cdot}COOH$

$$CH_2$$

Lysine $H_2N{\cdot}CH_2{\cdot}CH_2{\cdot}CH_2{\cdot}CH_2{\cdot}CH{\cdot}COOH$
$$|$$
$$NH_2$$

Fischer had also shown that amino-acid molecules could react (or 'condense') with each other to give water plus molecules of more complex substances (called peptides), as for example with glycine:

$$H_2N \cdot CH_2 \cdot COOH + H_2N \cdot CH_2 \cdot COOH \longrightarrow$$
$$H_2N \cdot CH_2 \cdot CO \cdot NH \cdot CH_2 \cdot COOH + H_2O$$

and that peptide molecules, being still amino-acids, could undergo still further inter-reaction either with more amino-acid molecules or with other peptide molecules to give *polypeptides*. He had accordingly concluded that proteins must be complex intercombinations of polypeptides, but he and other chemists of his day were prevented from going much beyond this generalization, not only by the inherent complexity of the subject, but also by the general inhibition at the time against conceiving of really large molecules. With this inhibition removed by Staudinger's work, Carothers set out to pursue the notion of synthesizing macromolecular compounds from simple amino-acids to form 'models' of the complex processes of natural protein-formation (in natural materials like skin, wool, and silk) in much the same way that Staudinger's polystyrene work and Carothers's own neoprene work could be thought of as synthetic models for the natural process of rubber-formation.

In particular, he recognized that the interaction between amino-acid molecules to form peptides and polypeptides exemplified exactly the same principle as that which Staudinger had identified in the polymerization of double-bonded compounds, namely, the principle of a chain-reaction in which the product at every stage has the power of further reaction of the same kind as that which produced it. Carothers expressed this by saying that double-bonded compounds and amino-acids are both *bifunctional*, by which he meant that their molecules have—for rather different reasons— the ability to react readily in two directions at once. And in putting the matter this way, he was able to embrace under the same general principle many other kinds of bifunctional material which could, by implication, act as the starting-points for chain-reactions leading to macromolecular substances. The most obvious cases in point are *hydroxy-acids*, substances containing —OH and —COOH groups in every molecule. The condensation of hydroxy-compounds (normally known as alcohols) with acids was one of the very earliest of all reactions to be studied in organic chemistry back in the nineteenth century, a reaction in many ways analogous to the reaction of alkalis with acids to form salts and water in ordinary inorganic chemistry. The products of the reaction are normally

known as esters, and a typical simple example would be methyl
acetate, or methyl acetic ester, formed from acetic acid and methyl
alcohol by the equation

$$CH_3 \cdot COOH + HO \cdot CH_3 \longrightarrow CH_3 \cdot CO \cdot OCH_3 + H_2O$$

Acetic acid   Methyl alcohol   Methyl acetate

Hydroxy-acids, Carothers reasoned, should in principle be capable
of intermolecular reactions giving rise to macromolecular chain
compounds which might be called *polyesters*—and the same kind of
effect might be achieved by interacting two different bifunctional
compounds, namely a double (or 'dibasic') acid with two —COOH
groups in each molecule and a double (or 'dihydric') alcohol with
two —OH groups in each molecule. This explained the interesting
range of resinous materials that had for some years been used in the
paint industry, made by mixing phthalic acid and glycerol: these
would react to form a complex ester which is also a hydroxy-acid and
therefore capable of further inter-reaction, thus:

Glycerol   Phthalic acid

Water + Complex hydroxy-acid

On the same lines, Carothers reasoned that the kind of chain-
formation that happens with amino-acids in the polypeptide
reaction might equally well be brought about by inter-reacting a
dibasic acid with a di-amine (a material with two —NH$_2$ groups in
each molecule), and it was this that led him to nylon.

In modern chemical jargon the term 'nylon' refers, not to any one
specific material but to any macromolecular material made by
inter-acting dibasic acids with diamines: such materials are sometimes also called *polyamides*, since in organic chemistry generally
the condensation of acids with amines is known as amide-formation,
as in the simple example of acetic acid condensing with methylamine to give methylacetamide and water:

$$CH_3 \cdot COOH + H_2N \cdot CH_3 \longrightarrow CH_3 \cdot CO \cdot NH \cdot CH_3 + H_2O$$

Acetic acid   Methylamine   Methylacetamide

Since acetic acid and methylamine are merely monofunctional, i.e. have only one reactive group in each molecule, their inter-reaction does not offer the possibility of continuing reaction to yield macro-molecular chains, but this possibility exists in principle whenever a dibasic acid is reacted with a diamine. Carothers's great invention came when he reacted hexamethylenediamine with adipic acid, both of these being materials which had the prospect of being made cheaply on the industrial scale:

$$H_2N-(CH_2)_6-NH_2 + HOOC-(CH_2)_4-COOH$$

Hexamethylene diamine   Adipic acid

$$H_2O + H_2N-(CH_2)_6-NHOC-(CH_2)_4-COOH$$

Complex amide which is also an amino-acid capable of
further reaction at both ends of each molecule

The technical name for Carothers's polymer in modern jargon is Nylon 6:6, because each of its components contains six carbon atoms. No other nylon has ever been quite so successful as a fibre-forming material, although Nylon 6:10 has found application as a plastic: this is made by reacting hexamethylenediamine, i.e. the diamine with 6 carbon atoms, with a dibasic acid containing 10 carbon atoms, of formula $HOOC(CH_2)_8COOH$. The only serious rival to Nylon 6:6 as a fibre-forming material is Nylon 6, which has only one component—i.e., it is a true polypeptide formed from an amino-acid containing six carbon atoms, aminocaproic acid, $H_2N\cdot CH_2\cdot CH_2\cdot CH_2\cdot CH_2\cdot CH_2\cdot COOH$. Nylon 7, a polypeptide made from the corresponding amino-acid with seven carbon atoms, $H_2N\cdot(CH_2)_6\cdot COOH$, has also some use in fibre-making, and nylons 11 and 12, polypeptides made from the corresponding 11- and 12-carbon atom amino-acids, are used as plastics on a small scale.

Carothers's original invention (not then called Nylon 6:6) was dated 1935, and his tragic death two years later meant that he never saw the full commercial realization of it. It is typical of modern industrial chemistry that the Du Pont company had to spend years of intensive development work, involving hundreds of scientists and engineers and costing something like ten million pounds, before the new fibre could be fully launched on to the market—and then the Second World War delayed its really massive exploitation still further. Nevertheless both Du Pont and their competitors in various parts of the world realized it was a winner, and intensive research was devoted to searching for other fibre-forming materials. One of the most important inventions to come out of this work in the 1930s, from the laboratories of I. G. Farbenindustrie in Germany, was 'Perlon U', which in the Second World War fulfilled the same role for German women as Nylon 6:6 did for women in America and other Allied countries. This was produced in 1937, the year of Carothers's death, by an application of his functionality principle which he had not himself considered at all.

Carothers had remained content to identify just two kinds of reaction that could bring about macromolecular chain-formation, namely the addition of double-bonded molecules, which he called the A-method, and condensation between bi-functional substances like alcohols, acids, or amines, which he called the C-method. The German chemists started with a dihydric alcohol and a substance containing two 'isocyanate' groups in each molecule, that is to say, groups containing nitrogen atoms bonded to CO groups as in the formula of hexamethylene di-isocyanate,

$$OC{=}N{-}CH_2 \cdot CH_2 \cdot CH_2 \cdot CH_2 \cdot CH_2 \cdot CH_2{-}N{=}CO$$

Alcohols react with isocyanates by the transfer of a hydrogen atom to form a compound containing the *urethane* group, $-O \cdot CO \cdot NH-$, and so when the dihydric alcohol butan-1, 4-diol reacts with hexamethylene di-isocyanate the result is a urethane with active groups at both ends of each molecule which are capable of further reaction of the same kind, thus:

$$HO \cdot CH_2 \cdot CH_2 \cdot CH_2 \cdot CH_2 \cdot OH + OC{=}N{-}(CH_2)_6{-}N{=}CO$$

butan-1, 4-diol | hexamethylene di-isocyanate

$$HO \cdot (CH_2)_4 \cdot O \cdot CO \cdot NH \cdot (CH_2)_6 \cdot N{=}CO$$

Urethane molecule with hydroxyl group at one end and isocyanate group at the other, each capable of further reaction to form longer-chain urethanes

This was the reaction that led to Perlon U (U for urethane), and in the years after the war many other polyurethanes were developed for use as plastics. The reaction came to be known as the 'rearrangement method' for producing long-chain molecules.

Polyurethanes resemble polyamides in having macromolecular chains in which nitrogen atoms are interspersed with groups of carbon atoms, and so maintain a certain analogy with natural protein fibres like wool and silk. The other important natural fibres like cotton and flax are based on cellulose which contains no nitrogen, and this led other research workers in the 1930s to pursue the possibility of making synthetic fibre-forming materials from condensation reactions of the polyester type (p. 279). The known polyesters based on phthalic acid and glycerol—technically called *alkyd resins*—were useless for this purpose precisely because of the property that made them useful in the paint industry, namely the property of hardening into rigid, brittle masses on exposure to air: this is a valuable, indeed almost essential feature when the need is for a material which can be painted on to a surface to give it a hard protective coating, but it is the very thing that must not happen if the need is for a material that can be drawn out and spun into fibres. Perhaps the greatest importance of Carothers's theory of functionality was that it not only pointed the way towards identifying, in a completely general way, chemicals which might in principle provide starting-materials for synthesizing macromolecular substances, but also identified the features which cause some structural materials to have this property of hardening irreversibly—rather as clay hardens on baking—while others can be melted, or softened with solvents, for re-moulding into new shapes as desired, somewhat on the analogy of metals.

The essential point (worked out by Carothers, by scientists studying alkyd resins in the laboratories of the American General Electric Company and elsewhere, and also to some extent by Staudinger himself) is that if any of the components of a macromolecular chain have a functionality higher than two, then the chain-molecules contain reactive groups all along their length which can, in appropriate conditions, react again so as to join the chains together into a single rigid mass. In alkyd resins this happens because the chains have —OH groups all along their length, arising from the fact that glycerol is actually a trihydric alcohol (see the formula on p. 279). Similarly rubber can be 'vulcanized' into a hard, horny substance by treatment with sulphur or other chemicals, because isoprene has not just one but two double bonds in each molecule, so that rubber chains have double bonds all along their length (see the formula on p. 271) which can be broken open by sulphur atoms or other bifunctional molecules so that the chains get knitted together. The vegetable oils like linseed oil on which paints were based from ancient times will harden on exposure to air because they too consist of hydrocarbon chain-molecules (quite short chains in this case) with double bonds in the chains, which get knitted together by oxygen molecules. This principle came to be known among the new generation of 'high polymer technologists' as the principle of *cross-linking*, and those macromolecular materials which harden irreversibly because of cross-linking came to be known as *thermosetting resins*. Macromolecular materials with no facility for cross-linking, like polystyrene, polythene, polymethyl methacrylate, polyvinyl chloride, and nylon, came to be known as *thermoplastics*.

With this understanding of the matter, it followed that the search for a fibre-forming polyester meant finding a thermoplastic polyester, which could come about only by inter-reaction of a dibasic acid with a strictly dihydric alcohol (as opposed to glycerine which is trihydric). The first successful material of this kind was discovered in the laboratories of the British Calico Printers' Association in 1941, as the result of reacting a near relative of phthalic acid, called terephthalic acid, with ethylene glycol, thus:

$$HOOC - \langle \rangle - COOH + HO \cdot CH_2 \cdot CH_2 \cdot OH$$

Ethan-1, 2-diol
(Ethylene glycol)

Terephthalic
acid

$$HOOC - \langle \rangle - CO \cdot O \cdot CH_2 \cdot CH_2 \cdot OH$$

· Ethylene terephthalate, an ester
which is also a hydroxy-acid and
so capable of further reaction

This invention was taken up and developed by Imperial Chemical Industries Ltd. to emerge in the immediate postwar years as the fibre known variously as 'Terylene' or 'Dacron'.

Of the vast number of other macromolecular materials invented in the 1930s, two deserve special mention by virtue of embodying new principles. One was the use of elements like chlorine—known generically as the halogens—to confer greater chemical resistance to high polymers, this being one of the most valuable features of the two chlorine-containing polymers already mentioned, P.V.C. and 'Neoprene'. Several other chlorine-containing double-bonded compounds were found to give rise to useful polymers in the early 1930s, notably *vinylidene chloride*, $CH_2{=}CCl_2$, but the most striking invention in this field was made by accident in an American industrial laboratory when a gas cylinder containing a compound of carbon and fluorine, tetrafluoroethylene, $CF_2{=}CF_2$, was opened and found to be apparently empty. When the cylinder was cut open it was found to be lined with a white solid which was very highly resistant indeed to chemical reaction, and this marked the discovery of *polytetrafluoroethylene*, or P.T.F.E., which is the plastic known to the general public in non-stick utensils under such trade names as 'Teflon' or 'Fluon'.

The other 1930s invention worthy of special mention was also a case of making use of the special properties of an element other than carbon, namely the element which most closely resembles carbon, silicon (Si). In this case the chemists' efforts to find structural substances embodying silicon had the best possible natural precedent, in that this element forms the basis both of nature's commonest structural materials, rocks, and of mankind's oldest artificial materials, clay and glass. One important outcome of Staudinger's establishment of the macromolecule concept was to make chemists appreciate that the solidity of materials like these arises from the fact that their molecules contain immense chains or networks of atoms all linked together—in this case not carbon atoms at all, but silicon and oxygen atoms with various metal atoms in attendance: indeed, modern theory recognizes that the concept of a molecule really does not apply to materials like rocks or clays, inasmuch as the silicon–oxygen–silicon–oxygen links often extend throughout whole masses of the material. (The same applies, of course, to cross-linked masses of thermosetting resins: since the chemical bonding extends throughout the mass, there is no real sense in speaking of molecules of these substances.) The great virtue of clay, glass, and rock for making any kind of heavy structure from a pot to a palace, is their fire-resistance. Materials based on carbon atom chains, whether natural ones like wood or rubber or silk or wool or skin, or artificial ones like the synthetic high polymers so far described, are much lighter and subtler than mineral materials but are inevitably subject to burning or charring, because carbon and hydrogen atoms start to react with the oxygen of the air as soon as the temperature gets much above a couple of hundred-odd degrees centigrade, whereas silicon atoms joined to oxygen atoms

are practically immune to attack in this way. It was natural, therefore, that some chemists in the 1930s should set out to see whether
other materials might be made from silicon, perhaps trying to get
the best of both worlds by using compounds involving both silicon
and carbon. The groundwork had already been laid for this by the
extensive researches of Professor F. S. Kipping (1863–1949), who
at Nottingham University had worked since the beginning of the
century on parallels between the chemistry of silicon and that of
carbon.

That the two elements were chemically similar had been known
since the nineteenth century: both, for example, form dioxides
(carbon dioxide, CO_2, and silica, SiO_2) and tetrahydrides
(methane, CH_4, and silane, SiH_4). It had indeed often been specu-
lated that conditions might be found under which silicon would
become the basis for vast ranges of complicated chain- and ring-
compounds as carbon does in organic chemistry, and this notion is
still sometimes used by science-fiction writers who want to posit the
existence of life on very hot planets. Professor Kipping found no
way of making silicon as versatile as this, but he did succeed in
making a large number of compounds in whose molecules silicon
atoms are joined to complex carbon-based groupings, for example:

Trimethylsilanol   Ethyltriphenylsilane   Trichloromethylsilane

He seems to have been utterly uninterested, however, in the resinous
gums that sometimes formed in the course of his experiments, and
to his dying day believed that the 'organic' chemistry of silicon had
turned out to be of purely academic interest. It was left to the
research workers of the Corning Glass Company in the United
States to make the first artificial silicon-based polymers in 1931,
by treating dichlorosilane derivatives with water thus:

$$\underset{\text{Dichlorodimethylsilane and water}}{\overset{\displaystyle CH_3}{\underset{\displaystyle CH_3}{Cl-Si-Cl}} + H_2O + \overset{\displaystyle CH_3}{\underset{\displaystyle CH_3}{Cl-Si-Cl}} \longrightarrow}$$

$$2HCl + \overset{\displaystyle CH_3 \qquad CH_3}{\underset{\displaystyle CH_3 \qquad CH_3}{Cl-Si-O-Si-Cl}}$$

Silicon - oxygen - silicon compound with two chlorine atoms capable of further reaction to give long-chain polymers

These materials, known as silicone polymers, have since found considerable applications as lubricants, greases, and rubber-substitutes where their distinctive properties of heat-resistance, water-repellency, and non-stick character are sufficiently needed to justify the high cost of the synthetic process.

At the outbreak of the Second World War it was clear that chemical science and technology had entered a new phase in which synthetic structural materials of many widely different kinds could be produced almost as required from whatever raw materials happened to be available at the right prices. It was an era in which most discoveries were made by teams of research workers rather than by brilliant individuals: that is why only the few spectacular giants have been singled out for individual mention here—the complete record even of major discoverers would be immensely long. Staudinger's work had indeed opened the floodgates—not to chaos, as his early critics had feared, but to a vast new era of human knowledge and invention. Yet the actual volume of production of synthetic structural materials was still in those days minute in comparison with what we have come to take for granted in the second half of the twentieth century. The war in many cases acted as a forcing-house for the new developments—P.V.C. production being stepped up by new methods because of rubber shortages; polyethylene development being undertaken as a crash programme because a new light electrical insulating material was needed for the development of radar; polymethyl methacrylate being developed to provide unshatterable windows for military aircraft—yet at the same time hostilities prevented the opening up of mass consumer markets and put restrictions on the raw material which was eventually to prove the great prime source of high polymer manufacture, namely petroleum. It is doubtful whether anyone but a few visionaries even dreamt in 1945 that the new materials would soon be produced in tens of millions of tons a year.

II. ON THE FRONTIERS OF CHEMISTRY AND BIOLOGY

Another development which was instrumental in improving the public image of chemistry dramatically in the period between the end of the First World War and that of the Second was the remarkable advance of medicinal chemistry, described in newspaper parlance as the discovery of 'wonder drugs' for treating infection, most notably of penicillin. And this too involved a conceptual revolution in which a long-held scientific prejudice had to be discarded.

The establishment, towards the end of the nineteenth century, that infectious diseases are caused by bacteria and other microorganisms, was rapidly followed by the discovery that various chemicals could be used to keep diseases at bay by disinfectant action, and in the years leading up to the First World War some of the milder of these germ-killing chemicals were developed as antiseptics to restrict infection in wounds and surgical operations. It was taken for granted, however, that any chemical that was toxic to bacteria would of necessity also be toxic to large organisms such as human beings. Hence when Alexander Fleming (1881–1955) made his famous observation at St. Mary's Hospital, Paddington, in London in 1929, that a bacterial culture accidentally contaminated by a mould blown in on the wind was rapidly cleared of its bacteria, the scientific world took it as no more than an interesting discovery about the mould, *Penicillium notatum*.

The fact that micro-organisms can sometimes be chemically antagonistic to one another had been known for nearly forty years, and the great pioneer of bacteriology, Louis Pasteur, had even been inspired to hope that this might provide the basis for new advances in medicine. But all the bacteria-antagonistic chemicals subsequently isolated from cultures of moulds or other bacteria had followed the expected pattern of being equally antagonistic to human health. So Fleming's discovery was regarded as remarkable only inasmuch as it showed *Penicillium notatum* to be capable of producing an especially powerful anti-bacterial chemical. The implications for medicine were almost totally ignored for nearly a decade, and when chemists failed to isolate the active principle it was felt as no more than an academic disappointment.

In the 1930s, however, medical scientists were led, by discoveries quite unrelated to penicillin, to realize that their ancient dilemma about the necessary toxicity to man of all substances that are toxic to bacteria was a complete fallacy. This realization came as a largely accidental result of research undertaken by German dyestuffs chemists in following up the idea of the great Paul Ehrlich (1854–1915) that a way might be found between the horns of the dilemma by utilizing the fact that some dyes stain bacterial tissue without staining other kinds of tissue. Ehrlich reasoned that if a bacteria-staining dye could be found which also rendered the bacteria incapable of multiplying, a way of attacking bacteria without harming the host-organism might be developed. Except for Salvarsan, he had little success in his own search for this 'magic bullet' for killing bacteria selectively, but his idea remained an inspiration to chemists, especially in the laboratories of the great German company I. G. Farbenindustrie, and in 1935 a minor breakthrough seemed to have been made by the discovery that a dye known as Prontosil Red could be used to treat streptococcal infections such as puerperal fever (sepsis following childbirth). This dye has the formula

The real break-through came when French biochemists studied what happened to Prontosil in the body and found that its anti-bacterial action had nothing to do with its dyeing action at all, inasmuch as it was converted at once by the body's metabolism into a simpler chemical, sulphanilamide, which was not a dye. Sulphanilamide, known as a laboratory chemical since 1908, has the formula

and tests soon showed that its medicinal effects were similar to those of Prontosil.

It was the dawn of a new era in which chemists all over the world began to look in every conceivable direction for substances that might be useful in medicine. The search inevitably had a slow start, since the kind of research involved is necessarily both expensive and time-consuming: in particular, although it is no longer taken for granted that a substance which kills bacteria is necessarily harmful to human beings, there still have to be extensive, careful, and time-consuming tests made on every new prospective chemotherapeutic agent to ensure that it is not *in fact* harmful—tests that start with thousands of laboratory experiments on experimental animals of different kinds, and then proceed to careful trials with human volunteers. The first experiments to be made, in the late 1930s, were with chemicals closely related to sulphanilamide, and chemists of the May and Baker company in Britain found that replacement of one of the hydrogen atoms in the $-SO_2 \cdot NH_2$ group in sulphanil-amide molecules, with groups containing carbon, hydrogen, and nitrogen atoms, produced materials with greatly enhanced pharmaceutical effectiveness. The first of the 'wonder drugs', known as M & B 693, astonished the medical world with its effectiveness against two diseases which had hitherto been nightmare spectres, pneumonia and meningitis: chemically this drug is known as sulphapyridine because its formula has one of the hydrogen atoms of sulphanilamide replaced by a nitrogen-containing ring-group derived from the coal-tar product pyridine:

Pyridine, a stable ring-structure similar to benzene and normally written

Sulphapyridine, normally written

At first the general public remained suspicious of the new development, inasmuch as M & B 693 could sometimes produce unpleasant after-effects and also involved waking pneumonia patients up from sleep for regular doses of the drug in order to maintain a constant concentration in the system. Subsequent research, however, yielded a whole range of new 'sulpha-drugs' capable of being used against a wide variety of infectious diseases without these inconveniences of the first 'wonder-drug'. The formulae of some of the best-known are given below, where for simplicity the letter R is used to represent the sulphanilamide group, H_2N —⬡— $SO_2 \cdot NH$, which they all have in common:

Sulphathiazole   Sulphaguanidine   Sulphamerazine

Sulphamethazine   Sulphadiazine

Meanwhile the new climate of opinion led to a revival of Pasteur's old hope that the 'antibiotic' chemicals produced by micro-organisms themselves might sometimes be non-toxic to human beings and so have pharmacological uses. In 1938 Howard Florey (1898–1968) and Ernst Chain (b. 1906) began an intensive programme of research at Oxford, with particular interest in the remarkably strong antibacterial action which Fleming had observed in *Penicillium notatum,* and with this new interest and more refined chemical methods the active chemical penicillin, as it came to be called, was isolated. It was soon evident that it was a potential drug of immense power against a very wide range of infections, and with great numbers of war casualties needing protection against wound-infections and other diseases, there was every incentive for the pharmaceutical industries of the Allied countries to put great efforts into developing methods of large-scale manufacture. Chemical investigation showed that there were in fact several different varieties of penicillin in different species of the natural product, all having in common a basic chemical structure which, like that of the sulpha-drugs, contains both sulphur and nitrogen atoms in among complex carbon–hydrogen–oxygen groupings: the formula below shows the basic structure with the variable part denoted by X, X

being the group $-CH_2-\bigcirc$ in the variety known as Penicillin

G, the group $-CH_2-CH=CH-CH_2 \cdot CH_3$ in Penicillin F, and other groups in other varieties of penicillin:

In 1944 a laboratory synthesis of Penicillin G was achieved, but it was too complex a process for use in industrial production, which was carried out by developing a new and highly sophisticated variation of an age-old technology for producing chemicals from micro-organisms, namely fermentation. A large-scale fermentation process using *Penicillium notatum* in stainless steel vats made possible the production of sufficient quantities of the new 'super-wonder-drug' to treat all the Allied casualties on D-Day in 1944.

By the end of the Second World War it was evident that a new era had dawned for medicine, and for their decisive part in this, Fleming, Florey, and Chain shared a Nobel Prize (as well as being, at different times, knighted for their services). Another notable advance in chemotherapy in the war years was the discovery by research workers of Imperial Chemical Industries Ltd. of a synthetic chemical for the treatment of malaria, a chemical which was not merely a substitute for the ancient natural treatment, quinine, that was in short supply because of war conditions, but considerably more effective as a cure. This was given the name of Paludrine and has the formula

$$Cl-\bigcirc-NH-\underset{\substack{\parallel \\ NH}}{C}-NH-\underset{\substack{\parallel \\ NH}}{C}-NH-\underset{\substack{| \\ CH_3}}{\overset{\overset{\displaystyle CH_3}{|}}{CH}}$$

Equally important in the control of malaria, and indeed of a number of other tropical diseases, was the development of powerful new insecticides for killing off insects that act as carriers. The war also provided additional incentive for this development with the need to protect scarce crops against insect-pests. The first synthetic insecticide was the compound which subsequently became known as D.D.T., from its chemical name, dichlorodiphenyltrichloroethane: its formula is

$$\begin{array}{c} Cl-\bigcirc \\ CH-CCl_3 \\ Cl-\bigcirc \end{array}$$

It was first made in the course of a general programme of laboratory synthesis of chlorine-containing organic chemicals in 1874, but was rediscovered as a potential insecticide in the laboratories of the Geigy company in Switzerland in the mid-1930s and first used on a large scale as a weapon against the ravages of the Colorado beetle just before the outbreak of war. Then in the mid-1940s chemists working for ICI rediscovered an even more venerable chlorine-containing material as an insecticide. This was benzene hexachloride, $C_6H_6Cl_6$, originally made by Michael Faraday by reacting benzene with the newly-discovered gas chlorine in 1825. In 1912 it was dis-covered that benzene hexachloride as prepared in the laboratory is a mixture of four 'isomers' all of which have precisely the same formula if it is merely drawn out in two dimensions, namely

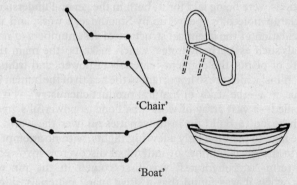

The difference between the four is explainable only by drawing out the formula in three dimensions, whereupon it becomes apparent that molecules composed of a ring of six ⁻CHCl⁻ groups can be either boat-shaped or chair-shaped, and that both shapes can have different mutual arrangements of hydrogen and chlorine atoms in relation to the adjacent carbon atoms. An idea of the two basic forms is given in the diagrams below, where each knob represents a CHCl group:

'Chair'

'Boat'

Precise understanding of which isomer corresponded to which molecular shape did not come until after the war, by which time the subject had gained practical as well as theoretical significance from the ICI chemists' discovery in 1943 that one and only one of the four—the 'gamma' isomer, corresponding, it was found, to one of the chair-shaped configurations—was an extremely powerful insecticide. They developed a method of separating it in large-scale manufacture and it has since proved particularly valuable against locusts; it has the advantage of being less likely than D.D.T. to be accumulated, in the bodies of animals that feed on plants sprayed with it, into large concentrations that may have unpleasant effects.

This discovery of the unique importance of molecular shape in producing biological activity served to confirm a general hypothesis that had been developing among biochemists for many years, that many biochemical processes work on the analogy of a 'lock and key' mechanism between different chemical molecules in the living organism. At that stage, however, almost nothing was known about the precise mechanisms involved in any particular case. The possibility of more specific detailed understanding had to await the discovery, in the decades following the war, of the exact chemical structure of the immensely complicated materials at the heart of every living cell that actually determines its future pattern of growth and reproduction, by controlling in minute detail the processes of protein synthesis that go on inside the cell or at its surface. In the 1930s and the war years few people imagined that this epoch-making discovery—the discovery of how 'genetic codes' for cell growth are carried in the DNA (deoxyribose nucleic acid) of the cell nucleus—was so close. In all kinds of ways, however, the foundations were being laid for it, both in the general understanding of very large molecules opened up by Staudinger's work, and also in the elucidation of the chemical structure of vast numbers of natural chemicals such as 'carbohydrates' which make up the main tissue-structure of plants, the pigment-materials of flowers and fruits, and the 'vitamins' which are so important to the health of the human body.

In this area—the study of 'natural product chemistry', as it came to be called—a vast array of work was done as powerful schools of research began to build up in universities all over the world. It is possible here to mention only a few highlights, with no attempt to do justice to the great number of individual discoverers involved.

The term 'carbohydrates' was first coined in the nineteenth century when it was found that a great many materials extracted from plant-tissues had formulae which looked like some kind of combination between elementary carbon and molecules of water— notably glucose and various other sugars with formulae $C_6H_{12}O_6$, cane sugar with formula $C_{12}H_{22}O_{11}$, and the starches and celluloses which make up the bulk of plant tissue and were apparently polymers of the unit $C_6H_{10}O_5$. The basic foundations for an understanding of these materials were laid in the early years of the century by Emil Fischer, who showed that they were all polyhydric alcohols of various kinds, based on chains of $—HC\cdot OH—$ units. Fischer

suggested that glucose might have a structural formula something
like this:

$$
\begin{array}{c}
CH_2 \cdot OH \\
| \\
CH \cdot OH \\
| \\
CH \cdot OH \\
| \\
CH \cdot OH \\
| \\
CH \cdot OH \\
| \\
CH = O
\end{array}
$$

but although this was consistent with many of the properties of
glucose, there remained the difficulty that glucose does not show any
of the chemical reactions normally associated with the aldehyde
group, —CH=O. This prompted more detailed investigations by
various methods in the 1930s, eventually leading to the recognition
that carbohydrates in their more stable form exist as ring-
compounds: for example, the crystalline form of glucose has the
structure

but, in solution, a small amount of the open-chain form co-exists
in equilibrium with the ring form. In the macromolecular carbohydrates the repeating unit in the chain-molecules is a ring-unit,
so that the natural celluloses are composed of long-chain molecules
with formulae something like this:

The manufacture of plastics from cellulosic materials can be understood on this basis as a modification of the natural cellulose macromolecules by converting some of the $—OH$ groups into ester groups, $—O·NO_2$ groups in the case of cellulose nitrate, or $—O·CO·CH_3$ groups in the case of cellulose acetate. A wide range of different kinds of cellulose-based plastics is clearly possible, by controlling the amount of 'esterification' that takes place, and with this new understanding the manufacture of these plastics was able to keep pace, all through the 1930s and 1940s, with the manufacture of the new synthetics.

The study of the beautiful and subtle pigments of flowers had engaged the attention of chemists for more than a century, and the identification of a particular class of chemical involved, capable of producing various colours by combination with different kinds of cell-sap, goes back to work done in the first half of the nineteenth century by the German chemist Ludwig Marquart, who called these pigments *anthocyanins*. In the early years of the twentieth century methods of extracting these pigments in pure form were developed, and the problem of their chemical structure began to be investigated by many chemists, most notably in the school of Professor R. M. Willstätter (1872–1942) at Munich. Already a Nobel Prize-winner in 1915, Willstätter and his pupils made notable contributions to this and several other fields of natural product chemistry over forty years. Eventually seven separate anthocyanin pigments were isolated, each capable of producing a range of colours by combining with different carbohydrate, mineral, or other constituents of cell sap. All are derivatives of the compound flavonol, which has the formula below, showing three rings of atoms in each molecule:

Another class of vegetable pigments first identified in the 1830s are called carotenoid, because they are all related to the yellow pigment which H. W. F. Wackenroder isolated from carrots and called carotene. Many of the yellow pigments of fruits and flowers were subsequently found to be closely related to carotene, as were also the red pigments of tomatoes, rose hips, and other fruits. In the 1930s carotene was shown to be a complex hydrocarbon with the symmetrical formula:

The commonest of all plant pigments, the green chlorophyll which is essential to the plant's ability to build up its structure from the carbon dioxide of the air, was first subjected to chemical study in the 1880s by H. E. Schunck, and was the object of intensive research by Willstätter's school and others all through the first third of the twentieth century. It turned out to be a very complicated compound indeed, with the extremely unusual feature that each of its molecules contains a single atom of the metal magnesium (Mg). The formula, finally established in 1934, is where the group $C_{20}H_{39}$ is simply a long chain of carbon atoms with a full complement of attendant hydrogens. The presence of the magnesium atom seemed at that time something of an oddity, although it was suspected that it might be a significant kind of oddity in view of the fact that Emil Fischer had already found a similar feature in the red colouring-matter of blood, haemin, which has a structure analogous to that of chlorophyll built round an atom of iron at the centre of each molecule. Research since the Second World War has shown what the significance is: the metal atom in compounds like these plays a vital part in bringing about chemical synthesis in the living organism, by providing an electronically active site on which molecules of other substances are brought together in a way that would never otherwise occur, with their component atoms in an excited state which leads to reaction. The general principle of using metal compounds as 'chemical marriage-brokers' in this way—the principle technically known as catalysis—had been known both in the laboratory and in industrial chemistry from the early nineteenth century, but it was only during the Second World War and the following decade that chemists began to appreciate how this principle could be applied to achieve immensely subtle chemical syntheses by using organic compounds containing metal atoms, in which the electronic structure on the surface of each metal atom is modified into an active site of just the right shape needed in each particular synthesis. In the case of chlorophyll, for example, the complicated structure around the magnesium atom in each molecule forms a kind of cage of exactly the shape that will catch molecules of carbon dioxide and water and bring them together to form sugars—a process that has never yet been elegantly simulated by ordinary laboratory synthesis. Where chemists *have* been able to employ the principle, with metal-organic compounds somewhat simpler than chlorophyll, they have achieved remarkable results, including the eventual successful imitation of the rubber tree's synthesis of rubber from isoprene.

Because of the need to supply iron-atoms for the continuous renewal of the vital chemicals of the blood, iron salts form an essential part of human diet, and in the early years of the twentieth century it was established that many other substances were also needed in small quantities in diet to preserve health, alongside the basic body-building and energy-supplying substances that form the bulk of diet (the proteins, the fats, and the carbohydrates). The work of Sir Frederick Gowland Hopkins (1862–1947) at Cambridge was particularly important in establishing the need not only for certain vital mineral salts but also for a mixed bag of organic materials which came to be called vitamins. It was only in the inter-war years, however, that chemists were in a position to make a really serious attack on the investigation of their precise nature, and it then became apparent that they were indeed a motley collection of substances, varying widely in complexity, with little or no apparent connection one with another. Some turned out to be relatively simple substances; for example ascorbic acid, the 'Vitamin C' which occurs in fresh fruit and vegetables and prevents scurvy, was found to have the sugar-like formula

$$
\begin{array}{c}
CH_2OH \\
| \\
HO\text{-}CH \\
\end{array}
$$

and to be capable of ready synthesis on the industrial scale. 'Vitamin A', which occurs in fish-liver oil, green plants, tomatoes, etc., and is essential to the growth of young animals, turned out to be a rather more complicated compound related to carotene—in fact the formula shows that it can be (and under natural conditions normally is) derived from carotene by splitting open the molecules and adding a molecule of water to each half so as to put a $-CH_2 \cdot OH$ group in place of the $CH=$ groups that are joined together in the middle of the carotene structure:

'Vitamin D', the constituent of fish-liver oil which prevents rickets, was found to be a more complex material still, while 'Vitamin B', originally identified in wheat germ and yeast, turned out to be a whole mixture of quite different substances, some simple, some complex, and each with its own definite role to play in preserving the organism's health. One of these B-vitamins, subsequently called Vitamin B_{12}, was found to be essential to prevent pernicious anaemia, and turned out in due course to be another of those compounds whose complex organic molecules contain metal atoms—in this case, the metal cobalt.

Another highlight of natural product chemistry in the 1930s was the elucidation of the chemical structure of cholesterol, a substance widely distributed in animal tissues and closely related to the hormones which control both male and female sex-functions. This was shown to have the formula

$$
\begin{array}{c}
CH_3 \quad CH_2 \\
CH \quad CH_2 \\
CH_3 \mid \quad \mid \quad CH_3 \\
CH_2 \quad CH \quad CH_2-CH \\
CH_2 \quad C \quad CH_2 \quad CH_3 \\
CH_3 \mid \quad \mid \quad \mid \\
CH_2 \mid \quad CH \quad CH-CH_2 \\
CH_2 \quad C \quad CH \\
\mid \quad \mid \\
CH \quad C \quad CH_2 \\
OH \quad CH_2 \quad CH
\end{array}
$$

a multi-ringed type of structure which came to be known as *steroid* structure. Other hormones—glandular secretions which act as 'chemical messengers' to control many different kinds of biological function, including some growth-functions—were also investigated intensively during this period, but some turned out to involve macromolecular protein structures, the full elucidation of which had to await the postwar years. On the other hand the substances which exercise somewhat similar vital control-functions in plants, known as auxins, proved to be of rather simpler chemical constitution, as typified by one known as auxin-A which was shown in 1933 to have the formula

$$CH_3-CH_2-\overset{\overset{\displaystyle CH_3}{|}}{CH}-CH-CH$$
$$\underset{\overset{\displaystyle |}{CH_2}}{}\quad\|$$

$$CH_3-CH_2-\underset{\underset{\displaystyle CH_3}{|}}{CH}-CH-C-\underset{\underset{\displaystyle OH}{|}}{CH}-CH_2-\underset{\underset{\displaystyle OH}{|}}{CH}-\underset{\underset{\displaystyle OH}{|}}{CH}-COOH$$

In developments like these the term 'organic chemistry', which for a century had been considered merely a convenient archaism for the chemistry of carbon compounds, began to recapture something of its ancient significance as the chemistry of life.

III. DEVELOPING THEORIES AND TECHNIQUES

Few of the discoveries and inventions described in the two previous sections would have been possible without the continuous development throughout the inter-war period of the basic theory of chemical reactions and of techniques of chemical manipulation. In this field too the period was characterized not so much by brilliant individual discovery (although there were many highly distinguished individuals) as by the work of schools building up in universities all over the world—in this case, schools of 'physical chemistry'. Research workers in industrial laboratories also made notable contributions to this aspect of chemical science.

One constant problem for the chemist, both in research and in industrial manufacture, is that of separating out mixtures into their component pure substances. The standard techniques such as distillation (whereby mixtures of liquids are separated by virtue of the components boiling at different temperatures) and fractional crystallization (whereby mixtures that dissolve in water or other liquids are separated into their components by virtue of the fact that each component crystallizes out at a different temperature when the solution is cooled) are often inapplicable if only tiny quantities of material are available, as is commonly the case in biochemical work or in trying to check the results of a complicated synthesis with very small product-yield. The tremendous advances of organic chemistry in the inter-war years would have been impossible without the development of a much subtler separation technique called *chromatography*, based on the principle that is exemplified whenever a spot of ink on blotting paper spreads out into two or more rings of colour, with a dark spot at the centre and a lighter area surrounding it. This happens because most inks are composed of mixtures of different pigments, whose solutions diffuse into paper at different rates, so that the faster-diffusing pigment gets carried farther out from the centre before drying out. The idea of using this phenomenon as a way of separating the colouring-matters extracted from plants by solvents was first mooted in the nineteenth century, and at the turn of the century several chemists in different parts of the world began to use the method by passing solutions of coloured mixtures along columns of absorbent chalky powders, chopping the resultant bands of colour out separately and then soaking out the absorbed material from each section in turn. It was only in the 1930s and 1940s, however, that the technique was developed really systematically into one of the chemist's most powerful laboratory tools, and at this stage ways were found of using it to separate substances with no colour differentiation at all, by using electrical measurements to detect where the different components of a mixture are distributed along an absorbing column or on a sheet of absorbent paper. So, by one of those linguistic paradoxes that abound in science, the term 'chromatography', which means literally 'colour writing', has come to be used to refer to separation processes that often have nothing to do with colour.

Another technicality of chemical terminology which should be mentioned in this context is the use of a special term, *ad*sorption rather than *ab*sorption, for the process whereby particles of a substance are taken out of a solution or a vapour by solid materials like blotting paper or chalk or powdered charcoal. The technical term is used to indicate that what happens in these cases (of which chromatography is just one instance) is not a general absorption of the dissolved material or vapour right into the solid, but a collection of molecules of the dissolved material or vapour *on the surface* of the individual fibres of the paper or the individual grains of the powder. A full understanding of this process depends on an understanding of the electronic interlocking of atoms in molecules, and the resultant electrical forces that develop around the molecules, and a great deal of research was done on this subject in the 1930s. The body of theory which was developed had practical applications over a wide field quite apart from chromatography, from the understanding of catalysts (which usually work by adsorbing molecules on the surface of grains of the catalyst material) to the improvement of practical chemical processes such as the use of electric current to split up compounds into their component elements, the process known as *electrolysis*.

This process, originally discovered by Faraday, had been used since the nineteenth century to extract metals from mineral salts, by virtue of the fact that when an electric current is passed into a salt solution or melt through electrodes, atoms of the metal component of the salt are extracted and deposited at one electrode while the non-metallic components of the salt are collected round the other electrode. In the early twentieth century this became a major industrial process, not only for metal extraction but also for the manufacture of chlorine from common salt, which is sodium chloride: in this case the metal component of the electrolysis is not deposited at the electrode because metallic sodium reacts with water to give caustic soda, so that the electrolytic process is normally used to make chlorine and 'caustic' (although it can be adapted to make metallic sodium if molten salt is used instead of salt solution). The development of the electronic theory of atomic constitution in the years before the First World War made a much fuller understanding of the electrolytic process possible, based on a recognition that atoms can join together to form molecules in two distinct ways. In one case, known as *covalent bonding*, there is an actual meshing of the outer electron shells of the atoms, so that the combined atoms in effect share a new single outer electron shell: this is what happens in the majority of organic compounds. In the case of compounds like mineral salts, however, the atoms exchange electrons and so acquire electric charges of opposite sign, which subsequently hold them together by a kind of electrostatic attraction: this is known as *ionic bonding*. When an ionically bonded substance melts or dissolves in water, its component electrically-charged atoms, known as *ions*, separate completely and drift around almost independently, so that when an electric current is applied to the liquid the ions simply drift apart under the attraction of the two electric poles—in fact it is this physical movement of the ions that actually conveys the current from one electrode to the other. In the 1930s a great deal of research was done on the detailed dynamics of the movement of ions in solutions and melts, and this provided the basis for the development of more sophisticated electrolytic manufacturing plants as the industrial demand grew, not only for metals like nickel and chromium but also for more and more chlorine to be used in making chlorine-containing plastics and insecticides.

Alongside this development of the theory of liquids went a corresponding growth in understanding of the behaviour of solid materials. It came to be recognized that in spite of the ease with which the ions of a salt split up in solution, a solid crystal of such a material with ionic bonds running right through it can be immensely strong, just as can a macro-molecule of an organic high polymer consisting of a chain or cross-linked mat of covalently bonded atoms. It has accordingly become possible to develop a comprehensive theory of the structural behaviour of solid materials, based on a detailed understanding of how their component crystals or macro-molecules are packed together in any given specimen. The elastic behaviour of rubber-like materials, for example, is seen to derive from the fact that their individual chain-molecules, each a reasonable fraction of a millimetre long (as contrasted with the molecules of non-macromolecular substances, which are measured in millionths of a millimetre), are of coiled, spring-like shape, so that a mass of them woven together has both solid cohesion and springiness. Again, crystalline mineral solids have considerable potential strength in so far as ionic bonding can run right through the solid mass, but in practice weaknesses are introduced by the fact that there are almost always faults in the crystal structure, which lead to cracking and eventually to crumbling: when near-perfect crystals can be made their strength is immense, and the post-war years have seen the development of materials many times stronger than steel, made by stiffening plastics with perfect crystals of carbon fibre.

Another outcome of the developing electronic theory of chemical bonding in the 1930s was a steady growth in chemists' ability to work out the inner molecular structure of compounds by observing and measuring the effects of light or X-rays on solutions or crystals of a material and interpreting the results mathematically in terms of interactions between the waves (of light or X-rays) and the inter-linked atoms inside each molecule. The basic techniques here, known as *spectroscopy* and *X-ray diffraction*, were developed in the early years of the century, but the 1930s saw many new ideas— for example, the use of infra-red radiation in various ways to investigate the nature of bonding between atoms, and the use of beams of electrons (which in this context behave like waves) to gain information quickly by virtue of the speed with which electrons, as contrasted with other kinds of radiation, affect photographic plates or films. Only by using methods of this kind was there any chance of elucidating the chemical structure of such complicated organic materials as plant-pigments and steroids, which in addition to presenting formidable difficulties to the ordinary chemical analyst, are usually available only in tiny quantities into the bargain, so that consumption of material in chemical analysis needs to be avoided wherever possible.

During the war years and in the immediate postwar period the branch of chemistry known as *radiochemistry* received an enormous boost as a result of the revolution in nuclear physics, a phenomenon which required the participation of chemists at every point, notably in devising methods for extracting and purifying the special materials involved, including radioactive elements like uranium and thorium. Perhaps the greatest impact of nuclear research on chemistry, however, came from the physicists' and engineers' need to develop electronic computers to carry out elaborate calculations quickly. In the postwar years this development enabled chemical theorists to achieve a leap forward in the development of their subject which had seemed impossible before, by enabling calculations that had hitherto taken months or years to be carried out in a few hours. This, probably more than any other single factor, was to enable chemical science after the Second World War to fulfil the hopes and promises of the inter-war years far more quickly than most people dreamt at the time.

FOR FURTHER READING: SCIENCE

For a descriptive bibliography in physics, chemistry, and biology from 1900 forward, see *The Twentieth-Century Mind*, vol. I, pp. 357–9. From among the works listed there it may be helpful to repeat certain titles relevant to the period covered by the present volume.

GENERAL: *The Origins and Growth of Physical Science*, ed. D. L. Hurd and J. J. Kipling (1964), biographical essays on scientists in physics and chemistry.

PHYSICS: H. Margenau, *The Nature of Physical Reality* (New York, 1949); M. Planck, *A Survey of Physics* (1925); P. W. Bridgman, *The Nature of Physical Theory* (Princeton, 1936); M. Born, *Experiment and Theory in Physics* (Cambridge, 1943) and *The Restless Universe* (1935); B. Hoffmann, *The Strange Story of the Quantum* (1947); E. Zimmer, *The Revolution in Physics* (1936); Sir James Jeans, *The Mysterious Universe* (Cambridge, 1930). On the philosophical background of physics: L. S. Stebbings, *Philosophy and the Physicists* (1937). On the historical context: H. S. Lipson, *The Great Experiments in Physics* (Edinburgh, 1968). On mathematical thought: E. T. Bell, *Men of*

Mathematics, 2 vols. (1937). For advanced reading in physics: G. Joos, *Theoretical Physics* (1934); P. G. Bergmann, *Basic Theories of Physics* (New York, 1949); and the seven-volume Pergamon Press series by L. Landau and E. M. Lifschitz, *Theoretical Physics*.

CHEMISTRY: A. Findlay, *A Hundred Years of Chemistry* (1965); T. M. Lowry, *Historical Introduction to Chemistry* (1936); F. S. Taylor, *A History of Industrial Chemistry* (1957); B. C. Saunders and R. E. D. Clark, *Order and Chaos in the World of Atoms* (rev. ed., 1948).

10

Poetry

JOHN WAIN

I

T. S. Eliot (1888–1965), the most influential poet of the English-speaking world during the time-span covered by this chapter, is now seen in retrospect as a poet of the religious sensibility. His conversion to Christianity, which he announced in 1928, took him formally into the Christian camp, and for the rest of his life he was the leading non-clerical member (some would say, the leading member *tout court*) of the Anglo-Catholic intelligentsia, which numbered such variously interesting figures as C. S. Lewis, Charles Williams, and Dorothy L. Sayers. His greatest poem, *Four Quartets*, appeared between 1935 and 1943: this is, during the years in which intellectual Anglo-Catholicism reached the crest of its short but very real period of influence on English life.

We must guard, however, against any tendency to present Eliot as a devout churchman who happened also to be a poet, or to see his greatest poem as a kind of lofty poetic version of the *Screwtape Letters*. Eliot was a major poet whose symbols were, for the most part, those traditionally associated with Christian belief and whose mood, both before and after his conversion, was penitential.

These thoughts are directly relevant to a consideration of Eliot's early poetry as presented in *Prufrock and Other Observations* (1917) and *Ara Vos Prec* (1920). We have already seen * that the title poem of *Prufrock*, which dominates the volume and sets its tone, can be taken as an expression of that longing to break through the concrete paving of 'real' life and come at the truth, as it lay there waiting to be embodied, grasped, and uttered in the metaphors of the Symbolists. In *Ara Vos Prec*, Eliot takes us into the same world of outward squalor and triviality, and intense inner longing. The volume takes its title from a passage in Dante's *Purgatorio* which clearly haunted Eliot's imagination. Here (Canto XXVI), among those whose sin on earth was lustfulness, Dante encounters Guido Guinicelli, a widely influential Florentine poet, who in turn indicates to him the Provençal troubadour Arnaut Daniel as 'a better craftsman in the

* See *The Twentieth-Century Mind*, vol. I, p. 408.

mother tongue' (*miglior fabbro del parlar materno*). Arnaut, a poet
who excelled in the highly opaque style known as *trobar clus*,
represents a personal preference of Dante's in which subsequent
taste has been unwilling to follow him, but Eliot evidently sees no
such difficulty, and when in the dedication to *The Waste Land* he
calls Ezra Pound *il miglior fabbro*, the comparison with Arnaut is
obviously intended to honour both poets. In the *Purgatorio*, Dante
holds speech with Arnaut Daniel, who makes the moving plea,

> 'Ara vos prec, per aquella valor
>   que vos guida al som de l'escalina,
>   sovegna vos a temps de ma dolor.'

('Now I pray you, by that Goodness which guides you to the
summit of the stairway, be mindful in due time of my pain.') In
allowing Daniel to speak in his own Provençal tongue rather than
in the Italian of the rest of the poem, Dante was for a moment
anticipating the polyglot method of Eliot's own work; but obviously
what attracted the poet to this passage was its penitential mood.

Throughout *Ara Vos Prec*, Eliot continues the practice of
speaking through a *persona* or Browningesque dramatic fiction;
here, the successors to Prufrock are 'Sweeney' and the unnamed
speaker of 'Gerontion'. Sweeney is a figure who recurs in Eliot's
poetry and is finally given the star role in the unfinished *Sweeney
Agonistes* (1926–7); he is the human being as animal, seen always in
a satirical light and yet not without sympathetic qualities; many
people like animals and many people would probably like Sweeney.
The other dramatic invention is the old man who utters the major
poem in the volume, 'Gerontion' (γερων is Greek for an old man:
'Gerontion' is the diminutive, a little old man). He has grown old
among the same unrealities that beset Prufrock; his experience
seems to have taught him nothing. Several lines foreshadow the
opening of *The Waste Land*: the challenge to new life appears as
terrible and devouring to the spiritually dead and dying.

> Signs are taken for wonders. 'We would see a sign!'
> The word within a word, unable to speak a word,
> Swaddled with darkness. In the juvescence of the year
> Came Christ the tiger.

The old man, caught in the spiral of decline and exasperation which
Eliot many years later was to describe, ironically, in 'Little Gidding'
as 'the gifts reserved for age/To set a crown upon your lifetime's

effort', longs like Prufrock to break free and find some meaning
that will make his life worth having lived, but he sinks back at last
into the indifference of exhaustion:

> Tenants of the house,
> Thoughts of a dry brain in a dry season.

No other poem in *Ara Vos Prec* is as important as 'Gerontion',
though the slighter pieces are memorable in their tight, dry way.
In fact what we chiefly notice, today, about this volume is the
originality of its idiom. We have Eliot's own testimony that when
he started out as a poet he found nothing in the English poetry of
the immediate past that helped him to find his own voice. Searching
in that commodious 'mind of Europe' to which his early studies
had given him the key, he found two moments in the history of
poetry which seemed to offer what he needed. One was the French
poetry of the later nineteenth century, the other the English poetry of
the early seventeenth. These two kinds of poetry are not really
similar; they come together in Eliot's work because of the white
heat of the imagination that forges them into unity; in themselves
they are separate, but Eliot's poetic mind is strong enough to fuse
them into something that retains the basic features of both and yet
is entirely his own. In *Ara Vos Prec* we see this process beginning:
both the French and the English influences are there, but they
have not yet come together. The two French poets most drawn on
are Tristan Corbière and his successor Jules Laforgue, both of
whom developed an idiom in which satiric colloquialism came into
abrupt collision with tenderness and occasional grandeur. Both
these poets are full of metrical *élan*, of a kind that is very much to
seek in the English poetry of the period. They combine a typically
French skill in formal arrangement with an exuberant freedom;
they bring the rhythms of everyday speech into counterpoint with
those of formal verse in a way that can hardly be paralleled in
English poetry later than Shakespeare. In particular, both poets
showed a fondness for the strict octosyllabic quatrain (examples:
Corbière's *A L'Etna* or *Paysage Mauvais*, Laforgue's *Complainte de
Cette Bonne Lune* or, with an even tighter six-syllable line, *Complainte de l'Oublie des Morts*), which provided a direct model for
poems like 'Whispers of Immortality' and 'Sweeney Among the
Nightingales', as they did for Ezra Pound's roughly contemporary
Hugh Selwyn Mauberley. Amid all this, Eliot never seems less than
his own man. Although he makes no attempt to cover up what he

has learnt from other poets, he never suggests any one of them in particular. Similarly in 'Gerontion' the movement is that of late Elizabethan or Jacobean blank verse, and yet Eliot nowhere seems to be echoing Shakespeare, or Webster, or Middleton, too directly. He is in search of a tradition; but he knows that it is also a tradition, among poets, to be original.

These early poems had attracted 'fit audience, though few'. But it was Eliot's next work, *The Waste Land* (1922), which established him immediately as a major poet. Appearing in the same year as Joyce's *Ulysses*, Proust's *Sodom et Gomorrhe*, Yeats's *Later Poems*, Lawrence's *Aaron's Rod*, and Rilke's *Sonette an Orpheus*, Eliot's poem took its place among a whole galaxy of major works that embodied the new sensibility of Europe. But from the beginning that place was seen as a central one.

The importance of *The Waste Land* was many-sided. To begin with one of the most obvious of its facets, it broke through into a whole range of new subject-matter by deriving its sustaining metaphors from the world of anthropology. In his search for a concrete way of presenting the situation of modern mankind, Eliot was drawn to the wide-ranging symbolism of the medieval legend of the quest for the Holy Grail. Under the scrutiny of a generation of anthropologists presided over by Sir J. G. Frazer, this legend had revealed a complex and ever-ramifying ancestry. Eliot must have been attracted to it for many reasons. At the outset, its eclectic nature must have appealed to a young scholar-poet who found interest and relevance in so many areas. Eliot abandoned his early studies in Indian philosophy because he felt that they were taking him out of sight of the Western tradition which was his true home; this was due not to timidity but to a realization that the Western tradition can best be carried on by people who have studied it in all its richness and identified their own development with it. A few years before *The Waste Land*, he had argued in his essay 'Tradition and the Individual Talent' that 'the mind of Europe . . . is a mind which changes, and that this change is a development which abandons nothing *en route*, which does not superannuate either Shakespeare, or Homer, or the rock drawing of the Magdalenian draughtsmen'. To Eliot, anything worthy to be called civilization was the interaction of so many ideas, so many places and people, that he must have found his poetic imagination enormously liberated by the panoptic labours of an anthropologist like Frazer. Then there was the blend of Christian and non-Christian elements in this bundle of legends; the exact point at which Eliot's mind began to turn towards Christianity is not established, but many of its elements claimed his attention and respect from the beginning, and to see Christian folklore embedded in vegetation myths and nature-worship generally would please his sense of the drama of human ideas.

Another very attractive feature of this material was its fragmentary nature. Nowhere in Europe have collectors been able to find a show-case version of the Grail story in which all the habitual elements are present. Instead, as usual with folklore, element *a* is found with elements *d* and *e*, *b* with *c* and *a*, etc. Eliot actually took most of his material from a short and highly readable semi-popular account by Jessie L. Weston, *From Ritual to Romance* (1920), in which Miss Weston, who had written many books on medieval legend, was concerned to argue that the seemingly discrete parts of the Grail myth had a common origin in ritual and therefore in religious worship. She began by drawing particular attention to the fact that the legend, originally whole, was disassembled so that a certain scholarly and imaginative effort was needed to see it properly at all: 'A prototype, containing the main features of the Grail story—the Waste Land, the Fisher King, the Hidden Castle, with its solemn Feast, and mysterious Feeding Vessel, the Bleeding Lance and Cup—does not, so far as we know, exist.'

These words evidently jumped off the page to the eye of the young Eliot. For *The Waste Land* might be described in just those words: a prototype containing the main features of the Grail story. Another passage in Miss Weston's book which obviously riveted the poet's attention is her description, in chapter 6, of the ancient and mysterious Tarot pack of cards, which number 78 and contain 22 bearing a special symbolism and known as 'the Keys'. 'To-day', says Miss Weston, 'the Tarot has fallen somewhat into disrepute, being principally used for purposes of divination. . . . Traditionally it is said to have been brought from Egypt.' Hence the presence in Eliot's poem of Madame Sosostris, with her Egyptian-sounding and doubtless self-bestowed name. Starting from this satirical episode, the symbolism of the Tarot thrusts outwards to all parts of the poem, culminating in an association, which Eliot himself admits to be 'quite arbitrary', of The Man with Three Staves with the Fisher King—so that the 'three staves' become the three virtues inculcated in the thunder's message, and thus prop the dying king into a dignified readiness for his sacrifice.

Miss Weston, having quoted an expert on the Tarot to the effect that 'many of the words are of Sanskrit, or Hindustani, origin', goes

on to invoke the authority of W. B. Yeats, 'whose practical acquaintance with Medieval and Modern Magic', she says primly, 'is well
known', and to quote from a personal letter in which Yeats assures
her that various elements of the Tarot 'have never lost their mystic
significance, and are today a part of magical operations'. Here we
are at one of the flash-points in the history of modern poetry; the
two greatest poets of their age stand for an instant on the same
ground; and Eliot, like Yeats, hears a voice which says, 'We are
come to give you metaphors for poetry.'

We are now ready to see *The Waste Land* in Yeatsian terms as 'a
fardel of stories' capable of being quickened by poetic meditation
into metaphors that could make sense of the world and man's place
in it. The legends provided both distancing and immediacy. They
brought the contemporary scene—the postwar life of the big city—
into strikingly clear focus because the modern world, with its
smashed cultures and dried-up faiths, *is* the Waste Land and its
inhabitants *are* both seeking for, and fearing, a renewal of life. It also
held that scene at arm's length and prevented it from flooding the
imagination with a deluge of meaningless detail. Not that these
sources of symbolism are altogether absent from Eliot's earlier
poetry. The death of Phlebas, not yet assimilated to its appropriate
Tarot card but seen as the cleansing of someone soiled by life,
occurs in his French poem 'Dans le Restaurant' (1918). But this
symbolism is worked out freshly and fully in *The Waste Land*.

I shall not offer a description of the poem, whose details have
been shredded out over the years by numerous commentators. *The
Waste Land* was at once accepted as a classic statement of the
situation of modern Western man, and particularly so by younger
readers. Edmund Wilson tells us in *Axel's Castle* that 'where some
of even the finest intelligences of the older generation read *The
Waste Land* with blankness or laughter, the young had recognized
a poet'. In fact, this recognition amounted mainly to the acknowledgement of a common sense of frustration; the element of positive
questing and affirmation in the poem was largely ignored, and it was
received by its first public as an expression of despair.

It was, in short, the poignant evocation of loss, rather than the
search for a way upward from loss, that came across to that first
generation of readers: what struck them was the landscape within
the Waste Land rather than the plotting of routes out of the Waste
Land. This was the more pardonable in view of the poem's densely
cryptic nature. It was first printed in the opening number of the
Criterion, an international review launched in 1922 under Eliot's

editorship, and in this original guise it was unaccompanied by notes. Only when the publishers of the first American edition, Boni and Liveright, found the poem too short to publish in book form and asked for additional material (the Hogarth Press in England seems to have raised no such objection), did Eliot sit down and write the notes, which, unsatisfactory as they are, do at least provide the essential pointer to Miss Weston's book without which the poem would scarcely be intelligible at all to many readers.

Before leaving *The Waste Land*, it is important to drive home a fact not so far mentioned: that the poem as we have it is so modified in response to the criticism of a fellow-poet that it could perhaps almost be described as a collaboration between the two men. This fellow-poet was Ezra Weston Loomis Pound (b. 1885), whom Eliot had met in 1914 and whose influence on his own practice was at this time at its height.

Since Eliot gave away the manuscript of *The Waste Land* to his lawyer friend John Quinn more or less as soon as he had finished working on it, and since it remained generally unknown among Quinn's papers until 1968, there were many years in which the details of Pound's reshaping of the poem remained a matter for speculation. Eliot, consulting his memory, could testify only that 'It was in 1922 that I placed before him in Paris the manuscript of a sprawling, chaotic poem called *The Waste Land* which left his hands, reduced to about half its size, in the form in which it appears in print' (statement in *Poetry*, 1946).

When the manuscript finally turned up, it was at once put on view in the New York Public Library and was made the subject of a detailed article in the London *Times Literary Supplement* by the bibliographer Donald Gallup (7 November 1968). It appeared from Gallup's account that Eliot had remembered correctly the general drift of Pound's criticism: whole sections of the poem had been tossed out, making it more difficult (because connecting links had disappeared) but also more cinematic in its abrupt changes of focus and its rapid tracking and panning alternating with sudden close-ups. In its pre-Poundian form, *The Waste Land* was an Ovidian poem; Eliot had studied Latin at Harvard under E. K. Rand, a scholar with a special interest in Ovid, and indeed the Ovidian poetic universe, with its constant shifting of shapes and boundaries, was very congenial to the poetic mind of the 1920s; it is worth recalling that there is a strong Ovidian influence in Pound's Cantos, beginning as early as Canto II, and that the small publishing house which issued the first edition of *Hugh Selwyn Mauberley* was called

The Ovid Press. In the original *Waste Land*, there is a set of Popean couplets describing the way a certain Lady Fresca, attended by her maid Amanda, prepares to face the day. During the 69-line passage, the scene changes from the eighteenth to the twentieth century; this sense of flowing and changing is in line with the generally Ovidian flavour of the poem—the way Tiresias, for instance, experiences the action through the sensibility of all the other characters at once.

The original poem had dramatic juxtapositions, which on the whole Pound sharpened by his harsh cutting, though a rather fine one was lost in the 'Death by Water' section when *il miglior fabbro* threw out a 71-line passage describing a shipwreck. After Pound had finished with it, *The Waste Land* was still an Ovidian poem, but now it was also cinematic and abrupt in the modern manner. Pound had, in fact, brought it into line with his own practice in *Mauberley* —a poem we shall be considering a few pages further on—and the early Cantos.

Since Ezra Pound has irrupted, in his boisterous way, into our narrative, we can no longer postpone a discussion of the man and his work. He was born at Hailey, Idaho, of pioneer stock—exactly that stock which, having tamed the American continent, had to stand by and watch the fruits of its achievement eaten up by a multi-racial swarm of immigrants in the years around 1900, a fact which may go some way to explaining Pound's later political attitudes. Hailey, Idaho, with its natural beauty, its rooted rural community, and its vivid though short historical tradition, was an excellent place for a poet to be born in, and Pound's misfortunes may be said to have started when he was taken away in babyhood. The family moved to a suburb of Philadelphia, and the poet's wanderings had begun.

After graduating, Pound held a fellowship in romance languages at the University of Pennsylvania (1905-7), then, briefly, a teaching post at Wabash College, Crawfordsville, Indiana, which ended after a few months with the recognition on both sides that he was 'too much the Latin quarter type'. Still in 1907, he sailed for Europe and tramped through Spain, Italy, and Provence before arriving in London, his headquarters for the next thirteen years.

Convinced of the puritan provinciality of America ('a half-savage country, out of date'), Pound was blissfully receptive to Europe. His scholarly equipment, while nothing like as good as Eliot's, was

enough to get him started on his lifelong voyage of polyglot exploration. He became interested in the troubadours, in medieval poetry
generally, and published in 1910 a critical survey of this area, *The
Spirit of Romance*. He also admitted various formal elements from
these poets into his own verse: a good example would be the spirited
'Sestina: Altaforte', composed at about this time.

In these early days, Pound might have been mistaken for a
typical Edwardian-romantic worshipper of the Middle Ages like
Chesterton or Belloc, and in fact his early verse is even more pre-
Raphaelite than theirs, though with more rhythmical vitality. But
Pound's impulse, from the beginning, was to modernize. He ran-
sacked the past because he wished to use its materials to build a new
present.

Roughly, Pound's position was the same as that which Eliot had
reached independently—which was why they greeted one another
with such pleasure when, in 1914, their paths finally crossed.
Pound had longed for the richness of Europe, but when he got there
he found that the treasures were lying about unnoticed and unused.
Europe seemed to him moribund in so many ways: moribund in
politics, in social attitudes, and above all in art and literature. The
great river of European letters had shrunk to a filtered trickle tame
enough to decorate a gentleman's garden.

Pound's attack on this state of affairs was two-pronged. In the
first place he strove to revitalize the tradition by massive injections
from the usable past. (Naturally, his ideas about what was, and what
was not, usable from the past were very much his own.) At the same
time he sought out, and propagated with tireless energy and
generosity, those writers and artists who seemed to him to express
a genuinely modern consciousness. The conservative literary
'establishment', much more sure of itself and much more heavily
organized than it is today, dominated most of the newspapers,
magazines, and publishing houses. But Pound, exasperated and
indomitable, hammered away wherever he could, disdaining no
outlet that would allow him to make a few converts, pouring out
ceaseless argumentation, expostulation, and encouragement. In
poetry, he exerted himself particularly on behalf of Eliot: in prose,
of James Joyce (who would certainly have languished in neglect for
many more years if Pound had not done so much to draw attention
to him—cf. the full story in *Pound/Joyce*, edited by Forrest Read,
1968); in music, of George Antheil; in sculpture, of Henri Gaudier,
the young French artist who was known as Gaudier-Brzeska,
having added to his own the name of the Polish lady who was his

soul-mate and Ægeria; in painting, of Wyndham Lewis, whom he also praised as a novelist.

In 1917–19 Pound acted as London editor of *The Little Review*, the explosive and enthusiastic magazine run by two Chicago ladies (cf. Margaret Anderson's entertaining memoir, *My Thirty Years' War*, 1930), and supplied it with much of its most interesting material, including some sections of Joyce's *Ulysses*, for which the magazine was to feel the heavy hand of the law. Later, from Paris, he was foreign correspondent of *The Dial*. And, intermittently through all those years, he struggled to get the poets he approved of into the dignified pages of Harriet Monro's *Poetry: A Magazine of Verse* (Chicago).

The full intricate story of Pound's alliances, ardours, and enthusiasms during these years, c. 1907–20, would involve us in too much detail; his relationship with various groups—the Imagists, the Vorticists—his fiery quarrels and equally glowing friendships. The story has been told many times. What concerns us in a general history of poetry is that Pound's main critical drive was towards uncluttered statement, directness and swiftness of utterance. His most frequent complaint against English and American writing of the recent past, both in prose and verse, was that it was squashy, inflated, over-ornamented: he was for a clean, surgical precision, and he wanted it on social and political grounds as well as 'literary':

It is very important that there should be clear, unexaggerated realistic literature. It is very important that there should be good prose. The hell of contemporary Europe is caused by the lack of representative government in Germany, *and* by the non-existence of decent prose in the German language. Clear thought and sanity depend on clear prose. They cannot live apart. . . . A nation that cannot write clearly cannot be trusted to govern, nor yet to think.[1]

It was this that underlay Pound's sympathy with Imagism ('an Image', he said, 'is that which presents an emotional or intellectual complex in an instant of time') and his excitement over Ernest Fenollosa's *The Chinese Written Character*, which offered the Western reader an introduction to the ideogram. As Pound understood it, the ideogram, by its visual nature, could present an idea with that simultaneity and bareness which the Imagists sought in 'the image'.

At this distance of time both notions are apt to seem slightly threadbare: Chinese scholars, such as the late Arthur Waley, dealt harshly with the Pound/Fenollosa assessment of the ideogram, while as for the doctrines of Imagism, they seem today too thin and superficial to be of serious help to a poet. At the time, however, they must have seemed liberating, to an ear tired of Newbolt, Bridges, and Gordon Bottomley. The Imagists maintained that poetry must present the unadorned object without moralizing or other forms of discourse; and they favoured free verse because, to them, a pre-defined verse form suggested a pre-defined emotion, and they held that a poem ought to spring fire-new from the unique emotion that precipitated it. As a theory of poetry this has its weaknesses, but the Imagists made their contribution during the years 1912–14.

In moving towards an appreciation of Pound's poetry, it is helpful to start as far back as *A Lume Spento* (Venice, 1908), even though these very early poems are heavily ornamented, 'literary', and given to the medievalizing of an enthusiastic amateur. When the book was re-issued in 1965, the elderly Pound contributed a brief, dismissive foreword describing it as 'A collection of stale creampuffs'. The poems, he added, revealed nothing except 'the depth of ignorance, or rather the superficiality of non-perception—neither eye nor ear'. A man has surely the right to say what he likes about his own work, and much of this we may admit: but *A Lume Spento*, when read with sympathetic hindsight, still seems a promising beginning, worthy of an important poet. There is a rhythmical *élan*, a buoyancy and zest, which do not consistently achieve lightness and grace, but often approach this ideal and, perhaps once in five or six poems, achieve it. What is even more important is that the characteristic Poundian blend of the singing voice and the speaking voice can be heard thus early. Amid pages of a merely pre-Raphaelite rhythm, one finds the beginning of that characteristic flexible manner, somewhere between the conversational and the lyrical, able at any moment to modulate fully into either. Such a blend seems to me to be present in this poem, of which I quote the whole:

THRENOS

> No more for us the little sighing,
> No more the winds at twilight trouble us.
>
> Lo the fair dead!
>
> No more do I burn.
> No more for us the fluttering of wings
> That whirred the air above us.
>
> Lo the fair dead!

No more desire flayeth me,
No more for us the trembling
At the meeting of hands.

Lo the fair dead!

No more for us the wine of the lips,
No more for us the knowledge.

Lo the fair dead!

No more the torrent,
No more for us the meeting-place
(Lo the fair dead!)
Tintagoel.[2]

'The unseizable magic of poetry is in the queer paper volume, and words are no good at describing it.' So wrote a reviewer of that day, in, of all places, the *Evening Standard*, and his review was quoted with cool approbation in an elegant pamphlet, unsigned, which appeared in New York in 1917: *Ezra Pound his Metre and Poetry*. The author of this pamphlet was T. S. Eliot. Thus early did the acknowledgement and the repayment begin, for Eliot had already learnt crucial lessons from Pound—or, we might more accurately say, been sustained and prompted by Pound in achieving crucial insights.

The year 1913 was an important one for Pound; he took over the leadership of the Imagists (their manifesto published in the April number of *Poetry* was probably drafted by him) and published *Personae and Exultations*, his most important collection so far. *Personae*, the masks of the Roman actor, exactly describes Pound's mode of working at this time. He was always interested in translation, and his original work is often close to translation in that it models itself on some style, some set of attitudes, that has caught his fancy in Anglo-Saxon or Provençal or (after 1915, when he published *Cathay*) Chinese. No poet has ever written in so many different styles as Pound, and yet there is always something essentially Poundian, some aroma of his personality and some rhythm of his voice, that binds these poems together as the work of one man.

But occasional forays into this or that area of sensibility, scattered exercises in different styles, were beginning to be insufficient for Pound. In 1917, he took an important step forward by linking a series of *personae*-pieces into a coherent whole. This was *Homage to*

Sextus Propertius, in which Pound partly translated and partly recreated a number of poems by the Latin elegist, and put them together to form a lively and memorable sequence on the theme of the poet's life; what he can expect, what he hopes for, what brings him happiness and sorrow, what he feels to be his place in society. His chief happiness is in the love of women; his chief hope, the immortality of his verses. There is a gaiety, a light-hearted irony, a lyrical zest and a delicate balance in Pound's *Propertius*, making it the most purely enjoyable of all his works. But it also strikes a serious note. The problems of the poet are real problems. He is too earthy and at the same time too erudite for 'the populace', who want empty respectabilities from their poets:

> For the nobleness of the populace brooks nothing below
>   its own altitude.
> One must have resonance, resonance and sonority . . .
>   like a goose.

There are hints, and more than hints, that the poet behind the *persona* is finding his life-style incompatible with that of the society he lives in.

Pound left England for good in 1920, and in that year he published *Hugh Selwyn Mauberley*, his farewell to the Anglo-Saxon world which he had come to feel was so unsatisfactory. This is a sequence of eighteen poems, falling into two parts. The first part consists of twelve poems followed by an 'Envoi' dated 1919; the second part is headed 'Mauberley' and dated 1920. Taken together, the poems tell the story of a poet and his attempt to survive, as man and artist, in a basically hostile environment. This environment is the England of *circa* 1910, and the poet's fate is to drift into hedonistic solipsism. His attempts to come to an understanding with his age, or to mount a successful opposition to it, fail equally, and he vanishes into a refined oblivion.

Even this bald account of the poem's subject-matter, however, is confronted at once by serious difficulties of interpretation. Is Mauberley meant to be Pound himself? To F. R. Leavis, the poem is 'quintessential autobiography'; to G. S. Fraser, Mauberley is 'not wholly Pound; but he is a real aspect of Pound'. On this view, the poem would be a farewell to that period of Pound's life in which he had lived and worked as an aesthete, a man primarily concerned with shapes, colours, sounds, and rhythms. As Dr. Leavis reads the poem, it 'offers, more particularly, a representative experience of the phase of English poetry in which it became plain that the

Romantic tradition was exhausted'. Hugh Selwyn Mauberley, as a minor poet whose work is insufficiently grounded in reality, fails to produce memorable work and dissolves in a cloud of aesthetic velleities. His life is emblematic of the difficulties that beset people in his situation; he is a poetic Everyman.

As against this view, we have the opinion of John J. Espey, whose *Ezra Pound's 'Mauberley': a Study in Composition* (1955) is the most thorough study of the poem yet made, that Pound and Mauberley are to be strongly contrasted. Mr. Espey sees the poem as having an essentially dramatic structure. The first part concerns 'E.P.'; the second, the more dimly focused figure of 'Mauberley'. The two come together only in having a common world and a common set of 'contrasts'; so that the vignettes of 'Monsieur Verog', 'Brennbaum', and 'Mr. Nixon', all types who illustrate the deadness of contemporary civilization, reveal a frustration which afflicts both figures equally. But they react in different ways; 'E.P.' leaves in order to survive, Mauberley stays on and is sucked under.

The gap between these two interpretations can probably be bridged. Mauberley goes on making the mistakes that 'E.P.' is determined to make no longer. He clings to an 'aesthetic' position, living on the scraps of an exhausted tradition, whereas 'E.P.' is determined to move forward into a more active role. From now on, Pound will see art as directly arising from the circumstances of life and directly affecting them in turn. He is moving towards the point he is to reach in the mid-thirties, when he can write to a friend: 'I can tell the bank rate and component of tolerance for usury in any epoch by the quality of *line* in painting. Baroque, etc., era of usury becoming tolerated.'

The objection to Mr. Espey's interpretation, that Pound and Mauberley are two distinct characters and that one goes while the other stays, is that it is difficult to point to any passage in the poem that unambiguously *says* that 'E.P.' is going to take himself off to fresh woods and pastures new. We know, as a matter of biographical fact, that he did, and this fact influences our reading of the poem; but that hardly seems enough. Still, there is some indication of a departure in the opening poem of the sequence, a mock-epitaph which speaks of 'E.P.' in the third person:

> Unaffected by 'the march of events',
> He passed from men's memory in *l'an trentiesme*
> *De son eage;* the case presents
> No adjunct to the Muses' diadem.

And perhaps that is enough. What is attractive about Mr. Espey's theory, once one has accepted it, is that it makes *Mauberley* a better poem, with an effective dramatic structure to add to its witty vignettes and its tone of mocking yet tragic irony.

Coming two years before *The Waste Land*, *Hugh Selwyn Mauberley* anticipates many of the main features of Eliot's poem. It uses a dizzying multiplicity of literary reference; it changes focus and direction with ferocious abruptness; it speaks through oblique ironies, punctuated by sudden utterances of a disconcerting directness. Like all Pound's work, *Mauberley* arouses hostility and revulsion in some readers, fanatical devotion in others; there is not, and perhaps never will be, a critical consensus about any of Pound's major works. But we can say without being controversial that it is an extraordinarily *accomplished* poem. The shifts of rhythm and tone, the modulation in and out of parody and burlesque, the irreverent humour and the sombre invective, all help to give the poem a range and elasticity which enable it to deal with a large area of life in a few pages.

There are, really, three fixed points in *Mauberley*, and the poem is a series of forked lightning-flashes in the triangular space between them. One is Pound himself, another is the London *milieu* which obstinately refused to learn what he so much desired to teach; and the third is the shadowy figure of Mauberley, who does not succeed by the standards of either of the other two. Mauberley, as Pound sees him, is the kind of twilight aesthetic poet, with no firm grip either on life or art, who must be superseded. On the other hand, he has values of his own which at least are not those of Mr. Nixon, Brennbaum, and the Lady Valentine; he also has 'mildness amid the neo-Nietzchean clatter', which would set him apart from the rather bullying knot of intellectual roughnecks (Wyndham Lewis, T. E. Hulme, Pound himself) who were associated with Lewis's magazine *Blast*.

Pound's rejection of the London of 1919 is harsh and satiric; his rejection of Mauberley is elegiac. Perhaps Mauberley represents an outgrown part of himself. At the moment of reshaping his life and art, Pound looks with dismay and yet with a kind of tenderness on the path that he might easily have trodden, and the kind of man he might easily have become. And all this gives *Mauberley* a range of tone and feeling that makes it, whatever our reservations, a major poem.

Reservations, of course, there must be. Pound's analysis of Victorian and Edwardian London is the analysis of an outsider, a brilliant and sharp-eyed outsider who for all his brilliance will make mistakes that an insider would not make. For this reason, the 'vignettes' that dramatize Pound's discontents are better if we take them as simple cartoons; once we discover whom they are meant to be portraits *of*, we cannot help protesting, for instance, that Arnold Bennett was not a vulgarian like 'Mr. Nixon', but an artist who had given years to the struggle to enrich English fiction by importing French techniques and attitudes, thus fulfilling one of Pound's major commandments, to break down English insularity: and also a critic whose generous enthusiasm for quality, wherever he found it, was ill rewarded by Pound's sneer: ' "I never mentioned a man but with a view/Of selling my own works." ' As for the portrait of Max Beerbohm as 'Brennbaum', a man who knew Edwardian London from the inside, rather than the outside, would have known that Beerbohm was not a Jew but of German Baltic stock, so that 'The heavy memories of Horeb, Sinai and the forty years' could hardly be expected to show in his face. For all his wit and insight, one is left with the impression that Pound did not really *know* the society he was damning.

The point is of some importance because the poet was entering a phase of his life and work in which the claim to know society, to understand what made it work, was to seem to him more and more worth making. In 1948, when a selection of his poems was issued by the American firm of New Directions, Pound contributed a page or so of notes on his career under the heading 'Autobiography'. One of these notes runs: '1918: Began investigation of causes of war, to oppose same.' If we take the date 1918 seriously, and there seems no reason why we should not, we can place the most important change in Pound's interests and attitudes within the few months separating *Propertius* from *Mauberley*. From this time on, he is interested in what makes a society sick or healthy; and everything he writes is directed, ultimately or immediately, to preaching what he thinks needful for health. This is why Mauberley, with his eye on evanescent aesthetic tints, will not do. On the other hand, democracy will not do either. In section III of *Hugh Selwyn Mauberley*, Pound is scathing about the kind of popular democracy that was emerging:

> Even the Christian beauty
> Defects—after Samothrace;
> We see τὸ καλὸν
> Decreed in the market place.

> Faun's flesh is not to us,
> Nor the saint's vision.
> We have the press for wafer;
> Franchise for circumcision.
>
> All men, in law, are equals.
> Free of Pisistratus,
> We choose a knave or an eunuch
> To rule over us.[3]

Perhaps most readers, in 1920, took at least some of this as mere verbal flourishing. After all, 'the press' and 'franchise', though they may not be as impressive as the saint's vision or as close to the primal mysteries as circumcision, are the machinery by which democracy works. But Pound, as he was increasingly to reveal, was in deadly earnest. He really did dislike the free press and the universal vote. His trust in the judgement of the average man, either in art or in politics, was nil. (This could be inferred from his critical writings, with their determined insistence that only the opinion of a tiny enlightened minority is worth having. He rejects outright the idea that a great culture can spring from a people as a whole: 'The Greek populace was PAID to attend the great Greek tragedies, and darn well wouldn't have gone otherwise, or if there had been a cinema.')

Against such a background we must set Pound's disgust at seeing 'τὸ καλὸν/Decreed in the market place'. The Greek expression means literally 'beauty', but Pound connected beauty with health and order in the social and personal spheres (as who does not?), and a mere thirteen years later he was declaring his faith in Mussolini's Fascism in the same terms: 'I assert again my own firm belief that the Duce will stand not with despots and the lovers of power but with the lovers of ORDER, τὸ καλὸν.'

That quotation comes from *Jefferson and/or Mussolini* (1933). Up to the point of writing it, Pound had experience of Fascism only as an Italian phenomenon; the infinitely more businesslike German version was just, at that moment, coming to power. Pound had chosen Italy as his home in 1924, and by 1933 he was so deeply committed to supporting Fascism that even the rise of Nazism, even the outbreak of war between the Fascist countries and the democracies, did not halt him. He made an attempt to return to the United States when that country entered the war in 1941, but this was frustrated (by American officialdom, the story goes), and he remained in Rome throughout the war, broadcasting his views.

These views were a hotch-potch of economic and social theories, much the same as he had been propagating for at least the previous ten years. They were opposed to the American war effort and were therefore, technically, treason; but what is likely to seem most offensive in them today is their anti-Semitism, which continued unabated during the terrible agony of Europe's Jews, and the open worship of Fascist dictatorship.

This, however, is to anticipate. Pound himself gives 1918 as the year in which his attention turns to economics and politics. Three years earlier, he had begun work on his long poem, or sequence of poems, *The Cantos*. And the Cantos were designed, from the beginning, to live up to Pound's definition of an epic poem: 'a poem that includes history'.

We noted earlier that there is no critical consensus about Pound's work. To say this of *The Cantos* would be an understatement. Some respectable judges of literature regard the whole vast work as a monument of incoherent nonsense. Others give their testimony that it is one of the great poems of the world. And always, in the background, is the patient swarm of academic commentators who, without pausing to judge one way or the other, get on with the job of explaining the poem's thousands of allusions.

Pound may now, in extreme old age, have laid aside *The Cantos*, but he was still actively at work on them as late as 1959. Since he began them in 1915, this gives 44 years of continuous work—rather more than twice the time it took Shakespeare to write his complete plays. In view of this huge time-span, and the cataclysmic things that have happened to Pound within it, there seems little point in looking for a single coherent structure to which all the parts can be related. Pound told Yeats that when the hundredth Canto was written, the whole would be seen to have a unity 'like that of a Bach fugue'. The hundredth Canto was written some time in the late 1950s, but long before then it was obvious that this prophecy would not be fulfilled. What we have, instead, is an enormous tapestry in which certain motifs occur again and again. Who is the wise ruler? What are the links between private happiness and the public good? Under what conditions (social, political, economic above all) can art flourish and men live fulfilled lives? Pound gives his answer to these questions not directly, as 'I', but according to the method he had developed in his work up to and including *Mauberley*. He speaks through masks; he dramatizes through emblematic personages. Certain historical figures become nodes for speculation and exhortation: Thomas Jefferson, Confucius, Mussolini, John Adams,

Alexander Hamilton, Sigismondo Malatesta. In Cantos LII–LXI the scene shifts to China, and Pound investigates the health or otherwise of the Chinese world under several dynasties. In *The Pisan Cantos* (LXXIV–LXXXIV), written when he was incarcerated and had no access to books, he falls back on reminiscence, his mind playing especially on those key years between 1910 and 1920: Canto LXXIV brings in Ford Madox Ford, Yeats, Maurice Baring, James Joyce, and Henry James. Not only figures but themes recur obsessively: usury is bad; the Jews are bad because many of them practise usury; 'freedom of speech' in mass democracies is an illusion.

Pound hammers away at these themes until they become, for me at least, boringly overstated. But there are refreshments, and surprises, in *The Cantos* sufficient to keep one turning the pages. Among the scraps of dialogue, quotations from official documents, little jokes, snatches of reminiscence, and the ever-recurring Chinese ideograms, one comes across delicate passages of lyric verse, or sustained denunciations that recall the War passage in *Mauberley*. In the later sections, *Rock-Drill* (LXXXV–XCV) and *Thrones* (XCVI–CIX), these oases are very rare, and one has the impression that the strong Poundian personality which has held the whole structure together for forty years is now in deliquescence.

The attempt to find a single unifying structure in *The Cantos* must now, I think, be given up. But the whole, with all its obscurities and its maddening repetitions, is impressive. It is the record of a poet's struggle with the artistic and social problems with which the twentieth century confronted him, and with which it confronts all poets. Pound's answers may not be our answers (they are certainly not mine), and yet the record of a struggle so long, and sustained with such determination, must stand as an example. And, on the merely technical level, *The Cantos* provided a model for the modern long poem and quite possibly, in so doing, saved the long poem from extinction in our time.

Pound the man fared rather worse than Pound the poet. With the collapse of the Italian war effort in 1944, he was taken into custody by the American military authorities and in due course, after a spell at a maximum-security internment camp where his fellow-prisoners were mostly hardened criminals and where he spent three weeks in a steel mesh cage, flown to Washington, D.C. to stand trial for treason to his country. He was never actually tried for this, because four psychiatrists had unanimously testified that he was of unsound mind and unfit to plead, but there was a public hearing on the question of his sanity or otherwise which had very much the atmosphere of a trial for treason. He was found to be of unsound mind, and confined in St. Elizabeth's Hospital, Washington, for twelve years. During this period he continued to work at *The Cantos* and also to receive visitors from all over the world. These visitors came away with conflicting reports about Pound's mental condition; some maintained that he was perfectly sane and was only being held in an asylum so that he would not have to be executed; others found him abnormal in speech and behaviour. (On the day I visited him, in August 1957, he was capable of connected and logical speech but not of conversation; he took no notice of anything said to him, but continued a steady monologue for hours on end. My impression was that, in his own interests, I would not have allowed him out of the hospital grounds by himself.) Finally, in 1958, after years of agitation from fellow-poets and liberals, it was decided that Pound, though still not sane enough to be tried, was not too dangerous to be let out, under his wife's care. He returned to Italy, and made his home first at Schloss Brunnenburg, near Merano in the Italian Alps, with his daughter Mary and her family, and later in Venice. At first, he worked on at *The Cantos*, but soon fell silent; in his rare, and short, conversations with visitors he belittled his own work and expressed 'profound remorse'; but mostly he said nothing. 'I did not enter into silence,' he said on his eightieth birthday. 'Silence captured me.' The long monologue was over at last.*

Pound's immersion in 'ideas' was at least serious to this extent, that it involved him in practical action and led to the tragic suffering of his later years. And yet it would be generally admitted that, despite the power and originality of his mind, something of the amateurish and the home-made clings to his thinking whenever it leaves the strictly defined territory of the writer's art. By contrast Eliot, though his general opinions were often at no great distance from Pound's, shows a combination of total seriousness and rigorous intellectual discipline which makes his criticism far the most important written by any poet in our century. The difference between Eliot and Pound might be indicated by a remark about Pound which Eliot let drop, more or less as an aside, in one of the

* I wrote these words too soon. Pound has published another substantial slab of *The Cantos* (*Drafts and Fragments of Cantos CX–CXVII*, 1970); and has occasionally been heard in Venice and elsewhere, talking away as he did in his prime.

lectures which he later printed as *After Strange Gods* (1934), to the effect that Pound was 'attracted to the Middle Ages, apparently, by everything except that which gives them their significance'.

The remark is penetrating because Pound, for all his wonderful sensitiveness to cadence, to the aesthetic quality of a poem and how that quality is achieved, often gives the impression of being un-interested in the loam in which the flower is rooted; the Middle Ages were first and foremost a period of religious faith, and in Pound's scattered pronouncements on medieval writers there is rarely—I had almost written, never—a sentence that shows any awareness of this fact. From the beginning, Eliot's critical prose is as much alive to social, historical, and philosophical implications as to 'purely' literary ones (whatever *they* may be). In fact, the first thing we notice when we begin to distinguish Eliot's criticism from that of Pound and of most other poets is its sensitive but powerful historicity. Possibly because of his family background, Eliot's mind had from early youth been accustomed to think in historical terms; where Pound, and most poets, ransack the past for what can be seized and put to immediate use, or in gentler moods wander in its gardens like nectar-sucking bees guided only by an instinct for making honey, Eliot was fascinated by the sheer amount that had happened in the past and was never tempted to think that literature and art had 'just growed', like Topsy. Intensely aware of his own point on the time-chart, aware also of the different rate of develop-ment and growth in different countries, he was always sensitive to the exact dimensions of the task that needed to be done, and in seeking help from the past he was always clear about what *kind* of help was needed.

Eliot's first full-scale critical book was *The Sacred Wood* (1920), a group of essays whose main thrust was towards a clearer way of thinking about poetry; as the Preface to the second edition put it retrospectively, 'the problem appearing in these essays, which gives them what coherence they have, is the problem of the integrity of poetry, with the repeated assertion that when we are considering poetry we must consider it primarily as poetry and not another thing.'

If this gives the impression that Eliot was proposing to fence off a limited area which could safely be called 'poetry' and then cosily operate within that area, the essays speedily demonstrate the contrary. Eliot wishes to avoid confusion and to oppose the vague habit, developed during the nineteenth century, of speaking of poetry as if it were religion, or philosophy—and of speaking of these things as if they were poetry. He does not at all consent to be sealed off within 'literature'. Above all, in the famous essay 'Tradition and the Individual Talent', Eliot makes a frontal assault on the problems arising from his own procedure as a poet and his preoccupations as a man. Everyone has always known, he argues, that the past influences the present; but it is not so generally realized that the present also influences the past. The backward look modifies the object; the past exists in the collective mind of the present, and if something happens to alter that mind, the past changes its appearance, the objects grouped there enter upon a different relationship with one another, and the landscape takes on a new life. Hence re-assessment of previous masterpieces can be effected only by artists, or by critics writing in the wake of art.

In this important manifesto (which, characteristically, avoids any direct reference to the fact that he himself writes poetry) Eliot not only indicated that the historical bias of his mind was central to his imaginative inspiration, but paved the way for most of the developments in his thinking and writing over the next quarter-century. When he said, for instance, that the practising poet 'must be very conscious of the main current, which does not at all flow invariably through the most distinguished reputations', he was justifying in advance the quietly iconoclastic note that would shortly become apparent. In the 1920s, when such opinions were not by any means the commonplaces that they are now, Eliot was making firmly limiting judgements on most of the English Romantic poets, and even more so on their Victorian successors, and in their place exalting Donne and Dryden, whom the Victorians had hardly considered as poets at all; he was disrespectful to Milton while giving powerful support to the tendency, already well in evidence, to exalt the seventeenth-century 'Metaphysicals' into major poets.

Eliot did these things because it was of vital importance to him to trace 'the main current'. He disliked eccentricity; it was not enough for him, as it has been enough for some English poets of our time, to declare independence and proceed on his own picturesque way. Like Matthew Arnold, from whom in other respects he sharply dissented, Eliot admired 'the tone of the centre'. To his mind, with its ingrained historicity and its conservative habit, the main current was where the finest energies of a nation were to be traced. And he looked for this main current not only in art and literature, but in those religious and social institutions to which a citizen is free to give, or not to give, his loyalty.

Not that these considerations pushed him towards conformism.

Eliot was very much his own man, and the proof of it is that he managed, despite his unfailing courtesy and reticence, to offend just about every shade of opinion in the English-speaking world in some way and at some time. In 1928 he announced, in the Preface to a small book of essays entitled *For Lancelot Andrewes*, that he had firmly adopted three positions: classicist in literature, royalist in politics, Anglo-Catholic in religion. None of these endeared him at all to the mass of left-wing, radical, and free-thinking 'progressives' who made up the bulk of the readership for modern poetry; so that at one stroke he alienated the sympathies of the people who had given him his fame. And if his newly defined stance seemed likely to placate those literary and intellectual tories who had hitherto so fiercely denied him even a vestige of talent, he made no effort to form any alliance with these people in his literary and historical views. The academic world, where his political and religious convictions would be likely to meet with sympathy, was overwhelmingly hostile to Eliot's reputation as a man of letters until well into the 1940s. It had to be, since Eliot had single-handedly overthrown the main pillar of the academic position, which is that literary reputations, once established, are immutably fixed and that textbooks must not go out of date or they will also go out of print. Books like John Sparrow's *Sense and Poetry* (1934) and F. L. Lucas's *Decline and Fall of the Romantic Ideal* (1936), both defensively contemptuous of all that Eliot stood for as a poet, provide convincing evidence that the academic mind was not prepared to welcome him merely because his political and social ideas were conservative.

Eliot continued on his way unmoved. 'Many people', said Blake, 'are not capable of a firm persuasion of anything'; those who are, can usually find—in a free society—the courage to voice their opinions. Eliot, having settled in England during the First World War, took British nationality in 1927, largely (we may suppose) because he was looking for his own roots; he came of seventeenth-century English stock on both sides, and England would not have attracted him if it had contained nothing but the Waste Land of postwar London. Like Henry James, he came in search of an England that was a repository of living tradition. And the astringency of many of his criticisms of English life and institutions arose from his desire that England should live up to these traditions and not lose them in a wash of international 'modernity'.

Like Yeats, like Pasternak, like Robert Graves, Eliot has no interest in a life drained of religious significance. His ideal is a human existence illuminated by spirituality. In his poetry, after the naked despair of *The Hollow Men* (1925), which is far more truly a Waste Land than *The Waste Land* itself, he moves, after his conversion, to the penitential optimism of *Ash Wednesday* and thence to *Four Quartets*. In his critical writing, he advances on a broad front. Seventeenth-century Anglicanism is the temper of mind that attracts him; that brief, glorious age when the Church of England could muster the wit of Donne, the piety of Andrewes, the learned subtlety of Hooker. For this reason, he dislikes Cromwell; and, since he dislikes Cromwell, he also dislikes Milton. That earlier, finer phase of English sensibility, when thought and emotion flowed together, had been interrupted by Puritanism, and Eliot sometimes appears to be on the verge of saying that it was a national misfortune that Milton should have been such a great poet; if Puritanism had relied for its literary expression on feeble poets, there might have been no final closing of that Eden; but Milton, in Eliot's well-known phrase, erected 'a Chinese wall'. After him, it remained only to pick up the pieces and start again; and Dryden, whom he admits to have been a much coarser poet than Donne or Herbert, yet has Eliot's admiration because he established order and started things moving in an intelligible direction.

Unlike many literary critics who have a strong social tendency— unlike F. R. Leavis, for example—Eliot at no time hesitates to fill in the background of his positions. He assents to the Anglican Church, for instance, because he finds 'the main current' in it: 'In its persistence in finding a mean between Papacy and Presbytery the English Church under Elizabeth became something representative of the finest spirit of England of the time. It came to reflect not only the personality of Elizabeth herself, but the best community of her subjects of every rank.' Again, 'in both Hooker and Andrewes—the latter the friend and intimate of Isaac Casaubon— we find also that breadth of culture, at ease with humanism and Renaissance learning, which helped to put them on terms of equality with their continental antagonists and to elevate their Church above the position of a local heretical sect.'

This kind of consideration was of importance to Eliot. He could not have borne the notion that the form of religion he subscribed to was 'local' or 'heretical'. And his work as a literary critic was as important to the twentieth century as Samuel Johnson's to the eighteenth, and in the same way. It discouraged solipsism, faddiness, and the slippered cosiness that loves to wax eloquent over some minor master while neglecting the giants. It introduced standards;

it was firmly anchored to a political, religious, and philosophical base. Eliot is not universal in his sympathies (and even Johnson was unfair to Milton and Gray), but no other modern critic has anything like his range. He is wonderful on Dante; on Shakespeare, he is illuminating in sudden flashes; his essays on the Metaphysical poets and the Elizabethan dramatists marked a turning-point in the study of these authors; he is full of passionate insight on Baudelaire and Pascal, Virgil and Goethe.

What Eliot valued in English society was its comparatively stable and rooted character. Himself a child of dynastic, Puritan, intellectual New England (though born in St. Louis, his roots were mostly on the Eastern seaboard), he must have realized early in life that the new America—since the Civil War, since mass immigration, since the uprooting of rural life by industrialization—was no longer hospitable to the culture to which he belonged. But his transfer to England was no mere exchange of one chauvinism for another. He considered himself, first and last, a European in his allegiances. If English society attracted him by its homogeneity and rootedness, it repelled him by its insularity and philistinism. Not only Harvard and New England, but America as a whole, is far more open to continental European ideas than England is. Eliot, in this respect, was like Pound: an opener of windows. But unlike Pound, he operated not on the surface but from deep within the society he had adopted. As an Anglican and a royalist, he was openly committed to those features of English society most despised by the modern-minded, to whom he seemed a respect-worthy but comical figure, in well-creased uniform on the bridge of a sinking ship. Yet, inasmach as these people were 'modern', they were his offspring; his sensibility presided over all modern verse in English, except that of Yeats.

As a literary and social critic, as an editor, as an influential publisher, Eliot would have made a sufficient mark if he had never written a line of poetry. What gives his criticism the added dimension of excitement is that it is geared closely to his practice. Though he virtually never refers to his own work, he is always facing, in his criticism, the kind of problem that confronts him in the writing of his poetry. We read his essays with a double interest: because we are concerned with the subjects, and because we enjoy watching Eliot battle with the problems involved in forming a style, making a poetry that will draw strength from tradition while remaining uncluttered by the mere debris of the past. And if we keep his poetry freshly in mind while reading his prose, we shall be rewarded by many accretions of richness. In 1929, he remarks that 'the poetry of Dante is the one universal school of style for the writing of poetry in any language . . . he is safer to follow, even for us, than any English poet, including Shakespeare'. After this, anyone who fails to pick up the Dantesque echoes in Eliot's verse can hardly blame the poet. And, for the reader who has been willing to take what Eliot gives him, the famous *terza rima* passage in 'Little Gidding' (section II), comes as the repayment of a whole series of debts.

For anyone wishing to become acquainted with Eliot's critical mind, the central book is *Selected Essays* (1932). Most of the really important work is there, mapping the direction of Eliot's mind during the years from *Prufrock* to *Ash Wednesday*. Even the last phase, when in the 1940s and '50s Eliot was working entirely as a dramatist, is illuminated by the Drydenian 'Dialogue on Dramatic Poetry' in this volume. Only two essays of vital importance, to my mind, need to be sought elsewhere, and these are two lectures that Eliot gave during the early forties, 'The Music of Poetry' and 'The Social Function of Poetry', both collected in *On Poetry and Poets* (1957). Each is an example of Eliot's ability to take some central, much-discussed subject and cut through the tangle of confusion surrounding it. But their significance goes beyond that. 'The Music of Poetry', in particular, clarifies a point that is central to our understanding of Eliot's achievement.

Eliot's early reputation was as a modernizer. He repeatedly made the point that the way a nation uses its language is perpetually changing. Idioms, speech-rhythms, cadences, alter from day to day, and linguistic strategies that worked well twenty-five years earlier will simply not suffice to express what people are thinking and feeling today. The language of poetry, in particular, needs to be periodically dismantled and rebuilt, and to this effort the generation of Pound and Eliot addressed themselves. But it is obvious to anyone who reads Eliot's poems in their order of composition that this rebuilding instinct grew weaker in him as time went on. In his later work the search is for a dense, settled, solid diction that will express the strength of positive convictions, as opposed to the explosive diction of quest and dismay in *Prufrock* or *The Waste Land*. Some readers, connecting this change with Eliot's conversion and with certain changes in his literary convictions (notably the great difference between his first lecture on Milton in 1936 and his second eleven years later), put it down to a dully predictable movement from Left to Right; Eliot had become conformist, stuffy, a lost leader. In fact, the change was connected with his sensitive alertness to history. His was a long career, and it spanned two distinct phases of literary history. Let Eliot himself take up the story:

... the task of the poet will differ, not only according to his personal constitution, but according to the period in which he finds himself. At some periods, the task is to explore the musical possibilities of an established convention of the relation of the idiom of verse to that of speech; at other periods, the task is to catch up with the changes in colloquial speech, which are fundamentally changes in thought and sensibility.

Then, as usual, Eliot describes his own practice by fastening on some past poet who did something similar:

The poet who did most for the English language is Shakespeare: and he carried out, in one short lifetime, the task of two poets. I can only say here, briefly, that the development of Shakespeare's verse can be roughly divided into two periods. During the first, he was slowly adapting his form to colloquial speech: so that by the time he wrote *Antony and Cleopatra* he had devised a medium in which everything that any dramatic character might have to say, whether high or low, 'poetical' or 'prosaic', could be said with naturalness and beauty. Having got to this point, he began to elaborate. The first period—of the poet who began with *Venus and Adonis*, but who had already, in *Love's Labour's Lost*, begun to see what he had to do—is from artificiality to simplicity, from stiffness to suppleness. The later plays move from simplicity towards elaboration. The late Shakespeare is occupied with the other task of the poet—that of experimenting to see how elaborate, how complicated, the music could be made without losing touch with colloquial speech altogether, and without his characters ceasing to be human beings. This is the poet of *Cymbeline*, *The Winter's Tale*, *Pericles*, and *The Tempest*.[4]

This is true of Shakespeare. And it is even more true of Eliot. It has the inward-and-outward relevance that marks all Eliot's best criticism; and it is the perfect defence against those who regard his change of mind about Milton, or the consolidation of manner in his later poetry, as mere apostasy. The other essay, 'The Social Function of Poetry', from which I shall be quoting later, carries on the examination of language, notably as regards the relationship of the poet's language to the ordinary man's, and is a subtle, and final, restatement of the reasons why a living tradition, such as Eliot's own work postulates, is essential to the health of a society.

Both those essays were written during the years of Eliot's last great effort as a poet. That is, he was still grappling hard with the problems of a practitioner. After *Four Quartets*, he turned to a different field, that of drama, and the problems of verse-writing appeared to him in a different light. He was content, on the whole, with the solutions he had arrived at during the long march from *Prufrock* to 'Little Gidding'. He continued to write criticism, but the later essays, though always interesting and illuminating, have lost that sting of urgency; we are no longer watching an artist building his own world in the guise of a critic making refined distinctions. This double practice could, of course, lead Eliot astray; there are times when his judgements seem irrelevant to the text under discussion, and his academic opponents have not been slow to attack these weak points; but we may doubt whether any great criticism has ever been entirely disinterested, entirely without a personal motive underlying the impersonal one of service to the author under discussion. And at all times, even when the personal bias is at its strongest, Eliot is saved from mere idiosyncrasy (such as we find so often in, say, the criticism of Robert Graves) by the pull of his mind towards the centre, towards orthodoxy, towards 'the main current'.

II

All through his lifetime, Eliot's reputation was very high, and his influence (even reckoned by the most mechanical standard of all, the sheer number of other poets who tried to write like him) was enormous. Still, there were times, particularly in what Auden later called the 'low, dishonest decade' of the thirties, when his hold on younger poets was temporarily weakened, and this 'main current' of his seemed to many of his juniors to be a backwater. Eliot himself, looking back, spoke of 'Twenty years largely wasted, the years of *l'entre deux guerres*', and it is a fact that, after his brilliant start in the twenties, we have to wait till the forties before Eliot again emerges clearly as a great poet. Not that the work he did in the thirties is without value. But it seems to be marking time. After *The Waste Land* with its unforgettable images of questing through a doomed and haunted landscape, there is the utterly poignant despair of *The Hollow Men* (1925), where the suffering seems to be without alleviation or hope; after this abyss, we climb up to the specifically religious dawn of *Ash Wednesday* in 1930. And there, for some years, Eliot remains. We, who know that the austere splendours of the *Four Quartets* are yet to come, can see this period for what it is: a rock-strewn plateau which the poet had to traverse before assaulting the final peaks. But to younger eyes at the time, it often seemed that Eliot had wandered away from the path of the true ascent. Much of his energy at this time went into controversy and social criticism. As editor of the *Criterion* (1922–39) and as author of such books as *Thoughts After Lambeth* (1931), *After Strange Gods* (1934), and *The Idea of a Christian Society* (1939), he threw his weight on the side of a conservative attitude towards social problems. In criticism, he stressed the importance of tradition; the scholarship with which he sought to give weight and solidity to the insights of a poet was a traditional scholarship. And in the 1930s, this conservatism and tradition were enthusiastically rejected; the call was for 'new styles of architecture, a change of heart'.

Eliot, as we noted earlier, encouraged the younger poets; his office in Russell Square was the nerve centre of 'modern poetry' in England for some twenty years. But he necessarily stood rather apart from them. Besides the fact that he was Christian and conservative while they were 'progressive' and sceptical, there was also the fact of their Englishness.

Modern poetry, up to this point, had been international. Its idiom was strikingly similar in all the languages in which it was written, and it was an idiom that owed little to the speech-habits or literary traditions of any particular nation. As far as English was concerned, the main technical work had been done by two expatriate American poets, drawing heavily on the work of an earlier generation of Frenchmen. Eliot's early poetry contains turns of phrase that are obviously influenced by French ('They will say: but how his arms and legs are thin!') as well as a few Americanisms (e.g. 'the gashouse' for what we English would call 'the gasworks'). For verse that used a purely English idiom—English in its vocabulary, English in its rhythms and intonations—one would have to look, in the 1920s, among the more traditional poets who carried on the line marked out by the Georgians of a decade earlier. And these poets numbered in their fraternity no poet as interesting and original as Eliot or Pound. This, no doubt, was largely due to the First World War. If Edward Thomas had lived, if Owen, Rosenberg, Sorley, even Rupert Brooke, had lived, the more native English idiom might have emerged in a stronger and more adaptable form that would have enabled it to offer a counter-attraction to international modernity. But these poets died, and the survivors, though they included poets of the stature of Blunden and Graves, were in no state to initiate a new poetic tradition; they were too few, too scattered, and too shaken by their trench experiences. Robert Graves, the best of the returned soldiers, did not hammer out a strong personal idiom till about 1926, by which time the Eliot–Pound school was firmly in possession of the public ear.

So the international accent of 'modern' poetry dominated the scene, or at any rate the most interesting part of the scene, until a new generation of poets, too young to have been involved in the war or to remember the world before 1914, grew up and began to publish. This happened towards the end of the twenties. Auden and Day Lewis both brought out their first volumes in 1928, MacNeice and Spender in 1929. With these four names, we meet for the first time a 'modern' poetry whose accent is distinctively English and which deals primarily with English experience.

Since England is a small, compact country in which people of the same social background tend to have very similar formative experiences, it is not surprising that the young poets who emerged together at the end of the twenties should have found it natural to write, and think, as a group. They were not only English, but English of the upper-middle class; their education was similar, their world was a shared one; moreover, the situation they faced in the larger world was urgent, and its urgencies pressed on them all in a similar way.

The twenties had been, in some respects, an optimistic decade. It is true that the world had been through the terrible blood-spilling and faith-spilling of the First World War, and that no one could any longer believe in the myth of automatic progress. But, for a few years at least, many people found it possible to believe that they lived in a new world, that the nations had learnt their lesson from 'the war to end war', that problems would really be solved by the League of Nations and by international socialism, which had already come to power in Russia and seemed to indicate that a new form of society, outlawing fear and greed, might be possible. The twenties were uncomfortable if you lived in Germany and lost everything during the inflation, or if you were a member of the working class in almost any country; but if you had a little money in the bank, an interest in the arts, and a 'modern' outlook, it was difficult not to enjoy life. In Greenwich Village, in Chelsea, on the Left Bank, new ideas were stirring; the cheapness of paper and printing made this the heyday of the Little Magazine, and every poet could get into print somehow, somewhere; meanwhile the parties went on till dawn, the emancipated girls were pretty, and the small private incomes were still enough to live on. This was the decade of Picasso and Gertrude Stein, of E. E. Cummings and George Antheil, of Diaghilev and Jean Cocteau. It was ended by the stock market crash of 1929, the slump in world trade, and the disappearance of that atmosphere of easy living and innocent experimentation that had fostered so much rubbish and a few masterpieces.

'Macspaunday', as Roy Campbell mockingly dubbed the composite poet of the thirties, came to birth in a world chilled by economic depression and appalled by the reappearance of the grim spectre of war. In Italy, Mussolini had already established a Fascist regime which openly glorified violence. In Germany, the chaos and decadence of a sick society were soon to throw up a grimmer and more Teutonically thoroughgoing version of the same thing. The 1930s poets were young men and they had the idealism of youth. Inevitably, they rejected any notion that art could be its own justification. They looked for social solutions and they advocated those solutions in their verse. This much would have been true in any case. There would have been, we may confidently speculate, a politically-flavoured school of English poetry in the thirties whether these particular poets had existed or not.

What caused this school to take the shape it actually took, and write the poems it actually wrote, was the presence in it of Wystan Hugh Auden (b. 1906). Both for good reasons (he was the best poet of the group) and for bad reasons (his idiom was fatally easy to imitate, and his worst poems were his most imitable), Auden was the acknowledged leader from first to last.

There were many reasons for this. To begin with, Auden was, in his background and the kind of experience that had shaped him, the archetype or diagram of the young upper-middle-class poet. Coming from a solid professional background in the Midlands (he describes himself somewhere as 'Son of a nurse and doctor, loaned a dream'), he was exposed to the routine influences at a minor public school and at Oxford. Then followed a spell of teaching at a school not much different from the one where he had been a pupil. In such a life, the main events are books and conversations; one's knowledge of hunger, violence, manual work, loneliness, comes through the imagination. Auden had this imagination. He understood from the beginning that he was living in a world threatened by ruthless destructive forces. His early poems were brisk and challenging; they also had a dimension of nightmare. The combination was irresistible.

The thirties, though in historical terms they happened only yesterday, are a very remote period. English society has changed so much since then that it is no wonder so much of the literature of the thirties has dated badly. For one thing, it was unequal to a degree that can hardly be imagined today. The society we have now is by no means a just one, but at least we do not have a fat and lethargic middle class resting on the back of a working class who have to count every halfpenny and think themselves lucky if they are able to keep one jump ahead of unemployment. Nor do we have a huge coolie empire on whose sweat we live while taking care to know nothing whatever about them or their problems. English life in the 1930s was grim and narrow for the working class who made up three-quarters of the population; for those above, it was soft and pampered. And this naturally affected the youthful poets. Young men do not like to feel soft and pampered. They like to feel that their lives are real and meaningful. Hence the attraction for these poets of anything that seemed spare, purposeful, resolute.

Auden was certainly all these things. More than any other single quality, it was his dynamism that drew his generation about him. He was sternly contemptuous of fripperies or out-moded ways; both in public and private life, he saw problems and he drove hard towards solutions. His poetry, though haunted by nightmares, was positive, even optimistic, in its determination to

> Publish each healer that in city lives
> Or country houses at the end of drives.

As well as being positive and energetic, Auden's poetry was satisfyingly 'modern'. For decades past, poets had felt a duty to write about the modern world, to incorporate specifically modern objects (aeroplanes, machines, skyscrapers) into their verse. Marinetti and the Futurists in Italy, Mayakovsky in Russia, had pointed the way, and many poets had dutifully followed. But it is hard to escape the impression, on re-reading many of those poets of the twenties, that they were bowing to a convention rather than obeying an inner impulse. They write of steel and glass and concrete, but one feels that left to themselves they would be happier writing about primroses. In Auden, a poet had arisen who seemed to write about the modern world naturally; he introduced machinery and Nissen huts and mine-shafts not because these things were *de rigueur*, but because they were the natural properties of his world. As a child, he had wanted to be an engineer, and his interests had retained a scientific and practical tinge. His poetry promised an escape from the over-civilized drawing-room of the purely literary.

Third, and perhaps most important of all, was the ease with which Auden had naturalized an idiom taken over from Eliot. The starting-point of his verse was Eliot's; yet, where Eliot had been cautious and magisterial, publishing very little and preaching the virtues of a rigorous poetic discipline, Auden seemed a purely 'English' poet in that he wrote as fast, and as confidently, as Byron or Browning. If Eliot and Yeats had made poetry once more the vehicle for major statements, Auden, while accepting the changes they had brought about, lowered the tension and set before younger poets the ideal of a poetry which, while speaking from the centre of the stage, should do so in a tone that was relaxed, colloquial, and (for all its occasional over-terseness) not difficult to understand.

To some of his disapproving elders—to F. R. Leavis, for example —Auden's poetry seemed remarkable chiefly for its self-confidence. Yet this self-confidence was immensely exhilarating to poets of his own generation. Auden's pages were a hotch-potch; one never knew what one would find there; his mind, powerful, unsystematic, and insatiably curious, picked up one subject after another and explored the world from a series of rapidly changing angles. He seemed to be interested in everything, provided only that it promised some release from the padded cell of habit and convention into which 'the old gang' had led us. He took, as he has always taken, panoramic views:

> Consider this and in our time
> As the hawk sees it or the helmeted airman.

The world of Auden's early poetry *is* the world of the thirties, where dictators yell threats, armaments pile up in the factories, frontiers turn back desperate refugees, millions rot on the dole while food is dumped in the sea to keep prices high, and where at the same time the forces of hope are at work, planning a new world. Auden is always aware of the world outside the window, at the same time that he writes unabashedly personal letters to his friends, mentioning them by name and bringing in private jokes like any prep school boy. His elegies on Freud and Yeats, probably the two greatest men to die in the 1930s, emphasize the contribution of each to the larger life of the world. With equal naturalness he can address his friends:

> I miss you, Christopher,
> Your short squat body and enormous head.

In all this, Auden is typical of the class, and nation, from which he comes. England is too small, and too civilized, to be a country of loneliness. The isolation in which the American or Russian writer faces his problems is unknown in our little window-box of a country. The basic assumption of English life is that a man has his assured place within his own 'set' (the word is revealing, with its association of a row of plates on a Welsh dresser or a shelf of toby jugs). Sometimes English writers feel annoyed at this quality in their own society, as Lawrence was annoyed, or Wyndham Lewis. In which case, the best solution is to emigrate. This is one respect in which English life will not, because it cannot, be changed. Auden makes no attempt to rebel against this particular feature of English society; on the contrary, he exploits it and turns it into a strength. His large and generous concern for the problems of the world can coexist easily with a central point of reference that is unself-consciously English, and within England, of his own class and type, and within the class and type, of his own circle. They are like the concentric rings in a tree-trunk. Each adds solidity to the next.

Eliot's poetry was set in a generalized 'modern world' which was largely assimilated to symbol. It developed recognizable landscapes with great skill (the London of *The Waste Land* is as solid and tangible as the London of Dickens), but by the use of a cinematic technique of cutting, tracking, and panning, it moved from the Thames to the Ganges, via an entirely imaginary landscape of drought and desert, so that in the total impression it takes place everywhere and nowhere. Auden's, by contrast, takes off on long flights but always starts and ends in the landscape, physical and social, that English people recognize as theirs.

> It is later than you think; nearer that day
> Far other than that distant afternoon
> Amid rustle of frocks and stamp of feet
> They gave the prizes to the ruined boys.

One feature of the English is that they make a tremendous fuss about their education; a man will actually classify himself through life according to the kind of school he went to for five years of his adolescence. The young Auden, like a great many other people, was convinced that the more elaborate and expensive 'public' (sc. private) schools had their values wrong, so that the boys who most eagerly soaked up their ethos and absorbed their attitudes were incapacitated for happiness or usefulness in later life. All this he says, memorably and succinctly, in the line 'They gave the prizes to the ruined boys'—a line which, in its direct simplicity and effectiveness, might have been written by Kipling.

In politics, naturally, Auden was Left. Naturally, because when a young man looked at the world from the vantage-point of England in the 1930s, all the most reactionary forces he saw were Right, from Fascism with its tie-up with big business and in some cases with the Church, to British Conservatism with its inert and selfish determination to do nothing about anything. Socialism, on the other hand, had the virtue of never having been tried, so that its large promises could not be checked against any disappointing performance and it was the natural repository for idealism. It is true that a regime describing itself as socialist had been in power since 1917 in Russia. But Russia was a long way away and its frontiers were closed to all visitors except those who could be trusted to see what they were told to see and repeat what they were told to repeat. The occasional miscalculation, when someone was invited who came back with misgivings about the way things were going, and even had the bad taste to make these misgivings public, as Gide did in *Retour de l'U.R.S.S.*, could safely be left to the propaganda machine, which covered the offender with stinking mud.

All this explains why, in the 1930s, the Soviet Union became the node of socialist fantasies, and its official philosophy, Marxist-Leninism, so attractive at a distance to many writers who would not have survived a fortnight if they had actually had to live under the Russian system, with its ruthless party machine backed by a secret police. Russia was the only large country where socialism had been put into effect; therefore it *must* be believed in. And if anyone argued that what Russia had was not in fact socialism but a particularly repressive kind of state capitalism, that the urban proletariat in whose name the revolution had been made had lost everything, even the right to strike—well, it was easy enough to reply that such people were merely selfish conservatives who were afraid that the Russian experiment might succeed, in which case they would lose their comforts and privileges.

To argue against the Soviet system, to maintain that there might be some truth in the persistent stories of terror and bloodshed and forced confessions, was to find oneself arguing on the same side as the *Daily Mail*. What is more, the Marxist case seemed, in the thirties, inherently credible. Marx had predicted that before the capitalist nations finally collapsed they would run mad; and the thirties, with their hunger marches, slumps, private armies, and grotesque inequalities of wealth, seemed intent on proving him right. From that point of view, there was no difference, or only a difference in degree, between England and Germany, or France and Italy. Given this picture, Russia *had* to be right, and Communism *had* to be the answer. So the reports of purges and mass deportations were ignored, young poets like John Cornford and Christopher Caudwell flocked into the Communist party, and one set of illusions was confronted by another.

Auden, to do him justice, was very far from being the simple-minded Marxist of that time. He accepts that the social and economic system of England is worn-out and useless; he accepts the general Marxist position that people who live in such a society, and accept its values, become unable to cope with the world. To him, these people are sick. He habitually represents them in his poems by images of actual physical disease—

> the liar's quinsy
> And the distortions of ingrown virginity.

But his recipe for dealing with the problem varies according to his mood. Sometimes he speaks as if these sick people who encumber the earth must be killed off like house-flies—though, to be sure, the writings in which he seems to be making this suggestion, such as *The Orators* (1932), are heavily facetious in tone, full of schoolboy jokes and a general air of farcical unreality, as if Auden wished to say and unsay his message in the same breath. At other times he talks as if the victims of this illness could cure themselves by opening their natures to 'love'. Where official Marxism sees nothing for these pathetic relics except to be ground down in the class struggle, Auden has moods in which he holds out the promise of salvation to them. In a prose utterance of this period, he speaks of 'that art which shall teach man to unlearn hatred and learn love'.

In the work of the 'English Auden', the cruelty of official Marxist-Leninism is softened by the persistent suggestion that we are all schoolboys playing jokes on one another; and also, at other times, by Auden's interest in psychoanalysis, which Communist doctrine dismisses as a mere indulgence of the decadent rich. Auden often combines psychoanalysis with Marxism in his images of a diseased world, 'this England where nobody is well'; from Groddeck, and from Homer Lane, he had imbibed the theory that physical illness is caused by disharmony with one's environment, and this dovetailed neatly with the Marxist notion of a sick, decadent capitalist world. But even Auden, in the poem he wrote about the Spanish Civil War, could permit himself the phrase 'necessary murder', could speak of the liquidation of one's political opponents quite in the glib tone of a *New Statesman* reader dismissing the Russian purges with, 'You can't make an omelette without breaking eggs.' Ah, those famous eggs that are so easy to break when you don't have to watch the

yolk running in the gutters! Auden's facetiousness, his tendency to
squirt out a cuttle-fish ink of irony or buffoonery, has not diminished
through the years, though in almost every other respect the poet
has changed almost out of recognition.

The poetic stage-properties of modernity and socialism are used
more crudely, sometimes with an embarrassingly self-conscious
brio, in the early work of Cecil Day Lewis (b. 1904). The Day Lewis
of *Transitional Poem* (1929) and *From Feathers to Iron* (1931) is apt
at any moment to lapse into conventionally 'progressive' imagery
imitated from Auden but applied without Auden's wit: in a poem
celebrating the birth of a child, he heaps up stanzas of this kind of
thing:

> Now shall the airman vertically banking
> Out of the blue write a new sky-sign;
> The nine tramp steamers rusting in the estuary
> Get up full pressure for a trade revival;
> The crusty landlord renew the lease, and everyone
> Take a whole holiday in honour of this.

The result is sometimes endearing but seldom successful. Day
Lewis was, in fact, unfortunate in his early influences. By nature he
is a quiet poet, dealing in low tones and gradual hues, and the later
phase of his work, which lies outside the scope of this chapter, has
seen him wisely revert to a pre-modern tradition of sober, well-
shaped verse, orbiting round the central star of Hardy's lyric poems.
In the thirties, when he was imitating Auden, and through Auden
the poets such as Hopkins and Eliot who had formed Auden's style,
he gave the impression of a gifted writer whose gift was continually
being pulled slightly out of shape. There are good passages embedded in the mass of his early work, and he often writes entertainingly
and neatly, as in his description of Auden as

> the tow-haired poet, never done
> With cutting and planing some new gnomic prop
> To jack his all too stable universe up:—
> Conduct's Old Dobbin, thought's chameleon.

But it is not until the volume of wartime poems, *Word Over All*
(1943), that one can point to a Day Lewis who has come into his
own, as a strong, unspectacular poet of the middle range, no longer
pausing to run after Auden's golden apples.

Stephen Spender (b. 1909) has always had a tinge of the pure,
Shelleyan lyric poet. Like Shelley, he has some genius but no talent

—using these as convenient shorthand words, 'genius' being the quality that suddenly declares itself in flashes of achievement far beyond the normal range, and 'talent' being the ability to keep up a consistent, respectable standard. Spender made an excellent beginning: his *Twenty Poems* (1930) contains a number of poems ('Discovered in Mid-Ocean', for instance, or 'Beethoven's Death-Mask') as good as anything he has done since, and when an augmented edition was issued three years later, the additional poems include at least one of his best, the lyric beginning

> What I expected was
> Thunder, fighting,
> Long struggles with men
> And climbing.

At the same time, there were the disconcerting lapses to which Spender has always been prone, and which no merely talented poet would be guilty of. He is capable of letting pass a couplet like

> This lamp and wooden furniture are gracious,
> All other times and places seem atrocious.

And in these early poems, he is always embarrassing when he gets into his forward-from-liberalism ultra-Left vein.

Though Spender's early work is blemished by patches of journalism-in-verse, it is fair to concede that some of the best of his early poems are very directly related to the immediate historical movement. The Spanish Civil War, which he watched with an agonized fascination, moved him to some excellent poems: 'War Photograph', for instance, a meditation on a picture taken in the instant of a soldier's death:

> I am that numeral which the sun regards,
> The flat and severed second on which time looks,
> My corpse a photograph taken by fate;
>
> Where inch and instant cross, I shall remain
> As faithful to the vanished moment's violence
> As love fixed to one day in vain.
>
> Only the world changes, and time its tense,
> Against the creeping inches of whose moon
> I launch my wooden continual present.[5]

Spender is, in academic parlance, an alpha–gamma poet; but perhaps his lack of ordinary talent, that unexpected and improvising quality which makes him write either above or below what should be his natural level, will prove in the end to be a redeeming quality; certainly he has kept some creative vitality, and seems, in the 1970s, likely to be less ossified, less sunk into a carapace of habitual idiom, than Auden.

Of all these socially-conscious, public-school-and-university poets who emerged in the 1930s, the best poetic craftsman was undoubtedly Louis MacNeice (1907–64). MacNeice, an Ulsterman, son of a bishop, was a good classical scholar who for a time taught Greek at Birmingham University, before joining the B.B.C. as a star writer of features and radio drama. He was like the other thirties poets in being very much a man of this world, involved in life, urban, gregarious, speaking with the voice of *l'homme moyen sensuel*, never claiming any special privilege or point of vantage on account of being a poet. He was unlike them in his greater detachment and irony, his ingrained suspicion of slogans and mass movements; his *Poems* (1935) contains several memorable statements of this attitude, notably 'Turf-Stacks' and 'The Individualist Speaks'. MacNeice was a poet with a deep instinct for form; in his case, the impulse to write in verse seems to have arisen from a need to express his thoughts elegantly, sparely, and with the maximum of memorable impact, rather than from a *furor poeticus*. The early MacNeice resembles the early Auden in his diagnosis of the choked-up inertia of English civilization in the thirties, his premonition of apocalyptic disaster, and his distaste for

The flotsam of private property, pekingese and polyanthus,
The good things which in the end turn to poison and pus,

but he has nothing like Auden's succession of panaceas; his remedy, if it is one, is simply to go on living from day to day: in his 'Eclogue for Christmas', a dialogue between townsman and countryman, both participants conclude that their way of life is dying, but find life worth living while they are spared, and its common abundances worth being grateful for.

MacNeice is the poet of everyday life, as it is lived among educated people of his generation; no one has ever written better documentary poetry. His *Autumn Journal* (1939) gives, better than anything else I know in prose or verse, the *feel* of those last months before the house of cards of the thirties collapsed into war. In describing it as documentary poetry, one gives full emphasis to both words; honest and satisfying as documentary, it never ceases to be poetry, albeit poetry of the kind that gets its effects by deliberately going close to prose.

The thirties movement, as a movement, ended neatly in 1940 with the publication of *Another Time*, the last volume by the 'English Auden'. Two years previously, the two strongest talents of that movement, Auden ('the poet') and Isherwood ('the novelist') had been together to China, to see the fighting on the Manchurian border which was one of the points at which the Second World War effectively started. (Their observations are recorded in *Journey to a War*, one of the most interesting of their collaborations.) On the way back, they passed through the United States, and both, it is said, decided then and there that they would return to stay permanently. They did so, both taking American citizenship. With the departure of Auden, the thirties poetic structure would in any case have crumbled, but the onset of the war finished it even more decisively; once the shooting had broken out, that kind of socially orientated discussion-poetry was dead and was seen to be dead. There was, however, no time for funeral obsequies. All the thirties poets continued to write, though they moved farther away from any discernible common centre, and at the same time a new 'movement' came into the foreground.

These writers were 'romantic' in one of its senses, that sense in which the romantic is concerned with the inner world rather than the outer, with the dream and the vision and the symbol rather than the political meeting and the steel-rolling mill. To say this is, of course, to simplify, since the major romantic artist always imposes his inner vision on the outward world; but it will do for a rough classification. During the Marxizing decade, poets whose imaginative world was subjective rather than objective—and there were many of them, at varying levels of achievement: Dylan Thomas, David Gascoygne, George Barker, Edith Sitwell, to jot down a few representative names—had tended to be crowded out of the centre of the stage; but with the collapse of that decade, something that could be called romanticism, that could be called visionary or subjective, became for a few years dominant in English poetry.

We might present the poetic history of two decades, then, in broad terms: first the Marxizing decade in which a group of poets claimed public attention with a kind of poetry that turned its attention outwards from the self and discussed the problems of the

West, and within those problems the specific problems of the English *bourgeoisie*, reverting to the personal identity only within that larger social framework; these poets had a definite programme for which they made overt propaganda—more socialism at home and more resistance to fascism abroad—and when the war came, fulfilling one part of that programme and inevitably postponing the fulfilment of the other half until 1945, the movement lost what cohesion it had had. Meanwhile, another line, traceable from Surrealism and beyond that from the larger root of European symbolism, with overtones added by the discoveries of Freud and the experimentation of Pound and Joyce, moved definitely into the gap left by the disappearance of the Auden generation. (For, while as poets they remained, as 'a generation' they disappeared, probably to their benefit as artists.) And this group remained dominant during the 1940s.

'Broad terms'—and perhaps the terms are a little too broad, even for such a survey as this. For, as usual, round the edges of the dominant school, whatever it might be at any given time, individual poets were working, poets formed in different generations and by different circumstances. Many of the Georgian poets from 1910 were still working thirty years later. A fine old Victorian like Robert Bridges was active right up to his death in 1930; Walter de la Mare held a large following with his fanciful, numinous verses. Even among young poets of the generation and social class of Auden and his friends, there was a counter-movement, which can be seen in the work of the young Cambridge poets of the time (Auden & Co. were Oxford products), notably those gathered in the remarkable anthology *Cambridge Poetry 1929*. The most outstanding of these was William Empson (b. 1906), who made a brilliant reputation before he was thirty both as a poet and a supersubtle critic of poetry. Empson's first poems, collected in *Poems* (1935), are far more cerebral than their Oxford counterparts; he had studied science for some years before taking up the study of English literature, and these early poems handle themes taken from scientific discovery and the modern world generally, with an ease and power that really does, at times, remind one of Donne. At a time when archaeological research into cave paintings is just getting under way, Empson will begin a love poem with, 'Searching the cave gallery of your face'—a metaphor which conveys in a flash the lover's sense of wonder and mystery, and also the slightly apprehensive search for clues as to what his beloved might be thinking and feeling, as the electric torch plays over the disconcerting and enigmatic cave paintings which have slept in darkness for thousands of years. The early Empson is full of these exciting poetic surprises; in his second volume, *The Gathering Storm* (1940), the themes are more often social, and the personal revelation more direct; images of travel, and of the approach of war, take precedence over the more intellectual themes. If the first volume might be briefly described as the flash-point where science and poetry meet—the effect on a strong young mind, trained in elementary science, of suddenly reading Sir Herbert Grierson's *Metaphysical Poems and Lyrics of the Seventeenth Century*, the second volume is, again speaking very roughly, an Empsonian counterpart of MacNeice's *Autumn Journal*.

The movement, then, had a counter-movement. And there were also poets working in sublime indifference to prevailing fashion. Of these Robert Bridges is perhaps the foremost of those survivors from the late-Victorian days who added richness and variety to the scene by continuing to write a poetry that was either not 'modern' at all, or 'modern' very much on their own terms. Bridges, whose lyrical poems are delicate and yet have considerable tensile strength, had always had a hankering for the more or less 'experimental' long poem; much of his experimentation looks from this distance like mere tinkering, as when he devised a system of spelling and a type-face for himself, and had his *Collected Essays* so printed, thus rendering them unreadable. His culminating long work, *The Testament of Beauty*, was not likely to seem very daringly experimental when it came out in 1929, at least not to a public who had got used to Eliot, Pound, and Joyce; but Bridges's personal variant on the long twelve-syllable line—the 'loose alexandrine', as he liked to call it—can be read with interest and pleasure.

To revert to the main line of our narrative. The swing of the pendulum towards a more prophetic/subjective/romantic mode was signalled by the rise of a group calling themselves 'The Apocalyptics', who came before the public with two anthologies, *The New Apocalypse* (n.d. but probably 1941) and the more elaborate *White Horseman* (1941). This group had an acknowledged affinity with Surrealism, which had been exerting a general underground influence on all the arts since it evolved from the more purely 'protest' movement of Dada in 1922. In *The New Apocalypse*, Henry Treece, who with J. F. Hendry was the chief instigator of the movement, has a manifesto, 'An Apocalyptic Writer and the Surrealists', which gives what rationale the movement was felt to need; though in *The White Horseman*, perhaps looking for corroboration from outside the immediate circle, Hendry and Treece invited the rising young critic G. S. Fraser to write a general theory of the movement, under the title 'Apocalypse in Poetry'.

Amid the uncertainties of wartime, literature survived by a series of shifts and improvisations: faced with paper shortage and the collapse of normal conditions of publishing, poets published where their verse could find a home, without considering too curiously. It is this, one may speculate, that explains the presence among the 'apocalyptics' of two poets who, though romantic in tendency, had deeper and stronger roots: Vernon Watkins (1906–67) and Dylan Thomas (1914–53). Watkins, though much the lesser poet of these two, had staying power which came partly from a well-planted foundation in the richer soil of European symbolism: he is, though in a smaller and fainter way, 'subjective' in the way that Rilke is subjective.

To begin with, the patron saints of wartime romanticism were D. H. Lawrence (from whose writings the word 'apocalypse', used in this sense, was culled), and, among living writers, Herbert Read, who inspired the movement partly by his work as a propagandist for Surrealism and partly by his own practice, as a poet and in such prose works as *The Green Child*. But the leadership quickly passed to Dylan Thomas, who had already been well known for some six years as a young poet of prodigious attack and originality. Thomas's first collection, *18 Poems* (1934), would be an important volume to come from any poet; from a youth of twenty, collecting the work he had done over the previous three or four years, it is staggering. Most poets, even the greatest, begin by imitating someone else; even such brilliant early starters as Auden and Empson can be shown to have had guiding and sustaining models. Thomas, in adolescence, already sounds like no one but himself.

> Light breaks where no sun shines;
> Where no sea runs, the waters of the heart
> Push in their tides;
> And, broken ghosts with glow-worms in their heads,
> The things of light
> File through the flesh where no flesh decks the bones.

Anyone interested, in the mid-thirties, in sorting out poetry into 'schools' could see that Thomas's affiliations were not with the socially-conscious poets of debate and discussion, and certainly not with anything 'intellectual' in the manner of, say, William Empson, but rather with that exploration of the interior landscape that goes with Surrealism, Symbolism, and the modern phase of romanticism generally. (And here, after having turned away from him for so much of our narrative, we begin to lift our eyes once more towards the giant figure of Yeats.) When Thomas died, one phase of his life's work—that of the pure lyric poet—was probably over, and the signs are that another phase, more closely orientated towards the drama in one form and another, was beginning. Certainly his achievement as a lyric poet is complete and satisfying. By 1940, he had strengthened and purified his idiom until he stood ready to act as a magnetic centre for the new grouping of English poetry that inevitably followed, as we saw, on Auden's departure for America. Thomas's development, up to that point, had not been quite in a straight line; after the triumphant assurance of *18 Poems*, he entered a bad patch with *25 Poems* (1936) and *The Map of Love* (1939), though both these volumes contain splendid poems among much that is overstrained and falsely rhetorical.

The coming of the war, though it did nothing to solve Thomas's personal problems, seemed to add stature to him as a poet; amid the crash of destruction, he sang like a nightingale during an air raid. The Second World War did not have 'war poets' like the First; in 1914–18, the man in the trenches occupied a world so different from that of the population at home that they could barely imagine it, and if he happened to be a poet his work seemed to be coming back to them from a place as remote as Sirius and as terrible as hell. In 1939–45, this difference was largely ironed out; when 20,000 Londoners were killed by German bombs, one could no longer speak of the civilian life as 'sheltered'. Thomas is the major 'war poet' of 1939–45, and to say that is not to underestimate the many fine poets who were in uniform, such as his fellow-Welshman Alun Lewis, or Keith Douglas, or Sidney Keyes. (All of whom, incidentally, were killed.) It was Thomas who provided the poetry that went with the national mood of the early 1940s; amid death, it celebrated life; amid destruction, it *built*, raising a tower of words; amid lies and denials, it affirmed. To me, and to many others, to think of the London blitz is to think of such a poem as Thomas's 'Refusal to Mourn the Death, by Fire, of a Child in London'.

'The national mood of the early 1940s'—what was that mood? It was, I think, visionary and heroic, where the thirties had been pragmatic and rather cowed. Certainly the Marxizing decade was finally over. No one any longer tried to account for historical developments by economic explanations or to draw up tidy charts about 'progress' and 'reaction'. There was plenty of socialism, but it was socialism of an idealistic kind, and it was not (from my personal memories I can testify to this) in conflict with Christianity. Indeed, a distinctly religious mood was in the air.

> I pray—for fashion's word is out
> And prayer comes round again,

wrote Yeats in one of his last poems. And his instinct for the *Zeitgeist* had not deserted him. Prayer *had* 'come round again'. The mood of almost all English writing in the first half of the forties—the last years, that is, covered by this volume—was to a greater or lesser extent mystical or visionary; it was not rationalistic or anti-supernatural. The argumentative, politically-minded thirties had given place to the visionary forties. If Dylan Thomas was the poet who best summed up the general mood, it was the Eliot of *Four Quartets* who gave it its most lofty and durable statement. But, indeed, this frame of mind ran through all poets, from a great classic like Eliot to an interesting minor poet of the time like Henry Treece. In a summary of his aims during these years, *How I See Apocalypse* (1946), Treece wrote:

In my definition, the writer who senses the chaos, the laughter and the tears, the order and the peace of the world in its entirety, is an Apocalyptic writer. His utterance will be prophetic, for he is observing things which less sensitive men have not yet come to notice, and as his words are prophetic, they will tend to be incantatory, and so musical. At times, even, that music may take control, and lead the writer from recording his vision almost to creating another vision. So, momentarily, he will kiss the hem of God's robe.

In the years that followed 1946, this kind of attitude lingered on and was a protective cover for a deal of shockingly bad writing. In some of the minor poets of the late forties—in George Barker, say, or Edith Sitwell—the 'music' has 'taken control' in the most literal sense, producing a jumble of words that satisfy their author so long as they *sound* vaguely impressive. But this is the defect that inevitably accompanies any strength, the shadow cast by a light striking a solid object. The sense of mystery, the prophetic utterance that modulates easily into the incantatory—these are the marks of *Four Quartets* or the poems of Dylan Thomas or of the Yeats of *Last Poems*: and these are the touchstones of achievement for the poetry of the 1940s.

While thinking in this direction we may conveniently make brief mention of David Jones (b. 1895)—brief, because we cannot deal here with his great achievements as a painter and draughtsman,

while of his literary works only one, *In Parenthesis* (1937), falls within our present time-span. Jones is certainly a major artist; as a poet
alone, he is more important than all but two or three of the poets
we have been discussing. Not that 'poet' is exactly the right word;
there is no right word for David Jones; he is a seer who has used,
with consummate skill and patience, whatever means were fittest
for the communication of his vision. What particularly concerns us
in this context is that his vision is fundamentally a religious one (he
was converted to Roman Catholicism in 1921 and sees all life
through the lens of his faith), and that he is a 'modern' writer in the
classic sense, at one with the generation of Joyce, Pound, and Eliot
in that the tendency of his work has been to set contemporary life
in the dimension of myth. In Eliot, Tiresias foresuffers all; in Yeats,
Cuchulain fights the ungovernable sea; in Joyce, Mr. Bloom throws
the giant shadow of Odysseus; in David Jones, the Roman soldiers
on duty at the Crucifixion talk like British privates during the Boer
War, a battle on the Western Front takes on overtones of Welsh
heroic legend or of *Gawain and the Green Knight*; as in *The Cantos*,
but with a very different texture and effect, past and present slide
into one another, everything is true and everything happens at the
same time. Jones has gone some way towards defining his method
in his critical book, *Epoch and Artist* (1959): a modern man, he says,
might wish to escape from 'the sacramental' and treat the world
simply as the world and finite things as finite, but

no sooner does he put a rose in his buttonhole but what he is already in
the trip-wire of sign, and he is deep in an entanglement of signs if he
sends that rose to his sweetheart, Flo; or puts it in a vase by her portrait;
and he is hopelessly and up to his neck in that entanglement of Ars, sign,
sacrament, should he sit down and write a poem 'about' that sweetheart.
Heavens knows what his poem will really be 'about'; for then the 'sacramental' will pile up by a positively geometric progression. So that what
was Miss Flora Smith may turn out to be Flora Dea and Venus too and
the First Eve and the Second also and other and darker figures, among
them, no doubt, Jocasta. One thing at least the psychologists make plain:
there is a recalling, a re-presenting again, anaphora, anamnesis.

In Parenthesis is 'about', in this complex sense, the First World
War. So long marinated in the imagination, so original, and personal,
it must surely be accounted the finest work of imaginative literature
to concern itself with that war. It tells of the experiences of a private
soldier (emblematically named John Bull) in a Welsh regiment; how
he parades for embarkation, goes overseas, arrives in Flanders,

moves up to the front line, and finally takes part in a battle in which he is wounded and many of his comrades killed. The bare outline here suggested is filled in by a wonderful multi-dimensional imaginative mixture: there is Welsh history and legend; there is the Shakespeare of *Henry V*; there is the English Bible and the Vulgate; there is Malory and the Arthurian legends generally. If this were literary decoration, it would be nothing; but it is strong and integral, David Jones's way of seeing the world. The more complex pattern he later evolved in *The Anathemata* (1952) is best approached after the reader has fully absorbed *In Parenthesis* and *Epoch and Artist*.

Jones's living concern for myth reminds one that, only three years further on from our terminal date for this volume, Robert Graves (b. 1895) published *The White Goddess*, a work which bears the same relation to his poetry as *A Vision* does to Yeats's. Graves set out to reinterpret a large body of myth and legend, revealing, as he claims, its true significance and the interrelationship of the separate parts. His material is drawn from the Bible (both Old and New Testaments), classical Greek, Welsh, and Irish. Whether or not one takes the scholarly pretensions of *The White Goddess* with any seriousness, one recognizes it as Graves's personal contribution to the great collective effort made by so many modern poets, to divest life of the banalities of the merely rational and material, and set it once more in a religious dimension. In the years before 1945, Graves's poetry had not yet shown any signs of this effort; it was, in the main, sardonic and sceptical, with a tragic beauty that came from stoical acceptance of suffering, and a strength derived from joy in the natural world. Graves, who saw some of the worst of the trench warfare of 1914–18, said his say about that war in *Good-bye to All That* (1926), a brilliant piece of reporting and reminiscence, conveying in its laconic understatement so much about what Graves the poet later described as 'The inward scream, the duty to run mad.' During the twenties and thirties, Graves put himself through a rigorous poetic discipline, becoming a master of spare, dry (but not too dry) utterance. His full characteristic tone is first found in *Poems 1926–30* (1931), in which he showed himself master of a style that in many ways anticipated the manner of Auden and, through him, the other 'thirties poets': for instance, his poem from that volume, 'Sick Love':

> O Love, be fed with apples while you may,
> And feel the sun and go in royal array,
> A smiling innocent on the heavenly causeway,

Though in what listening horror for the cry
That soars in outer blackness dismally,
The dumb blind beast, the paranoiac fury:

Be warm, enjoy the season, lift your head,
Exquisite in the pulse of tainted blood,
That shivering glory not to be despised.

Take your delight in momentariness,
Walk between dark and dark—a shining space
With the grave's narrowness, though not its peace.[6]

So many of Graves's poems, before he discovered his new direction in the later 1940s, deal, as this one does, with negative states, with hard-won respite and precarious balance; when the new vein comes in, with poems like 'To Juan at the Winter Solstice', one feels that the fulfilment was worth waiting for; a unifying belief, something to make sense of the pattern of existence, has lifted the continual strain of 'taking one's delight in momentariness'.

There are other interesting poets one might mention, who show the same tendencies as we have noted in Vernon Watkins, Dylan Thomas, David Jones, or Robert Graves. But before our chapter draws to an end, we have still to explore two mountain ranges, overshadowing everything else within our chosen period: the Yeats of the final years, and the Eliot of *Four Quartets*.

III

Yeats's preoccupation with symbol, his trust in its power to embody and animate a knowledge that could not be expressed discursively, had remained constant since the 1880s. During the intervening years, he had consistently meditated on the symbols that most drew his mind, and his reward had been a greater and greater power to strike out symbols which held unquenchable vitality and relevance. So important was this effort to Yeats that he accepted, with astonishing docility, the unceremonious pragmatic criticism offered him by Ezra Pound during the period of their earlier association in 1911–14. Yeats was over twenty years Pound's senior and already a poet of great fame, but he allowed Pound to 'eliminate the abstract' from his work—the words are Yeats's own—without demur. The reason, I think, is that Yeats saw and respected Pound's instinctive drive towards what was clear, direct, unhampered, and above all concrete.

In his essay 'A Few Don'ts from an Imagiste' (1913) Pound was offering this advice to young poets: 'Don't use such an expression as "dim lands *of peace*". It dulls the image. It mixes an abstraction with the concrete. It comes from the writer's not realizing that the natural object is always the *adequate* symbol.'

An expression like 'dim lands of peace' might easily have come from the early work of Yeats: such expressions abound there. But Yeats, even without the help of Pound, was already moving towards a full trust in 'the natural object'—i.e. the object as seen objectively, in its own nature—as 'the adequate symbol'. From *The Wild Swans at Coole* (1919) through *Michael Robartes and the Dancer* (1921) to *The Tower* (1928) and the final flowering that lay beyond, his achievement was to make his symbols more and more inclusive, to grasp within them a greater and greater range of human experience.

This development can be seen in two of his most important poems, 'Sailing to Byzantium' (1927) and 'Byzantium' (1930), which serve to illustrate the ceaseless deepening of Yeats's symbols during the last two decades of his incredibly fertile career. In the first poem, Byzantium is the symbol of that immunity from change and passion that art offers to the contemplating mind. In the second, it is still that symbol, but it has been put into a relationship with 'all that man is', including his 'bitter furies of complexity', which are seen as the source of their power, the images which beget further images, so that Byzantium is as living as the natural world, living and changing amid its timelessness.

In such poems as these, Yeats has at last found the answer to the questions that so baffled his youth, when he was in the situation of 'The Man Who Dreamed of Faeryland' who could find no bridge from the actual to the ideal. His earlier work is haunted by the theme of incompatibility, of truths that will not be reconciled to each other. Now, with the strength that comes from much meditation and the weathering of much experience, he can endure the knowledge that

> ... Love has pitched his mansion in
> The place of excrement;
> For nothing can be sole or whole
> That has not been rent.

These late poems of Yeats are the most fully accepting, the most fully rejoicing, the most life-giving of any written in modern times. Not even Goethe accepted more, not even Baudelaire held his gaze steadier, not even Rilke distilled his symbols into so potent a truth.

Yeats was, in his personal philosophy, a tragic fatalist; he did not expect good to triumph; he foresaw no success for the art, the ideas, the institutions, on which his love had fastened. But he had won through, in these last twenty years, to an acceptance of human experience that found joy in all of it, even its tragedies and disappointments.

The account of the development of modern poetry in my chapter in volume I of this series began with Yeats, in his bedroom in the Hôtel Corneille, trembling at the power of the Savage God. As a counterbalancing picture, we might consider this poem, from his *Last Poems* (1939):

HIGH TALK

Processions that lack high stilts have nothing that catches the eye.
What if my great-granddad had a pair that were twenty foot high,
And mine were but fifteen foot, no modern stalks upon higher,
Some rogue of the world stole them to patch up a fence or a fire.
Because piebald ponies, led bears, caged lions, make but poor shows,
Because children demand Daddy-long-legs upon his timber toes,
Because women in the upper storeys demand a face at the pane,
That patching old heels they may shriek, I take to chisel and plane.

Malachi Stilt-Jack am I, whatever I learned has run wild,
From collar to collar, from stilt to stilt, from father to child.
All metaphor, Malachi, stilts and all. A barnacle goose
Far up in the stretches of night; night splits and the dawn breaks loose;
I, through the terrible novelty of light, stalk on, stalk on;
Those great sea-horses bare their teeth and laugh at the dawn.[7]

The savage exaltation here, the recklessness that welcomes the role of a mad performer both feared and needed, the surging strength of the verse, have nothing to fear from 'comedy, objectivity, the Savage God'. The image of a wild goose high in the sky at dawn, or of the sea-horses, might have occurred in one of Yeats's earliest poems in his 'Celtic Twilight' period, but the strength of the descriptive language lifts them to another level altogether: 'night *splits* and the dawn *breaks loose*'; the sea-horses are wild creatures which exult in the 'terrible novelty of light'. So does Malachi Stilt-Jack as he stalks on; and as we contemplate this grotesque, visionary figure on his 'timber toes', we realize that at last Yeats has found a place in his poetry for Ubu Roi and all his wild modern progeny, that he has beaten the Savage God, that the challenge thrown to him by Alfred Jarry has been triumphantly answered.

The later work of Yeats, both in verse and prose, shows him steadily moving towards the solution of those problems that had troubled him from the beginning: how to bring dream and reality into one steady view, and how to reconcile himself to Ireland.

We will take the second subject first. Yeats, as we saw in the previous volume, never succeeded in his youth in finding a workable relationship with his native land, though his sympathies were passionately rooted there and he felt himself a foreigner in England. His clashes with the supporters of the Young Ireland movement, with Sir Charles Gavan Duffy, with the audiences that howled down the work of Synge, had finally convinced him that in trying to influence the urban Catholic middle class he was beating his head against a brick wall. Only in such places as Coole Park, only in the company of such friends as Augusta Gregory, Edward Martyn, and the Gore-Booth family, did he find himself truly at home in an Irish setting. Not that this brought him any nearer to the levers of power. The land-owning gentry were evidently despised by the people who actually governed Ireland; their values counted for nothing. Coole House itself, so much loved by Yeats and so important in the story of his life, could not survive the narrow, grasping hostility of the central bureaucracy. Despite her struggle to maintain the house and grounds, Lady Gregory was forced to sell both to the government in 1927; a little later, Coole House was pulled down.

The power in Ireland was not held then, and is not held now, by such as Yeats. Not only that: he was never in the confidence of the revolutionaries who led the rebellion against England; 1916 took him by surprise, and the whole movement that led to the founding of a Republic, and the establishment in power of De Valera, went forward without him.

Nevertheless, a relationship was slowly forged. In his autobiographical writings, notably *The Trembling of the Veil*, Yeats re-lived the story of his part in the struggle of the late nineteenth century towards the formation of an Irish consciousness and an Irish pride. The award of the Nobel Prize in 1923 was welcome to him chiefly because it increased his influence at home. Then there were the six years he spent as a member of the Irish Senate, a position he did not much enjoy, but which gave him opportunities to speak out in defence of literature and the arts and to safeguard their place in Irish life. Better still, there was his marriage to George Hyde-Lees in

1917, the birth of his son and daughter, and his purchase in 1922 of
the Norman tower Thor Ballylee (for £35!) as a family home. A
settled man, a husband, and father, with a reputation beyond the
reach of fashion, he was rooted—almost. The only need that
remained was for an intellectual pedigree, something to demonstrate
that anglicized, Protestant Irishmen such as he had played a role
in the shaping of the country.

How seriously he traced this pedigree, how important it was in his
thinking and feeling, we can see from both prose and verse. There
is, for instance, the long and important preface to *The Words Upon
the Window-Pane* (1934) with its passionate claim that the eighteenth
century was the pivot of Irish civilization, 'that one Irish century
escaped from darkness and confusion', when Swift in his *Drapier
Letters* 'created the political nationality of Ireland', and when minds
of an Irish cast dominated a great age of literature.

I divine an Irish hatred of abstraction likewise expressed by that fable
of Gulliver among the inventors and men of science, by Berkeley in his
Commonplace Book, by Goldsmith in the satire of *The Good-Natured Man*,
in the picturesque, minute observation of *The Deserted Village*, and by
Burke in his attack upon mathematical democracy.

And in a footnote he defends the Protestant ascendancy against the
charge of being mere colonizing 'English': 'the newest arrivals soon
inter-married with an older stock, and that older stock had inter-
married again and again with Gaelic Ireland.'

This tradition became assimilated into the central stream of
Yeats's imagination, and he linked himself and his tower with these
Anglo-Irish names in the marvellous sequence of poems, 'Blood and
the Moon' (1933). We may smile at his concern for ancestors, as
we may smile at Eliot's devotion to the Anglo-Catholic pieties of
East Coker and Little Gidding, or for that matter Shakespeare's
aggrandizing of his family by applying for a coat of arms. But
perhaps when we come to understand poets better we shall find
that their interest in roots, in local association and family tradition,
is part of that tactile and organic approach to life which, having
made poets of them in the first place, causes them to wish their
'days to be/Bound each to each by natural piety'.

When we contemplate this side of Yeats's life-work there are,
then, no serious difficulties. Its other main facet, his immersion in
magic and the occult, raises more delicate issues. Its explicit expression is mostly in his prose works, and we shall find it useful to
approach his late work through the prose writings contained in

Mythologies (1959) and, of course, *A Vision* (1925, much revised and altered up to the final edition brought out in 1955).

In trying to make up our minds as to the value and relevance of Yeats's mystical theories and the prose works in which he expressed them, the most important thing to recognize is that the poet remained entirely faithful to the position he adopted in the 1880s. At that time, feeling as he did that Victorian science had barred the way to Christian belief, Yeats never for a moment considered living a life based on materialism alone; he never wavered in his belief that the physical world, however much the investigations of science might illuminate its laws and processes, was not sufficient unto itself, that true power and significance and value lay elsewhere and that the human mind, if it underwent the right discipline, might hope to perceive them. What Irishman, once he has parted company with the priest, can resist the impulse to make his own religion? Even Samuel Beckett, who has set up as the prophet of utter nihilism and despair, cannot help preaching that despair with all the fervour of a new doctrine, investing it with lyricism, filling his emptiness with an energy and savage delight that belie his message that inertia and helplessness are all.

Once Yeats's long search had begun—through theosophy, the Golden Dawn, Rosicrucianism, Swedenborg, Blake, the Upanishads, alchemy, mediumism, etc., etc.—it could have only one ultimate goal: the construction of a complete system, a building with many doors and windows, which his mind could wander into and out of, always with delight and refreshment. This structure, when it finally arose, was *A Vision*. It was significant that he never finished this book, never reached a point at which he could sit back and say that it was finished; he was revising and rebuilding all his life; to be at work on such a system was more important to him than to be the owner of the finished construction.

The story of how Yeats came to write *A Vision* is familiar enough, even to people who will never trouble to read the book. Four days after his marriage in 1917, his wife George suddenly began to produce automatic writing:

What came in disjointed sentences, in almost illegible writing, was so exciting, sometimes so profound, that I persuaded her to give an hour or two day after day to the unknown writer, and after some half-dozen such hours offered to spend what remained of life explaining and piecing together those scattered sentences. 'No', was the answer, 'we have come to give you metaphors for poetry.' [8]

After a time, Mrs. Yeats gave up writing and uttered aloud what she heard, her husband taking it down and storing the material for arrangement and study. In the introductory chapters of *A Vision*, Yeats has made an enthralling story of the whole process; how the incorporeal guides took turns at the work, often interrupted by a rival team known as Frustrators, and sometimes sowing doubt amid their genuine messages by such remarks as, 'Remember that we will deceive you if we can'; how they demanded to be prompted with questions, and chided Yeats for his slowness and confusion in formulating them; how once, when an owl hooted in the garden, the dictating spirit broke off and asked for a few minutes' silence, because 'Sounds like that give us great pleasure'; how the Frustrators later attacked the health of his children.

This account is characteristically Yeatsian in its blend of high mystical dignity with a dash of earthy shrewdness and even irreverence. The second, amplified version of *A Vision* also includes a piece of prose fiction, *Stories of Michael Robartes and his Friends: an extract from a record made by his Pupils*, which introduces the two characters Michael Robartes and Owen Aherne, whom Yeats had invented as long ago as 1896 and who typify two contrasting attitudes towards experience: Robartes is a visionary, in love with mystery and danger, capable of saintliness and of evil; Aherne is prudent and conventional, yet also better attuned to solitude and meditation. By bringing in this emblematic pair, Yeats signalled the subjective nature of the experience he was expounding. He was illuminating and explaining one imaginative experience in terms of another. In the same spirit, at about this time, he wrote a general note to accompany three poems, 'The Phases of the Moon', 'The Double Vision of Michael Robartes', and 'Michael Robartes and the Dancer'. This note is highly relevant to *A Vision*:

Years ago I wrote three stories in which occur the names of Michael Robartes and Owen Aherne. I now consider that I used the actual names of two friends, and that one of these friends, Michael Robartes, has but lately returned from Mesopotamia, where he has partly found and partly thought out much philosophy. I consider that Aherne and Robartes, men to whose namesakes I had attributed a turbulent life or death, have quarrelled with me. They take their place in a phantasmagoria in which I endeavour to explain my philosophy of life and death. To some extent I wrote these poems as a text for exposition.[9]

The word 'consider' is interesting in that passage; Yeats used it where another writer might more bluntly put 'imagine' or 'assume'; it is the *donnée* behind the 'phantasmagoria'. He does not make up things about Robartes and Aherne; he 'considers' them. The word provides an approach to the whole question of belief and imagination in Yeats. The phantasmagoria exists to expound the 'philosophy'; the dream colours and animates a perception of reality; *A Vision* contains not only the story of Robartes and Aherne, but also two of Yeats's greatest poems, 'Leda and the Swan' and 'All Soul's Night'.

With these considerations in mind, we are ready to approach the central passages of *A Vision*, in which Yeats set out what the spiritual voices actually told him. It turns out to be an elaborate exposition of human psychology and history in terms of the phases of the moon. These are 28 in number, but, according to the psychological part of the theory, two of them are non-human, so that we are left with 26. Each phase is described in detail, with examples from history of the type of character produced by its influence. Soon, on 6 December, a new element was added: the 'gyres', or spirals, two whirling cones which, interpenetrating and spinning one inside the other, symbolized the persistent principle of flux between antithetical extremes. Not only the individual soul, but the whole movement of history, is seen as moving ceaselessly from left to right and back from right to left; one cone represents the objective, the other the subjective, and as soon as the fullest realization of one is achieved, the movement towards the other begins. Yeats's thinking had always been dominated by the idea of antithesis, of the fruitful interpenetration of opposites, as when he elaborated the theory of the Anti-self, the Mask, which made all achievement possible. Applying his symbol of the 'gyres' (the *g*, incidentally, is hard) to history, he came up with the theory that the length of time necessary for an historical process to move completely across from subjective to objective, or back again, was 2,000 years. This meant, of course, that in our century the Christian era, which had begun as a swing from objective to subjective, was coming to an end and history was going into reverse, turning back to an era of objectivity. He found ample evidence of this in historical fact—naturally, since he found what he was looking for—and claimed in particular that the rise of large, impersonal mass movements like democracy and totalitarianism were evidence of the impending movement towards objectivity and the submergence of the individual.

The question at once arises, How seriously did Yeats take all this? The answer is that he took it seriously with his own kind of seriousness. By satisfying his lifelong need for a system of beliefs that would bind together the fragments of human life, it allayed many of the anxieties that had driven him from society to society, from séance to séance, without ever bringing him much illumination. By being shared with his wife, whom he loved and who had brought him happiness and serenity, it confirmed his feeling that in marriage he had at last found himself. By giving full play to his strong imaginative bias towards the idea of creative tension between opposites, it released new energy into his art. And literal belief? Yeats was a modern man, and what modern man gives literal belief to any intellectual system? 'The best in this kind are but shadows'; they are all metaphors, the concrete expression of abstract realities too fine for human perception, unless Yeats is correct in his belief that these things will become plain to us after death, for

> it is a ghost's right,
> His intellect is so fine
> Being sharpened by his death,
> To drink from the wine-breath
> While our gross palates drink from the whole wine.

None of this is my invention; Yeats has explained, within *A Vision* itself, the nature of his relationship to the theories he outlines there.

Some will ask whether I believe in the actual existence of my circuits of sun and moon. Those that include, now all recorded time in one circuit, now what Blake called 'the pulsaters of an artery', are plainly symbolical, but what of those that fixed, like a butterfly upon a pin, to our central date, the first day of our Era, divide actual history into periods of equal length? To such a question I can but answer that if sometimes, overwhelmed by miracle as all men must be when in the midst of it, I have taken such periods literally, my reason has soon recovered; and now that the system stands out clearly in my imagination I regard them as stylistic arrangements of experience comparable to the cubes in the drawing of Wyndham Lewis and to the ovoids in the sculpture of Brancusi. They have helped me to hold in a single thought reality and justice.[10]

'Stylistic arrangements of experience': where have we heard this kind of language before? Often, of course, in Yeats. One thinks of those words in *Estrangement*: 'Style, personality—deliberately adopted and therefore a mask—is the only escape from the hot-faced bargainers and the money-changers.'

It seems to me that *A Vision* is a work in the tradition of those dialogues of Plato's in which Plato is frankly inventing, though using his inventions to convey things close to the heart of his view of the world. 'Some will ask', Yeats wrote in 1928, 'if I believe all that this book contains, and I will not know how to answer. Does the word belief, used as they will use it, belong to our age, can I think of the world as there and I here judging it?' To me, it is a mistake to prod *A Vision* with a broomstick until it falls into its component parts of literal belief, symbol, and invention, and then take up these components one at a time for analysis. It is an imaginative work, no less than his poems, though inferior to the poems, and rightly so, since it exists to serve them.

All the evidence points to the conclusion that Yeats was very shrewdly aware of what dreams could do and what they could not do. If his entire life had been dominated by his experience as a visionary and his immersion in occult tradition, we might expect to find those preoccupations in everything he did. In fact, he was in most areas very clear-cut. We know exactly where he stood on every practical point; we know his politics, his views on art and literature (his critical essays are excellent, not nearly as subjective as Eliot's and quite as well argued), his assessment of the characters of various notable men of his day. Clearly, he was no mystagogue; he knew what mystical reverie could do for him, and he acknowledged its power in his life; but the symbols that animate his poetry are symbols that do their work in the world of human experience rather than in the world of shadow and divination.

IV

After all the majesty of Yeats, there is nowhere to go but down: unless one goes to Eliot. In concentration and power, *Four Quartets* is the only work in modern poetry written in English that one can pick up after Yeats without the sensation of breathing much more common air.

Beyond a doubt, *Four Quartets* is the crown of Eliot's work as a poet. After the early diagnosis of fever and bewilderment, after the concrete and even bellicose argumentation of the middle years, we arrive at this series of intertwined lyrical meditations—on faith and the search for faith, on self-forgetfulness and self-fulfilment, on the nature of man as a creature of plural consciousness, living always at the point of intersection between time and eternity—with the sense of having broken from the timber-line and gained at last the uncluttered peaks. All the features of Eliot's previous work are here, but all refined and intensified by long meditation and experience into a poetry stripped of all tricks and ornaments, a style so pure and strong as to make us assent once more, from a different angle, to Yeats's conclusion that 'there's more enterprise in walking naked'. Lofty and severe, yet intensely human in their evocation of the always-renewed struggle of man to shake free of death and mount towards life, these poems speak directly out of the courage and earnestness, the noble sense of purpose and dedication, which the poet shares with those seventeenth-century ancestors to whom his thoughts so continually recur: men like Andrew Eliot of East Coker, or Isaac Stearns who was one of the first generation of settlers in Massachusetts: men of action whose lives were fortified by reflectiveness, learning, and piety. In the language and rhythms of *Four Quartets* there is a direct plainness and a delicate exactness that testifies to the same qualities, somehow preserved intact through three centuries to speak out again in the battered England of the early 1940s—that same England which, after years of debilitating indecision in the epoch of inferior leadership and 'a thousand lost golf balls', had at last found the courage to turn and stand against the evil of totalitarianism.

Each of the Four Quartets can be read separately, and all were published separately before they were issued in one volume in 1944; nevertheless, they are conceived and written as a whole, with a complex interchange of echoes. They progress, not like a vehicle moving along a road, but like a wheel revolving about a hub. Each of them is intensely concrete in its evocation of a locale; equally, each of them is able at any moment to depart from this fixed point, to move backwards and forwards in time, or sideways into a universal dream-landscape.

Taking a bearing on the fixed and known in order to explore that which is beyond our normal gaze, *Four Quartets* continues a tradition of Eliot's poetry that goes back as far as *The Waste Land* and even *Prufrock*. One of its main themes might almost be summed up in Shelley's lines from *Adonais*:

> The One remains, the many change and pass:
> Heaven's light for ever shines, Earth's shadows flee:
> Life, like a dome of many-coloured glass,
> Stains the white radiance of Eternity,
> Until Death tramples it to fragments.

Eliot's concern is with the fragments as they lie discarded, and also with the 'white radiance': the 'dome', the shaped and continuing individual life, is to him an illusion.

To speak of the artistry of *Four Quartets* is to take cognizance of a stylistic range, a variety of expedients and strategies, beyond the scope of all but a very few poets in history. Here, as in the earlier phases of his career, Eliot set himself to organize multiplicity into unity, to say much and to suggest more, to make his intensely pregnant statements not only by means of what was said but also by the form in which it was said, so that the changes of rhythm and the alternation of densely intricate passages with more relaxed and conversational sections is always a contribution to the total meaning. To write like this is not given to a youthful poet, nor to a poet of any age who has been content with superficial thought and slipshod practice. The perfect assurance with which Eliot moves from intricate formal verse-patterns (such as the beautiful lyric passage at the beginning of section II of 'The Dry Salvages', which seems to be a personal adaptation of the sestina form and, I take it, Eliot's own invention) to something that might, if by this date the term had any meaning left in it, be described as 'free verse', verse in which the speaking voice, as it moves through soliloquy and medita-tion towards discovery, imposes the rhythm of its thought on the movement of the words—all this, clearly, is the fruit of many years of patient donkey-work and recalls an earlier prescription of Eliot's, that the poet, however little he publishes, must keep his skill alive by 'some hours' work every week of his life'. Or, as Milton put it, that he must 'strictly meditate the thankless Muse'.

Eliot's devoted self-discipline to the poetic art is not seen only, or even primarily, in the page-by-page expertness of the verse. It appears even more clearly in his power of sustaining a large struc-ture. Though their total number of lines is small, the Quartets are built like a cathedral into a structure large enough for the purpose of a lifetime. And this building is carried out on principles that Eliot discovered and elaborated through profound and original poetic thinking. It owes nothing to any previous poem, of his or anyone else's. If the basic organizing procedure of *The Waste Land* was cinematic, here, as the name indicates, it is musical. Shortly after completing the Quartets, Eliot gave his lecture on 'The Music of Poetry', in which he mentioned with typical impersonality and modesty some of the thoughts which must have guided his practice.

There are possibilities for verse which bear some analogy to the development of a theme by different groups of instruments; there are possibilities of transitions in a poem comparable to the different move-ments of a symphony or a quartet; there are possibilities of contrapuntal arrangement of subject-matter. It is in the concert room, rather than in the opera house, that the germ of a poem may be quickened.[11]

The reference to 'contrapuntal arrangement of subject-matter' reminds us that musical construction will carry a poem only for a certain distance, and that the larger unity of the *Four Quartets* is built with the more familiar stuff of imaginative literature: with symbols and images, echoed from one passage to another and always with some new facet displayed, some new accretion of meaning. As well as the evocation of times and places, each of the poems centres its imagery in one of the four elements: 'Burnt Norton' in air, 'East Coker' in earth, 'The Dry Salvages' in water, and 'Little Gidding' in fire; and to examine the way this symbolism is woven into the poems is to come close to the secret of Eliot's quiet and unspectacular mastery. Other binding devices are also used. Each of the four poems begins with a general statement, evoking a place and a state of mind, and then goes on, in section II, to a lyric of delicate formality, followed by a more extended passage which repeats in less compressed language the theme of the lyric and usually offers some comment on it. Another strictly formed lyric occurs in each poem as section IV. Each Quartet has five sections, and it is worth noting that the fifth and concluding section, in every case except 'East Coker' and to some extent even there, ends with a tighter rhythm and shorter lines than it begins with; a system of reverberating echoes that reminds us how deeply pondered, in this poem, are the analogies with musical form.

In addition to these rhythmic and, as it were, melodic structural devices, *Four Quartets* also uses variations of linguistic texture as a shaping and steadying force. Passages of considerable concentration, which almost defy paraphrase, alternate with passages that offer up their meaning with the greatest docility on a first reading. The degree of difficulty itself, that is, can be seen as a structural scaffolding. The reader rises to his full intellectual height, then sinks back, then rises again, in a continuous shifting of mental posture, so that the experience of reading *Four Quartets* is exactly the opposite of what we find in one of those amorphous long poems that go on and on and finally cease when the author runs out of material. The music of words, the music of metrical patterns, the music of ideas, all combine to make the four parts unite in one larger statement, giving it an aesthetic unity more satisfying than that of any other long poem of modern times.

One result of this is that the poem as a whole takes in, without strain, a remarkable range of subject-matter. The sheer number of things that are said in the *Four Quartets*, when you come to write them out in prose, is quite staggering. Apart from the central theme, the exploration of faith and the rediscovery of a tradition that will give a personal foundation for faith, Eliot has also managed to bring in the problems that confront him as a poet—and without irrelevance, since the struggle to perceive and understand is always bound up with the struggle to communicate. Eliot, as we have seen, was at one with the other major poets of his age in rejecting any merely decorative function for poetry; to him the act of poetic creation is always 'a raid on the inarticulate', a moving towards new perception, finer adjustment, deeper awareness, and hence one of the few activities capable of raising men (sometimes, and in some places) above the level of savagery. We must not be surprised, then, to find that in this, his greatest poem, he manages to give us a very complete statement of his view of the nature and function of the poetic art.

In 1943, between the completion of the *Quartets* and their appearance in book form, Eliot gave his lecture on 'The Social Function of Poetry', which must have seemed to him of some importance, since he later expanded it and delivered it again in Paris in 1945, and later printed it in a magazine and then in his volume *On Poetry and Poets*. The whole essay is profoundly stimulating and suggestive; it has a continuity with Eliot's earlier utterances on this theme while correcting the imbalance or incompleteness of some of these utterances (one thinks particularly of the famous remark in *The Sacred Wood* that poetry is 'a superior form of amusement'). In 'The Social Function of Poetry', while beginning with a firm directive that poetry must give pleasure, Eliot goes straight to the heart of the poet's task: his concern with language.

We may say that the duty of the poet, as poet, is only indirectly to his people: his direct duty is to his *language,* first to preserve, and second to extend and improve. In expressing what other people feel he is also changing the feeling by making it more conscious; he is making people more aware of what they feel already, and therefore teaching them something about themselves. But he is not merely a more conscious person than the others; he is also individually different from other people, and from other poets too, and can make his readers share consciously in new feelings which they had not experienced before.

This statement of the connection between the poet and the *res publica* is developed in various ways throughout the essay, one of these ways being a reassertion, in slightly different form, of the need for a continuing tradition in poetry, the need for the present and the past to interact, which had been one of the main planks in Eliot's platform since 'Tradition and the Individual Talent'.

. . . if we have no living literature we shall become more and more alienated from the literature of the past; unless we keep up continuity, our literature of the past will become more and more remote from us until it is as strange to us as the literature of a foreign people. For our language goes on changing; our way of life changes, under the pressure of material changes in our environment in all sorts of ways; and unless we have those few men who combine an exceptional sensibility with an exceptional power over words, our own ability, not merely to express, but even to feel any but the crudest emotions, will degenerate.[12]

At the same time, Eliot also met a possible objection to this view. In modern mass society, even the greatest poet has a very small audience, and if we are to rely on poetry to keep our language, and therefore our consciousness, in repair, how will his efforts avail when the bulk of the society is unaware of it? To counter this, Eliot made use of a homely illustration. The poet has a small, highly conscious audience (many of whom, we might add on our own account, will be other poets); his use of language, that cleaned and restored language which alone can show the true dimensions of thought and feeling, will influence first this small, active minority, and then filter outwards, being taken up first by more popular writers and journalists, and then by the society at large, by which time the true poet and his attendant *avant-garde* will again be some distance ahead. To perceive the influence of a poet on the language and sensibility of his time, said Eliot, is like trying to follow the flight of a bird or an aeroplane through a clear sky. If we were watching it when it was near us, we can hold it in sight, long after it has become a mere speck which could never be found by someone who began to search for it at that stage.

From here, our thoughts naturally go back to the last of the Quartets, 'Little Gidding', in whose second section occurs the famous passage, written in English blank verse that has the same movement as Dante's *terza rima*, which describes the meeting of Eliot and the ghost of some dead master. This master, in whose composite features we may discern traces of personal mentors of Eliot's such as George Santayana and Ezra Pound, as well as of masters of the European tradition such as Dante himself, reminds Eliot that

> our concern was speech, and speech impelled us
> To purify the dialect of the tribe.

As so often at a crucial point of his argument, Eliot here chooses to speak through someone else's mask, and the line is his translation of Mallarmé's description of the poet's task, *Donner un sens plus pur aux mots de la tribu.* This willingness to quote, at a crucial point, evidently springs from the same part of Eliot's mind that makes him uphold the discipline of an impersonal 'tradition'; he is always saying, with complete sincerity, that his own individual personality only takes on its true value when blended harmoniously with something greater than itself—the mind of Europe, the discipline of the Church. So that this statement about the poetic language, taking the form of a translation from Mallarmé and occurring in a passage in which Eliot gracefully merges his own poetic personality with that of Dante, comes over with the authority of something believed and uttered by European poets generally and not merely an idiosyncratic opinion of Eliot's. It is a triumphant justification of his method.

Four Quartets was published in volume form in 1944. Dylan Thomas's wartime poems, collected as *Deaths and Entrances,* appeared in 1946. In halting at 1945, then, we are ending our survey at a point where the tide is still running strongly. The later forties, in poetry as in much else, were disappointing years; but the years between 1939 and 1945 had seen the publication of enough masterpieces and near-masterpieces to make the forties, as a whole, memorable as a good decade. (Decisively better, one is tempted to speak out of turn and add, than anything that has come since.)

In coming to an end, one regrets, inevitably, the interesting poets who have been crowded out from an already long chapter. In particular, the absence of American poets will be noticed. But the fact is that, before 1945, there was not much traffic between English and American poetry. In Victorian times, indeed, an American poet, Longfellow, had conquered the English public, and Whitman had his discerning admirers in England well before he enjoyed any reputation at home. But, between the two World Wars, the American poets who made an impression in England were those who came here. A few names crossed the Atlantic; Cummings, largely owing to the devoted propaganda work of Robert Graves, was appreciated as an amusing oddity; the literary, allusive, ironic style of Allen Tate, John Crowe Ransom, and their companions of the 'Fugitive Group' may have had a few readers in university circles; Hart Crane's brilliant but smoky and guttering flame was clearly visible; as for Robert Frost, he made his first reputation in England and was consistently well-known here. But, on the whole, the diversity and variety of American poetry were not appreciated in

England before 1945. The one stay-at-home American poet of unquestionably major status, Wallace Stevens, had to wait until 1953 for an English edition, though he had been respected in America since the publication of *Harmonium* thirty years previously.

England, before 1945, was much more of an island than she will ever be again. And the mood of England, after the long stalemate of the thirties, had blazed out into something prophetic. Poets of very different styles and temperaments were agreeing in their passionate desire to 'kiss the hem of God's robe'. During those years of privation and danger, their object was to make

> Soul clap its hands and sing, and louder sing
> For every tatter in its mortal dress.

Not all these poets were 'religious' in any formal sense. The prophetic mood runs the entire gamut from Eliot's orthodox Anglo-Catholicism to the home-made constructions of Yeats or Graves, and the almost pantheistic reverence for life, the mere process of life, in Dylan Thomas. Across the Atlantic, Auden, who in his earlier years as an American still seemed to be within the gravitational pull of England, experienced Christian conversion and wrote his two most explicitly Christian works, *New Year Letter* (1941) and *For the Time Being* (1945).

There need be no quarrel here between 'Christians' and 'humanists'. All these poets, by expressing their instinctive belief that life is not a mere biological accident but a sacrament, were pointing to the path that man must follow if he is to avoid being swallowed up by his political systems and enslaved by his technology. The attitude they share, a fundamentally religious approach to the wonder of life, is not merely the best way, but the only way, of giving back dignity and meaning to human existence.

NOTES

[1] Ezra Pound, in *The Egoist*, IV, 2 (Feb. 1917), 22–4.
[2] Ezra Pound, *Collected Shorter Poems* (1968), 17. Quoted by permission of Faber & Faber Ltd.
[3] Ibid., 207.
[4] T. S. Eliot, *On Poetry and Poets* (1957), 35–6.
[5] Stephen Spender, *Selected Poems* (1940), 46.

[6] Robert Graves, *Collected Poems 1965* (1965), 63. Quoted by permission of the author.

[7] W. B. Yeats, *Last Poems and Plays* (1940), 73. Quoted by permission of Mr. M. B. Yeats and Macmillan & Co. Ltd.

[8] W. B. Yeats, *A Vision* (1961), 8.

[9] W. B. Yeats, *Collected Poems* (1939), 446.

[10] Yeats, *A Vision*, 24–5.

[11] Eliot, *On Poetry and Poets*, 38.

[12] Ibid., 20–1.

FOR FURTHER READING

Among the many books on Eliot, the best are probably Hugh Kenner, *The Invisible Poet: T. S. Eliot* (1960) and Helen Gardner, *The Art of T. S. Eliot* (1946), the latter including a brilliant pioneer study of *Four Quartets*. Kenner's book is a stimulating and perceptive study, especially illuminating on 'Eliot's long struggle, in the years after *Prufrock*, to arrive at a criterion of relevance and a self-sufficient logic of structure—a struggle not consummated until *Four Quartets*'. George Watson, 'The Triumph of T. S. Eliot', in *The Critical Quarterly* (Winter, 1965), deals with the growth of Eliot's early reputation; this article disposes finally of the idea that it was only a few lonely and 'courageous' people who admired him in the 1920s.

A reading list for Yeats is given in volume I of *The Twentieth-Century Mind* (p. 412).

Noel Stock, *The Life of Ezra Pound* (1970) is copious and sensible. Donald Davie, *Ezra Pound: Poet as Sculptor* (1965) is a highly intelligent appraisal. J. P. Sullivan, *Ezra Pound and Sextus Propertius: A Study in Creative Translation* (1964) contains parallel texts of Propertius's original and Pound's re-creation, with an interesting commentary from one of the few professional classical scholars to be basically in sympathy with Pound's aims. See also Noel Stock, *Reading the Cantos: A Study of Meaning in Ezra Pound* (1967), J. E. Edwards, *Annotated Index to the Cantos* (1959), J. J. Espey, *Ezra Pound's 'Mauberley', a Study in Composition* (1955), *New Approaches to Ezra Pound*, ed. Eva Hesse (1969), and Christine Brooke-Rose, *A ZBC of Ezra Pound* (1970).

C. K. Stead, *The New Poetic* (1964) and Frank Kermode, *Romantic Image* (1957) are both excellent analyses of modernism in poetry. Francis Scarfe, *Auden and After* (1942) is a journalistic survey of poets in the 1930s; also useful as background are Stephen Spender's autobiographical volume, *World within World* (1951), Julian Symons, *The Thirties* (1960), and D. E. S. Maxwell, *Poets of the Thirties* (1969). The latter is useful on Auden, and on the political background of the thirties poets.

Monroe K. Spears, *The Poetry of Auden: The Disenchanted Island* (New York, 1963) is a most useful general book. The chapters are interspersed with 'chronologies' which are the nearest thing yet published to a biography of Auden. The 'Index of first lines' resolves the bibliographical chaos that so frequently surrounds the poems. Joseph Warren Beach, *The Making of the Auden Canon* (Minneapolis, Minn., 1957) discusses Auden's revisions: Auden as self-critic and self-disguiser. John Fuller, *A Reader's Guide to W. H. Auden* (1970) has good analyses of the poems.

Constantine Fitzgibbon, *The Life of Dylan Thomas* (1966) is large and solid, the 'authorized' biography, done with tact and truthfulness. J. M. Brinnin, *Dylan Thomas in America* (1956) gives a moving account of the poet's last months and of his death. Bill Read and Rollie McKenna, *The Days of Dylan Thomas* (1965) is a fascinating collection of photographs, virtually a Thomas family album, connected by a wispy commentary. For criticism, see W. Y. Tyndall, *A Reader's Guide to Dylan Thomas* (New York, 1962) and *Dylan Thomas: A Collection of Critical Essays*, ed. C. B. Cox (Englewood Cliffs, N. J., 1966).

Two volumes of Lawrance Thompson's biography of Robert Frost have appeared, *Robert Frost: The Early Years 1874–1915* (1966) and *Robert Frost: The Years of Triumph 1915–1938* (1971). See also Thompson's *Fire and Ice: The Art and Thought of Robert Frost* (1961) and Louis Untermeyer, *Robert Frost: A Backward Look* (Washington, D.C., 1964).

Some poets who were working during this period, but whose most important poems were written after 1945 (e.g. Edwin Muir, Hugh MacDiarmid, and Stevie Smith) are missing from the chapter and this reading list.

11

The English Novel

G. S. FRASER

I

There are five major English figures in this period who need, it
seems to me, to be treated in short blocks: Joyce as an inventor
and as a great comic novelist, D. H. Lawrence as a searcher, a
novelist of the ego, Virginia Woolf for a peculiar delicacy of mind
and spirit, E. M. Forster as the author of the last great 'traditional'
English novel, a moralist whose gentle manners disguise a neo-
Calvinistic rigour of judgement: and Ford Madox Ford as a great
impersonative, impressionistic showman, whose technical virtuosity
cannot quite disguise the fact that his characters are conceived very
simply, as types of virtue and vice, and that he is writing a kind of
Christian allegory, illustrated moral theology rather than social
history. Conrad who survived into this period was also a major
novelist, but his major works had been written before 1918, and
what needs to be said about him has been said in the previous
volume by Alan Friedman. The element of romance, the wistfulness
for the romantic past and for youth, is the strongest strand in later
fictions like *The Rover* and *The Arrow of Gold*.

All these writers were great individualists, who resist grouping.
There is a group of satirical novelists, satirizing social folly from a
stance of privilege which is almost one of complicity: Norman
Douglas, Ronald Firbank, Aldous Huxley, the early Evelyn Waugh,
the early Anthony Powell. They should be contrasted with a more
massively ambitious writer, Wyndham Lewis, whose satire is that
of the 'outsider' and who at his best, in *Tarr* and *The Revenge for
Love*, say, is a Dostoevskian novelist of the 'insulted and injured',
of alienation: his real affinities are with a French writer like Céline,
and in some of his non-fictional books he appears to share Céline's
Fascist, or semi-Fascist, attitudes. In *The Childermass*, which was
to be enlarged after 1945 as *The Human Age*, he writes a kind of
allegory of hell.

Apart from Ford Madox Ford's tetralogy about Christopher
Tietjens, the First World War produced no major fiction in England. Its best prose records are books of memoirs and disguised
memoirs like Robert Graves's *Good-Bye to All That*, Siegfried

Sassoon's *Memoirs of a Fox-Hunting Man* and *Memoirs of an Infantry Officer*, Frederic Manning's *Her Privates We*, and the war passages in the various versions of Herbert Read's autobiography. Richard Aldington's *Death of a Hero*, though it became a best-seller, is not in this class, and is at its best in fact, like Aldington's only other really interesting novel, *The Colonel's Daughter*, in its bitter double-edged satire, first on the shams, prudery, and snobbery of English middle-class philistinism and then, in reverse, on the hollowness and nastiness of the London literary and artistic life. Aldington could be partly classed with the group of satirical novelists I have mentioned except that, like Wyndham Lewis, he has the bitterness of the outsider.

One thinks of the best fiction of the 1920s as certainly individualist and in a broad sense experimental. One could very crudely say that the 1920s were a decade of genius, the 1930s of talent: the best new writers are in some sense disciples, but disciples with an eye, which their masters had not, for the popular market, and often with a simple story-telling power which their masters lacked. Graham Greene comes out of Stevenson, Conrad, and Henry James, seeing the last, in a rather simple-minded way, as a novelist of betrayal and treachery (he sees that the Prince and Charlotte, in *The Golden Bowl*, can be said to betray Maggie and Adam, that Kate and Densher, in *The Wings of the Dove*, can be said to betray Millie, but not that there is another sort of betrayal, the betrayal of renunciation; that Charlotte and the Prince, beautiful objects accessible to wealth, are isolated and crushed by the Ververs' magnanimity, and that Millie's will acts as a kind of posthumous revenge, dividing Kate and Densher for ever, holding Densher for ever).

Christopher Isherwood comes essentially out of E. M. Forster, with a much lighter light-comedy touch, but with an equally rigorous separation of sheep and goats. Very good women novelists like Elizabeth Bowen and Rosamund Lehmann lose something when read in the shadow of Virginia Woolf, though both are natural story-tellers in a sense that she is not. Joyce Cary's considerable impersonative techniques lose something when they are compared with Ford Madox Ford's.

L. P. Hartley, a delicate and sensitive novelist, with a special feeling for childhood, for the shocks that come upon innocence, for the delicacies of family relationships, again owes much to James, the James of *What Maisie Knew* and *The Awkward Age*. The general standard of intelligence and sensibility in fiction went up in the 1930s, as it is steadily going up today. But there seemed a lack of great masters. Isherwood, the voice that one most willingly listened to in the 1930s, the voice with the unaffected wit of stringent humanity, has not quite fulfilled his early splendid promise, perhaps betrayed by a too special interest in the bizarre situation, the 'camp' situation, the sexual or social oddball. He remains a writer to whom one turns, as one turns to Virginia Woolf, for the distinction of his spirit and the casual masterfulness of his prose; Evelyn Waugh, his rival for elegance of style among the novelists of the 1930s, is perhaps in comparison always a little too wary of close contact with the reader, a little too much *en robe de parade*.

Graham Greene's style translates exactly into cinematic images, makes a montage of metaphor and presented scene, sometimes almost appals one with its efficiency, though one remembers no sentence: but if he has not lived on to be exactly our greatest master, he has lived on to be our greatest pro. Expecting the bag of tricks as before, one is always in fact gripped and held. All these novelists of the 1930s could be contrasted with Henry Green, an innovator in his special handling of syntax, in his use of dialogue, in his ability to give scenes of industrial life, accurately notated, a strange air of remote pastoral comedy; but Green's overmastering interest in the shaping of the novel, a certain enclosedness in his work, deprived him of the wide popularity of Graham Greene, and left him very much a novelist's novelist, in the sense that one speaks of a poet's poet.

We are left with a broad picture of the 1920s as a period dominated by a few great individualists, and of the 1930s and 1940s as a period of much more widely diffused talent in the novel, without any such outstanding figures. The great figures of the 1920s are very much highbrows; the notable figures of the 1930s and early 1940s have a much broader appeal, and are not ashamed to use some of the techniques of the popular novel. Graham Greene owed much of his formation to historical thrillers like Marjorie Bowen's *The Viper of Milan*, and wrote appreciative articles on writers like Rider Haggard, Anthony Hope, A. E. W. Mason. Waugh's handling of farcical situations and stock farce characters, like the old Colonel in *Vile Bodies*, owes a great deal to P. G. Wodehouse. Greene's handling of foreign settings owes something to Somerset Maugham, about whom again he wrote appreciatively, and his thrillers or 'entertainments' have affinities with the contemporary, and very good, political thrillers of Eric Ambler, though a more important and distinguished source is probably Conrad's *The Secret Agent*.

The period was a very distinguished period in European and American fiction, but it is very difficult to trace direct influences.

Proust, in Scott Moncrieff's translation, enjoyed enormous esteem, and there is obviously an element of Proustian sensibility in Virginia Woolf: in the trembling openness of her sensibility, in her humour, in her *mystique* about parties, Clarissa Dalloway has something in common with the young Marcel. But it was on the whole Proust as the comic and satirical social observer, seeing grotesque figures swimming past him at parties, obsessed with the sudden revealing detail, that influenced English novelists, rather than the Proust engaged on his mystical or metaphysical quest for the total reconstitution of time in memory: Joyce's handling of time and memory was quite different and at their only meeting in Paris he and Proust found nothing to say to each other.

But Proust's social comedy strongly influenced even an anti-Proustian like Wyndham Lewis, in the huge set scenes of receptions and dinner parties in *The Apes of God*: from Proust also Wyndham Lewis perhaps got his obsession with homosexuality, a subject that did not interest other novelists of the period, though there is of course a strong element of latent and sublimated homosexuality in Lawrence, and Waugh uses the topic, in passing, for effects of farce. Aldous Huxley leant heavily on Gide's *Les Faux-Monnayeurs* for *Point Counter-Point*. But other important novelists translated in this period, and highly praised, Thomas Mann, Hermann Broch, Lady Murasaki in Arthur Waley's magnificent version of *The Tale of Genji*, had little direct influence. Kafka had perhaps some influence on the allegorical romances of Rex Warner but Warner's tough left-liberalism is very different from Kafka's ironic metaphysical despair, nor are the talents commensurate.

If they could be considered as a novel, the various volumes of Sir Osbert Sitwell's autobiography are very much a Proustian novel, but by a very unFrench Proust; rather Sir Osbert delved down to some of Proust's English sources, Ruskin for the elaborate and detailed passages of scenic and architectural description, Dickens (the Dickens of the Veneerings' dinner parties in *Our Mutual Friend*) for social comedy and the presentation of grotesques. It should be noted in passing how much distinguished fictive talent (Siegfried Sassoon is another example) went in this period directly into autobiography or memoirs; just as much autobiographical material, as in Lawrence's *Aaron's Rod* and *Kangaroo*, went directly into fiction.

American fiction had perhaps less direct influence even than European fiction. In the 1920s and 1930s the United States was much more of a *terra incognita* than Europe. Even good English critics often failed to spot the best American talent, and E. M. Forster praised too highly the essentially second-rate gift of Sinclair Lewis, though Lawrence, in a perceptive review, saw the point of Hemingway and T. S. Eliot saw at once that Scott Fitzgerald's *The Great Gatsby* was a work of genius. Wyndham Lewis, who had a more widely ranging intellectual curiosity than any other critic of his time, wrote interestingly but polemically about Gertrude Stein in *Time and Western Man* and rather more appreciatively about Hemingway as the 'dumb ox' of literature and about Faulkner's slightly mechanical atmospherics and monotonous vocabulary in *Men Without Art*, but on the whole English novelists seemed to think of the United States with a certain humorous condescension: an attitude that survived as late as Waugh's *The Loved One*, which falls outside our period.

The European settings and the atmospheres of *The Sun Also Rises* and *Tender Is The Night* have some affinities, perhaps, with the atmospheres of some novels with a European setting by D. H. Lawrence and Aldous Huxley, *Aaron's Rod* and *Those Barren Leaves*, but the differences are more important than the similarities. One American writer who had a certain subterranean influence towards the end of the 1930s was Henry Miller, with the publication in Paris of *Tropic of Cancer*, which inspired the young English poet, Lawrence Durrell, to a similar book, then unprintable in England, *The Black Book*. But this had only a limited circulation and Durrell's full development as a novelist belongs to the next volume.

George Orwell was much impressed by Miller's honesty, his total uncritical though often disgusted immersion in experience, and wrote a fine essay about him, 'Inside the Whale': but he had no influence on Orwell's own fiction, which was essentially an extension of his polemical social and political journalism. Orwell lacked the patience with 'alien modes of being' that is necessary for a good novelist; of the novels that he wrote in this period, the best probably is *Burmese Days*, which can be read as a kind of parody of *A Passage to India*, differing from Forster's great novel in having no noble or even sympathetic characters, and in extending critical dislike as much to the natives as to the white colonial administrators. Orwell's important development in fiction was not to be as a 'straight' novelist, but as a fabulist and Swiftian satirist, in *Animal Farm* and *1984*. *Down and Out in Paris and London*, not a novel, though it is not a literally true autobiography either, has the bitter feeling for the underdog which he admired in Miller.

I have been mentioning writers who seem to matter retrospectively. The period was also that of the great middlebrow bestsellers, Hugh Walpole, Charles Morgan, Clemence Dane, Compton Mackenzie, Somerset Maugham, J. B. Priestley, and others, who got more critical acclaim at least from the Sunday reviewers than most of the writers I have mentioned; and of more popular writers, of romance, comic fiction, or detective fiction, P. C. Wren, P. G. Wodehouse, Agatha Christie, Dorothy L. Sayers, some of whom appealed to more intellectual writers. T. S. Eliot reviewed new detective stories appreciatively in *The Criterion*: Wodehouse received an Oxford doctorate. In spite of Virginia Woolf's sharp distinction between highbrow, lowbrow, and middlebrow tastes, worked out more sharply and methodically by Q. D. Leavis in *Fiction and the Reading Public*, we have seen that popular fiction had a considerable influence on some of the best novelists of the 1930s, like Evelyn Waugh.

One should add also that writers whose early fame belongs to the Edwardian or early Georgian period, Arnold Bennett (very influential as a reviewer of fiction), John Galsworthy, and H. G. Wells went on writing fiction, though with diminished force: Galsworthy's sentimentality, a touch of the mechanical in Bennett, the straggly and improvisatory side of Wells became more obvious. The public had a great appetite for fiction (there was no television, sound radio was unsophisticated, the cinema was considered as a lower-middle-class kind of entertainment and was not, until the 1930s, beginning to be seriously considered as an art). Best-selling fiction fed fantasy interests, daydreams, that are now more abundantly catered for elsewhere. The novelist who thought of himself or herself as primarily an artist was throughout the period a lonely figure; and in the 1930s art was beginning to disguise itself very effectively, in Waugh, Isherwood, and Greene, say, as entertainment.

II

James Joyce's (1882–1941) *Ulysses* was published in Paris in 1922, after parts of it had come out in *The Little Review*, the brilliant New York literary magazine, from 1918 onwards. Though it did not achieve English or American publication till the 1930s, it became at once a controversially famous book. Early responses to it were odd and mixed. Richard Aldington, who had admired *Dubliners* and *Portrait of the Artist as a Young Man*, reacted to it rather as Thackeray had reacted to the fourth book of *Gulliver's Travels*, seeing it as an attack on human nature. T. S. Eliot agreed that the approach was Swiftian, but said that he thought the fourth book of *Gulliver's Travels* was one of the great achievements of the human spirit; he saw the book as ending the history of the novel in the traditional sense, as transforming fiction into myth. Virginia Woolf, though she was to learn some lessons from Joyce, expressed in her diaries lady-like distaste. She saw Stephen Dedalus as an irritating autodidact, like her own Charles Tansley, a boring cultural show-off. Shaw thought the book a work of documentation rather than art, and a tremendous indictment of the squalor of Dublin civilization. The humour and sympathy of the book were hardly noted by early critics at all.

Stuart Gilbert's still very useful commentary on *Ulysses*, for good tactical reasons (since *Ulysses* had been especially assailed for indecency), concentrated on the Homeric parallels and the elaborations of construction. D. H. Lawrence found the book a stinking *olla podrida*. In his pages on *Ulysses* in *Time and Western Man*, Wyndham Lewis, though writing polemically, made a few very useful points: that the tradition of verbal comedy through loose association of words and ideas, for instance, has its roots in Sterne, in the Smollett of Tabitha Bramble's and Winifred Jenkins's letters in *Humphry Clinker*, in the jerky speech of Mr. Jingle in *Pickwick*. He rightly saw that Bloom is, and is meant to be, a richer and more sympathetic character than Stephen, and much more like his middle-aged creator. Lewis's criticism is off balance, however: his favourite novelists were the great Russians; in the Stephen of *Ulysses* he found a vein of shabby-genteel snobbery and self-conscious self-pity that distressed him, and he failed to see that Stephen is not intended to be a heroic figure, in the sense in which the Stephen of *Portrait of the Artist* genuinely is. He claimed also that Bloom was not a real Jew but a compendium of music-hall jokes about Jews. But, as very often in his polemical criticism (one might refer to his essays on Pound, on Faulkner, on Hemingway), Lewis, while ostensibly bulldozing, put his finger on many positive qualities.

Today, *Ulysses* no longer shocks and is no longer seen as either ending or renovating the tradition of the novel. In an interesting lecture on *Ulysses* (see below, p. 416), Miriam Allott has crystallized the view of many sensitive modern readers. The parallels with the Odyssey, the many parodic devices, the variations on the stream-of-consciousness technique, are all there primarily to disguise the fact that *Ulysses* is anything but a formal masterpiece, is rather, in the Jamesian sense, a baggy monster or a fluid pudding of a book:

they are there to disguise a Dickensian obsession with detail, detail often irrelevant to what there is of plot, to what, problematically, there is of general theme. *Ulysses* is, as it were, a bulgy parcel, full of mixed goodies, which Joyce keeps from bursting open and scattering on the pavement by tying it together with various kinds of matching coloured string.

Ulysses, Mrs. Allott feels, is a masterpiece of untidy energy and of rich and scattering comic sympathy: sympathy with men, with places, with the diverse grandeurs and absurdities of human language. It is a comedy of style as much as of episode and character. If it is the greatest of Joyce's works, this is because it has, in a crude, old-fashioned sense, most life in it: life of a lavish and wasteful, but in the end self-justifying sort.

Joyce was, of course, capable of exquisite formal construction. This is evident in every individual story of *Dubliners* and in the placing and balancing of the stories in relation to each other. *A Portrait of the Artist as a Young Man* is exquisitely economical in its elimination of the irrelevant: about the young man, except about what makes him an artist in the end, we learn nothing. The discarded first version, *Stephen Hero*, of which the surviving fragment was edited by T. Spencer in 1944, shows how much rich background material, material of extreme documentary and personal interest, Joyce was willing to discard in *A Portrait* for the sake of thematic singleness. But *Ulysses* is much more like the pre-*Dombey* novels of Dickens; thematic singleness is far to seek.

Ulysses is a human comedy, sympathetic rather than satirical, not at all Swiftian; the mood is a little like Sterne's, in *Tristram Shandy*, though Joyce lacks both Sterne's sentimentality and his genuine tenderness. Bloom is a likeable character, but not so likeable as My Uncle Toby; Stephen's pedantry, in his lecture on Shakespeare, is not so engaging as My Uncle Toby's pedantry about war or My Father's about the magic of names. There are touches of brutal comedy, as in the episode of the Citizen, that are more like Smollett than Sterne, but like Smollett at his mellowest, most Sterne-like, as in *Humphry Clinker*. The most common modes of purely verbal humour are the parodic (as in the use of headline language in the scene in the newspaper office, of the language of romantic novelettes and of advertisements in the thoughts of Gerty MacDowell), the burlesque and the mock-heroic.

Ulysses is partly a deflation of the epic mode, Leopold Bloom is like Ulysses a father seeking a son, Stephen like Telemachus a son seeking a father, Molly Bloom a Penelope but an unchaste one,

Gerty MacDowell a crippled and pathetic Nausicaa, the Citizen a yet more grotesque Polyphemus. Yet the effect is not wholly deflationary, for Bloom has some of the virtues of Ulysses, patience and tenacity, and some modern virtues, kindness and good nature, that are unheroic, but none the worse for that; Stephen, as Wyndham Lewis noted, is not a heroic figure, and also rather imperfectly a comic one.

Joyce was no longer utterly identified with Stephen, as he had been in *A Portrait*, but could not quite hold him at a sympathetically comic distance either; Stephen is the least satisfactory character in *Ulysses*, his self-pity and egotism repel, we feel a pity for him bordering on irritation or even contempt, though there is a certain tenacity in him which is admirable. But he is somehow always a little out of perspective with the general comic mode, without quite satisfactorily introducing a lyrical or a tragic mode. Stephen's pedantry also affects his creator: the long passage in the lying-in hospital, where the styles of English prose from its beginnings are used to symbolize the gradual development of the foetus in the womb, is a self-indulgence on Joyce's part as are the speculations about *Hamlet*. But where Bloom and Molly Bloom are the centres of consciousness the mode of sympathetic comedy triumphantly prevails. Stephen needed, what he was granted in *A Portrait* and not here, a predominantly lyrical mode to carry over to the reader a convincing sense of his youthful genius. The Stephen of *Ulysses* observes nothing accurately, outside his own feelings, and to that extent is something much less than his creator.

Some passages in *Ulysses* are mock-heroic, accounts of low doings in high language (Gerty MacDowell on the beach for a central example, the contrasts of style and content in the successive parodies of the hospital passage for another), but others are burlesque: accounts of high feelings, or at least deep and serious feelings, in low language, as at Paddy Dignam's funeral, or perhaps fairly generally throughout Molly Bloom's soliloquy. Burlesque deflates traditionally noble episodes and characters by a use of low diction and vulgar detail: and what it aims at is an unsolved critical problem—does it appeal to the desire in all of us to see the noble taken down a peg or two, the desire to draw a moustache on the Mona Lisa, or does it satirize that desire, or perhaps in a queer way does it humanize the heroic, giving it more breadth if less height? Breadth of scope and sympathy is certainly a central characteristic of *Ulysses*. The burlesque and the mock-heroic are, in any case, only two elements in a continuing display of stylistic virtuosity which might be called, in Pevsner's sense, *manneristic*: the showy display of stylistic devices in deliberately inappropriate or unexpected contexts, for an effect of surprise, in this case mainly comic surprise. If one thinks, as Mrs. Allott does, in reading *Ulysses*, of Dickens, one should think also of Steven Marcus's new emphasis on Dickens's great gift, first fully ripened in *Martin Chuzzlewit*, for exploiting the comedy of language: Pecksniff, Sairey Gamp, the fire-eating or transcendental Americans.

Nowhere else does Joyce use language with such grossly human comic richness. But there is an odd sense in which there is less 'poetry' in *Ulysses* than in *Dubliners*, *A Portrait*, or *Finnegans Wake*. Joyce has purged himself of that feeling of fastidious disgust with life, that fine and hopeless compunction, that feeling of wistful yearning, which brings again and again into his earlier fictions what Matthew Arnold called 'the eternal note of sadness'. He has almost but not quite purged himself (the failure of the portrait of Stephen shows that he has not *quite* purged himself) of youthful self-importance and over-seriousness. Becoming grosser in some ways, he has also become more human. The banal has acquired its own sort of sacredness. Leopold Bloom masturbates on the beach while the crippled Gerty MacDowell, leaning back to watch the fireworks, shows him all she has got. This episode exactly matches that in *A Portrait* where Stephen Dedalus is rescued from a Jesuit-instilled masturbatory guilt by seeing a beautiful young girl, long-legged like a bird, her skirts tucked up above her knickers, wading on the beach. Fireworks broke and popped around Leopold, above his head in the sky, as he finally spilled his seed: a new and lovely sense of the erotic as the lyrical, the unshameful, invaded the merely contemplative Stephen. But basically it is the same episode: and Leopold's experience does not destroy or undermine Stephen's. It merely reinforces a new and charitable comic sense.

The device of interior monologue, of which contemporary critics made so much, seems today merely one of a whole battery of stylistic devices. It is skilfully varied in handling; Stephen's associations are not really loose, he composes elaborate moodscapes in sub-Paterian prose; Bloom in his short, jerky passages recalls Dickens's Mr. Jingle: Molly's unpunctuated erotic meditations have what Henry James called a 'terrible fluidity'. Stuart Gilbert felt that 'silent monologue' would be a better term than 'interior monologue'. The monologues are artistically effective and indeed this is their main importance. They are not a real transcription of what goes on in one's head in directionless reverie; this is usually non-verbal, though it can be readily verbalized when somebody asks us, 'A penny for your thoughts!' But they are an artistically effective way of transcribing or perhaps of creating a kind of equivalent for the half-conscious ground-base of our more conscious willing and striving and thinking: in dreams, this ground-base takes over completely, and it was natural enough that Joyce should go on from *Ulysses* to *Finnegans Wake* (1939), to an attempt to create a verbal texture completely equivalent to the loose drowned confusion of dreams.

T. S. Eliot likened Joyce to Milton as 'a great blind musician'. Already, in *A Portrait*, the young Stephen, short-sighted, with a perfect musical ear, has confessed that the music of the sentences he invents to evoke the visual world around him, the flight of birds, is more important to him than the intrinsic beauty of that visual world. Sight makes artistic sense for him only when translated or transcribed into verbal cadences. Joyce's sight, never good, was becoming desperately bad as he worked on *Finnegans Wake*. He overlaid an original fairly simple folk-tale structure with an endless palimpsest of multi-lingual puns. Here and there prose becomes music, as at the end of the great Anna Livia Plurabelle passage, of which Joyce himself made a magnificent recording. In my own struggles with the book, however, the musical and poetic concentration there is unique. Much more typical is an engaging cosmic jokiness, as in the passage about the Wellington Museum in Dublin. A fully adequate 'reader's companion' to *Finnegans Wake* would be a work of many volumes.

One does not want to take a philistine attitude towards the last achievement, no doubt considered by Joyce himself as the crowning achievement, of a very great writer. Joyce was a good man. No writer that I know of has left a more moving record of the isolation of the young artist in a bigoted and passionate and philistine society, which nevertheless is to supply the sole raw material of his art. Joyce was gentle, he abhorred violence, he had room in his heart for all sorts and conditions of men; his bitterness is a very compassionate bitterness; his deepest emotions were family and local loyalties, totally stripped of sentimentality. Pound thought him not an intelligent man, except in relation to his art, but to most readers he will seem a much better and wiser man than Pound or than the most penetrating of his early critics, Wyndham Lewis.

Yet his treasure was his youth. Much as I admire *Ulysses*, I find myself going back in Joyce's work, for the assurance of complete success, to *Dubliners*, to those two unsurpassable short stories, 'Ivy

Day in the Committee Room' and 'The Dead', sometimes, for its documentary honesty, to *Stephen Hero* rather than to *A Portrait of the Artist as a Young Man*, and in *A Portrait* particularly and most often to the great dramatic scene (the only properly dramatic scene in all Joyce) of the Christmas dinner row about the Bishops and Parnell—a passage in which the child Stephen is recorder rather than participant, and which one could call, in its fusion of comedy and tragedy, of the splendid and the pathetic, Shakespearian.

The more fully he developed what was unique in him, as no doubt he did in *Finnegans Wake*, as he had begun to do in *Ulysses*, the more Joyce stepped outside the history of the novel proper. His gift, lyrical and comic, was the poet's gift; and it is among the great word-obsessed men of this century, the makers, the celebrators, that I would number him, passing on with regret, since poetry rather than the novel has been my 'ruling passion', to the drabber tribe of novelists proper. Yet drab, of course, is not the word for our next major figure, D. H. Lawrence.

III

Joyce and Lawrence are the two giants of our period. Lawrence (1885–1930) like Joyce was a poetic novelist, and like Joyce, in a secondary way, a distinguished poet in verse: a much more vigorous, copious, and penetrating poet in verse than Joyce, though in fact never such a 'finished' poet. On his first meeting with Ezra Pound, Lawrence wrote to the Leicester schoolmistress to whom he was half-engaged that his guiding star was life, Pound's was art: the same contrast applies as strikingly to himself and Joyce, though it is a paradoxical fact that there is nowhere in Lawrence such a massive and complete acceptance of life as Molly Bloom's soliloquy, and that there is nowhere in Joyce the hatred and fear of human society, modern industrial society, as a whole, which is a recurrent theme in Lawrence. Lawrence was as great an artist in the Protestant tradition as Joyce in the Catholic (this was what T. S. Eliot meant when, in *After Strange Gods*, he praised Joyce, in contradistinction from Lawrence, for his 'orthodox imagination'). Joyce belonged, in a phrase to which Sir Kenneth Clark has recently called attention, a phrase of H. G. Wells's, to the community of obedience: Lawrence to the community of will.

Perhaps Joyce's greatest central quality as a writer was his 'societal' sense, and this Lawrence himself admitted to be the thing lacking in his life. Joyce could never unbelong to the Catholic, nationalist

Ireland of his childhood: he could only step back from it to belong to it in imagination more fully, to forge the uncreated conscience of his race. Lawrence could never belong fully and finally anywhere, to any class, to any region; a driving restlessness is at the root of his genius, a wish to be let alone, not to be tied, not to be imposed upon, a refusal to surrender himself to general conventions or mass purposes: fear, hate, antagonism he understands as Joyce never understood them. Belongingness, what Yeats called 'unity of being', he is sometimes wistful for, but the impulse of sensitive rejection, the wish to break away, to start again—and how many startings again!—is always stronger still. He is for the poppy, the useless and beautiful momentary flowering of life; not for the nourishing cabbage.

In 1914, after the great effort of the long novel *The Sisters*, which in the end split into *The Rainbow* and *Women in Love*, Lawrence set himself to write something popular, light-hearted, in the manner, say, of Arnold Bennett's *The Card* or H. G. Wells's *Kipps*, of the sub-Dickensian tradition that still lingered on into the Edwardian and early Georgian ages. The manuscript of this work was left in Germany all through the First World War, but was retrieved, and hastily finished off, in 1919, with a conclusion that made use of Lawrence's recent travels in Italy.

The Lost Girl is mainly interesting for the Italian passages at the end and for the efficiency, real if somewhat perfunctory, with which Lawrence earlier in the book exploits a traditional, indeed rather conventional vein of lower-middle-class comedy. His later novels have, until *Lady Chatterley's Lover*, mainly foreign settings, and use up material that Lawrence might have otherwise used up in travel books. The next two, *Aaron's Rod* (1922) and *Kangaroo* (1923), were very rapidly improvised and have been described as 'anti-novels'. Certain basic themes, emotionally very important to Lawrence at this time, run through both books, and give them what unity they have (there is not much unity of plot or story). One theme is the final decay, as Lawrence sees it, in the postwar years of the old Christian and liberal-humanist ideals. Words or ideas like love, liberty, justice, brotherhood have all gone bad. Political planning is a trap—any revolution would be pointless, since it would leave the mass of men just the unsatisfactory creatures they are—and so are the traditional routines and loyalties, one's place in a community, one's family. What is valuable for Lawrence at this stage is masculine independence, separateness: not 'giving in' to society, to political movements, above all to women. Nevertheless, some man-to-man, male-to-male relationship is necessary. Lawrence, or his spokesmen or representatives in these novels, sees this relationship as a leader–follower, master–disciple one, based not on love (one of the words that, for Lawrence, has gone bad) but on frank recognition of charisma—on authority or power of a personal rather than a political sort. The apostle of power in *Aaron's Rod* is a boring and dogmatic character—who can, however, be shown as absurd and can sometimes even laugh at himself—called Lilly. Lilly is Lawrence the prophet as Aaron, the other hero, is Lawrence the artist. (Moses, in the Pentateuch, has no gift of speech and needs the eloquence of Aaron to get his message across to the chosen people.)

Lawrence was impotent during the last few years of his life and his relationships with men, unlike his relationships with women, were always tense and emotionally difficult. It is doubtful if there was a single man friend, with the exception of Aldous Huxley, with whom he achieved the easy and equal relationship of proper friendship. So it is difficult to see *Aaron's Rod* as not being fundamentally about both the male fear of impotence, indeed about the castration-complex, the *vagina dentata*, about a sublimated and idealized homosexual relationship as a safe substitute for the gaping mouth of marriage. The destruction of Aaron's flute, a beautiful but slim and frail instrument, oddly anticipates the accident that renders that other artist, Sir Clifford Chatterley, permanently impotent.

There is a remarkable emphasis throughout this novel also, as later throughout *Kangaroo*, on physical fear. Aaron's wallet is stolen in Italy (and if the flute is a symbol for the penis, the wallet might be a symbol for the testicles: money is quite a frequent symbol in literature, used a lot for instance in Henry James's *The Golden Bowl*, for sexual desirability and potency). Aaron sets himself a rule that henceforth he must be tensely, one might say paranoiacally, on guard against all his fellow-men:

Fool, you might have known beforehand, and then you needn't have paid at all. You can ill afford pounds sterling, you fool. But since you have paid, then mind, mind the lesson is learned. Never again. Never expose yourself again. Never again absolute trust. It is blasphemy against life, is absolute trust. Has a wild creature ever absolute trust? It minds itself. Sleeping or waking, it is on its guard. And so must you be, or you'll go under. Sleeping or waking, man or woman, God or devil, keep guard over yourself. Keep guard over yourself lest worse befall you. No man is robbed unless he attracts a robber. No man is murdered unless he attracts a murderer. Then be not robbed: it lies within your own power. And be not murdered. Or if you are, you deserve it. Keep guard over yourself, now, always, and forever. Yes, against God quite as hard as against the devil. He's fully as dangerous as you. . . .

The passage, with its Biblical rhythms combined with working-class syntax ('It is blasphemy against life, is absolute trust'), its seeking of salvation on the bedrock of despair, its achievement of utter concentration through maddening repetition, is a very great passage of late Protestant prose: alive in every nerve. It is wonderful in its twisted muscular self-agony: sublime and horrible, bitterly honest, strangely, also, with a kind of humour in it (the humour of the Book of Job).

Yet in Lawrence at this time that hard, near-hysterical inner tension, that paranoiac terror of life and one's neighbours alternated with an easy, fluent, and yet uncommitted sympathy with all kinds of creatures and modes of being, including even human creatures and their modes. That sympathy, as the finally commanding stress, is the special mark of *Kangaroo*, a novel just as unorthodox as *Aaron's Rod* but far more rewarding: to me, in the end, *Kangaroo* for all its hastiness, for all its many obvious weaknesses of structure, is Lawrence's greatest achievement after his masterpiece, *Women in Love*. Somers, the hero of *Kangaroo*, is not a schizoid separation of two aspects of his creator, like Lilly and Aaron, but Lawrence himself, with Lawrence's saving power, at the end of his most fussily hortatory passages, of humorous self-deflation. Somers also has Lawrence's sane readiness, having worried duly about an insoluble problem, to leave it unsolved. He is Lawrence's most complete and self-accepting self-portrait.

Somers and his wife Harriet (a straight and very attractive rendering of Frieda Lawrence) come to Australia, as Lawrence and Frieda had done, to escape from postwar England. But, unlike Lawrence and Frieda, they are caught up in a political melodrama. This is a conflict between socialists and an ex-service group of idealistic— more or less—proto-Fascists, 'the Diggers'. There was no such movement in Australia, and Lawrence was probably drawing on his memories of the pre-Mussolini period in Italy. Somers responds sympathetically to the personalities of the leaders of both Diggers and socialists, but does not want to be drawn in. He will not be tied even to the brilliant leader of the Diggers, Ben Cooley, a Jewish lawyer called by his followers 'Kangaroo'. Cooley's movement is based on the idea of absolute love: Somers's creed is based on his certitude about his own personal charisma or legitimate and effective authority. Cooley threatens Somers, says he must leave Australia, and Somers is also threatened by Cooley's followers.

The fear that these threats arouse touches off a very long passage of agonizingly relived memory, about Somers's—in fact, about Lawrence's—years of humiliation during the First World War: the time in Cornwall, the suspiciousness of the neighbours and the authorities, the three medical examinations by the Army authorities, climaxing in the last one in something, a fingering and probing of his most private parts, that Lawrence or Somers feels almost like a rape. The growing personal persecution feeling is paralleled by a feeling that the fall of Old England, in the person of Asquith, to the Welsh rat Lloyd George and to Jewish financiers meant an absolute destruction of the true English tradition. Readers of Lawrence must learn to tolerate prejudices which we would today call racialist or Fascist.

The tone of these war reminiscences is intense, hysterical (Somers several times admits that every male of military age had to go through the same sort of thing, but that it is what it meant to *himself*—to his very exceptional, virginal and creative self—that matters to him). In the end, these pages are like the bursting of a boil, a squeezing out of pus, a very painful but in the end healing self-analysis. Having got it all out of his system, Somers (or Lawrence) realizes that his wartime agony has maimed him with a terrible deep fear and with, still deeper, a desire for violent revenge. He has suffered, and he wants others to suffer also.

The political melodrama, which composes the outer plot or framework of *Kangaroo*, is at once a projection and exorcism of this vindictiveness and this relived anger and fear. After the bursting of the boil, the real, non-melodramatic Australia (which slowly, without his being aware of it, is having a healing effect on Somers) comes out in the delightfully funny and casual chapter called 'Bits', largely an anthology of lively and inconsequential items from the *Sydney Bulletin*. Somers longs for revenge, like a character in Jacobean drama: but the genuine Australian is a cheery, jaunty, undeep being. It is impossible to dislike him, to fear him, to take him too seriously, or to wish to take revenge on him. Yet the Australian has not the dignity, he has not the weight of the old Europe . . . Lawrence now suddenly remembers that he must bring his novel to an end.

The end reconstitutes the earlier, and long interrupted, political melodrama. The Diggers break up a socialist meeting violently and, in the rumpus, Ben Cooley is shot in the guts. In hospital, he sends several times for Somers. Somers is compassionate but cannot bring himself to say, even when Cooley is dying, that he 'loves' Cooley. Jack, Cooley's tough henchman, who has earlier threatened Somers, thinks this is a typical English, prissy, perhaps even old-maidish attitude. We feel some strength in what Jack is saying: but we remember also how Jack smashed up several socialists with an iron bar at the meeting where Cooley was shot, and told Somers that the experience of killing is even more exciting than the experience of sex.

It should be emphasized that Somers's rejection of Cooley is not a 'tragic' scene: Lawrence was very suspicious of the whole notion of tragedy. The scene is rather an extreme version of the comedy of the very awkward social situation, the situation that seems to force a main character into insincerity. More broadly, in the plot the violence and the deaths have no tragic or violently epic consequences. Life will go on in Australia, cheery, shallow, and inconsequential, much as usual. Somers, for instance, will go on in the (purely and finely rendered) comedy of his domestic life talking about his need to dominate Harriet, to have what Chaucer called the 'maistrye', but like most wives Harriet will judge his feelings and not listen much to the content of what he is saying, nor give his opinions much weight: Harriet is the great centre of comic sanity in the book.

Both Harriet and Somers grasp, in the last few pages of the novel, the peculiar attraction, lonely, straggly, moonlike, undemanding, of the Australian landscape, but life, Somers feels—Lawrence feels —is too short to devote to enjoying calmly only one place. Harriet and Somers move off to America, not because Somers expects much from it, but because it is the next place. Harriet will follow Somers around, making wholesome fun of him: because she is like that, or perhaps because he has the mastery over her, about which he is always nagging, without realizing it. A sort of healing has taken place in Somers (and in Lawrence). It is this healing, a healing through landscape and the half-unwillingly resurgent sense of comedy, that *Kangaroo* is centrally about. The violent melodrama has minor importance in the true thematic pattern. Somers's violent, and then self-criticized, opinions—in his monologues here 'the Dark Gods' become for the first time important—are again minor items in what is essentially a therapeutic comedy.

Kangaroo is generally thought the most slapdash of Lawrence's novels. I believe it has a formal pattern, in that the use of the invented melodramatic plot is to put Somers in a state of fear and crisis that will start off the flow of his terrible wartime memories, and bring his hatred of his fellow men, his desire for revenge, to the surface; and then the use of the chapter 'Bits' is to cool off that hot resentful feeling, to make Somers himself realize that it is swollen and disproportionate, and to stop us taking the violence at the meeting and the death of Cooley too tragically. But certainly this shaping need not have been conscious, where the shaping of the next novel is very conscious; and for that reason *The Plumed Serpent* lacks the humour and unpredictability that make *Kangaroo* such a *live* book.

Lilly, the ideologue, rather than Aaron, the artist, is too much in command in *The Plumed Serpent* (1926). The one great success in this romance about the revival of an ancient and cruel Central American religion is the character of the heroine, Kate. Lawrence, with so much of the feminine in his own nature (and with his tendency to get on easily with most women but to get bored or impatient with most men, except as potential disciples) could 'do' women in fiction, on the whole, much better than men. His male characters, the minor ones at least, tend to be external though vivid sketches of acquaintances, versions of himself (Somers or Birkin, or Aaron-and-Lilly, or Paul Morel, or Mellors): enemies for whom he feels a certain love–hatred (Gerald, Ben Cooley) or pure enemies to be destroyed (Sir Clifford). The male characters in the more romantic stories, Don Cipriano in *The Plumed Serpent* or Count Psanek in the long tale *The Ladybird*, can be symbols rather than people, but symbols that have a wish-fulfilment element, that are rather like Lawrence in fancy dress. Lawrence's women are some of the most interesting women in all fiction; he could get inside a wide range of different female consciousnesses, but with men he is either reminiscing, role-playing, or observing—observing often with an animus of suspicion, with mocking dislike. In *The Plumed Serpent* the cult of the Dark Gods is boring: the revived Mexican religion, its rites and its sacrifices, has all the unattractiveness of a fake antique. But the focus in Kate's consciousness, the rebirth of full life-feeling in a middle-aged woman through sex, that saves the romance—apart from Kate it is a romance rather than a novel—from tediousness. Even among Lawrence's most fervent admirers, however, *The Plumed Serpent* has tended to be their least favourite work.

In his last novel, *Lady Chatterley's Lover* (1928), Lawrence worked more carefully than he had done since *Women in Love*, writing three drafts. He also left foreign settings and returned to the scene of his earlier novels, the Nottingham–Derbyshire coalfield area, in which pastoral landscape and the landscape of the early Industrial Revolution blend. (A visitor today to England can find this contrastive blend at its most dramatic, not at Lawrence's own Eastwood, but farther north, in the Sitwellian village of Renishaw near Sheffield or at Atterley, also near Sheffield, where, as I write, a film of *Women in Love* is being shot.)

Lawrence thought of calling this novel, which was to be his last, *Tenderness*. What he established at once in the heroine Connie Chatterley is not a special attractiveness or distinction—in many ways Connie is the least vital and aggressive, the most 'put-upon' of Lawrence's heroines—but a pathetic, hurt, and touching quality. Connie's whole being has been bruised and numbed by a lack of tenderness in her husband or her world. Sir Clifford, a writer, a landowner, was blown up in the First World War, made impotent and a cripple, a few months after the honeymoon. He writes fiction, fairly successfully, of a rather clever, sterile sort. Confined to his wheel chair, he symbolizes a class system to which Lawrence would not have objected when it was a true system of virile dominance in feudal times, but which today works only from the head, not from the heart or the guts. Connie is told by him that she can have lovers, of course of his own class. But Sir Clifford's friend, the playwright Michaelis, complains that Connie is too demanding, not giving enough, in the sexual act. This demandingness of women was a topic, we remember, also widely aired in *Aaron's Rod*, where perhaps the destruction of Aaron's flute foreshadows Sir Clifford's castration. Both catastrophes are brought about by an explosion.

Though Michaelis is not meant to be in the least sympathetic, the hero of the novel, the gamekeeper Mellors, makes exactly the same complaint to Connie about the wife from whom he is estranged: she sets the pace, she keeps his climax waiting for her climax, she finishes when she wants to not when he does. For all that he has to say about 'life' and the life-standard, one of Lawrence's queerest strengths comes from his constant awareness of something that might seem to be the opposite of 'life', fear. Fears of castration, impotence, inadequacy are, of course, very profound male fears. Men fear women because women are always ready to make love, men may always fail. But in dealing with relations purely between men and men, Lawrence also stresses very much fear, the sense of latent hostility, of possible violence. The wish to be left alone, not intruded upon, not enclosed, is strong in Lawrentian heroes.

As with Hobbes (whose view of society has a great deal in common with Lawrence's), one might say that fear and Lawrence were brothers. Aaron's reflections on losing his wallet in *Aaron's*

Rod, his sense that all men are 'wild creatures', are very Hobbesian. The night of intercourse culminating apparently in anal intercourse, the burning out of the secret shames, in *Lady Chatterley's Lover,* is important in this context of male fear because it may be that it is only in this kind of intercourse that a male can feel he is wholly dominating a woman, not at the mercy of her own subtle rhythms, her eagernesses or her rejections which may not coincide with his own. By allowing Mellors to use her as an object, Connie perhaps achieves a full submission which she also has been seeking. It was Mr. John Sparrow who first made the nature and significance of this particular episode clear. Fear is somewhere in the background here, perhaps as something to be conquered by the deliberate breaking of a taboo. And Sir Clifford is treated, I would suggest, in this novel with such savage animus not because Lawrence hated aristocrats (he got on very well especially with women aristocrats, like his wife and like Cynthia Asquith, and gives an idealized picture of the aristocratic temperament in Count Psanek). Sir Clifford, rather, is hated because he embodies a fate Lawrence personally dreads. When he wrote *Lady Chatterley's Lover,* Lawrence, like Sir Clifford, was impotent; Frieda, like Connie, was taking lovers: Lawrence was like Sir Clifford a distinguished man of letters not, like Mellors, a gamekeeper. Mellors is no doubt partly a projection of Lawrence; but in his rough dominatingness he may also be a gesture of appeasement to Paul Morel's father, Lawrence's own father, the rough, honest man castrated by his children's contempt and by Mrs. Morel's or Mrs. Lawrence's obsessive gentility.

Yet though the element of fear needs stressing, because it has been so little stressed, there is also of course true tenderness in *Lady Chatterley's Lover.* When Connie comes upon Sir Clifford's game-keeper, the ex-ranker-officer, Mellors, watching over the hatching of pheasants' eggs, the sight of the little chicks makes her cry. It is as much out of compassion as desire that Mellors first makes love to her. Each time they meet, their love-making grows in tenderness, and gradually Connie hears all about Mellors's unhappy marriage, his demanding wife, his deepest thoughts and feelings, his disgust with the industrial world. Connie becomes pregnant: Sir Clifford, growing more and more petulant and babyish under the care of the village wise-woman, the comic and sinister Mrs. Bolton, refuses a divorce. But Mellors can now get a divorce from his estranged wife, and Connie and he will live together, not with a chance perhaps of very great and intense happiness, but with the chance of healing each other's hurts. Their minds, even, may grow together. Connie has been relieved to notice that Mellors reads books.

Other kinds of hurts, the hurts of the sick, the tired, the defeated (Sir Clifford or the dying Kangaroo) exacted from Lawrence at most a tired patience, often an angry exasperation. An invalid, and Lawrence was an invalid for most of his life, cannot perhaps afford the pity for the weak that is naturally felt by a robust man. People, for Lawrence, were to blame for being mentally or physically ill just as, for Aaron, they were to blame for being robbed or murdered. Behind the life-religion there is the moral arbitrariness and the stern rejection of an ancestral Calvinism. What Life (like the Calvinist God) rejects we must reject, too. This stern creed, this paganized Calvinism, is saved from inhumanity—as properly Calvinist writing, like Bunyan's *Grace Abounding*, is at its best also saved from inhumanity—by the fact that the hero and heroines, that the author himself, are so near loss, so often themselves on the verge of total despair; by the fact that loss and reprobation seem so nearly the general human condition. The picture of that general human condition, of the surrounding external world, at the end of *Lady Chatterley's Lover* is still bleak; but for these two at least, for Connie and Mellors, there seems the possibility, but still doubtful and chequered, of growth and calm.

Humour and tenderness, a sudden sense that one must not be 'too serious', too humourlessly in earnest, a sudden impatient turning on his own rhetoric, a willingness to discard one position impatiently and move on to another, all these things make Aaron (Lawrence the artist) more humane, more sympathetic than Lilly (Lawrence the antinomian moralist, the man with the will to dominate, the hell-fire preacher). Lawrence loved life, the life of nature and the creatures, of 'alien modes of being'. But it is also part of his strength that certain terrible extremities of human nature, fear, aggression, resentment particularly, are presented so nakedly.

I leave deliberately out of this brief survey of post-1918 Lawrence the short stories and novellas. The short stories are often more completely successful than the novels; the preacher, as it were, has not time to get his head of steam up. Of the novellas, Dr. Leavis thinks *St. Mawr* comparable to, better than, *The Waste Land*: for most readers its undoubted power is marred by a streak of deliberate brutality. *The Ladybird*, the novel arising from Lawrence's friendship with Lady Cynthia Asquith, is marred, Dr. Ronald Draper thinks, by its slightly cloying, deliberately 'beautiful' style. I like it

rather better than Dr. Draper does, and feel that the style fits in with
the sophisticated folk-tale pattern of the lovely lady and her dark
and fair lovers. Of the novels proper that I have dealt with, not one
is a 'great' novel: Lawrence's really great novels appeared before
1918. But they deserve the space I have given them here because
their author was the greatest English writer of his time, poet,
prophet, preacher as well as artist. Of them all, the unpopular and
untidy *Kangaroo* seems to me to come nearest to greatness: in its
brilliant carelessness, its incorporation of apparent brash or crass
irrelevance into what turns out in the end to be a coherent thematic
design: in its use also of long passages of apparently maundering
reflection, on the surface carrying no narrative flow, as in the end
real forward thrusts. The novel as loose soliloquy, the novel as a
long discussion of why a novel is being written, Henry Miller's
Tropic of Cancer, Saul Bellow's *Herzog*, have their roots perhaps in
Kangaroo. But the best way to take Lawrence's novels from *Aaron's
Rod* to *Lady Chatterley's Lover* is as Kierkegaardian 'stages on life's
way': records of the dialectic of a great soul's exploration of the
open road.

IV

Unlike Joyce and Lawrence, E. M. Forster (1879–1970) is primarily
a novelist, neither more, other, or less than that. He is not a poet,
not a prophet; as an essayist, a topographical writer, a biographer, a
critic, he has very great charm but is quite deliberately minor. In
the novel, however, he is on the grand trunk road. I have said that
none of Lawrence's novels after 1918 is a great novel: Joyce's
Ulysses is a great book but perhaps not a great novel and it is perhaps
only biographical convenience that makes us consider *Finnegans
Wake* in a chapter on the novel rather than, along with Pound's
Cantos, say, in a chapter on poetry. But *A Passage to India*, which
came out in 1924, fourteen years after *Howards End*, is undeniably
great, and undeniably a novel. It is the last really major English
'traditional' novel, the last rounded and complete, distanced and
exact portrait in our language of a rationally intelligible and morally
judgeable society. It is also a very middle-class book. The novel,
from its beginnings in the eighteenth century, is *par excellence* the
art form of the middle classes. Since 1918, the middle classes, in
England and elsewhere, have tended to lose their old self-confidence;
and many writers of fiction are moving back to the roots from
which the true novel grew, the idealizing romance of aristocratic

life and the picaresque tale of low life. Forster is the novelist of the middle-class mind both at its most confident and at its most sharply and honestly self-critical: only the confidence makes the sharp self-criticism possible.

To put this another way: *A Passage to India* is the last great English novel of unquestionable authorial authority. It is, as neither Joyce's nor Lawrence's later novels are, beautifully plotted. It has behind it a calm and unexcited grasp of the strengths and weaknesses of what we call 'civilization'. The moral stance is strong just because, unlike Lawrence's changing and always dramatized or rhetoricized moral stances, it is not assertive. Yet, more deeply, represented by the ambiguous boom, which fuses rejection and acceptance, of the echo of the Marabar Caves, by the mystical despair and hopeless sanctity, the flat uncaring honesty, of Mrs. Moore, this novel has an extra dimension, a height or depth—mystical, metaphysical, symbolical?—that questions all reasonable purposes and sensible attitudes, all codes and forms.

Civilization rests on fine discriminations, of feeling, responsiveness, more than of thought, but its framework or order—always, and this is something that Forster is saying from his earlier novels onwards, *itself* very imperfectly civilized—rests also on a certain rigidity and reliability: in *A Passage to India*, for instance, on Ronnie's public-school religion that, because it is inherently sterile, will not go bad even in the tropics. Great empires and great revolts cohere or are effective only because of unquestioned tribal loyalties, uncriticized prejudices. On the sub-civilized prejudices and loyalties of the many there rests, for the very few, the possibility of criticism, of the chosen and examined life.

The first page of *A Passage to India* is a wonderful condensation and transformation of traditional guide-book style (Forster himself had written an excellent guide-book to Alexandria). That page plants the main symbols, the crumbling shapelessness of the native Indian town, a sub-organic unity, falling away at the edges into the muddy Ganges, not here sacred, and the neat geometrical sterility of the English station, a sort of transplanted Aldershot. High civilization, aesthetic order, an enjoyable tone of life are things that have not begun to show themselves in India (the brief contrasts with Egypt, with Italy, when Fielding goes home on leave, underline this point). India is hopelessly and irremediably untidy like nature, a sort of muddle: and a joyous recognition of that muddle is what the Hindu religion (or at least its pre-Sanskrit, Dravidian, Krishna elements) can at times achieve. The English station keeps its order by keeping its distance, by keeping order sterile, free of the contagions of art, thought, and human spontaneity. But the English order is not quite so healthily sterile as Ronnie's religion: it can, under the stress of tribal fear, go bad.

Yet fear, panic fear, is not so important or terrifying for Forster as for Lawrence in *Kangaroo* or *Aaron's Rod*. Forster has not Lawrence's frequently expressed contempt (or the frequently expressed contempt of some of Lawrence's representative characters) for people in the mass, for man's efforts to achieve an orderly society. Aziz, Fielding, Miss Quested, all on the whole accept society—critically, of course—and try to build up personal and social virtue, even personal and social fulfilment, within the framework of social frustration and limitation. That this *is* an effort, a conscious, intelligent, always partly tiring and tedious effort, is one of Forster's main stresses. Forster's people have all certain responsibilities to institutions, traditions, and neighbours, and achieve themselves through these: whereas a Lawrence character, Somers or Aaron say, begins to achieve life, generally, when he cuts adrift from his old ties. Getting away, being let alone, this is the Lawrentian passion: not the Forsterian one.

Yet, as we have underlined, in the pursuit of the civilized good life there is also the sense of a strain, of effort, of the factitious. There is always the boom, boom, boom of the echo of the Marabar caves, the sense of the certainty of death, the inhuman ancientness of the geological world, the meaningless swarm of life in India dwarfing the classical human scale: the effort is not only factitious and precarious but perhaps in the end futile. Nevertheless, for Forster the individual effort is what centrally matters. Aziz moves effortfully away from group prejudice in trying to make friends with Mrs. Moore, Miss Quested, Fielding. Miss Quested finds the courage to recognize that her thought that Aziz had indecently touched her was an hallucination. Fielding has the courage to stand up for Aziz against the whole English community, and the decency not to mock or exult when he is proved right and Turton, who has had him expelled from the club, has to eat humble pie: to invite, indeed to command him to join again.

But Forster does not deal in perfect characters. Aziz turns against Fielding when Fielding begs him not to ruin Miss Quested by suing her for enormous damages. He mistrusts the sincerity of his friend, suspecting that Fielding intends to marry Miss Quested for her money. The root fault of all Indians, Forster notes, is suspiciousness, just as the root fault of all Englishmen, from the

Indian point of view, is insincerity, or polite hypocrisy. They are trained to expose only a little of their feelings. In the period preceding Aziz's trial, the English community is held together, given a certain strength, by a sullen, silent, controlled rancour: in the period succeeding Aziz's acquittal, the Indian community displays a contrasting weakness, becomes excited, hysterical, vindictive, childishly and foolishly insolent. Yet the Indians, even in the midst of their triumph, recognize the holiness of Mrs. Moore. She herself, previously a conventionally devout woman, has died in a state of spiritual bleakness, with a new awareness of Christianity as something provincial, with a feeling that life is meaningless: it is almost casually, and with indifference, that she asserts that Aziz is of course innocent. What does it matter anyway? But the old English lady, in her dark night of the soul, dying at sea, becomes a saint to the Indians. And her bleak negative mysticism is set by Forster against a positive mysticism: the creative muddle of the Hindu festival, the splashings with coloured water, the unbridled childlikeness, the motto 'GOD SI LOVE'.

Yet Godbole, the learned Hindu, the symbol of Brahmin wisdom, is, as many critics have noted, a morally ambiguous character. He does not help Aziz in any positive way. Aziz, a Muslim, himself belongs after all to a less puzzling, a more clear-cut tradition, that of the Moguls whose empire preceded England's and was to last about as long. That they both belong to conquering not submerged peoples, to the rulers of men, perhaps helps to make the friendship of Aziz and Fielding possible: that makes it seem possible on their last ride together, as their horses wheel together and apart, that there should be unity at some future time.

A Passage to India has a very clear story structure; at the same time, it seems to have inexhaustible layers of deeper meaning. 'God Si Love' may not be such a muddle as it seems: in French or Italian, 'si' means 'if': there is God for Forster, or a sense of a divine meaning in human affairs, *if* there is love . . . but it is a very big if. So often and so disastrously there is not love, and love for Forster is a habit of the mind not a mere emotional response, though it is that also; it is something involving conscience, intelligence, will. Thus, in the 1930s, in a period of social and political crisis, it was to Forster that writers like Auden and Isherwood turned as a moral mentor, not to Lawrence or to Joyce. The way in which he combines solidity of structure and sobriety of observation with a certain openness to the unexpected links Forster to the great past of the English novel, but also to some possibilities of the future. Perhaps the central moral quality of his art is a willingness to wait, a refusal to anticipate, an intelligent patience. He is not, like Lawrence, bored by the ordinary; he knows that the ordinary is never ordinary if one looks at it long and hard enough.

Yet what is also notable about Forster—and what has been disguised from many of his critics by his humour and gentleness of tone—is a peculiarly rigorous separation in all his novels of the sheep from the goats, of the elect from the reprobates. He, like Lawrence, is a kind of neo-Calvinist. The Agnes and Herbert Pembrokes, the worldly-wise Mrs. Fearings, Ronnie, who wants to be decent, the Wilcox sons and Mr. Wilcox (till, with a broken and a contrite heart, he is snatched by Margaret like a brand from the burning), are all as much victims or servants of the City of Destruction and the dark Prince of This World as Bunyan's neighbour Pliable, his Mr. Legality, his Mr. Worldly Wiseman. There are no villains in Forster, with the possible exception of Rickie's father in the most melodramatic of all the novels, the most melodramatic and the most implausibly plotted, *The Longest Journey*; but there are many characters who are firmly placed among the lost: like the clever Meredithian Mrs. Fearing (Meredith's clever characters are all 'anti-life') or like the brother of the Schlegel sisters, who studies Chinese, but cannot be saved by 'a little cold culture'. It is not enough to have some intelligence or to wish to behave with conventional propriety: the elect are also plucky, sensitive, warmhearted.

This puritanism has other manifestations. There are no hearty and enjoyable scenes of eating or drinking in Forster: the whiskies at the club in *A Passage to India* blacken rather than warm human hearts. Some characters, like Aziz or Gerald in *The Longest Journey*, may have sexual vitality, but Aziz's is stated rather than presented, and Gerald's is morally ambiguous. For Rickie, the sight of Agnes in Gerald's arms is a sudden glory: but for the reader it is inextricably bound up with Gerald's bullying of the schoolboy Rickie and Agnes's admiration for that, and with Gerald being all broken up (so implausibly, but Forster quite often kills people suddenly and implausibly when he wants to be rid of them) in the football game. The aesthetic response of the Schlegel sisters is to music, the art which is transportable and, as Auden says, 'does not smell': the aesthetic response of Fielding is to architecture, an art of mathematical proportion, whose final appeal is to the intellect rather than the senses. Even in *A Room with a View*, the novel of all Forster's novels nearest light comedy, the moral point is not a young girl's sudden awareness of the glory of a young man's healthy body but the Bunyanesque probation, the temptation to return to the City of Destruction, which for Forster is the City of Convention: the temptation to do what others, not oneself, feel to be proper, before Lucy Honeychurch can pluck up courage, enter by the Wicket Gate, and drop her Burden. All Forster's saved characters are tried and tested by having to stand alone. This concealed vein of iron in him should never be ignored.

V

Virginia Woolf (1882–1941) was a close friend of Forster's, and he has written a beautiful tribute to her, but her own rigour is of a very different kind. Her father, Leslie Stephen, was one of the great Victorian agnostics, extremely Victorian in the rigour of his agnosticism: the Stephen family, originally from Scotland, had made their name at the beginning of the nineteenth century in connection with the Evangelical agitation against the slave-trade and West Indian slavery. They had become one of the great professional, or mandarin, families of the Victorian age. Leslie Stephen's brother was a judge, noted for the severity of his sentences; Leslie Stephen himself, giving up a promising career in Cambridge because he could no longer subscribe to the Thirty-Nine Articles, even in a Broad Church sense, made a career in London, where he became a founder editor of the *Dictionary of National Biography*, wrote a definitive work on the rather dull English deist thinkers of the early eighteenth century, and wrote much criticism which, as A. E. Housman noted, is never unintelligent and never charming.

In his industry, in his severity, in the demands he made upon himself and his children, he was typically Victorian: Virginia, as her severe and exact but compassionate portrait of him as Mr. Ramsay in *To the Lighthouse* shows, respected the central quality of the mind but rejected the mixture of dominatingness and dependence, the self-pity leading to selfishness, which was the less agreeable aspect of her father's character. Obscurely, Leslie Stephen was aware of some lack in himself; for both his wives, the first a Thackeray, the second, Virginia's mother, from a family of artists, had the ease, the spontaneity, the vivid charm which he himself lacked. Virginia's mother died young, in 1895. In his loneliness, his disappointment with his own achievements, Stephen was a more demanding and overbearing father to the daughters who now kept house for him than, probably, he ever realized. Virginia's life-long

feminism, her hostile attitude to Victorianism and especially to the
Victorian idea of the submissive woman and the dominant male,
sprang mainly from her mixed feelings about her father; but she
had inherited from the Stephen side of her ancestry a scrupulous
and self-examining temper of mind, and a habit of tireless industry,
which prevented her from being a mere charmer, a delightful
amateur of letters, like her Thackeray aunt, Lady Ritchie. From
Leslie Stephen also came the recurrent fits of melancholia and
depression, and of doubts about the value of her own work, one of
which was to lead to her suicide at the beginning of the Second
World War.

One might say that Virginia Woolf accepted her father's agnosticism but rejected his Victorianism. There is no question in her, as
there is in Joyce, Lawrence, and Forster, of a concealed Christian
foundation. Indeed, she was an atheist rather than an agnostic, but
a mystical atheist. There was a side in her of worldliness and
frivolity, of gay bohemianism, deriving from the Thackerays and
the Jacksons. She loved parties and gaieties and aristocratic friends,
there was a good deal in her of the *maîtresse de salon*. But her
mysticism plays on Mrs. Ramsay's *bœuf en daube* and on Mrs.
Dalloway's party: the meal is a sacramental meal, the party is an
opening of the soul in poetic receptivity. Virginia Woolf uses a kind
of interior presentation which owes something to Joyce and something to Dorothy Richardson's (on the whole rather dull and
plodding) pioneer stream-of-consciousness series of novels, *Pilgrim-
age*. But the total effect of her own mode of stylized reverie is utterly
different.

In their most intimate self-communings, Mrs. Woolf's characters
do not, like Mr. Bloom, masturbate or go to the lavatory or, like
Molly Bloom, let their minds slide down a soft slope of easy erotic
memories. Mrs. Woolf was incurably a gentlewoman. She was also
incurably interesting, incurably a fine soul. Where Dorothy Richardson's good cow Miriam is a passive consciousness, on which events
impinge, unsorted, in linear temporal succession, the consciousnesses of Mrs. Ramsay, of Clarissa Dalloway, of all the characters
in *The Waves* are active, selective, poetic consciousnesses, not merely
recording the immediate event but reaching back and forward and,
in an emotional sense, outwards.

The Waves (1931), Mrs. Woolf's most original, perhaps her
greatest achievement, is like a prose prolongation of the theme of
Keats's odes, the attempt to grasp the eternal in the transient, the
attempt of the consciousness to give the awareness of things passing

lasting shape. No doubt Proust's great novel was one of the influences behind *The Waves*; and Mrs. Woolf (though not in *The Waves* particularly) is like Proust also in her gift for elaborate social comedy, the comedy of a fine feminine consciousness, *divers et ondoyant*, playing on the solid Podsnappian complacencies and unbudgingnesses of the male. In *To the Lighthouse* (1927), her 'solidest' novel by ordinary standards, the male in all his baffled exasperation and proud need is represented by Mr. Ramsay the very distinguished thinker and man of letters tormented by the consciousness that he is not in the very first rank: demanding from his wife and children not merely love, which they are very ready to give him, but a kind of reassurance about his centrality and importance which they and he both know to be false. Mrs. Ramsay, an even more wonderful portrait, based on Virginia's mother, is on the surface the ideal wife and mother, humorous, patient, coaxing, wonderfully beautiful and charming, aware of her own beauty and charm, aware also of irritations and exasperations, of damagingly comic perceptions, which she is wise enough not to express openly.

Is Mrs. Ramsay 'almost a saint', as we often say of women with difficult and distinguished husbands, or partly a great actress, a star and prima donna of the domestic scene, a little overpowering, annoyed when she does not bowl everybody over, a bit (as with Charles Tansley, the scholarship boy) of a snob? What she is certainly is one of the richest and fullest portraits of a really attractive woman in English literature. Critics who say that Mrs. Woolf can 'do' atmosphere but not character should reflect how much more fully we are given Mrs. Ramsay than, say, Forster's Mrs. Wilcox or Mrs. Moore whose peculiar charisma we have to take largely on Forster's say-so; just as there is a sense in which we know Clarissa Dalloway (in *Mrs. Dalloway*, if not in her first appearance in *The Voyage Out*) far more fully than we know, in Forster, Adela Quested or Margaret Schlegel. Forster confines himself to those aspects of character that lead to action, or failure to act. Virginia Woolf wants to present something like the total impact, the living flow, of a personality intimately known. Moments of choice, in the narrower sense, matter less in her novels than moments of achieved perception: as when Lily Briscoe completes her picture at the end of *To the Lighthouse*—as Virginia Woolf is completing her picture—with, after hesitation, the single necessary stroke.

The vein of iron in Virginia Woolf's writing comes from the combination of the lyrical yet selective delight in all experience with

the Keatsian awareness of loneliness, transience, death. She had
several severe nervous breakdowns, worked on her novels with
Flaubertian thoroughness, lived nobly on her nerves, drowned herself in the end like Ophelia. Her attractiveness is like that of one of
the great romantic poets, somehow inseparable from her personal
beauty and distinction. No doubt life is a coarse business, and some
other novelists have had a greater appetite for the coarse; but, very
much a gentlewoman, she is not in the least genteel. And in the
thematic structure of her novels, as in that long beautiful bony
face of hers, one salutes both an infinite capacity for suffering and
enjoyment, and an iron will. She has had a strong though indirect
influence on a number of subsequent women novelists, but her
importance is an individual one. The world she created may be
privileged and limited; but it expresses, or reflects, an extraordinary
fineness of soul. Almost any other writer, even of broader talent,
to whom one turns, after immersing oneself in her, seems at first
a little vulgar. Ford Madox Ford, our next major specimen, certainly
does, though in an endearingly comic way.

VI

Ford Madox Ford (1873–1939) is an odd critical case. Because of a
peculiar but lovable ineptitude, an extraordinary gift for playing his
own cards badly (while helping many other writers, Conrad with
whom he collaborated, the young Pound, the young Lawrence, to
play theirs well) he was consistently underestimated throughout his
lifetime. He was always misjudged. He collaborated with Conrad
loyally, but was accused, by Conrad's stupid and petty-minded
widow, Jessie, of exploiting the collaboration for his own ends. As
editor of *The English Review* around 1910, he was one of the great
editors of the century: publishing Lawrence, Pound, Wyndham
Lewis, Hardy, Yeats. He was also a good editor in postwar Paris, in
the days of Gertrude Stein and the young Hemingway. But good
editors are not always loved; and Ford irritated many of his fellow-
writers by playing, with too much gusto, the part of the old English
gentleman. Hemingway in that ill-natured posthumous work about
Paris, *A Moveable Feast*, has a portrait of a fat, snobbish, pompous
Ford, smelling so much of food and drink and tobacco that, in a
room with him, Hemingway always wanted to open a window.

Ford's books of memoirs, wonderfully readable, also weakened
his reputation during his lifetime. They are factually unreliable. His
method, in memoir as in fiction, was that of the impressionist; his

impressions of the important writers he had known are extraordinarily vivid, and essentially true, but the anecdotes about them are largely invented. His early English career was interrupted by the First World War and before that by a libel case brought by his first wife, whom he thought he had divorced in Germany but had not, against Violet Hunt, his mistress, who was now calling herself Mrs. Ford Madox Hueffer (he changed his German surname to Ford after the First World War). His greatest technical *tour de force* in the novel, *The Good Soldier*, came out in 1915: and was savagely slanged by patriotic reviewers who, because of the title, expected a war story and instead found a gripping, tragic, and yet partly comic novel about upper-class adultery.

After the war, Ford lived partly in Paris, partly in the United States, partly in Provence, writing copiously, so that the four novels about Christopher Tietjens did not stand out as the single masterpiece they are. Poets praised him after his death, Pound in the *Pisan Cantos* and Robert Lowell in a moving memorial poem. But it is in the years since his death that his reputation has gradually grown, through memoirs and biographies, and through the work of critics and editors like Robie Macauley, Mark Schorer, and Graham Greene. Perhaps it has grown a little too much. There was in Ford an extraordinary combination of flair, technical ingenuity, goodheartedness, and a certain central *naïveté*, which could be almost obtuseness. There was nothing vulgar in his heart; but he had some characteristics, the name-dropping, the naïve superiority, the simple and whole-hearted admiration for what is left of Christian toryism, of the ethos of the English landed gentry, that can sometimes seem vulgar in other people. And he was, technically, a show-off: a wizard of display. And he is never really sentimental, but one often fears that he will become so.

The son of a German-born music critic of *The Times*, and descended on his mother's side from the pre-Raphaelite painter, Ford Madox Brown, Ford was in the thick of the literary and artistic world from his 'teens in the late 1890s. He admired Henry James and Conrad; but from his pre-Raphaelite background, there came also a taste for romance (*Romance* was the title of the rather Stevensonian story which he and Conrad published in collaboration in 1903). As much as Conrad, he was the inventor of that method of narration in which events are presented, not in their order of occurrence, but in the order in which they acquire significance, in informal retrospect, for a narrator. In *The Good Soldier*—which Ford had originally wished to call, more wisely, *The Saddest Story*, but that was not thought a selling title for wartime—the narrator, an apparently mild and benevolent Philadelphia Quaker, an apparently helpless and rather stupid looker-on at a tragic series of events in which he cannot helpfully intervene, is gradually shown to be something more interesting and more full of pathos, more formidable, perhaps even more sinister.

The Good Soldier is memorable for its narrative structure and as an impersonation. The cautious and precise tone of the Philadelphia Quaker makes a beautiful comedic counterpoint to the violent passions involved; so also does the rigid social correctness, in an outward sense, of the characters caught up in the passions. And what about the narrator himself, whom Graham Greene sees as saintly, Mark Schorer as an ignoble figure of unconscious envy and self-deception? He is perhaps impotent, he is certainly a cuckold; in his soldier hero's helpless violence and power in love he sees—lovingly, enviously?—something which in his own timidity and propriety he would half like to be. He seems largely a fool, a figure of fun, yet his passing remarks are full of bitter penetrating humour, which may or may not be conscious. Is it mere pity, or some more sinister combination of emotions, that makes him in the end quietly go away, leaving 'the good soldier' to cut his throat? And is the whole moral pattern of the book a tribute to English upper-class society, tragic but heroic, or an indictment of a tradition that has kept its manners but lost its moral core?

Ford's greatest achievement, however, is not *The Good Soldier* but the tetralogy of novels about Christopher Tietjens, a 'good soldier' in a more straightforward sense than Captain Ashburnham, which came out between 1924 and 1928: *Some Do Not* (1924), *No More Parades* (1925), *A Man Could Stand Up* (1926), and *The Last Post* (1928). The last novel was an afterthought, and Ford thought it a mistake, Graham Greene (who does not include it in his Bodley Head edition of Ford) agreeing with him. But the American critic, Robie Macauley, who brought all four novels together in one volume in 1950 with the title *Parade's End*, thinks, and I agree with him, that *The Last Post* is an indispensable coda. It is a novel of forgiveness and reconciliation, and that note reverberates, in retrospect, through the earlier three books.

Though Tietjens was modelled on Ford's friend, Arthur Marwood, a member of the Yorkshire squirearchy, a brilliant mathematician, too proud, too self-assured to dream of making a name or a career for himself, Christopher, whom his mistress, Valentine, calls her 'dear, meal-sack elephant' is physically and emotionally more like Ford himself: no doubt a somewhat idealized and romanticized Ford. He is, like Ford, a man who is always kind, brave, dutiful, self-sacrificing, but who infuriates people by his very patience and goodness, his refusals to retaliate, and even more by a suspicion that these are not motivated purely by Christian charity but also by a conscious or unconscious arrogance. Christopher, the last surviving English Tory gentleman, would not dream of demanding from his inferiors what he automatically demands of himself. The world he belongs to really died out in the eighteenth century. Assailed by a new England of managerial careerists, typified by his friend the restless, uneasy civil servant, McMasters, by his disloyal wife, Sylvia, by his godfather General Campion, Christopher refuses to fight back. There is a kind of gross silent complacency in this lumpy elephantine creature.

Parade's End then turns perhaps a little too much into a kind of Spenserian allegory; the beautiful impersonative and impressionistic technique cannot wholly disguise the fact that the characters are conceived in very broad and simple moral outline, almost as personifications of vices and virtues. We are reading something like a morality play, fleshed out. The skill, also, does not quite enough conceal itself: we are at a firework show. Yet there is wonderful range, life, and the most generous human sympathy. Ford was a very great craftsman and a very good man whose goodness comes across perhaps most touchingly when it is tinged with his absurd and pardonable vanity.

VII

There is a long tradition in English fiction of Menippean satire. The first pure example of this mode is Thomas Love Peacock, but there are elements of the mode also in Swift and Fielding. Menippean satire seems to flourish in periods when many subversive or deleterious ideas are in the air, but when these hardly seem to effect practically a traditional privileged mode of life, and can be considered mainly as odd and entertaining. Aldous Huxley (1894–1963), one of the great masters of the mode in our period, talked in his first novel, *Crome Yellow* (1921), about ideas 'bombinating in a vacuum', and this is the effect of Menippean satire at its best. The mode also lends itself, as it did in the pioneer modern work of this kind, Norman Douglas's *South Wind*, to picturesque description and a fantastic and comical display of learning. Huxley's two masterpieces in the mode were his first two novels, *Crome Yellow* and *Antic Hay* (1923), which, for wit, lightness, and gaiety, he never excelled. In his third novel, *Those Barren Leaves* (1925), the theme of mystical awareness, which was to haunt Huxley, makes its first important appearance. The character of the elderly nymphomaniac hostess, still clinging desperately to the illusion that she is sexually attractive, is handled superficially with comedy, but more deeply with compassion: so is the character of the committed elderly sensualist Cardan (modelled on Norman Douglas), growingly haunted, as old age and poverty draw near, by the thought of illness and death. The writing is more diffuse in this novel than in the first two, but it is also richer, particularly in the evocations of Italian landscape.

Huxley's fourth novel, *Point Counter-Point* (1928), was also his first great popular success, and was more ambitious than the earlier ones. It wears less well. There are portraits of Middleton Murry, D. H. Lawrence, Sir Oswald Mosley, Augustus John, and Huxley himself appears as the crippled novelist, the intellectual unable to get emotionally close to anybody, Philip Quarles. One character, Spandrell, is Baudelaire (Baudelaire with the intelligence, but without the genius) transferred to a London literary milieu of the 1920s. In its structure, the novelist within the novel, the shifting kaleidoscope, the book as I have noted owes something to Gide's *Les Faux-Monnayeurs*. The plot, as an English B.B.C. television version revealed, has a gripping quality not to be found in Huxley's earlier fictions. But D. H. Lawrence was right to find Huxley's version of himself, Mark Rampion, the Life-Forcer, boring, and Wyndham Lewis in *Men Without Art* was right to find the style clear but thin and undistinguished. Huxley in all his later writings presents the paradoxical spectacle of a man whose feeling for his art grows thinner as his human sympathies and his religious intuitions become more profound. He spreads himself thin; the cleverness becomes a little mechanical, the learned allusions too clearly out of the *Encyclopaedia Britannica*, the prose, always graceful and lucid, becomes a little prolix, ceases to bite. One reads Huxley's later work out of affection and respect for a noble and distinguished spirit rather than in the expectation (which the later Huxley would in any case have thought a trivial and narrow expectation) of pure literary pleasure.

Ronald Firbank (1886–1926), a slightly older contemporary, who died after an irregular, self-indulgent, and lonely life in the 1920s, had nothing like Huxley's range of mind. His books seem almost as if they might have been written by a naughty child: with their bad spellings, their giggling suggestiveness, their vein of pure fantasy or make-believe combined with moments of jabbing malice, they might seem to belong on the same shelf with Daisy Ashford's *The Young Visiters*—or, a nearer American relation, Anita Loos's *Gentlemen Prefer Blondes*—rather than with *Nightmare Abbey*, *The New Republic*, or *Crome Yellow*. Like Anita Loos, Firbank is scandalous and fundamentally innocent. Anthony Powell, in his useful introduction to the *Complete Ronald Firbank*, suggests that what makes up for the lack of maturity and toughness in Firbank and the lack of structural ability is his gift for disciplining his wish-fulfilment myths, gaily, into 'hard . . . sparkling words' and presenting us, in the end, with a completely original world. In a phrase or two he can, better than many more 'professional' novelists, conjure up an interior or a person; his use of choric speech, Powell thinks, can be set not absurdly alongside Hardy's, the West Indians in *Prancing Nigger* alongside the rustics in *The Return of the Native*.

Anthony Powell himself, like that other distinguished Menippean satirist of the 1930s, Evelyn Waugh (1903–66), clearly owes something to Firbank: in their use of dialogue both are closer to Firbank than to Huxley, whose dialogue may have struck them as too artificial; though the German architect who would like to build houses without people, people being a messy and disturbing element, in Waugh's first novel, *Decline and Fall* (1928), is very much a Huxley character. But, in an interesting tribute to Huxley in *The London Magazine*, Waugh admired the swiftness, zest, and comic invention of the earlier novels, but confessed himself bored by the occasional intrusions of the essayist and not too enthusiastic about the Peacockian 'discussion' element.

As well educated in his way as Huxley, Waugh was anxious nevertheless not to appear an 'intellectual': the world of his early novels with its raffishness, its bucks and rakes and rooks and heavy swells and innocent butts, is in some ways (but for his lack of interest in the 'sporting life') more like Pierce Egan's world or Surtees's than Peacock's. Nearer his own time, the farcical elements —the old Colonel and his film about the life of Wesley in *Vile Bodies* (1930)—owe a great deal to a popular contemporary writer whom he adored, P. G. Wodehouse. The pure gaiety, the dis-interested comic destructiveness, of *Decline and Fall* he never quite recaptured; his young wife left him as he was writing *Vile Bodies*, and henceforth the farce and the satire conceal a sense of indignation and pain. The best of these early novels, *A Handful of Dust* (1934), uses a technique of dry comedy to emphasize the pain of futile adultery and pointless betrayal, the pain of heartlessness; the decent

hero at the end is left in a hut in the Amazonian jungle reading the
works of Dickens (whom Waugh detested) over and over again to
a madman with a rifle.

To combine the farcical with the painful, in an almost vindictive
way, became typical of Waugh: as when, in *Black Mischief* (1932),
Basil Seal, the rogue hero, finds that he has eaten the girl he loves
at a cannibal feast. In the end, after the Second World War, Waugh
was to attempt a straight romantic novel, though of course with
some comic and satirical trimmings, in *Brideshead Revisited* (1945):
what is most moving there is the picture of self-destructive innocence in Sebastian Flyte. He was to become a 'straight' novelist of
the first rank with his war trilogy *The Sword of Honour* (1952–61):
this should be compared with Ford's Tietjens tetralogy: it comes
out much less thick and rich but sharper in moral outline. Waugh
there probes and questions his own romantic Christian toryism as
Ford never did; he is not, like Ford, in danger of sentimentality.
Guy Crouchback was the last embodiment of his typical comic hero,
the holy fool or inept knight-errant, baffled and tricked by the
world, but baffling the world by his own innocence. One could not
have predicted that novel from *Decline and Fall*, his one masterpiece
of pure comic enjoyment, as gay and apparently heartless as
Voltaire's *Candide*. But the innocent hero, Paul Pennyfeather, is
already established there.

Underneath Waugh's farce and satire there lay an extremely
romantic vision of life. Anthony Powell (b. 1905), an Oxford
contemporary of Waugh's, a friend, though never a close friend, is
oddly parallel and different. His greatest achievement, the long
series of novels, *The Music of Time*, belong to our next volume. His
novels of the 1930s resemble Waugh's in their social background,
in their wit, but in little else. This is comedy of the dry mock, in
which Powell displays futility, ineptness, petty treachery: the Bright
Young People have no glamour for him, as they have for Waugh
even at his most satirical. Waugh loves his fools, like the Colonel
in *Vile Bodies*, and his rogues, like Captain Grimes in *Decline and
Fall*: Powell presents his rogues and fools in a dry, exact way
without sympathy, though possibly not without a certain concealed
pity. Where Waugh is impressed by the wildness, silliness, and
wickedness of a section of upper-class society, Powell is impressed
by a drabness, dryness, lack of life or love. Less brilliantly farcical
than Waugh's early novels, already marked by that obsessional
exactness in recording incident and dialogue, however apparently
trivial, that is a distinguishing feature of *The Music of Time*, these

early novels, *Afternoon Men* (1931), *Venusberg* (1932), *From a View to a Death* (1933), *Agents and Patients* (1936), and *What's Become of Waring* (1939), are funny in a dry and disabused way. There are no characters, as in Waugh, grander and simpler than life, no flights into fantasy, no youthfulness, and no romanticism: the satire and the comedy come from the dry exaggeration of the all too possible. The books are corrective comedy, very negative in feeling; for the development of Powell's more positive values we had to wait for *The Music of Time*.

Wyndham Lewis (1884–1957), an anguished, isolated figure who straddled all the arts, thought of himself as primarily a satirist, a non-moral satirist, a novelist of the external eye: his view of humour was roughly Bergson's that men, being free and organic creatures, are funny when they behave like machines. But his real gift as a novelist sprang, like Dostoevsky's, from his own discontent and isolation; his best two 'pure' novels in our period are *Tarr* (1918), his first novel, and a novel of the 1930s, *The Revenge for Love* (1937). In both, the hard satirical tone masks, and barely masks, an obsession with human madness, treachery, and violence, the dangerousness and brutality of the human creature. He treats as funny what has ceased to be funny, treats tragedy in terms of farce, creates (whether consciously or not) sympathy for his creatures by apparently so brutally withholding it. His own pure satire *The Apes of God* (1930) is weakened by its length and top-heaviness, and by his megalomania, which robs his attack on the London literary world of that 'coolness at the centre' which, in writing of Dryden, he rightly saw as essential to satire.

At his own centre, as a later novel, *Self-Condemned* (1954), shows clearly, there burned ashy fires: a devouring and insatiable egotism, a rancour, gives an unmistakable personal flavour to everything he writes, but also tilts it off the balance of sanity. He is heavily scabrous in dealing with sexual episodes, and here, also, we cannot believe that the approach is really external. *The Childermass* (Book I, 1928), a brilliant fantasy, is partly an attack on democracy (embodied in the sinister figure of the Bailiff) and partly a vision of the antechambers of a new kind of hell: it was completed after the war as *The Human Age*, and belongs really to our next volume. In one sense, Lewis belongs less with the Menippean satirists whom we have considered so far than with a French writer like Céline or with some aspects of Henry Miller. His vision of life is a fierce, Gothic one, powerful and distorted. He was a man of genius, paranoiac genius; his fictions, for all their extraordinary vigour, are more

interesting in the end for the light they throw on his own strange
mind than as a critical mirror of the social life of his time. Yet he is
a major figure in the literary, artistic, and ideological life of his time:
not quite, however, a major novelist.

VIII

Major novelists have, on the whole, tended either to take a retrospective view of life and time (*Middlemarch* and *War and Peace*,
for instance, are 'historical' novels) or what may be called a 'classical'
view: it does not occur to Jane Austen, for instance, that the stable
society of respectable, well-educated and religious country gentle-
folk, which is her scene, is a precarious and passing condition of
society. She takes it as the civilized norm. The years of the 1930s
till the end of the Second World War in 1945 were a peculiar period
in English literary history in that immediately current social and
political events pressed very hard on the creative writer, and made
it difficult for him to take either a retrospective or a classical view.
The external factors have often been classified: the Wall Street
crash, the slump, and widespread unemployment in Britain, the rise
to power of Hitler, the Abyssinian war, the Spanish Civil War, the
failure of sanctions, the final outbreak of the Second World War in
1939, after the pact between Germany and the Soviet Union. In
these precarious years an attitude like James Joyce's, of abstract
dedication to art, or an attitude of poetic introspection, like Virginia
Woolf's, seemed for younger writers no longer valid. These were
the years of political commitment of one sort or the other, to the
Peace Pledge Union, often for young poets more than young
novelists to the Communist party or to the idea of a Popular or
United Front, of the Left Book Club: there was a Right Book Club,
also, and these years saw the rise of Sir Oswald Mosley's British
Union.

But the committed, or partly committed, young writers belonged
inescapably by birth and upbringing to the English upper-middle
classes, and were, whether they liked it or not, heirs of the liberal
tradition. The need to make some sort of stand against Hitlerism,
against the Axis, was combined both with a profound horror of war
and with a distrust of the kind of political and military leaders a
war was likely to throw up. The actual war against Hitler, when it
came about, was not the simple crusade the young poets had
imagined. The Labour Government, just, efficient, but irremediably
prosaic, and largely indifferent to the arts, which came into being

in 1945 did not bring about that kind of transformation of the quality of life which, in the 1930s, young socialists had imagined. The moral relief of victory over the Axis was blunted by the use of the atom bomb and the beginnings of the Cold War and the achievement of peace through a Balance of Terror. The drab English world of the war and immediately postwar scene did not lend itself to the transforming efforts of the imagination. Novelists like Evelyn Waugh in *Brideshead Revisited* or L. P. Hartley in *The Go-Between* (which falls a little outside our period, being published in 1949) looked romantically backwards. It was not till the early 1950s that a new generation of writers, Kingsley Amis, John Wain, Iris Murdoch, and others, were to attempt to take in the immediately contemporary world, a world of non-mandarin culture. And they were perhaps not in the straight tradition of the novel: Amis and Wain were tending towards the picaresque, Miss Murdoch towards romance and covert allegory. Retrospect was in danger of becoming sentimental: the 'classical' attitude, assuming a certain representative permanence in human manners and institutions, was in danger of seeming utterly unreal.

Nevertheless, the 1930s and early 1940s constituted a period of much more widespread high talent in the novel than the 1920s: Christopher Isherwood, Graham Greene, Elizabeth Bowen, Rosamund Lehmann, Henry Green, L. P. Hartley, all these, much more accessible (except Henry Green, perhaps) to the ordinary reader than Joyce or Virginia Woolf, were nevertheless dedicated artists and craftsmen, with a care for the simplest element in fiction, the element of 'story', which an older generation had lacked.

In retrospect, Christopher Isherwood (b. 1904) seems to me to have been the most promising of all these new talents, though as I have said, for a variety of reasons the promise was never quite fulfilled; his long and ambitious postwar novel, *The World in the Evening* (1954), was generally felt even by his warmest admirers to be an honourable failure. His earliest novels, *All the Conspirators* (1928) and *The Memorial* (1932), enjoyed at most a *succès d'estime*: the subject-matter was in a sense traditional, the stranglehold of family tradition, middle-class tradition, on the young male, the oppressiveness of the mother-dominated family, the gulf between social classes. Isherwood achieved fame with his highly topical works with a setting in Berlin, the set of stories *Good-Bye to Berlin* (1939) and the novel *Mr. Norris Changes Trains* (1935; in the United States, *The Last of Mr. Norris*). What made the Berlin books fascinating was the use of a narrator, borrowing something from but not identical with Christopher Isherwood the person, who was essentially a character of sympathetic comedy: receptive, observant, deceptively naïve, devastatingly accurate and habitually politely understating his emotions. Cool-headed but warm-hearted, this narrator had Forsterian virtues, but could also seem at times an engaging farce figure, a Bertie Wooster of the liberal Left. This narrator was the spectator of, but failed always to become completely involved in, the tragedy and melodrama of pre-Hitlerian Germany; he could not divest himself of a certain detachment, a certain English feeling that all this excessive German behaviour was a little unreal. (I have noticed that readers from East Europe do not share the admiration of English and American critics for these books: they find in them an element of English hypocrisy or superiority, the 'sense of humour' being used in an evasive way.)

Isherwood presents European tragedy in the vein of English comedy; his Mr. Norris is frightfully treacherous and corrupt, but the narrator's attitude to this extraordinary old creature remains to the end that of an appalled connoisseur of the absurd. The balance which made this achievement possible was precarious. It totters, rather, in the short novel *Prater Violet*, about the film industry: it had been diluted and sentimentalized in *The World in the Evening*. But it is there again in a volume of stories of the 1960s, revisiting the 1930s scene, *Down There on a Visit*. The sheer economy, disguising an extraordinary density of observation, of presentation, the unobtrusive grace and wit of style, the ease with which the comedy of surprise is handled, will make the two Berlin books classics long after their topical or historical interest has become of minor moment.

Isherwood conquers by the flexible ease with which he establishes rapports (between himself and his characters, between himself and his readers) around his fictive identity: by charm. We read even his slighter pieces because they enable us to know, or have the illusion of knowing, Isherwood. Graham Greene (b. 1904), an equally compelling writer, who can make use occasionally of a comparable sort of comedy (in *Our Man in Havana*, for instance) is perhaps more purely and objectively a novelist in that the power of his narratives does not depend on his establishing a feeling: 'How pleasant to know Mr. Greene!' He makes, more broadly, an interesting contrast morally. He understands Catholics, Communists, black sheep: is fascinated by betrayal, especially self-betrayal, by the sudden heroisms of the abject, narrative patterns of pursuit and turning. He is as much a novelist in a European Catholic tradition (the tradition of Mauriac and Bernanos, say) as Isherwood, like Forster, is in an Anglo-Saxon liberal Protestant tradition. He likes extreme situations. What has worried many non-Catholic readers about his Catholicism is how far in his fiction (leaving his purely personal spiritual life, of which of course one knows nothing, aside) it is in danger of becoming a plot-making device. Similarly, his morality, with its sharp distinction between the good/evil dichotomy (sacred) and the right/wrong dichotomy (secular, and inauthentic) is very simplified, and would not stand up to much philosophical probing by, say, a distinguished Jesuit philosopher like Father Coplestone.

Greene's crudities, his extremes, are, at any rate, the deliberately chosen crudities and extremes of an extremely intelligent man, and out of them he has created a world of his own, Greeneland, whose general patterns become, indeed, increasingly predictable, but which has a gripping vitality. He observes also, like a first-rate journalist: of the novels of the period we are concerned with, *It's A Battlefield* (1934) and *England Made Me* (1935) reflect the social tensions, the personal involvements, of the 1930s in a rich, dense, dramatically mobile way; we have the double feeling, in reading Greene, of being caught up in a very thrilling story and of admiring, as in reading a good thriller also, the skill and verve with which the author keeps the story moving. One might call Greene, in this sense, an honest illusionist. Though one can predict his devices (the fusion, for instance, of image or impression and metaphor) and knows roughly his range of characters and typical situations, his own integrity and involvement, his tough intelligence, prevent the devices, the characters, the situations from ever becoming mechanical. The fastidiousness of some critics comes perhaps from a tension between immediate emotional conviction, which the novels carry, and latent intellectual resentment against the implied point of view: or, more meanly and guiltily, from a worry that a work of literature should also be, in Kingsley Amis's phrase, a 'good read'.

In retrospect, as I say, these two novelists seem to dominate the English novel of the 1930s and some years onwards, to dominate it perhaps because of a representative quality. In a changed way, Isherwood stands for the Forsterian tradition, of the scrupulous and ironical individual conscience: Greene stands for a kind of new tribalism, and the grandeurs and miseries of the Communist ethic have, in fact, fascinated him almost as much as those of the Roman Catholic faith. No other novelist of the 1930s has this representative quality. Technically, Henry Green is remarkable, as I have said earlier 'a novelist's novelist': but his extraordinary powers of narrative organization through a prose which makes much use of asyndeton and an ear for dialogue, for the rhythms and repeated phrases of non-affective communication—in his handling of dialogue, he anticipates Harold Pinter—do not, for the ordinary reader, make up for a kind of opacity, or for a feeling that the verbal patterning is possibly more important to Green than the people. Elizabeth Bowen and Rosamund Lehmann combine an awareness of inward sensibility, deriving something from Virginia Woolf, with a direct old-fashioned story-telling power. In her powerful novel of the Second World War in London, *The Heat of the Day*, Miss Bowen remarkably combines Woolfian atmospherics with a plot of suspense, violence, blackmail, and betrayal which owes a great deal, in its general handling, to Graham Greene.

L. P. Hartley really belongs in his formation to the 1920s, when he published his first short novel, *Simonetta Perkins*. His Eustace and Hilda trilogy is set back in the 1920s and hardly reflects at all the pressures of the 1930s. It is a study of relations between a brother and sister who, between them, represent two traditions of English middle-class life: the brother, Eustace, the tradition of Paterian aestheticism and, a little, of Jamesian social climbing: the sister, Hilda, the other tradition of puritan self-sacrifice and social service. But it is Eustace, with his apparently self-indulgent philosophy, who sacrifices himself again and again to Hilda, whose philosophy of unselfishness is combined with a remarkable will to dominate: and it is Hilda, not Eustace, who is bowled over, and breaks her heart, for a right-wing, near-Fascist aristocrat who stands for everything she disapproves of. A basic charity, an unbreakable childish love for the strong and hard young sister—really not so strong as himself—is something far more deep in Eustace than aestheticism, vanity, or snobbery. The pictures of Oxford and of country-house life are done with an insider's assurance. If one had a criticism at all, it would be that the total flavour, in the end, is a little bland: but there is bite and pain, though it is a cunningly concealed bite.

At the end of such a survey as this, one wonders, of course, if one has built up one's discrete observations into a pattern of any general significance. Literary history can never be related in a crude, simple, and direct fashion to social and political history. The formation of the older writers with whom I have been dealing here, Joyce, Lawrence, Forster, Virginia Woolf, Ford Madox Ford, belonged to an earlier period, the late Victorian and Edwardian age:

for Joyce particularly, nothing that had *happened* in the world since the year 1904 in Dublin mattered much. The Menippean satirists observed the world around them, but from a stance of social or intellectual privilege. Wyndham Lewis observed it from an embittered and polemical point of view. On the writers of the 1930s, current events—because they were more urgent, dramatic, and threatening—had a greater impact, yet in Isherwood and in Graham Greene it is their art and craft that matters more to us now than their documentary impact. If there is any large generalization that one could make it is that the novel is *par excellence* the art form of a society in which the standards, needs, and desires of the educated middle classes provide a sort of norm of expectation. Between the two wars, the middle classes were in the saddle in England, though in politics and social life older traditions, aristocratic traditions, still carried weight. Of the figures whom I have dealt with, only Lawrence came from the working classes, only Joyce from the lower-middle classes. The others might criticize their privileges, but were irremediably possessed of them. These are artists of a liberal society, a liberal society much shaken by the First World War, by the Russian revolution, by a reaction against the moral certainties of the Victorian age, artists recoiling from the general philistinism of the society around them, but they criticize a liberal society from within it. The society has a sort of cohesion which they do not always quite consciously allow for. The Second World War, more than the First, was a watershed. In the next volume we shall see the novelist speaking in a different kind of social voice.

FOR FURTHER READING

(Dates after novels are those of first publication)

Perhaps further reading should begin with European and American novels of the same period. The major European novels include Marcel Proust, *Remembrance of Things Past* (1917–27), André Gide, *The Counterfeiters* (1926), Jean-Paul Sartre, *Nausea* (1937), Franz Kafka, *The Castle* (1930) and *The Trial* (1937), Thomas Mann, *The Magic Mountain* (1924), Italo Svevo, *The Confessions of Zeno* (1923), and Ignazio Silone, *Bread and Wine* (1936).

Major American novelists are William Faulkner, Ernest Hemingway, and Scott Fitzgerald, who all published several important novels during this period. See particularly Faulkner's *Sartoris* (1929), *The Sound and the Fury* (1929), *As I Lay Dying* (1930), *Sanctuary* (1931), *Light in August* (1932), *Absalom, Absalom!* (1936), *The Wild Palms* (1939), and *The Hamlet* (1940); Hemingway's *The Sun Also Rises* (1926), *A Farewell to Arms* (1929), and *For Whom the Bell Tolls* (1940); and Fitzgerald's *The Great Gatsby* (1925), *Tender is the Night* (1934), and *The Last Tycoon* (1941).

Other important novels are Sinclair Lewis, *Main Street* (1920) and *Babbitt* (1922); Theodore Dreiser, *An American Tragedy* (1925); Sherwood Anderson, *Winesburg, Ohio* (1919); Willa Cather, *My Antonia* (1918), *A Lost Lady* (1923), and *Death Comes for the Archbishop* (1927); Thornton Wilder, *The Bridge of San Luis Rey* (1927); Elinor Wylie, *The Venetian Glass Nephew* (1925); Thomas Wolfe, *Look Homeward, Angel* (1929); Carson McCullers, *The Heart is a Lonely Hunter* (1940) and *Reflections in a Golden Eye* (1941); John Dos Passos, *The 42nd Parallel* (1930); Henry Miller, *Tropic of Cancer* (1934) and *Tropic of Capricorn* (1939); and John Steinbeck, *Of Mice and Men* (1937) and *The Grapes of Wrath* (1939).

General books on the novel are listed in *The Twentieth-Century Mind*, volume I (pp. 444–6), where reading lists on E. M. Forster, James Joyce, and D. H. Lawrence are also given. The lecture on *Ulysses* by Miriam Allott, cited on p. 379, is unpublished; Mrs. Allott's essay 'James Joyce: The Hedgehog and the Fox', in *On the Novel* (1971), a *festschrift* for Walter Allen, partly derives from this lecture but is not identical with it.

Virginia Woolf's *A Writer's Diary* (1953) provides invaluable material for the understanding of her novels. Leonard Woolf's autobiography throws light on the biographical background; the five volumes are *Sowing* (1960), *Growing* (1961), *Beginning Again* (1964), *Downhill All the Way* (1967), and *The Journey Not the Arrival Matters* (1969). Good background studies are Quentin Bell, *Bloomsbury* (1968) and J. K. Johnstone, *The Bloomsbury Group* (1954). Among the many books on Virginia Woolf, the best are probably A. D. Moody, *Virginia Woolf* (1963) and Jean Guiguet, *Virginia Woolf and Her Works* (1965). Erich Auerbach, *Mimesis* (Princeton, 1953) includes a famous analysis of a passage from *To The Lighthouse*.

There are good critical analyses in Richard A. Cassell, *Ford Madox Ford: A Study of His Novels* (1961) and John A. Meixner, *Ford Madox Ford's Novels: A Critical Study* (1962). The latter is probably the best introduction to Ford's work.

12

Drama

WALTER STEIN

I

Indubitably, the theatre in England from 1918 to 1945 continues to have George Bernard Shaw (1856–1950) as its presiding figure. Even towards the end of this period, when Shaw's most decisive work was clearly behind him, he continued to add significantly to his canon; while his influence is apparent not only at various levels of comedy and the social problem play but, more surprisingly, even in T. S. Eliot's poetic drama. (Eliot himself has noted that, in writing the prose epilogue to *Murder in the Cathedral*, 'I may, for aught I know, have been slightly under the influence of *Saint Joan*'; and there are many other features—from the Third Tempter in the same play to much of Eliot's later comic material—that seems at any rate to have caught something of Shaw's characteristic tone.)

Nevertheless—though Shaw has distinguished critical advocates, like Eric Bentley, and has enjoyed considerable popular stage successes in recent years—it is at least open to question whether he still connects vitally with our concerns in the sort of way in which Ibsen, Chekhov, and Strindberg continue to be important to us, or in which both Beckett and Brecht, in all their extreme oppositeness, are now helping us to find ourselves. There is something about Bernard Shaw's more ambitious plays that is now liable to generate a sense of distance, of intellectual or emotional disconnection, which no amount of verbal and theatrical brilliance can properly bridge.

That this cannot be simply due to the passage of time is evident, if only since Shaw's contemporaries and immediate predecessors have not all been thus affected. On similar evidence, it cannot be merely due to 'naturalism' (indeed, whatever his theoretical affiliations, Shaw is rarely naturalistic in technique); nor to its opposite, theatrical artifice—for we are now thoroughly acclimatized to stage conventions of many kinds. Nor, again, can a sufficient explanation be found in Shaw's largely comic approach: much of our most telling recent drama is 'largely comic'. If Shaw seems in danger of erosion as a serious power in our awareness, the causes must lie deeper within the particular character of his work.

There are two aspects of this work that seem crucial in this connection—the one more abstract and intellectual, concerned with social and cosmic beliefs, the other more immediately personal, flowing from temperament or emotional culture. Of course these two aspects are closely related: it is just the manner of their inter-action in Shaw's sensibility that gives rise to 'Shavianism'—that mixture of continuous eclectic improvisation on themes by Marx, Ibsen, Butler, Nietzsche, and Bergson (among others), and his sustained theatrical paradox and verbal clowning—providing a much more justifiable basis for turning Shaw's name into an 'ism' than ever existed for the 'Ibsenism' he had proclaimed as the quintessence of Ibsen's art.

'In Shavianism, we can see—just as clearly as in the technological vision of H. G. Wells—the utter bankruptcy of the progressive Victorian temper in an age of confusion, upheavals, and ominous threat.' To agree with this judgement of Robert Brustein's, in *The Theatre of Revolt*, is not necessarily to endorse the temper of histori-cal absurdism of which Brustein's own book is an instance. Both these approaches and tempers—Utopian aspirations and fascinated fixations upon their collapse—are essential components of modern experience. Both recur, in a variety of guises, and in varying strengths, throughout our epoch. The potent, unstable tension between them spans the whole field of modern awareness: from private to social, from national to international relations, from action to contemplation, from secular to religious concerns.

Those who now feel Shavianism as indeed indicative of the 'bankruptcy' of a certain type of 'progressive temper' need not, therefore, align themselves with any simple recoil from radical, forward-looking commitments. The profound dynamic polarity between historical hopes and despairs cannot properly be reduced to such mechanical, stereotyped disjunctions. Indeed, is it not fair to submit that the struggle towards human maturity—towards man's renewed self-awareness—in our time is essentially defined by this dialectic of hope and despair, both within our shifting forms of belief (or unbelief) and within history's just as drastically shifting responses to our responses?

All this is itself thoroughly 'dramatic'. And if Bernard Shaw's theatre of ideological debate now largely seems to by-pass our really experienced dilemmas and concerns, this could be because, in the relevant sense, his theatre is in fact not dramatic enough. This is not a matter of 'talk' versus 'action', of 'cerebration' versus 'feel-ing': Brecht's epic theatre, with its insistent, direct buttonholing of the audience and its elaborate traps against spontaneous dramatic emotion, can yet be total in its demands on our dramatic involvement; and even Beckett's ultimate abandonment of 'plot' in any traditionally recognizable sense can hold us suspended within a deeply enforced, intimately explosive inaction. If Shaw now falls short in the power to probe us in depth, this is because of what actually happens (or fails to happen) *within* his dialogue—or plots— or intellectual dialectic—or emotional resolutions—and because of the ways in which these elements relate to each other. And here, in the concrete quality of Shaw's dramatic imagination, we can observe how essentially the type of 'progressive temper' he exemplifies and Shaw's personal emotional attitudes converge.

Within the limits of this brief account, we can only glance at a couple of major examples of Shaw's later plays. Although *Heartbreak House* and *Back to Methuselah* are both, in their different ways, exceptional works, they are at the same time highly characteristic of their author. Shaw himself describes *Heartbreak House*—which he began in 1913, finished in 1916, but withheld 'from the footlights during the war; for the Germans might on any night have turned the last act from play into earnest'—'as a fantasia in the Russian manner on English themes'. The five plays that constitute the 'metabiological Pentateuch', *Back to Methuselah*, were published in 1921. The underlying unity of sensibility between these two works is all the more revealing in view of their apparently totally divergent forms, subject-matter, and dominant moods.

Though the stage directions scrupulously describe Heartbreak House as situated in 'the middle of the north edge of Sussex', it is soon apparent that its real, essential location is that familiar cultural landscape which was soon to be named the Waste Land. There, the members of a symbolically representative upper-class family— brilliant, eccentric, trapped within their own febrile stagnation— collide with each other in a criss-cross of rituals of resignation or despair. They entertain friends or acquaintances, to whom they would like to give—they hardly know what, and from whom they would like to elicit some sort of meaning for their own lives. They compulsively flirt, talk, tease—and break hearts. Their dottily impressive patriarch, Captain Shotover, delivers fragmentary off-beat jeremiads, concerning his family, or the need to re-establish control over the ship of state and civilization (the architecture of the house itself resembles a ship). Slowly, within this multiple focus, there emerges a central emphasis upon Ellie, a visitor brought to 'heartbreak' by her accidental contact with the family, and upon

Captain Shotover's anguish and fury in the face of the destructiveness ripening within the House—even, indeed, within his own being.
The play ends with the menace—and subsequent relief—of bombers
passing over, a near-by explosion, and, as the curtain drops, an
equivocal, fascinated contemplation of the possibility of their
coming again 'tomorrow night'.

The play has a kind of appeal hardly matched by anything else in
Shaw. Driven by Shaw's own Shotover-impulses in the face of
radical cultural dissolution and the war, and under the technical
guidance of Chekhov, it exposes some deeply vulnerable nerves,
which Shaw's 'progressive' and 'comic' temper had hitherto kept
consistently hidden—especially from himself. Yet there is something
brittle, something defectively realized about the play, as if the habitual attitudes or pressures that had hitherto served as safeguards
against 'heartbreak' were unconsciously sabotaging the new work.
We need only to place it by the side of *Uncle Vanya*, say, or *Three
Sisters*, to see how heavily it leans on Chekhov as a model, and yet
how superficially Shaw has made Chekhov's 'manner' his own. The
essential point was made, as early as 1921, by Desmond MacCarthy,
in a basically sympathetic review of the play: 'Mr. Shaw does not
know what heartbreak is.' And this—it is worth repeating—is not
at all a point against 'comedy' as such: given its special seriousness
of intention, *Heartbreak House* might have been a 'savage farce' like
Ben Jonson's *Volpone*; or a desperately gay fantasy like Aristo-
phanes' *Lysistrata*; or, like Molière's *Misanthrope* or Chekhov's own
masterpieces, it might have pushed comedy to a point where it
centrally fuses with tragedy. Instead, we get a mere jumble of
tones. (What on earth is that tritely farcical burglar doing in the
play, or—still more perplexing—how are we to react to his and the
capitalist Mangan's, no doubt symbolic, deaths during the air raid?)
And, though some of the scenes are genuinely poignant, too often
the evident neo-Chekhovian and poetic aspirations remain unfulfilled. Ellie Dunn's 'heartbreak', and rapid heartbroken maturing,
are at once trivial, sentimental, and portentously stiff-upper-lipped.
Captain Shotover's sibylline grandeur hovers between intended
poetic mystery and theatrical Grand Old Man appeal. Randall and
Mangan are, in their different ways, conventional stock caricatures.
The most solidly created character is Lady Hushaby; she is perhaps
the only truly Chekhovian re-creation within Shaw's play. But the
play as a whole, for all its ironies, lacks the controlling, central ironic
poise of its models. And its high-pitched passages beyond workaday
prose often seem perilously overstretched.

Yet, one only needs to read Shaw's Preface to have brought home to one the reality and passion of his responses to the historical situation the play deals with. What is it that impairs this theatrical virtuoso's theatrical embodiment of these responses?

I think we may answer in the terms already suggested: that the answer lies partly in Shaw's personal sensibility, partly in the composition of his beliefs. On the personal plane, that shrinking from any deep emotional probing most often concealed, in Shaw's work, by virtuosities of distancing paradox but occasionally betraying itself in sheer, unguarded conventional sentimentalities, may account for the play's inability to dramatize private 'heartbreak' with imaginative authority. And this equally holds on the plane of social and cosmic shock: though the Preface eloquently confronts the spiritual landslide of the war, the play itself vainly strives to probe such a confrontation in depth through a proportionate dramatic 'poetry'. It is in this sense that 'Mr. Shaw does not know what heartbreak is'—and also that a certain kind of 'progressive temper'— unable to see the unbearable steadily and whole—may now seem 'bankrupt'.

Thus, *Back to Methuselah* is, for all its differences from *Heartbreak House*, its direct imaginative complement. For the 'heartbreak' not really measured by the earlier play is, in *Back to Methuselah*, transcended without taking its measure. That is, it is not really transcended. 'I am not blaming you', says Franklyn Barnabas to Burge and Lubin (Shaw's Lloyd George and Asquith figures) in 'The Gospel of the Brothers Barnabas':

Your task was beyond human capacity. What with our huge armaments, our terrible engines of destruction, our systems of coercion manned by an irresistible police, you were called on to control powers so gigantic that one shudders at the thought of their being entrusted even to an infinitely experienced and benevolent God, much less to mortal men whose whole life does not last a hundred years.[1]

The leap from Captain Shotover's 'Navigation. Learn it and live; or leave it and be damned' to Barnabas's 'Your task was beyond human capacity' is equally facile in its desperation and in its hope. For the everyday business of human living lies within the area spanned by this leap. If we are indeed trapped in heartbreaking impossibilities, how could any prospective Superman *ex machina* here and now save us from damned heartbreak? There is an intelligible live relevance in visions of sheer human catastrophe or farcical entrapment or, alternatively, of tragic triumph or divine redemption. But Shaw's 'metabiological' religion, like his personal creative sensibility, ultimately eludes the challenge of radical tragedy—and so cannot authentically offer itself as a source of relevant hope within radical tragic facts.

The five playlets of *Back to Methuselah*, though they have moments of spontaneous dramatic life, are for the most part cripplingly yoked to their didactic scheme; and what we are taught, as the scheme unfolds, is a sell-out of human values and meanings. 'In the Beginning' recasts the Genesis myth into a fable of Shavian Creative Evolution. Its surprises have style and point. And, though Eve's 'expression of overwhelming repugnance' when the Serpent reveals the 'secret' (sexual reproduction), and Cain's cry: 'I revolt against the clay, I revolt against the food', give warning of what Shaw's imagined future has in store, Eve's final words to Adam seem unexceptionable:

Man need not always live by bread alone. There is something else. We do not yet know what it is; but some day we shall find out; and then we will live on that alone; and there shall be no more digging nor spinning, nor fighting nor killing.

She spins resignedly; he digs impatiently.[2]

But in the second playlet, 'The Gospel of the Brothers Barnabas'— the only one set within the actualities of the postwar years—positive aspirations give way, as already noted, to a sort of bankrupt present investment in future human longevity. Longevity is what happens in 'The Thing Happens', in the year A.D. 2170. It continues to happen, in the year 3000, in 'Tragedy of an Elderly Gentleman'; which, though hardly a 'tragedy' by any dramatic standards, marks the beginning of the end of mankind as we know it. The 'discouraged' old gentleman—it is important that, for all his ludicrous feebleness, he is clearly superior to other shortlivers still at large in the world—is finished off by a kind of psycho-physical euthanasia. (We gather that 'tertiaries'—longlivers in their third century— 'are not at all squeamish about killing': 'Poor shortlived thing!' concludes the tertiary as she looks down on the gentleman's body. 'What else could I do for you?') And so we are set for 'As Far as Thought Can Reach', in the year 31,920; by when longevity has become even longer—indeed, but for the statistical certainty of eventual accidents, it is now unlimited—and Shaw's drift becomes finally explicit.

Longevity is salvation: not only from present social and political ills, but from any recognizably human sort of aliveness at all. Nature, friendship, sexual love, and art are all abandoned as adolescent toys as the longlivers mature and grow bald. We are shown a group of adolescents in the process of growing up—that is of tiring of each other and of 'these childish games—this dancing, and singing and mating'. (One of them declares: 'My heart is broken', but fortunately the She-Ancient is able to tell him that he is only at the beginning of it all.) Eventually we gather from the He-Ancient how he himself had ceased to look for 'perfection in friends, in lovers, in nature, in things outside myself':

And I, like Acis, ceased to walk over the mountains with my friends, and walked alone; for I found that I had creative power over myself but none over my friends. And then I ceased to walk on the mountains; for I saw that the mountains were dead.[3]

No doubt, such superhuman self-sufficiency is calculated to dispose of the shocks that flesh is heir to—if at a cost. Even so, however, it does not dispose of the ultimate shock: that flesh is flesh. Already, for the longlivers, eating and drinking are no longer associated with excretion. Birth is no longer from human bodies but from prodigious eggs delivering Newly Borns 'who would have been guessed at seventeen in our day'. The body, which 'always ends by being a bore', has become simply an irrelevance and threat to survival. Ultimately, therefore, even longevity is not enough. Ultimately, 'the day will come when there will be no people, only thought.' 'And that will be life eternal.' Lilith, reappearing in the play's conclusion, muses how she 'brought life into the whirlpool of force, and compelled my enemy, matter, to obey a living soul'. Now life is to 'press on to the goal of redemption from the flesh'.

This, then, is where Eve's 'there is something else', those endemic 'childish games' that fulfil or break human hearts, and our present political tasks 'beyond human capacity' finally tend. A final solution of human problems: of the human problem in fact. There could be no more clairvoyant explication of Shaw's habitual 'comic' evasion of human facts. We have noted the precarious polarization of Shaw's vision between uncritical sentiment and an equally facile, farcical detachment. This polarity could be traced in works as diverse as *Candida*, *Heartbreak House*, and *Saint Joan*, as well as in *Back to Methuselah* itself. But the farther Shaw's thought sets out to reach, the more nearly wholesale his evasion of human meanings appears. *Back to Methuselah* disowns human meanings twice over: first, in taking the hypothetical future as a warrant for not taking the actual present really seriously; and, secondly, in stripping that future itself of any relevant human content. A 'progressive temper' reduced to such shifts can only confuse and evade. Its grasp of human ills lacks tragic absoluteness. Its associated farcical tolerances lack comic discrimination. Its very idea of redemption is a form of human surrender. To 'live on that alone'—as Shaw's Eve longs to—is to contract out of humanity altogether.

If observations like these are sound, they may help to explain the recent decline of 'Shavianism' as a cultural force; as they might also help to diagnose some still highly pertinent tensions between rival assessments of human potentiality, and within radicalism itself, in our time. But they do not imply that Shaw's theatre may now have to be written off as merely a monument of its period. Whatever the ultimate verdict on Shaw as a focal consciousness of human dilemmas should be, we only need to recall such works as *Arms and the Man, You Never Can Tell, The Devil's Disciple, Captain Brassbound's Conversion, Pygmalion, Too True to Be Good, Village Wooing*, and, supremely perhaps, *Man and Superman*, to acknowledge a comic creativeness that will always enrich men with sheer, celebrating high spirits—a subtly renewed capacity for 'these childish games—this dancing, and singing and mating'.

The presence of *Man and Superman* (1901) in such a list should help to give further definition to what is most likely to keep Shaw's drama alive. In his 1944 Postscript to *Back to Methuselah*, written as an introduction to the World's Classics edition, Shaw himself, insisting on the centrality of this work ('*Back to Methuselah* is a world classic or it is nothing'), refers to the 'pot-boilers' he had been obliged to write 'until I was rich enough to satisfy my evolutionary appetite (or, as they say, give way to my inspiration).' And the Preface to the original edition, of 1921, describes *Man and Superman* as an earlier 'dramatic parable of Creative Evolution', which, however, was 'decorated . . . too brilliantly and lavishly' by way of a compromise with 'the sweetshop view of the theatre' that was then in vogue. He now finds himself 'inspired to make a second legend of Creative Evolution without distractions and embellishments'. Shaw saw himself as essentially an 'artist-philosopher', and it is easy to understand his feelings. But for us the question must be: which, really, is the 'inspiration' in Shaw's plays? Intellectual rapier sparkle and emotional high jinks, or the charting of metaphysical depths? *Arms and the Man* or *Heartbreak House*? *Man and Superman* or *Back to Methuselah*? His ubiquitous comic exuberance, or his ultimate confrontations with 'the bottomless pit of an utterly discouraging pessimism'?

Is it not a clinching consideration that what, for 'the goal of redemption's' sake—redemption 'from the flesh'—is glibly written off as 'these childish games' is precisely what, in Shaw's most realized drama, is celebrated with vitally serious playfulness? So long as Shaw is willing to draw a bold line around his dramatic representations, in recognition of their essential abstraction from life as a whole, his work has dramatic solidity and completeness. But the more he seeks to reflect, or transcend, 'the bottomless pit', the more inadequate his drama becomes as imaginative reflection. I have suggested a possible diagnosis of these dispositions in Shaw (and in the stream of 'progressive' optimism which flows through him): an inability, or unwillingness, to focus, in relevant depth, the endemic human facts of 'heartbreak'—and pulls of the 'pit'. So long as he is content to stop short of sounding these depths, he triumphs with masterly ease. Beyond this, however, he can only unleash an unfocused, indulgent emotionalism, or shrink back into a correspondingly indulged nostalgia for total withdrawal from being human.

It is here, where Shaw is at his weakest, that the work of Sean O'Casey (1880–1964) during the twenties shows up best. Their strengths and weaknesses are strikingly complementary. O'Casey's evocations of the Irish Troubles and civil war—*The Shadow of a Gunman* (1923), *Juno and the Paycock* (1924), and *The Plough and the Stars* (1926)—are, basically, just blown-up anecdotes, with no pretension to intellectual finesse. Indeed, his handling of Dublin slum life under 'the shadow' of these political upheavals runs altogether counter to analytic niceties. His appeal lies essentially in bold juxtapositions: of character types, of situations, of naturalism and heightened forms of language, and, above all, of comic and tragic currents of tone. Most centrally, the thrust of his plays is thus towards relentlessly maturing catastrophes engulfing devious comic energies that play up against their approach. This is a type of dramatic interplay especially characteristic of our era; and we have already noted some of its potentialities and pitfalls in the context of *Heartbreak House*. O'Casey deploys it with a much more integral attunement of vision. A degree of genuine modern tragedy is thus achieved.

This achievement is, however, limited and flawed by serious bluntnesses at every level of dramatic realization. Too often O'Casey's boldness, of structure and texture, reveals not so much an uninhibited imaginative vigour as a determined manipulative demonstrativeness. Thus there is a certain mechanical quality about the ways in which the actions of *Juno and the Paycock* and *The Plough and the Stars* unfold. Everything in *Juno* is calculated to converge towards the final compound collapse: one cannot help sensing this convergence as 'calculated' in a literal sense since there is no apparent connection—either factual or thematic—between the social catastrophe of Johnny's execution by the Irregulars and the burst bubble of the expected legacy, together with the 'fallen' Mary's abandonment by Jerry. In a different way, the famous second act of *The Plough and the Stars*, interweaving an earthy comic pub scene with the grandiloquent patriotic seductions of a speaker addressing a meeting outside, is equally patently milked for its effects. And the 'pity and terror' of its conclusion—Nora's loss of her baby, her Ophelia-like madness, the news of her husband's death, and the accidental shooting of Bessie—are luxuriantly laid on. Again, there is a crucial disproportion between O'Casey's requirements for heightened expression and the quality of his 'poetic' resources. Much of the comedy draws attention to itself, like disconnected music-hall turns (Brendan Behan was to push this approach to its logical conclusion, but here it has to work within a naturalistic convention). And the absence of any framework of radical tragic stock-taking—or questioning—deprives the emotional demands so insistently made upon us of any proportionate yield of significance.

The new technical departures in *The Silver Tassie* (1928) suggest that O'Casey himself was aware of these tendencies within his work, and that he was searching for means to focus and discipline the inner imaginative thrust of his emotive assaults. The play—an outcry against the dehumanizations of the First World War—introduces Expressionist elements into an action still resting upon a naturalist groundwork. The resulting dramatic experiment is of considerable interest, but it does not resolve O'Casey's problems as a dramatist, and his subsequent work hardly adds anything essential to his standing.

II

O'Casey's problems, like Shaw's, are both in part problems of dramatic form universal to dramatists in our century. Following the great nineteenth-century naturalists, Ibsen, Strindberg, and Chekhov, but increasingly aware of imaginative needs pulling against the grain of photographic theatrical illusion, modern dramatists are thus constantly brought back to the problem of relevant form. Chekhov had created a unique, subtle method of orchestrating 'slice of life' moments, so as to generate a sort of subterranean poetry profoundly transcending its surface restrictions. It is to the standards set by him that one must inevitably refer when confronted with undertakings like *Heartbreak House* or *Juno and the Paycock*. Ibsen and Strindberg, potent as their naturalistic work can be (as in *Ghosts*, or *The Father*), were themselves in their own ways concerned to break through the limits of illusionist dramatic conventions. Strindberg's break-through was the more total and systematic; and with works like his *To Damascus* plays, *A Dream Play*, and *The Ghost Sonata* (1898-1907) he emerged as the fountainhead of dramatic Expressionism.

Strindberg's focus had been essentially introspective and metaphysical, but the Expressionist movement, especially as it developed in Germany, during and after the war, was centrally a reaction to the prevailing climate of social and cultural dissolution. Writers like Frank Wedekind (1864-1918), Ernst Toller (1893-1939), Georg Kaiser (1878-1945), and the Czech dramatist Karel Čapek (1890-1938) employed a variety of satirical shock-tactics, fantasies, and symbolic simplifications to convey their vision of communal crisis. A somewhat related movement had developed in Italy, the *teatro del grottesco*—whose 'grotesqueness' was associated with a special conjunction of private and social elements, reflected in the title of its best-known play, *The Mask and the Face*. This work, by Luigi Chiarelli (1884-1947), staged in 1916, powerfully enforces a confrontation between 'the mask' of moribund social standards and the emergent realities of personal experience. One of the characters' ironic remark, 'People should never be forced to face their own convictions', pinpoints the source of the movement's 'grotesque' doubleness of tone—its special contribution to our century's growing interchange between comic and tragic forms of perception. It was from here that Pirandello's work took its start; as Brecht's has to be seen against the background of German Expressionism.

The crucial place that Luigi Pirandello (1867-1936) holds within the development of the modern theatre may be seen in three distinct, related ways: technically, as the point where naturalism becomes fully self-conscious as a dramatic convention, and explodes against itself; socially, as implying a vision for which any sort of communal hope seems both irrelevant and illusory; and metaphysically, as a critical undercutting of the most apparently rock-bottom solidities of personal, and inter-personal, existence. Though there are other dramatists of our age who may finally be more decisive for us than

Pirandello, his impact upon our period's emerging dramatic consciousness is massive, and his challenge remains inescapable.

Pirandello's explosion of naturalism from within was most directly enacted in his plays-about-plays, *Six Characters in Search of an Author* (1921), *Each in His Own Way* (1924), and *Tonight We Improvise* (1930). The technical basis of these plays is essentially simply the projection into quasi-literal fact of the naturalist theatre's postulate that the characters we watch on the stage are real people, and an elaborate deadpan investigation of the clashing 'facts' and 'realities' thus set before us. Given that 'willing suspension of disbelief' which constitutes us a theatre audience, it is only necessary to extend the conventional fiction of real-life-reality on the stage into a fully 'real' fiction of fiction-as-real-life, to have our heads spinning with infinitely multiplying clashes of reality and appearance. The irruption of the Six Characters whose author is said to have failed to bring them to life (he 'either couldn't or wouldn't put us materially into the world of "art"') into a 'real' play-rehearsal (of one of Pirandello's own earlier plays) opens the way to a radical subversion of our footholds within the categories of being and seeming.

If this kind of assault, exposing the paradoxes of the naturalist theatre's make-believe life pretending to actual life, were all that Pirandello had to offer, his interest would be little more than technical—an intriguingly ironic culmination of the aesthetics of naturalism. But the theatre has for centuries been recognized as a deeply suggestive symbol of the world—a human creation which not only holds 'the mirror up to nature' but which is itself charged with searching potential analogies to human existence—from Jaques's stage, in *As You Like It*, where men and women 'have their exits and their entrances', Lear's 'great stage of fools', or Macbeth's 'poor player/That struts and frets his hour upon the stage', and from Calderón's *El gran teatro del mundo* (*The Great Theatre of the World*), to Anouilh's 'it's all a matter of what part you are playing' and Beckett's 'circus' or 'music-hall'. And it is the re-activating of this profound source of poetic analogies, in twentieth-century terms, that endows Pirandello's plays about naturalist plays with a much more substantial imaginative importance:

FATHER. Now just consider the fact that we [*pointing quickly to himself and to the other* FIVE CHARACTERS] as ourselves, have no other reality outside this illusion!

PRODUCER [*in utter astonishment, looking round at his actors who show the same bewildered amazement*]. And what does all that mean?

FATHER [*the ghost of a smile on his face. There is a brief pause while he looks at them all*]. As I said. . . . What other reality should we have? What for you is an illusion that you have to create, for us, on the other hand, is our sole reality. The only reality we know. [*There is a short pause. Then he takes a step or two towards the* PRODUCER *and adds*] But it's not only true in our case, you know. Just think it over. [*He looks into his eyes.*] Can you tell me who you are? [*And he stands there pointing his index finger at him.*][4]

This probing gesture, whose real target is of course our own complacent self-identification, is the central, persistent thrust within Pirandello's theatre. Its thrust is already implicit in such relatively straightforward plays as *The Pleasure of Honesty* (1917) and *The Rules of the Game* (1918), where 'the mask and the face' of Chiarelli's formula separate out as shocking and ludicrous contradictions between received social roles and personal immediacies. But in Pirandello's hands the imagery of theatrical illusion, of mask-wearing realities, of role-playing identification, is developed into a comprehensive metaphysical vision—a dramatic master-key to the human situation.

Accordingly, it is not merely that society—through its institutions, established beliefs, and traditions—imposes upon us functions and aims that are alien to the inner logic of our personal existence, but that this existence is also constantly in the process of being falsified by the images we cannot but project upon each other in our personal relations—and even upon ourselves, for the sake of self-recognition. These contradictions and falsifications are diagnosed as inevitable—built absolutely into the structure of human life. Language itself, the very medium of human awareness, communication, and self-understanding, is, thus, doubly estranging. The Father, in *Six Characters*, exclaims in despair:

How can we understand each other if into the words which I speak I put the sense and the value of things as I understand them within myself. . . . While at the same time whoever is listening to them inevitably assumes them to have the sense and value that they have for him. . . . The sense and value that they have in the world that he has within him? We think we understand one another. . . . But we never really do understand!

Given such mutual falsifications, we can only play out our lives as 'characters' helplessly interlocked in each other's mental productions:

FATHER. Look at this situation, for example! All my pity, all the pity I feel for this woman [*pointing to the* MOTHER] *she* sees as the most ferocious cruelty.

MOTHER. But you turned me out of the house!
FATHER. There! Do you hear? I turned her out! She really believed that
I was turning her out![5]

No social structure could remedy, or prevent the occurrence of, this sort of failure. For Pirandello, defects of perception and communication are so built into the structure of human existence that the only authentic alternatives open to us are either a sort of shoulders-shrugging submission to these defects, or an obsessive kicking against them verging on madness. The first of these options is pressed to its limits in *Right You Are (If You Think So)* (1917), the second in *Henry IV* (1921). *Right You Are (If You Think So)*, making a virtue of necessity, insists that there are contexts in which the cultivation of fictions may be an essential condition of decent survival (the theme can be seen as a development from Ibsen's *The Wild Duck*); *Henry IV* engages the reciprocal pressures of fact and fiction, literally, in a struggle to the death—and in maddeningly naked encounters with mortal limits.

Henry IV is surely Pirandello's most intensely charged work— one of the definitive peaks of twentieth-century drama. Its, on the face of it, almost wilfully eccentric plot—bordering, like so many of Pirandello's plots, on sheer melodrama—succeeds in distilling a profound, complex despair in the face of indubitably central human problems. A young nobleman, cheated of love, is involved in an accident that precipitates insanity. We gather that he was thrown from his horse when someone behind him—perhaps his friend, though rival in love, Baron Belcredi—treacherously caused the horse to rear. He identifies himself with the medieval German Emperor Henry IV, whom he had impersonated in a fancy-dress Carnival pageant. For twenty years he maintains a fancy-dress court which improvises meticulous re-enactments of Henry's traumatic suit to Pope Gregory VII at Canossa. The play opens when 'Henry'— significantly, we never discover his real-life name—is visited by his nephew Di Nolli, the Marchioness Matilda, whom he had wished to marry, Baron Belcredi, Donna Matilda's daughter Frida, and a psychiatrist, with a view to effecting a cure. This is to take the form of suddenly confronting the man who has become fixed in a single moment of his past—a moment identified with his role as Henry IV —with 'a sensation of the distance of time', through the double appearance of the now middle-aged Donna Matilda and of her daughter (who exactly resembles her youthful self) in the guise of the Marchioness of Canossa, in which Donna Matilda had accompanied Henry at the pageant. Thus the doctor hopes 'to set him going again, just like a watch that has stopped at a certain time', which is given a shake. But things do not go according to plan. Henry is no watch. Indeed, he is no longer the madman he has been thought to be. It emerges that some eight years ago he recovered his sanity, but—his own real passionate desires and hopes meanwhile irremediably defeated by life—he had chosen 'the pleasures of history' (where you can 'even scratch yourself in character when you feel your shoulder itching') in preference to rejoining his actual contemporaries, 'torturing themselves, in an absolute agony of anxiety, to know how things will work out'. But can this indeed be sanity? The play moves, with relentlessly growing terror and multiple shifts of clues, to its still radically equivocal conclusion, when Henry, duly 'shaken', first claims Matilda's daughter as his love—

You're mine! You're mine! Mine! Mine in my own right! [*He clasps her in his arms, laughing like a madman, while all the others cry out in terror*]—

and then, as Belcredi protests: 'Let her go! Let her go! You're not mad!', snatches a sword:

So I'm not mad, eh? Take that, you . . .! [*And he drives* LANDOLPH's *sword into* BELCREDI's *belly.*]

No summary can, however, suggest the massive, functional intricacy of the action, correlating the three temporal planes of present, personal past, and historical role-playing (itself on several planes), and the extraordinary concentration of poetic-dramatic significances thereby achieved. Pirandello's fondness for cerebral encounters has led to his frequently being coupled with Shaw. But this is a very superficial emphasis. Nothing could be further from Shaw than Pirandello's insistent, voraciously single-minded inquisitions into a central inspiring anguish. Pirandello's dramatic dialectic, at its best, offers (as T. S. Eliot said of Chapman and Donne) 'a direct sensuous apprehension of thought, or a recreation of thought into feeling'. He thus relates much more intimately to Ibsen or Strindberg—or Beckett. Indeed, in *Henry IV* we may, without strain, refer back to Shakespeare—the Shakespeare of *Troilus and Cressida* and *Hamlet*. Pirandello succeeds here in holding together, in a masterly creative unity, encounters of being and seeming, life-flow and conceptual awareness, time and arrested meanings, spontaneity and role-acting, reality as the natural and reality as art or artifice—all suspended within a maddening central limitation:

I would never wish you to think, as I have had to do, of that horrible thing which really drives you out of your mind. . . . You're there, very close to someone, looking into his eyes, just as, one day, I looked into someone's eyes . . . and you see yourself mirrored there. . . . But it's not really yourself! No, you see yourself as a beggar, standing before a door through which you will never pass. The man who goes through that door will not be you . . . you with that secret life, that world you have within you . . . the familiar world of sight and touch. . . . It will be someone quite unknown to you who will pass in at that door. . . . The man *he* sees you as . . . The one he, in his own personal, impenetrable world, sees and touches.[6]

How much in the visions of Sartre, Camus, Anouilh, T. S. Eliot, Samuel Beckett, Ionesco, or even Tennessee Williams and John Osborne is already latent in this terrible image! Do 'reality' and 'sanity' lie in determined contemplations of its mirroring windows, or in determinedly blindfold passages through its doors? Or can we authentically transcend these conditions altogether?

Contradiction, falsification, 'deafness', self-estrangement: these have always been the stuff of drama. In Pirandello, however, these endemic dramatic potentialities proclaim themselves sovereign finalities within the human tragi-comedy. It is here—even more than in his associated critique of naturalist theatrical illusion—that Pirandello constitutes the decisive turning-point of modern drama. No serious writer will henceforth be able to by-pass these proclaimed sovereignties. Many—this is one of the roots of the Theatre of the Absurd—will essentially be concerned to pay them ritual tribute. Any serious revolution against them must start from a recognition of their authentic power—and must appeal to a higher reign.

Bertolt Brecht (1898–1956) and T. S. Eliot (1888–1965) are complementary key figures in this ongoing process of human self-diagnosis in our time. Both are poets as well as dramatists, both are as consciously concerned with problems of dramatic form as with specific expressions of their visions; and what they offer in their dramatic works beyond the 'sovereignties' we have noted is sharply divergent in outlook and feeling.

Brecht's name is so closely associated with Communism that it can be surprising to discover that, in its opening phase, his work had quite a different emphasis. Although social and political facts make themselves felt almost from the start, his initial preoccupations are much more private than social. Indeed, Brecht's first play, *Baal* (1918), is wholly uninterested in social values, portraying—essentially uncritically, it seems—a poet of ravenous sensuality, whose nihilistic rebelliousness and wilfully brutal egoism are reflected in the brutal lyricism of the play. Brecht's second play, *Drums in the Night* (*Trommeln in der Nacht*), written in 1919, and set within the German Communist rising after the war, directly poses a choice between private happiness, however imperfect, salvaged from the ruins, and revolutionary self-sacrifices—and it is private values that win. But it is in the two works, *In the Jungle of Cities* (*Im Dickicht der Städte*, 1921–4)—and *Man is Man* (*Mann ist Mann*, 1924–6)— that the foundations of Brecht's creative personality are most deeply revealed.

From the bizarre, fictitious 'Chicago' of *In the Jungle of Cities* there emerges a vision not only of Brecht's own, European experience of postwar society but, more radically, a sense of intimate personal relations closely akin to writers with whom Brecht is so often supposed to have absolutely nothing in common. The play centres on an 'absurd' love–hate relationship between two men, as violent and metaphysically despairing as anything in Pirandello's vision; and indeed, as Martin Esslin has noted, it in many respects anticipates the form and burden of the drama of Beckett, Ionesco, and Adamov—or, we might add, the sado-masochistic world of Sartre. In the penultimate scene, clinching the progression of grotesque, enigmatic intensifications of the 'fight' to the death between the two men, there is a passage that might form part of the nightmare world of Henry IV. Shlink, the initial 'aggressor' in the relationship, on the point of death confesses to his 'enemy', Garga:

Man's infinite isolation makes enmity an unattainable goal. But even with the animals understanding is not possible. . . . I've observed the animals. Love, the warmth of bodies in contact, is the only mercy shown us in the darkness. But the only union is that of the organs, and it can't bridge over the cleavage made by speech. Yet they unite in order to produce beings to stand by them in their hopeless isolation. And the generations look coldly into each other's eyes.[7]

Brecht here acts unmistakably as one of the links in the line that connects Strindberg and Pirandello with our still obsessive, cumulative emphases upon human isolation and the impotence of speech. No doubt, Brecht's later work is very different, both in subject-matter and in approach, but is it not just because 'man's infinite isolation' remains so radically active within it—as a *challenge* at least—that it is able to go on challenging us, as Shaw cannot?

Thus, together with *Man is Man*, which follows it, *In the Jungle of Cities* defines Brecht's sense of 'the human condition' from which his later work starts. *In the Jungle of Cities* simply declares man's essential, insupportable citizenship of the jungle. *Man is Man* postulates a complementary, in a sense perhaps contradictory, diagnosis: that things are never simply what they are; that man is essentially a response to his city's conditions. So totally is he a product of particular circumstances, so exhaustively is he reducible to his social roles, that the timidly inoffensive labourer, Galy Gay, can be processed before our eyes into a prodigy of soldierly prowess. The personality-change is accomplished, with farcical plausibility, by three soldiers in imperial India who are obliged to produce a substitute for a fourth who got left behind while robbing a temple with them. (A complementary episode features a sergeant who cures his own incurable sexual compulsions by self-castration.) The implications are irreducibly equivocal. If man is infinitely open to human manipulation, is this a fact for better or for worse? And, in view of the findings of *In the Jungle of Cities*—and, for that matter, of the sergeant's final solution of his sexual problems in *Man is Man* itself—how far is it, after all, implied that man is master of his fate, how far does the jungle appear as in fact built into manhood as such—including man's capacity for asserting himself over his manhood?

One could, indeed, say that it is these equivocal emphases of Brecht's early work that generate the developing tensions of his entire career. At best, Brecht is able to draw from these tensions a power and authority far beyond any merely didactic projection of conscious ideas. At worst, they are liable to tempt him into quagmires of shifting irony. *The Threepenny Opera* (1928), by which Brecht rose to international recognition, manifests both these tendencies side by side.

At this stage, Brecht has clearly committed himself to a drama of social purpose, and, going with this, a search for appropriate theatrical methods. The techniques of 'epic theatre', which Brecht took over and developed from innovators like the Communist producer Erwin Piscator, are stratagems to disrupt any self-sufficient dramatic empathy—whether on the actors' part or the audience's—and to encourage a distancing critical responsiveness in place of a 'spell-bound' emotional self-identification. Open-ended, episodic construction, short-cuts in exposition and character-drawing, non-realistic décor, loosely inserted musical interludes, projected scene and song titles, and a battery of incidental '*Verfremdungs* effects' (to 'give distance to' or 'make strange' what we habitually take for granted)—all confess, and insist on, the theatre's theatricality; they explode any temptation to naturalist illusionism—as Pirandello exploded (as well as exploited) naturalist illusion for his own purposes.

The Threepenny Opera employs a further, central control of its implications: a satirical irony rooted in parody. The ironic satire already at work in John Gay's eighteenth-century 'ballad-opera', *The Beggar's Opera*, is subjected to a savage and wildly comic redoubling, so that Gay's genteel-lower-class mirror of an aristocratic society (and its fastidious operatic culture) is shaped into a *lumpenproletariat* reflector of the capitalist jungle (and *its* operatic and literary tastes). The ebbing and flowing fortunes of Macheath—gangboss, bigamist, and insatiable frequenter of brothels—and the complementary organization of beggars ruled, with something of an ecclesiastic touch, by his father-in-law, Jonathan Jeremiah Peachum—rationalizing social misery into a sort of monopolistic milking of 'human pity' (or guilt feelings)—hold the mirror up to more familiar manifestations of the free enterprise ethos. The whole liberal economy, the play suggests—with a levity as essentially serious as Ben Jonson's comic hyperboles in *Volpone*—is compounded of criminal lawlessness and moral hypocrisy.

'We will not keep the people waiting,' says Macheath in his affecting set-piece when he seems irreversibly destined for execution (though, a few moments later, a Mounted Messenger from the queen will announce a last-minute 'rescue' for the finale):

Ladies and gentlemen, you see here the vanishing representative of a vanishing class. We bourgeois artisans, who work with honest jemmies on the cash boxes of small shopkeepers, are being swallowed up by large concerns backed by the banks. What is a picklock to a bank share? What is the burgling of a bank to the founding of a bank? What is the murder of a man to the employment of a man? Fellow citizens, I herewith take my leave of you. . . .[8]

Not only the structure of economic relations: the entire culture built around these relations—religiosity, art, government, justice, friendship, love, sexuality, family life—are shown as carrying within themselves corresponding self-contradictions, compromises, and betrayals. These many-levelled ironic significances continually reveal themselves as the work's hidden pursuit, teasing us with its implacable ferreting out of only too patently familiar targets, or luring us into outrageous moral booby-traps. For, of course, it is we, the audience, who are most directly (and most insidiously) under attack—above all, through the very form of the work. As Brecht himself puts it in one of his notes to *The Threepenny Opera*: 'It is a sort of summary of what the spectator in the theatre wishes to see of life. Since, however, he sees, at the same time, certain things that he does not wish to see and thus sees his wishes not only fulfilled but also criticized (he sees himself not as a subject, but as an object), he is, in theory, able to give the theatre a new function.'

To complete this insidious dramatic superweapon, Brecht suspends his narrative within a sequence of songs and ballads, themselves partly ironic in implication, partly impinging as direct, prophetic calls to revolutionary repentance. These, as set to Kurt Weill's potent music, are—whatever the theory—certainly apt to cast 'spells' of their own. Vulgarly full-blooded, precious, jaunty, and poignant by turns, they strike home with the weight of the whole 'savage farce' behind them, climaxing in a number of direct evocations of smouldering rebellion. It is not unduly paradoxical to suggest that, with Weill's brashly ominous orchestration, these songs initiate us into a sort of cult—a ritual participation in intense, dissonant awarenesses: shock, indignation, guilt, an almost apocalyptic terror, and a revivalist hunger and thirst for justice and human renewal.

We cannot doubt that we have here a major break-through in the drama of our time. Both in vision and in technique, Brecht, assisted by Weill, is pushing beyond the frontiers of previous dramatic worlds—including the worlds of Shaw's 'progressive Victorian temper' and of Pirandello's fixations on human self-imprisonment; and so, too, beyond Brecht's own brooding upon 'man's infinite isolation' only a few years before. Nevertheless, *The Threepenny Opera* is, in several ways, a flawed achievement. Its emergent revolutionary commitments are too trigger-happy in identifying each and every tragic human fact with remediable social circumstances, while at the same time it continues to recognize apparently permanent fatalities in human existence—without acknowledging the resulting contradiction (unable, therefore, to hold these visions together within a coherent dialectical structure). And the extraordinary technical prodigality of the work has its own dangers in this context, its rich complexities aiding and abetting this underlying confusion— with apparently irresistible invitations to emotional or moral assent apparently cancelled by devious hints of satirical mockery, satirized

characters suddenly holding forth with the most direct authorial
licence, one elusive complex of ironies impenetrably double-crossing
another.

But the measure of Brecht's success can be kept most sharply in
view by bearing in mind on the one hand the various limits he broke
through, and on the other hand the perils of conventional didactic
art—not least those of 'socialist realism'. In this light, even the
grave indisciplines within *The Threepenny Opera* are marks of a
deeply active integrity and creative potential. The drive to diagnose,
and to incite to action, is not allowed to short-circuit perceptions
beyond Brecht's own urgently favoured theoretical model. The
tensions originally staked out by the respective emphases of *In the
Jungle of Cities* and *Man is Man* are (however unwillingly, perhaps)
kept in being—and, indeed, these tensions are going to enforce
themselves with increasing centrality in Brecht's most mature work,
of the period just before and during the Second World War—most
directly in *The Good Woman of Setzuan*. It is precisely their dialectic
within Brecht's later plays, partly by direct design, partly in more
subterranean ways—that ensures Brecht's pivotal stature, with a
handful of other writers, within the consciousness of our age.

The great plays written between 1937 and 1945, *The Life of
Galileo*, *Mother Courage and her Children*, *The Good Woman of
Setzuan*, *Puntila* (*Herr Puntila und sein Knecht Matti*), and *The
Caucasian Chalk Circle*, only began to make themselves properly
felt in the years following the war. Meanwhile, Brecht passed
through a period of systematic ideological didacticism. The idiom
of *The Threepenny Opera*—re-employed in *Happy End* and *Rise
and Fall of the Town of Mahagonny* (both 1928–9)—gave way to
what Brecht himself called *Lehrstücke*, teaching-plays, whose
avowed 'purpose' was to assist in the education of revolutionary
left-wing groups; and later, in exile, to a number of anti-fascist
works, including the naturalistic *Fear and Misery of the Third
Reich* (1935–8). Some of the *Lehrstücke*, the most important of
which is *The Measures Taken* (*Die Massname*), of 1930, are of
great power, with a stylized concentration modelled on the Japanese Nō play tradition. Here it must suffice to note Brecht's repeated insistence upon the total subordination of individual human
rights and responsibilities to an impersonal social 'necessity' un-
comfortably suggestive of Stalinism. In *The Measures Taken* a
Communist agent, whose irrepressible human compassion en-
dangers three of his comrades during a vital secret mission, is shot
by them with his consent—and with the subsequent approval of

the party on their return. Under one aspect these resolute ideological certainties can be seen as pointing to the persistent human
dilemmas of *The Good Woman of Setzuan*. Under another, the
inconvenient comrade's readiness for his own disposal touches on
questions concerning the rationale of self-sacrifice—such as
Kattrin's death in *Mother Courage* will keep in view. Brecht seems to
have arrived at an ideological 'solution' to every problem. But it is
the problems, rather than the solutions, that take hold of and survive
in us—and survive within Brecht's own continuing dramatic
inquisitions.

It is here that T. S. Eliot can be seen as a relevant complement
to Brecht. Though sharply opposed in moral, political, and cosmic
outlook, they both—from their different diagnoses of cultural
failure—are determined to expose all residual illusions and evasions,
to break through beyond states such as those the Chorus in *Murder
in the Cathedral* describes as 'Living and partly living'. There are
even some telling parallels in their dramatic techniques—at any
rate up to *Murder in the Cathedral* (1935) and *The Family Reunion*
(1939). (Eliot's later plays, to be examined in Volume III, are quite
another matter.)

Long before he entered the theatre, Eliot had been much concerned with the idea of a reborn poetic drama. As a critic, he
constantly returned to stress the inherent mutual relevance of
poetry and drama. For, on the one hand, poetic drama can be a
direct instrument of a poetic vision—and an indispensable link
between the poet and a wider audience. And, on the other hand, a
theatre dissociated from poetry may be emotionally and spiritually
deprived. More especially, the 'prose'—or rather, the prosaic
imitation of 'fact'—which constitutes the conventions of the naturalistic theatre, is perilously cut off from imaginative resources,
mechanically recording the surfaces of human behaviour, or lending
itself to an illustrative role within some discursive social-thesis
framework.

Eliot's poetic practice itself points consistently in the direction
of a full-scale poetic drama. From his early monologues, 'Prufrock'
and 'Portrait of a Lady', to 'Gerontion' and the elaborate interplay
of voices and memories in *The Waste Land*, his poetry is already
intensely dramatic. 'The Hollow Men' and the 'Ariel' poems may
be seen as dramatic poems of conversion, obliquely related to
Sweeney Agonistes (1926–7), an experimental, fragmentary 'melodrama' (as Eliot himself describes it), hovering between secular

satire and religious terror mystery, which impresses itself with a
haunting, disciplined flamboyance of its own. *Ash Wednesday*
evolves a liturgical idiom (which is, at the same time, intensely
personal)—put to use, in a simplified and severely impersonal form,
in the sermon-like pageant sequence *The Rock* (1934), to which
Eliot contributed a series of Choruses. A year later *Murder in the
Cathedral* was staged—or, one could almost say, ritually enacted—
at the Canterbury Festival, in the Cathedral's Chapter House: an
ideal occasion for Eliot's full emergence as a Christian poetic
dramatist.

At any rate, the occasion was ideal for achieving that fusion of
poetic modernity, classical dramatic resources, and Christian
perceptions in a post-Christian age which is of the essence of Eliot's
aims as a dramatist. The re-enactment of the martyrdom of Thomas
Becket in close proximity to its actual historical location is comparable to Aeschylus's *Oresteia*, celebrating Athens's reception of the
Furies as transfigured participants in its civilized system of justice.
And just as Aeschylus's drama ends with a procession out of the
theatre drawing in members of the audience, *Murder in the Cathedral*
is rounded off with a *Te Deum* and Chorus clearly embracing the
audience in its thanksgiving and rejoicing in a renewed faith.

Formally, *Murder in the Cathedral* is carved with a Greek
statuesqueness, astonishingly at ease with its associated medieval
morality tone and modern attack—with something of Shaw and
Pirandello and Brecht about it. It is, one might say, a literary re-
affirmation of a ritual tradition in decline; as Brecht's work so often
turns into a sort of counter-ritual, prefiguring a future that calls for
creation. In this sense, neither Eliot nor Brecht stands within a fully
operative culture. And both, caring not only for personal integrity
in such a world but for the renewed integrity of a whole way of life,
are driven to technical innovations—or revivals—which will re-
enfranchise the audience within the drama, and, conversely, allow
the dramatist to enter into direct, dialectical commerce with it. This
is why allegory (as well as 'ritual') is re-emergent in both writers;
and why, where Brecht has recourse to flaunted theatricalities,
ironic equivocations, and frontally direct lyrical assaults in full
musical strength, Eliot offers a parallel range of stratagems: the
four Tempters, verbal repetitions, the structurally central sermon
Thomas delivers, straight at the audience, a few days before his
death, the farcical, aggressively anachronistic scene in which the
murderers step forward to justify themselves—again straight at the
audience—in outrageous twentieth-century clichés, or the moment

when Thomas, having surmounted his temptations—including that
of 'the greatest treason:/To do the right deed for the wrong reason'—
turns his mind outwards again, suddenly turns on *us*:

> I know
> What yet remains to show you of my history
> Will seem to most of you at best futility,
> Senseless self-slaughter of a lunatic,
> Arrogant passion of a fanatic.
> I know that history at all times draws
> The strangest consequence from remotest cause.
> But for every evil, every sacrilege,
> Crime, wrong, oppression, and the axe's edge,
> Indifference, exploitation, you, and you,
> And you, must all be punished. So must you . . . [9]

Thus our participation in the pattern of sacrificial rebirth—where
'action is suffering/And suffering is action'—is both vicarious, by
identification with the Chorus, and immediate, as we are increasingly
implicated in 'an eternal action, an eternal patience' wherein 'we
can rejoice and mourn at once and for the same reason'.

Murder in the Cathedral is, by any standards, an outstanding work
of art. Apart from a few local lapses—in one or two places the
Chorus's language breaks disconcertingly loose from the play's taut
economy of structure and speech—it achieves a rare and original
perfection, enacting vast, elusive significances with a distilled,
sharp-edged lucidity. (Placed by its side, Shaw's *Saint Joan*, for
all its forensic vitality, appears as luxuriant and soft-centred.) And
though, as we have seen, the play owes much to the special conditions of its first performance, it is not at all dependent upon these
conditions. Again and again it has proved its power to generate its
own equivalents to these conditions, whatever the actual context of
performance, recruiting its audiences to re-create them. In these
terms, it is unsurpassed.

Nevertheless, Eliot felt that, both in matter and form, *Murder in
the Cathedral* was too essentially a thing of its own to be able to lead
the way to further developments. Its remote, costume-dress setting,
its quasi-liturgical atmosphere, the whole overtly 'religious drama'
approach (whatever the bridges thrown across towards our contemporary, secular world)—all this seemed to him dramatically a dead
end. What, he felt, was now needed was a meeting of sacred and
secular meanings on more neutral, and on contemporary, ground—
preferably, indeed, altogether avoiding the use of any ready-made
Christian sign-posts and references. For not only is 'religious drama'

in an increasingly secular culture liable to come through only to believers; but, in so far as it seems to offer itself as a specialized Christian cultural package, it will have less and less vital relevance even to Christian believers themselves—who, after all, inhabit the same pluralist world as their secular humanist contemporaries.

Accordingly, *The Family Reunion* (1939) seeks to break through towards a form that can give equal dramatic presence to these divergent contemporary options, and bring them into decisive confrontation. The return of Harry, Lord Monchensey, after many years of absence abroad, to his family country home, his critical encounters both with members of his family and with his own problematic identity, and his decision to leave again immediately— which precipitates his mother's death through heart-failure—form the groundwork of a dramatic structure as essentially complex and riddling as that of *Murder in the Cathedral* is simple. Harry's murder of his wife (in desire, at least; there are strong suggestions that her death may actually have been an accident) is illuminated by deeper and deeper insights into his own and his family's past (the play's method, in this respect, seems clearly indebted to Ibsen), and ultimately connects up in his consciousness with hints of a universal disorder—and universal potentialities of redemption.

It is these hints, and their intricate convergence towards a pattern revealing 'not a story of detection,/Of crime and punishment, but of sin and expiation' which form the poetic heart of the play. But it is no less essential to its poetic purpose that these animating religious meanings should have to emerge from, and beat against, 'a story of detection' set within a *milieu* of modern unbelief, invincibly resistant to the signals transcending its secular commonplaces.

Eliot, therefore, has recourse to a number of further experimental devices, which determine the play's special dramatic impact: a half-submerged structural parallel to Aeschylus's *Oresteia*; a sharp disjunction of characters into sheep and goats of awareness or lack of awareness; a spasmodic gathering of four of the least 'aware' characters into an *ad hoc* Chorus of invincible spiritual banality; and a continual interplay of shifting levels of poetic intensity, reflecting corresponding shifts of vision. All this serves the single, strategic purpose of enforcing the confrontation of rival conceptions of 'reality', so as to bring the most banal modes of consciousness into relation to the most mysterious. It insidiously sets out to trap our contemporary common-sense reflexes—eroding our confidence in the solidity of isolated 'facts' with signals from the roots of our Western inheritance, and threatening (if we should fail to rise to the challenge) to convict us ignominiously of complicity with the Chorus.

It is not surprising that such a complex dramatic strategy might be in danger of becoming impenetrable. And since, on top of this, there are indications that the play is at once concerned to give vent to perceptions intimately private to the author and to preserve this privacy under a protective dramatic mask, this danger is vastly multiplied; while, at the same time, the two most 'aware' characters —Harry and Agatha—are inclined to become so shrilly over-assertive that they are liable to appear essentially as mystery-mongering snobs. One cannot, therefore, help having some sympathy with those who are repelled by the play.

Whether such dislike is warranted or no, it is a crucial fact in the history of modern drama that Eliot himself came to feel radically dissatisfied with this play. For, coupled with his sense that *Murder in the Cathedral* 'was a dead end', his own strictures against *The Family Reunion* (set out in his Spencer Memorial Lecture, 'Poetry and Drama', of 1951) led him to drastic changes of approach in his last three plays, written between 1949 and 1958. Thus, he found the play permeated by 'a failure of adjustment between the Greek story and the modern situation. I should either have stuck closer to Aeschylus or else taken a great deal more liberty with his myth.' Also, he had fallen out of sympathy with his hero—who now struck him 'as an insufferable prig'. He doubted whether his intermittent Chorus of minor characters and two scenes involving Harry —'lyrical duets', in a special kind of verse, 'beyond character'—were workable. And he concluded that, in general, the verse forms employed were unsuitable for the purposes of a modern poetic drama—being too obtrusively 'poetic' and at times insufficiently integrated with the action.

Eliot was undeniably right with regard to his handling of the *Oresteia* theme and the characterization of Harry. But it is at any rate open to doubt whether he may not have been unjust to himself in his assessment of *The Family Reunion*'s Chorus and verse idioms; and, similarly, whether *Murder in the Cathedral* really need have been the 'dead-end' Eliot took it to be. Indeed, it may be held that his greatest dramatic achievements lie precisely here: that *Murder in the Cathedral* not only remains his finest play, but might—subject to relevant adjustments—still serve as a formal prototype; and that *The Family Reunion*, too, with all its faults, is sufficiently impressive —precisely in its many-levelled poetic form and choric conventions in a modern setting—to be both worthy of intrinsic admiration and to remain a potential model for further developments. In the light of the resulting alternatives, represented by his *The Cocktail Party*, *The Confidential Clerk*, and *The Elder Statesman*, Eliot's retreat from *Murder in the Cathedral* and *The Family Reunion* may in fact be seen as a major set-back for modern drama.

Eliot had come to believe that 'if the poetic drama is to reconquer its place, it must . . . enter into overt competition with prose drama':

What we have to do is to bring poetry into the world in which the audience lives and to which it returns when it leaves the theatre; not to transport the audience into some imaginary world totally unlike its own, an unreal world in which poetry is tolerated. What I should hope might be achieved, by a generation of dramatists having the benefit of our experience, is that the audience should find, at the moment of awareness that it is hearing poetry, that it is saying to itself: '*I* could talk in poetry too!' Then we should not be transported into an artificial world; on the contrary, our own sordid, dreary daily world would be suddenly illuminated and transfigured.[10]

At first sight, this has great force; and it certainly locates with clarity the central problem of modern dramatic form—which is merely a special aspect of the hiatus in modern culture generally between 'prose' and 'poetry': between facts and meanings, surface 'realities' and 'real' human truths, human limits and the heroic, secularism and sacred claims. But the problem cannot be met by an 'overt competition' which actually just seems to disown the hiatus. Indeed, to what purpose should poetic drama pretend to walk on as prose, at a time when 'prose drama' is itself so largely intent on pushing beyond naturalistic perceptions? What precisely does 'prose drama' mean in this context? Brecht's kind of theatrical shock-treatment of 'our own sordid, dreary daily world'? Or Pirandello's shattered naturalistic mirror of 'the world in which the audience lives'? Expressionism? O'Casey's 'poetic' stage-Dublin vernacular? Or Shaw's dramatic prose—the Shaw whom Eliot had once described as a stillborn poet?

III

The most basically naturalistic dramatist of major importance in this period is Eugene O'Neill (1888–1953). Is *this* the type of 'prose drama' to which Eliot's programme would assimilate contemporary poetic drama? Hardly. (A much more likely candidate would seem to be Noel Coward! Though whether such a starting-point could be said to avoid transporting us into an 'artificial world' is another question.) A study of O'Neill's career—both its successes and its failings—should, however, throw further light on the fallacy behind Eliot's conclusions.

For Eugene O'Neill, too, though a 'prose dramatist', sought to 'illuminate' and 'transfigure' 'our own sordid, dreary daily world'. Indeed, in a phrase strikingly akin to Eliot's emphases, he once spoke of his concern 'to see the transfiguring nobility of tragedy, in as near the Greek sense as one can grasp it, in seemingly the most ignoble, debased lives' (letter to Thomas Hobson Quinn). It is this, closely related to his often avowed commitment to dramatizing 'mystery', that most sharply marks off O'Neill from other American dramatists of the period such as Elmer Rice and Clifford Odets, and would seem to place him in the great line of Ibsen, Strindberg, and Pirandello.

But O'Neill's metaphysical aims are by no means consistently realized; to some critics they in fact seem only a symptom of blown-up ambitions. In the letter just referred to O'Neill continues:

And just here is where I am a most confirmed mystic, too, for I'm always, always trying to interpret Life in terms of lives, never just lives in terms of characters. I'm always acutely conscious of the Force behind (Fate, God, our biological past creating our present, whatever one calls it— Mystery certainly) and of the one eternal tragedy of Man in his glorious, self-destructive struggle to make the Force express him instead of being, as an animal is, an infinitesimal incident in its expression. And my profound conviction is that this is the only subject worth writing about. . . .

Quoting this passage, Eric Bentley, in his incisive essay, 'Trying to Like O'Neill', asks with a pertinent astringency just what O'Neill's phrases mean:

Reading them several times over, we find that we could give them a meaning—but without any assurance that it is O'Neill's. What is interpreting 'Life in terms of lives' and what is 'mystical' about it? What does it mean to be 'expressed' by a Force—as against being an incident in 'its expression'? Isn't O'Neill comforting himself with verbiage? For what connection is there—beyond the external ones of *Mourning Becomes Electra*—between his kind of drama and the Greek? How could one be ennobled by identifying oneself with any of his characters?[11]

These questions probe all that is most suspect in O'Neill. The plays themselves, just as much as O'Neill's stated aims, constantly force them upon us. And yet, is it not evident that O'Neill's career includes moments of authentic 'transfiguring' tragic grandeur?

It is a career of extraordinary scope—in subject-matter, technique, and degree of achievement. Between 1914, when he began his series of one-act plays, *S. S. Glencairn*, and his last completed work, *A Moon for the Misbegotten* (1943), O'Neill continually alternated between theatrical naturalism and a variety of stylistic reactions against (as he once put it) 'the banality of surfaces'. Both his concern to exhibit the interaction of obscure, subconscious forces in human life and his insistent, shifting metaphysical searches, led him to cut methodically through 'surfaces'. Thus *The Emperor Jones* (1920), *The Hairy Ape* (1921), and *All God's Chillun Got Wings* (1923) deploy bold Expressionist stage imagery, sound effects, and speech conventions—side by side with O'Neill's characteristic reproduction of closely observed American dialects and personality 'surfaces'; *The Great God Brown* (1925) separates out its characters into social and psychological types, overlaid by removable—and even interchangeable—masks, on Pirandellian lines; *Lazarus Laughed* (1926) is a bulging Nietzschean morality spectacle; *Strange Interlude* (1926) qualifies its dialogue with asides and interior monologues, at a length which required its New York production in 1928 to run from 5.30 to 11 p.m. (including an interlude for dinner); *Mourning Becomes Electra* (1930) elaborates its Civil War parallel to the Oresteia cycle with a scrupulous 'banality of surfaces' —and at vastly greater length than Eliot was to require in *The Family Reunion*; and *Days Without End* (1934), a drama of religious conversion, has a hero literally split into two, until his final arrival at a crucifix in a church. But naturalism retains a steady grip upon O'Neill's work—not only in reproducing the 'surfaces' he set out to cut through, but often directly, as a dominant principle. It is there, from the start, in his one-act plays of the sea and remains dominant in *Anna Christie* (1921), *Desire Under the Elms* (1925), *Ah, Wilderness!* (1933), *The Iceman Cometh* (1939), *Long Day's Journey into Night* (1940–1), and *A Moon for the Misbegotten* (1943) —though non-naturalistic elements enter into some of these in various degrees.

O'Neill's themes reflect his insistent, desperate quest for alternatives to his lost Catholic faith (or, in *Days Without End*, a fugitive *rapprochement* with this faith). And, notwithstanding a certain lack of intellectual cutting-edge—and his tendency to compensate for this lack with trite mystery-mongering and pretentious histrionics— which often impaired, or even undid, his work, there is a core of authentic tragic intensity and cosmic seriousness.

Two recurrent emphases in O'Neill's work may help to define

this core. The first is a sense of intolerable enclosure. This already has a double realization in *The Emperor Jones*: in the factual, spatio-temporal closing in of a man-hunt, at night in a forest, to the accompaniment of an unceasing, steadily quickening tom-tom beat; and intensively, in a sequence of Expressionist terrors within the fleeing Negro dictator's mind, culminating in potent evocations of primordial entrapment—which first identify him with a ship-load of African slaves, crushed together under 'a low ceiling about five feet from the ground', swaying together in unison to the rhythm of the tom-tom, wailing in naked desolation; and at last, still further back in time, casting him as a chosen sacrificial victim in a Congolese rite, pulsing and pressing towards the edge of a crocodile-haunted river. *The Hairy Ape*—an Expressionist parable about human homelessness in industrial civilization and, ultimately, within the universe itself—opens in the 'cramped space in the bowels of a ship, imprisoned by white steel' where the stokers, crushed down by the ceiling, emit 'a confused, inchoate uproar, swelling into a sort of unity, a meaning—the bewildered, furious, baffled defiance of a beast in a cage'; and later shifts to the stokehole, where, against 'the monotonous throbbing beat of the engines' and a conjunction of other noises, the men are 'outlined in silhouette in the crouching, inhuman attitudes of chained gorillas'. Eventually the aroused stoker, Yank—following his abortive efforts to come to terms with the alien alternative of sophisticated New York—lands himself in prison, whose atmosphere is strongly evoked; and, on his release, visits a zoo and liberates a gorilla—who hugs him to death, and shuts the cage on his expiring body. Again, *All God's Chillun Got Wings* underwrites the neurotic conflicts between a young Negro and his white wife with images of social confinement (at their wedding they have to plow through 'two racial lines on each side of the gate, rigid and unyielding, staring across at each other with bitter hostile eyes') and of domestic contraction (as their marriage builds up its pressures, their home shrinks and shrinks, as in an Ionesco play, until the ceiling 'barely clears the people's heads' and 'the furniture and the characters appear enormously magnified'). In *Desire Under the Elms* the claustrophobia is rural and cosmic: the elms of the title brood with a 'sinister maternity' over a New England farmhouse, trailing their branches over its roof; while the characters—trapped between Puritan harshness and irrepressibly insurgent passions (so that the youngest son's eyes 'remind one of a wild animal's in captivity')—constantly find themselves staring at the sky, whether with 'puzzled awe', or 'a numbed appreciation', 'rebelliously', 'with hard defiant eyes', or crying: 'God A'mighty, call from the dark!' Emotional and spiritual claustrophobia is, again, what lies behind the 'white Greek temple portico' of the Mannons' house in *Mourning Becomes Electra* ('Each time I come back after being away', says the Clytemnestra figure, Christine, 'it appears more like a sepulchre! The "whited" one of the Bible—!') and, in direct opposition to its Aeschylean prototype, the trilogy ends with an ultimate shutting in—or burial alive—Lavinia's (Electra's):

I'm the last Mannon. I've got to punish myself! Living alone here with the dead is a worse act of justice than death or prison! I'll never go out or see anyone! I'll have the shutters nailed close so no sunlight can ever get in. . . . It takes the Mannons to punish themselves for being born! . . . You go now and close the shutters and nail them tight.[12]

A decade later, among O'Neill's last plays, we return to the same kind of imaginative emphasis. *The Iceman Cometh* is set, throughout, in a drinking-den, the habitat of a group of psychological exiles who are virtual fixtures there—though it is the 'real' world outside, rather than their 'pipe-dream' saloon, that, in effect, closes in upon them. And *Long Day's Journey into Night* takes place in a single room of an isolated summer home, enveloped in deepening fog (as well as night) as the play approaches its conclusion.

To this instinctive, and often intensely potent, evocation of physical, psychological, and spiritual entrapment, O'Neill's drama joins a sense of relentlessly deepening causal perspectives, defining the present (and future) as the revealed compulsions of the past. This Ibsenite—and classical Greek—sense of the direct, controlling presentness of the past is as basic to works like *The Emperor Jones* or *The Hairy Ape* (whose technique of stringing together discrete dramatic tableaux is, in some ways, much closer to Büchner or Wedekind) as to *Mourning Becomes Electra* or *Long Day's Journey into Night*, which are directly continuous with Greek and Ibsenite methods of 'exhuming the past'. O'Neill can be impressive in both these modes. But he is constantly in danger of overstretching himself. At his best he offers genuine modern tragic perceptions, interpreting 'Life in terms of lives'. But at his (unfortunately frequent) worst he falls back on biological, social, or psychoanalytic commonplaces in place of dramatic insight, melodramatic bludgeoning in place of tragic penetration, or mechanical, wilful pointers to larger 'meanings' in place of emergent patterns of meaning.

Thus, O'Neill is usually on much safer ground where he is simply projecting his sense of life as a trap than in his efforts to trace the trap's origins and significance (or to point the way towards escape). He is at his worst not only in works like *The Great God Brown, Lazarus Laughed*, and *Days Without End* but, even in plays that have much to commend them, such as *The Hairy Ape, All God's Chillun Got Wings*, and *Desire Under the Elms*, precisely at those points where diagnostic emphases take over. *The Hairy Ape* has a concentrated original power which very remarkably anticipates the idiom of Beckett and Ionesco. Thus it survives its tiresomely literal plugging of its man-the-too-ape-tied-advancer motive, but just misses being the great pioneer work it might have been. *All God's Chillun Got Wings* mingles its strengths and weaknesses much more drastically. On the sociological plane, it has an uncanny prophetic grasp of those aspects of the American colour problem that, in our own time, were to give rise to Black separatism. And, technically, as already noted, it too sports elements of Ionescian stage imagery. But it rides its miscegenation theme to death; irrelevantly surrounds it with stock problem-of-evil questions; and rounds off its increasingly melodramatic conflict with one of the most sentimentally facile last-minute resolutions in all drama. The balance of achievement in *Desire Under the Elms* is again more positive. It is a measure of its success that a plot which, in summary, could hardly avoid sounding like melodrama pure and simple in fact elicits truly tragic resonances. But, just as *The Hairy Ape* is marred by its obtrusive biological moralizing, so *Desire Under the Elms* overplays its Freudian explication of an illicit sexual passion in terms of a dead mother's continuing influence (a mixture of Oedipal drives, cosmic fatality, and plain spookish hoo-ha).

O'Neill's insistent concern, then, with 'the Force behind' human lives ('Fate, God, our biological past creating our present, whatever one calls it—Mystery certainly') somehow lacks a proportionate sureness of resources. The more determined he is to define the 'Mystery', the more blotted—or else wilfully touched up—his dramatic definitions are apt to become. This appears most fully in *Mourning Becomes Electra*—in many ways his most ambitious work—in which so many of the tendencies we have been noting converge. We have seen how rooted in immediate personal awarenesses is O'Neill's sense of tragic limits, and his 'Greek' (and Ibsenite) probing of fatalities pressing in from the past. Yet when, in *Mourning Becomes Electra*, he directly addresses himself to parallelling Aeschylus's trilogy of an inherited archetypal disorder with a sequence of unusual crimes and punishments in an American stately home, the effect is simply to sensationalize 'banality' while confusing a jumble of well-worn modern commonplaces with ancient religious mysteries. A background of Puritan guilt-consciousness, an exhaustive criss-cross of incestuous attractions, and an ominous stress on the characters' mask-like resemblances to each other, set the scene for a chain of murderous compulsions. But they are the stuff of melodramatic extremism, not of tragic extremity.

Nevertheless, O'Neill vindicates his pursuit of 'Mystery'—not only in qualified successes like *The Hairy Ape* and *Desire Under the Elms* but, at least twice in his career, in fully achieved realizations of his sense of tragic fatality. At one end of his career, it seems to me, *The Emperor Jones* (though its form is altogether remote from anything we could fit into the established category, 'tragedy') is much more than a theatrical *tour de force*. It is indeed, through and through, an achievement of the theatrical imagination—its incantatory sounds and movements, and sequence of deepening nightmare states largely undercutting articulate language. But its theatrical potency is an index of genuine, primitively articulate intuitions. Perky common-sense self-sufficiencies crack and crumble in a forest of 'formless fears'—'Woods, is you tryi' to put somethin' ovah on me?' And deeper and deeper traces of buried traumas, ultimately continuous with an inherited communal anguish, are activated to paroxysm as the present catastrophe closes in. This simple, plotless structure—almost the whole play is at one and the same time simply a catastrophe throbbing towards its finish and, conversely, a simple regress of antecedents towards an ultimate origin—generates an almost mythical suggestiveness. It is as if O'Neill had here almost accidentally stumbled upon what he was to go on searching for, with such strenuousness, throughout his career: an archetypally active tragedy. The fatal conjunctions which *The Hairy Ape* protests (in an idiom halfway between didactic melodrama and the coming conventions of the Theatre of the Absurd) and which *Desire Under the Elms* and *Mourning Becomes Electra* seek to retrace by reference to Greek prototypes (tacitly, and generically, in the former case; by sustained, specific elaboration in the latter), *The Emperor Jones* recreates—with a wholly modern, but also timeless, economy and directness.

It was not until towards the end of his work for the theatre that O'Neill was to find again a comparable perfection of expression. And when he did so, in *Long Day's Journey into Night*, this was at once an utterly opposite kind of undertaking and one that bears remarkably close analogies to the inner imaginative structure of *The Emperor Jones*. *The Emperor Jones* is anthropological, historically discursive, and strung out between collective and purely solitary experiences (by-passing the whole dimension of personal relations); while *Long Day's Journey into Night* is intimately domestic, classically unified, and—notwithstanding its great length—a distilled single movement of compulsively interlocking love–hate miseries. Or rather, this tragic impetus, among four members of a single family, towards a more and more lucidly intolerable interdependence, is counterpointed by a backward movement—of recrimination and self-diagnosis—that finally coincides, in its ultimate revelations, with the definitive night and fog into which they are 'journeying'. At the same time the drama contracts from dialogue (however tortuously knotted) and drinking rituals among the three men (spiralling towards alcoholic desperation) into the absolute solitude of soliloquy—and of soliloquy appallingly witnessed by those excluded. The last scene of the play thus clinches, and recapitulates, the whole tangle of relationships as a journey into soliloquy—the benighting relapse of a drug-addict—and finally locks the past and the present within a single continuum of endemic catastrophe: 'That was in the winter of senior year', Mary concludes her drugged total recall.

Then in the spring something happened to me. Yes, I remember. I fell in love with James Tyrone and was so happy for a time.
  (*She stares before her in a sad dream.* TYRONE *stirs in his chair.* EDMUND *and* JAMIE *remain motionless.*)
CURTAIN

The greatness of this late, directly autobiographical work (set in the year 1912) is clearly as much a triumph of self-confrontation as of its achieved mastery of dramatic form. Its late-matured, painfully bared directness of gaze surely reveals the root of O'Neill's variously projected patterns of entrapment, of the recurrent idea of a 'curse', of the usurpation of a present condition by the past.

It is only in *The Emperor Jones* and *Long Day's Journey into Night* that the pattern of catastrophic fusion of past and present elements is fully realized: in the one case, obliquely, remotely, and in a sense at a level wholly below explicit utterance; in the other case with an articulate autobiographical immediacy. Both could be said to generate modern archetypes of an at once pursuing and static fate. (Not only Sartre's demonstrative model of 'hell is other people' in *Huis Clos*, but Beckett's metaphysical farces and Genet's rituals of violence are, so to speak, anchored in 'the banality of surfaces' through the tradition consummated by *Long Day's Journey into Night*.) In both works, however, it is neither a play-back of ancient myths nor any sort of verbal renewal that do the job. The poetry is in the facts.

The 'banality of surfaces', then, is not only, after all, an important aspect of human experience, but capable—in privileged creative perspectives—of yielding irreplaceable insights, in depth. One need but note that human consciousness is an embodied consciousness to see why this is only to be expected. To react against naturalism with the indiscriminate rejection that has often seemed obligatory in our time can be a disabling cultural snobbery. Equally, however, it remains a central human fact that 'facts'—the facts of human 'surfaces'—are not enough: that those deep-seated needs in man which have generated myth, ritual, incantation, poetry retain their hold on us—if anything, bind us all the more radically because they now threaten to leave us shrivelled. As Yeats wrote, in his 'Three Movements':

> Shakespearean fish swam the seas, far away from land;
> Romantic fish swam in nets coming to the hand;
> What are all those fish that lie gasping on the strand?

Much more is involved, of course, than problems of artistic form; more, indeed, than the whole sphere of activities we call art: the sea of existence itself; and the renewal of our capacity to swim it. We must swim in the facts as they are. The facts are what they are, but our meanings must meet them.

While, however, all this implies some sort of creative convergence between 'banality' and poetic depth, it seems inherent in present conditions that such approaches, from either of these poles, must, by and large, retain their distinctness. For Shakespeare—at any rate in his central tragic period—there was hardly a conscious break between surface fidelities and poetic confrontation: Othello, Hamlet, even Macbeth, inhabit universes just as hospitable to 'naturalistic' as to 'symbolic' approaches. But even his own major contemporaries like Marlowe, Jonson, and Tourneur, at their most effective operated within emphatically non-naturalistic conventions. And Shakespeare's own pivotal quest for affirmative depths within the utmost reduction to bankruptcy, *King Lear*, is—with all its mastery of psychological realities—essentially, patently 'symbolic' (in some measure anticipating the last romances). In this light, and within the further perspectives of Greek drama, it is highly doubtful whether *any* such quest for ultimate affirmations can be other than 'symbolic': its world symbolically 'made strange', or made new: a 'poetic', or 'ritual', renewal. Negative visions as ultimates are another matter. A sort of negative poetry—unique in its peculiar reach—can, as we saw, be more readily generated in naturalistic terms. At a certain spiritual pressure and temperature, the surface 'banalities' of human anguish can themselves be crystallized into translucent meanings. Thus the poetry of *Long Day's Journey into Night* worthily fulfils the idiom of Ibsen's *Ghosts* and Strindberg's *The Father*. This may well be as far as it is—in principle—possible to go in these terms. (Unless we should place Peter Weiss's 'oratorio', *The Investigation* (1965), carved out of the records of the Auschwitz trial, in the same line: but this would be to press the notion of 'banality' into areas where it is not only aesthetic categories that explode in our time.) Romanticism took the opposite route—as in Blake's incantatory and mythical descent into the inner depths of imaginative vision, or the early poetic drama of Ibsen—seeking to bring outer facts under renewed human control, the rule of human meanings. But halfway through Ibsen's career, 'the facts'—the starkness of physical, biological, social, and psychological processes —declared themselves sovereign; and the naturalistic theatre strove to acknowledge this sovereignty. Yet soon (as in *Ghosts* or *The Father*) its search for 'reality' advanced—or reverted—to showing forth 'deeper' or 'higher' realities through its facts. And so, as in Ibsen's last plays and in Strindberg's Expressionist pioneer works, the naturalist masters themselves were led to press again beyond 'surface' verisimilitude. We have seen this process carried further in the work of Pirandello and Brecht—as Beckett was to open up yet further dramatic idioms within this post-naturalist tradition. All, in their various ways, witness that the essential identification of reality with factual verisimilitude falls short of human reality. The more factually orientated a culture becomes, the more—rather than the less—important the capacity to transcend mere verisimilitude will be. And this capacity cannot be adequately sustained merely by crystallizing the facts into factual poetry. A twofold convergence is needed: a scrupulous adherence to 'facts', eliciting their potential inherent meanings; and a bold confidence in imaginative meanings transcending these facts—though indeed pointing back to these facts with transfiguring potency. These approaches are essentially complementary. As Sir Henry Harcourt-Reilly remarks, in a somewhat different context, in *The Cocktail Party*:

> Neither way is better.
> Both ways are necessary. It is also necessary
> To make a choice between them.

For it is in the world of 'facts' that we exist; it is this world with which we must come to terms. But the sense of being stranded in this world points beyond this empirical world's own terms: whether in metaphysical despair, as in Pirandello, O'Neill, and the early Brecht; or, as in Brecht's subsequent work, demanding revolutionary transformation; or, as with Eliot, in Christian faith and hope.

From the 'illusion of reality' to a 'vision of reality'; and from freely creative 'vision' to respect for matters of fact: both ways are necessary. It is also necessary to make a choice between them: because only thus are the critical breaks within our culture properly acknowledged; and only through such acknowledgement—in the very 'techniques' of creative expression—can a really creative dialectic take place.

Is this not at least a large part of the explanation of the respective strengths and weaknesses in the dramatic careers of O'Neill and Eliot? O'Neill's most authentic, and deepest, poetry emerges from verisimilitude. The more he busies himself with advancing grand interpretations of 'Life in terms of lives', the less he is usually present to us at all. Where he would reveal, he merely declares; where he would relate modern lives to mythology, he only man-handles and inflates his material; where he would rise to mysterious grandeur, he falls into melodrama. It is precisely in fidelity to 'surfaces' that his life-long pursuit of 'mystery' really finds itself. Even *The Emperor Jones*—which so tellingly breaks through 'surfaces'—owes much to verisimilitude, in language and events. And it surely cannot be an accident that his immeasurably greatest play should have the centrally direct verisimilitude of autobiography. Eliot, on the other hand, is most himself when he most frankly seeks to transcend the Waste Land, when he directly draws on resources beyond the 'sordid, dreary daily world' that needs to be 'trans-figured'. *Murder in the Cathedral* is, so to speak, a direct extension—and appropriation—of the Christian 'myth'—at once historic and contemporary with us; its ritual idiom is an essential element in its dialectic. *The Family Reunion* uneasily strives to identify Christian with classical meanings, over against contemporary matters of fact; and again, its structural and linguistic forms are an integral part of the undertaking. Though there are deep-seated flaws in the outcome, it touches authentic 'mystery'; the charge of pseudo-profundity would be much more applicable to *Mourning Becomes Electra*. Eliot's subsequent efforts to let his poetic drama 'enter into overt competition with prose drama' by toning down its overt poetic characteristics could only blur the point of the 'competition'; while

O'Neill so often, conversely, fell between 'the banality of surfaces' and an only too 'overt competition' with the resources of poetic drama. Not only *Mourning Becomes Electra* but, in a different way, *The Iceman Cometh* seems to me a monument of such falling between two idioms. The problem of naturalist limits and the problem of making traditional 'poetic' resources relevant within the contemporary world are indeed part of a single cultural crisis. But the crisis cannot be met—for, indeed, it cannot be faced—by compromises blurring its symptoms.

The writers we have examined offer a suitable focus for a study of modern drama in the inter-war years, in which so many modern tensions intersect. But it certainly is not intended to imply that these careers exhaust the period's major dramatic writing. We may conveniently divide the most important of the writers whose work we have not been able to explore into two loose groups. The first is the relatively coherent school of French prose dramatists from Cocteau (1889–1963) and Giraudoux (1882–1944) to Anouilh (b. 1910) and Sartre (b. 1905). The second consists of three outstanding, sharply contrasting international poets: France's Paul Claudel (1868–1955), Spain's Garcia Lorca (1898–1936), and Ireland's W. B. Yeats (1865–1939). Both groups are vitally involved in the crisis of dramatic form and vision which we have been concerned to understand. Many of their preoccupations parallel those informing the work of their contemporaries we have here surveyed. But of course there is much that is uniquely their own.

What is passed on to the period that follows—the period we are now living through—is a twofold set of challenges: the dialectic between apparent fatality and redemptive imperatives; and, going with this, the continued challenge of creative form. Essentially, as I hope to have shown, these are really one and the same challenge.

NOTES

[1] G. B. Shaw, *Back to Methuselah*, Standard Edition (1921, rev. and reprinted 1931), 67–8.
[2] Ibid., 33.
[3] Ibid., 243.
[4] L. Pirandello, *Six Characters in Search of an Author*, trans. F. May (1954), 55–6.
[5] Ibid., 17.

⁶ L. Pirandello, *Henry IV*, in *Three Plays*, ed. E. Martin Browne, trans. F. May (1962), 231.

⁷ B. Brecht, *In the Jungle of Cities*, in *Collected Plays*, vol. I, ed. J. Willett and R. Manheim (1970), 172.

⁸ B. Brecht, *The Threepenny Opera*, in *Three German Plays* (Penguin Books), 222.

⁹ T. S. Eliot, *Murder in the Cathedral*, in *Collected Plays* (1962), 30–1.

¹⁰ T. S. Eliot, 'Poetry and Drama', in *On Poetry and Poets* (1957), 82.

¹¹ E. Bentley, *In Search of Theater* (1952), 241–2.

¹² E. O'Neill, *Mourning Becomes Electra* (1932), 287–8.

FOR FURTHER READING

John Gassner and Edward Quinn, *The Reader's Encyclopedia of World Drama* (1970) is a very useful reference book. Eric Bentley, *The Playwright as Thinker* (New York, 1946) is an informative and stimulating discussion of the development of drama since Ibsen. Robert Brustein, *The Theatre of Revolt* (1965) and Raymond Williams, *Modern Tragedy* (1966) are among the most challenging critical works on the period—interestingly divergent in their approaches. Brustein concentrates mainly on extended analyses of a number of dramatists, starting with Ibsen—Shaw, Pirandello, O'Neill, and Brecht among them; Williams's emphasis is more theoretical—providing a Marxist diagnosis—though he also comments directly on the work of individual writers. Williams's *Drama from Ibsen to Brecht* (1969), a revised and expanded version of *Drama from Ibsen to Eliot* (1952), is a wider critical survey. Francis Fergusson, *The Idea of a Theater* (New York, 1949), a distinguished series of essays ranging from Sophocles to Eliot, is relevant not only because it includes discussions of Shaw, Pirandello, and Eliot, but because of the light it throws on the whole nature of drama and the evolution of dramatic forms.

Archibald Henderson, *George Bernard Shaw: Man of the Century* (New York, 1956), is a vast factual compilation; Henderson was regarded by Shaw as his official biographer. The collection of short reviews in Desmond MacCarthy's *Shaw* (1951), written between 1904 and 1945, conveys something of the flavour of Shaw's impact on his contemporaries—and, at its best, is remarkably far-sighted. Edmund Wilson's 'Shaw at Eighty', in *The Triple Thinkers* (rev. ed., New York, 1948), while respecting Shaw's art, questions his claims as a 'thinker' —which were so important to Shaw himself. Saros Cowasjee, *O'Casey* (1966) is a competent introduction. On Pirandello, see Domenico Vittorini, *The Drama of Luigi Pirandello* (Philadelphia, 1935) and Oscar Büdel, *Pirandello* (1966). Martin Esslin, *Brecht—A Choice of Evils* (1959) and John Willett, *The Theatre of Bertolt Brecht* (2nd ed., 1960) provide important scholarly background; Ronald Gray, *Brecht* (1961) is a compact and lively critical introduction. Helen Gardner, *The Art of T. S. Eliot* (1949) gives a balanced general picture of Eliot's work; D. E. Jones, *The Plays of T. S. Eliot* (1960) examines each play in considerable detail; Denis Donoghue, *The Third Voice* (1959) assesses Eliot's development as a playwright within the general context of modern poetic drama in

English. Arthur and Barbara Gelb, *O'Neill* (New York, 1962) is a thorough biographical study; John H. Raleigh, *The Plays of Eugene O'Neill* (Carbondale, Ill., 1965) a sympathetic critical account. Eric Bentley, 'Trying to Like O'Neill', in *In Search of Theater* (New York, 1952) is a powerful attack—somewhat blunted through its failure to give due weight to its own recognition that O'Neill, nevertheless, 'was a good playwright insofar as he kept within the somewhat narrow range of his own sensibility'. (In fairness, it should also be noted that Bentley's essay was written before the—posthumous—publication of *Long Day's Journey into Night*.) Joseph Chiari, *The Contemporary French Theatre* (1958) is a helpful series of essays on dramatists, ranging from Claudel to Anouilh and Montherlant.

13

Literary Criticism

A. R. JONES

I

The history of literary criticism in English has been dominated since the time of Ben Jonson more by personalities than by theories, affected by eccentricities of taste and fashion, by prejudice and pre- disposition of character rather than by any coherent attempt to achieve even a partial structure within which discussions of purely literary questions could take place. At best English literary criticism is so strongly rooted in empiricism that discussion of the subject turns always away from the subject towards discussion of particular critics.

In England aesthetics as a subject of study has failed significantly to establish itself in spite of the fact that many of the most influential aesthetic theorists have been British. Their influence has been felt mainly not in England but on the Continent and, in particular, in America. At one end of the scale there is a point at which mere book-reviewing shades into criticism and at the other end a point where criticism becomes mere metaphysics and the middle ground is mainly confusion.

With the rise of English studies in the universities, firmly established within the period 1918–45, a new professionalism entered the field of criticism. Never was criticism so active or so militantly pursued, never before had such claims been made on its behalf. Looking back on those twenty-odd years, it is impossible not to be impressed by the quality and subtlety of mind of the critics of the period, by the variety of points of view represented, by the erudition displayed with such passion, and the passion expressed with such fitful clarity. In this period literary criticism seems to have become what theology had been in the sixteenth and seven- teenth centuries—the area that engaged the attention of many of the best minds of the age although, as in theological dispute, these minds often seemed to be at the service of deeply entrenched convictions.

In this new theology questions of literature and morality were inextricably linked and the discussion of literature, even at a textual level, was likely to set off arguments of a distinctly theological nature, that is an argument concerning the nature of morality. There was little or no attempt to establish anything like an art-for-art's-sake position but the discussion of literature became a free-for-all discussion of the purpose and morality of all human activities. Even those (perhaps particularly those) who called for discipline and rigorous standards of inclusion seemed to be overwhelmed by the weight of their undertaking, for from the 1930s onwards the term literature was inseparably linked to the word life. The field of the literary critic was no longer literature alone but literature *and* life. The terms of reference within which literature was discussed were so widespread as to be almost totally inclusive. Anthropology, sociology, psychology, philosophy, the old and the new disciplines, were pressed into the service of literary criticism, and if criticism itself seemed urgently motivated by a sense of impending social and cultural crisis it also generated an atmosphere of intellectual excitement. As an activity, literary criticism ceased to be merely an adjunct to literature and claimed attention as a new, creative activity in its own right. Although for the most part literature and literary works remained at the centre of the discussion, the subject of literary critical discussion was not only literature but was now literary criticism. Indeed some of the most distinguished and most characteristic literary criticism of the period is devoted to exploring and defining literary criticism.

In spite of a war that killed off a generation, in the 1920s the old did not suddenly give way to the new. The Victorian tradition of belles-lettres was strongly entrenched and the idea of the aristocracy of letters was slow to give way. Literature and its ancillary activities, such as the writing of essays and the editing of journals, were still regarded as the embodiment of gracious, leisured, beautiful living, the pursuit of which distinguished the gentlemen from the players. Yet a real attempt had been made before the war, particularly by the Imagists, to restore the centrality of literature, and this attempt was vindicated by T. S. Eliot (1888–1965), whose poem *The Waste Land* symbolized in an uncompromising way the culmination of those pre-war efforts to re-establish a direct and powerful connection between literature and contemporary society. Published in 1922, Eliot's poem confronted contemporary England with its own spiritual and cultural desolation. The poem dramatically, artistically, and even technically, enacted the breakdown of the whole structure of traditional values at every level. *The Waste Land* seems to have destroyed the last illusions of a postwar generation already disillusioned. Yet if in this poem Eliot so successfully demonstrated the death of traditional values, he had already in his critical essays begun a re-examination of the tradition of English poetry in an attempt to find some living principle of continuity relevant to the situation in which he found himself. Convinced that it 'is part of the business of the critic to preserve tradition—where good tradition exists', he set about the rigorous examination of the poetry of the past in order to restore the 'good tradition' to the present. Thus, *The Sacred Wood*, a collection of essays written between 1917 and 1920, is the starting-point for much of the critical activity that followed.

Both as poet and critic T. S. Eliot dominated the postwar generation. His poetry seemed an affront to those whose taste in poetry was formed on nineteenth-century expectations, and his critical essays took little regard for the accepted opinions of the orthodox. But for the younger poet and critic Eliot was both spokesman and liberator. He seemed to recognize their common situation with complete authenticity and to indicate a way out. Moreover, at least in so far as the intellectuals of his generation were concerned, he demonstrated as poet and critic the crucial significance of literature to the cultural, intellectual, moral, and spiritual life of the time. More than anyone else, he was responsible for re-establishing literary activity as the focus of all other human activity. In *The Waste Land* he uses mainly literary allusions in this very literary poem to illustrate the decline from a meaningful past to a meaningless present. In his critical essays he tends to assume that the poetry he is discussing also indicates aspects of the period other than purely literary ones. So in defining or isolating the sensibility of a particular poet we are also establishing the sensibility of a period or culture. (As he grew older so he wrote about culture and society more directly and increasingly generalized about poetry.)

For the most part the early criticism of T. S. Eliot is probing and tentative in spite of what often seems to be the authoritative tone of the essays themselves. In 'Tradition and the Individual Talent' he argues for an increased objectivity in poetry, attacking the idea of poetry as a statement or expression of personal feeling. Indeed, he argues for the 'impersonality' of the poet, poetry being not an expression of personality but an escape from it, the poet being so concerned with the form and style of the poem as to be completely immersed in the business of the poem's making. In his essays on individual writers it is the style and form of their poetry that holds his interest. He examines the literature of the past in order to discover a tradition of what is valuable in English poetry which would itself establish an art of objective value. Throughout these early essays we can see Eliot deliberately rejecting those assumptions and objectives that stem from English Romanticism, and he is continually stressing those attributes in poetry that the Romantics themselves rejected. In his critical writings he is both implicitly and explicitly rejecting the nineteenth-century romantic tradition and all that implied, and restating the classical, formal, virtues of structure, rhythm, natural grace of language, ironic detachment, intelligence, and awareness of social and historical values. He attacks the vague and the lyrical and praises the precise, urbane, witty, and elegantly formal. As he makes clear in his essay, 'The Metaphysical Poets' (1921), he seems to have found many of the qualities he most admired in the poetry of Donne and his followers.

He admired the formal structure of their poems, their ability to maintain the idiom of speech, their interest in the free play of intelligence, the way in which they turned experience, however disparate, into sensory images that brought the physical, spiritual, and intellectual together with easy immediacy. His feeling of affinity with these poets led him to identify with them to the point where he stressed their modernity, his strong feeling that they had faced up to problems similar to those that he saw confronting the modern world. They were the direct successors of the dramatists of the sixteenth century: they possessed to the same degree that unified sensibility that enabled them to comprehend the complexity and variety of experience; to express thought as sensory feeling and recreate thought into feeling in a poetic form of an intensely analytic, urbane, and formal kind. In spite of his admiration for the virtues of Dryden and Pope (but particularly Dryden), Eliot in his criticism returns time and time again to the dramatists and poets of the late sixteenth to early seventeenth century. In his writings on poets and poetry Eliot never really manages, except perhaps in his essay on Marvell, to reconcile his admiration for the virtues of classical formalism with his admiration for the unified sensibility, the line of 'wit', that ran out, be believed, between the time of 'Donne or Lord Herbert of Cherbury and the time of Tennyson and Browning'. Certainly it was this aspect of his critical writings, this emphasis he placed on the early dramatists and the Metaphysical poets, that was most influential.

He was the first critic since the time of Matthew Arnold to present a complete re-examination of the English poetic tradition and while *The Waste Land* was largely responsible for changing the direction of English poetry, his critical writings undoubtedly changed the direction of English criticism. Nevertheless, it must be said that T. S. Eliot never attempted to formulate a complete and systematic theory of poetry; the theoretical basis of his criticism gradually emerges in his individual essays although it never becomes anything approaching consistent, let alone systematic. His strength as a critic resides largely in his ability to recognize, to respond to, and to evaluate, good poetry wherever he finds it, irrespective of any theory of poetry. In this respect he is firmly part of the great tradition of English empirical criticism almost, like Dryden, *in spite* of his social, cultural, and artistic theories, to say nothing of his admiration, also shared by Dryden, for continental, particularly French, theorists. Many of his theories have long since been rejected, particularly his theory of the impersonality of poetry* and the poet. His theories of art and culture no longer command the kind of magisterial respect they appear to have exercised in the 1920s and 1930s. In his *T. S. Eliot* (1963) in the *Writers and Critics* series, Northrop Frye contends that Eliot in his critical writing mastered the art of passing off critical polemic in the disguise of objective, disinterested criticism. In other words he is insisting that Eliot's criticism is a much more personal exercise than was generally thought and that his critical judgements are impaired by certain prejudices and preferences that he does not openly reveal.

This may well be the case as, indeed, it is with other major critics of the past such as Johnson or Coleridge. The fact remains, however, that Eliot's essays opened up critical discussion to his generation in a way that was vitally creative. If his criticism was motivated by any animus against Romanticism, then it was an animus he inherited from critics such as Irving Babbitt and T. E. Hulme which was shared also with many of the best minds of his age. Also, we might argue, it was absolutely necessary at that period that poetry and criticism should be freed from the dead hand of the nineteenth century in order to establish themselves, centrally, in the changed context of the twentieth. Literary revolutions, after all, generally define themselves in direct opposition to the orthodoxy of the immediate past and a reappraisal of the past appears to be a necessary preliminary to any movement forward. Certainly in his criticism T. S. Eliot turned attention towards those areas of literature that had been unjustly neglected for more than a century and away from those on which critical attention had been

---

* E.g. it is now widely recognized that *The Waste Land* is quite as personal an expression of the poet's feelings as, say, 'Tintern Abbey'.

lavished for so long. Even his essay on *Hamlet*, a strangely misguided reading of the play in so many ways, drew attention to
other aspects of Shakespeare's work, in *Coriolanus* in particular, that
had long been overlooked.

Always in his critical work he concentrated attention on the
structure, the words on the page, the poem or drama as a whole,
the craft of literature, not the personality of the poet. He selected
his quotations with an unerring felicity to establish his argument
and his argument was always challenging even when at its most
cryptic. So many of the phrases and so much of the terminology of
his essays have passed into the critical language of the time that on
these grounds alone we might establish their influence. The style
of these essays is often elliptic, sometimes opaque, the approach
often oblique, but in reading them we are made constantly aware
of a precise and sensitive intelligence responding to literature.
Whatever Eliot's inconsistencies, whatever his strengths and his
failings, as a critic he commands respect even from his dissenting
readers. There can really be no doubt that his critical work was
seminal and it would be hard to see where or how modern criticism
would have developed without the impetus of his writings.

II

I. A. Richards (b. 1893) is best considered as a literary theorist
rather than a literary critic, and as a theorist his work has undoubtedly been vastly influential though, it should be said, his
influence has been more obviously apparent in the field of aesthetics
generally, and mainly on the Continent and in America where such
things are often taken more seriously. His interest was largely in
semantics and psychology and his objective was to establish a
methodology. So far as poetry is concerned he had no historical
sense at all; indeed his whole methodology actually depends on *not*
having such a sense, for it ignores entirely all idea of the context of
literature. His interest in the psychology of art is apparent enough
in his first book, *The Foundations of Aesthetics* (1922), in which he
collaborated with C. K. Ogden and James Wood in investigating
the concept of beauty in art by analysing its effect on its audience.
The Meaning of Meaning, which he published in 1923 and which
was written with C. K. Ogden, is more literary in so far as it
attempts some kind of semantic distinction between the language of
science (i.e. prose), 'symbolic' language, and the language of poetry,
'emotive' language. However, it is in his books *Principles of Literary*

Criticism (1924), and *Practical Criticism* (1929), that his work in semantics and psychology is focused upon the criticism of poetry. He assumes that a poem is a 'piece of experience' and furthermore that that experience is communicable; he devoted his study to exploring the process of communication between the poem and the reader. His attempt was no less than to establish criticism as one of the applied sciences paying due attention both to interpretation and evaluation and achieving in criticism a high degree of scientific objectivity.

Richards's *Principles of Literary Criticism* was planned as the theoretical foundation of a critical method that was built upon in experimental terms in *Practical Criticism*. There can be no doubt that Richards's work re-directed attention to the text of the particular poem and that so far as his theory of analysis goes he put into the hands of critics a large number of useful critical tools and significantly increased the terminology of criticism. He attempted to distinguish the various elements that make up a poem, such as tone, feeling, and intention, and raised a number of the most important problems that must confront a reader of poetry. He emphasized particularly the ambiguous nature of poetic language and suggested ways in which this ambiguity could be dealt with. He was not, however, at all concerned with the form of poetry except in so far as form is meaning, verbally and linguistically that is, and he denied any concept of aesthetic value as such.

He was concerned primarily with the effect of the poem as experience on the mind of the reader and not with the poem as an objective aesthetic structure. Indeed, he insists (Chapter 2) that 'When we look at a picture, or read a poem, or listen to music, we are not doing something quite unlike what we were doing on our way to the Gallery or when we dressed in the morning. The fashion in which the experience is caused in us is different, and as a rule the experience is more complex and, if we are successful, more unified. But our activity is not of a fundamentally different kind.' A poem to I. A. Richards is merely 'a strictly limited piece of experience', perhaps more complex and better organized than most other experiences, but none the less no different from the ordinary experiences 'of the street or of the hillside', except perhaps that it is communicable.

The emphasis of his work is to analyse *how* an experience in language communicates and *what* it is that is communicated. Such an analysis leads him to explore the psychology of the reader. When he comes to discuss the value of experience gained through poetry he, again, does so in psychological terms and can see this value only as a kind of psychotherapy in inducing in the reader a more organized 'patterning of impulses'. None the less, it is not his psychological theories that have been so influential but his analytic methodology as demonstrated and discussed in *Practical Criticism*. What he undertook was in fact an educational experiment. Over a period of years he distributed to his Cambridge students a number of printed sheets of poems disguising their period and author by modernizing the spelling and omitting the names of the authors. The poems distributed ranged from Shakespeare and Donne to Ella Wheeler Wilcox and Philip James Bailey. The students were asked to read the poems carefully and to comment on them freely. Richards collected these comments, which he called 'protocols', and discussed them with his audience taking care not to evaluate the poems or to divulge their authorship. In *Practical Criticism* he published the 'protocols' on thirteen poems, analysed the problems they give rise to, and made a number of specific recommendations. Although he does not himself specifically analyse any of the poems directly, he does allow, by implication, something like a relevant interpretation to emerge.

The comments he publishes make nonsense of the poems, virtually inverting their real value—Donne received many more unfavourable comments than favourable and J. D. C. Pellew's poem 'The Temple' was the poem that was most widely approved—but the ways in which the poems were commented upon seem to demonstrate a general inability to read poetry at all. Indeed, in his Introduction, Richards lists his primary objectives in conducting and publishing such an experiment:

First, to introduce a new kind of documentation to those who are interested in the contemporary state of culture whether as critics, as philosophers, as teachers, as psychologists, or merely as curious persons. Secondly, to provide a new technique for those who wish to discover for themselves what they think and feel about poetry (and cognate matters) and why they should like or dislike it. Thirdly, to prepare the way for educational methods more efficient than those we use now in developing discrimination and the power to understand what we hear and read.

If the experiment proved anything—and there are those who hold that it proved nothing at all—it must be the need to develop a more careful and attentive reading of poetry. Richards lists and comments on what he believes to be the ten most common failings of his readers, ranging from an inability to make out the plain sense to the introduction of critical preconceptions. But the book itself really has little bearing on literary criticism as such, except in so far as the general reader is concerned where we may be justified in assuming that the understanding of the poem is a necessary preliminary to dealing with it critically. As an educational method aimed at improving a student's ability to read poetry, a kind of remedial reading course, and also to help in analysing what he is reading, Richards's book has had an undeniably beneficial influence. This is not to suppose, however, that this kind of exercise should be seen as any more than an exercise.

There were those, however, who supposed that examination of individual poems, ignoring author and literary history entirely, was the proper business of criticism. Richards's method while wildly unhistorical was never recommended by him as anything more than methodology, but particularly in America, the 'New Critics'* adopted a theory of criticism that assumed the text of a poem to be self-sufficient. The text and only the text is the object of analysis, according to these critics who are the true heirs to Richards even if they are developing his work in a way he never intended and even if they are attempting to maintain the body of his work intact while rejecting the eccentric psychology on which it is founded and from which it draws its life. None the less, his emphasis on the linguistic structure of poetry and his drawing psychological concepts into literary criticism generally, have been vigorously infectious on all criticism since his time. Literary criticism since the 1920s could not afford to ignore the work of either T. S. Eliot or I. A. Richards whether in accord or in disagreement.

The most obvious and immediate influence of Richards was on the work of William Empson (b. 1906), who by largely ignoring Richards's psychology, demonstrated how his analytic method could be used to yield surprising results. Richards was Empson's director of studies at Magdalene College, Cambridge, when he changed from mathematics to read English literature in his last undergraduate year, and is on record as saying that Empson was mainly influenced in the writing of *Seven Types of Ambiguity* (1930) by the example of Robert Graves's and Laura Riding's analysis of Shakespeare's Sonnet CXXIX in their book, *A Survey of Modernist Poetry* (1927). There is also the suggestion that Empson was helpful to Richards. Whichever the case in personal terms, Empson's practice of criticism as exemplified by *Seven Types of Ambiguity* follows the linguistic,

* Cf. in particular John Crowe Ransom, *The World's Body* (1938); Cleanth Brooks, *The Well Wrought Urn* (1947); W. K. Wimsatt, *The Verbal Icon* (1954).

analytic pattern of *Practical Criticism*. Part of the success of Empson's book must be attributable to the fact that he neatly turned the tables on those who dismissed poetry as being too vague and imprecise to be really meaningful in a modern scientific age, for he seizes on vagueness and imprecision of meaning as being poetry's chief strength, a significant and perhaps the only honest way to record the complexities of experience.* He defines ambiguity as 'an indecision as to what you mean, an intention to mean several things, a probability that one or other or both of two things has been meant, and the fact that a statement has several meanings'. In poetry he sees ambiguity most effectively operating at the most crucial and climactic points of the poem and lending the poem what he calls a quality of tension: 'if there is contradiction, it must imply tension; the more prominent the contradiction, the greater the tension; in some way other than by the contradiction, the tension must be conveyed, and must be sustained. An ambiguity, then, is not satisfying in itself, nor is it, considered as a device on its own, a thing to be attempted; it must in each case arise from, and be justified by, the peculiar requirements of the situation.'

Empson distinguishes seven types of ambiguity ranging in 'stages of advancing logical disorder'; the ambiguities are most tense where the texture of the poetry is densest. He demonstrates an amazing dexterity in unravelling verbal intricacies and in discovering ambiguity where all seemed plain and straightforward. It is not only the adroitness and subtlety of his intelligence that the reader admires, not only the brilliance with which he confronts verbal difficulties; also the reader finds himself carried forward, not only because of a sense of problems faced and solved, but because of the enthusiastic performance of sheer inventiveness that is being laid on for his benefit. No other work of close linguistic analysis of poem after poem gives anything like such pleasure to the reader and this fact alone seems some justification for the analytic, linguistic method. In a real sense William Empson is in his book producing a whole series of 'protocols' of the quality and perceptiveness that I. A. Richards's other students so dismally failed to demonstrate.

Yet in his second book *Some Versions of Pastoral* (1935), there is a growing suspicion that Empson enjoys the discussion of literature at this level because of the way in which it acts as a stimulus for a display of his omnivorous intelligence and that his pleasure derives

* It is interesting to compare T. S. Eliot in this respect writing on 'difficult' poetry, cf. *The Use of Poetry and the Use of Criticism* (1933).

not from the literature ostensibly under discussion but from the more or less free play of eclectic learning and intelligence activated by such a discussion. In this second book he draws on a tremendous range of materials, on linguistics, anthropology, philosophy, theology, physics, Marx, Freud, Darwin, and Frazer, to list just some. He defines pastoral, ambiguously, as 'simple people expressing strong feelings in learned and fashionable language' and comments elsewhere that in literature 'If you choose an important member of a class the result is heroic; if you choose an unimportant one it is pastoral.' In his book he is concerned chiefly with structural rather than linguistic analysis, though because he covers such an enormous amount of ground—proletarian literature, the sub-plot in drama, a sonnet by Shakespeare, Marvell's 'The Garden', *Paradise Lost*, *The Beggar's Opera*, and *Alice in Wonderland*—the organization of the book, which is in any case disjointed, is not sufficiently coherent to support any thematic argument. The book, divided as it is into a discussion of seven types of pastoral, tends to fall into its separate parts. Moreover, the reader is more obviously conscious of the ingenuity of the various arguments and exegeses than of their justness. In *Seven Types of Ambiguity* Empson's analyses often lose sight of the text and bury themselves in some interesting corner of the author's own very interesting world, but in *Some Versions of Pastoral* the reader is too often left wondering why the author felt the need to go through the motions of discussing a text or developing an argument at all. This is not to say that the work is anything but interesting for, to misuse Dr. Johnson's famous dictum, even when William Empson's ideas are far-fetched, they are often worth the carriage—'great labour', we recall, 'directed by great abilities, is never wholly lost'.

III

Although the writings of Freud and the doctrines of Marx were widely disseminated during the 1920s and 1930s and both were highly influential, colouring the writing of the period, none the less little or no thoroughgoing Freudian or Marxist literary criticism was produced in England. This is particularly surprising when we take into account the fact that so many writers and intellectuals at this time professed Marxist principles. Certainly William Empson in *Some Versions of Pastoral* deployed Marxist assumptions in his discussion of the social implications of the pastoral mode; he also discusses Ernest Jones's Freudian reading of *Hamlet* and does his own Freudian analysis of *Alice in Wonderland*. Nevertheless, Empson is accustomed to taking his ideas from wherever he can find them and cannot really be described as either a Marxist or a Freudian critic. Not until Christopher Caudwell's *Illusion and Reality* (1937) was any thoroughgoing Marxist literary theory fully expounded, although in fact the attempt in that book to derive poetry from tribal emotions and to confine literature to the bourgeois 'illusion' of individualism is remarkably unpersuasive. In point of fact L. C. Knights's book, *Drama and Society in the Age of Jonson* (1937), which investigates the relations between culture and economics in Elizabethan and Jacobean society, is a much more intelligent application of Marxist ideas to literature, although Knights undoubtedly owed more to R. H. Tawney's *Religion and the Rise of Capitalism* (1926), itself indebted to Max Weber, than he ever owed to Marx or Marxism.

Perhaps, however, the influence of Marx has been more pervasive than might be suspected in so far as his concept of the relation of literature and society has been generally incorporated into the attitudes of the period as a whole. The same is probably also true of the influence of Freud, for although there has been little specific Freudian literary criticism, his ideas, and his vocabulary, have been widely incorporated and absorbed in our thinking about literary questions. Jungian psychology has, however, been more directly influential particularly through Maud Bodkin's discussion of 'archetypes' in her book *Archetypal Patterns in Poetry* (1934), and has given rise to something like a school of 'mythological' criticism. This Jungian approach to literature was, of course, prepared for by the interest in the 1920s in anthropology and it is of importance in this respect to recall the influence of Frazer's *The Golden Bough* and the fact that T. S. Eliot drew largely on Jessie Weston's *From Ritual to Romance* in writing *The Waste Land*. The strength of Maud Bodkin's book, particularly apparent in her analysis of *The Ancient Mariner*, is that she uses Jungian concepts of recurring patterns of death and rebirth to illuminate the poem rather than the poem to illustrate Jungian ideas. She avoids undue mysticism and uses her concepts with a proper respect for the poetry under discussion. The difficulty, of course, inherent in this kind of 'mythological' criticism is that the method tends to reduce all poems to one poem, all patterns to one archetypal pattern. Thus in literary criticism the tools it places in the hands of the critic are extremely blunt instruments and unsuitable probably for the purposes of analysis, comparison, or

evaluation. The best that can be done with archetypes is to recognize
them and catalogue them.*

The critic who best characterizes the period as a whole, however,
is probably Dr. F. R. Leavis (b. 1895), who in 1932, together with
his wife Q. D. Leavis and other critics in Cambridge at the time,
founded the critical journal *Scrutiny*. In his first book of literary
criticism, *New Bearings in English Poetry* (1932), Leavis was quick
to recognize the achievement of T. S. Eliot both as a poet and as a
critic but, perhaps more importantly, he realized that the changed
sensibility of the age brought with it a new challenge to criticism as
well as fresh dangers to the English cultural tradition. From the
outset he concerned himself with larger issues than those generally
acknowledged by his contemporaries as being literary. Literary
values cannot be isolated from the values of the culture from which
it emerges or from those of the audience to which it is addressed.
Like Arnold, Leavis was all too conscious of the philistines but he
was also aware of the danger of literary standards falling into the
hands of those who would corrupt them from within, so to speak,
and he clearly indicted the intellectual élite of his time whether
centred on Bloomsbury or in his native Cambridge. From the outset
Leavis made plain his passionate concern for literature and his
belief that critical activity was vitally creative and necessary to the
living continuity of all that was best in the culture of the past. He
saw the function of criticism as involving the health and life of the
intellectual and spiritual climate of the times, and at the same time
was fully aware of the way in which commercial pressures had
produced a Grub Street larger and more densely populated
than anything Pope imagined. He was careful to avoid labels of
any kind, except to insist that the object of *Scrutiny*'s contributors was to ensure 'the free play of intelligence on the underlying issues'. Indeed, looking back it is evident that *Scrutiny* did
not speak with one voice but with the distinctive voices of its
individual contributors; this in itself seems to have aroused a
strange antagonism.

Yet Leavis is recognizably an empirical critic whose position
emerges from his critical activity only gradually; no doubt, he could
reply to those who demanded he define his position, that the proper
activity of a literary critic is the practice of literary criticism and by
the end of the 1930s he could certainly point to a large and influential

---

* This is the procedure recommended by the Canadian critic Northrop Frye
as a valid critical programme; cf. his *Anatomy of Criticism* (1957).

body of critical work. René Wellek has defined his critical antecedents in the following terms:

F. R. Leavis . . . has applied the methods of Richards with much sensitiveness and has combined them with a revaluation of the history of English poetry begun, with dogmatic assurance, in the essays of T.S. Eliot. Without giving up Richards's methods of interpreting poetry, Leavis has abandoned his pseudo-scientific apparatus. Without giving up Eliot's critical attitude towards modern civilization, Leavis has refused to follow him into the camp of Anglo-Catholicism. His stress on the unity of a work of art, his conception of tradition, his sharp rejection of an artificial distinction between literary history and criticism are all leading traits of the anti-positivistic movement. (*Concepts of Criticism*, ed. S. G. Nichols (1963), 266.)

It is difficult to know how far, if at all, Leavis is indebted to I. A. Richards for, in fact, he seldom practises practical criticism in the latter's manner. His debt to T. S. Eliot is clear enough and freely acknowledged by him. It is worth emphasizing that René Wellek also singles out F. R. Leavis's achievement as an 'influential teacher', and noting that he has always seen criticism as a dialogue between teacher and taught, an exploratory and co-operative enterprise properly conducted within the educational community of a university. Yet his insistence on the wide social and cultural context of literature has always ensured that criticism for him has never become a remote, ivory-tower preoccupation.

In his book, *Revaluation* (1936), he establishes the tradition and development of the line of wit in English poetry from the time of Donne (filling out T. S. Eliot's work in this direction). As he promises in his introduction, he invariably relates his judgements to 'producible texts' and certainly the book as a whole illustrates a grasp of particularities and a series of insights that demonstrate just how fully and with what disinterestedness Leavis responded to literature. Just how serious a critic and moralist he is emerges most clearly in his later work on the novel but, none the less, in the 1930s the accomplishment of *Scrutiny*, as a platform for literary criticism of the most incisive and provocative kind, stands out clearly. It must not be forgotten, however, that *Scrutiny* was a co-operative enterprise and published Q. D. Leavis's work on the novel, particularly her work on Jane Austen,* D. A. Traversi's essays on Shakespeare, John Speirs's work on medieval literature, and much else that has

* Vol. X, 1941–2. Her work on the novel generally, particularly *Fiction and the Reading Public* (1932), has been neglected and pillaged.

since proved its value. When *Scrutiny* was recently reprinted, it was surprising to notice just how widely it had spread its net and just how *un*doctrinaire it was; it is difficult to sustain the charge of its being merely the work of an 'in-group',* although the flexibility of Leavis's criticism has sometimes revealed, to their discomfort and disadvantage, the inflexibility of those who claim to be his followers.

IV

The work of T. S. Eliot, I. A. Richards, William Empson, and F. R. Leavis, undertaken for the most part in the 1920s and 1930s, profoundly changed the critical climate of the whole period 1930–60. Their work has so changed the way in which we regard literature that we should be justified in claiming that they changed the whole ethos (to borrow one of Leavis's terms) of their own and their subsequent generation. This is not to deny, however, the importance of other critics or to underestimate the influence of others. This is not to say, either, that the 'amateur' critic does not continue to flourish in the same areas where Leavis found him thriving in 1932.

The period saw the founding of *The Criterion*, in 1922 under the editorship of T. S. Eliot, which was published as a quarterly magazine and which apart from publishing work by its editor and other notable creative writers of the period also published a good deal of foreign, particularly French, material. Two collections of Virginia Woolf's brilliantly impressionistic criticism appeared as *The Common Reader* (1925 and 1932); her gifts as a critic were directly related to her ability as a novelist to recreate the feeling and atmosphere of a writer, a book or a period. The 'New Cambridge Shakespeare' edited by Quiller-Couch and Dover Wilson began to appear in 1921 (complete 1931) and C. H. Herford and Percy and Evelyn Simpson's monumental edition of Ben Jonson in 1925 (11 vols., complete 1952). Perhaps the most significant work of criticism in the field of Shakespearian studies, however, was G. Wilson Knight's book *The Wheel of Fire*, which was published in 1930 with an introduction by T. S. Eliot, and which, instead of discussing Shakespearian tragedy in terms of plot and character, looks for 'the pattern below the level of plot and character'. His work encouraged the study of the plays concentrating on the symbolic images, treating each work within the canon as having theme, structure, and recurring imagery, and giving the plays the same kind of close verbal and thematic attention they deserve as *poetic* drama. Wilson Knight

* Made by G. Watson in *The Literary Critics* (1962), 213.

seems to have been indebted to Middleton Murry's analysis of Shakespeare's imagery in *The Problem of Style* (1922) and certainly Wilson Knight having extended his analysis over the range of Shakespeare's tragedies, from *Hamlet* to *Timon of Athens*, appears to have corrupted his own methodology by oversimplification and, more importantly, by drawing in material of a mystical, or at least fantastic, kind of irrelevance. It is, none the less, this method that L. C. Knights employs, more effectively perhaps, in his now classic essay 'How Many Children had Lady Macbeth?' (1933); though it will not be overlooked that Knights was one of the editors of *Scrutiny* and possibly, as his essay on George Herbert (1944)* demonstrates, one of the finest textual critics contributing to that journal.

Altogether the field of literary studies both in criticism and in scholarship underwent a profound change in the 1920s and 1930s (with the exception perhaps of Old English and medieval studies which proved stubbornly resistant on the whole to new methods and ideas). By 1945 English studies were institutionalized in the universities and rapidly becoming the centre of humane liberal studies. Indeed, the very professionalism of literary criticism bred its own dangers. In particular, criticism among professional critics tends always towards the parochial; the audience for academic criticism is largely academic critics. This specialized, ingrown quality of literary criticism becomes especially apparent in the decades that followed, leaving the common reader more than ever at the mercy of the reviewer, the amateur, and the commercial pressures of Grub Street. Yet, it must be insisted, literary criticism is a transitory art and like culture itself needs to be renewed for each succeeding generation. Our debt to the critics of the 1920s and 1930s resides largely in the fact that they recognized literary criticism as a vital and creative activity, central to the health of our culture as a whole. No longer could it be considered merely a by-product of a leisured class browsing among private libraries. While they offered no easy answers, and handed over no quick solutions, they raised the pertinent questions, opened up relevant lines of inquiry, and defined the framework of reference within which the discipline of literary criticism, as we understand the activity at the present time, has struggled to establish itself. Subsequent criticism has been largely an elaboration and development of their work.

* Both these essays were collected in Knights's book *Explorations* (1946). He acknowledges his indebtedness to G. Wilson Knight.

FOR FURTHER READING

With regard to this chapter, further reading should be mainly confined to the works themselves. The major books of criticism in this period include T. S. Eliot, *Selected Essays 1917–1932* (1932), I. A. Richards, *Principles of Literary Criticism* (1924) and *Practical Criticism* (1929), William Empson, *Seven Types of Ambiguity* (1930) and *Some Versions of Pastoral* (1935), L. C. Knights, *Drama and Society in the Age of Jonson* (1937), Maud Bodkin, *Archetypal Patterns in Poetry* (1934), F. R. Leavis, *New Bearings in English Poetry* (1932) and *Revaluations* (1936), Virginia Woolf, *The Common Reader* (1925 and 1932), and G. Wilson Knight, *The Wheel of Fire* (1930). The magazine *Scrutiny* has been reprinted by the Cambridge University Press, and its pages demonstrate the vitality of criticism at this time.

14

The Other Arts

EDWARD LUCIE-SMITH

I

Before the war, it often seemed that artists could not wait for the conflict, that only a vast blood-letting would satisfy their own personal fantasies and desires. Marinetti, the prophet of Futurism, glorified not only speed and the machine, but warfare, which he described as 'the only hygiene of the world'. Even in the midst of the conflict, Guillaume Apollinaire wrote a poem which began with the line: *'Dieu, que la guerre est jolie!'* It would have been difficult to discover such enthusiasm among the war-weary artists of 1918.

For many painters, the Cubists in particular, the period 1914–18 had been one of experiment. Now the mood of the time encouraged them to consolidate their gains rather than to go further. Picasso (b. 1881), inevitably, was a partial exception to this. He continued for a while to explore Cubist ideas. The two versions of the 'Three Musicians' (1921) are probably the most elegantly logical Cubist pictures ever painted. The forms are reduced to their simplest denominators—the flat patches of colour originally suggested by collage. Cubism is no longer 'analytic' but 'synthetic'. That is, it aims to create, by means of a consistent vocabulary of form, a universe which parallels the real one while still remaining separate from it. In the 'Three Musicians', flat strips of colour overlap in a shallow, arbitrarily compressed space. From these flat areas, monumental figures are created. Picasso has succeeded in creating a world which is completely under the painter's control, which is about nothing but itself. At the same time as he painted the 'Three Musicians', however, Picasso was busy with a completely different sort of picture. His visit to Rome, to work with Diaghilev and the Ballets Russes in 1917, had renewed his interest in the forms of classic art: in Roman wall-paintings, for example. He now set out to create a classicism in his own image. The pictures of Picasso's 'neo-classical' period reimpose the order which their author had once rejected. Indeed, they exaggerate classical characteristics, such as material density and roundness. The mood is one of deliberate calm, deliberate solidity. In Picasso's case, such a mood could not possibly last for long. Already, by the time he painted the 'Three Dancers' of 1925, the classic order and logic have dissolved and the picture is frenzied and Dionysiac.

The case of Georges Braque (1882–1963), Picasso's closest collaborator in the Cubist experiment, was different, and perhaps more typical of the time. Braque never rejected Cubism; he remained faithful to the style throughout his career. Already, by 1917, we find him moving towards a more flexible and personal version of it. The forms are loosened to allow for a renewed interest in colour and texture. Braque reverts towards the tradition of Cézanne, and beyond that, to the tradition of Chardin. The painter is intent on making a beautiful object, something which can be generally understood and appreciated, and which will at the same time express his own feeling about the order which underlies the world. Braque invented some very daring compositions in the twenties—notably the still-lifes where the whole weight of the composition lies at the very top of a tall, thin canvas, but they never give us a feeling of strain or exaggeration.

The same avoidance of exaggeration is to be found in the work which Matisse (1869–1954) was doing at the same period. Matisse had moved to Nice in 1917, and, except for brief journeys abroad, the town was to remain his home for the rest of his life. The Mediterranean warmth and the Mediterranean light induced a feeling of hedonism. The artist turned with renewed relish to the material world. Especially characteristic of this phase of Matisse's art are the compositions showing women in interiors, sometimes clothed, sometimes unclothed. Often the paintings have an oriental flavour, which makes them the successors of the Moroccan paintings of Delacroix. For Matisse, this period of consolidation was to continue almost throughout the years between the wars, though occasionally large compositions showed that he had not entirely lost his wish to experiment. Particularly daring was the decoration which he made for the Barnes Foundation, in Merrion, Pennsylvania. This exists in two versions, as faulty measurements made it impossible to fit the first attempt in its appointed place. With its radical simplification of line and tone, this decoration, which dates from 1931–3, was at least as extreme as anything which the artist had executed previously.

There was a likeness between the kind of work which Matisse did between the wars and that of a superficially very different artist, Pierre Bonnard (1867–1944). Bonnard had been a founder-member of the Nabis, and he and Edouard Vuillard (1868–1940) were the two principal 'intimist' painters, 'intimism' being a style which was neither Impressionist nor post-Impressionist, but had some of the characteristics of both. All his life long Bonnard was a master of the domestic atmosphere and of the domestic interior. A constant subject was his neurasthenic wife, who was reluctant to venture into the outside world. Many of these late works by Bonnard, which count among his greatest, were painted at his house at Le Cannet, near Cannes, where the couple spent their summers. Like the Matisses of the same period, they are flooded with Mediterranean light, and the compositions have a more than superficial likeness to the characteristic Matisse interiors of the time.

Another senior artist who continued to explore his vocation was the great Impressionist, Claude Monet (1840–1926), whose career just laps over into the postwar epoch. Grown old and blind, Monet struggled with the very last of the 'series' which dominated the latter part of his career. He had embarked on the first of these in the nineties. On huge canvases, he depicted the water-lilies which floated on the ponds in his garden at Giverny. Traditional rules of composition were ignored, all that mattered were the drifts of colour which the artist conjured up. At the time when they were painted, these pictures were an isolated phenomenon, alien to the mood of the time. Later, with the arrival of 'free abstraction', they were to be thought of as some of the most daring and original works of their epoch.

Far more typical of the epoch were the tough, hard, architecturally solid canvases of artists such as Fernand Léger and Juan Gris. Léger (1881–1955) had been a Cubist almost as daring and almost as distinguished as Braque and Picasso. His painting of the Cubist period shows him to have been fascinated with the image of the city. During the war, he served with an engineering unit, which further modified his vision of modern life, and he developed a heroic conception of the machine. His postwar paintings were deliberately 'mechanistic'—hard, cold, rationally organized. His subjects were the invented objects of modern industrial civilization.

The short-lived Juan Gris (1887–1927) was a second-generation Cubist, who carried the synthetic Cubist argument to the limits of purity and precision. Gris remarked, revealingly, that 'it is not a certain picture X which tries to enter into agreement with an object, but an object X, which strives to coincide with my picture.'

Léger and Gris represent the best side of twenties classicism. The forms they used were extremely influential, and were to be popularized and debased as the vocabulary of the Art-Deco style in furnishings and fabrics. But they were only one aspect of the complicated pattern of development in the School of Paris at this time. Some of the leading modern masters faltered and compromised. The work of André Derain (1880–1954), who had once been considered the most promising of the Fauves, suffered a set-back from which it never quite recovered. As the cult of the modern became part of fashionable life, painters such as Raoul Dufy (1877–1953) and Kees van Dongen (b. 1877) found themselves being taken up by fashionable patrons. In neither case was the process much resisted, as both of them felt a real attraction for the *douceur de vivre*, and slipped easily enough into the kind of niche which Boucher had provided for himself in the eighteenth century.

Elsewhere, the tensions were fiercer. In Germany, for example, the social and financial collapse which was the aftermath of defeat left artists with two choices which seemed sharply enough defined. Either they could become social commentators, bitterly chronicling the folly and the wickedness of mankind, or they could try and build a new society more or less from the ground up. The first choice was that made by Georg Grosz (1893–1959), whose name will always be associated with the savage caricatures which he made of life in Weimar Germany. If we want to capture the atmosphere of the Berlin of the period, we have only to turn to Grosz's drawings, and it is significant that, when Nazism forced him into exile, his work lost its power. The world he lampooned had in some way sustained him.

The other path was that chosen by the artists who were associated with the Bauhaus. The Bauhaus was founded in Weimar in the spring of 1918, by the architect Walter Gropius (b. 1883). It lasted, with several changes of location, until the Nazis came to power in 1933. Gropius's views, and the broad policy of the Bauhaus, are summed up in the Bauhaus Manifesto, which dates from the year of the foundation:

Architects, sculptors, painters, we must all turn to the crafts. Art is not a 'profession'. There is no essential difference between the artist and the craftsman. The artist is an exalted craftsman. In rare moments of inspiration, moments beyond the control of his will, the grace of heaven may cause his work to blossom into art. But proficiency in his craft is essential to every artist. Therein lies a source of creative imagination.

Let us create a new guild of craftsmen, without the class distinctions which raise an arrogant barrier between craftsman and artist. Together let us conceive and create the new building of the future, which will embrace architecture and sculpture and painting in one unity and which will rise one day towards heaven from the hands of a million workers like the crystal symbol of a new faith.

These lofty sentiments would have been without effect but for the fact that, throughout its history, the Bauhaus enjoyed the services of a very remarkable group of teachers. Some of them started as the pupils of the institution, and later graduated to teaching others. Among the most notable were the painters Paul Klee (1879–1940), Vassily Kandinsky (1866–1944), Lyonel Feininger (1871–1956), Lazlo Moholy-Nagy (1895–1946), Oskar Schlemmer (1888–1943), and Josef Albers (b. 1888), and the architect Ludwig Mies van der Rohe (1886–1970).

This roll-call of names makes it clear that the tendency of the Bauhaus was towards the systematic, the abstract, and the rational. Bauhaus teaching put a great deal of emphasis on the exploration of form and also of materials, and the preliminary course (perhaps the most novel and experimental part of Bauhaus teaching) was designed to bring a fresh awareness of these to the students.

In its desire to provide a complete aesthetic, which would serve for the crafts as well as the arts, the Bauhaus had been narrowly preceded by an initiative in Holland. In 1917 Theo van Doesburg (1883–1931) and Piet Mondrian (1872–1944) founded a magazine which they called *De Stijl*—as the title indicates, those who were connected with the magazine and with the movement which centred upon it wanted to create a new style of art based upon principles of order which would possess a universal validity. Proportion was to replace form, synthesis analysis, logic irrational lyricism, mechanical perfection the thumbprint of the craftsman. Collectivity was to replace individualism. The purest expression of these principles are the entirely abstract and geometric pictures of Mondrian's developed style, where the colours are all primaries, where all the lines are straight, and the only angle is the right angle. Using this restricted formal vocabulary, Mondrian produced some of the principal classical masterpieces of twentieth-century painting.

If Mondrian was the genius of De Stijl, van Doesburg was its principal propagandist. In January 1921 he visited the Weimar Bauhaus, and was to return for longer or shorter periods in succeeding years. Van Doesburg was later to claim that he alone had turned the young German painters away from 'moody expressionism', and that it was the intervention of De Stijl, which had 'brought the young artists back to order and discipline'. While acknowledging his influence, the Bauhaus rejected so large a claim.

Indeed, one has only to look at some of the work produced by those who were associated with it to perceive that it was possible for a great diversity of approaches to exist within the framework which the Bauhaus provided. Kandinsky, for instance, explored an almost mystical notion of universal order. Klee produced paintings which were never entirely abstract, and which were filled with his own brand of wry humour. Schlemmer, too, remained a figurative painter, and his work was influenced by his interest in the theatre, and especially in the dance. The importance of the Bauhaus lay, not in any rigorous doctrine, but in the positive quality of its approach to art, and in its desire to involve the artist with the problems of society. This political aspect of its work was clearly understood by its opponents, and it was political trouble which forced its removal from Weimar to Dessau in 1925, and from Dessau to Berlin in 1932, and its final dissolution under pressure from the Nazis in 1933.

If modern art suffered a check in Germany, it also suffered another and more permanent one in Russia. At first sight, this may seem surprising because the Russian Futurists had very often been fervent supporters of the Revolution, and at first there was an alliance between the artists and the new regime. The artists organized pageants and demonstrations. Vladimir Tatlin (1885–1953) produced the most ambitious scheme of all, his model for a 'Monument to the Third International'. In finished form, it was to have been twice the height of the Empire State Building. Its three parts, a cylinder, a cone, and a cube, were all meant to revolve: respectively once a year, once a month, and once a day. Altogether, it was a typical expression of the extravagant hopes and plans of the years of 'heroic Communism'. Meanwhile artists were locked in passionate debate about what their role was to be in the society which was being created by Communism. In conditions of the bitterest material hardship, the Utopia of the years to come was envisaged and planned for. The debate was between those, such as Casimir Malevich (1878–1935), who thought of art as essentially a spiritual activity, and those such as Tatlin and Alexander Rodchenko (1891–1956) who adopted the concept of the artist-engineer, who saw the machine as something which could release man from labour, and transform his whole life into art. It was Rodchenko and his followers who moved towards the last phase of Russian modernism—the Constructivist movement. Constructivism aimed to replace the concept of 'style' with that of 'technique'. A Constructivist manifesto published in the magazine *Lef* in 1923 states that: 'The material formation of the object is to be substituted for its aesthetic combination.' Artists therefore began to devote themselves to problems of practical industrial design. As with the Bauhaus, there was no longer to be a division between the craftsman, or designer, and the fine artist.

And, as with the Bauhaus, architecture was regarded as the culminating point, the crown of the other arts, though due to the economic situation in Russia, nearly all the ambitious architectural projects of the time remained on paper. By a supreme irony, the one major surviving building in Constructivist style in Russia is the Lenin Mausoleum in Red Square in Moscow, designed in 1924.

Many Constructivist projects were ephemeral by their very nature. A major field of activity was theatrical design. Vsevolod Meyerhold, the theatrical director, was a convert to the movement, and the influence of Constructivism is also to be seen in Eisenstein's early films. Constructivism also had a marked impact on typography and on poster design—El Lissitzky (1890–1941) was a major influence, and it was he who designed the famous 'abstract' poster, 'The Red Wedge'. Rodchenko and Lissitzky both experimented with photo-montage.

But Constructivism had two basic weaknesses, which in combination proved fatal to modern art in Russia. The first was something which sprang from the very philosophy of the movement. The independent work of art, painting or sculpture, was at a discount as compared to art which could be made to serve some practical social purpose. The artist was accepted as a 'working' member of society—but asked to surrender control over his art. Most of the leading Constructivists gradually drifted away from the fine arts—Rodchenko became interested in the possibilities of photography; in the early thirties Tatlin was already at work on the Letatlin glider, a project which never came to fruition.

Meanwhile, the political climate grew steadily more difficult. The political authorities had never been wholly in favour of the work done by their *avant-garde* allies. What Lenin had tolerated, thanks to the influence of his Commissar for Education, Lunacharsky, Stalin cordially disliked. In 1932 the doctrine of socialist realism was finally imposed, and, so far as Russia was concerned, the adventure was over. The Nazi regime followed suit a year later, and suppressed what it labelled, with unintentional irony, 'cultural bolshevism'.

So far I have spoken of the positive, consciously rational contribution made by artists in the decade following the war. Logically enough, one reaction to war's destruction was to consolidate and systematize what had already been gained. The neo-classicism of the École de Paris, the doctrines of the Bauhaus, and those of Constructivism all basically represent a similar reaction to a common situation. But it was not the only possible reaction. The real dialogue in the years between the wars, so far as the visual arts were concerned, was one between the protagonists of reason, and those of unreason. It is a debate which has continued right up to the present day.

What one may describe as the 'irrationalist' strain had its roots in the Dada Movement, which began in Zurich in 1915. Few important art movements have been so widely misunderstood as Dada, possibly because few are so totally resistant to art-historical explanations. In part, Dada was a simple protest against the criminal folly of the war. The Dadaists acted out, in their cabaret performances, the absurdity they saw surrounding them, much as the Russian Futurists had done in their own cabarets a little earlier. Dada was also the child of pre-war German Expressionism—a point which one can most easily prove by calling attention to the similarity between Dada texts and certain Expressionist poems, such as those written by Alfred Lichtenstein, which bear a strong resemblance to the writings produced by the sculptor-poet Hans Arp (1887–1966).

The leading spirits of Zürich Dada included the poet Hugo Ball (1886–1927), Tristan Tzara (1896–1963), Francis Picabia (1878–1953), and Arp himself. The movement was as much literary as artistic, and it was essentially cosmopolitan rather than narrowly nationalistic. Its purposes were summed up in a letter written by Ball in November 1916:

What we call Dada is foolery, foolery extracted from the emptiness in which all the higher problems are wrapped, a gladiator's gesture, a game played with the shabby remnants . . . a public execution of false morality.

One of the attractions of the new movement was that, in however strange a way, it did embody a moral imperative: it proclaimed the artist's freedom to do as he pleased, and the necessity of breaking down the old order. One of the instruments of demolition was a new concept, that of 'anti-art'.

The honour of inventing 'anti-art' probably belongs about equally to the Zürich Dadaists and to Marcel Duchamp (1887–1968). The laughing philosopher of modern art, Duchamp will probably be best remembered for his concept of the 'ready-made'—the everyday object which the artist lifts out of its normal context and transforms into a work of art merely by naming it as such. 'The choice', Duchamp remarked, 'was based on a reaction of *visual indifference* with a total absence of good or bad taste . . . in fact a complete anaesthesia.' The scene of Duchamp's activity during the war was New York. He went there in 1915, and was soon the centre of a small group of kindred spirits, which included the photographer Alfred Stieglitz (1864–1946) and Man Ray (b. 1890). Picabia, who visited America in 1915 and again in 1917, helped to unite the two groups, which had this much in common: that both stood on the fringes of the war, fascinated and horrified spectators who were unable to do anything about it. In each case, there was a hothouse atmosphere; isolation made it easier to go to extremes.

As soon as the war ended, Dada burst from its confines. It made itself felt in Berlin, where its protagonists were swiftly involved in the revolutionary politics of the time. Max Ernst (b. 1891) linked up with Arp in Cologne in 1919; Kurt Schwitters (1887–1948) emerged in Hanover. Schwitters is perhaps the purest expression of the Dada personality. His collages, made of strange scraps of material—bus-tickets, wrapper-fragments, buttons, pieces of cloth —are attempts to create a private domain of fantasy. This activity, to which the artist gave the generic title MERZ, was also undertaken on a larger scale. Schwitters's own house became a vast collage-environment, a MERZbau which was always growing and changing. Schwitters was a strange mixture of naïveté and sophistication. His experiments often seem to have been undertaken for the simple reason that a possibility had crossed his mind, and all possibilities were to be pursued. The logic of Dada was the logic of capricious desire.

Dada's conquests in Germany in the long run counted for less than the impression which it made in Paris, the traditional capital of the *avant-garde*. Its apostle was Tristan Tzara, who already had numerous contacts there. He had contributed to periodicals such as Pierre Reverdy's *Nord-Sud* and Pierre Albert-Birot's *Sic*. And in 1918 leading members of the Paris literary *avant-garde*, such as André Breton (1896–1966) and Louis Aragon (b. 1897), were contributors to the Dada magazine in Zürich. Meanwhile, Picabia was doing a great deal of advance propaganda for the new movement. By the time Tzara himself arrived in Paris in 1919, the scene was already set.

Tzara, Breton, and a group of kindred spirits immediately set about organizing a spate of Dadaist events, each more deliberately outrageous than the last. But here problems arose. The Dadaists found themselves trapped by their own extremism. Nothing new was being produced—there is, for example, no 'Paris Dada' style or school of painting. The leaders of the movement quarrelled among themselves.

The quarrel was not wholly fruitless, because a new movement was born from the ashes of Dada, under the leadership of the implacable André Breton. By the force of Breton's will, Dada became Surrealism.

It is important to emphasize, as Maurice Nadeau does in his excellent *History of Surrealism*, that:

The movement was envisaged by its founders not as a new artistic school, but as a means of knowledge, a discovery of continents which had not yet been systematically explored: the unconscious, the marvellous, the dream, madness, hallucinatory states—in short, if we add the fantastic and the marvellous as they occurred throughout the world. The accent, perhaps in reaction to Dada's destructive anarchism, was on the systematic, scientific, experimental character of the new method.

Breton defined Surrealism, in the First Surrealist Manifesto of 1924, as

pure psychic automatism, by which an attempt is made to express, either verbally, in writing, or in any other manner, the true functioning of thought. The dictation of thought, in the absence of all control by the reason, excluding an esthetic or moral preoccupation.

The major contributing factor to the doctrine of Surrealism—in addition, that is, to the elements taken from Dada—was the teaching of Freud. Freud's theory of the unconscious provided a way of systematizing the insights which Dada had provided. It also suggested a way of linking Dada to an older and more specifically French tradition, that of the *voyant*, which could be traced to nineteenth-century writers such as Rimbaud and Lautréamont.

So far as the visual arts were concerned, Surrealism meant a renewed emphasis on the content of the work of art rather than on its formal organization. There are, however, two main varieties of Surrealist painting. One tries to give a 'realistic' version of fantasies drawn from the unconscious; the other deals, not in solidly three-dimensional forms set in real space, but in a kind of cursive hand-writing. It was the first group which attracted the lion's share of public attention and comment in the movement's heyday; but the second was ultimately to prove more influential.

The leading members of the first group included Max Ernst, Yves Tanguy (1900–55), Salvador Dali (b. 1904), and the Belgian painter René Magritte (1898–1968), and they represent a considerable diversity of styles. Ernst gives a hallucinatory view of nature—crawling, swarming, bejewelled, and menacing. The whole tradition of German painting contributes to his work, from Altdorfer in the sixteenth century to Caspar David Friedrich in the nineteenth. Dali paints transformed objects in a laborious style derived from the academic painting of the nineteenth century. His by now familiar repertoire of images—soft watches, grotesquely elongated limbs and buttocks—is deliberately and slyly Freudian.

Like Tanguy, Dali owes a good deal to the *Pittura Metafisica* of Giorgio de Chirico (b. 1888). The empty, echoing desert space which is so characteristic of Tanguy's pictures as well as of Dali's derives from Chirico, whose contribution to twentieth-century painting was this feeling of ominous stillness. Tanguy is more abstract than Dali. His objects are not recognizable—they are soft, amorphous things, fungi from an alien planet.

Magritte, too, was very much influenced by Chirico, but what he took over from *Pittura Metafisica* was essentially its feeling for visual paradox. A famous picture by Magritte shows a canvas on an easel in front of a window. The landscape seen through the window and the landscape on the canvas match one another—the view continues without a break. Illusion is reality and reality illusion.

The second group of Surrealist painters was headed by André Masson (b. 1896) and the Spaniard Joan Miró; a later convert to this method of painting was the Chilean Roberto Matta (b. 1912). Both Masson and Miró have a debt to Klee. Like Klee, Masson is a calligrapher; it is the line which gives life to his paintings; a line which no sooner creates one image than it is off in pursuit of another. Miró, again like Klee, is a creator of hieroglyphs, simplified graphic signs, sometimes figurative, sometimes abstract, which seem instinct with mysterious meanings. Miró, like other modern painters, has made intelligent use of the art of children as an ingredient in his own style (an interest in child art and in the creations of people who were mentally disturbed was something suggested to artists by basic Surrealist doctrine).

Because Surrealism was a new way of looking at life, rather than merely a new style of art, it was able to attract towards itself painters who were already established. The most notable convert was Picasso, who soon reacted against the tranquillity of his own brief neo-classical period. In the late twenties, he began to paint pictures of women bathing which were a grotesque, insulting deformation of the figures which had appeared in the neo-classical works. Throughout the thirties he pursued this new interest in the savage deformation of form. The culminating work of this phase is his vast composition, 'Guernica', an anguished outcry in protest against the cruelty of the Spanish Civil War.

Yet 'Guernica' was exceptional in Surrealist art because it made successful use of a political event. Throughout the late twenties and thirties, as the political climate darkened, the Surrealists became increasingly obsessed with politics. In particular, the movement felt the attraction of Communist doctrine, yet could never (by its very nature) surrender its autonomy as the Communists demanded. Aragon was lost to the movement after he went to a literary congress in Russia in 1930, and returned a whole-hearted convert.

In addition to this, Breton's dictatorial nature led to perpetual rows and expulsions, accompanied by much public vilification, which robbed Surrealism of many of the abler writers and artists who had originally been attracted to it. All things considered, the thirties were not a good decade for the visual arts, and when war broke out in 1939, the Surrealist movement was battered and exhausted. Many would have described it as a spent force. Yet an astonishing resurrection was to take place.

At the fall of France, many of the leading Surrealists fled to America, and set up a kind of government in exile in New York. Emigrating thus, they followed the example of other Europeans who had chosen America as a refuge from the Nazi terror. Albers, for instance, had been teaching in the United States since 1933. What the original exiles lacked was the Surrealist sense of solidarity, which had survived all their quarrels. The political issue was, in a sense, settled by events. Helpless to influence these, Breton and his followers were able to return undistracted to the arts. Peggy Guggenheim, then married to Max Ernst, founded the Art of this Century Gallery in 1942, and this became a centre for Surrealist manifestations. It also became an important meeting-place for European artists and their American colleagues.

American painting, during the twenties and thirties, had been essentially provincial. American experimentalists found it even harder to win acceptance from the public than did foreign ones, who had something of the glamour of the exotic about them. There was a temptation to set up a double standard for American and foreign artists. This began to change with the coming of the Depression. Artists were hit hard, and the Federal Art Project was set up in order to try and alleviate the situation. Painters, sculptors, and graphic artists were employed by the government, and paid a monthly wage. A characteristic means of expression were murals, painted for housing projects, bus and airline terminals, schools, and other institutions. The idea for these came from Mexico, where Diego Rivera (1886–1957) and others had created a popular school of mural painting. Rivera's work, despite its aggressively left-wing content, was much admired in the United States at this time.

Most of the work done under the auspices of the Federal Art Project has since been destroyed, and much of it was never worth saving. But two things were accomplished under its auspices. First of all, a new feeling of solidarity was created among American artists. Secondly, as no distinction was made between abstract and figurative painting, abstract art obtained a foothold which it might never otherwise have got.

Among those involved in the Federal Art Project were Arshile Gorky (1905–48) and Jackson Pollock (1912–56). Gorky is the most important transitional figure between Surrealism and Abstract Expressionism. As an American provincial, Gorky had tended to recapitulate in his own work the whole course of modernist develop-ment. He was particularly attracted to Picasso, and some of his figurative paintings in the style of Picasso are undoubtedly very beautiful. But it was contact with Roberto Matta, and later with Breton himself, which drew him towards Surrealism. He was the last painter to be fully accepted into the movement.

Gorky's final style makes a soft, fluid use of biomorphic forms. It combines both realistic and calligraphic elements. Gorky made use of preliminary drawings, and did not insist on the complete calligraphic freedom which was later to be the hallmark of Pollock. But basically Gorky's Surrealism was painterly, an exploration of a path already marked out by Masson, Matta, and Miró.

Pollock was also associated with the New York Surrealist group, and had his first one-man show at the Art of this Century Gallery in 1943. Other American artists who showed there included Robert Motherwell (b. 1915) and Mark Rothko (1903–70), who were to be leading Abstract Expressionists.

Abstract Expressionism, in fact, represented a return to Surrealist sources. The obsession with politics was abandoned, the importance of psychic automatism was once again emphasized. Harold Rosen-berg, one of the leading critical advocates of the new school, once described it as a 'conversion phenomenon', something akin to a religious experience. Surrealism had been that too, in its time.

This astonishing revival of influence in the United States during the war made sure that Surrealism would be the main medium of transmission for modernist doctrines. It also made sure that American art would have a tremendous impact in Europe as soon as hostilities ceased. The war drove European artists back upon themselves. In countries occupied by the Nazis, they survived as best they could, working in isolation under a regime they knew to be hostile. In Britain, beleaguered but free, the tendency was for art to follow a national rather than an international tradition. Modernist artists began to feel that it was their patriotic duty to make what they did more accessible to the bulk of the population. British painting went into a figurative, neo-romantic phase. This hothouse style, the product of special circumstances, did not long survive the war. America was the only country with a new and unified art movement, ready to spread its wings as soon as things returned to normality.

So far, I have said little about sculpture. The reason is that modern painting shows a continuous process of evolution; modern sculpture only an intermittent one. The great modernist discoveries were made by painters rather than sculptors, and many of the leading painters were also important for their sculptural work—among them Matisse, Braque, and Picasso. Their work in three dimensions has a freedom and an inventiveness often lacking from that of their 'professional' colleagues.

Naturally, sculptors felt the impact of the new ideas in painting. This was especially true of Cubism, because Cubism concerned itself with an investigation of three-dimensional form. Among the sculptors connected with the movement were Henri Laurens (1885–1954), who owed much to his friendship with Braque and Picasso; Jacques Lipchitz (b. 1891); Ossip Zadkine (b. 1890); and Alexander Archipenko (b. 1897). The three first named all evolved away from Cubism during the twenties and thirties towards a kind of modernist baroque—a style which, on the whole, has worn rather badly.

Drier and more intellectual was the work done by the brothers Antoine Pevsner (b. 1884) and Naum Gabo (b. 1890). Pevsner and Gabo were members of the Constructivist movement in Russia, driven abroad by political events. They remained the great champions of a wholly abstract sculpture, and their work often seems to have a greater affinity to the architecture of the period than to the rest of its art.

A handful of sculptors, however, stand out for their orginality. The greatest is probably the Rumanian, Constantin Brancusi (1876–1957). Brancusi began his career under Rodin's influence, and gradually moved to the farthest possible extreme from Rodin's impressionism. Already, by 1910, when he made the first version of 'The Kiss', Brancusi had established a style of rigorous simplification.

He was to pursue simplicity all his life. His aim was to get at
the essence of things—to express the inner life of a bird or a fish in
absolutely pure and final form. He had a very small stock of basic
images, and used them over and over again, seeking always to reach
a yet more convincing finality.

Another highly original artist was Julio Gonzalez (1876–1942).
Gonzalez began as a painter, and it was not until as late as 1927
that he finally gave up painting to devote himself entirely to sculpture. His medium was metal—usually, for preference, iron. Where
Brancusi's work is tight and dense, that of Gonzalez stretches out to
embrace the surrounding space. He uses thin rods, and sheets of
metal, joined by welding. His attitudes to sculpture, and the
processes which he pioneered, made little impact at the time, but
were to have immense importance in the years after 1945.

Linked to Gonzalez by some of his techniques, and also by the
change in status he has undergone, is the American, Alexander
Calder (b. 1898). Calder's invention of the mobile, in the early
thirties, was important for modern art. These fragile-seeming
constructions of wire and sheet metal introduced an aleatory element
which was something new. As the parts turned and twisted into new
relationships, the spectator felt a change in his attitudes towards
such things as volume and space. At the same time, the airiness and
lightness of Calder's work called into question the monumental
nature of sculpture, hitherto taken for granted.

Original contributions to the development of sculpture were also
made by Hans Arp and Henry Moore (b. 1898). The two men came
from very different artistic backgrounds. Arp, thanks to his involvement with Dada, sprang into prominence early. Moore made his
way slowly and painfully in the provincial England of the twenties
and thirties. What both men were concerned with was much the
same, however. Both were 'vitalists', convinced that the natural
unity should be represented by a unity of forms. The shapes they
use are biomorphic, and we seem always to catch them in the process
of evolution. Without Surrealism neither Arp's work, nor Moore's,
would have taken precisely the course it did, but they were able to
demonstrate that the special qualities of sculpture—in this case, its
denseness and earthiness, could produce effects which were outside
the range of painting.

II

Where architecture is concerned, it is customary to think of the twenties and thirties as the years when the so-called 'international style' established itself. This is true, but certain qualifications must be made. Architects suffered perhaps even more than painters and sculptors from the political catastrophes of the time. They also suffered, especially in the thirties, from unfavourable economic conditions. The two decades between the wars were the time when new architecture made its mark, but completed buildings, as opposed to projects which remained on paper, are scarce. Yet these buildings, together with the projects (which were published and widely discussed), were enough to revolutionize architectural thinking.

The purist architecture of the twenties and thirties corresponds in one sense to the neo-classicism which was again making its appearance in painting and music. Mies van der Rohe, perhaps the most important of all the International Style architects, acknowledges the influence upon him of the nineteenth-century Berlin classicist, Karl Friedrich von Schinkel. In a more general sense, it is possible to trace a resemblance between a man such as Le Corbusier and the visionary architects of the end of the eighteenth century, such as Ledoux.

Architecture, however, had not suffered the kind of revolution which painting had been undergoing from 1905 onwards, and the proposals of the new school of architects seemed correspondingly shocking, though in many ways they simply represented an acceptance of the technological progress of the nineteenth century. Among the key figures, Mies and Le Corbusier have just been mentioned. Another, perhaps less great as an architect but just as important as an organizer and theorist, was Walter Gropius. Gropius had already designed important buildings before the war, notably the Fagus shoelace factory (1911), built in collaboration with Adolph Meyer, and the Administrative Office Building at the Deutscher Werkbund Exhibition in 1914, built with the same collaborator.

Gropius's real breakthrough, however, came with the building he designed for his own Bauhaus at Dessau, completed in 1926. This demonstrated his idea that architecture was the rational interpretation of human needs. Other characteristic ideas were his insistence on teamwork, and his interest in the possibilities of pre-fabrication and standardization.

Though Gropius has had a long and distinguished architectural career, first in Germany and later in England and in the United States, the Bauhaus still summarizes the aims which he constantly put before himself, which were as much those of a sociologist as of an architect. We do not get the sense of aesthetic excitement from Gropius's buildings that we do from those of the man who eventually succeeded him as director of the Bauhaus, Mies van der Rohe.

Mies had worked with Gropius in the office of Peter Behrens (1868–1940), whose industrial architecture in particular anticipated some of the ideas of the International Style. Mies was at this time more influenced by the neo-classicism of Behrens's domestic projects. But after the war came an abrupt conversion. Two projects for glass skyscrapers (1919 and 1920–1) put Mies in the forefront of the new architecture. But it was not until the late twenties that Mies got the chance to put some of his ideas into practice. He was director of the large outdoor exhibition of housing sponsored by the Deutscher Werkbund at Stuttgart in 1927, and built a notable apartment block as his own contribution. And in 1929 came his German Pavilion for the International Exhibition at Barcelona. This exquisite small building made an immense, if delayed, impression. With its construction, modern architecture seemed suddenly to come of age. It was followed in 1930 by the Tugendhat House at Brno in Czechoslovakia. Shortly thereafter, Mies found himself in increasing difficulties with the Nazis, and in 1937 he left for the United States, there to begin a new architectural career.

America brought him the opportunities which Europe had refused. In 1938 he accepted an offer to teach at the Illinois Institute of Technology, by 1940 he was busy drawing up a campus plan for his new employers, and in 1942–3 the first buildings of this ambitious project were put up. With the I.I.T. project Mies established his American style—reticent, subtle, spare—which was to have such an immense impact on the postwar architecture of the United States, chiefly because it so perfectly expressed American building technology.

Mies and Gropius were not alone in making the westward journey. Among the other distinguished European architects who went to the United States were the Hungarian Marcel Breuer (b. 1902) and the Austrian Richard Neutra (b. 1892). Breuer had been among the first generation of students at the Bauhaus, and later turned his attention to furniture design—the furniture used in the Dessau Bauhaus was designed by him. Between 1928 and the advent of Nazism he designed some radical houses and apartments which were particularly notable for their practicality. Later he emigrated to England, and finally to America, where he joined forces with Gropius, and taught with him at Harvard.

Neutra moved to the United States much earlier, in 1923, where he made contact with Wright. In 1926 he settled in California, and soon embarked on the first of a long series of notable private houses. These were often distinguished by the boldness of their technical experimentation, as if the 'new' society of the West Coast set the architect free to take a fresh and unprejudiced look at structural problems. Meeting with fewer frustrations than his peers (he was able to go on building during the war, for instance, though wartime shortages forced him to try different materials), Neutra was in 1946, when he built the Kaufmann Desert House at Palm Springs, one of the most mature and sophisticated of the International Style architects.

Not all architectural pioneers made their way across the Atlantic, however. Among those who stayed put were the Dutchman, J. J. P. Oud (1890–1963), and the Finn, Alvar Aalto (b. 1898). Oud is the less important of the two. He progressed from an association with Van Doesburg and De Stijl to a position as the apostle of Functionalism. The radical nature of his work can be appreciated in a number of housing schemes built in Holland during the twenties, for example in the workers' housing estate built at the Hook of Holland in 1924, where the smooth, sleek shapes are purist in the extreme. Later, in the middle thirties, Oud tended to retreat from the position he had originally taken up.

Aalto has been responsible for some of the classics of modern architecture. His first really important buildings were put up in the late twenties and early thirties, notably the Paimio Sanatorium (1929–33), a classic statement of Functionalism and one of the most elegant and persuasive buildings of its epoch. Since his fellow-countrymen showed little prejudice against advanced architecture, Aalto was able to pursue an active career during the thirties, designing, among other buildings, the Finnish pavilions at the International Exhibitions in Paris (1937) and New York (1939). These helped to establish the Finnish reputation for modern design. Aalto's work, even in this first phase of his career, was notable for its feeling of ease and naturalness, and the architect's sympathy for the landscape within which his buildings were set was always evident.

This account has so far left undiscussed the two towering, difficult, unclassifiable geniuses of modern architecture, Frank

Lloyd Wright (1867–1959) and Le Corbusier (b. 1887). The years between the wars were stormy ones for Wright—his personal life was disrupted by tragedies and scandals; his architecture, with its sometimes fussy detailing, looked old-fashioned when it was compared to the work of the new men in Europe. Wright's technical genius and his feeling for setting and space remained, however. Perhaps the most striking example of the former was the Imperial Hotel in Tokyo, built between 1916 and 1922. Wright devised a structural system for this which enabled him to build on a spongy site, and at the same time to produce a structure which would resist earthquake shocks. His success in doing this was dramatically proved by the great earthquake which struck Tokyo two years after the hotel was completed, which left the building undamaged. A dazzling example of the latter is the famous house Falling Water, built at Bear Run, Pennsylvania, in 1936. Cantilevered out over a waterfall, this is perhaps the most spectacularly picturesque house of the twentieth century, and it shows the simplicity of form and detail which Wright had now begun to attain in the wake of his younger rivals. It was followed by the S. G. Johnson & Son administration building in Racine, Wisconsin, an entirely individual solution to a commonplace modern problem.

Great though these achievements were, Wright was not quite the leader during these years that he had been earlier. That honour now belonged to the Swiss-born architect-painter, Le Corbusier. Le Corbusier settled in Paris in 1917, after contact with the leading French and German architects of the time. In Paris itself, he had a decisive encounter with Cubism. A year later, he founded Purism, with the painter and theorist Amédée Ozenfant (1886–1966). In 1923 he published his influential manifesto, *Vers une architecture*.

Le Corbusier was too original and above all too abrasive a personality to find the path made easy for him, and the result was that he built little during the period under review. But what he did build was decisive. Among the most important of his commissions were the Cook house of 1926, the Villa Stein of 1929, two apartment houses for the Weissenhof exhibition at Stuttgart (organized by Mies van der Rohe), the Villa Savoye at Poissy (1927–31), and the Maison Suisse in the Cité Universitaire in Paris (1930–2). These demonstrated many of the architect's fundamental ideas: pure forms achieved by the use of continuous window-strips, glass walls, flat roofs; the lightness which came from raising the structure on *pilotis*. The buildings of this period of Le Corbusier's career have a smooth, sleek finish which often proved vulnerable to the elements—

one reason why the architect changed to a different sort of texture in the work he did after the war. But less important than the finish (though it caused a great stir at the time) was their creator's mastery over interior space.

Le Corbusier also devoted much thought to larger projects—town planning, the apartment blocks of the future—but here he found it more difficult to realize his ideas. He came very close to winning the competition for the Palace of the League of Nations in 1927, and was cheated of the commission at the last moment. It is clear that the plan he submitted influenced the structures which were finally put up, though they do not have a tenth of the distinction which he could have brought to them.

Perhaps because he was an original thinker about society as well as about architecture, Le Corbusier found himself apparently frustrated at every turn. Yet the very controversies in which he found himself engaged helped to spread the doctrines which he wished to propagate, in the teeth of opposition. The power of both his personality and his ideas can best be demonstrated by what took place in Brazil. He paid a brief visit there in 1936 to act as a consultant on the new Ministry of Education and Health building in Rio de Janeiro, which was then being designed by a team of Brazilian architects. His intervention was decisive, and the building (his first skyscraper) bears the unmistakable Le Corbusier stamp, with many devices, such as the sun-control louvres, which have since been used in similar buildings all over the world. This office-block exercised a decisive effect on Brazilian architecture, as the Brazilians themselves were not slow to acknowledge. One of Le Corbusier's colleagues on this occasion was Oscar Niemeyer (b. 1907) who has since gone on to become the most important single force in his country's architectural development. Niemeyer, like Neutra in California, was lucky in missing the full consequences of the war, which called a halt to so many architectural careers elsewhere, and it was in his hands that the International Style continued to develop during the early forties.

The reason for the importance of modern architecture during the years 1918 to 1945, and in particular for the importance of Le Corbusier, lay in the fact that architectural thinking became one of the channels through which men began to think about society in general. Everywhere that totalitarianism triumphed, architectural development ground to a halt and was replaced by a sterile and inhuman academic classicism. Even Russia, which saw some brilliant architectural projects inspired by Constructivism, and which attracted the attention and sympathy of progressive architects in a way that the Nazis could not, finally committed herself to the horrors of the Stalinist style of building, which proved all too faithful an image of the regime that sponsored it. The close link between architecture and politics made architecture seem especially vital in an increasingly political era.

III

Music, by contrast, did not serve so readily as a means for the exploration of political and social questions, though attempts were certainly made to make it serve social ends. In some ways, what happened to it provides a distinct parallel with developments in painting and sculpture. Stravinsky, the central figure in the fashionable *avant-garde* of the immediately pre-war years, turned towards classicism. The Russian revolution cut his roots in his native country, and in 1920 he settled in France, where he was to remain until 1939. This perhaps had an influence on the new direction taken by his work. His neo-classical period begins with the Symphony for Wind Instruments, of 1920, which, despite its dedication to Debussy's memory, is treated in distinctly anti-impressionist style. There followed the Piano Sonata, the Concerto for piano and wind instruments, and the Serenade in A, all representing a return to the eighteenth-century tradition, and all dating from 1924–5. Stravinsky did not insist that his sources should be eighteenth century only— he also paid tribute to composers such as Weber and Tchaikovsky. Everything Stravinsky wrote at this time is elegant and inventive, so much so as to reassure his Parisian audience that modern music had now 'come of age'. But little of it is as powerful as the two major works of the decade immediately following the war, the *Oedipus Rex* of 1927, a setting of a text by Cocteau which was afterwards translated into Latin, because of the composer's wish to set 'a language of convention', and the Symphony of Psalms of 1930. Here we see Stravinsky not merely playing with classical devices, but trying to get at the very core of classicism, of the hieratic, impersonal art which music can become.

Stravinsky's decision to return to classical roots was a creative decision valid for himself, but it did tend to remove him from the mainstream of musical development. Few composers had anything like his gift for inhabiting past styles, possessing them, and making them viable again. Less protean musicians had to choose a different course, and the apparent range of choice was wide.

There was, first of all, the music of the French *avant-garde*—of the generation which followed in the footsteps of Erik Satie. In fact, the music of the group which was promptly dubbed *Les Six*—Louis Durey, Germaine Tailleferre, Georges Auric, Darius Milhaud, Arthur Honegger, Francis Poulenc. It was the three latter who counted for most. Milhaud (b. 1892) and Poulenc (1899–1963) show a lightness, a charm, a wit, a bitter-sweet romanticism which makes what they write a constant pleasure to listen to. Milhaud, in particular, felt the attraction of jazz, which had also appealed to Stravinsky. Honegger (1892–1955) was a more traditionalist composer, fonder of the large canvas than the other two, tending to avoid the deliberate fragmentation of much of their work. The result was highly professional and ambitious music which somehow fails to excite the ear.

Hostile to the neo-classical point of view, and ultimately to be a much more important composer than any of the members of *Les Six*, was Olivier Messiaen (b. 1908). Messiaen first began to make a reputation in the late twenties and early thirties, with works such as *Le Banquet eucharistique* (1928), which tended to be as expansive as those of the neo-classicists were terse. Messaien's musical sources are varied but coherent—Debussy's impressionism, medieval music, Hindu music, and nature herself—especially bird-song. Particularly characteristic is his tendency towards rhythmic experimentation (the influence of Hindu music is here especially evident). Messaien has always been conscious that what he wrote was in a special idiom—one reason why he published the treatise *Technique de mon langage musical* in 1944. But he has been equally sure that his methods could be used by other people. This belief has been justified by his growing influence among younger composers in the postwar years.

Neo-classicism was only one of the solutions which musicians proposed to themselves in the years 1918–45. Nationalism—a return to the roots—was another. It has often been pointed out that twentieth-century musical nationalism was more 'scientific' than the equivalent phenomenon in the nineteenth century. Composers began to research seriously into the heritage of folk-tunes, and to treat their discoveries with a new respect. But nationalism was more self-conscious in some milieux than in others.

In Russia, for example, the nationalism of the nineteenth century lapped over into the twentieth, and even Stravinsky began his career as a consciously Russian composer. Soviet composers found it easier than Soviet painters and sculptors to maintain continuity, to keep their links with the immediate past, because Soviet Communism was not, in the end, hostile to the nationalist spirit. Soviet composers certainly had their troubles with the government—a notorious example was the official condemnation of the opera by Dimitri Shostakovitch (b. 1906), *Lady Macbeth of Mzensk*. *Pravda* launched a violent attack on this work in 1936. Nevertheless, Russian music continued to develop, and preserved, in a quite extraordinary way, the full musical apparatus of the nineteenth century, not barrenly, but as a living thing.

Shostakovitch himself is perhaps the best example of this. His use of symphonic form puts him in the great line of development which runs through Beethoven and Brahms, and which seems to finish in non-Communist countries with Mahler and Bruckner. The epic note rings out in the Symphony No. 5, of 1937, which Shostakovitch wrote in reply to the critics of his opera.

Sergei Prokofiev (1891–1943), the other great composer of the Soviet era, was also fairly successful in adjusting himself to the demands of the regime, though he, too, was to meet with official criticism. Prokofiev had just begun to establish his reputation as a composer at the time of the revolution. In 1918 he emigrated, and went first to the United States, where he met with mixed fortunes, and later to Paris. Diaghilev took him up, and produced his ballet *Chout*. But, though he made a large European reputation, Prokofiev could never quite reconcile himself to the loss of his homeland, and in 1934 he went back to Russia again. Prokofiev admitted that there was a strong 'neo-classical' element in his musical style. One early work is called simply the *Classical Symphony* (1917), and is composed, Prokofiev said, 'as Haydn might have written it had he lived in our day'. Prokofiev's output after his return to Russia is marked by greater lyricism, greater seriousness, less grotesquerie. In fact, he moves from the musical ambience of Stravinsky (the arch-fiend of the Soviet musical demonology—at least, until very recently) to a much more orthodox position. There is an acute contrast, for instance between the early opera, *The Love of Three Oranges*, written just after Stravinsky left Russia, and the late *War and Peace* (1941–2)—the one rejoices in absurd and humorously exaggerated effects, the other keeps as close to Tolstoy's text as possible.

England proved almost as resistant to musical innovation as Soviet Russia. Vaughan Williams (1872–1958), the representative musical figure of the time, stated roundly that 'the greatest artist belongs inevitably to his country as much as the humblest singer in a remote village'. He was very conscious of the lack of a continuous musical tradition in England, except at the level of folk-song; con-

scious, too, of his own lack of technical equipment. He tried, nevertheless, to revive the best elements of the golden age of English
music, which stretches from the Elizabethan madrigalists to Purcell.

Benjamin Britten (b. 1913), a more sophisticated and perhaps a
more durable composer than Vaughan Williams, writes music which
has certain elements at least in common with his—notably, he shares
Vaughan Williams's interest in the madrigalists and in Purcell.
But he also shares characteristics with middle-period Stravinsky,
notably the fact that he is deeply interested in the craftsmanship of
music, and still finds life in the classical tradition. One of Britten's
great strengths as a composer lies in his response to words—equally
evident in *Our Hunting Fathers* (1936), based on a collection of old
poems assembled by the poet W. H. Auden, and in his settings of
Rimbaud's *Les Illuminations* (1939). The opera *Peter Grimes* (1945),
based on a poem by George Crabbe, shows Britten, as much as
Shostakovitch and Prokofiev, as the writer of a deliberately 'national'
music. The opera expresses the spirit not only of the Borough which
Crabbe wrote about, but of England itself. It is important to remember that the opera was composed just at a moment when the English
sense of national identity was particularly strong.

The man who towers over all the other national composers of the
century is the Hungarian, Béla Bartók (1881–1945). By 1918, Bartók
was already a mature composer, with important works to his credit.
But the greatest music belongs to the latter part of his life—a time
when Bartók was increasingly at odds with the pro-Nazi regime of
Admiral Horthy. He exiled himself to New York in 1940, and died
there of leukemia five years later. Among Bartók's most notable
scores are the piano pieces in *Mikrokosmos* (1926–37), the later
string quartets (the last dates from 1939), the Music for String
Instruments, Percussion and Celesta (1936), and the Third Piano
Concerto (1945). These show Bartók absorbing and using all the
varied musical influences of his time: he experimented with poly-
tonality, but at one point (early in the twenties) felt the attraction of
Viennese atonalism; he was at moments expressionist and at
others neo-classical.

As a Hungarian, Bartók was in touch, like Liszt before him, with
the German musical tradition, and it was still this which remained
the main current of musical development in the years between the
wars. Basically, two choices seemed to be open to the composers
brought up in this tradition. They could try to check the luxuriance
of the late nineteenth century, and to reach the audience more
directly—a desire prompted by the political events of the time—or

else they could try to find a new road for music altogether. On the whole, it was German composers who made the first choice, and Austrians who made the second.

Kurt Weill (1900–1950) will certainly not rank as the most important composer of the period, but it is still his plangent jazz-influenced settings of the words of Bertolt Brecht (1898–1956) which sum up the atmosphere of the Weimar Republic. The *Threepenny Opera*, *Mahagonny*, and *Happy End* have proven surprisingly durable, and the jazzy 'Ballad of Mack the Knife' became a hit-tune when someone revived it after the war. Paul Hindemith (1895–1963) is a less limited musician than Weill, but he does not have Weill's gift for tunes that catch the ear. But he, like Weill, was also a partisan of *Gebrauchsmusik*, a term which has been defined as meaning 'simple, practical music designed for use in the home and the community'. Hindemith was really yet another neo-classicist, but with a strong practical and pedagogical bent. The tradition of simplicity and popular appeal continued even under the Nazis, with the tuneful directness of Carl Orff (b. 1895). Orff's best-known work is the *Carmina Burana*, a dramatic cantata which dates from 1936.

The most significant musician of the time, and perhaps of the century, was Arnold Schoenberg (1874–1951). It was Schoenberg who presided over the dissolution of the old tonal system, and who proposed a new system of composition, the twelve-tone method, which entails basing every composition on an arbitrarily chosen arrangement of the twelve chromatic tones. The 'tone row' or basic set is the essence of the composition, and is peculiar to that composition and no other. The twelve tones, once selected, are always used in the same order, but the row itself may be inverted, or used backwards, or even in retrograde inversion. And any of these variants may start with any note of the row, so long as the order itself is not tampered with. This gives total unity to the composition, and yet 'perpetual variation'. It can be seen that there is at least one resemblance between Schoenberg's method and Stravinskian neo-classicism—both are abstract and formal.

Schoenberg was, of course, already an established composer at the outbreak of war, though acceptance of his talent was fairly recent, and had come with the first performance of the expressionist *Gurrelieder* in 1913. After this Schoenberg fell silent for seven years —from 1915 to 1923. The twelve-tone method was initiated with the Five Piano Pieces of Opus 23. The last of these is a fully developed example of the new style, which was essentially Schoenberg's way of organizing the intuitions which had come to him during the writing of earlier, atonal works. The power which could be generated by the new way of composing music was exemplified is the famous Variations for Orchestra, Opus 31 (1927–8). Nazism forced Schoenberg to emigrate to America, like so many other European artists, and it was there that he continued his career as a teacher and composer. Gradually, doctrines which had seemed far-fetched and outlandish began to dominate the whole musical scene. Schoenberg's victory was more complete even than that of the Cubists in painting. At the same time, Schoenberg himself relaxed the strictness of his dodecaphonic procedures. He even remarked: 'It seems urgent to warn my friends against orthodoxy. Composing with twelves tones is not nearly as forbidding and exclusive a method as is popularly believed.'

But Schoenberg did not have to wait for disciples until he reached America. Among the earliest were Alban Berg (1885–1935) and Anton von Webern (1883–1945). Berg was Schoenberg's friend and pupil long before the invention of dodecaphonic music. The work which made Berg's reputation was the opera *Wozzeck*, completed in 1921 and first performed in its entirety in 1925. *Wozzeck*, based on the play by Georg Büchner (1813–37), is perhaps the most striking opera of the period under discussion. By seizing upon the latent expressionism of the operatic form, it gave a new lease of life to a genre which already seemed in danger of dying on its feet. *Wozzeck* is an atonal work, but Berg was inevitably drawn towards fully developed dodecaphonic procedures. The beautiful Violin Concerto of 1935 shows him trying to reconcile the two systems— the new and the old. The tone row itself has traditional tonal im-plications. For many listeners, this work was to form the easiest means of approach to the rigours of the new music.

Webern's name has only become of international importance since his death. His own retiring nature made him shun the lime-light, and the Nazis banned his music and even forced him to lecture in secret. Webern's music is characterized by its extreme concision. Each separate sound is lovingly examined, and silence counts for as much as sound. He had an enormous sensitivity to unusual sonori-ties. The thing which holds his music together, and gives it its structure, is the dodecaphonic method, which he had already adop-ted by 1924. Unlike Berg, he did not try to loosen the bonds, but carried them to extremes of strictness—not only pitches, but timbre and rhythm were brought within the confines of the method. This combination of radicalism and logic appealed greatly to many of the young musicians who established themselves after the Second

World War. Webern is the point from which music took its start again in 1945, and even Stravinsky, once so scornful of the dodecaphonic school, was to feel the fascination of Webern's legacy.

IV

The music of Schoenberg, Webern, and Berg gives music the claim to be both the most advanced and esoteric of the arts during the period 1918–45. By contrast, the most popular was the new art of the cinema. Film-making was marked off from the other arts by two quite special factors. First of all, the movie audience was in no sense a minority. By the mid-thirties, the movie audience was almost everybody, though certain films might exercise only a minority appeal. On the other hand, films, to a much greater extent than the other arts at this period, were at the mercy of technological changes. The coming of the talkies (1927) marks a break in the history of the cinema which is not to be found in the history of any of the other arts.

The limitations of the silent film did, now we look back, make it easier to combine artistry and popularity. At the same time, the newness of the art, the lack of an established tradition, made it easy for film-makers to experiment. No one had a settled idea of what a film should be. The famous early horror film, *The Cabinet of Dr. Caligari* (1919), shows the influence of both Cubism and Expressionism. Eisenstein, as I have already said, felt the attraction of Constructivist ideas.

At the same time, the novelty of the film made it a good medium for expressing the new political ideas—one reason, perhaps, for the brilliance of the early Russian cinema, with works such as *Battleship Potemkin* (1925), *Ten Days That Shook The World* (1928), and *Storm over Asia* (1928). The film audience experienced the collectivity of emotion which the painters and sculptors who supported the revolution struggled to attain.

Yet the silent film did not have to be deliberately serious, or to concern itself with novelty, to create art. Among the classic achievements of the twenties must surely figure the silent screen comedies, and especially those of Charlie Chaplin, made with an artistry at once pure and unpretentious.

Naturally the film attracted the attentions of the professional *avant-garde*. Hans Richter's *Rhythmus 21* (1921) is an early example of an abstract film, made by one of the founder-members of Zürich Dada. In 1924 Fernand Léger made the abstract *Ballet Mécanique*—a film which works directly on the physical reflexes of the spectator.

The Surrealists were particularly fascinated by the possibilities which the film offered for the juxtaposition of images. Perhaps the two most famous *avant-garde* films ever made are *Un Chien Andalou* (1929) by Luis Bunuel and Salvador Dali, and *L'Age d'Or* (1930), and it is arguable that *Un Chien Andalou* carries out Dali's artistic aims more completely than any picture he has ever painted because we get not just the static juxtaposition of dream images, but a continuous sequence of images, moving at a pace chosen by the creators of the film.

The coming of sound tended to rob the film of its own special virtues. Films became photographed plays; trick sound effects were used to excess. The story of the cinema in the thirties is not only the story of a mass entertainment phenomenon, but of the search for ways of mastering the means of expression that technology had made available to movie-makers. The struggle to master an unruly and complex medium can be traced in many films of the period, and sometimes the problems are triumphantly surmounted. Orson Welles's *Citizen Kane* (1941) showed that the talking cinema at last had a fully developed vocabulary of effects and of methods of narration.

The cinema stands apart from the other arts, however, in most of its preoccupations. It remained obstinately romantic and experimental where things such as painting, sculpture, and music showed a tendency to revert to the concepts of classicism.

For the modern movement, the period 1918–45 was on the whole a period of consolidation. The immense euphoria which had prevailed before the war was gone for ever. The artists, like the rest of the world, emerged shaken from the holocaust. At the same time, all the arts were affected by the political struggles which dominated the two decades before the world was again plunged into war. Modernism began to consider its duty towards society—one reason for the rapid progress made by architecture, which is pre-eminently an art where the creator must think in social terms. At the same time, artists found that the equivalence which they had assumed would be found between radical art and radical politics was often the product of their own too-hopeful imaginations. The tension within the Surrealist movement often sprang from this particular misunderstanding.

At the same time, Surrealism (surely the most important of all the artistic movements which flourished in the time under review) directed attention once more to the importance of the inner life of the artist. The importance of the period as a whole is still difficult to judge, because artistic developments were cruelly at the mercy of political events. At the same time, it is true to say that political urgencies directed the attention of creative people towards the social problems which had hitherto been ignored. *Avant-garde* art tried to reintegrate itself with society as a whole—not always successfully, it is true. At the same time, the period of the *entre-deux-guerres* saw a kind of codification of modernist doctrine. People began to ask themselves what it meant to be 'modern', and this kind of self-questioning has continued ever since. At the same time, there was a certain flagging of purely creative energies—even the most advanced arts drew back a little from innovation. The area of possible activity was defined and explored in more detail, without (except in architecture and to some extent in music) going beyond the frontiers which had already been set. Given the tension of the time, its economic and political storms, its achievements are surprisingly solid, but they do not rival those of the heroic age of modernism.

FOR FURTHER READING

    Useful general books include the *Encyclopaedia of Modern Architecture* (1963), Joseph Machlis, *Introduction to Contemporary Music* (New York, 1961), *Twentieth Century Music*, ed. Rollo Myers (1960), and Werner Haftmann's two-volume *Painting in the Twentieth Century* (1965). *Ise Gropius and Walter Gropius—Bauhaus, 1919-1928*, ed. Herbert Bayer (Boston, 1959), Maurice Nadeau, *The History of Surrealism* (New York, 1965), John Willett, *Expressionism* (1971), and Hans Richter, *Dada* (1965) provide a wide range of background material. For treatment of individual figures, see Arnold Haskell, *Diaghileff* (1935) and Eric W. White, *Stravinsky* (1966). Other useful general books are Wilfred Mellers, *Music in a New Found Land* (1964), L. Moholy-Nagy, *Vision in Motion* (Wheaton Ill., 1961), and Paul Rotha, *The Film Till Now* (1949).

Index